The Vinogradoff Institute
Dickinson School of Law
Pennsylvania State University

# CIVIL CODE OF THE REPUBLIC KAZAKHSTAN

**Translated & Edited By**

**William E. Butler**

John Edward Fowler Distinguished Professor of Law
Dickinson School of Law
Pennsylvania State University
Foreign Member, National Academy of Sciences of Ukraine
and Russian Academy of Natural Sciences
Professor Emeritus of Comparative Law in the
University of London

**Wildy, Simmonds & Hill Publishing**

Civil Code of the Republic Kazakhstan

British Library Cataloguing-in-Publication Data:
A catalogue record for this book is available from The British Library

ISBN 9781898029984



First published in 2008 by

Wildy, Simmonds & Hill Publishing Ltd.
58 Carey Street, London WC2A 2JB
England

# THE CIVIL CODE OF KAZAKHSTAN

**W. E. Butler**

The Republic Kazakhstan acquired its own first civil code in 1963. Prior to then the 1926 Civil Code of the Russian Soviet Federated Socialist Republic had operated on the territory of the Kazakh SSR together with general legislation of the former USSR regulating civil-law relations. Uniquely in Central Asia, a strong school of civilists emerged in the Kazakh SSR, individuals of all-union stature who made their individual contributions from the early 1960s to Soviet civil law generally. When the Kazakh SSR became an Independent State after 1991, these individuals played a significant role in shaping the present Code, both at the initial stage and during discussions of subsequent amendments.

Just as in the other former union republics of the Soviet Union, the dissolution of the former USSR had a minimal impact in and of itself upon civil-law relations in Kazakhstan. The Civil Code adopted on 28 December 1963 and in force as from 1 July 1964 remained fully in place, replicating in all material respects the 1961 Fundamental Principles of Civil Legislation of the USSR and Union Republics.

Kazakhstan, moreover, followed the Russian Federation in introducing into force the 1991 Fundamental Principles of Civil Legislation of the USSR and Republics (adopted 31 May 1991 and scheduled to enter into force in the USSR from 1 January 1992, but not doing so because the USSR was by then nonexistent). These 1991 Fundamental Principles were introduced into force with effect from 28 January 1993 and operated side by side with Kazakhstan market-oriented legislation on ownership, lease, enterprises, pledge, and others.

The Republic Kazakhstan adopted its Civil Code in a two-stage process. The General Part was enacted on 27 December 1994 and the Special Part on 1 July 1999; each Part entered into force respectively on 1 March 1995 and 1 July 1999.

On 6 March 1995, less than a week after the 1994 Civil Code entered into force, the Constitutional Court of the Republic Kazakhstan ruled that the elections held in 1994 for the Supreme Soviet of the Republic Kazakhstan were illegally conducted in several key respects. After reconsideration of the position at the request of the President of the Republic Kazakhstan, the Constitutional Court reaffirmed its position in a ruling and decree issued on 10 and 11 March 1995. Accordingly, the Supreme Soviet was dissolved, and with its dissolution, all of the laws and decrees which it had enacted were called into doubt.

On 23 March 1995 the President of the Republic Kazakhstan issued an Edict (translated in relevant part below) on the basis of a Law adopted 10 December 1993 granting him interim powers to adopt edicts having the force of a law pending the election of the new Supreme Soviet pursuant to the 1993 Constitution of the Republic Kazakhstan. The Civil Code and the Decree on its introduction into operation were confirmed by the said Edict as being in force.

In Kazakhstan the draftsman have followed in considerable measure the Model Civil Code developed within the Inter-Parliamentary Assembly of the Commonwealth of Independent States, but subsequent amendments to the Code have increasingly departed from that model. Family law is regulated by its own code, following the Soviet tradition; Kazakhstan is among the majority of CIS countries to incorporate private international law into the Civil Code.

The translation is from the official Russian language text.

*status juris*: 16 November 2007

# Contents

GENERAL PART

SECTION 1. GENERAL PROVISIONS

[AS AMENDED BY LAW OF 20 DECEMBER 2004, NO. 13-III]



SECTION 2. RIGHT OF OWNERSHIP AND OTHER RIGHTS TO THING



SECTION 3. LAW OF OBLIGATIONS

[AS AMENDED BY LAW OF 20 DECEMBER 2004, NO. 13-III]

SUBSECTION 1. GENERAL PROVISIONS ON OBLIGATION

SUBSECTION 2. GENERAL PROVISIONS ON CONTRACT



SPECIAL PART

SECTION 4. INDIVIDUAL TYPES OF OBLIGATIONS

[AS AMENDED BY LAW OF 20 DECEMBER 2004, NO. 13-III]

SECTION 5. LAW OF INTELLECTUAL PROPERTY



SECTION 6. INHERITANCE LAW



SECTION 7. INTERNATIONAL PRIVATE LAW

# Detailed Contents

## General Part

## Section 1. General Provisions

[as amended by Law of 20 December 2004, No. 13-III]

### Chapter 1. Regulation of Civil-Law Relations



### Chapter 2. Subjects of Civil Rights

### §1. Citizens of Republic Kazakhstan and Other Natural Persons

§2. Juridical Persons

§3. Participation of State and Administrative-Territorial Entity in Relations Regulated by Civil Legislation

Chapter 3. Objects of Civil Rights

§1. General Provisions



§2. Securities



§3. Personal Nonproperty Rights

Chapter 4. Transactions



Chapter 5. Representation and Power of Attorney



Chapter 6. Calculation of Periods



Chapter 7. Limitations

Chapter 14. Termination of Right of Ownership
and Other Rights to Thing



Chapter 15. Defense of Right of Ownership
and Other Rights to Thing



Section 3. Law of Obligations
[as amended by Law of 20 December 2004, No. 13-III]
Subsection 1. General Provisions on Obligation
Chapter 16. Concept of and Grounds of Arising of Obligation



Chapter 17. Performance of Obligation

Chapter 18. Securing Performance of Obligation

§1. General Provisions



§2. Penalty



§3. Pledge

§4. Guarantee and Suretyship



§5. Deposit



§6. Withholding
[added by Law of 12 January 2007, No. 225-III]



Chapter 19. Change of Persons in Obligation

Chapter 20. Responsibility for Violation of Obligation



Chapter 21. Termination of Obligation



Subsection 2. General Provisions on Contract

Chapter 22. Concept and Conditions of Contract

§3. Delivery



§4. Agricultural Procurement Contract



§5. Electric Power Supply



§6. Sale of Enterprise

§5. Peculiarities of Independent-Work for Scientific-Research,Experimental-Construction Design, and Technological Work



Chapter 33. Compensated Rendering of Services



Chapter 34. Carriage

Chapter 44. Trust Management of Property



Chapter 45. Integrated Entrepreneurial License (Franchising)



Chapter 46. Competition Obligations

Chapter 47. Obligations Arising as a Consequence of Causing Harm

§1. General Provisions



§2. Compensation of Harm Caused to Life and Health of Citizen

# CIVIL CODE OF THE REPUBLIC KAZAKHSTAN

[Adopted 27 December 1994 as amended by Edict of 31 August 1995; Edict of 5 October 1995, No. 2489; Edict of 27 January 1996, No. 2835; Law of 15 July 1996, No. 30-I; Law of 7 December 1996, No. 50-I; Law of 21 January 1997, No. 68-I; Law of 5 March 1997, No. 80-I; Law of 19 June 1997, No. 132-I; Law of 19 June 1997, No. 134-I; Law of 2 July 1997, No. 144-I; Law of 11 July 1997, No. 154-I; Law of 2 March 1998, No. 211-I; Law of 22 April 1998, No. 221-I; Law of 29 June 1998, No. 238-I; Law of 10 July 1998, No. 282-I; Law of 10 July 1998, No. 283-I; Law of 16 December 1998, No. 320-I; Law of 16 July 1999, No. 436-I; Law of 16 July 1999, No. 440-I; Law of 4 November 1999, No. 472-I; Law of 8 November 2000, No. 96-II; Law of 18 December 2000, No. 128-II; Law of 15 January 2001, No. 141-II; Law of 2 March 2001, No. 162-II; Law of 11 July 2001, No. 239-II; Law of 24 December 2001, No. 276-II; Law of 17 January 2002, No. 285-II; Law of 21 May 2002, No. 323-II; Law of 7 January 2003, No. 372-II; Law of 16 May 2003, No. 416-II; Law of 20 May 2003, No. 417-II; Law of 3 June 2003, No. 426-II; Law of 10 July 2003, No. 483-II; Law of 13 October 2003, No. 486-II; Law of 8 April 2004, No. 542-II; Law of 11 May 2004, No. 552-II; Law of 7 July 2004, No. 577-II; Law of 20 December 2004, No. 13-III; Law of 18 May 2005, No. 50-III; Law of 8 July 2005, No. 72-III; Law of 23 December 2005, No. 107-III; Law of 10 January 2006, No. 115-III; Law of 31 January 2006, No. 125-III; Law of 20 February 2006, No. 127-III; Law of 5 May 2006, No. 139-III; Law of 5 June 2006, No. 146-III; Law of 22 June 2006, No. 147-III; Law of 5 July 2006, No. 164-III; Law of 12 January 2007, No. 222-III; Law of 12 January 2007, No. 224-III; Law of 12 January 2007, No. 225-III; Law of 19 February 2007, No. 230-III; Law of 7 August 2007, No. 321-III.

Introduced into operation by Decree of the Supreme Soviet of the Republic Kazakhstan, 27 December 1994, No. 269-XII. By Edict of the President of the Republic Kazakhstan Having the Force of a Law "On Acts of the Supreme Soviet of the Republic Kazakhstan" of 23 March 1995 the Code was deemed to be operating and to have legal force from the day of introduction into operation]

GENERAL PART

## SECTION 1. GENERAL PROVISIONS
[AS AMENDED BY LAW OF 20 DECEMBER 2004, NO. 13-III]

### *Chapter 1. Regulation of Civil-Law Relations*

**Article 1. Relations Regulated by Civil Legislation**

1. Goods-money and other property relations based on equality of participants, and also personal nonproperty relations connected with property [relations], shall be regulated by civil legislation. Citizens, juridical persons, the State, and also administrative-territorial entities, shall be participants of relations regulated by civil legislation.

2. Personal nonproperty relations not connected with property [relations] shall be regulated by civil legislation insofar as is not provided otherwise by legislative acts or does not arise from the essence of the personal nonproperty relation.

3. Civil legislation shall apply to family and labor relations and relations relating to the use of natural resources and protection of the environment which meet the indicia specified in point 1 of the present Article in instances when these relations are not regulated respectively by family and labour legislation and legislation on the use of natural resources and protection of the environment.

4. Civil legislation shall not apply to property relations based on administrative or other power subordination by one party to the other, including to tax and other budget relations, except for instances provided for by legislative acts.

**Article 2. Basic Principles of Civil Legislation**

1. Civil legislation shall be based on recognition of the equality of the participants of the relations regulated by it, the inviolability of ownership, the freedom of contract, the inadmissibility of arbitrary interference by anyone in private matters, and the necessity for the unobstructed effectuation of civil rights, ensuring the restoration of rights violated, and the judicial defence thereof.

2. Citizens and juridical persons shall acquire and effectuate their civil rights by their own will and in their own interest. They shall be free in establishing their rights and duties on the basis of contract and in determining any conditions of a contract which are not contrary to legislation.

3. Goods, services, and money shall move and circulate freely throughout the entire territory of the Republic Kazakhstan. Limitations on the movement of goods and services shall be introduced in accordance with legislative acts if this is necessary in order to ensure safety, defence of human life and health, and the protection of nature and cultural valuables [as amended by Law of 11 July 1997, No. 154-I].

**Article 3. Civil Legislation of Republic Kazakhstan**

1. Civil legislation of the Republic Kazakhstan shall consist of the present Code, other laws of the Republic Kazakhstan, edicts of the President of the Republic Kazakhstan having the force of a law, decrees of the Parliament, decrees of the Senate and Mazhilis of the Parliament (legislative acts) adopted in accordance with it, and also edicts of the President of the President of the Republic Kazakhstan and

decrees of the Government of the Republic Kazakhstan regulating relations specified in Article 1(1) and (2) of the present Code.

2. In the event of a contradiction of norms of civil law contained in acts of legislation of the Republic Kazakhstan, except those which have been specified in Article 1(3) of the present Code, to provisions of the present Code, the provisions of the present Code shall apply. Norms of civil law contained in legislation of the Republic Kazakhstan and contrary to norms of the present Code may be applied only after the making of respective changes in the Code.

3. Relations connected with the creation, reorganization, bankruptcy, and liquidation of banks and grain-acceptance enterprises, control over banking activity and the audit verification there, control over the activity of grain-acceptance enterprises, and the licensing of individual types of banking operations and effectuation of operations with warehouse certificates of grain-acceptance enterprises shall be regulated by the present Code in the part which is not contrary to legislative acts regulating banking activity and the activity of grain-acceptance enterprises [added by Edict of the President of the Republic Kazakhstan Having the Force of a Law, No. 2447, 31 August 1995]

Relations between banks and their clients, and also relations between clients through banks, shall be regulated by civil legislation in the procedure established by point 2 of the present Article.

4. Civil relations may be regulated by customs, including customs of business turnover, unless they are contrary to civil legislation operating on the territory of the Republic Kazakhstan.

5. Ministries and other central executive agencies and local representative and executive agencies may issue acts regulating civil relations in the instances and within the limits provided for by the present Code and other acts of civil legislation.

6. The rights of citizens and juridical persons established by the present Code and other legislative acts of the Republic Kazakhstan may not be limited by acts of agencies of State administration and local representative and executive agencies. Such acts shall be invalid from the moment of their adoption and must not be applied.

7. Foreign natural and juridical persons, and also stateless persons, shall have the right to acquire the same rights and shall be obliged to fulfil the same duties as have been provided for by civil legislation for citizens and juridical persons of the Republic Kazakhstan unless provided otherwise by legislative acts.

8. If other rules have been established by an international treaty to which the Republic Kazakhstan is a participant than those which are contained in civil legislation of the Republic Kazakhstan, the rules of the said treaty shall apply. International treaties of which the Republic Kazakhstan is a participant shall apply to civil relations directly, except for instances when it follows from the international treaty that the publication of an intra-Republic act is required for the application thereof [Article 3 as amended by Laws of 2 March 1998, No. 211-I, and of 15 January 2001, No. 141-II].

### Article 4. Operation of Civil Legislation in Time

1. Acts of civil legislation shall not have retroactive force and shall apply to relations which arose after the introduction thereof into operation. The legal force of an act of civil legislation for relations which arose before the introduction thereof into operation shall be extended in instances when this is expressly provided for thereby.

2. With regard to relations which arose before the introduction into operation of an act of civil legislation, it shall apply to the rights and duties which arose after the introduction thereof into operation. Relations of parties under a contract concluded before the introduction into operation of an act of civil legislation shall be regulated in accordance with Article 383 of the present Code.

**Article 5. Application of Civil Legislation by Analogy**

1. In instances when relations provided for by Article 1(1) and (2) of the present Code have not been expressly regulated by legislation or by agreement of the parties and there are no customs applicable to them, norms of civil legislation regulating similar relations (analogy of lex) shall apply to such relations insofar as this is not contrary to the essence thereof.

2. When it is impossible to use analogy of lex in the said instances, the rights and duties of the parties shall be determined by proceeding from the general principles and sense of civil legislation and the requirements of good faith, reasonableness, and justness (analogy of jus).

**Article 6. Interpretation of Norms of Civil Legislation**

1. Norms of civil legislation must be interpreted in accordance with the literal significance of their verbal expression. If various understandings of the words used in the text of legislative norms are possible, preference shall be given to the understanding which corresponds to the provisions of the Constitution of the Republic Kazakhstan and to the basic principles of civil legislation set out in the present Article, above all in Article 2 thereof.

2. When eliciting the precise sense of a norm of civil legislation it shall be essential to take into account the historical conditions under which it was introduced into operation and its interpretation in judicial practice, unless this violates the requirements set out in point 1 of the present Article.

**Article 7. Grounds for Civil Rights and Duties to Arise**

Civil rights and duties shall arise from the grounds provided for by legislation, and also from the actions of citizens and juridical persons, which although not provided for by it but by virtue of the basic principles and sense of civil legislation give rise to civil rights and duties.

In accordance therewith civil rights and duties shall arise:

(1) from contracts and other transactions provided for by legislation, and also from transactions which, although not provided for by it, are not contrary to legislation;

(2) from administrative acts which give rise, by virtue of legislation, to civil-law consequences;

(3) from a judicial decision which has established civil rights and duties;

(4) as a result of the creation or acquisition of property on the grounds permitted by legislative acts;

(5) as a consequence of the creation of inventions, industrial designs, works of science, literature, and art and other results of intellectual activity;

(6) as a consequence of the causing of harm to another person, and likewise as a consequence of the unfounded acquisition or saving of property at the expense of another person (unfounded enrichment);

(7) as a consequence of other actions of citizens and juridical persons;

(8) as a consequence of events with which legislation connects the ensuing of civil-law consequences.

**Article 8. Effectuation of Civil Rights**

1. Citizens and juridical persons shall at their discretion dispose of the civil rights belonging to them, including the right to the defense thereof.

2. The refusal of citizens and juridical persons to effectuate rights belonging to them shall not entail the termination of these rights except for instances provided for by legislative acts.

3. The effectuation of civil rights must not violate the rights and the interested protected by legislation of other subjects of law and must not cause damage to the environment.

4. Citizens and juridical persons must act in good faith, reasonably, and justly when effectuating the rights which belong to them, complying with the requirements contained in legislation and moral principles of society, and entrepreneurs also with the rules of business ethics. This duty may not be excluded or limited by a contract. The good faith, reasonableness, and justness of actions of the participants of civil legal relations shall be presupposed.

5. The actions of citizens and juridical persons directed towards causing harm to another person, towards an abuse of a right in other forms, and also towards the effectuation of a right contrary to its purpose, shall not be permitted. In the event of the failure to comply with the requirements provided for by points 3-5 of the present Article, a court may refuse to a person the defense of a right belonging to him.

**Article 9. Defense of Civil Rights**

1. Defense of civil rights shall be effectuated by a court, arbitrazh court, or arbitration court by means of: recognition of the rights, restoration of the situation which existed before the violation of the right; the suppression of actions which violate the right or create a threat of violating it; awarding the performance of a duty in kind; recovery of losses or a penalty; deeming a transaction to be invalid; contributory compensation of moral harm; termination or change of legal relations; recognition as invalid or as not subject to application the act of a State agency of administration or local representative or executive agency which does not correspond to legislation; recovery of a fine from a State agency or official for obstructing a citizen or juridical person in the acquisition or effectuation of a right, and also by other means provided for by legislative acts.

2. Recourse for the defense of a violated right to an agency of power or administration shall not prevent recourse to a court with a suit to defend the right unless provided otherwise by legislative acts.

3. In the instances specially provided for by legislative acts the defense of civil rights may be effectuated directly by actual or legal actions of the person whose right has been violated (self-defense).

4. A person whose right has been violated may demand full compensation for losses caused to him unless provided otherwise by legislative acts or by contract.

By losses is understood expenses which have been made or must be made by the person whose right is violated, loss or damage of his property (real damage), and also revenues not received which this person would have received under ordinary conditions of turnover if his right had not been violated (lost advantage).

5. Losses caused to a citizen or juridical person as a result of the publication of the act of an agency of State power or other State agency which does not correspond to a legislation, and also actions (or failure to act) of officials of these agencies, shall be subject to compensation by the Republic Kazakhstan or respectively by the administrative-territorial entity.

6. If the ensuing of legal consequences of a violation is dependent upon the fault of the offender, his fault shall be presupposed except for instances when provided otherwise by legislative acts.

**Article 10. Defense of Rights of Entrepreneurs and Consumers**

1. Entrepreneurship – is the initiative activity of citizens and juridical persons, irrespective of the form of ownership, directed towards the receipt of net revenue by means of satisfying the demand for goods (or work, services), based on private ownership (private entrepreneurship) or on the right of economic jurisdiction of a State enterprise (State entrepreneurship). Entrepreneurial activity shall be effectuated in the name, at the risk, and under the financial responsibility of the entrepreneur [as amended by Law of the Republic Kazakhstan, 11 July 1997].

2. The State shall guarantee the freedom of entrepreneurial activity and ensure the defense and support thereof.

3. The rights of entrepreneurs effectuating activity not prohibited by legislation shall be defended by:

(1) the possibility of the effectuation of entrepreneurial activity without receiving any authorizations whatever except for the types of activity being licensed;

(2) the maximally simple registration procedure without prior arrangement of all types of entrepreneurship in all spheres of the economy in one registering agency;

(3) the limitation by legislative acts of verifications of entrepreneurial activity being effectuated by State agencies;

(4) the compulsory termination of entrepreneurial activity only by decision of a court rendered on a grounds provided for by a legislative act;

(5) the establishment by legislative acts of a list of work and types of goods and services which have been prohibited for private entrepreneurship or prohibited or limited for export or import;

(6) the bringing of State agencies, officials, and also other persons and organizations, to the property responsibility established by legislation for unlawfully obstructing the activity of entrepreneurs;

($6^1$) the prohibition by executive control and supervisory agencies to enter into contractual relations with subjects of entrepreneurship on the subject of the fulfilment of duties which are the functions of these agencies;

(7) other means provided for by legislation.

4. The introduction of a licensing procedure with regard to individual types of activity shall be established for the purposes of national security, ensuring legal order, defense of the environment

or the ownership, life, and health of citizens. The licensing of individual types of activity shall be established in instances when requirements established by laws of the Republic Kazakhstan for a product, requirements for obligatory confirmation of the confirmation of individual types of products, processes, and/or State control over activity is insufficient for achieving the purposes of State administration. [point as amended by Law of 12 January 2007, No. 222-III].

5. A commercial (or entrepreneurial) secret shall be protected by a law. The procedure for determining the information constituting a commercial secret, the means of defense thereof, and also the list of information which must not comprise a commercial secret, shall be established by legislation.

6. The defense of the rights of consumers shall be ensured by the means provided for by the present Code or by other legislative acts. Every consumer shall have, in particular, the right to:

free conclusion of contracts for the acquisition of goods and the use of work and services;

proper quality and safety of goods (or work, services);

full and reliable information concerning goods (or work, services);

combining into social organizations of consumers [Articled 10 as amended by Law of 10 July 1998, No. 283-I].

**Article 11. Inadmissibility of Abuse of Freedom of Entrepreneurship**

1. Monopolistic and any other activity directed towards the limitation or elimination of legal competition, receiving unjustified privileges, and impinging upon the rights and legal interests of consumers shall not be permitted.

2. The use by entrepreneurs of civil rights for the purposes of limiting competition shall not be permitted except for instances provided for by legislative acts, including:

(1) abuse by entrepreneurs of their dominant position in the market, in particular, by means of the limitation or termination of production or withdrawal of goods from circulation or the creation of a shortage thereof or increase of prices;

(2) conclusion and performance by persons effectuating analogous entrepreneurial activity of agreements concerning prices, division of markets, elimination of other entrepreneurs, and other conditions materially limiting competition;

(3) performance of actions not in good faith directed towards impinging upon the legal interests of a person conducting analogous entrepreneurial activity and consumers (unfair competition), in particular, by means of deceiving consumers relative to the manufacture, purpose, means, and place of manufacture, quality, and other properties of the good of another entrepreneur and by means of inaccurately comparing goods in advertising and other information, copying the external design of another's good, and by other means.

Measures relating to the struggle against unfair competition shall be established by legislative acts.

## *Chapter 2. Subjects of Civil Rights*

### *§1. Citizens of Republic Kazakhstan and Other Natural Persons*

**Article 12. Concept of Natural Person**

By natural persons are understood citizens of the Republic Kazakhstan, citizens of other States, and also stateless persons. The provisions of the present Chapter shall apply to all natural persons unless established otherwise by the present Code.

**Article 13. Legal Capacity of Citizens**

1. The capacity to have civil rights and to bear duties (civil legal capacity) shall be recognized in equal measure for all citizens.

2. The legal capacity of a citizen shall arise at the moment of his birth and be terminated by death.

**Article 14. Basic Content of Legal Capacity of Citizen**

A citizen may have property by right of ownership, including foreign currency, both within the limits of the Republic Kazakhstan and beyond its boundaries; inherit and bequeath property; freely move about the territory of the Republic and select a place of residence; freely leave the limits of the Republic and return to its territory; engage in any activity not prohibited by legislative acts; create juridical persons autonomously or with other citizens and juridical persons; conclude any transactions not prohibited by legislative acts and participate in obligations; have the right to intellectual property in inventions, works of science , literature, and art, and other results of intellectual activity; to demand compensation for material and moral harm; and have other property and personal rights.

**Article 15. Name of Citizen**

1. A citizen shall acquire and effectuate rights and duties under his own name, including surname and forename, and also at his wish – patronymic.

2. Instances of the anonymous acquisition by citizens of rights and the effectuation of duties or the use of a pseudonym (fictitious name) may be provided for by legislation.

3. The forename received by a citizen at birth, and also a change of forename, shall be subject to registration in the procedure established by legislation on the registration of acts of civil status.

4. A citizen shall have the right to change his name in the procedure established by legislative acts. The change of name shall not be grounds for the termination or change of his rights and duties acquired under the previous name, anonymously, or under a pseudonym.

5. A citizen shall be obliged to take necessary measures to inform his debtors and creditors about the change of his name and shall bear the risk of the consequences caused by those persons lacking information about the change of his name.

6. A citizen who has changed name shall have the right to demand the making of respective changes in documents formalized in his previous name.

7. The acquisition of rights and duties under the name of another person shall not be permitted.

8. A citizen shall have the right to demand the prohibition of the use of his name when this has been done without his consent.

9. Harm caused to a citizen as a result of the unlawful use of his name shall be subject to compensation in accordance with the provisions of the present Code.

In the event of the distortion or of the use of the name of a citizen by means or in a form affecting his honor, dignity, and business reputation, the rules provided for by Article 143 of the present Code shall apply [Article 15 as amended by Law of 12 January 2007, No. 225-III].

**Article 16. Place of Residence and Legal Address of Citizen [as amended by Law of 12 January 2007, No. 224-III]**

1. That population centre where a citizen permanently or primarily resides shall be deemed to be the place of residence.

2. The place of residence of persons who have not attained fourteen years of age or citizens under trusteeship shall be deemed to be the place of residence of their parents, adoptive parents, or trustees.

3. A citizen shall have a legal address to be used in relations with natural and juridical persons, and also the State.

The place of his registration shall be deemed to be the legal address of a citizen.

The procedure for the registration of a citizen shall be determined by the Government of the Republic Kazakhstan [point 3 added by Law of 12 January 2007, No. 224-III].

**Article 17. Dispositive Legal Capacity of Citizens**

1. The capacity of a citizen by his own actions to acquire and effectuate civil rights, to create civil duties for himself, and to perform them (civil dispositive legal capacity) shall arise in full with the ensuing of majority, that is, upon attaining eighteen years of age.

2. When by legislative acts entry into marriage is permitted before attaining eighteen years of age, a citizen who has not attained eighteen years of age shall acquire dispositive legal capacity in full from the time of entering into marriage.

3. All citizens shall have equal dispositive legal capacity unless established otherwise by legislative acts.

**Article 18. Inadmissibility of Deprivation and Limitation of Legal Capacity and Dispositive Legal Capacity**

1. No one may be limited in legal capacity and dispositive legal capacity other than in the instances and in the procedure provided by legislative acts.

2. The failure to comply with the conditions and procedure established by legislative acts for the limitation of legal capacity and dispositive legal capacity of citizens or of their right to engage in entrepreneurial or other activity shall entail the invalidity of the act of the State or other agency establishing the respective limitation.

3. The full or partial renunciation by a citizen of legal capacity or dispositive legal capacity and other transactions directed towards a limitation of legal capacity or dispositive legal capacity shall be invalid except for instances when such transactions are permitted by legislative acts.

**Article 19. Entrepreneurial Activity of Citizens**

1. Citizens shall have the right to engage in entrepreneurial activity without the formation of a juridical person, except for instances provided for by the present Code and by other legislative acts [as amended by Law of 2 July 1997, No. 144-I].

2. The State registration of individual entrepreneurs shall be without prior arrangement and shall consist of being recorded as an individual entrepreneur.

3. The rules of the present Code which regulate the activity of juridical persons which are commercial organizations shall apply respectively to the entrepreneurial activity of citizens effectuated without the formation of juridical person unless arises otherwise from legislation or the essence of a legal relation.

4. Individual entrepreneurs who meet one of the following conditions shall be subject to obligatory State registration:

(1) use the labor of hired workers on a permanent basis;

(2) have from entrepreneurial activity aggregate yearly revenue calculated in accordance with tax legislation in an amount exceeding the amount of aggregate yearly revenue nonleviable with tax established for natural persons by legislative acts of the Republic Kazakhstan;

The activity of the enumerated individual entrepreneurs without State registration shall be prohibited except for instances provided by the Tax Code of the Republic Kazakhstan [as amended by Law of 2 July 1997, No. 144-I, and by Law of 24 December 2001, No. 276-II].

5. If an individual entrepreneur effectuates activity subject to licensing, he shall be obliged to have a license for the right to effectuate such activity. The license shall be issued in the procedure established by legislation on licensing.

The license shall be issued in the procedure established by legislation on licensing [added by Law of 24 December 2001, No. 276-II]

The Government of the Republic Kazakhstan shall have the right to establish a simplified procedure for the issuance of licenses to individual entrepreneurs [as amended by Law of 2 July 1997, No. 144-I].

**Article 20. Property Responsibility of Citizen**

1. A citizen shall be liable for his obligations with all of the property belonging to him except for property against which execution may not be levied in accordance with legislative acts.

2. A List of the property of citizens against which execution may not be levied shall be established by Code of Civil Procedure of the Republic Kazakhstan.

**Article 21. Bankruptcy of Individual Entrepreneur**

1. The insolvency of an individual entrepreneur (Article 52 of the present Code) shall be grounds for deeming him to be a bankrupt.

2. The bankruptcy of an individual entrepreneur shall be deemed in a voluntary or compulsory procedure according to the rules established for juridical persons, taking into account the peculiarities provided for by points 4 and 5 of the present Article. From the moment of deeming an individual entrepreneur to be a bankrupt, his registration as an individual entrepreneur shall lose force.

3. When applying the procedures of bankruptcy to an individual entrepreneur, his creditors with regard to obligations not connected with entrepreneurial activity also shall have the right to present their demands if the period of performance with regard to such obligations has ensued. The demands of the said creditors not declared by them in such procedure, and also demands which were not satisfied in full from the bankruptcy mass, shall retain force and may be presented for recovery after the completion of the procedures of bankruptcy to the debtor as to a natural person. The amount of such demands shall be reduced by the amount of satisfaction received in the process of bankruptcy of the debtor.

4. Court expenses shall be covered from the bankruptcy mass before the satisfaction of demands of creditors, and also expenses relating to the payment of remuneration to the bankruptcy and rehabilitation administrator, on condition of the appointment thereof. The satisfaction of the demands of creditors of an individual entrepreneur in the event of the deeming him to be a bankrupt shall be effectuated at the expense of property belonging to him in the following priority:

(1) in the first priority shall be satisfied demands relating to the recovery of alimony, and also demands relating to compensation of harm caused to life and health;

(2) in the second priority the settlement of accounts shall be made for the payment of labor and payment of contributory compensation to persons working under a labor contract, indebtedness for social deductions to the State Social Insurance Fund, payment withheld from the revenue of a person for obligatory pension contributions, and also payment of remuneration relating to author's contracts;

(3) in the third priority shall be satisfied the demands of creditors secured by the pledge of property belonging to the individual entrepreneur within the limits of the amount of security;

(4) in the fourth priority indebtedness for taxes and other obligatory payments to the budget shall be repaid;

(5) in the fifth priority the settlement of accounts shall be made with other creditors in accordance with legislative acts.

5. After completing the settlement of accounts with creditors, the debtor deemed to be a bankrupt shall be relieved from the performance of residual obligations connected with entrepreneurial activity, except demands of citizens to whom the person who has been declared to be a bankrupt bears responsibility for causing harm to life or health, and also other demands of a personal character provided for by legislative acts of the Republic Kazakhstan [as amended by Laws of the Republic Kazakhstan of 2 July 1997, No. 144-1; of 2 March 1998, No. 211-I; of 31 January 2006, No. 125-III; and of 12 January 2007, No. 225-III].

**Article 22. Dispositive Legal Capacity of Minors from Fourteen to Eighteen Years of Age**

1. Minors in age from fourteen to eighteen years shall conclude transactions with the consent of parents, adoptive parents, or guardians. The form of such consent must correspond to the form which has been established by legislation for a transaction concluded by a minor.

2. Minors in age from fourteen to eighteen years shall have the right to autonomously dispose of their earnings, stipend, and other revenues, and of objects of the right of intellectual property created by them, and also to conclude petty domestic transactions.

3. When there are sufficient grounds, a trusteeship and guardianship agency may limit or deprive a minor of the right to autonomously dispose of his earnings, stipend, other revenues, and objects of the right of intellectual property created by him.

4. Minors in age from fourteen to eighteen years shall autonomously bear responsibility for transactions concluded by them in accordance with the rules of the present Article and shall bear responsibility for harm caused by their actions according to the rules of the present Code.

**Article 22$^1$. Declaration of Minor to Fully Have Dispositive Legal Capacity (Emancipation)**

1. A minor who has attained sixteen years of age may be declared to fully have dispositive legal capacity if he works under a labor contract or with the consent of parents, adoptive parents, or guardian engages in entrepreneurial activity.

2. The declaration of a minor to fully have dispositive legal capacity (emancipation) shall be made by decision of the trusteeship and guardianship agency with the consent of both parents, adoptive parents, or guardian or in the absence of such consent by decision of a court.

3. An emancipated minor shall possess civil rights and bear duties (including under obligations which arose as a consequence of harm caused by him), except for those rights and duties for the acquisition of which an age limit has been established by legislative acts of the Republic Kazakhstan.

Parents, adoptive parents, and a guardian shall not bear responsibility for obligations of an emancipated minor [added by Law of 12 January 2007, No. 225-III].

**Article 23. Dispositive Legal Capacity of Minors Up to Fourteen Years of Age**

1. For minors who have not attained fourteen years of age transactions shall be concluded in their names by parents, adoptive parents, or trustees unless provided otherwise by legislative acts.

2. Minors in age up to fourteen years shall have the right to autonomously conclude only petty domestic transactions corresponding to their age which are performed when they are concluded.

**Article 24. Consent of Trustee and Guardianship Agencies to Conclusion of Transactions by Minor and For Minor**

Instances may be established by legislative acts when the preliminary consent of a trustee and guardianship agency is required for the conclusion of the transaction by a minor and for a minor.

**Article 25. Right of Minors to Make Deposits in Banks and Dispose of Deposits**

1. Minors shall have the right to make deposits and autonomously dispose of the deposits made by them.

2. Deposits made by anyone in the name of minors who have not attained fourteen years of age shall be disposed of by their parents or other legal representatives, but a minor who has attained fourteen years of age shall autonomously dispose of the deposits made by anyone in his name.

**Article 26. Deeming of Citizen to Lack Dispositive Legal Capacity**

1. A citizen who as a consequence of mental illness or feeble-mindedness can not understand the significance of his actions or direct them may be deemed by a court to lack dispositive legal capacity, in connection with which a trusteeship shall be established over him.

2. Transactions in the name of a citizen deemed to lack dispositive legal capacity shall be concluded by his trustee.

3. In the event of the recuperation or significant improvement in the health of a person who does not have dispositive legal capacity, a court shall deem him to have dispositive legal capacity, after which the trusteeship shall be removed.

**Article 27. Limitation of Dispositive Legal Capacity of Citizen**

1. A citizen who as a consequence of abusing alcoholic beverages or narcotic substances places his family in a grave material position may be limited in dispositive legal capacity by a court in the procedure established by the Code of Civil Procedure of the Republic Kazakhstan. A guardianship shall be established over him. He shall have the right autonomously to conclude petty domestic transactions. He may conclude other transactions, and also receive earnings, pension, and other revenues and dispose of them only with the consent of the guardian.

2. If the citizen terminates the abuse of alcoholic beverages or narcotic substances the court shall vacate the limitation of hi s dispositive legal capacity. The guardianship established over the citizen shall be vacated on the basis of the decision of a court.

**Article 28. Deeming of Citizen to be Missing**

1. A citizen may, upon the application of interested persons, be deemed by a court to be missing if within one year there is no information at his place of residence concerning him.

2. When it is impossible to establish the day of receipt of the last information concerning the absent person, the commencement of the absence of the missing person shall be considered to be the first date of the month following that in which the last information was received concerning the missing person, and when it is impossible to establish this month, the first of January of the following year.

**Article 29. Protection of Property of Missing Person**

1. A trusteeship shall be established on the basis of the decision of a court over the property of a person deemed to be missing. From this property maintenance shall be issued to persons whom the missing person was obliged to maintain, and indebtedness shall be repaid for taxes and other obligations of the missing person.

2. Upon the application of interested persons a trusteeship and guardianship agency may appoint a trustee to protect and manage property also before the expiry of one year from the day of receipt of the last information concerning the whereabouts of the missing person.

**Article 30. Vacating Decision on Deeming Person to be Missing**

In the event of the appearance or discovery of the whereabouts of a person deemed to be missing a court shall vacate the decision deeming him to be missing and concerning the establishment of a trusteeship over his property.

**Article 31. Declaration of Citizen to be Deceased**

1. A citizen may, upon the application of interested persons, be declared by a court to be deceased if there is no information at his place of residence about him in the course of three years, and if he was missing under circumstances threatening death or giving grounds to suppose he perished from an accident, within six months.

2. A military serviceman or other person who is missing in connection with military actions may be declared to be deceased not earlier than upon the expiry of two years from the day the military actions end.

3. The day of death of a person declared to be deceased shall be considered to be the day of entry into legal force of the decision of the court declaring him to be deceased. In instances of the declaration of a person to be deceased who is missing under circumstances threatening death or giving grounds to suppose he perished in an accident, the court may deem the day of death of this person to be the day of his presupposed perishing.

4. On the basis of the decision of a court declaring a person to be deceased which has entered into legal force, an entry shall be made concerning his death in the books for entries of acts of civil status. The consequences of the entry shall be the same as an entry concerning an actual death.

**Article 32. Consequences of Appearance of Person Declared to be Deceased**

1. In the event of the appearance or discovery of the whereabouts of a person declared to be deceased, the respective decision shall be vacated by the court.

2. Irrespective of the time of his appearance, a citizen may demand from any person the return of property preserved which passed to this person without compensation after the declaration of the citizen to be deceased.

3. If the property of a person declared to be deceased was alienated by his legal successor to third persons who at the moment of the appearance of the person had not paid in full the purchase price, then the right of demand of the unpaid amount shall pass to the person who has appeared.

4. Persons to whom property of a citizen declared to be deceased has passed under compensated transactions shall be obliged to return this property to him, and if they do not have the property – to compensate the value thereof, if it is proved that at the moment of acquisition of the property they knew that the citizen declared to be deceased was alive.

5. The alienator of property who knew at the moment of alienation that the person declared to be deceased was alive shall bear jointly and severally with the acquirer the duty to return or compensate the value of the property.

6. If the property of a person declared to be deceased has passed by right of inheritance to the State and was realized, then after the vacating of the decision concerning the declaration of the person to be

deceased to him shall be returned the amount derived from the realization of the property, taking into account the retail value thereof on the day of payment.

*§2. Juridical Persons*

**I. General Provisions**

**Article 33. Concept of Juridical Person**

1. A juridical person shall be deemed to be an organization which has solitary property by right of ownership, economic jurisdiction, or operative management and is liable with such property for its obligations, may in its own name acquire and effectuate property and personal nonproperty rights and duties, and be a plaintiff and defendant in court. A juridical person must have an autonomous balance sheet or estimate.

2. A juridical person shall have a seal with its own name.

**Article 34. Types and Forms of Juridical Persons**

1. A juridical person may be an organization pursuing the deriving of revenue as the basic purpose of its activity (commercial organization) or not having the deriving of revenue as such purpose and not distributing net revenue received among the participants (noncommercial organization) [as amended by Law of 11 July 1997, No. 154-I].

2. A juridical person which is a commercial organization may be created only in the form of a State enterprise, economic partnership, joint-stock society, or production cooperative.

3. A juridical person which is a noncommercial organization may be created in the form of an institution, social association, joint-stock society, consumer cooperative, social foundation, religious association, and in another form provided for by legislative acts.

A noncommercial organization may engage in entrepreneurial activity only insofar as this corresponds to its charter purposes.

$3^1$. A juridical person which is a non-commercial organization and maintained only at the expense of the State budget may be created solely in the form of a State institution [added by Law of 16 December 1998, No. 320-I].

4. Juridical persons may create associations (Article 110 of the present Code).

5. A juridical person shall operate on the basis of the present Code, the law on each form of juridical person, other legislative acts, and constitutive documents [Article 34 as amended in accordance with Laws of 11 July 1997, No. 154-I, of 2 March 1998, No. 211-I, of 10 July 1998, No. 282-I, 16 December 1998, No. 320-I, and of 12 January 2007, No. 225-III].

**Article 35. Legal Capacity of Juridical Person**

1. A juridical person may have civil rights and bear duties connected with its activity in accordance with the present Code. Commercial organizations, except for State enterprises, may have civil rights and bear civil duties necessary for the effectuation of any types of activity not prohibited by legislative acts or constitutive documents.

In instances provided for by legislative acts for juridical persons effectuating determined types of activity the possibility to engage in another activity may be excluded or limited.

A juridical person may engage in individual types of activity, a List of which shall be determined by legislative acts, only on the basis of a license.

2. The legal capacity of a juridical person shall arise at the moment of its creation and shall terminate at the moment of the completion of its liquidation. The legal capacity of a juridical person in the sphere of activity to engage in which it is necessary to receive a license shall arise from the moment of receipt of such license and shall terminate at the moment of the withdrawal thereof, expiry of the period of operation, or being deemed invalid in the procedure established by legislative acts.

3. The legal capacity of a juridical person which is a non-commercial organization and maintained only at the expense of the State budget (State institution) shall be determined by the present Code and other legislative acts of the Republic Kazakhstan [point 3 added by Law of 16 December 1998, No. 320-I; Article as amended by Law of 2 March 1998, No. 211-I].

**Article 36. Rights of Founders (or Participants) to Property of Juridical Persons Created by Them**

1. With respect to solitary property of a juridical person, the founders (or participants) thereof may have rights of obligations or rights to a thing.

2. Economic partnerships, joint-stock societies, and cooperatives shall be relegated to juridical persons to whose property the participants (or founders) thereof retain rights of obligations.

3. Organizations possessing property by right of economic jurisdiction or right of operative management shall be relegated to juridical persons to whose property the founders thereof retain the right of ownership or other right to a thing.

4. Social associations, social foundations, and religious associations shall be relegated to juridical persons to whose property the founders (or participants) thereof do not retain property rights.

5. The rights of founders (or participants) to property of juridical persons created by them of other organizational-legal forms shall be determined by legislative acts of the Republic Kazakhstan [Article as amended by Laws of 10 July 1998, No. 282-I, and of 12 January 2007, No. 225-III].

**Article 37. Organs of Juridical Person**

1. A juridical person shall acquire civil rights and assume duties through its organs operating in accordance with legislative acts and the constitutive documents.

2. [point 2 repealed by Law of 2 March 1998, No. 211-I].

2. The types, procedure for appointment of or election of organs of a juridical person, and the powers thereof shall be determined by legislation and the constitutive documents [renumbered by Law of 2 March 1998, No. 211-I].

**Article 38. Name of Juridical Person**

1. A juridical person shall have its own name enabling it to be distinguished from other juridical persons. The name of a juridical person shall include its name and an indication of the organizational-legal form. It may include additional information provided for by legislation.

The name of a juridical person shall be specified in the constitutive documents thereof.

The use of names which are contrary to the requirements of legislation or to norms of social morality, own names of persons if they do not coincide with the names of the participants or if the participants have not received the authorization of these persons (or their heirs) for the use of the own name, shall not be permitted in the name of a juridical person [as amended by Edict of the President of the Republic Kazakhstan Having the Force of a Law of 15 July 1996, No. 30-I].

2. The name of a juridical person which is a commercial organization after registration of the juridical person shall be the firm name thereof. A juridical person shall be entered in the unified State register of juridical persons under the determined firm name.

A juridical person shall have the exclusive right of use of the firm name. A person unlawfully using another's firm name shall, at the demand of the possessor of the right to the firm name, be obliged to terminate the use of such name and to compensate losses caused.

The rights and duties of a juridical person connected with the use of the firm name shall be determined by legislation.

3. [repealed by Law of 24 December 2001, No. 276-II].

4. The use in firm names, service marks, and trademarks of juridical persons which are not State agencies of indications to official names of State agencies of the Republic Kazakhstan established by legislative acts and acts of the President and Government of the Republic Kazakhstan shall be prohibited [Article as amended by Laws of 15 July 1996, No. 30-I, of 2 March 1998, No. 211-I, and of 16 July 1999, No. 440-I].

**Article 39. Location of Juridical Person**

1. The location of a juridical person shall be deemed to be the location of its permanently operating organ.

2. The location of a juridical person shall be specified in its constitutive documents with an entry of the full postal address.

3. In relations with third persons a juridical person shall not have the right to refer to the failure of its actual address to conform to the address entered in the unified State register of juridical persons. In so doing a third person shall have the right to send to the juridical person postal and other correspondence both to the address entered in the State register and to the actual address [point 3 added by Law of 2 March 1998, No. 211-I]

**Article 40. Founders of Juridical Person**

1. A juridical person may be founded by one or several founders.

2. The founders of a juridical person may be the owners of the property or agencies or persons empowered by them, and in instances specially provided for by legislative acts – other juridical persons. In so doing juridical persons which possess property by right of economic jurisdiction or operative management may be founders of other juridical persons with the consent of the owner or agency empowered by it.

3. The founders of a juridical person may not have any preferences over other participants of a particular juridical person who are not the founders thereof, except for instances provided for by legislative acts of the Republic Kazakhstan [Article as amended by Law of 16 May 2003, No. 416-II].

**Article 41. Constitutive Documents of Juridical Person**

1. A juridical person shall effectuate its activity on the basis of a charter and constitutive contract, or if the juridical person is founded by one person, a charter and decision formalized in written form concerning the founding of the juridical person (or decision of the sole founder), unless provided otherwise by the present Code and legislative acts of the Republic Kazakhstan. In the instances provided for by legislative acts of the Republic Kazakhstan, a juridical person which is a noncommercial organization may operate on the basis of a General Statute on organizations of the particular type.

A juridical person which is a subject of small entrepreneurship may effectuate its activity on the basis of a model charter whose content shall be determined by the Government of the Republic Kazakhstan [added by Law of 19 June 1997, No. 132-I].

2. The constitutive contract of a juridical person shall be concluded, and the charter confirmed, by its founders. The constitutive contract shall not be concluded if a commercial organization is founded by one person.

3. The subject and purposes of activity of a juridical person must be determined in the constitutive documents of a noncommercial organization and State enterprise.

The subject and purposes of their activity may be provided for by the constitutive documents of an economic partnership, joint-stock society, and production cooperative.

4. In a constitutive contract the parties (or founders) shall be obliged to create a juridical person and determine the procedure for joint activity relating to its creation and the conditions for the transfer to its ownership (or operative management) of their property and participation in its activity. The conditions and procedure for distribution among the founders of net revenue, the management of the activity of the juridical person, and the withdrawal of founders from the composition thereof also shall be determined by the contract, and the charter thereof shall be confirmed unless provided otherwise by the present Code or legislative acts on individual acts of juridical persons [as amended by Law of 11 July 1997, No. 154-I].

Other conditions also may be included in the constitutive contract with the consent of the founders.

$4^1$. The decision of a sole founder must contain the decision concerning the appointment of persons who will effectuate actions with regard to registration of a juridical person, conditions of the transfer in ownership (or economic jurisdiction, operative management) of property and other decisions not contrary to legislation of the Republic Kazakhstan.

The decision of a sole founder-juridical person shall be adopted by the organs thereof possessing the right to adopt such decisions in accordance with legislation of the Republic Kazakhstan and charter of the particular juridical person.

5. There shall be determined in the charter of a juridical person: its name, location, procedure for the formation and competence of the organs thereof, conditions of reorganization and termination of its activity.

If a juridical person is founded by one person, then the procedure for the formation of the property and the distribution of revenues also shall be determined in its charter. The charter also may contain other provisions which are not contrary to legislation [as amended by Edict of the President of the Republic Kazakhstan Having the Force of a Law, 15 July 1996, No. 30-1].

6. In the event of contradictions between the constitutive contract and charter of one juridical person the conditions must be applied:

(1) of the constitutive contract if they relate to internal relations of the founders;

(2) of the charter, if the application thereof may have significance for relations of the juridical person with third persons.

7. All interested persons shall have the right to familiarize themselves with the charter of a juridical person [Article 41 as amended by Laws of 15 July 1996, No. 30-I, of 19 June 1997, No. 132-I, of 11 July 1997, No. 154-I, of 2 March 1998, No. 211-I, of 22 April 1998, No. 221-I, of 10 July 1998, No. 282-I, of 16 May 2003, No. 416-II, and of 12 January 2007, No. 225-III].

**Article 42. State Registration and Reregistration of Juridical Persons**

1. A juridical person shall be subject to State registration in justice agencies, except for instances provided for by legislative acts of the Republic Kazakhstan. The procedure for State registration shall be determined by legislation.

2. The data of State registration, including for commercial organizations the firm name, shall be incorporated in the unified State register of juridical persons.

3. A juridical person shall be considered to be created from the moment of the State registration thereof.

4. Branches and representations shall be registered in the procedure established by legislative acts. Branches and representations shall be subject to reregistration in the event of a change of name.

5. A violation of the procedure established by a law for the formation of a juridical person or the failure of its constitutive documents to conform to law shall entail the refusal of the State registration of the juridical person. A refusal of registration for reasons of inadvisability of the formation of the juridical person shall not be permitted.

The refusal of State registration, and also the evasion of such registration, may be appealed to a court.

6. A juridical person shall be subject to reregistration in instances of:

(1) a reduction of the amount of the charter capital;

(2) a change of name;

(3) a change of the composition of the participants in economic partnerships (except for economic partnerships in which the keeping of the register of participants of an economic partnership is effectuated by a professional participant of the securities market having a license for the effectuation of activity with regard to keeping the system of registers of holders of securities).

The changes made in constitutive documents with regard to the said grounds without the reregistration of a juridical person shall be invalid.

In the event of making other changes in and additions to the constitutive documents a juridical person shall notify the registering agency thereof within a month's period [Article 42 as amended by Edict of the President of the Republic Kazakhstan Having the Force of a Law of 15 July 1996, No. 30-I, Law of 11 July 1997, No. 154-I, of 2 March 1998, No. 211-I, of 10 July 1998, No. 282-I, of 16 May 2003, No. 416-II, of 8 July 2005, No. 72-III, and of 5 June 2006, No. 146-III].

**Article 43. Branches and Representations**

1. A solitary subdivision of a juridical person situated outside the location thereof and effectuating all or part of its functions, including the function of representation, shall be a branch.

2. A solitary subdivision of a juridical person situated outside the location thereof and effectuating the defence and representation of the interests of the juridical person and concluding transactions and other legal actions in its name shall be a representation, except for instances provided for by legislative acts of the Republic Kazakhstan.

3. Branches and representations shall not be juridical persons. They shall be endowed with property of the juridical person which created them and operate on the basis of Statutes confirmed by them.

4. The directors of structural subdivisions (or branches and representations) of social associations shall be elected in the procedure provided for by the charter of a social association and the statute on its branch or representation.

The directors of structural subdivisions (or branches and representations) of religious associations shall be elected or appointed in the procedure provided for by the charter of a religious association and the statute on its branch or representation.

The directors of branches and representations of other forms of juridical persons shall be appointed by the empowered organ of a juridical person and operate on the basis of its power of attorney [as amended by Edict of the President of the Republic Kazakhstan Having the Force of a Law, 15 July 1996, No. 30-I, and Law of 23 December 2005, No. 107-III].

**Article 44. Responsibility of Juridical Person**

1. Juridical persons, except special financial companies being financed by the founder of institutions, State institutions, and treasury enterprises, shall be liable for their obligations with all of the property belonging to them.

An institution shall be liable for obligations with the money at its disposition. In the event of the insufficiency thereof, responsibility for obligations of the institution shall be borne by the founder thereof.

A State institution shall be liable for its obligations with money at the disposition thereof.

In the event of the insufficiency of money at a State institution responsibility for the obligations thereof shall be borne by the Government of the Republic Kazakhstan or respective local executive agency.

A treasury enterprise shall be liable for its obligation with the money at the disposition thereof.

In the event of the insufficiency of money at a treasury enterprise the Government of the Republic Kazakhstan or respective administrative-territorial entity shall bear subsidiary responsibility for the obligations thereof. With regard to contractual obligations responsibility shall ensue in the procedure established by legislative acts on the State enterprise.

Civil-law transactions concluded by State institutions shall be subject to registration in the procedure determined by the Government of the Republic Kazakhstan.

Civil-law transactions concluded by State institutions not provided for the expenditure of budgetary means shall not be subject to registration.

Civil-law transactions of State institutions shall be subject to payment after the registration thereof.

A special financial company shall be liable for its obligations in the procedure provided for by legislation of the Republic Kazakhstan on securitization.

2. The founder (or participant) of a juridical person or owner of its property shall not be liable for its obligations, and the juridical person shall not be liable for the obligations of the founder (or participant) of the juridical person or owner of the property thereof, except for instances provided for by the present Code, other legislative acts, or the constitutive documents of the juridical person.

3. If the bankruptcy of a juridical person has been caused by the actions of its founder (or participant) or owner of the property thereof, then in the event of the insufficiency of means of the juridical person the founder (or participant) or respective owner of the property thereof shall bear subsidiary responsibility to creditors.

4. A juridical person shall bear responsibility to third persons for obligations assumed by the organ of the juridical person in excess of its powers established by constitutive documents except for instances provided for by Article 159(11) of the present Code [Article as amended by Laws of 11 July 1997, No. 154-I, of 2 March 198, No. 211-I, of 16 December 1998, No. 320-I, of 4 November 1999, No. 472-I, of 20 May 2003, No. 417-II, of 20 February 2006, No. 127-III, and of 12 January 2007, No. 225-III].

**Article 45. Reorganization of Juridical Person**

1. The reorganization of a juridical person (merger, accession, division, separation, transformation) shall be by decision of the owner of its property or agency empowered by the owner, the founders (or participants), and also by decision of the agency empowered by the constitutive documents of the juridical person, or by decision of judicial agencies in the instances provided for by legislative acts. Other forms of reorganization also may be provided for by legislation.

The reorganization of a juridical person-cumulative pension fund, insurance (or reinsurance) organization, and special financial company shall be effectuated by taking into account the peculiarities provided for by legislation on pension security, insurance activity, and securitization.

The reorganization of joint-stock societies shall be effectuated by taking into account the peculiarities established by the legislative act of the Republic Kazakhstan on joint-stock societies.

2. Reorganization may be conducted voluntarily or compulsorily.

3. Compulsory reorganization may be effectuated by decision of judicial agencies in the instances provided for by legislative acts.

If the owner of the property of a juridical person, agency empowered by them, founders, or organ of the juridical person empowered to reorganize it by its constitutive documents does not effectuate the reorganization of the juridical person within the period determined in the decision of the judicial agency, the court shall appoint an administrator of the juridical person and charge him with effectuating the reorganization of this juridical person. From the moment of appointment of the administrator to him shall pass the powers relating to managing the affairs of the juridical person. The administrator shall act in the name of the juridical person in court, draw up the separation balance sheet and transfer it for confirmation of the court together with the constitutive documents arising as a result of the reorganization of the juridical persons. The confirmation by the court of the said documents shall be the grounds for the State registration of the newly arisen juridical persons.

4. A juridical person shall be considered to be reorganized, except for instances of reorganization in the form of accession, from the moment of registration of the juridical persons which have newly arisen.

In the event of the reorganization of a juridical person by means of accession thereto of another juridical person, the first of them shall be considered to be reorganized from the moment of making an entry in the State register of juridical persons concerning the termination of the activity of the juridical person which has acceded [Article as amended by Laws of 19 June 1997, No. 134-I, of 18 December 2000, No. 128-II, of 8 July 2005, No. 72-III, of 20 February 2006, No. 127-III].

**Article 46. Legal Succession in Event of Reorganization of Juridical Persons**

1. In the event of the merger of juridical persons the rights and duties of each of them shall pass to the juridical person which newly arises in accordance with the act of transfer.

2. In the event of the accession of a juridical person to another juridical person, to the last shall pass the rights and duties of the acceding juridical person in accordance with the act of transfer.

3. In the event of the division of a juridical person its rights and duties shall pass to the juridical persons which newly arise in accordance with the division balance sheet.

4. In the event of separation from a juridical person of one or several juridical persons, to each of them shall pass the rights and duties of the reorganised juridical person in accordance with the division balance sheet.

5. In the event of the transformation of a juridical person of one type into a juridical person of another type (change of organisational-legal form), to the juridical person which arises anew shall pass the rights and duties of the reorganised juridical person in accordance with the act of transfer.

**Article 47. Act of Transfer and Division Balance Sheet**

1. The property rights and duties of a reorganized juridical person shall pass to the juridical person which newly arose; in the event of merger and accession – in accordance with the act of transfer, and in the event of division and separation – in accordance with the division balance sheet.

The act of transfer and division balance sheet must contain provisions concerning legal succession regarding all obligations of the reorganized juridical person with respect to all creditors and debtors thereof, including obligations being contested by the parties.

2. The act of transfer and division balance sheet shall be confirmed by the owner of the property of the juridical person or by the agency which adopted the decision concerning reorganization of the juridical

person and shall be submitted together with the constitutive documents for the State registration of the juridical persons which newly arose or the making of changes in the constitutive documents of existing juridical persons.

The failure to submit with the constitutive documents the act of transfer or division balance sheet respectively, and also the absence therein of provisions concerning legal succession with regard to the obligations of the reorganised juridical person, shall entail a refusal of State registration of the juridical persons which newly arose.

3. The property (or rights and duties) shall pass to the legal successor at the moment of its registration unless provided otherwise by legislative acts or by the decision concerning the reorganization.

**Article 48. Guarantees of Rights of Creditors of Juridical Person in Event of its Reorganization**

1. The owner of the property of a juridical person or agency which adopted the decision concerning the reorganization of a juridical person shall be obliged to inform in writing the creditors of the juridical person being reorganized thereof.

2. In the event of division or separation, the creditor of a juridical person being reorganized shall have the right to demand the termination of an obligation before time, the debtor with regard to which this juridical person is, and compensation of losses .

3. If the division balance sheet does not make it possible to determine the legal successor of the reorganised juridical person, the juridical persons which newly arose, and also the juridical person from the composition of which the other juridical person was separated, shall bear joint and several responsibility for the obligations of the reorganised juridical person to its creditors [Article as amended by Law of 2 March 1998, No. 211-I].

**Article 49. Grounds for Liquidation of Juridical Person**

1. By decision of the owner of its property or agency empowered by the owner, and also by decision of the organ of the juridical person empowered by the constitutive documents for this, a juridical person may be liquidated on any grounds.

The liquidation of a juridical person-cumulative pension fund, insurance (or reinsurance) organization, and special financial company shall be effectuated by taking into account the peculiarities provided for by legislation on pension security, insurance activity, and securitization.

2. By decision of a court a juridical person may be liquidated in instances of:

(1) bankruptcy;

(2) deeming the registration of a juridical person to be invalid in connection with violations of legislation permitted during the creation thereof which are of an ineradicable character;

(3) systematic effectuation of activity which is contrary to the charter purposes of the juridical person;

(4) effectuation of activity without proper authorization (or license) or activity prohibited by legislative acts, or with repeated or flagrant violation of legislation, including the failure to submit a declaration concerning corporate income tax (or aggregate yearly revenue and deductions made) or simplified declaration upon the expiry of one year after the period for submission established by

a law, the absence of the juridical person at the location or actual address, and also of the founders (or participants) and officials without which a juridical person may not function during one year;

(5) in other instances provided for by legislative acts.

3. A demand concerning liquidation of a juridical person on the grounds specified in point two of the present Article may be presented to a court by the State agency to which the right to present such demand has been granted by legislative acts, and in instances of bankruptcy, also by a creditor.

Duties relating to the effectuation of the liquidation of a juridical person may be entrusted by decision of a court concerning the liquidation of a juridical person to the owner of its property, agency empowered by the owner, or organ empowered to liquidate the juridical person by its constitutive documents, or other agency (or person) appointed by a court.

4. If the value of the property of a juridical person with respect to which a decision has been adopted in the procedure established by point 1 of the present Article concerning liquidation is insufficient in order to satisfy the demands of creditors, such juridical person may be liquidated in the procedure established by legislation on bankruptcy.

5. The liquidation of individual types of juridical persons shall be possible by decision of the respective agency empowered by the State on the grounds provided by legislative acts [Article as amended by Laws of 21 January 1997, No. 68-I; of 19 June 1997, No. 134-I; of 2 March 1998, No. 211-I; of 18 December 2000, No. 128-II; of 24 December 2001, No. 276-II; of 20 February 2006, No. 127-III; and of 12 January 2007, No. 225-III].

**Article 50. Procedure for Liquidation of Juridical Person**

1. The owner of the property of a juridical person or agency which adopted the decision concerning liquidation of the juridical person shall be obliged immediately to notify in writing the justice agency thereof effectuating the registration of juridical persons and tax agency at the place of registration.

2. The owner of the property of a juridical person or agency which adopted the decision concerning the liquidation of the juridical person shall appoint the liquidation commission and establish, in accordance with the present Code, the procedure and periods of liquidation.

From the moment of appointment of the liquidation commission to it shall pass powers relating to the management of property and affairs of the juridical person. The liquidation commission shall act in court in the name of the juridical person being liquidated.

3. The liquidation commission shall publish information concerning the liquidation of a juridical person, and also concerning the procedure and period for the declaration of claims by its creditors in official printed publications of the central justice agency. The period for the declaration of claims may not be less than two months from the moment of the publication concerning the liquidation.

The liquidation commission shall take measures to elicit creditors and receive indebtedness, and also inform creditors in writing concerning the liquidation of a juridical person.

4. After the expiry of the period for the presentation of claims by creditors, the liquidation commission shall draw up the interim liquidation balance sheet, which shall contain information concerning the composition of the property of the juridical person being liquidated, a list of claims declared by creditors, and also the results of their consideration.

The interim liquidation balance sheet shall be confirmed by the owner of the property of the juridical person or agency which adopted the decision concerning the liquidation of the juridical person.

When drawing up the interim liquidation balance sheet allotted assets within the composition of property of the juridical person being liquidated shall not be included which are security for bonds issued in accordance with legislation of the Republic Kazakhstan concerning securitization, and pledge property which is the next security under mortgage bonds: the rights of demand under contracts of a mortgage housing loan (including mortgage certificates), and also State securities of the Republic Kazakhstan in instances when the right of ownership to the said bonds arose with the holders thereof or passed to them under transactions or other grounds provided for by legislative acts of the Republic Kazakhstan. The said property and allotted assets which are security for bonds issued in accordance with legislation on the Republic Kazakhstan on securitization shall be transferred by the liquidation commission to a representative of the holders of mortgage bonds or bonds issued in accordance with legislation of the Republic Kazakhstan on securitization for settlement with creditors-holders of the said bonds in accordance with legislation of the Republic Kazakhstan on the securities market.

5. If the money which the juridical person being liquidated (except State institutions) is insufficient to satisfy the demands of creditors, the liquidation commission shall effectuate the sale of the property of the juridical person at public sales in the procedure established for the execution of judicial decisions.

6. The money shall be paid to creditors of the juridical person being liquidated by the liquidation commission in the sequence of priority established by Article 51 of the present Code in accordance with the interim liquidation balance sheet, commencing from the day of its confirmation. The peculiarities of the distribution of property of joint-stock societies shall be established by legislation on them.

7. After the completion of the settlement of accounts with creditors, the liquidation commission shall draw up the liquidation balance sheet, which shall be confirmed by the owner of the property of the juridical person or by the agency which adopted the decision concerning the liquidation of the juridical person.

8. The property remaining after the satisfaction of the demands of creditors shall be directed towards the purposes specified in the constitutive documents.

9. If the property of a treasury enterprise being liquidated is insufficient, and of an institution being liquidated, the money to satisfy the demands of creditors, the last shall have the right to bring suit in a court to satisfy the remaining part of the demands at the expense of the owner of the property of this enterprise or institution.

$9^1$. State enterprises whose property complex has been privatized shall be liquidated in the procedure established by a law of the Republic Kazakhstan on privatization.

10. The liquidation of a juridical person shall be considered to be completed and the juridical person to have terminated existence after the making of entries thereof in the State register of juridical persons [Article as amended by Laws of 15 July 1996, No. 30-I; of 11 July 1997, No. 154-I; of 2 March 1998, No. 211-I; of 10 July 1998, No. 282-I; of 3 June 2003, No. 426-II; of 10 January 2006, No. 115-III; of 20 February 2006, No. 127-III; and of 12 January 2007, No. 225-III].

**Article 51. Satisfaction of Demands of Creditors**

1. When liquidating a juridical person the demands of its creditors shall be satisfied in the following priority:

(1) in the first priority – the demands with regard to the payment of alimony withheld from earnings and/or other revenue, and also demands of citizens to whom the juridical person being liquidated bears responsibility for the causing of harm to life or health by means of capitalizing the respective time payments shall be satisfied;

(2) in second priority – accounts shall be settled with regard to the payment of labor and payment of contributory compensation to persons working under a labor contract, indebtedness for social deductions to the State Social Insurance Fund, for payment of obligatory pension contributions withheld from earnings, and also remuneration under authors' contracts, except for instances when part of the amounts of demands in accordance with a legislative act regulating questions of bankruptcy are satisfied in the fifth priority;

(3) in third priority – the demands of creditors relating to obligations secured by the pledge of property of the bankrupt being liquidated shall be satisfied within the limits of the amount of the security, except for demands of creditors-holders of mortgage bonds secured by the pledge of the rights of demand under contracts of a mortgage housing loan (inclujding the pledge of mortgage certificates), and also State securities of the Republic Kazakhstan in instances when the right of ownership to the said bonds arose with the holders thereof or passed to them under transactions or on other grounds provided for by legislative acts of the Republic Kazakhstan;

(4) in fourth priority – the indebtedness relating to taxes and other obligatory payments to the budget;

(5) in fifth priority – accounts shall be settled with other creditors in accordance with legislative acts.

2. The demands of each priority shall be satisfied after the full satisfaction of demands of the preceding priority.

3. In the event the property of a juridical person being liquidated is insufficient, it shall be distributed among the creditors of the respective priority in proportion to the amounts of demands subject to satisfaction, unless established otherwise by a law.

4. In the event of the refusal of the liquidation commission to satisfy the demands of a creditor or the evasion of the consideration thereof, a creditor shall have the right before confirmation of the liquidation balance sheet of the juridical person to bring suit against the liquidation commission in court. By decision of the court the demands of the creditor may be satisfied at the expense of the residual property of the liquidated juridical person.

5. The property of a juridical person remaining after satisfaction of the demands of the creditors shall be transferred to its owner or founders (or participants) having the rights to a thing in such property or rights of obligations with respect to the juridical person, unless provided otherwise by legislation or by the constitutive documents of the juridical person.

6. Claims of creditors not satisfied because of the insufficiency of the property of the juridical person being liquidated, and also not declared before confirmation of the liquidation balance sheet, shall be considered to be paid.

Demands of creditors not recognized by the liquidation commission, if the creditor has not brought suit in court, and demands whose satisfaction has been refused to a creditor by decision of a court, also shall be considered to be paid [Article as amended by Laws of 21 January 1997, No. 68-I; of 2 March 1998, No. 211-I; of 11 July 2001, No. 239-II; of 3 June 2003, No. 426-II; of 8 April 2004, No. 542-II; and of 12 January 2007, No. 225-III].

**Article 52. Bankruptcy**

Bankruptcy is the insolvency of a debtor which is grounds for the liquidation thereof recognized by decision of a court.

By insolvency is understood the inability of the debtor – individual entrepreneur or juridical person – to satisfy the demands of creditors with regard to monetary obligations, to settle accounts with regard to the payment of labor with persons working under a labor contract, and also to ensure obligatory payments to the budget and extrabudgetary funds [Article as amended by Laws of 21 January 1997, No. 68-I; of 29 June 1998].

**Article 53. Deeming of Bankruptcy**

1. The deeming of bankruptcy shall be possible in a voluntary or compulsory procedure.

2. The deeming of bankruptcy in a voluntary procedure shall be effectuated on the basis of the application of a debtor to a court.

3. The deeming of bankruptcy in a compulsory procedure shall be effectuated on the basis of the application of a creditor to a court, and in the instances provided for by legislative acts, also other persons [Article as amended by Law of 21 January 1997, No. 68-I; of 29 June 1998, No. 238-I].

**Article 54. Rehabilitation Procedure in Bankruptcy Cases**

Any measures not contrary to legislation and directed toward the restoration of its solvency for the purpose of averting liquidation may be applied to an insolvent debtor.

The said measures shall be realised within the framework of a rehabilitation procedure, the procedure and periods for the effectuation of which shall be determined by legislation on bankruptcy [Article as amended by Law of 21 January 1997, No. 68-I].

**Article $54^1$. External Observation**

The procedure of external observation may be introduced by a court for the purposes of:

ensuring the preservation of property of the debtor;

eliciting the indicia of deliberate and false bankruptcy;

conducting an analysis of the financial state of the debtor and actions (or failure to act) with regard to evading the performance of obligations to creditors;

control on the part of creditors over the state of financial-economic activity of the debtor and conducting of reorganization by him;

control over the conclusion of transactions for the alienation of basic means, transfer of property on pledge or lease, and also other transactions at prices significantly lower than market or without sufficient grounds whose performance may entail losses for the debtor.

The application of external observation shall be effectuated in the procedure established by legislative acts of the Republic Kazakhstan [Article added by Law of 10 January 2006, No. 115-III].

**Article 55. Consequences of Initiation of Bankruptcy Proceeding [as amended by Law of 29 June 1998, No. 238-I]**

1. From the moment of the initiation of a bankruptcy proceeding:

(1) the insolvent debtor shall be prohibited from the alienation (except for instances when authorization for alienation has been given by the meeting of creditors) or transfer of property and the payment of obligations;

(2) the periods of all debt obligations of the insolvent debtor shall be considered to have expired;

(3) the calculation of penalty and remuneration (interest) regarding all types of indebtedness of the insolvent debtor shall terminate;

(4) all legislative limitations against the levy of execution against the property of the insolvent debtor shall be lifted;

(5) disputes of a property character with the participation of an insolvent debtor being considered in a court shall terminate if the decisions adopted regarding them have not entered into legal force.

2. All demands of a property character from this moment may be filed against the debtor only within the framework of a bankruptcy proceeding [Article as amended by Laws of 11 July 1997, No. 154-I; and of 29 June 1998, No. 238-I].

**Article 56. Relieving Insolvent Debtor of Debts**

1. After the sale of property and distribution of monies received from the sale among creditors an insolvent debtor shall be relieved from the performance of remaining obligations and other demands filed for execution and taken into account when deeming a juridical person to be bankrupt.

2. An insolvent debtor shall not receive relief from obligations if he concealed or transferred for the purpose of concealment to another person part of his property within three years before the commencement of the liquidation proceeding or secreted or falsified necessary report information, including bookkeeping books, accounts, and documents [Article as amended by Laws of 2 March 198, No. 211-I; 11 July 2001, No. 239-II; and 10 January 2006, No. 115-III].

**Article 57. Termination of Activity of Juridical Person-Bankrupt**

1. The deeming of a juridical person to be bankrupt by a court shall entail the liquidation thereof.

2. The activity of a bankrupt enterprise shall be considered to be terminated from the moment of the excluding thereof fro m the State register of juridical persons.

## II. Economic Partnership

### 1. General Provisions

**Article 58. Basic Provisions on Economic Partnership**

1. A commercial organization with charter capital divided into participatory shares (or contributions) of the founders (or participants) shall be deemed to be an economic partnership. The property created at the expense of contributions of the founders (or participants), and also produced and acquired by the economic partnership in the process of its activity, shall belong to the partnership by right of ownership.

2. Economic partnerships may be created in the form of a full partnership, kommandit partnership, limited responsibility partnership, and additional responsibility partnership.

3. An economic partnership, except a full partnership and kommandit partnership, may be created by one person who becomes the sole participant thereof.

Only citizens may be participants of a full partnership and full partners in a kommandit partnership.

4. The constitutive contract and charter shall be the constitutive documents of an economic partnership.

The charter shall be the constitutive document of an economic partnership which has been founded by one person (or one participant).

5. The constitutive documents of an economic partnership (charter and constitutive contract) shall be subject to notarial certification.

6. The constitutive documents of an economic partnership must contain, besides the information specified in Article 41(4) and (5) of the present Code, conditions concerning the amount of the participatory shares of each of the participants; the amount, composition, periods, and procedure for the making of contributions by them to the charter capital of the partnership; on the responsibility of the participants for a violation of duties relating to the making of contributions to the charter capital of the partnership, and also other information provided for by legislative acts.

7. [repealed by Law of 2 March 1998, No. 211-I].

8. An economic partnership may be the founder of other economic partnerships except for instances provided for by legislative acts.

9. An economic partnership shall have the right to conclude a contract with a professional participant of the securities market having a license to effectuate activity with regard to conducting the system of registers of holders of securities to keep the register of participants of an economic partnership.

The operation of a constitutive contract shall terminate from the day of forming the register of participants of the economic partnership. An extract from the register of participants of an economic partnership shall be the document confirming the right to a participatory share in the charter capital of an economic partnership, keeping the register of participants of which is effectuated by a professional participant of the securities market having a license for the effectuation of activity with regard to conducting the system of registers of holders of securities.

In the event of the transformation of a joint-stock society into an economic partnership, the keeping of the register of participants of which will be effectuated by a professional participant of the securities market having a license for the effectuation of activity with regard to conducting the system of registers of holders of securities, a constitutive contract shall not be concluded.

Rights to a participatory share of participation in the charter capital of an economic partnership, keeping the register of participants of which is effectuated by a professional participant of the securities market having a license for the effectuation of activity with regard to conducting the system of registers of holders of securities shall arise from the moment of registration of these rights in the register of participants of the economic partnership.

The procedure for forming, conducting, and keeping the register of participants of an economic partnership shall be established by legislation of the Republic Kazakhstan [Article as amended by Laws of 11 July 1997, No. 154-I; of 2 March1998, No. 211-I; of 10 July 1998, No. 282-I; of 16 May 2003, No. 416-II; of 8 July 2005, No. 72-III; and of 12 January 2007, No. 225-III].

**Article 59. Contribution to Charter Capital of Economic Partnership. Participatory Share of Participant in Charter Capital and Property of Economic Partnership**

1. The contribution to the charter capital of an economic partnership may be money, securities, things, property rights, including rights to the results of intellectual activity, and other property (except for special financial companies created in accordance with legislation of the Republic Kazakhstan on securitization, whose charter capital is formed exclusively by money).

The contributions of founders (or participants) to the charter capital in kind or in the form of property rights shall be valued in money form by agreement of all the founders or by decision of the general meeting of all participants of the partnership. If the value of such contribution exceeds the amount equivalent to twenty thousand amounts of monthly account indicators, the valuation of which must be confirmed by an independent expert.

In the event of reregistration of an economic partnership, the monetary valuation of the contribution of its participant may be confirmed by bookkeeping documents of the partnership or by an auditor report.

The founders (or participants) of a partnership within five years from the moment of such valuation shall bear joint and several responsibility to creditors of the partnership within the limits of the amount by which the valuation of the contribution was increased.

In instances when the right of use of property is transferred as a contribution to the partnership the amount of this contribution shall be determined by the payment for use of such property calculated for the entire period specified in the constitutive documents.

The making of contributions shall not be permitted in the form of personal nonproperty rights and other nonmaterial benefits, and also by means of set-off of demands of participants against the partnership.

2. The participatory shares of all participants in the charter capital and respectively their participatory share in the value of property of the economic partnership (or participatory share in property) shall be proportionate to their contributions to the charter capital unless provided otherwise by the constitutive documents.

The participant of an economic partnership shall have the right to pledge and to sell his participatory share in the property of a partnership unless provided otherwise by legislative acts or the constitutive documents.

3. The procedure and periods for making contributions to the charter capital, and also responsibility for the failure to perform the obligations relating to the formation of the charter capital, shall be established by legislative acts and/or constitutive documents.

4. A reduction of the charter capital of an economic partnership shall be permitted after notification of all the creditors thereof. The last shall have the right in this event to demand the termination before time of the partnership or performance of respective obligations and compensation of losses to them.

A reduction of charter capital in violation of the procedure established by the present point shall be grounds for liquidation of the partnership by decision of a court upon the application of interested persons [Article as amended by Law of 15 July 1996, No. 30-I; 11 July 1997, No. 154-I; of 2 March 1998, No. 211-I; of 20 February 2006, No. 127-III; and of 5 May 2006, No. 139-III].

**Article 60. Management of Economic Partnership**

1. The general meeting of the participants thereof shall be the highest organ of an economic partnership.

In economic partnerships, except a full and kommandit partnership, founded by one person the powers of the general meeting shall belong to the sole participant thereof.

2. An executive organ (collegial and/or one-man) effectuating the current direction of its activity and accountable to the general meeting of its participants shall be created in an economic partnership. A one-man management organ may be selected not from among the participants thereof.

There may be created as collegial organs of the partnership:

(1) board (or directorate);

(2) supervisory council;

(3) other organs in instances provided for by legislative acts or by decision of the general meeting of participants of the economic partnership.

3. The competence of the organs of an economic partnership, the procedure for selecting (or appointing) them, and also the procedure for the adoption of decisions by them, shall be determined in accordance with the present Code, by legislative acts, and by the constitutive documents.

4. An economic partnership may enlist an auditing organization for the verification and confirmation of the correctness of the financial report which is not connected with property interests with the partnership or participants thereof (external audit).

An auditor verification of an economic partnership must be conducted at any time at the demand of one or several participants of the partnership at the expense of its or their means.

The procedure for conducting an auditor verification of activity of an economic partnership shall be determined by legislation and the constitutive documents of the partnership [Article as amended by Laws of 2 March 1998, No. 211-I; of 22 April 1998, No. 221-I; of 5 May 2006, No. 139-III; and of 12 January 2007, No. 225-III].

**Article 61. Rights and Duties of Participants of Economic Partnership**

1. The participants of an economic partnership shall have the right to:

(1) participate in the management of the affairs of the economic partnership in the procedure determined by the constitutive documents;

(2) receive information concerning the activity of the economic partnership and familiarize themselves with the documentation thereof in the procedure established by the constitutive documents;

(3) take part in the distribution of net profit. The conditions of constitutive documents providing for the elimination of one or several participants from participation in the distribution of net revenue shall be invalid;

(4) receive in the event of the liquidation of an economic partnership the part of its property corresponding to the participatory share thereof in the property of the partnership remaining after the settlement of accounts with creditors or the value there of;

(5) [repealed by Law of 2 March 1998, No. 211-I].

The participants of an economic partnership may also have other rights provided for by legislative acts and the constitutive documents.

2. The participants of an economic partnership shall be obliged to:

(1) comply with the demands of the constitutive documents;

(2) make contributions in the procedure, amounts, means, and within the periods provided for by the constitutive documents;

(3) not divulge information which has been declared by the economic partnership to be a commercial secret.

The participants of an economic partnership may also bear other duties provided for by legislative acts of the Republic Kazakhstan and the constitutive documents [Article as amended by Laws of 11 July 1997, No. 154-I; and of 19 February 2007, No. 230-III].

**Article 62. Transformation of Economic Partnerships**

1. Economic partnerships of one type may be transformed into economic partnerships of another type or into joint-stock societies or production cooperatives by decision of the general meeting of participants in the instances and in the procedure established by legislative acts.

2. In the event of the transformation of a full or kommandit partnership into a joint-stock society, limited responsibility partnership, or additional responsibility partnership, each full partner who has become a participant of a joint-stock society or limited or additional responsibility partnership shall for two years bear subsidiary responsibility with all of its property for obligations which passed to the joint-stock society or limited or additional responsibility partnership from the full or kommandit partnership. The alienation by a former full partner of stocks (or participatory shares) belonging to him shall not relieve it from such responsibility [Article as amended by Laws of 15 July 1996, No. 30-I; of 16 July 1999, No. 436-I].

## 2. Full Partnership

### Article 63. Basic Provisions on Full Partnership

1. A partnership whose participants bear, in the event of the insufficiency of property of the full partnership, joint and several responsibility for its obligations with all of the property belonging to them shall be deemed a full [partnership].

2. A citizen may be a participant only of one full partnership.

### Article 64. Charter Capital of Full Partnership

1. The amount of the charter capital of a full partnership shall be determined by its founders, but may not be less than the minimum amount established by legislative acts [as amended by Law of 11 July 1997, No. 154-I].

2. [repealed by Law of 2 March 1998, No. 211-I].

### Article 65. Conducting Affairs of Full Partnership

1. The highest organ of a full partnership shall be the general meeting of participants. A decision regarding internal questions of the full partnership shall be adopted by the common agreement of all the participants. Instances may be provided for by the constitutive contract of the partnership when a decision shall be adopted by a majority vote of the participants. Each participant of a full partnership shall have one vote unless another procedure has been provided for by the constitutive contract for determining the number of votes of the participants thereof. It may be provided by the constitutive contract that the number of votes which participants dispose of shall be determined commensurately with their participatory share in the charter capital.

2. The management of a full partnership taking into account the provisions of point 1 of the present Article shall be effectuated by the executive organs of the full partnership. The types, procedure for formation of the management organs, and their competence shall be determined by the constitutive documents.

3. The participant of a full partnership shall not have the right without the consent of the other participants to conclude in its name and in their interests or in the interests of third persons transactions of the same kind as those which constitute the subject of activity of the partnership. In the event of a violation of this rule a partnership shall have the right at its choice to demand of such participant either compensation for losses caused to the partnership, or the transfer to thepartnership of all advantage acquired under such transactions.

4. Organs of a full partnership to which conducting the affairs of the partnership have been entrusted shall be obliged to submit to all participants at their demand complete information on its activity.

5. A participant who has acted in the general interests without having powers, in instances when his actions are not approved by all the other participants, shall have the right to demand compensation from the partnership for expenditures made by hi m on condition that if it is proved that thanks to his actions the partnership saved or respectively acquired property exceeding in value the expenses incurred by the partnership [Article as amended by Law of 11 July 1997, No. 154-I].

**Article 66. Transfer of Participatory Share (or Part of Participatory Share) of Participant of Full Partnership**

1. The transfer by a participant of his participatory share (or part of participatory share) to other participants of the full partnership or to third persons shall be possible only with the consent of all the other participants.

2. In the event of the transfer of the participatory share (or part of the participatory share) to a third person the transfer shall simultaneously occur of the passing of the entire aggregate of rights and duties which belonged to the participant who withdrew from the full partnership.

3. In the event of the death of the participant of a full partnership the legal successor (or heir) may with the consent of all the other participants join the partnership.

4. The legal successor (or heir) shall bear responsibility for the debts of the participant to the full partnership, and also for the debts of the partnership to third persons which arose during the entire time of activity of the partnership.

5. In the event of the refusal of a legal successor (or heir) to join the full partnership or the refusal of the full partnership to accept the legal successor (or heir) he shall be paid the value of the participatory share in the property of the partnership which belonged to him on the basis of legal succession as determined on the day of death of the participant.

In these instances respectively the amount of property of the partnership specified in the constitutive contract (or charter) shall be reduced within the period provided for in the constitutive contract (or charter), but not later than three months.

**Article 67. Withdrawal of Participant from Full Partnership**

1. The participant of a full partnership may at any time withdraw from the partnership, having warned the remaining participants thereof by not less than the period provided for by legislative acts or by the constitutive contract.

2. If in the event of the withdrawal of a participant the full partnership is preserved, to the withdrawing participant shall be paid the value of his participatory share in the property of the partnership in proportion to the contribution made in accordance with the balance sheet drawn up on the date of the withdrawal. At the demand of the participant and with the consent of the partnership the contribution may be returned wholly or partially in kind. To the withdrawing partner shall also be paid the portion of the net revenue due to him received by the partnership in the particular year for the period of his being in the partnership in that year [as amended by Law of 11 July 1997, No. 154-I].

The property transferred by the participant of the partnership only for use shall be returned in kind without remuneration .

**Article 68. Expulsion of Participant from Full Partnership**

1. The participants of a full partnership shall have the right to demand in a judicial procedure the expulsion of one or several participants from the partnership upon the unanimous decision of the other participants and where there are justifiable reasons for this, in particular, a flagrant violation by him (or them) of his duties or having discovered an inability to conduct affairs.

2. To a participant expelled from a full partnership shall be paid the value of the part of the property in the procedure determined by Article 67(2) of the present Code.

**Article 69. Levy of Execution Against Participatory Share of Participant in Full Partnership**

1. Levying execution against the participatory share of a participant in the property of a full partnership regarding his personal debts shall be permitted only when his other property is insufficient to cover the debts. Creditors of such a participant shall have the right to demand of the full partnership the partition of the part of the property of the partnership proportionate to the participatory share of the debtor in the charter capital for the purpose of levying execution against this property. The part of the property of the partnership subject to apportionment or the value thereof shall be determined according to the balance sheet drawn up at the moment of the creditors presenting the demand concerning the apportionment [as amended by Law of 11 July 1997, No. 154-I].

2. The levy of execution against the participatory share of a participant in the property of a full partnership shall terminate his participation in the partnership and entail the consequences provided for by Articles 70 and 71 of the present Code.

**Article 70. Responsibility of Participants for Debts of Full Partnership**

1. If in the event of the liquidation of a full partnership it turns out that the cash property is not enough to cover all of its debts, the participants thereof shall bear joint and several responsibility for the partnership in the portion which is short with all of their property against which in accordance with legislative acts execution may be levied.

The participant of a full partnership shall be liable for the debts of the partnership irrespective of whether they arose after or before his joining the partnership unless provided otherwise by legislative acts.

2. A participant who has paid debts of the full partnership in a part exceeding his participatory share in the property of the partnership shall have the right to bring a regressive demand for the respective part against the remaining participants, who shall bear participatory share responsibility to him proportionate to the amount of their participatory shares in the property of the partnership.

3. A participant who has paid debts of the full partnership at his own wish or was expelled from the partnership by decision of a court, and also the legal successor (or heir) of a deceased participant who has refused the proposal to join the partnership, shall be liable for the obligations of the partnership which arose before the moment of their withdrawal for two years from the day of confirmation of the report on the activity of the partnership for the year in which they withdrew from the partnership.

4. A participant who has withdrawn from a full partnership by way of transfer of the participatory share to another participant or to a third person, by way of levy of execution against his participatory share in the property of the partnership by a creditor(s), and also the legal successor (or heir) of a deceased participant who was refused admission to the partnership by the other participants, shall not be liable for the obligations of the partnership.

5. After the termination of a full partnership, the participants shall bear responsibility for obligations of the partnership which arose before the moment of its termination for two years from the date of termination of the partnership.

6. Agreements of the participants changing the procedure for their responsibility for obligations of the full partnership provided for by the present Article shall be invalid [Article as amended by Law of 2 March 1998, No. 211-I].

**Article 71. Liquidation of Full Partnership**

1. A full partnership, in addition to the grounds specified in Article 49 of the present Code, shall also be liquidated when a sole participant remains in the partnership unless he within six months transforms the partnership or does not accept new participants.

2. In instances of the withdrawal or death of any of the participants of a full partnership, deeming one of them to be missing, to lack dispositive legal capacity, or to have limited dispositive legal capacity, or to be bankrupt or of the levy of execution by creditors of one of the participants against the property corresponding to his participatory share in the charter capital, the partnership may continue its activity if this has been provided for by the constitutive documents of the partnership or agreement of the remaining participants [as amended by Law of 11 July 1997, No. 154-I].

3. If one of the participants withdrew from the partnership on the grounds specified in point 2 of the present Article, the participatory shares of the remaining participants in the charter capital of the partnership shall increase proportionately to their contributions unless provided otherwise by the constitutive documents [as amended by Law of 11 July 1997, No. 154-I].

**3. Kommandit Partnership**

**Article 72. Basic Provisions on Kommandit Partnership**

1. A partnership which includes together with one or more participants bearing additional responsibility for the obligations of the partnership with all of their property (full partners) also one or more participants whose responsibility is limited by the amount of the contribution made by them to the property of the full partnership (contributors) and who do not take part in the effectuation of entrepreneurial activity by the partnership shall be deemed to be a kommandit [partnership].

2. The legal status of the full partners participating in the kommandit partnership and their responsibility for the obligations of the partnership shall be determined by the rules on participants of the full partnership.

3. A citizen may be a full partner only in one kommandit partnership.

A full partner in a kommandit partnership may not be a participant of a full partnership.

4. The rules of the present Code on the full partnership shall apply to the kommandit partnership insofar as this is not contrary to the provisions of the present Code on kommandit partnerships [Article as amended by Law of 2 March 1998, No. 211-I].

**Article 73. Contributor of Kommandit Partnership**

1. The contributor of a kommandit partnership shall be obliged to make the initial contribution and additional fees (or contributions) in the amount, by the means, and in the procedure provided for by the constitutive documents.

2. The contributor of a kommandit partnership shall have the right to:

(1) receive part of the net revenue of the partnership due to his participatory share in the charter capital in the procedure provided for by the constitutive documents [as amended by Law of 11 July 1997, No. 154-I];

(2) familiarize himself with the financial report of the partnership, and also demand the ensuring of the possibility of verifying the correctness of the drawing up thereof;

(3) transfer his participatory share to the charter capital or part thereof to another contributor or to a third person in the procedure provided for by legislative acts and constitutive documents of the partnership. The transfer by the contributor of all his participatory share to another person shall terminate his participation in the partnership [as amended by Law of 11 July 1997, No. 154-I];

(4) withdraw from the partnership in the procedure provided for by legislative acts and constitutive documents.

Other rights of a contributor also may be provided for by the constitutive documents of a kommandit partnership.

Waiver of the rights provided for by the present Code and other legislative acts for contributors of a kommandit partnership, or the limitation thereof, including by agreement of the contributors and full partners, shall be invalid.

3. If the contributor concludes a transaction in the interests of the kommandit partnership without proper powers, then in the event of the approval of his actions by the partnership it shall be liable for the transaction to creditors in full. If approval is not received, the contributor shall be liable to a third person autonomously with all of his property against which execution may be levied according to legislation [Article as amended by Laws of 11 July 1997, No. 154-I and of 2 March 1998, No. 211-I].

**Article 74. Charter Capital of Kommandit Partnership**

1. The charter capital of a kommandit partnership shall be composed of the contributions of its participants. The charter capital may be changed in the process of economic activity. The charter capital without taking into account the contributions of the contributors shall determine the participatory share of the full partners in the property of the kommandit partnership [as amended by Law of 11 July 1997, No. 154-I].

2. The amount of the charter capital shall be determined by the full partners of a kommandit partnership and may not be less than the minimum amount established by legislative acts. [as amended by Law of11 July 1997, No. 154-I].

3. A reduction of the charter capital of a kommandit partnership shall be permitted after informing all of its creditors. The last shall have the right in this event to demand the termination before time or performance of the respective obligations and compensation to them of losses. A reduction of the charter capital in violation of the procedure established by the present Article shall be grounds for liquidation of the kommandit partnership by decision of a court upon the application of interested persons [as amended by Law of 11 July 1997, No. 154-I].

**Article 75. Management of Affairs of Kommandit Partnership**

The management of the affairs of a kommandit partnership shall be effectuated by the full partners. The procedure for management and the conducting of affairs of a kommandit partnership by its full partners shall be established by them according to the rules on the full partnership. The contributors shall not have the right to participate in the management of affairs of the kommandit partnership, nor to act in its name other than under a power of attorney. The contributors of a kommandit partnership shall not have the right to contest the actions of full partners with regard to the management of affairs of the partnership.

**Article 76. Termination of Kommandit Partnership**

1. A kommandit partnership shall terminate in the event of the withdrawal of all the contributors who participated in it. T he full partners shall have the right instead of liquidation to transform the kommandit partnership into a full partnership. The kommandit partnership shall be liquidated also on the grounds provided for liquidation of a full partnership.

2. In the event of liquidation of a kommandit partnership the contributors shall have a preferential right before the full partners to receive contributions from the property of the partnership remaining after satisfaction of the demands of its creditors. The property of the kommandit partnership remaining after this shall be distributed among the full partners and contributors proportionate to their contributions in the property of the partnership unless another procedure has been established by the constitutive documents.

## 4. Limited Responsibility Partnership

**Article 77. Basic Provisions on Limited Responsibility Partnership**

1. A limited responsibility partnership shall be deemed to be a partnership founded by one or several persons, the charter capital of which is divided into participatory shares in amounts determined by the constitutive documents; the participants of a limited responsibility partnership shall not be liable for its obligations and shall bear the risk of losses connected with the activity of the partnership within the limits of the value of the contributions made by them. Exceptions from this rule may be provided for by the present Code and legislative acts.

The participants of a limited responsibility partnership who have not made contributions in full shall bear joint and several responsibility for its obligations within the limits of the cost of the unpaid portion of the contribution of each of the participants.

2. The number of participants of a limited responsibility partnership shall not be limited.

A limited responsibility partnership may not have as a sole participant another economic partnership consisting of one person.

3. An audit verification of the activity of a limited responsibility partnership must be conducted at the demand of any of its participants.

The public accountability of a limited responsibility partnership shall not be required except for instances provided for by legislation or by the constitutive documents.

4. A limited responsibility partnership may be voluntarily reorganized or liquidated upon the unanimous decision of its participants. Other grounds for the reorganization and liquidation of a limited responsibility partnership shall be determined by the present Code and by legislative acts.

A limited responsibility partnership shall have the right to be transformed into another economic partnership, a joint-stock society, or production cooperative.

5. [repealed by Law of 2 March 1998, No. 211-I].

6. The legal status of a limited responsibility partnership and the rights and duties of its participants shall be determined by the present Code and by legislative acts [as amended by Laws of 15 July 1996, No. 30-I; of 11 July 1997, No. 154-I; of 2 March 1998, No. 211-I; of 22 April 1998, No. 221-I; of 16 July 1999, No. 436-I; of 16 May 2003, No. 416-II].

**Article 78. Charter Capital of Limited Responsibility Partnership**

1. The amount of the charter capital shall be determined by the founders (or participants) of the limited responsibility partnership and may not be less than the minimum amount established by legislative acts [as amended by Law of 11 July 1997, No. 154-I].

2. [repealed by Law of 2 March 1998, No. 211-I].

**Article 79. Management in Limited Responsibility Partnership**

1. The competence of the management organs of a partnership, and also the procedure for the adoption by them of decisions and acting in the name of the partnership, shall be determined in accordance with the present Code and the charter of the partnership.

2. There shall be relegated to the exclusive competence of the general meeting of participants of a limited responsibility partnership:

(1) a change of the charter of the partnership, including a change of the amount of its charter capital [as amended by Law of 11 July 1997, No. 154-I];

(2) the election (or appointment) of a member(s) of the executive organ and termination before time of his (or their) powers, and also the adoption of a decision concerning the transfer of the partnership or the property thereof to trust ownership and determination of the conditions of such transfer;

(3) the confirmation of financial report of the partnership and distribution of its net revenue [as amended by Law of 11 July 1997, No. 154-I];

(4) a decision concerning reorganization or liquidation of the partnership;

(5) the election and termination before time of the powers of the supervisory council and/or internal audit commission (or internal auditor) of the partnership, and also confirmation of the reports and opinions of the internal audit commission (or internal auditor) of the partnership;

(6) the confirmation of internal rules, procedures for the adoption thereof, and other documents regulating the internal activity of the partnership, except for instances provided for by legislative acts of the Republic Kazakhstan;

(7) the decision concerning participation of the partnership in other economic partnerships, and also in non-commercial associations;

(8) the appointment of the liquidation commission and confirmation of the liquidation balance sheets;

(9) the decision concerning the compulsory purchase of the participatory share from a participant of a limited responsibility partnership in accordance with Article 82 of the present Code.

The deciding of other questions also may be relegated by the charter of the partnership to the exclusive competence of the general meeting.

3. The questions relegated to the exclusive competence of the general meeting of participants of the partnership may not be transferred by it for decision of the executive organ of the partnership [as amended by Laws of 11 July 1997, No. 154-I; of 2 March 1998, No. 211-I; of 22 April 1998, No. 221-I; of 12 January 2007, No. 225-III; and of 19 February 2007, No. 230-III].

**Article 80. Transfer of Participatory Share in Charter Capital of Limited Responsibility Partnership to Another Person**

1. The participant of a limited responsibility partnership shall have the right to sell or otherwise assign its participatory share in the charter capital of the partnership or part thereof to one or several participants of the particular partnership, except for instances provided for by the present Code [as amended by Laws of 11 July 1997 and 7 August 2007, No. 154-I and No. 321-III].

2. The alienation by a participant of a limited responsibility partnership of its participatory share (or part thereof) to third persons shall be permitted unless provided otherwise by the charter of the partnership or legislative acts [as amended by Law of 7 August 2007, No. 321-III].

The participants of a limited responsibility partnership shall enjoy a preferential right of purchase of the participatory share of a participant (or part thereof),except for instances provided for by the present Code. Unless provided otherwise by the constitutive documents or agreement of the participants of the partnership, the preferential right of purchase of the participatory share (or part thereof) shall be effectuated by the participants in proportion to the amounts of their participatory shares in the charter capital of the partnership [as amended by Law of 7 August 2007, No. 321-III].

In the event of the sale of a participatory share (or part thereof) in violation of the preferential right of purchase any participant of the limited responsibility partnership shall have the right within three months from the day of sale to demand in a judicial proceeding the transfer to it of the rights and duties of the purchaser.

3. If in accordance with the constitutive documents of a limited responsibility partnership the alienation of the participatory share of a participant (or part thereof) to third persons is impossible, and the other participants of the partnership refuse to purchase it, the partnership shall be obliged to pay the participant its real value or to issue him property in kind corresponding to such value.

4. The participatory share of a limited responsibility partnership may be alienated before being paid up in full only in that portion in which it has already been paid up.

5. In the event of the acquisition of the participatory share of a participant (or part thereof) by the limited responsibility partnership itself, it shall be obliged to realize it to the other participants or to third persons within the periods and in the procedure provided for by legislative acts and by the constitutive documents of the partnership, or to reduce its charter capital. During this period the distribution of net revenue, and also voting in the highest organ, shall be without taking into account the participatory share acquired by the limited responsibility partnership [as amended by Law of 11 July 1997, No. 154-I].

6. Participatory shares in the charter capital of a limited responsibility partnership shall pass to the heirs of citizens and to the legal successors of juridical persons who were participants of the partnership unless it is provided by the constitutive documents that such transfer is permitted only with the consent

of the other participants of the partnership. Refusal of consent to the transfer of a participatory share shall entail the duty of the partnership to pay the heirs (or legal successors) of the participant the real value thereof in the procedure and on the conditions provided for by legislative acts and the constitutive documents of the partnership [as amended by Law of the Republic Kazakhstan, 11 July 1997, No. 154-I].

The peculiarities of the transfer of participatory shares to the legal successors of juridical persons may be provided by legislative acts [Article as amended by Laws of 11 July 1997, No. 154-I; and of 2 March 1998, No. 211-I].

**Article 81. Additional Contributions of Participants of Limited Responsibility Partnership**

Unless provided otherwise by the charter of a limited responsibility partnership, the general meeting of participants may adopt a decision concerning the making of additional contributions by the participants to the property of the partnership. The decision shall be adopted by a majority of three-quarters of the votes of all participants of the partnership [as amended by Law of 22 April 1998, No. 221-I].

**Article 82. Compulsory Purchase of Participatory Share from Participant of Limited Responsibility Partnership [as amended by Law of 2 March 1998, No. 211-I]**

In the event of a violation by a participant of a limited responsibility partnership of his duties to the partnership established by legislative acts or constitutive documents, the partnership in accordance with the decision of the general meeting shall have the right through a court to demand the compulsory purchase of the participatory share of such participation at a price determined by agreement of the partnership with the participant. In the event of failure to reach agreement the price of the participatory share to be compulsorily purchased shall be established by the court [as amended by Law of 2 March 1998, No. 211-I].

**Article 83. Levy of Execution on Participatory Share of Participant in Limited Responsibility Partnership**

In the event the property of the participant of a limited responsibility partnership is insufficient to cover personal debts, creditors may demand the apportionment in the established procedure of the participatory share of the participant-debtor [as amended by Law of 2 March 1998, No. 211-I].

## 5. Additional Responsibility Partnership

**Article 84. Basic Provisions on Additional Responsibility Partnership**

1. An additional responsibility partnership shall be deemed to be a partnership whose participants are liable for its obligations with their contributions to the charter capital, and in the event these amounts are not sufficient, additionally with the property belonging to them in the amount of a multiple to the contributions made by them [as amended by Law of 11 July 1997, No. 154-I].

2. The maximum amount of responsibility of the participants shall be provided for in the constitutive documents.

In the event of the bankruptcy of one of the participants his responsibility for the obligations of the partnership shall be distributed among the remaining participants in proportion to their contributions unless a different procedure for the distribution of responsibility has been provided for by the constitutive documents.

3. The rules of the present Code on the limited responsibility partnership shall apply to the additional responsibility partnership insofar as not provided otherwise by the present Article [Article as amended by Laws of 11 July 1997, No. 154-I and of 22 April 1998, No. 221-I].

### III. Joint-Stock Society

**Article 85. Concept of Joint-Stock Society**

1. A juridical person issuing stocks for the purpose of attracting means in order to effectuate its activity shall be a joint-stock society. The stockholders of a joint-stock society shall not be liable for its obligations and shall bear the risk of losses connected with the activity of the society within the limits of the value of the stocks belonging to them, except for instances provided for by legislative acts.

2. A joint-stock society shall possess property solitary from the property of its participants, bear responsibility for its obligations within the limits of its property, and not be liable for the obligations of its participants.

The stockholders of corporate cumulation pension funds shall bear joint and several responsibility relating to obligations of the said funds in the procedure and on the conditions established by legislation on pension security.

3. A joint-stock society may be created by one person or consist of one person in the event of the acquisition by one stockholder of all the stocks of the society unless provided otherwise by legislative acts.

4. The legal status of a joint-stock society and the rights and duties of stockholders shall be determined in accordance with the present Code and by legislative acts. The peculiarities of the legal status of joint-stock societies created by means of privatization of State enterprises or control packet of stocks which belongs to the State shall be determined by legislative acts of the Republic Kazakhstan.

5. In instances provided for by legislation non-commercial organizations may be crated in the organizational-legal form of a joint-stock society [Article as amended by Laws of 19 June 1997, No. 134-I; of 11 July 1997, No. 154-I; of 2 March 1998, No. 211-I; of 10 July 1998, No. 282-I; and of 13 October 2003, No. 486-II].

**Article 86. Open and Closed Joint-Stock Societies** [repealed by Law of 16 May 2003, No. 416-II]

**Article 87. Constitutive Documents of Joint-Stock Society**

1. The constitutive contract (or decision of sole founder) and charter shall be the constitutive documents of the joint-stock society.

The constitutive documents of a joint-stock society must contain information determined by the present Code and other legislative acts of the Republic Kazakhstan.

Constitutive documents of a joint-stock society shall be subject to notarial certification.

2. The operation of a constitutive contract (or decision of a sole founder) shall terminate from the day of State registration of the issue of declared stocks.

3. The procedure for confirmation of the charter of a joint-stock society shall be established by legislative acts of the Republic Kazakhstan [Article as amended by Laws of 11 July 1997,No. 154-I; of 2 March 1998, No. 211-I; of 10 July 1998, No. 282-I; and of 16 May 2003, No. 416-II].

**Article 88. Charter Capital of Joint-Stock Society**

The minimum amount and procedure for forming the charter capital of a joint-stock society, and also the procedure for an increase thereof, shall be determined by legislative acts of the Republic Kazakhstan [Article as amended by Laws of 11 July 1997, No. 154-I; of 10 July 1998, No. 282-I; of 16 May 2003, No. 416-II; of 8 July 2005, No. 72-III].

**Article 89. Increase of Charter Capital** [repealed by Law of 16 May 2003, No. 416-II]

**Article 90. Reduction of Charter Capital** [repealed by Law of 16 May 2003, No. 416-II]

**Article 91. Issuance and Distribution of Securities**

1. The types of securities to be issued by a joint-stock society shall be determined by legislative acts.

2. The procedure for State registration of the issuance of declared stocks and the placement thereof shall be determined in accordance with legislative acts of the Republic Kazakhstan.

3. A joint-stock society shall have the right to issue secured bonds and bonds without security. A joint-stock society shall have the right to issue coupon and discount bonds. The conditions and procedure for the issuance of bonds shall be determined by legislation on the securities market.

4. The form, means, and procedure for the payment of revenue on securities shall be determined by the charter of the joint-stock society or prospectuses for the issuance of securities, taking into account the peculiarities provided by legislative acts.

5. A joint-stock society shall not have the right to pay dividends on stocks of the society:

(1) in the event of a negative amount of own capital or if the amount of own capital of the society becomes negative as a result of the payment of dividends on its stocks;

(2) if it meets the indicia of inability to pay or insolvency in accordance with legislation of the Republic Kazakhstan on bankruptcy or the said indicia appear at the society as a result of the payment of dividends on its stocks.

Other grounds prohibiting the payment of dividends on stocks of a joint-stock society may be provided for also by legislative acts of the Republic Kazakhstan.

6. A joint-stock society shall have the right to issue derivative securities, options, and convertible securities in the procedure determined by legislation [Article as amended by Laws of 11 July 1997, No. 154-I; of 2 March 1998, No. 211-I; of 10 July 1998, No. 282-I; of 16 May 2003, No. 416-II; of 20 February 2006, No. 127-III; and of 19 February 2007, No. 230-III].

**Article 92. Management of Joint-Stock Society**

1. The highest management organ of a joint-stock society shall be the general meeting of its stockholders.

2. The exclusive competence of the general meeting of stockholders shall be determined by legislative acts.

3. The deciding of questions relegated to the exclusive competence of the general meeting of stockholders may not be transferred to other organs of the joint-stock society.

4. A council of directors shall be created in a joint-stock society which shall effectuate general direction of the activity of the society except for the deciding of questions relegated by the present Code, legislative acts, and the charter of the joint-stock society to the exclusive competence of the general meeting of stockholders. Questions relegated by the present Code, legislative acts, and the charter of the joint-stock society to the exclusive competence of the council of directors may not be transferred for decision to the executive organ of the joint-stock society.

In instances established by legislative acts of the Republic Kazakhstan the possibility may be provided in a joint-stock society with one stockholder by the charter of the society for the management of the joint-stock society without the creation of a council of directors.

5. The executive organ of a joint-stock society may be collegial (board) and/or one-man (director, director-general, president). It shall effectuate current direction over the activity of the joint-stock society and be accountable to the council of directors and the general meeting of stockholders.

To the competence of the executive organ of the joint-stock society shall be relegated the deciding of all questions which do not constitute the exclusive competence of other organs of the society determined by legislation or by the constitutive documents.

6. Other organs may be created in a joint-stock society in accordance with legislative acts.

7. The competence of organs of a joint-stock society, and also the procedure for the adoption of decisions by them and of acting in the name of the society, shall be determined in accordance with the present Code, legislation, and the constitutive documents.

8. [repealed by Law of 16 May 2003, No. 416-III].

**Article 93. Reorganization and Liquidation of Joint-Stock Society**

1. A joint-stock society may be reorganized or liquidated by decision of the meeting of stockholders. Other grounds and the procedure for reorganization and liquidation of a joint-stock society shall be determined by the present Code and other legislative acts.

2. A joint-stock society shall have the right to be transformed into an economic partnership or production cooperative [Article as amended by Laws of 15 July 1996, No. 30-1; and of 16 May 2003, No. 416-II].

### IV. Subsidiary and Dependent Partnerships

**Article 94. Subsidiary Organization [as amended by Law of 16 May 2003]**

1. A juridical person the predominant part of whose charter capital another juridical person (hereinafter: principal organization) has formed shall a subsidiary organization, or if in accordance with a contract (or otherwise) concluded between them the principal organization has the possibility to determine decisions to be adopted by the particular organization.

2. A subsidiary organization shall not be liable for the debts of its principal organization.

The principal organization which under a contract with the subsidiary organization has the right to give to the last instructions which are binding upon it shall be liable subsidiarily with the subsidiary organization with regard to transactions concluded by the last in performance of such instructions.

In the event of the bankruptcy of the subsidiary organization through the fault of the principal organization the last shall bear subsidiary responsibility for its debts.

3. The participants of a subsidiary organization shall have the right to demand compensation by the principal organization for losses caused through its fault to the subsidiary organization unless established otherwise by legislative acts.

4. The peculiarities of the status of subsidiary organizations not provided for by the present Article shall be determined by legislative acts [Article as amended by Laws of 11 July 1997, No. 154-I; of 10 July 1998, No. 282-I, and 16 May 2003, No. 416-II].

**Article 95. Dependent Joint-Stock Society**

1. A joint-stock society shall be deemed to be dependent if another (participating, predominant) juridical person has more than 20% of the voting stocks thereof.

2. The predominant (or participating) juridical person shall be obliged immediately to publish information concerning the acquisition by it of the respective part of the stocks of the dependent joint-stock society in the procedure provided for by legislative acts.

3. The mutual participation of joint-stock societies in the charter capital of one another may not exceed 25% of each of their charter capital unless provided otherwise by legislative acts. Joint-stock societies mutually participating in one another's charter capital may not use more than 25% of the votes at the general meeting of stockholders of one another.

4. The peculiarities of the status of dependent and joint-stock societies mutually participating in one another's charter capital which are not provided for by the present Article shall be determined by legislative acts [as amended by Laws of 11 July 1997, No. 154-I; of 10 July 1998, No. 282-I; and of 16 May 2003, No. 416-II].

### V. Production Cooperative

**Article 96. General Provisions on Production Cooperative**

1. A production cooperative shall be deemed to be a voluntary association of citizens on the basis of membership for the purpose of joint entrepreneurial activity based on their personal labor participation and the combining of property contributions by the members thereof.

2. The members of the cooperative must be not less than two.

3. The members of a production cooperative shall bear for obligations of the cooperative additional (or subsidiary) responsibility within the amounts and in the procedure provided for by the Law on the Productive Cooperative.

4. The legal status of the production cooperative and of the members thereof shall be determined in accordance with the present Code by legislative acts [Article as amended by Law of 2 March 1998, No. 211-I].

**Article 97. Charter of Production Cooperative**

The charter of a production cooperative must contain, besides the information specified in Article 41(5) of the present Code , the conditions concerning the amount of the share of the members of the cooperative; the composition and procedure for the making of contributions by members of the cooperative and their responsibility for a violation of the obligation to make a contribution; the character and procedure of labor participation of its members in the activity of the cooperative and their responsibility for a violation of the obligation relating to personal labor participation; the procedure for the distribution of net revenue of the cooperative; the composition and competence of the management organs of the cooperative and the procedure for the adoption of decisions by them, including on questions the decisions regarding which shall be adopted unanimously or by a qualified majority of votes [as amended by Law of 11 July 1997, No. 154-I; and of 2 March 1998, No. 211-I].

**Article 98. Property of Production Cooperative**

1. Property in the ownership of a production cooperative shall be divided into shares of its members in proportion to their contributions unless established otherwise by the charter of the cooperative.

2. The net revenue of a cooperative shall be distributed among its members in accordance with their labor participation unless another procedure has been provided by the charter of the cooperative.

3. In the event of the liquidation of a production cooperative or the withdrawal therefrom of a member of a cooperative, the last shall have the right to a partition of his participatory share [Article as amended by Laws of 11 July 1997, No. 154-I; and of 2 March 1998, No. 211-I].

**Article 99. Management of Production Cooperative**

1. The highest management organ of a production cooperative shall be the general meeting of its members.

A supervisory council which shall effectuate control over the activity of executive organs of the cooperative may be created in a production cooperative. The members of the supervisory council shall not have the right to act in the name of the production cooperative.

The executive organs of a cooperative shall be the board and/or its chairman. They shall effectuate current direction over the activity of the cooperative and shall be accountable to the supervisory council and the general meeting of the members of the cooperative.

Only members of the cooperative may be members of a supervisory council and board of the production cooperative. A member of a cooperative may not simultaneously be a member of the supervisory council and a member of the board.

2. The competence of the management organs of a production cooperative, and also the procedure for the adoption of decisions by them and acting in the name of the cooperative, shall be determined by legislative acts and by the constitutive documents.

3. There shall be relegated to the exclusive competence of the general meeting of members of the production cooperative:

(1) change of the charter of the cooperative;

(2) formation of the executive and internal audit organs and the supervisory council and the recall of the members thereof;

(3) admission and expulsion of members of the cooperative;

(4) confirmation of the financial reports of the cooperative and distribution of its net revenue;

(5) decision concerning the reorganisation and liquidation of the cooperative.

The deciding of other questions also may be relegated to the exclusive competence of the general meeting by legislative acts and by the constitutive documents.

Questions relegated to the exclusive competence of the general meeting or supervisory council of a cooperative may not be transferred by them for decision of the executive organs of the cooperative.

4. A member of a cooperative shall have one vote when decisions are adopted by the general meeting [Article as amended by Law of 11 July 1997, No. 154-I].

**Article 100. Termination of Membership in Production Cooperative**

1. The member of a production cooperative shall have the right at his discretion to withdraw from the cooperative. In this event his share must be paid or issued to him, and also other payments provided for by the charter effectuated.

The issuance of the share and other property to a withdrawing member of a cooperative shall be done at the end of the report period and confirmation of the financial report of the cooperative.

2. A member of a production cooperative may be expelled from a cooperative upon the decision of the general meeting in the event of the failure to perform or the improper performance of the duties placed on him by the charter of the cooperative, and also in other instances provided for by legislative acts and by the constitutive documents.

The expulsion of members of the production cooperative may be appealed to a court.

A member of the production cooperative may be expelled from it by decision of the general meeting in connection with membership in an analogous cooperative.

A member of a cooperative expelled therefrom shall have the right to receive the share and other payments provided for by the charter of the cooperative in accordance with point 1 of the present Article.

3. A member of a production cooperative shall have the right to transfer his share or part thereof to another member of the cooperative unless provided otherwise by the present Code, other legislative acts, and by the constitutive documents [as amended by Law of 7 August 2007, No. 321-III].

The transfer of a share (or part thereof) to a citizen who is not a member of the production cooperative shall be permitted only with the consent of the cooperative unless provided otherwise by legislative acts. In this event the other members of the cooperative shall enjoy the preferential right of purchase of this share (or part thereof), except for instances provided for by the present Code [as amended by Law of 7 August 2007, No. 321-III].

4. In the event of the death of a member of a production cooperative his heirs may be admitted as members of the cooperative unless provided otherwise by the charter of the cooperative. In the event of the refusal of the heir of the deceased member of the cooperative to joint the cooperative or the refusal of the cooperative to accept the heir, he shall be paid the poarticipatory share in the property proportional to the share of the deceased member of the cooperative, and also the net revenue of the

cooperative and remuneration for personal labor participation in the activity of the cooperative due to the deceased.

5. The levying of execution against the share of a member of a production cooperative shall be permitted with regard to his personal debts only if his other property is insufficient to cover such debts in the procedure provided for by legislative acts or by the constitutive documents of the cooperative [Article as amended by Law of 2 March 1998, No. 211-I].

**Article 101. Reorganisation and Liquidation of Production Cooperative**

1. A production cooperative may be voluntarily reorganised and liquidated by decision of the general meeting of its members.

Other grounds and the procedure for the reorganisation and liquidation of a production cooperative shall be determined by the present Code and by other legislative acts.

2. A production cooperative may, by unanimous decision of its members, be transformed into an economic partnership.

## VI. State Enterprise

**Article 102. Basic Provisions on State Enterprise**

1. Enterprises relegated [to the category of] State shall be:

(1) based on the right of economic jurisdiction;

(2) based on the right of operative management (treasury enterprise);

2. The property of a State enterprise shall be indivisible and may not be distributed according to contributions (or participatory shares, shares), including among the workers of the enterprise.

3. The firm name of State enterprises must contain an indication of the owner of the property thereof.

4. A State enterprise shall be created, liquidated, and reorganized by decision of the empowered State agency.

5. The director, who is appointed by the empowered State agency and accountable to it, shall be an organ of the State enter prise.

6. [repealed by Law of 2 March 1998, No. 211-I].

7. The legal status of a State enterprise shall be determined by the present Code and other legislative acts.

**Article 103. Enterprise Based on Right of Economic Jurisdiction**

1. The constitutive document of an enterprise based on the right of economic jurisdiction shall be its charter, confirmed by the founder.

2. An enterprise based on the right of economic jurisdiction shall be liable for its obligations with all of the property belonging to it.

An enterprise based on the right of economic jurisdiction shall not bear responsibility for the obligations of the State.

The State shall not be liable for the obligations of an enterprise based on the right of economic jurisdiction except for instances provided for by the present Code and other legislative acts [Article as amended by Law of 2 March 1998, No. 211-I].

**Article 104. Treasury Enterprise**

1. A treasury enterprise shall be an enterprise possessing State property by right of operative management.

2. A treasury enterprise shall be created by decision of the Government of the Republic Kazakhstan or by a local executive agency.

3. The constitutive document of a treasury enterprise shall be its charter, confirmed by the founder.

4. The firm name of an enterprise based on the right of operative management must contain an indication of that fact that the enterprise is a treasury enterprise.

5. The economic activity of a treasury enterprise shall be determined by its purposes and tasks fixed in the charter.

6. The Republic Kazakhstan or administrative-territorial entity shall bear subsidiary responsibility for the obligations of a treasury enterprise. Responsibility shall ensue under contractual obligations in the procedure established by legislative acts on the State enterprise [Article as amended by Law of 16 December 1998, No. 320-I]

## VII. Noncommercial Organizations

**Article 105. Institution**

1. An institution shall be deemed to be an organisation created and financed by the founder thereof in order to effectuate management, socio-cultural, or other functions of a noncommercial character.

2. A State institution shall be deemed to be an institution created by the State in accordance with the Constitution and laws of the Republic Kazakhstan or normative legal acts of the President of the Republic Kazakhstan, Government of the Republic Kazakhstan and akimats of the regions (or cities of republic significance, capitals), district (or city of regional significance) and maintained only at the expense of the State budget or budget (or estimate of expenses) of the National Bank of the Republic Kazakhstan if additional sources of financing have not been established by legislative acts.

3. A State institution may not create nor act as the founder (or participant) of another juridical person except for those institutions to which the right of possession, use, and disposition of State ownership has been transferred in the established procedure.

$3^1$. The acceptance by a State institution of contractual obligations exceeding the confirmed plan of financing for the respective financial year shall not be permitted.

4. The rights of an institution and State institution to property consolidated to them shall be determined in accordance with Articles 202 to 208 of the present Code [Article as amended by Laws

of 16 December 1998, No. 320-I; of 21 May 2002, No. 323-II; of 20 May 2003, No. 417-II; of 10 July 2003, No. 483-II; of 11 May 2004, No. 552-II].

**Article 106. Social Association**

1. Political parties, trade unions, and other associations of citizens created on a voluntary basis for the achievement by them of common purposes which are not contrary to legislation shall be deemed to be social associations in the Republic Kazakhstan.

The participants (or members) of social associations shall not have the rights to property transferred by them to these associations, including membership dues. They shall not be liable for the obligations of social associations in which they participate as members thereof, and the said associations shall not be liable for the obligations of their members.

2. [paragraph repealed by Law of 2 March 1998, No. 211-I].

3. [paragraph repealed by Law of 2 March 1998, No. 211-I].

4. [paragraph repealed by Law of 2 March 1998, No. 211-I].

5. [paragraph repealed by Law of 2 March 1998, No. 211-I].

6. [paragraph repealed by Law of 2 March 1998, No. 211-I].

7. The property of a social association liquidated by decision of the congress (or conference) or general meeting shall be directed to the purposes provided for by its charter.

The property of a social association liquidated by decision of a court shall be used in accordance with the present Code and other legislative acts.

8. The legal status of a social association shall be determined in accordance with the present Code and by legislative acts [Article as amended by Laws of 5 October 1995, No. 2489; and of 11 July 1997, No. 154-I].

**Article 107. Social Foundation**

1. A social foundation shall be deemed to be a noncommercial organization not having membership, founded by citizens and /or juridical persons on the basis of voluntary property contributions, and pursuing social, philanthropic, cultural, educational, and other socially-useful purposes.

2. A social foundation shall be a juridical person, represented in civil turnover by organs of the foundation, and have an autonomous balance sheet and bank account.

3. The property transferred to the social foundation by its founders shall be the ownership of the foundation.

The founders of the foundation shall not have property rights in the property of a social foundation.

4. The financial source of a social foundation shall be money and also other property of the founders, sponsorship, voluntary donations, and other legal proceeds.

[paragraph two repealed by Edict of the President of the Republic Kazakhstan Having the Force of a Law, 5 October 1995, No. 2489].

5. The procedure for the management of a social foundation and the procedure for forming its organs shall be determined by its charter confirmed by the founders.

The charter of a social foundation must, besides the information contained in Article 41(5) of the present Code, contain indications concerning the organs of the foundation, the procedure for the appointment of officials of the foundation and of relieving them, and the fate of the property of the foundation in the event of its liquidation.

6. The foundation shall be obliged annually to publish reports on the use of its property in official printed publications.

7. By decision of a court the social foundation may be liquidated in instances of:

(1) if the property of the foundation is insufficient to effectuate its purposes and the likelihood of receiving the necessary property is unrealistic;

(2) if the purposes of the foundation can not be achieved and necessary changes in the purposes of the foundation can not be made;

(3) in the event the foundation evades in its activity the purposes provided for by the charter;

(4) in other instances provided for by legislative acts or the constitutive documents.

8. The property remaining after the liquidation of a social foundation shall be directed to the purposes provided for by its charter [Article as amended by Laws of 5 October 1995, No. 2489; of 11 July 1997, No. 154-I; and of 16 July 1999, No. 436-I].

**Article 108. Consumer Cooperative**

1. A voluntary association of citizens on the basis of membership for the purpose of satisfying material and other requirements of participants effectuated by means of combining the property (or share) contributions of the members thereof shall be deemed to be a consumer cooperative.

In instances provided for by legislative acts juridical persons may join a consumer cooperative.

2. Members of a consumer cooperative shall be obliged within three months after confirmation of the annual balance sheet to cover losses which have formed by means of additional contributions. In the event of the failure to fulfil this duty, the cooperative may be liquidated in a judicial proceeding at the demand of the creditors.

Members of a consumer cooperative shall bear jointly and severally subsidiary responsibility for its obligations within the limits of the uncontributed portion of the additional contribution of each member of the cooperative.

3. The charter of a consumer cooperative must contain, besides the information specified in Article 41(5) of the present Code, conditions concerning the amount of shares of the members of the cooperative; the composition and procedure for the contributing of shares by members of the cooperative and their responsibility for a violation of the obligation relating to the contributing of the share; the composition and competence of the management organs of the cooperative and the procedure for the adoption of decisions by them, including on questions, the decisions regarding which are adopted unanimously or by a qualified majority of votes; and the procedure for the covering by members of the cooperative of losses incurred by it.

4. The revenues received by the consumer cooperative may not be distributed among its members and shall be directed towards charter purposes.

5. In the event of the liquidation of a consumer cooperative or the withdrawal of a member of the cooperative therefrom, he shall have the right to the apportionment of his participatory share in the property of the consumer cooperative in proportion to his share.

In the event of the death of a member of a consumer cooperative, his heirs shall have a priority right to be admitted as members of the cooperative unless provided otherwise by the charter of the cooperative. In the last instance the cooperative shall p ay the heirs for the participatory share in the property of the consumer cooperative in proportion to his share.

6. The legal status of a consumer cooperative, and also the rights and duties of their members, shall be determined in accordance with the present Code by legislative acts.

7. Rural consumer cooperatives may be created for the satisfaction of material and other requirements not only of their members, but also of other citizens residing in the rural locality.

The peculiarities of a rural consumer cooperative shall be determined in accordance with the present Article by special legislation.

8. The peculiarities of activity of consumer cooperatives-mutual insurance societies shall be determined by legislative acts of the Republic Kazakhstan [Article as amended by Laws of 2 March 1998, No. 211-I; of 5 July 2006, No. 164-III].

**Article 109. Religious Association**

1. A religious association shall be deemed to be a voluntary association of citizens who have combined in the procedure established by legislative acts on the basis of a community of their interests in order to satisfy spiritual requirements.

2. [repealed by Law of 2 March 1998, No. 211-I].

3. Religious associations in the Republic Kazakhstan having directing centers beyond the limits of the Republic shall be subject to registration in justice agencies. The charters (or statutes) of directing centers may be placed as the basis of the charters (or statutes) of such religious associations if they are not contrary to legislation of the Republic Kazakhstan.

4. [paragraph repealed by Law of 2 March 1998, No. 211-I].

5. [paragraph repealed by Law of 2 March 1998, No. 211-I].

6. [paragraph repealed by Law of 2 March 1998, No. 211-I].

7. [paragraph repealed by Law of 2 March 1998, No. 211-I].

8. [paragraph repealed by Law of 2 March 1998, No. 211-I].

9. A religious association shall have the right of ownership to property acquired or created by it at the expense of own means donated by citizens, organizations, or transferred by the State or acquired on other grounds not contrary to legislative acts.

10. The participants (or members) of a religious association shall not retain the rights to property transferred by them to this organization, including membership dues. They shall not be liable for

obligations of the religious association, and the religious association shall not be liable for the obligations of their members.

11. The peculiarities of the legal status of a religious association shall be determined in accordance with the present Code by legislative acts of the Republic Kazakhstan [Article as amended by Law of 5 October 1995, No. 2489; of 2 March 1998, No. 211-I].

**Article 110. Association of Individual Entrepreneurs and/or Juridical Persons in the Form of Association (or Union)**

1. Individual entrepreneurs and/or juridical persons may for the purposes of coordinating their entrepreneurial activity, and also of representing and defending common interests, create associations (or unions).

The peculiarities of the creation of associations (or unions) of juridical persons effectuating activity on the financial market and participation therein shall be established by legislative acts of the Republic Kazakhstan.

2. Social associations and other noncommercial organizations, including institutions, may voluntarily combine into associations (or unions) of these organizations.

3. An association (or union) shall be a noncommercial organization.

4. Members of an association (or union) shall retain their autonomy.

5. An association (or union) shall not be liable for the obligations of its members. Members of an association (or union) shall bear subsidiary responsibility for its obligations in the amount and in the procedure provided for by the constitutive documents of the association (or union) [Article as amended by Laws of 2 March 1998, No. 211-I; of 16 May 2003, No. 416-II; and of 12 January 2007, No. 225-III].

*§3. Participation of State and Administrative-Territorial Entity in Relations Regulated by Civil Legislation*

**Article 111. Participation of Republic Kazakhstan in Civil-Law Relations**

1. The Republic Kazakhstan shall act in relations regulated by civil legislation on equal principles with other participants of these relations.

2. Agencies of State power and administration of the Republic Kazakhstan within the framework of their competence established by legislative acts, statutes, and other acts determining the status of these agencies may in the name of the Republic Kazakhstan by their actions acquire and effectuate property and personal nonproperty rights and duties and appear in court.

In the instances and in the procedure provided for by legislation other State agencies, juridical persons, and citizens may act by special assignment of the Republic Kazakhstan in its name.

3. Civil-law disputes with the participation of the Republic Kazakhstan shall be settled by courts.

**Article 112. Participation of Administrative-Territorial Entity in Civil-Law Relations**

1. An administrative-territorial entity shall act in relations regulated by civil legislation on equal principles with other participants of these relations.

2. Local representative and executive agencies within the framework of their competence established by legislative acts, statutes, or other acts determining the status of these agencies may in the name of the administrative-territorial entity by their actions acquire and effectuate property and personal nonproperty rights and duties and appear in court.

In the instances and in the procedure provided for by legislation local State agencies, juridical persons, and citizens may act by special assignment of the administrative-territorial entity in its name.

3. In the instances determined by legislation an administrative-territorial entity may act in civil-law relations in the name of the State.

4. The provisions of the present Code concerning the participation of the State and its agencies in relations regulated by civil legislation shall extend to an administrative-territorial entity and its agencies unless it arises otherwise from legislation.

5. Civil-law disputes with the participation of an administrative-territorial entity shall be settled by courts.

**Article 113. Levy of Execution for Obligations of Republic Kazakhstan and Administrative-Territorial Entity**

1. The Republic Kazakhstan shall be liable for its obligations with the property of the State treasury, and an administrative -territorial entity shall be liable for its obligations with the property of the local treasury.

2. The Republic Kazakhstan and an administrative-territorial entity shall not be liable for the obligations of one another, and also for the obligations of citizens and juridical persons, and citizens and juridical persons shall not be liable for the obligations of the Republic Kazakhstan and an administrative-territorial entity, except for instances provided for by the present Code and legislative acts.

**Article 114. Application to State and Administrative-Territorial Entity of Norms on Juridical Persons**

Norms determining the participation of juridical persons in relations regulated by civil legislation shall, unless it follows otherwise from legislative acts, apply to the State and to administrative-territorial entities.

## *Chapter 3. Objects of Civil Rights*

### *§1. General Provisions*

**Article 115. Types of Objects of Civil Rights**

1. Property and personal nonproperty benefits and rights may be objects of civil rights.

2. To property benefits and rights (property) shall be relegated things, money, including foreign currency, securities, work, services, objectified results of creative intellectual activity, firm names,

trademarks, and other means of the individualization of manufactures, property rights, and other property.

2[1]. To money and rights (or demands) with regard to a monetary obligation (or rights of demand for the payment of money) shall apply respectively the legal regime of things or property rights (demands) unless provided otherwise by the present Code, other legislative acts of the Republic Kazakhstan, or arises from the essence of the obligation.

3. To personal nonproperty benefits and rights shall be relegated: life, health, dignity of the individual, honour, good name, business reputation, inviolability of private life, personal and family secrecy, right to name, right to authorship, right to inviolability of work, and other nonmaterial benefits and rights [Article as amended by Law of 12 January 2007, No.225-III].

**Article 116. Circulability of Objects of Civil Rights**

1. Objects of civil rights may be freely alienated or be transferred from one person to another by way of universal legal succession (inheritance, reorganization of juridical person) or by other means unless they have been withdrawn from turnover or are limited in turnover.

2. Types of things the alienation of which is not permitted (things withdrawn from turnover) must be expressly specified in legislative acts.

3. Types of things which may belong only to determined participants of turnover or whose acquisition or alienation is permitted by a special authorization (things of limited circulability) shall be determined by legislation.

4. Personal nonproperty benefits and rights shall be inalienable and nontransferable by other means, except for instances established by legislative acts.

**Article 117. Immovable and Movable Property**

1. To immovable property (or immovable things, immovable) shall be relegated: land plots, buildings, installations, perennial plantings, and other property that is firmly connected with the land, that is, objects whose movement without incommensurate damage to the purpose thereof is impossible.

2. To immovable things there also may be equated: aircraft and sea-going vessels subject to State registration, vessels of internal water navigation, vessels of "river-sea" navigation, and space objects. Other property also may be relegated by legislative acts to immovable things.

3. Property which is not relegated to immovable, including money and securities, shall be deemed to be movable property. The registration of rights to movable things shall not be required except for instances specified in legislative acts [Article as amended by Law of 2 March 1998, No. 211-I].

**Article 118. State Registration of Immovable**

1. The right of ownership and other rights to immovable things, limitations of these rights, the arising thereof, transfer, and termination shall be subject to State registration.

2. The right of ownership, right of economic jurisdiction, right of operative management, right of land use for a period exceeding a year, right of use for a period exceeding a year, pledge

of immoveable, rent for immoveable property, and right of trust management shall arise from the moment of State registration.

3. Transactions with an immovable shall be subject to State registration while complying with the rules of Chapter 4 of the present Code.

4. The agency effectuating State registration of rights to an immovable and transactions with it shall be obliged upon the petition of the rightholder to certify the registration made by means of the issuance of a document concerning the registered right or transaction or by making inscriptions on the document submitted for registration.

5. The State registration of rights to an immovable and transactions therewith shall be public. The agency effectuating registration shall be obliged to provide information concerning the registration made and the rights registered to any person.

6. A refusal of State registration of the right to an immovable or transaction therewith or the unfounded evading of registration may be appealed to a court.

7. The procedure of State registration and the grounds for refusal of registration shall be established in accordance with the present Code by the Law of the Republic Kazakhstan on the Registration of the Rights to Immovable Property and Transactions Therewith [Article as amended by Law of 2 March 1998, No. 211-I].

**Article 119. Enterprise**

1. An enterprise as an object of rights shall be deemed to be a property complex used to effectuate entrepreneurial activity.

An enterprise as a whole, as a property complex, shall be deemed to be an immovable.

2. Within an enterprise as a property complex shall be all types of property designated for its activity, including buildings, installations, equipment, tools, raw material, products, right to land plot, rights of demand, debts, and also rights to designation which individualise its activity (firm name, trademarks), and other exclusive rights, unless provided otherwise by legislative acts or contract.

3. An enterprise as a whole or part thereof may be the object of a purchase-sale, pledge, lease, and other transactions connected with the establishment, change, and termination of rights to a thing.

4. When transferring debts within the composition of an enterprise as a property complex the rights of creditors shall be guaranteed in the procedure provided by Article 48 of the present Code [point added by Law of 2 March 1998, No. 211-I]

**Article 120. Divisible and Indivisible Property**

1. Property may be divisible and indivisible.

Divisible property is property, parts of which as a result of division do not lose their purpose (or functions).

Indivisible property is that property which can not be divided without changing its economic purpose (or functions) or is not subject to division by virtue of the prescriptions of a legislative act.

2. The peculiarities of indivisible things as objects of a right shall be determined by legislation.

**Article 121. Complex Things**

1. If various kinds of thing form a single whole enabling it to be used for its purpose determined by the essence of the formation, they shall be considered to be one thing (complex thing).

2. The operation of a transaction concluded with regard to a complex thing shall extend to all of its constituent parts unless established otherwise by a contract.

**Article 122. Principal Thing and Appurtenance**

An appurtenance, that is, a thing designated to serve a principal thing and connected therewith by a common economic purpose, shall follow the fate of the principal thing unless established otherwise by legislation or by contract.

**Article 123. Fruits, Products, and Revenues**

Proceeds received as a result of the use of property (fruits, product, revenues) shall belong to the person using this property on legal grounds unless provided otherwise by legislation or by the contract concerning the use of this property.

**Article 124. Fauna**

To fauna shall apply the general rules on things insofar as not established otherwise by legislation.

**Article 125. Intellectual Property**

1. In the instances and in the procedure established by the present Code and other legislative acts an exclusive right of a citizen or juridical person shall be recognized to the results of intellectual creative activity and the means of individualisation of the juridical person equated to them or of a product of a natural or juridical person or the work or services fulfilled by them (firm name, trademark, service mark, and others).

2. The use of the results of intellectual creative activity and means of individualisation which may be the object of exclusive rights (intellectual property) may be effectuated by third persons only with the consent of the possessor of the right [Article as amended by Law of 2 March 1998, No. 211-I].

**Article 126. Employment and Commercial Secret**

1. Information comprising an employment or commercial secret when the information has real or potential commercial value by virtue of its being unknown to third persons, there is no free access to it on legal grounds, and the possessor of the information takes measures to protect its confidentiality shall be defended by civil legislation.

2. Persons who have received such information by illegal methods, and also employees who, contrary to the labor contract, or contracting parties who contrary to a civil-law contract, have divulged an employment or commercial secret, shall be obliged to compensate the damage caused.

**Article 127. Money (Currency)**

1. The tenge shall be the monetary unit of the Republic Kazakhstan.

2. The tenge shall be the legal means of payment obligatory for acceptance at face value throughout the entire territory of the Republic Kazakhstan.

3. Payments on the territory of the Republic Kazakhstan shall be effectuated in the form of cash and noncash settlement accounts.

4. The instances, procedure, and conditions for the settlement of accounts in foreign currency on the territory of the Republic Kazakhstan shall be determined by legislation of the Republic Kazakhstan.

**Article 128. Currency Valuables**

1. The types of property deemed to be currency valuables and the procedure for transactions with them shall be determined by legislative acts.

2. The right of ownership in currency valuables shall be defended in the Republic Kazakhstan on the general grounds.

*§2. Securities*

**Article 129. Securities**

1. A security shall be the aggregate of determined entries and other designations certifying property rights.

2. To securities shall be relegated stocks, bonds, and other types of securities determined in accordance with the present Code and other legislative acts of the Republic Kazakhstan.

3. Securities by form of issuance shall be subdivided into:

(1) documentary and paperless;

(2) emission and non-emission;

(3) inscribed, bearer, and order.

Documentary securities shall be securities issued in documentary form (on paper or other material carrier with the possibility of direct reading of the content of the security without the use of special technical means).

Paperless securities shall be securities issued in paperless form (or in the form of the aggregate of electronic entries).

Emission securities shall be securities possessing within the limits of one issue homogeneous indicia and requisites and placed and circulating on the basis of conditions uniform for the particular issue.

Non-emission securities shall be securities not corresponding to the indicia specified in paragraph four of the present point.

Inscribed security shall be a security confirming the affiliation of the rights certified by it to the person named thereon.

Bearer security shall be a security confirming the affiliation of the rights certified by it to the bearer of the security.

Order security shall be a security confirming the affiliation of the rights certified by it to the person named thereon, and in the event of the transfer by him of these rights in the procedure provided by Article 132(3) of the present Code, – to another person.

4. The possibility of the issuance of a determined type of securities in a particular form may be excluded by the present Code and other legislative acts of the Republic Kazakhstan [Article as amended by Law of 5 March 1997, No 80-I; and of 16 May 2003, No. 416-II].

**Article 130. Confirmation of Rights to Security**

1. The security itself shall be confirmation of the rights to a documentary security. In the event of the transfer of a documentary security for keeping to a professional participant of the securities market empowered for such keeping in accordance with a license issued to it the confirmation of the right to this security shall be an extract from the account opened by this professional participant for the purposes of the recording thereof. In the event of a divergence between the documentary security and the extract from the said account, the extract shall have priority.

2. Confirmation of the right to a paperless security shall be an extract from the account opened for the purposed of the recording thereof with a professional participant of the securities market which is empowered to register securities transactions in accordance with a license issued thereto.

3. The procedure for opening and conducting of accounts by professional participants of the securities market intended for recording securities, and also requirements for the maintenance and formalization of extracts from such accounts, shall be determined by legislation of the Republic Kazakhstan [Article as amended by Laws of 11 July 1997, No. 154-I; of 10 July 1998, No. 282-I; and of 16 May 2003, No. 416-II].

**Article 131. Requirements for Securities**

1. The types of rights which shall be certified by securities, the obligatory requisites of securities, the requirements for the form of a security, and other necessary requirements shall be determined by legislative acts or in the procedure established by them.

2. The absence of obligatory requisites of a security or the failure of the security to conform to the form established for it shall entail the invalidity thereof.

**Article 132. Transfer of Rights Relating to Security**

1. In order to transfer to another person the rights certified by a bearer security it shall be sufficient to hand over the security to this person.

2. The rights certified by an inscribed security shall be transferred in the procedure established for the assignment of a demand (cession). In accordance with Article 347 of the present Code a person who has transferred the right relating to a security shall bear responsibility for the invalidity of the respective demand, but not for its performance. When transferring rights under an inscribed security to another person, the security being transferred shall be annulled, and another security shall be issued in the name of the new possessor.

$2^1$. The peculiarities of the transfer of rights with regard to emission securities and confirmation of the rights with regard to them shall be determined by legislative acts of the Republic Kazakhstan.

3. The rights relating to an order security shall be transferred by means of making an endorsement of transfer on this security. The person transferring rights under an order security (endorser) shall bear responsibility not only for the existence of the right, but also for the effectuation thereof except for instances established by a legislative act of the Republic Kazakhstan on the mortgage of immoveable property.

An endorsement made on a security shall pass all the rights certified by the security to the person to whom or to the order of whom the rights relating to the security are transferred – the endorsee. An endorsement may be in blank (without specifying the person to whom performance must be made).

An endorsement may be limited only to a commission to effectuate the rights certified by the security without the transfer of these rights to the endorsee (endorsement of entrustment). In this event the endorsee shall act as a representative [Article as amended by Laws of 2 March 1998, No. 211-I; of 16 May 2003, No. 416-II; and of 3 June 2003, No. 426-II].

**Article 133. Performance Relating to Security**

1. The person who has issued a security and all the persons who have endorsed it shall be liable to the legal possessor thereof jointly and severally except for instances established by a legislative act of the Republic Kazakhstan on the mortgage of immoveable property. In the event of the satisfaction of the demand of the legal possessor of the security concerning the performance of the obligation certified by it by one or several persons from among those who are obliged according to the security, they shall acquire the right of reverse demand (regression) against the other persons who were previously obliged with regard to the security.

2. A refusal to perform an obligation certified by a security by referring to the absence of grounds of the obligation or to its invalidity shall not be permitted.

3. The possessor of a security who has discovered a forgery or a counterfeit security shall have the right to present to the person who transferred the security to him a demand for proper performance of the obligation certified by the security and for compensation of losses.

4. The rights relating to a security which is with an illegal possessor shall not be subject to effectuation [Law of 3 June 2003, No. 426-II].

**Article 134. Reinstatement of Security**

The rights relating to lost bearer securities and order securities shall be reinstated by a court in the procedure provided for by procedural legislation.

**Article 135. Paperless Securities** [repealed by Law of 16 May 2003, No. 416-II]

**Article 136. Bond**

1. A bond shall be a security with a period of circulation established beforehand when it is issued certifying the right to receive from the person who issued the bond in accordance with the conditions of issue remuneration with regard to it and upon the ending of the period of the circulation thereof – the par value of the bond in money or other property equivalent.

2. Bonds shall be issued only as inscribed emission securities.

3. The Government of the Republic Kazakhstan, National Bank of the Republic Kazakhstan, and commercial organizations shall have the right to issue bonds.

4. The types of bonds and procedure for the issuance thereof shall be established by legislation of the Republic Kazakhstan [Article as amended 11 July 1997, No. 154-I; of 10 July 1998, No. 282-I; of 16 May 2003, No. 416-II; of 20 December 2004, No. 13-III].

**Article 137. Cheque** [repealed by Law of 11 July 1997, No. 154-I].

**Article 138. Bill of Exchange** [repealed by Law of 11 July 1997, No. 154-I].

**Article 139. Stock**

1. A stock shall be a security issued by a joint-stock society and certifying the rights to participate in the management of the joint-stock society, receive a dividend with regard to it and part of the property of the joint-stock society in the event of its liquidation, and also other rights provided for by legislative acts of the Republic Kazakhstan.

2. Stocks shall be issued only as inscribed emission securities.

3. Types of stocks shall be established by legislative acts of the Republic Kazakhstan.

The procedure for the issuance of stocks shall be established by legislation of the Republic Kazakhstan on the securities market.

4. Noncommercial organizations created in the organizational-legal form of a joint-stock society shall not effectuate the payment of dividends on their stocks.

5. The possibility of the purchase of stocks by decision of a court from a stockholder violating by his actions or failure to act the interests of the joint-stock society may be provided for by legislative acts of the Republic Kazakhstan.

The possibility and grounds for compulsory purchase of stocks of banks and organizations effectuating individual types of banking operations, and also insurance (or reinsurance) organizations in the event they have a negative amount of own capital calculated in the procedure established by legislative acts of the Republic Kazakhstan may be provided by legislative acts of the Republic Kazakhstan [Article as amended by Laws of 11 July 1997, No. 154-I; of 2 March 1998, No. 211-I; of 10 July 1998, No. 282-I; of 21 May 2002, No. 323-II; of 16 May 2003, No. 416-II; and 8 July 2005, No. 72-III].

**Article 139$^{1}$. Bank Deposit Certificate**

A bank deposit certificate shall be an inscribed non-emission security certifying the rights of the holder thereof to receive upon the expiry of the period of circulation established for it by the conditions of the issue or upon the expiry thereof the par value and also remuneration in the amount established by the conditions of issue [added by Law of 12 January 2007, No. 225-III].

**Article 140. Bank Certificate** [repealed by Law of 11 July 1997, No. 154-I].

*§3. Personal Nonproperty Rights*

**Article 141. Defense of Personal Nonproperty Rights**

1. A person whose personal nonproperty rights have been violated shall have the right, in addition to the measures provided for by Article 9 of the present Code, to compensation for moral harm according to the rules of the present Code.

2. The defense of personal nonproperty rights shall be effectuated by a court in the procedure provided for by civil procedure legislation.

3. Personal nonproperty rights shall be subject to defense irrespective of the fault of the person who violated the right unless provided otherwise by the present Code. The person who has presented the demand concerning defense must prove the fact of the violation of his personal nonproperty right.

4. The person whose nonproperty right has been violated may at his choice demand the elimination of the consequences of the violation from the violator or at the expense of the violator autonomously perform the necessary actions or to entrust their performance to a third person [Article as amended by Law of 2 March 1998, No.211-I].

**Article 142. Personal Nonproperty Rights Connected with Property [Rights]**

In the event of the simultaneous violation of personal nonproperty and property rights the amount of compensation for property harm shall be increased by taking into account the contributory compensation due to the victim for the violation of personal nonproperty rights.

**Article 143. Defense of Honor, Dignity, and Business Reputation**

1. A citizen or juridical person shall have the right to demand through a court the refutation of information defaming his honor, dignity, or business reputation, unless the disseminator of such information proves that it corresponds to reality.

2. If information defaming the honor, dignity, or business reputation of the citizen or juridical person has been disseminated in the mass media, it must be refuted in the same mass media free of charge.

If the said information is contained in a document emanating from an organisation, the document shall be subject to replacement or recall with the obligatory communication to the addresses of the failure of the information contained in this document to conform to reality.

The procedure for refutation in other instances shall be established by a court.

3. A citizen or juridical person with respect to whom the mass media have published information impinging upon his rights or legal interests shall have the right to publication of his reply in the same mass media free of charge.

4. The demand of a citizen or juridical person concerning the publication of a refutation or a reply in the mass media shall be considered by a court if the mass media organ refused such publication or within a month has not made publication, and also in the event of its liquidation.

5. If the decision of a court has not been fulfilled, the court shall have the right to impose a fine on the violator to be recovered to the revenue of the budget. The fine shall be imposed in the procedure and in the amounts established by civil procedure legislation. The payment of the fine shall not relieve the violator from the duty to fulfil the action provided for by the court decision.

6. A citizen or juridical person with respect to whom information has been disseminated which defames his honor, dignity or business reputation shall have the right, together with the refutation of such information, to demand compensation of losses and moral harm caused by the dissemination thereof.

7. If it is impossible to establish the person who has disseminated information defaming the honor, dignity, or business reputation of a citizen or juridical person, the person with respect to whom such information has been disseminated shall have the right to apply to a court with a statement concerning recognition that the information being disseminated does not correspond to reality.

**Article 144. Right to Protection of Secrecy of Personal Life**

1. A citizen shall have the right to protect the secrecy of personal life, including secrecy of correspondence, telephone conversations, diaries, notes, memoranda, intimate life, adoption, birth, medical and lawyer's secrecy, and secrecy of bank deposits [as amended by Law of 11 July 1997, No. 154-I].

The disclosure of a secret of personal life shall be possible only in the instances established by legislative acts.

2. The publication of diaries, memoranda, notes, and other documents shall be permitted only with the consent of their author, and letters – with the consent of their author and the addressee. In the event of the death of any of them, the said documents may be published with the consent of the surviving spouse and children of the deceased.

**Article 145. Right to Own Image**

1. No one shall have the right to use the image of any person without his consent, and in the event of his death, without the consent of the heirs.

2. The publication, reproduction, and dissemination of a work of fine art (picture, photograph, cinema film, and others) in which another person is depicted shall be permitted only with the consent of the person depicted, and after his death with the consent of his children and surviving spouse. Such consent shall not be required if this has been established by legislative acts or the person depicted posed for payment.

**Article 146. Right to Inviolability of Housing**

A citizen shall have the right to inviolability of housing, that is, the right to suppress any attempts to intrude into housing without his will, except for instances provided for by legislative acts.

## *Chapter 4. Transactions*

**Article 147. Concept of Transaction**

The actions of citizens and juridical persons directed towards the establishment, change, or termination of civil rights and duties shall be deemed to be transactions.

**Article 148. Unilateral Transactions and Contracts**

1. Transactions may be unilateral and bilateral or multilateral (contracts).

2. A transaction for the conclusion of which in accordance with legislation, or by agreement of the parties, the expression of the will of one party is necessary and sufficient shall be considered to be unilateral.

3. The expression of the concordant will of two parties (bilateral transaction), or three or more parties (multilateral transaction) shall be necessary for the conclusion of a contract.

**Article 149. Legal Regulation of Unilateral Transactions**

1. A unilateral transaction shall create duties for the person who has concluded the transaction. It may create duties for other persons only in the instances established by legislative acts or by agreement with those persons.

2. The general provisions on obligations and on contracts shall apply to unilateral transactions respectively insofar as this is not contrary to legislation or to the nature and essence of the transaction.

**Article 150. Transactions Concluded Under a Condition**

1. A transaction shall be considered to be concluded under a condition subsequent if the parties have made the arising of rights and duties dependent upon a circumstance relative to which it is unknown as to whether this will ensue or not.

2. A transaction shall be considered to be concluded under a condition precedent if the parties have made the termination of rights and duties dependent upon a circumstance relative to which it is unknown whether this will ensue or not.

3. If the ensuing of the condition is obstructed by a party not in good faith for whom the ensuing of the condition is disadvantageous, the condition shall be deemed to have ensued.

If the ensuing of the condition is facilitated by a party not in good faith for whom the ensuing of the condition is advantageous, the condition shall be deemed not to have ensued.

**Article 151. Form of Transaction**

1. Transactions shall be concluded orally or in writing (simple or notarial).

2. A transaction for which the written (simple or notarial) or other determined form has not been established by legislation or agreement of the parties may be concluded orally, in particular – all transactions to be performed when they themselves are concluded. Such a transaction shall be considered to be concluded also when from the behaviour of the person his will to conclude the transaction is manifest.

3. A transaction confirmed by the issuance of a token, ticket, or other usually accepted mark shall be deemed to be concluded orally unless established otherwise by legislation.

4. Silence shall be deemed to be an expression of will to conclude a transaction in the instances provided for by legislation o r by agreement of the parties.

5. Transactions in performance of a contract concluded in writing may, by agreement of the parties, be concluded orally unless this is contrary to legislation.

**Article 152. Written Form of Transaction**

1. Transactions must be concluded in writing:

(1) which are effectuated in the process of entrepreneurial activity, except for transactions performed when they are concluded, unless otherwise specially provided for by legislation for individual types of transactions or otherwise arises from customs of business turnover;

(2) for an amount higher than one hundred account indicators, except for transactions performed when they are concluded;

(3) in other instances provided for by legislation or by agreement of the parties.

2. A transaction concluded in written form must be signed by the parties or their representatives unless arises otherwise from the customs of business turnover.

When concluding a transaction the use of facsimile copying means of a signature shall be permitted unless this is contrary to legislation or the demand of one of the participants.

3. Bilateral transactions may be concluded by means of the exchange of documents, each of which shall be signed by the party from which it emanates.

To the conclusion of a transaction in written form shall be equated, unless established otherwise by legislation or by agreement of the parties, the exchange of letters, telegrams, telephonegrams, teletypegrams, faxes, or other documents determined by the subjects and the content of their expression of will.

Additional requirements may be established by legislation or by agreement of the parties to which the form of the transaction must correspond, in particular, conclusion on the letterhead of a specified form and the affixing of a seal, and the consequences of failure to comply with these requirements shall be provided for.

4. If a citizen as a consequence of physical defect, illness, or illiteracy can not sign in his own hand, then at his request another citizen may sign the transaction. The signature of the last, unless provided otherwise by legislation, must be certified by a notary or by another official having the right to perform such a notarial action, specifying the reasons by virtue of which the person concluding the transaction could not sign it in his own hand.

5. The party who has performed a transaction concluded in written form shall have the right to demand a document from the other party confirming the performance.

The party who has performed an oral entrepreneurial transaction shall have the same right, except for transactions performed when they are concluded [Article as amended by Law of 2 March 1998, No. 211-I].

**Article 153. Consequences of Failure to Comply with Simple Written Form of Transaction**

1. The failure to comply with the simple written form of a transaction shall not entail its invalidity, but shall deprive the parties of the right in the event of a dispute to confirm the conclusion, content, or performance thereof by witness testimony.

The parties, however, shall have the right to confirm the conclusion, content, or performance of a transaction by written or other evidence, except witness testimony.

2. In instances expressly specified in legislative acts or in the agreement of parties, the failure to comply with the simple written form of a transaction shall entail its invalidity.

3. The failure to comply with the simple written form of a foreign economic transaction shall entail the invalidity of the transaction.

**Article 154. Notarial Certification of Transaction**

1. In the instances established by legislative acts or agreement of the parties, written transactions shall be considered to be concluded only after their notarial certification. The failure to comply with such a requirement shall entail the invalidity of the transaction with the consequences provided for by Article 157(3) of the present Code.

2. If a transaction requiring notarial certification has actually been performed by the parties or by one of the parties, by its content is not contrary to legislation, and does not violate the rights of third persons, the court shall have the right upon the application of the interested party to deem the transaction to be valid. In this event subsequent notarial certification of the transact ion shall not be required.

**Article 155. Registration of Transactions**

1. Transactions subject in accordance with legislative acts to State or other registration, including transactions creating, changing, or terminating rights enumerated in Article 118(2), paragraph one, of the present Code, shall be considered to be concluded after their registration unless provided otherwise by legislative acts.

A refusal of registration must be formalized in written form and shall be possible only with a reference to the violation of the requirements of legislation.

2. If a transaction requiring State registration has been concluded in the proper form, but one of the parties avoids the registration thereof, the court shall have the right at the demand of the other party to render a decision concerning registration of the transaction. In this event the transaction shall be registered in accordance with the decision of a court [Article as amended by Law of 2 March 1998, No. 211-I].

**Article 156. Exchange Transactions**

1. Exchange transactions shall be transactions whose subject is property permitted to circulate on the exchange and which are concluded on the exchange by participants of public sales conducted by it in accordance with legislation of the Republic Kazakhstan concerning the respective exchanges (goods, stock, and others) and the rules of exchange trade.

2. Exchange transactions shall be formalized by documents issued by the exchange in conformation of the conclusion of the said transactions.

3. The rules concerning the respective contract (purchase-sale, commission agency, and others) shall apply to exchange transactions, depending upon the content thereof, unless it arises otherwise from legislation, agreement of the parties, or the essence of the transaction.

4. The conditions of exchange transactions comprising a commercial secret of the parties and not subject to divulgence without their consent may be provided for by legislation or rules of exchange trade.

5. Disputes connected with the conclusion of exchange transactions shall be considered in the exchange arbitration tribunal attached to the respective exchange, the decision of which may be contested in a court.

6. [repealed by Law of 2 March 1998, No. 211-I]. [Article as amended by Law of 2 March 1998, No. 211-I; of 15 May 2003, No. 416-II].

**Article 157. Invalid Transactions and Consequences of Invalidity**

1. In the event of a violation of the requirements for the form, content, and participants of a transaction, and also the freedom of the expression of will, the transaction may be deemed to be invalid at the suit of the interested persons, the proper State agency, or a procurator.

2. The grounds for the invalidity of a transaction, and also a list of persons having the right to demand it be deemed to be invalid, shall be established by the present Code or other legislative acts.

3. When a transaction is deemed to be invalid, each of the parties shall be obliged to return to the other party everything receive under the transaction, and if it is impossible to return in kind – to compensate the cost in money.

4. If the transaction is directed towards the achievement of a criminal purpose, then if both parties have intent everything received by them under the transaction or intended for receipt shall, by decision or judgment of a court, be subject to confiscation. In the event of the performance of this transaction by one party, everything received by it from the other party shall be subject to confiscation, and everything due from it under the transaction to the other party. If neither of the parties commenced performance, everything provided for by the transaction for performance shall be subject to confiscation.

5. If there is intent to achieve a criminal purpose only on the part of one party, everything received by it under the transaction shall be subject to return to the other party, and that received by the last or due to it under the transaction shall be subject to confiscation.

6. Taking into account the specific circumstances, a court shall have the right not to apply partially or wholly the consequences provided for by points 4 and 5 of the present Article with respect to the confiscation of property received or subject to receipt with regard to the invalidity of the transaction. The consequences provided for by point 3 of the present Article shall ensue in this respect.

7. Besides the consequences provided for by points 3-6 of the present Article, a court may recover from the party guilty of committing the actions which gave rise to the invalidity of the transaction to the benefit of the other party which incurred losses connected with the transaction being deemed to be invalid.

8. An invalid transaction shall not entail legal consequences except for those which are connected with its invalidity and shall be invalid from the moment of its conclusion.

9. In deeming a transaction to be invalid, a court shall have the right, taking into account specific circumstances, to limit its elf to a prohibition of the further performance thereof.

**Article 158. Invalidity of Transaction Whose Content Does Not Correspond to Requirements of Legislation**

1. The invalidity of a transaction whose content does not correspond to the requirements of legislation, and also concluded for a purpose knowingly contrary to the fundamental principles of legal order or morality shall be invalid.

2. A person who has knowingly concluded a transaction which violates the requirement of legislation, the charter of a juridical person, or the competence of its organs shall not have the right to demand the transaction to be deemed to be invalid if such demand was caused by mercenary motives or the intention to evade responsibility.

3. If one of the participants of a transaction has concluded it with the intention of evading performance of the obligation or responsibility to a third person or the State, and the other participant knew or should have known about this intention, the interested person (or State) shall have the right to demand the transaction to be deemed invalid.

**Article 159. Grounds for Invalidity of Transactions**

1. A transaction concluded without receiving the necessary license or after the end of the period of operation of the license shall be invalid.

2. A transaction pursuing the purpose of unfair competition or violating the requirements of business ethics shall be invalid .

3. A transaction concluded by a person who has not attained fourteen years of age, except transactions provided for by Article 23 of the present Code, shall be invalid.

4. A transaction concluded by a minor who has attained fourteen years of age without the consent of his parents (or adoptive parents) or guardians, except for transactions which he by law has the right to conclude autonomously, may be deemed by a court to be invalid at the suit of the parents (or adoptive parents) or guardian.

5. A transaction concluded by a person deemed to lack dispositive legal capacity as a consequence of mental illness or feeble-mindedness shall be invalid. A transaction concluded by a citizen subsequently deemed to lack dispositive legal capacity (Article 26 of the present Code) may be deemed by a court to be invalid at the suit of his trustee if it is proved that at the moment of concluding the transaction this citizen was in a state of mental disturbance.

6. At the demand of the guardian a court may deem invalid a transaction concluded by a person with dispositive legal capacity limited by a court.

7. A transaction concluded by a citizen, although having dispositive legal capacity but at the moment of concluding it was in a state when he could not understand the significance of his actions or guide them, may be deemed by a court to be invalid upon the suit of this citizen, but if while the citizen was alive it was impossible to bring the suit, after the death of the citizen – upon the suit of other interested persons.

8. A transaction concluded as a consequence of delusion having material significance may be deemed by a court to be invalid upon the suit of the party who acted under the influence of the delusion. Delusion relative to the nature of the transaction, the identity or such qualities of its subject which significantly reduce the possibility of using it for its purpose shall have material significance. Delusion

relative to motives may serve as grounds for the invalidity of the transaction only when such motive is incorporated into the content thereof as condition subsequent or precedent (Article 150 of the present Code).

If the delusion was a consequence of gross negligence of the participant of a transaction or is encompassed by his entrepreneurial risk, the court taking into account the specific circumstances and interests of the other participant of the transactions, shall have the right to reject the suit to deem the transaction to be invalid.

9. A transaction concluded under the influence of fraud, coercion, or threat, and also a transaction which a person was force d to conclude as a consequence of the confluence of grave consequences on conditions extremely disadvantageous for himself which the other party took advantage of (cabalistic transactions) may be deemed by a court to be invalid upon the suit of the victim.

10. A transaction concluded as a consequence of the ill-intentioned agreement of the representative of one party with the other may be deemed by a court to be invalid upon the suit of the victim of the party. Compensation of losses incurred by the victim party (Article 9(4) of the present Code) may be placed subsidiarily on the representative not in good faith.

11. A transaction concluded by a juridical person which is contrary to the purposes of its activity specifically limited by the present Code, other legislative acts, or by constitutive documents, or with a violation of the charter competence of an organ thereof, may be deemed to be invalid upon the suit of the owner of the property of the juridical person or its founder (or participant) if it is proved that the other party in the transaction knew or knowingly should have known about such violations.

12. Transactions provided for by points 3 and 5 of the present Article may, at the demand of the parents, adoptive parents, or trustees of young persons or persons who lack dispositive legal capacity, by decision of a court be deemed to be valid if they were concluded to the advantage of the said persons [Article as amended by Laws of 2 March 1998, No. 211-I; of 12 December 2007, No. 225-III].

**Article 160. Fictitious and Sham Transactions**

1. A fictitious transaction concluded only for form, without the intention to give rise to legal consequences, shall be invalid.

2. If a transaction was concluded for the purpose of concealing another transaction (sham), the rules relevant to that transaction which the parties actually had in view shall apply.

**Article 161. Consequences of Invalidity of Part of Transaction**

The invalidity of part of the transaction shall not entail the invalidity of its other parts if it is possible to suppose that the transaction would have been concluded also without including the invalid part thereof.

**Article 162. Periods of Limitations Regarding Invalid Transactions**

1. [repealed by Law of 2 March 1998, No. 211-I].

2. The limitations regarding disputes connected with the invalidity of a transaction on the grounds provided for by Article 159(9) and (10) of the present Code shall constitute a year from the day of the termination of the coercion or threat under whose influence the transaction was concluded (Article

179[1]), or from the date when the plaintiff knew or should have known about other circumstances which are the grounds for deeming the transaction to be invalid.

### *Chapter 5. Representation and Power of Attorney*

**Article 163. Representation**

1. A transaction concluded by one person (representative) in the name of another person (person represented) by virtue of a power based on a power of attorney, legislation, decision of a court, or administrative act shall directly create, change, and terminate civil rights and duties of the person represented.

A power also may be manifest from the situation in which the representative acts (seller in retail trade, cashier, and others).

2. The rights and duties shall arise directly with the person represented in regard to a transaction concluded by the representative.

3. A representative may not conclude transactions in the name of the person represented either with respect to himself personally or with respect to another person whose representative he is simultaneously.

4. Persons acting, although in the interests of another but in their own name (commercial intermediaries, executors in the e vent of inheritance, and others), and also persons empowered to enter into negotiations relative to possible future transactions, shall not be representatives.

5. The conclusion through a representative of a transaction which by its character may be concluded only personally, and al so other transactions provided for by legislative acts, shall not be permitted.

**Article 164. Representation of Persons Lacking Dispositive Legal Capacity**

Legal representatives – parents (or adoptive parents) and trustees – shall conclude transactions in the name of citizens lacking dispositive legal capacity.

**Article 165. Representation Without Power**

A transaction concluded in the name of another person by a person not empowered to conclude a transaction or in excess of the power shall create, change, and terminate civil rights and duties for the person represented only in the event of the subsequent approval by him of this transaction.

The subsequent approval by the person represented shall make the transaction valid from the moment of its conclusion.

**Article 166. Commercial Representation**

1. A person who permanently and autonomously is representing in the name of entrepreneurs when they conclude contracts in the sphere of entrepreneurial activity (commercial representative) shall operate on the basis of a written contract containing an indication of the powers of the representative, and in the absence of such indications – also the power of attorney.

2. A commercial representative may simultaneously represent the interests of various parties to a contract concluded with h is participation. In so doing he shall be obliged to perform the commission given to him with the care of an ordinary entrepreneur.

3. A commercial representative shall have the right to demand the payment of stipulated remuneration and costs incurred by him when performing the commission from the parties to the contract in equal participatory shares unless provided otherwise by agreement between them.

4. A commercial representative shall be obliged to preserve the secrecy of the information made known to him concerning trade transactions also after the performance of the commission given to him.

5. The peculiarities of commercial representation in individual spheres of entrepreneurial activity shall be established by legislation.

**Article 167. Power of Attorney**

1. A power of attorney shall be deemed to be a written power of one person (principal) for representation in his name issued by him to another person (attorney).

2. A power of attorney to manage property or to conclude transactions requiring notarial certification must be notarially certified, unless established otherwise by legislation.

3. There shall be equated to notarially certified power of attorneys:

(1) powers of attorney of military servicemen and other persons being treated in military hospitals, sanatoriums, and other military treatment institutions certified by the heads or deputy heads for medical affairs, the senior or duty doctors of these military hospitals, sanatoriums, and other medical treatment institutions;

(2) powers of attorney of military servicemen, and in centres for the stationing of military units, formations, institutions, an d military training institutions where there are no State notarial offices and other agencies which perform notarial actions, also the powers of attorney of workers and employees, members of their families and members of the families of military servicemen certified by the commander (or head) of his unit, formation, institution, or educational institution;

(3) powers of attorney of persons in places of deprivation of freedom certified by the heads of the places of deprivation of freedom;

(4) powers of attorney of citizens who have reached majority and have dispositive legal capacity and who are in institutions for the social defense of the populace which are certified by the director of this institution or of the respective agency of social defense of the populace.

4. A power of attorney to receive correspondence, including monetary and parcel, to receive earnings and other payments from citizens and juridical persons may be certified by the apparatus of the akim of a district in city, city of district subordination, rural settlement, aul (or rural village), aul (or village) district where the principal resides, by the organization in which he works or studies, the housing operations organization at the place of residence, the administration of an inpatient medical institution in which he is situated for treatment, and also the command of the respective military units when the power of attorney is issued to a military serviceman. A power of attorney being sent by telegraph, and also by other types of communication when the despatch of the document is

effectuated by a communications worker, shall be certified by communications agencies [as amended by Law of 20 December 2004, No. 13-III].

5. Third persons shall have the right to consider genuine a power of attorney issued for the performance of actions with respect to them which is sent by the principal to the attorney by facsimile and other communications without the means of official communications agencies.

6. A power of attorney in the name of a juridical person shall be issued over the signature of its director or other person empowered by the constitutive documents to do so, with the seal of this organisation affixed.

7. A power of attorney in the name of a State agency, commercial or noncommercial organization to receive or issue money and other property valuables must be signed also by the chief (or senior) bookkeeper of this organisation.

8. The procedure for the issuance and the form of powers of attorney to perform operations in a bank and powers of attorney to conclude transactions in the domain of trade may be determined by special rules.

**Article 168. Period of Power of Attorney**

1. A power of attorney may not be issued for a term of not more than three years. If a longer period has been specified in the power of attorney, it shall be valid force for three years, and if the period of operation has not been specified therein – for one year from the date of the issuance thereof.

2. A power of attorney in which the date of its issuance has not been specified shall be invalid.

**Article 169. Transfer of Power of Attorney**

1. An attorney must perform personally perform those actions for which he is empowered. He may transfer the performance of them to another person only if empowered to do so by the power of attorney received or forced by virtue of circumstances in order to protect the interests of the principal.

2. The power of attorney under which the principal transfers powers to another person must be notarially certified, except for the instances provided for by Article 167(4) of the present Code.

3. The period of operation of a power of attorney issued by way of transfer may not exceed the period of operation of the initial power of attorney on the basis of which it was issued.

4. An attorney who has transferred the powers to another person must immediately notify the principal thereof and communicate to him the necessary information concerning this person and his residence. The failure to fulfil this duty shall place on the attorney responsibility for the actions of the person to whom he transferred the powers as for his own.

**Article 170. Termination of Power of Attorney**

1. The operation of a power of attorney shall terminate as a consequence of:

(1) expiry of the period of the power of attorney;

(2) effectuation of the actions provided for by the power of attorney;

(3) revocation of the power of attorney by the person who issued it;

(4) renunciation by the person to whom the power of attorney was issued;

(5) termination of the juridical person in whose name the power of attorney was issued;

(6) liquidation of the juridical person to whom the power of attorney was issued;

(7) death of the person who issued the power of attorney, deeming him to lack dispositive legal capacity, limited dispositive legal capacity, or to be missing;

(8) death of the citizen to whom the power of attorney was issued, deeming him to lack dispositive legal capacity, limited dispositive legal capacity, or to be missing.

2. A person who issued the power of attorney may at any time revoke the power of attorney or the transfer of the power of attorney, and the person to whom the power of attorney was issued, renounce it. An agreement concerning the waiver of this right shall be invalid.

**Article 171. Consequences of Termination of Power of Attorney**

1. A principal shall be obliged to notify the person to whom the power of attorney was issued about the revocation thereof (Article 170 of the present Code), as well as third persons known to him, with respect to whom the power of attorney was issued for representation. The same duty shall be imposed on the legal successors of the person who issued a power of attorney in instances of the termination thereof on the grounds specified in Article 170(5) and (7) of the present Code.

2. The rights and duties which arose as a result of the actions of the person to whom a power of attorney is issued before this person knew or should have known about its termination shall retain force for the person who issued the power of attorney and his legal successors with respect to third persons. This rule shall not apply if the third person knew or should have known that the operation of the power of attorney had terminated.

3. With regard to the termination of a power of attorney the person to whom it was issued or his legal successor must immediately return the power of attorney.

4. With the termination of a power of attorney the transfer of powers under this power of attorney to another person (transfer of power of attorney) also shall lose force.

## *Chapter 6. Calculation of Periods*

**Article 172. Determination of Period**

1. A period established by legislation, a transaction, or designated by a court shall be determined by a calendar date or by specifying an event which must inevitably ensue.

2. A period may also be established as a period of time which shall be calculated by years, months, weeks, days, or hours.

**Article 173. Commencement of Period Determined by Period of Time**

The running of a period determined by a period of time shall commence on the following day after the calendar date or ensuing of the event by which its commencement is determined.

**Article 174. Ending of Period Determined by Period of Time**

1. A period calculated by years shall expire in the corresponding month and date of the last year of the period.

The rules for periods calculated by months shall apply to a period calculated by a half-year.

2. To a period calculated by quarters of a year shall apply the rules for periods calculated by months. The quarter shall be considered to be equal to three months, and the quarters shall be calculated from the beginning of the year.

3. A period calculated by months shall expire on the corresponding date of the last month of the period.

A period determined as a half-month shall be considered as a period calculated by days and shall be considered to be equal to fifteen days.

If the ending of a period calculated by months comes in a month in which there is no corresponding date, the period shall expire on the last day of that month.

4. A period calculated by weeks shall expire on the corresponding day of the last week of the period.

**Article 175. Ending of Period on Non-Work Day**

If the last day of a period comes on a non-work day, the next work day following shall be considered to be the day of ending of the period.

**Article 176. Procedure for Performing Actions on Last Day of Period**

1. If a period has been established for performing any action whatever, it may be fulfilled up to 24:00 hours of the last day of the period.

However, if this action had to be performed in an organization, the period shall expire at the hour when in this organization the respective operations terminate according to the established rules.

2. Written applications and notifications handed in to the post, telegraph, or to another communications institution before 24:00 hours of the last day of the period shall be considered to be made within the period.

## *Chapter 7. Limitations*

**Article 177. Concept of Limitations**

1. A limitation is a period of time during which a suit demand may be satisfied which arose from violations of the right of a person or an interest protected by a law.

2. The periods of limitation and the procedure for calculating them shall be provided for by a law and may not be changed by agreement of the parties.

**Article 178. Periods of Limitation**

1. The general period of limitation shall be established as three years.

2. For individual types of demands special periods of limitation may be established by legislative acts reduced or longer in comparison with the general period.

3. The rules of Articles 177, 179-186 of the present Code shall also extend to special periods of limitation unless established otherwise by legislative acts.

**Article 179. Application of Limitations**

1. A demand concerning the defence of a violated right shall be accepted for consideration by a court irrespective of the expiry of the period of limitations.

2. Limitations shall be applied by a court only upon the application of the party to the dispute which was made before the rendering of the decision by the court.

3. The expiry of the period of limitations before the presentation of a suit shall be grounds for the court to render a decision to reject the suit.

With the expiry of the period of limitations relating to the principal demand, the period of limitations also relating to the supplementary demands shall expire (recovery of a penalty, responsibility of surety, and the like).

**Article 180. Running of Period of Limitations**

1. The running of the period of limitations shall commence from the day when the person knew or should have known about the violation of his right. Exceptions from this rule shall be established by the present Code and by other legislative acts.

2. With regard to obligations with a specified period of performance, the running of the limitations shall commence upon the ending of the period of performance.

3. With regard to obligations the period for the performance of which has not been determined or has been determined as the moment of demand, the running of limitations shall commence from the moment of presentation of the demand concerning t he performance of the obligation, and if the debtor is granted an exemption period for performance of such demand, the calculation of limitations shall commence upon the ending of the said period (Article 277(2) of the present Code).

4. With regard to regressive obligations the running of the limitations shall commence from the moment of performance of the principal obligation.

**Article 181. Period of Limitations in Event of Change of Persons in Obligation**

The change of persons in an obligation shall not entail a change of the period of limitations and the procedure for calculating it.

**Article 182. Suspension of Running of Period of Limitations**

1. The running of the period of limitations shall be suspended:

(1) if the bringing of suit has been obstructed by an extraordinary and unavoidable event under the particular conditions (insuperable force);

(2) by virtue of a deferral for the performance of obligations of a particular type (moratorium) declared by the President of the Republic Kazakhstan;

(3) if the plaintiff or defendant is in military subdivisions which are transferred to a military situation;

(4) if a person lacking dispositive legal capacity does not have a legal representative;

(5) by virtue of the suspension of the operation of legislation regulating the respective relation.

With regard to suits concerning compensation of harm caused to life or health of a citizen, the running of the period of limitations shall also be suspended in connection with the recourse of the citizen to respective organizations concerning the assignment and/or effectuation of pension payments or the assignment of a benefit, until the assignment and/or effectuation of pension payments or assignment of a benefit or refusal to assign and/or effectuate pension payments or assign a benefit [as amended by Law of 19 June 1997, No. 134-I].

2. The running of the period of limitations shall be suspended if the circumstances specified in the present Article arose or have continued to exist during the last six months of the period of limitations, and if this period does not exceed six months, the running of the period of limitations.

3. The running of the period shall continue from the date of termination of the circumstance which entailed the suspension. The remaining part of the period shall be lengthened up to six months, and if the period of limitations does not exceed six months, up to the period of limitations [Article as amended by Law of 19 June 1997, No. 134-I; of 2 March 1998, No. 211-I].

**Article 183. Interruption of Running of Period of Limitations**

1. The running of the period of limitations shall be interrupted by bringing suit in the established procedure, and also by the performance of actions by the obliged person which testify to recognition of the debt.

2. After the interruption, the running of the period of limitations shall commence anew; the time which elapsed before interruption shall not be calculated in the new period.

**Article 184. Running of Period of Limitations in Event of Leaving Suit Without Consideration**

1. If a suit has been left without consideration by a court, then the running of the period of limitations which commenced before bringing suit shall continue in the general procedure.

2. If a suit brought in a criminal case has been left by a court without consideration, then the running of the period of limitations which commenced before bringing suit shall be suspended until the entry into legal force of the judgment by which the suit was left without consideration. The time during which the limitation was suspended shall not be calculated in the period of limitations. In so doing if the remaining portion of the period is less than six months, it shall be lengthened up to six months.

**Article 185. Restoration of Period of Limitations**

1. In exceptional instances, when the court deems the reason for the lapsing of the period of limitations to be justifiable with regard to circumstances connected with the person of the plaintiff (grave illness, helpless state, illiteracy, and the like), the violated right of the citizen shall be subject to defense. The reasons for the lapse of a period of limitations may be deemed to be justifiable if they occurred in the last six months of the period of limitations, and if this period is equal to six months or to less than six months, the running of the period of limitations.

2. The period of limitations shall be restored and commence to run anew in instances when in accordance with legislative acts the plaintiff's right arises to present a new suit with regard to the same case in connection with a refusal to execute the judicial decision regarding this case.

**Article 186. Performance of Duty Upon Expiry of Period of Limitations**

A debtor or other obliged person who has performed a duty upon the expiry of the period of limitations shall not have the r ight to demand back that which has been performed, even though at the moment of performance the said person did not know a bout the expiry of the limitations.

**Article 187. Demands to Which Limitations Do Not Extend**

Limitations shall not extend to:

(1) demands concerning the defence of nonmaterial benefits and personal nonproperty rights, except for instances provided for by legislative acts;

(2) demands of depositors against a bank concerning the issuance of bank deposits [as amended by Law of 11 July 1997, No. 154-I];

(3) demands concerning compensation of harm caused to the life or health of a citizen. However, demands presented upon the expiry of the periods of limitations shall be satisfied for not more than three years preceding the bringing of suit;

(4) demands of the owner or other legal possessor concerning the elimination of any violations of his right, if such violations were not connected with a deprivation of possession (Articles 264 and 265 of the present Code);

(5) in the instances established by legislative acts, also other demands.

## SECTION 2. RIGHT OF OWNERSHIP AND OTHER RIGHTS TO THING

### *Chapter 8. Right of Ownership. General Provisions*

**Article 188. Concept and Content of Right of Ownership**

1. The right of ownership is the right of a subject which is recognized and protected by legislative acts at his discretion to possess, use, and dispose of property belonging to him.

The right of ownership shall be transferred to another person with all encumberments which existed at the moment of conclusion of the transaction.

2. The rights of possession, use, and disposition of his property shall belong to the owner.

The right of possession shall represent the legally ensured possibility of effectuating the actual possession of property.

The right of use shall represent the legally ensured possibility of deriving from the property its useful natural properties, and also to receive advantage from it. Advantage may take the form of revenue, increment, fruits, offspring, and other forms.

The right of disposition shall represent the legally ensured possibility of determining the legal fate of the property.

3. The owner shall have the right at his discretion to perform with respect to property belonging to him any actions, including to alienate this property in ownership to other persons, to transfer to them while remaining the owner his powers relating to possession, use, and disposition of the property, to pledge out property and to encumber it by other means, and to otherwise dispose of it.

4. The effectuation by the owner of his powers must not violate the rights and interests protected by a law of other persons and the State. A violation of the rights and legal interests may find expression, together with other forms, in the abuse by the owner of his monopoly or other dominant position.

An owner shall be obliged to take measures preventing damage to the health of citizens and the environment which may be inflicted when effectuating his rights.

5. The right of ownership shall be in perpetuity. The right of ownership to property may be compulsorily terminated only on the grounds provided for by the present Code.

6. In the instances, on the conditions, and within the limits provided for by legislative acts an owners shall be obliged to permit the limited use of his property by other persons [Article as amended by Law of 2 March 1998, No. 211-I].

**Article 189. Burden of Maintenance of Property**

1. The owner shall bear the burden of maintenance of the property belonging to him unless provided otherwise by legislative acts or by contract and may not unilaterally place this burden on a third person.

2. If property is lawfully situated with third persons, then the expenses incurred by them for the maintenance of another's property shall be subject to compensation by the owner unless provided otherwise by a contract.

Expenses for the maintenance of property shall not be compensated to the person who possessed a thing not in good faith and unlawfully (Article 263 of the present Code).

**Article 190. Risk of Accidental Perishing or Accidental Damaging of Property**

1. The risk of accidental perishing or accidental damaging of things being alienated shall be pass to the acquirer simultaneously with the arising of the right of ownership in him unless established otherwise by legislative acts or by contract.

2. If the alienator delayed with fault the transfer of a thing or the acquirer delayed with fault the acceptance thereof, the risk of accidental perishing or accidental damaging shall be borne by the party who delayed.

**Article 191. Concept and Types of Private Ownership**

1. Private ownership shall be both the ownership of citizens and/or non-State juridical persons and associations thereof [as amended by Law of 2 March 1998, No. 211-I].

2. Any property, except for individual types of property which in accordance with legislative acts may not belong to citizens or juridical persons, may be in private ownership.

The quantity and value of property in private ownership shall not be limited.

**Article 192. Right of State Ownership**

1. State ownership shall be in the form of Republic and municipal ownership.

2. Republic ownership shall consist of the State treasury and property consolidated to State Republic juridical persons in accordance with legislative acts.

The means of the Republic budget, the gold and hard currency reserve, and the diamond fund, objects of State ownership enumerated in Article 193 of the present Code, and other State property not consolidated to State juridical persons shall constitute the State treasury of the Republic Kazakhstan.

3. Municipal ownership shall consist of the local treasury and property consolidated to municipal juridical persons in accordance with legislative acts.

Means of the local budget and other municipal property not consolidated to State juridical persons shall constitute the local treasury.

3[1]. Municipal ownership shall be subdivided by levels of local State administration into regional (or cities of republic significance, capitals) and district (or cities of regional significance).

4. Property in State ownership may be consolidated to State juridical persons by right of economic jurisdiction or operative management.

5. The peculiarities of the legal regime of State property in the jurisdiction of individual State institutions shall be determined by legislative acts.

6. The transfer of State property from one type of State ownership to another shall be effectuated in the procedure determined by the Government of the Republic Kazakhstan.

The voluntary and uncompensated transfer of property from private ownership to State shall be effectuated in the procedure determined by the Government of the Republic Kazakhstan.

The transfer of property in municipal ownership from one level of local State administration to another shall be effectuated in the procedure determined by legislative acts on local State administration in the Republic Kazakhstan [Article as amended by Laws of 2 March 1998, No. 211-I; of 4 November 1999, No. 472-I; of 2 March 2001, No. 162-II; of 21 May 2002, No. 323-II; of 18 May 2005, No. 50-III; and of 12 January 2007, No. 225-III].

**Article 193. Ownership in Land and Other Natural Resources [as amended by Law of 2 March 1998, No. 211-I]**

Land, its subsoil, water, flora and fauna, and other natural resources shall be exclusively in State ownership. Land also may be in private ownership on the grounds, conditions, and within the limits established by legislative acts [as amended by Law of 2 March 1998, No. 211-I].

**Article 193[1]. Strategic Objects [added by Law of 7 August 2007, No. 1931]**

1. A strategic object is property having a socio-economic significance for the stable development of Kazakhstan society, the possession and/or use, and/or disposition of which will exert influence on the state of national security of the Republic Kazakhstan.

2. There may be relegated to strategic objects: main line railway networks; main line oil pipelines; main line gas pipelines; national electricity network; mainline communications lines; national postal

network; international airports; sea ports having the status of international significance; aero-navigation devices of air traffic management systems, devices and navigation marks regulating and guaranteeing safety of navigation; objects of use of atomic energy; objects of outer space branch; water-economy installations; motor vehicle roads of common use, and also blocks of stocks (or participatory shares, shares) in juridical persons in whose ownership strategic objects are situated, blocks of stocks (or participatory shares of participation, shares) of natural and juridical persons which have the possibility directly or indirectly to determine decisions or exert influence on the decisions of juridical persons to be adopted in whose ownership strategic objects are situated.

Strategic objects may be in State and private ownership in accordance with legislative acts of the Republic Kazakhstan.

3. The encumberment of strategic objects by the rights of third persons or the alienation thereof shall be possible on the basis of a decision of the Government of the Republic Kazakhstan concerning the issuance of an authorization and in the procedure determined by the Government of the Republic Kazakhstan.

4. In the event of a strategic object being in private ownership and the intention of the owner thereof to sell this object, the Government of the Republic Kazakhstan shall possess a priority right to purchase the strategic object at market value.

The market value of a strategic object shall be determined in accordance with legislation concerning evaluation activity.

The procedure for the use of a priority right of purchase of a strategic object shall be determined by the Government of the Republic Kazakhstan.

5. If the requirements of points 3 and 4 of the present Article have been violated by the owner of a strategic object, such transactions shall be deemed to be invalid from the moment of the conclusion thereof [Article 1931 added by Law of 7 August 2007, No. 321-III].

**Article 194. Right of Ownership and Other Rights to Thing in Housing**

The peculiarities of the effectuation of the right of ownership and other rights to a thing in housing shall be regulated by housing legislation.

**Article 195. Rights to Thing of Persons Who Are Not Owners**

1. There shall be relegated to the rights to a thing, together with the right of ownership:

(1) the right of land use;

(2) the right of economic jurisdiction;

(3) the right of operative management;

(4) other rights to a thing provided for by the present Code or other legislative acts.

2. Norms on the right of ownership shall apply to rights to a thing unless provided otherwise by legislation or not contrary to the nature of the particular right to a thing.

3. The transfer of the right of ownership in property to another person shall not be grounds for the termination of other rights to a thing to this property unless provided otherwise by legislative acts of

the Republic Kazakhstan [Article as amended by Laws of 2 March 1998, No. 211-I; and of 12 January 2007, No. 225-III].

## *Chapter 9. Right of Economic Jurisdiction*

### Article 196. Right of Economic Jurisdiction of State Enterprise

The right of economic jurisdiction shall be the right to a thing of a State enterprise which has received property from the State as owner and effectuated within the limits established by the present Code and other legislative acts, and the rights of possession, use, and disposition of this property [as amended by Law of 2 March 1998, No. 211-I].

### Article 197. Object of Right of Economic Jurisdiction

Any property, unless provided otherwise by legislation, may be the object of the right of economic jurisdiction.

### Article 198. Acquisition and Termination of Right of Economic Jurisdiction

1. The right of economic jurisdiction to property with respect to which the owner has adopted a decision to consolidate it to a State enterprise already created shall arise in this enterprise at the moment of consolidation of the property to the autonomous balance sheet of the enterprise unless established otherwise by legislation or by decision of the owner.

2. The fruits, products, and revenues from the use of property in economic jurisdiction, and also property acquired by an enterprise under contracts or other grounds, shall enter the economic jurisdiction of the enterprise in the procedure established by legislation for the acquisition of the right of ownership.

3. The right of economic jurisdiction to property shall terminate on the grounds and in the procedure provided for by legislation for the termination of the right of ownership, and also in instances of the lawful withdrawal of property from the enterprise by decision of the owner.

### Article 199. Rights of Owner With Respect to Property in Economic Jurisdiction

The owner of property in economic jurisdiction shall, in accordance with legislative acts, decide questions of the creation of the enterprise, determination of the subject and purposes of its activity, its reorganization and liquidation, effectuate control over the use for designation and the preservation of the property belonging to the enterprise.

The owner shall have the right to receive part of the net revenue from the use of property in economic jurisdiction of the enterprise created by it [as amended by Law of 11 July 1997, No. 154-I].

### Article 200. Conditions for Effectuation of Property Rights of State Enterprise

1. A State enterprise effectuating activity by right of economic jurisdiction, unless provided otherwise by legislative acts, shall not have the right without the written consent of the owner or State agency empowered by it to:

(1) alienate or by other means dispose (except for instances provided by the present Article) lease out on a long-term lease (more than three years), and grant for temporary use without compensation buildings, installations, equipment, and other basic means of the enterprise;

(2) create branches, representations, and subsidiary enterprises, found jointly with private entrepreneurs enterprises and joint production entities, and invest production and monetary capital in them;

($2^1$) dispose of stocks belonging to it (except for instances provided by the present Article), and also debtor indebtedness;

(3) grant loans;

(4) issue a suretyship or guarantee for the obligations of third persons.

2. A State enterprise, unless provided otherwise by legislation, shall autonomously dispose of movable property consolidated to it by right of economic jurisdiction not relegated to basic means.

A State enterprise by right of economic jurisdiction shall not have the right to sell and conclude transactions of gift with respect to property relegated to basic means of the State enterprise, nor to stocks belonging to it [Article as amended by Laws of 11 July 1997, No. 154-I; of 2 March 1998, No. 211-I; and of 21 May 2002, No. 323-II].

**Article 201. Extension of Provisions on Right of Ownership to Relations with Participation of State Enterprises**

The provisions of the present Code on the right of ownership shall, unless arises otherwise from the present Code and other legislative acts, extend to property relations with the participation of State enterprises.

## *Chapter 10. Right of Operative Management*

**Article 202. Concept and Content of Right of Operative Management**

The right of operative management shall be the right to a thing of an institution and State institution financed at the expense of assets of the owner and a treasury enterprise which has received property from the owner and effectuated within the limits established by legislative acts in accordance with the purposes of its activity, assignments of the owner and purpose of the property and the rights of possession, use, and disposition of this property [Article as amended by Laws of 2 March 1998, No. 211-I; of 16 December 1998, No. 320-I].

**Article 203. Acquisition and Termination of Right of Operative Management**

The acquisition and termination of the right of operative management shall be effectuated on the conditions and in the procedure provided for by Chapters 13 and 14 of the present Code unless established otherwise by legislation.

**Article 204. Rights of Owner of Property Transferred in Operative Management**

1. The owner of property in operative management shall, in accordance with legislative acts, decide questions of the creation of the institution, State institution, or treasury enterprise, the determination of the subject and purposes of its activity, and possess the right to determine the legal fate of the institution,

State institution, or treasury enterprise and the content of its activity [as amended by Law of 16 December 1998, No. 320-I].

2. The owner shall effectuate control over the effectiveness of the use and preservation by the institution, State institution, or treasury enterprise of property transferred by the owner.

3. If an institution is created by several owners, the relations between them and the rights of the owners to manage their property shall be determined by the constitutive contract or analogous agreement.

**Article 205. Right of Owner to Withdraw and Redistribute Property Transferred in Operative Management**

The owner of property consolidated to an institution, State institution, or treasury enterprise shall have the right to withdraw this property or to redistribute it between other juridical persons created by it at its discretion, unless established otherwise by legislative acts [as amended by Law of 16 December 1998, No. 320-I].

**Article 206. Disposition of Property of Institution, State Institution, or Treasury Enterprise [as amended by Law of 16 December 1998, No. 320-I]**

1. An institution or State institution shall not have the right autonomously to alienate or dispose by other means of property consolidated to it and property acquired at the expense of means allotted to it under the estimate unless established otherwise by a legislative act .

[paragraph two lost force by Law of 16 December 1998, No. 320-I]

2. A treasury enterprise shall have the right to alienate or by other means to dispose of property consolidated to it, and also to transfer and write off debtor indebtedness, only with the written consent of the owner of this property except for instances provided for by point 3 of the present Article.

A treasury enterprise shall autonomously realize products produced by it unless established otherwise by legislation. The procedure for the distribution of revenues of a treasury enterprise shall be determined by the owner of its property.

3. A treasury enterprise shall not have the right to sell and to conclude transactions of gift with respect to property relegated to its basic means [Article as amended by Laws of 16 December 1998, No. 320-I; of 2 March 2001, No. 162-II; of 21 May 2002, No. 323-II].

**Article 207. Responsibility of Founder for Debts of Treasury Enterprise, Institution, and State Institution [as amended by Law of 16 December 1998, No. 320-I]**

1. A treasury enterprise shall be liable for its obligations with money in its disposition.

In the event of the insufficiency of money at the treasury enterprise the Government of the Republic Kazakhstan shall bear subsidiary responsibility for its obligations or the respective local executive agency

Responsibility shall ensue for contractual obligations in the procedure established by legislative acts on the State enterprise.

2. Responsibility of an institution and State institution shall ensue in the procedure provided for by Article 44(1) of the present Code [Article as amended by Laws of 11 July 1997, No. 154-I; of 2 March 1998, No. 211-I; and of 16 December 1998, No. 320-I].

**Article 208. Transfer of Right of Ownership to Institution**

In the event of the transfer of the right of ownership to an institution to another person, this institution shall retain the rig ht of operative management to the property belonging to it.

## *Chapter 11. Common Ownership*

**Article 209. Concept and Grounds of Arising of Common Ownership**

1. Property in the ownership of two or several persons shall belong to them by right of common ownership.

2. Property may be in common ownership with the determination of the participatory share of each of the owners in the right of ownership (participatory share ownership) or without the determination of such participatory shares (joint ownership).

3. Common ownership to property shall be participatory share except for instances when the formation of joint ownership to property has been provided for by a law.

4. Common ownership shall arise when two or several persons enter into the ownership of property which can not be divided without changing its purpose (indivisible things), or is not subject to division by virtue of a law.

Common ownership in divisible property shall arise in the instances provided for by legislative acts or by contract.

5. By agreement of the participants of joint ownership, and in the event of not achieving consent, by decision of a court, the participatory share ownership of these persons may be established for common property.

6. Ownership in immoveable property may arise in the form of a condominium under which individual parts of the immoveable are in individual (or separate) ownership of citizens and/or juridical persons, and those parts of the immoveable which are not in separate ownership shall belong to the owners of parts of the immoveable by right of common participatory share ownership.

The participatory share of each owner in common property shall be inseparable from his separate ownership to the part of the immoveable belonging to him.

The amount of the participatory share of each owner in common property and the degree of participation in the expenses for its maintenance shall depend on the amounts of the parts of the immoveable in individual (or separate) ownership unless provided otherwise by legislative acts or contract.

The peculiarities of the legal regime of various types of condominium may be determined by legislative acts [point 6 added by Law of 2 March 1998, No. 211-I].

7. The peculiarities of the legal regime of common participatory share ownership to assets of a share investment fund shall be determined by legislative acts of the Republic Kazakhstan on investment funds [point 7 added by Law of 7 July 2004, No. 577-II].

**Article 210. Determination of Participatory Share in Right of Participatory Share Ownership**

1. If the amount of the participatory shares of the participants of participatory share ownership can not be determined on the basis of legislative acts and was not established by agreement of all of its participants, the participatory shares shall be considered to be equal.

2. The procedure for the determination and change of their participatory shares may be established by agreement of all the participants of participatory share ownership depending upon the contribution of each of them in the formation and growth of the common property.

**Article 211. Rights of Participant of Participatory Share Ownership Connected with Improvement Thereof**

1. A participant of participatory share ownership who has effectuated at his own expense while complying with the established procedure for the use of common property indivisible improvements of this property shall have the right to a corresponding increase of his participatory share in the right to common property.

2. Divisible improvements of common property, unless provided otherwise by agreement of the participants of the participatory share ownership, shall enter into the ownership of those participants who produced them.

**Article 212. Disposition of Property in Participatory Share Ownership**

1. The disposition of property in participatory share ownership shall be effectuated by agreement of all of its participants.

2. Each participant of participatory share ownership shall have the right at his discretion to sell, give, bequeath, or pledge his participatory share or to otherwise dispose of it while complying, in the event of alienation for payment, with the conditions provided for by Article 216 of the present Code.

**Article 213. Possession and Use of Property in Participatory Share Ownership**

1. The possession and use of property in participatory share ownership shall be effectuated by the consent of all of its participants, and if consent is not achieved, in the procedure established by a court.

2. Each participant of participatory share ownership shall have the right to grant part of the common property commensurate to his participatory share for possession and use, and if this is impossible, shall have the right to demand of the other participants who possess and use the property respective the payment of a respective monetary amount or other contributory compensation approximating his participatory share.

**Article 214. Fruits, Product, and Revenues from Use of Property in Participatory Share Ownership**

The fruits, product, and revenues from the use of property in participatory share ownership shall become part of the common property. The subsequent distribution of fruits, product, and revenues shall be made among the participants of participatory ownership commensurately with their participatory shares unless provided otherwise by an agreement between them.

**Article 215. Expenses for Maintenance of Property in Participatory Ownership**

Each participant of participatory share ownership shall be obliged commensurately to their participatory shares to participate in the payment of taxes, charges, and other payments relating to the common property, and also the costs for its maintenance and preservation.

**Article 216. Preferential Right of Purchase**

1. In the event of the sale of a participatory share in the right of participatory share ownership to an outside person the remaining participants of participatory share ownership shall have the preferential right of purchase of the participatory share being sold at the price for which it is being sold and on other equal conditions, except for sales at public sales. The public sales for the sale of the participatory share in the right of participatory share ownership may, in the absence of consent thereto of all the participants of participatory share ownership, be held in the instances provided for by Article 222(2) of the present Code, and in the other instances provided for by legislative acts.

2. The seller of a participatory share shall be obliged to notify in written form the remaining participants of participatory share ownership of the intention to sell his participatory share to an outside person, specifying the price and other conditions on which he is selling it. If the other participants of participatory share ownership refuse to purchase or do not acquire the participatory share being sold in the right of ownership to immovable property within a month, and with respect to other property, within ten days from the date of receipt of notification, the seller shall have the right to sell his participatory share to any person.

3. In the event of the sale of a participatory share in violation of the preferential right of purchase, any other participant of participatory share ownership shall have the right within three months to demand in court the transfer to him of the rights and duties of the purchaser.

4. The assignment of a preferential right of purchase of the participatory share shall not be permitted.

5. The rules of the present Article shall apply also when alienating a participatory share under a contract of barter.

6. The rules of the present Article shall not extend to instances of alienation of strategic objects [point 6 added by Law of 7 August 2007, No. 321-III]

**Article 217. Moment of Transfer of Participatory Share in Right of Participatory Share Ownership to Acquirer Under Contract**

The participatory share in the right of participatory share ownership shall pass to the acquirer under a contract from the moment of conclusion of the contract unless provided otherwise by an agreement of the parties.

The moment of transfer of a participatory share in the right of participatory share ownership under a contract subject to St ate registration or notarial certification shall be determined in accordance with Article 238(2) of the present Code.

**Article 218. Division of Property in Participatory Share Ownership and Partition of Participatory Share Therefrom**

1. Property in participatory share ownership may be divided between its participants by an agreement between them.

2. A participant of participatory share ownership shall have the right to demand the partition of his participatory share from the common property.

3. If the participants of participatory share ownership do not reach agreement concerning the means and conditions for the division of common property or partition of the participatory share ownership of one of them, the participant of participatory share ownership shall have the right to demand the partition of his participatory share in kind from the common property. If the partition of a participatory share in kind is not permitted by legislative acts or is impossible without incommensurate damage to property in common ownership, the partitioning owner shall have the right to payment to him of the value of his participatory share by the other participants of participatory share ownership.

4. The incommensurateness of property partitionable in kind to a participant of participatory share ownership on the basis of the present Article to his participatory share in the right of ownership shall be eliminated by the payment of a corresponding monetary amount or other contributory compensation.

The payment to a participant of participatory share ownership by the remaining co-owners of contributory compensation in place of the partition of his participatory share in kind shall be permitted with his consent. In instances when the participatory share of the respective owner is insignificant and can not be truly partitioned and he does not have a material interest in the use of the common property, a court may also, in the absence of the consent of this owner, oblige the other participants of participatory ownership to pay contributory compensation to him.

5. With the receipt of the contributory compensation in accordance with points 3 and 4 of the present Article the owner shall lose the right to the participatory share in the common property.

6. In the event of the evident inadvisability of dividing common property or partitioning a participatory share therefrom according to the rules set out in points 3-5 of the present Article, a court shall have the right to adopt a decision concerning the sale of the property at public sale with subsequent distribution of the amounts received among the participants of common ownership commensurate with their participatory shares.

**Article 219. Common Joint Ownership**

1. Common joint ownership shall exist in the form of:

(1) common ownership of spouses;

(2) common ownership of a peasant economy;

(3) common ownership in a privatized dwelling.

2. Other types of common joint ownership may also be provided for by legislative acts.

3. Common joint ownership shall be established and exist unless provided otherwise by a contract between the participants thereof [Article as amended by Law of 12 January 2007, No. 225-III].

**Article 220. Possession, Use, and Disposition of Property in Joint Ownership**

1. The participants of joint ownership, unless provided otherwise by agreement between them, shall possess and use common property in common.

2. The disposition of property in joint ownership shall be effectuated by the consent of all the participants, which shall be presupposed irrespective as to which of the participants has concluded the transaction with regard to disposition of the property.

3. Each of the participants of joint ownership shall have the right to conclude transactions relating to the disposition of common property unless it arises otherwise from the agreement of all the participants. A transaction concluded by one of the participants of joint ownership which is connected with the disposition of common property may be deemed to be invalid at the demand of the remaining participants for reasons that the participant who concluded the transaction lacked the necessary powers only if it is proved that the other party to the transaction knew or knowingly should have known about this.

When concluding transactions requiring notarial certification or State registration, the consent of the other participants of joint activity to conclude the transaction must be confirmed in a notarial procedure.

4. Points 1-3 of the present Article shall apply unless established otherwise for individual types of joint ownership by the present Code or other legislative acts.

**Article 221. Division of Property in Joint Ownership and Partition of Participatory Share Therefrom**

1. The separation of common property between participants of joint ownership, and also the partition of the participatory share of one of them, may be effectuated on condition of the preliminary determination of the participatory share of each of the participants in the right to common property.

2. In the event of the separation of common property and the partition of a participatory share therefrom, unless provided otherwise by legislative acts or by agreement of the participants, their participatory shares shall be deemed to be equal.

3. The grounds and procedure for the separation of common property and the partition of the participatory share therefrom shall be determined according to the rules of Article 218 of the present Code insofar as has not been established otherwise for individual types of joint ownership by the present Code and other legislative acts and does not arise from the essence of the relations of the participants of joint ownership [Article as amended by Law of 2 March 1998, No. 211-I].

**Article 222. Levying Execution Against Participatory Share in Common Property**

1. The creditor of a participant of participatory share or joint ownership shall, in the event that the latter's other property is insufficient, have the right to present a demand concerning partition of the participatory share of the debtor in the common property in order to levy execution against it.

2. In instances of the refusal of the remaining participants of common ownership to acquire the participatory share of the debtor, the creditor shall have the right to demand in court the levy of execution against the participatory share of the debtor in the right of common ownership by means of the sale of this participatory share at a public sale.

3. If in such instances the apportionment of the participatory share in kind is impossible or the other participants of participatory share or joint ownership object to this, the creditor shall have the right to demand the sale by the debtor of his participatory share to the other participants of common ownership at a price commensurate with the market value of this participatory share, with the means received from the sale being applied to repayment of the debt.

**Article 223. Common Ownership of Spouses**

1. Property acquired by spouses during marriage shall be their joint ownership unless provided otherwise by a contract between them that this property is the participatory share ownership of the spouses or belongs to one or in respective parts to each of the spouses by right of ownership.

2. The property which belonged to the spouses before entering into marriage, and also received by them during marriage as a gift or by way of inheritance, shall be the ownership of each of them.

Things of individual use (clothing, footwear, and others), except for jewellery and other articles of embellishment, although acquired during the marriage at the expense of the common means of the spouses, shall be deemed to be the ownership of that spouse who used them.

The property of each spouse may be deemed to be their joint ownership if it is established that during the marriage investments were made at the expense of the common property of the spouses which significantly increased the value of this property (capital repair, reconstruction, re-equipping, and others).

3. Execution may be levied with regard to the obligations of one spouse only against property in his ownership, and also against his participatory share in the common property of the spouses which would have been due to him in the event this property is separated.

4. The peculiarities of the right of common joint ownership of spouses shall be determined by legislation on marriage and the family of the Republic Kazakhstan.

**Article 224. Ownership of Peasant (or Farmer) Economy**

1. The property of a peasant (or farmer) economy shall belong to its members by right of joint ownership unless established otherwise by a contract between them.

The property of a farmer economy organized in the form of a simple partnership on the basis of a contract on joint activity shall belong to the members thereof by right of common participatory share ownership.

The property of a farmer economy based on personal entrepreneurship shall belong to him by right of private ownership.

2. In the ownership of members of a peasant or farmer economy may be land plots, plantings on a land plot, including plantings of the private forestry fund, wild fauna reared and maintained in captivity and/or semi-captivity conditions, economic and other structures, soil conservation and other installations, productive and working livestock, poultry, agricultural and other technology and equipment, means of transport, tools, and other property transferred by members of the economy and/or acquired for the economy from common means of its members.

3. The fruits, products, and revenues received as a result of the activity of the peasant (or farmer) economy shall be the common property of the members of the peasant (or farmer) economy and shall be used by agreement between them [Article as amended by Law of 12 January 2007, No. 225-III].

**Article 225. Separation of Property of Peasant (or Farmer) Economy**

1. In the event of the termination of a peasant (or farmer) economy in connection with the withdrawal therefrom of all of its members or on other grounds, the common property shall be subject to separation according to the rules provided for by Articles 218 and 221 of the present Code.

2. The means of production belonging to the peasant (or farmer) economy shall not be subject to separation in the event of the withdrawal of one of its members from the economy. The person withdrawing from the economy shall have the right to receive monetary contributory compensation commensurate with his participatory share in the common ownership in such property.

3. In the instances provided for by points 1 and 2 of the present Article, the participatory shares of members of a peasant (or farmer) economy in the right of joint ownership to the property of the economy shall be deemed to be equal unless established otherwise by an agreement between them [Article as amended by Law of 12 January 2007, No. 225-III].

**Article 226. Legal Regime of Property In Event of Reorganization of Peasant (or Farmer) Economy into Economic Partnership or Cooperative**

1. An economic partnership or production cooperative may be created by the members of a peasant (or farmer) economy on the base of the property of the economy. Such a reorganized peasant (or farmer) economy shall as a juridical person possess the right of ownership in the property transferred to it in the form of contributions and other dues by members of the peasant or farmer economy, and also in property received as a result of its activity and acquired on other grounds which are not contrary to legislation.

2. The amount of contributions of members of the peasant (or farmer) economy who are participants of the partnership or members of the cooperative shall be established by proceeding from their participatory shares in the right of common ownership of the property of the peasant (or farmer) economy determined in the procedure provided for by Article 218 and Article 225(3) of the present Code [Article as amended by Law of 12 January 2007, No. 225-III].

**Article 227. Common Ownership in Privatized Dwelling**

A dwelling in houses of the State housing fund purchased or acquired without compensation by the tenant in accordance with legislation on the privatization of housing shall pass into the joint ownership of the tenant and members of the family residing permanently with him, including minors and persons temporarily absent, unless provided otherwise by a contract between them.

The peculiarities of the right of joint ownership in a privatized dwelling shall be determined by legislative acts on housing relations [paragraph as amended by Law of 2 March 1998, No. 211-I].

## *Chapter 12. Contract on Joint Activity (Simple Partnership)*

**Article 228. Simple Partnership**

1. A simple partnership shall be formed on the basis of a contract on joint economic activity.

Under a contract on joint economic activity (or contract of simple partnership) the parties shall be obliged to act jointly in order to achieve revenues or to achieve a purpose which is not contrary to law [as amended by Law of 2 March 1998, No. 211-I].

A simple partnership shall not be a juridical person.

2. A contract on joint activity (or contract of simple partnership) shall be concluded between citizens, between citizens and juridical persons, and between juridical persons (consortium).

2. The obligations of the participants of a simple partnership connected with the contract on joint economic activity shall be joint and several to third persons unless provided otherwise by the contract on joint activity.

**Article 229. Conducting Common Affairs of Participants of Contract**

The conducting of the common affairs of the participants of a contract on joint activity shall be effectuated by their common consent. By an agreement between them they may commission the direction of joint activity and the conducting of common affairs to one of the participants operating in this event on the basis of a power of attorney issued by the other participants of the contract.

**Article 230. Common Property of Participants of Contract**

1. In order to achieve their purposes the participants of a contract on joint activity shall make contributions in money or other property or a labor contribution.

2. Monetary or other property contributions of the participants of a contract, and also property created or acquired as a result of their joint activity, shall be their common participatory share ownership.

3. [repealed by Law of 2 March 1998, No. 211-I].

4. The norms of the present Code on common participatory share ownership shall extend to the property of the participants of the contract unless provided otherwise by norms of the present Chapter, other legislative acts, or the contract on joint activity [point 4 added by Law of 2 March 1998, No. 211-I].

**Article 231. Common Expenses and Losses of Participants of Contract**

The procedure for covering common expenses relating to joint activity and losses which arose as a result thereof shall be determined by the contract of the participants. If such a procedure has not been provided for by the contract, the common expenses and losses shall be covered at the expense of the common property of the participants of the contract, and the amounts lacking shall be covered between them in proportion to their participatory shares in this property [as amended by Law of 2 March 1998, No. 211-I].

**Article 232. Transfer of Right and Renunciation of Participation in Joint Activity**

1. The transfer of the right to participate in joint activity may be effectuated only with the consent of the participants of a contract on joint activity (or contract of simple partnership).

2. The participant of a contract on joint activity (or contract of simple partnership) shall have the right at its discretion to renounce participation in the joint activity.

3. The losses of participants caused by the renunciation of any of them of participation in joint activity shall be recovered in full unless provided otherwise by the contract on joint activity (or contract of simple partnership).

**Article 233. Consortium**

1. A consortium is a temporary voluntary equal union (or association) on the basis of a contract on joint economic activity in which juridical persons combine particular resources and coordinate efforts in order to resolve specific economic tasks.

2. The participants of a consortium shall retain their economic autonomy and may take part in the activity of other consortiums or associations. Relations between the participants of a consortium shall be structured on a contractual basis.

3. The management of the consortium shall be effectuated in accordance with a consortium agreement of the participants of the consortium.

4. The participants of a consortium shall bear joint and several responsibility for obligations connected with the activity of the consortium unless stipulated otherwise by the consortium agreement [as amended by Law of 2 March 1998, No. 211-I].

5. The consortium shall terminate its activity upon the fulfilment of the tasks put or by decision of the participants thereof.

**Article 234. Rules on Individual Types of Joint Activity**

Individual types of joint activity shall be regulated in accordance with the present Code by legislation of the Republic Kazakhstan.

*Chapter 13. Acquisition of Right of Ownership and Other Rights to Thing*

**Article 235. Grounds for Acquisition of Right of Ownership**

1. The right of ownership in a new thing shall belong to the person who manufactured or created it unless provided otherwise by the contract or by legislation. The right of ownership to fruits, products, and revenues received as a result of the use of property shall be acquired in accordance with Article 123 of the present Code.

2. The right of ownership in property which an owner has may be acquired by another person on the basis of a contract of purchase-sale, barter, gift, or other transaction concerning the alienation of this property.

In the event of the death of a citizen the right of ownership to the property belonging to him shall pass by inheritance to other persons in accordance with the will or a law.

In the event of the reorganisation of a juridical person the right of ownership in the property belonging to it shall pass to the juridical persons-legal successors of the reorganized juridical person (Article 46 of the present Code).

The alienation of property from the owner to another person outside the will of the owner shall not be permitted except for instances provided for by the present Code.

3. In the instances and in the procedure provided for by the present Code, a person may acquire the right of ownership in property which has no owner, in property whose owner is unknown, or in property which the owner has renounced or to which he has lost the right of ownership on other grounds.

4. The members of a consumer cooperative (housing, housing-construction, dacha, garage, or other) other persons having the right to share-accumulation who have fully made their share contribution to an apartment, dacha, garage, or other premise granted to these persons by the cooperative for use shall acquire the right of ownership in the said property.

**Article 236. Arising of Right of Ownership in Newly Created Immovable Property**

1. The right of ownership in a building, installation, and other property complexes, and also other newly created immovable property, shall arise from the moment of the completion of the creation of this property.

2. If the acceptance of objects whose construction is completed has been provided for by legislative acts, the creation of the respective property shall be considered to be completed from the moment of such acceptance.

3. In instances when the immovable property is subject to State registration, the right of ownership to it shall arise from the moment of such registration.

4. Until the completion of the creation of immovable property, and in respective instances the State registration thereof, the rules concerning the right of ownership to materials and other property from which the immovable property is being created shall apply.

**Article 237. Converting**

1. Insofar as not provided otherwise by a contract, the right of ownership to a new movable thing manufactured by the person by means of converting materials which do not belong to him shall be acquired by the owner of the materials.

However, if the value of the converting materially exceeds the value of the materials, the right of ownership to a new thing shall be acquired by the person who, acting in good faith, has effectuated the converting for himself.

2. Unless provided otherwise by a contract, the owner of materials who has acquired the right of ownership in a thing manufactured from them shall be obliged to contributorily compensate the value of the converting to the person who has effectuated it, and in the event of the acquisition of the right of ownership to the new thing by this person, the last shall respectively be obliged to compensate the owner for the value of the materials thereof.

3. The owner of the materials who has lost them as a result of the actions not in good faith of the person who effectuated the converting shall have the right to demand the transfer of the new thing to his ownership and compensation of losses caused to him.

**Article 238. Moment of Arising of Right of Ownership in Acquirer under Contract**

1. The right of ownership in the acquirer of property by contract shall arise from the moment of the transfer of the thing unless provided otherwise by legislative acts or by a contract.

2. If the contract on the alienation of property is subject to State registration or notarial certification, the right of ownership in the acquirer shall arise from the moment of registration or notarial certification, and when both notarial certification and State registration of the contract are necessary, from the moment of the registration thereof.

**Article 239. Transfer of Thing**

1. The handing over of a thing to the acquirer shall be deemed to be the transfer, and likewise the handing over to a transport organization for dispatch to the acquirer, or to the post for the sending to the acquirer of a thing alienated without the obligation of delivery, unless provided otherwise by legislation or by a contract.

2. If at the moment of concluding a contract on the alienation of a thing it is already in the possession of the acquirer, the thing shall be deemed to be transferred to him from this moment. The transfer of a bill of lading or other disposition document f or a thing shall be equated to the transfer of a thing.

**Article 240. Acquisitive Prescription**

1. A citizen or juridical person who is not the owner of property but in good faith, openly, and uninterruptedly possesses immovable property as his own for fifteen years or other property for not less than five years shall acquire the right of ownership in such property (acquisitive prescription) [as amended by Law of 2 March 1998, No. 211-I].

The right of ownership in immovable and other property subject to State registration shall arise in the person who acquired this property by virtue of acquisitive prescription from the moment of such registration.

2. Until the acquisition of the right of ownership in property, the citizen or juridical person possessing the property as his own shall have the right to defend his possession against third persons who are not the owners of the property, and also who do not have the rights to possession thereof by virtue of another ground provided for by legislative acts or by contract.

3. A citizen or juridical person referring to the prescription of possession may combine to the time of his possession all of the time during which this property was possessed by he whom this person is the legal successor of.

4. The running of the period of acquisitive prescription with respect to property situated with a person from whose possession it may be demanded and obtained in accordance with Articles 260-263 and 265 of the present Code shall commence not earlier than the expiry of the period of limitations with respect to the corresponding demands.

5. If the person was refused recognition of his right of ownership in a court, the person who possesses the property shall become the owner.

**Article 241. Conversion to Ownership of Things Generally-Accessible for Gathering or Extraction**

When in accordance with legislation, local custom, or general authorization by a particular owner the gathering of berries, catching of fish, and gathering or extraction of other articles is permitted in forests, waters, or on other territories, the right of ownership in the respective things shall be acquired by the person effectuating the gathering or extraction thereof.

**Article 242. Masterless Things**

1. A thing which has no owner or whose owner is unknown, or a thing, the right of ownership in which has been renounced by the owner, shall be masterless.

2. Unless this is excluded by rules on the acquisition of the right of ownership to a thing which the owner has renounced (Article 243 of the present Code), on find (Article 245 of the present Code), on neglected animals (Article 246 of the present Code), and on treasure (Article 247 of the present Code), the right of ownership in masterless movable things may be acquired by virtue of acquisitive prescription (Article 240 of the present Code).

3. Masterless immovable things shall be accepted for recording by the agency effectuating State registration of immovable property upon the application of the apparatus of the akim of the distgrict in city, city of regional or district significance, rural settlement, aul (or village) and aul (or rural) national area on whose territory they are elicited. Upon the expiry of a year from the day of the masterless immovable thing being recorded, the agency empowered to manage municipal ownership may apply to a court with a demand to recognise this thing as having entered into municipal ownership.

The organization of work with regard to recording, keeping, valuation, further use, and realization of property which has entered municipal ownership shall be effectuated by the agency empowered to manage municipal ownership.

The procedure for the recording, keeping, valuation, further use, and realization of property which has entered State ownership shall be determined by the Government of the Republic Kazakhstan.

A masterless immovable thing not deemed by decision of a court to have entered into municipal ownership may be accepted anew into the possession, use, and disposition of the owner who left it, or acquired in ownership by virtue of acquisitive prescription (Article 240 of the present Code) [Article as amended by Laws of 24 December 2001, No. 276-II; of 20 December 2004, No. 13-III; of 22 June 2006, No. 147-III; and of 12 January 2007, No. 225-III].

**Article 243. Movable Things Which Owner Has Renounced**

1. Movable things which have been thrown away or otherwise left by him for the purpose of renouncing the right of ownership to them (things thrown away) may be converted by other persons into their ownership in the procedure established by point 2 of the present Code.

2. A person in whose ownership, possession, or use a land plot is situated where a thing thrown away is found whose value is clearly lower than the amount corresponding to twenty monthly account indicators or discarded scrap metals and defective product shall have the right to convert these things to his ownership, having embarked upon their use or having performed other actions testifying to the conversion of the thing to ownership.

Other things thrown away shall enter into the ownership of the person who took possession of them if upon the application of this person they have been deemed by a court to be masterless [Article as amended by Law of 2 March 1998, No. 211-I].

**Article 244. Arbitrary Structure**

1. A dwelling house, other structure, installation, or other immovable property created on a land plot not allotted for these purposes in the procedure established by legislation, and also created without obtaining the necessary authorizations for this, shall be an arbitrary structure.

2. A person who has effectuated an arbitrary structure shall not acquire the right of ownership in it. He shall not have the right to dispose of the structure – to sell, give, lease out, or conclude other transactions.

The arbitrary structure shall be subject to demolition by the person who effectuated it or at his expense, except for the instances provided for by points 3 and 4 of the present Article.

3. The right of ownership to an arbitrary structure may be recognized by a court for the person who effectuated the building on a land plot not belonging to him on condition that the particular plot will be granted to this person in the established procedure under the structure erected.

The right of ownership in an arbitrary structure also may be recognized by a court for the person in whose legal use the land plot is where the structure was effectuated. In this event the person whose right of ownership to the structure has been recognized shall compensate the person who effectuated it for the expenses for the structure in the amount determined by the court.

The right of ownership in the arbitrary structure may not be recognized for the said persons if retention of the structure entails a violation of the rights and the interests protected by a law of the other persons or creates a threat to the life and health of citizens.

4. In exceptional instances, taking into account socio-economic advisability, an arbitrary structure may be transferred to municipal ownership with compensation of expenses for the structure in an amount determined by a court.

**Article 245. Find**

1. The finder of a lost thing shall be obliged immediately to inform the person who lost it thereof or the owner of the thing or some other persons known to him as having the right to receive it and shall return the found thing to him.

If a thing has been found in a premise or on transport it shall be subject to being handed over to a person representing the possessor of this premise or transport. In this event this possessor shall acquire the rights and bear the duties of the person who found the thing.

2. If the person having the right to receive a found thing or his whereabouts are unknown, the finder of the thing shall be obliged to declare the find to the internal affairs agencies or the apparatus of the akim of the district in city or city.

3. The finder of a thing shall have the right to keep it himself or to hand it over for keeping to the internal affairs agencies or apparatus of the akim of the district in city, city of district significance, rural settlement, aul (or village), and aul (or rural) national area or person specified by them. A perishable thing or a thing whose costs for keeping are incommensurate in comparison with its value may be realised by the finder of the thing, receiving written evidence certifying the amount of the receipts. The money derived from the sale of a found thing shall be subject to keeping and return to the person empowered to receive the thing, or to transfer in ownership to other persons in the procedure and on the conditions established for this very thing.

The finder of a thing shall be liable for its loss or damage only in the event of his intent or gross negligence and within the limits of the value of the thing.

4. If upon the expiry of six months from the moment of declaring the find to the internal affairs agencies or apparatus of the akim of the district in city, city of district significance, rural settlement,

aul (or village), and aul (or rural) national area the person empowered to receive the lost thing has not been established and does not declare his right to the thing to the person who found it, or to the internal affairs agencies or apparatus of the akim of the district in city, city of district significance, rural settlement, aul (or village), and aul (or rural) national area, the finder of the thing shall acquire the right of ownership to it.

If the finder of a thing refuses to acquire the found thing in ownership, it shall pass to municipal ownership.

5. The finder and returner of a thing to the person empowered to receive it shall have the right to receive from this person, and in the event of the thing passing into municipal ownership, from the respective local executive agency, compensation of necessary expenses connected with keeping, handing over, or realization of the thing, and also expenditures for discovering the person empowered to receive the thing.

6. The finder of a thing shall have the right to receive remuneration from the person empowered to receive the thing in the amount of 30% of the value of the thing. If a found thing is of value only to the person empowered to receive it, the amount of remuneration shall be determined according to a valuation made by the parties.

The right to remuneration shall arise unless the finder of the thing has not performed his duty to declare the find or has performed other actions in order to conceal the find [Article as amended by Law of 20 December 2004, No. 13-III].

**Article 246. Neglected Animals**

1. A person who has detained neglected or stray livestock and other domestic or domesticated animals shall be obliged to return them to their owner, and if he or his whereabouts is unknown, not later than three days from the moment of such detention to declare the discovered animals to the internal affairs agencies or apparatus of the akim of the district in city, city of district significance, rural settlement, aul (or village), and aul (or rural) national area, which shall take measures to seek the owner.

During the period of search for the owner of the animals they may be left by the person who detained them with himself for maintenance and for use, or handed over for maintenance and use to another person having the necessary conditions for this. At the request of the person who detained the animals, the seeking of a person who has the necessary conditions for their maintenance and use and the transfer of the animals thereto shall be effectuated by the apparatus of the akim of the district in city, city of district significance, rural settlement, aul (or village), and aul (or rural) national area.

2. The person who has detained the animals and the person to whom they have been transferred for maintenance and use shall be liable for the perishing and spoilage to the animals only if there is fault and within the limits of the value of these animals .

3. If within six months from the moment of declaring the detention of working livestock or cattle and two months, other domestic animals, their owner is not discovered or does not declare his right to them, the right of ownership to these animals shall pass to the person with whom they are situated for maintenance and use.

If this person refuses to acquire in ownership animals maintained by him they shall enter into municipal ownership and be used in the procedure determined by the respective apparatus of the akim of the district in city, city of district significance, rural settlement, aul (or village), and aul (or rural) national area.

4. The person who detained animals and the person with whom they are situated for maintenance and use shall, in the event of the return of neglected domestic animals to the owner, have the right to receive compensation from this owner of their expenses connected with the maintenance of the animals, setting off the advantages derived from the use thereof.

5. The person who has detained neglected or stray livestock and other domestic or domesticated animals shall have the right to demand from their owner the payment of remuneration in accordance with Article 245(6) of the present Code.

6. In the event of the appearance of the former owner of animals after the transfer into the ownership of another person, the owner shall have the right when there are circumstances testifying to the retention of an attachment on the part of these animals towards him or the cruel or other improper treatment of them by the new owner to demand their return to him on the conditions determined by an agreement with the new owner, and in the event of the failure to reach agreement, by a court [Article as amended by Laws of 20 December 2004, No. 13-III; and of 12 January 2007, No. 225-III].

**Article 247. Treasure**

1. Treasure, that is, money and valuable objects buried in the earth or concealed by other means whose owner can not be established or by virtue of legislation has lost the right to them shall enter into the ownership of the possessor of the land plot or to the owner of the immovable thing in which the treasure was concealed, and the person who discovered the treasure, in equal participatory shares, unless established otherwise by a contract between them.

When a treasure is discovered by a person who has made diggings or searches for the valuables without the consent of the user of the land plot or the owner of the immovable property where the treasure was concealed, the treasure shall be subject to transfer to this owner.

2. In the event of the discovery of a treasure containing a thing relegated to monuments of history and culture, it shall be subject to transfer to the ownership of the Republic Kazakhstan. In so doing the user of the land plot or the owner of the immovable property in which the treasure was discovered and the person who discovered the treasure shall have the right to receive remuneration in the amount of 50% of the value of this treasure. The remuneration shall be distributed between these persons in accordance with the rules provided for by point 1 of the present Article.

**Article 248. Acquisition of Property Withdrawn from Owner**

If a person in the procedure and on the conditions established by legislative acts has acquired property withdrawn from the owner on legal grounds, this person shall acquire the right of ownership to the property.

## *Chapter 14. Termination of Right of Ownership and Other Rights to Thing*

### Article 249. Grounds for Termination of Right of Ownership

1. The right of ownership shall terminate in the event of the alienation by the owner of his property to other persons, renunciation of the right of ownership by the owner, the perishing or destruction of the property, and the loss of the right of ownership to property in other instances provided for by legislative acts.

2. The compulsory withdrawal from the owner of property shall not be permitted except for instances of:

(1) levying execution against property for obligations of the owner;

(2) compulsory alienation of property which by virtue of legislative acts can not belong to the particular person;

(3) requisition;

(4) confiscation;

(5) alienation of immovable property in connection with the withdrawal of a land plot;

(6) purchase of improvidently maintained cultural and historical valuables;

(7) in other instances provided for by the present Code.

3. In the instances, on the conditions, and in the procedure provided for by legislative acts on privatization, property in State ownership shall be alienated into the private ownership of citizens and juridical persons.

4. In the event of the adoption of the Law of the Republic Kazakhstan on the Conversion to State Ownership of Property in the Private Ownership of Citizens and Juridical Persons (Nationalization), losses shall be compensated to them in the procedure established by Article 266 of the present Code.

### Article 250. Renunciation of Right of Ownership

A citizen or juridical person may renounce the right of ownership in property belonging to him, so declaring or having performed other actions which specifically testify to the elimination of the possession, use, and disposition of the property without the intention to preserve any rights whatever to such property.

The renunciation of the right of ownership shall not entail the termination of the rights and duties of the owner with respect to the corresponding property until the moment of the acquisition of the right of ownership to the particular property by another person.

### Article 251. Levy of Execution Against Property of Owner

1. The levy of execution against property for obligations of the owner shall be done in a judicial procedure, unless otherwise provided for by contract [as amended by Law of 2 March 1998, No. 211-I].

2. The right of ownership in property against which execution is levied shall terminate in the owner from the moment the right of ownership arises in the withdrawn property in the person to whom the right of ownership passes in the procedure provided for by legislation.

**Article 252. Termination of Right of Ownership of Person To Whom By Virtue of Legislative Acts Property May Not Belong**

1. If on the grounds permitted by legislative acts property turns out to be in the ownership of a person which by virtue of legislative acts can not belong to him, this property must be alienated by the owner within one year from the moment the right of ownership arises in the particular property unless other periods have been established by legislative acts. If the property is not alienated by the owner within the specified period, it by decision of a court shall be subject to compulsory alienation with compensation to the owner of the value of the property less the expenditures for the alienation thereof.

2. If in the ownership of a citizen or juridical person on the grounds permitted by legislative acts there turns out to be a thing for whose acquisition a special authorization is necessary, the issuance of which has been refused to the owner, this thing shall be subject to alienation in the procedure established for property which can not belong to the particular owner.

**Article 253. Requisition**

1. In the event of natural disasters, wrecks, epidemics, epizootic, and other circumstances of an extraordinary character property may, in the interests of society by decision of State agencies be withdrawn from the owner in the procedure and on the conditions established by legislative acts with payment of the value of the property to him (requisition).

2. The valuation according to which the value of the requisitioned property shall be compensated may be contested by it in a judicial proceeding.

3. The person whose property was requisitioned shall have the right when the operation of the circumstances terminates in connection with which the requisition was made to demand in court the return to him of the property which has been preserved [Article as amended by Law of 2 March 1998, No. 211-I].

**Article 254. Confiscation**

In the instances provided for by legislative acts property may be withdrawn without compensation from the owner in a judicial proceeding in the form of a sanction for the commission of a crime or other violation of law (confiscation).

**Article 255. Termination of Right of Ownership to Immovable in Connection with Withdrawal of Land and Other Natural Resources**

1. The termination of the right of ownership to an immovable in connection with the decision of a State agency not directed expressly towards the withdrawal of property from the owner, including a decision concerning the withdrawal of a land plot on which a house, other structures, installations, or plantings belonging to the owner are situated, shall be permitted only in the instances and in the procedure established by legislative acts, presenting to the owner property of equal value and compensation of other losses incurred or compensation to him in full for losses caused by the termination of the right of ownership.

2. If the owner disagrees with the decision entailing the termination of the right of ownership, it may not be effectuated until settlement of the dispute in a judicial procedure. When the dispute is considered, all questions of compensation to the owner for losses caused also shall be decided.

3. The rules of the present Article respectively shall apply when terminating the right of ownership to immovable property in connection with the decision of a State agency concerning withdrawal of mining allotments, aquatory plots, and other plots on which property is situated.

**Article 256. Purchase of Improvidently Maintained Cultural and Historical Valuables**

In instances when the owner of cultural and historical valuables relegated in accordance with legislation to [the category of] specially valuable and protected by the State improvidently maintains these valuables, which threatens them with their losing their significance, such valuables may by decision of a court be withdrawn from the owner through purchase by the State or sale at a public sale.

In the event of the purchase of cultural valuables the owner shall be compensated their value in the amount established by agreement of the parties, and in the event of a dispute, by a court. In the event of the sale at a public sale the amount received from the sale shall be transferred to the owner less the expenses for holding the public sale.

**Article 257. Valuation of Property in Event of Termination of Right of Ownership**

In the event of the termination of the right of ownership, property shall be valued by proceeding from its market price.

**Article 258. Termination of Rights to Thing Which Belong to Non-Owner**

Rights to a thing which belong to a non-owner shall terminate according to the rules established by Articles 249-257 of the present Code, and also by decision of the owner in the procedure established by legislative acts, the charter of the juridical person, or by contract of the owner with the possessor of the property.

## *Chapter 15. Defense of Right of Ownership and Other Rights to Thing*

**Article 259. Recognition of Right of Ownership**

The owner shall have the right to demand recognition of the right of ownership.

**Article 260. Demanding and Obtaining Property by Owner from Another's Illegal Possession**

The owner shall have the right to demand and obtain his property from another's illegal possession.

**Article 261. Demanding and Obtaining Property from a Good-Faith Acquirer**

1. If property has been acquired for compensation from the person who did not have the right to alienate it, of which the acquirer did not know and should not have known (good-faith acquirer), then the owner shall have the right to demand and obtain this property from the acquirer only when the property has been lost by the owner or person to whom the property was transferred by the

owner in possession, or stolen from one or the other, or left the possession thereof by means other than the will thereof.

2. If property was acquired without compensation from a person who did not have the right to alienate it, the owner shall have the right to demand and obtain the property in all instances.

3. Demanding and obtaining property on the grounds specified in point 1 of the present Article shall not be permitted if the property was sold in the procedure established for the execution of judicial decisions [Article as amended by Law of 2 March 1998, No. 211-I].

**Article 262. Limitation on Demanding and Obtaining Money and Securities**

Money, and also bearer securities, may not be demanded and obtained from a good-faith acquirer.

**Article 263. Settlement of Accounts in Event of Return of Things from Illegal Possession**

1. When demanding and obtaining property on the basis of Articles 260 and 261 of the present Code, the owner also shall have the right to demand from a possessor not in good faith the return or compensation of all revenues which this person derived or should have been derived throughout the entire period of possession; and from a good-faith possessor, the return of compensation of all revenues which he derived or should have derived from the entire time of the possession; from a possessor in good faith – all revenues which he derived or should have derived from the time when he knew or should have known about the unlawfulness of the possession or receive a writ relating to the suit of the owner concerning the return of the property. A good faith possessor, in turn, shall have the right to demand from the owner compensation for necessary expenses made by him for the property from that time from which revenues from the property were due to the owner. A possessor not in good faith shall have the right to receive such compensation in full or in part only in instances when the demand of the possessor was deemed by a court to be well-founded.

2. An illegal possessor shall have the right to retain for himself improvements made by him if they can be separated without damaging the thing. If such a separation of the improvements is impossible, a good-faith possessor shall have the right to demand compensation for expenditures made for the improvement, but not more than the amount of the increase of the value of the thing. A possessor not in good faith shall not have this right.

**Article 264. Defense of Rights of Owner Against Violations Not Connected with Deprivation of Possession**

An owner shall have the right to demand the elimination of any violations of his right, even though these violations are not combined with deprivation of possession.

**Article 265. Defense of Rights to Thing of Person Who is Not the Owner**

The rights provided for by Articles 259-264 of the present Code shall belong also to a person who, although not the owner, is the possessor of the property by right of economic jurisdiction or operative management, permanent land use, or on another g rounds provided for by legislative acts or contract. This person shall have the right to the defense of his possession against the owner as well.

**Article 266. Defense of Interests of Owner in Event of Termination of His Rights on Grounds Provided by Law**

In the event of the adoption by the Republic Kazakhstan of legislative acts terminating the right of ownership, the losses caused to the owner as a result of the adoption of these acts shall be compensated to the owner in full by the Republic Kazakhstan.

**Article 267. Invalidity of Acts of Agencies of Power, Administration, and Officials Which Violate Right of Owner and Other Rights to Thing**

1. If as a result of the publication of a normative or individual act of an agency of State administration, local representative or executive agency, or official which does not correspond to legislation the rights of an owner or other persons with regard to the possession, use, and disposition of property belonging to them are violated, such act shall be deemed in a judicial proceeding to be invalid at the suit of the owner or the person whose right has been violated.

2. When decisions are rendered by a court with regard to a specific case, the acts of agencies of State administration and local representative or executive agency which are contrary to legislative acts shall not be applied.

Losses caused to the owner as a result of the publication of the said acts shall be subject to compensation in full by the respective agency of power or administration from the assets of the respective budget.

## SECTION 3. LAW OF OBLIGATIONS
[AS AMENDED BY LAW OF 20 DECEMBER 2004, NO. 13-III]

### SUBSECTION 1. GENERAL PROVISIONS ON OBLIGATION

### *Chapter 16. Concept of and Grounds of Arising of Obligation*

**Article 268. Concept of Obligation**

By virtue of an obligation one person (the debtor) shall be obliged to perform to the benefit of another person (the creditor) a determined action, that is, to transfer property, fulfil work, pay money, and the like or to refrain from a determined action, and the creditor shall have the right to demand from the debtor the performance of his duty. The creditor shall be obliged to accept performance from the debtor.

**Article 269. Parties to Obligation**

1. [repealed by Law of 2 March 1998, No. 211-I].

2. Several persons may participate simultaneously in an obligation as each of its parties – creditor or debtor. In these instances a participatory share, joint and several, or subsidiary obligation shall arise in accordance with the rules established by the present Code (Articles 286-288 of the present Code).

The invalidity of the demands of the creditor with respect to one of the persons participating in the obligation as a debtor, and likewise the expiry of the period of limitations with regard to the demand against such person, shall not in and of itself affect the demands of the creditor against the remaining such persons.

3. If each of the parties by virtue of an obligation bears a duty in favour of the other party, it shall be considered to be the debtor of the other party in that which it is obliged to do to its benefit, and simultaneously the creditor thereof in that which it has the right to demand from it [Article as amended by Law of 2 March 1998, No. 211-I].

**Article 270. Participants of Obligation**

1. The participants of an obligation shall be the parties (debtor and creditor) and third persons.

2. Persons connected by obligations or other legal relations with one of the parties of an obligation shall act as third persons.

3. An obligation shall not create duties for third persons. In the instances provided for by legislation or by agreement of the parties, an obligation may give rise to rights for third persons with respect to one or both parties of the obligation.

**Article 271. Grounds of Arising of Obligation**

Obligations shall arise from a contract, as a consequence of the causing of harm, or other grounds specified in Article 7 of the present Code.

## *Chapter 17. Performance of Obligation*

**Article 272. Proper Performance of Obligation**

Obligations must be performed duly in accordance with the conditions of the obligation and the requirements of legislation, and in the absence of such conditions and requirements – in accordance with the customs of business turnover or other usually presented requirements.

**Article 273. Inadmissibility of Unilateral Refusal to Perform Obligation**

A unilateral refusal to perform an obligation and a unilateral change of its conditions shall not be permitted except for instances provided for by legislation or by a contract.

**Article 274. Performance of Obligation in Parts**

A creditor shall have the right not to accept the performance of an obligation in parts unless provided otherwise by the conditions of the obligation, legislation, or does not arise from the customs of business turnover or the essence of the obligation.

**Article 275. Performance of Obligation to Proper Person**

Unless provided otherwise by agreement of the parties and it arises from the customs of business turnover or the essence of the obligation, the debtor shall have the right when performing the obligation to demand evidence that performance is accepted by the creditor himself or by a person empowered by him and shall bear the risk of the consequences of the failure to present such demand.

**Article 276. Performance of Obligation by Third Person**

1. The performance of an obligation may be entrusted as a whole or in part to a third person if this has been provided for by legislation or contract, and likewise if the third person is connected with one of the parties by a respective contract.

2. Unless the duty of the debtor to perform an obligation personally follows from legislation, the conditions of the obligation , or the essence thereof, the creditor shall be obliged to accept performance offered for the debtor by a third person.

3. A third person who is subject to the danger of losing his right to the property of the debtor (right of use, possession, pledge, and others) as a consequence of execution being levied by the creditor against this property may at his own expense satisfy the demand of the creditor without the consent of the debtor. In this event the rights of the creditor regarding the obligation shall pass to the third person and the rules of the present Code concerning the assignment of a demand shall apply (Articles 339-347 of the present Code).

**Article 277. Period for Performance of Obligation**

1. If an obligation provides for or enables the date of its performance or the period of time during which it must be performed to be determined, the obligation shall be subject to performance on that day or, respectively, at any moment within the limits of that period.

2. When an obligation does not provide for a period for its performance and does not contain conditions enabling this period to be determined, it must be performed within a reasonable period after the origin of the obligation.

An obligation not performed within a reasonable period, and likewise an obligation whose period of performance has been determined by the moment of demand, the debtor shall be obliged to perform within a seven-day period from the day of presentation by the creditor of the demand concerning the performance thereof unless the duty to perform within another period arises from legislation, the conditions of the obligation, the customs of business turnover, or the essence of the obligation.

**Article 278. Requirements for Equivalence of Performance of Obligation**

Obligations reckoned for prolonged periods of performance must be performed with equivalence, within periods reasonable for the particular type of obligation (day, ten days, month, quarter, and so forth), unless provided otherwise by legislation or the conditions of the obligation or follows from the essence of the obligation or customs of business turnover.

**Article 279. Performance of Obligation Before Time**

1. The debtor shall have the right to perform an obligation before the period unless provided otherwise by legislation or the conditions of the obligation, or does not arise from the essence thereof.

2. The performance of an obligation before time connected with entrepreneurial activity shall be permitted only in instances when the possibility to perform an obligation before the period provided for legislation or by the conditions of the obligation or arises from the customs of business turnover or the essence of the obligation.

**Article 280. Information on Course of Performance of Obligation**

The duty of the debtor to communicate to the creditor about the course of performance of an obligation may be provided for by legislation or conditions of the obligation.

**Article 281. Place of Performance of Obligation**

If the place of performance has not been determined by legislation or by the conditions of the obligation or is not manifest from the essence of the obligation or customs of business turnover, performance must be made:

(1) with regard to an obligation to transfer immovable property: at the location of the property;

(2) with regard to an obligation to transfer a good or other property with the use of carriage: at the place of handing over the property to the first carrier for delivery to the creditor;

(3) with regard to other obligations of an entrepreneur to transfer a good or other property: at the place of manufacture or storage of the property if this place was known to the creditor at the moment of origin of the obligation;

(4) with regard to a monetary obligation: at the place of residence of the creditor at the moment of arising of the obligation, and if the creditor is a juridical person – at its location at the moment of arising of the obligation; if the creditor at the moment of performance of the obligation has changed place of residence or location and notified the debtor thereof – at the new place of residence or location of the creditor, relegating to him all expenses connected with the change of place of performance to the account thereof [as amended by Law of 2 March 1998, No. 211-I];

(5) with regard to all other obligations: at the place of residence of the debtor, and if the debtor is a juridical person – at its location.

**Article 282. Monetary Obligation**

1. By virtue of a monetary obligation one person (debtor) shall be obliged to pay money to another person (creditor), and the creditor shall have the right to demand from the debtor the performance of his duty with regard to payment of money (or loan of money and other obligations). The rules concerning a monetary obligation, unless established otherwise by the present Code, legislative acts of the Republic Kazakhstan or arises from the essence of the obligation, shall apply to duties with regard to the payment of money under a compensated contract, obligations concerning compensation of losses and payment of a penalty, and also obligations arising as a consequence of the causing of harm or unfounded enrichment.

Monetary obligations on the territory of the Republic Kazakhstan must be expressed in tenge (Article 127 of the present Code) except for instances provided for by legislative acts of the Republic Kazakhstan.

The use of foreign currency, and also of payment documents in foreign currency, shall be permitted when effectuating the settlement of accounts on the territory of the Republic Kazakhstan with regard to obligations in the instances and on the conditions determined by legislative acts of the Republic Kazakhstan or in the procedure established by them.

The procedure and means for the effectuation of payments and transfers shall be established by legislation of the Republic Kazakhstan on payments and transfers of money and shall be determined by the parties in the respective contract.

2. The amount of payment made which is insufficient for performance of the monetary obligation shall, in the absence of another agreement of the parties, repay first of all the costs of the creditor relating to receiving the performance and then – penalty and remuneration (or interest), and thereafter, the principal amount of the debt.

3. In long-term obligations the indexation of the payment on the conditions stipulated by the parties may be provided for [Article as amended 11 July 1997, No. 154-I; of 16 June 1999, No. 436-I; of 24 December 2001, No. 276-II; of 10 July 2003, No. 483-II; and of 12 January 2007, No. 225-III].

**Article 283. Increase of Amounts Payable for Maintenance of Citizen**

An amount payable with regard to a monetary obligation directly for the maintenance of a citizen (in compensation of harm caused to life or health, under a contract of maintenance for life, and in other instances) shall be increased proportionately with an official increase of the minimum earnings.

**Article 284. Performance of Mutual Duties**

1. Mutual duties must be performed by the parties simultaneously unless it arises otherwise from legislation, customs of business turnover, conditions of the obligation, or the essence thereof.

2. The failure to perform or improper performance of the obligation by one party shall relieve the other party in the event of the performance of mutual duties and satisfaction of counter demands from the performance of his duties unless established otherwise by legislative acts or the conditions of the obligation.

**Article 285. Performance of Alternative Obligation**

The right of choice, unless it arises otherwise from legislation or the conditions of the obligation, shall belong to the debtor who is obliged to perform one of two or several actions.

**Article 286. Performance of Obligation in Which Several Creditors or Several Debtors Participate**

If several creditors or several debtors (obligation with multiplicity of persons) participate in an obligation, each of the creditors shall have the right to demand performance, and each of the debtors shall be obliged to perform the obligation in equal participatory share with the others insofar as it does not follow otherwise from legislation, or the conditions of the obligation (participatory share obligation).

**Article 287. Performance of Joint and Several Obligation**

1. An obligation with a multiplicity of persons by virtue of which each creditor has the right to demand, and each debtor is obliged to perform the obligation in full, shall be deemed to be a joint and several obligation.

A joint and several duty or a joint and several demand shall arise if this is provided for by the contract or has been established by legislative acts, in particular, in the event of the indivisibility of the subject of the obligation.

2. The duties of several debtors under an obligation connected with entrepreneurial activity, and likewise the demands of several creditors in that obligation, shall be joint and several unless provided otherwise by legislation or by the conditions of the obligation.

3. In the event of the joint and several duty of the debtors the creditor shall have the right to demand performance either from all of the debtors or from any of them individually, and for the debt either in full or in part. A creditor who has not received full satisfaction from one of the joint and several debtors shall have the right to demand that not received from the other joint and several debtors.

Joint and several debtors shall remain obliged until the obligation is performed in full.

The performance of a joint and several duty in full by one of the debtors shall relieve the other debtors from performance to the creditor.

4. In the event of the joint and severalness of a demand, any of the joint and several creditors shall have the right to present the demand to the debtor in full.

The performance of an obligation in full to one of the joint and several creditors shall relieve the debtor from performance to the other creditors.

5. In the event of a joint and several duty, the debtor shall not have the right to advance against the demands of the creditor objections based on those relations of other debtors against the creditor in which the said debtor does not participate.

In the event of the joint and severalness of demands, a debtor shall not have the right to advance against demands of one of the joint and several creditors objections based on those relations of the debtor with another joint and several creditor in which the said creditor does not participate [Article as amended by Law of 2 March 1998, No. 211-I].

**Article 288. Performance of Subsidiary Obligation**

It may be provided by legislative acts or by the conditions of an obligation between the creditors and debtors that in the event of the failure of the principal debtor to satisfy the demands of the creditor concerning the performance of the obligation, this demand may be declared in the unperformed part to another debtor (subsidiary debtor).

**Article 289. Regressive Demands**

1. A debtor who has performed an obligation of another person shall have the right of regressive demand against this person in the amount of the performed obligation.

A debtor who has not performed the obligation as a consequence of the actions of a third person shall have the right to demand compensation of losses from the said person.

2. A debtor who has performed a joint and several obligation shall have the right of regressive demand against each of the remaining debtors in equal participatory share, deducting the participatory share falling on him himself.

That unpaid by one of the co-debtors to the debtor who has performed the joint and several obligation shall fall in equal participatory share on this debtor and the remaining co-debtors.

The rules of the present point shall apply respectively in the event of the termination of a joint and several obligation for set-off of a counter-demand of one of the debtors.

3. A joint and several creditor who has received performance from the debtor shall be obliged to compensate other creditors the participatory shares due to them unless arises otherwise from relations between them.

**Article 290. Certification of Performance of Obligation**

1. A creditor shall be obliged, in accepting performance, at the demand of the debtor to issue him a receipt for the receiving of performance in full or in part.

If the debtor has issued a debt document to the creditor in certification of the obligation, the creditor must, in accepting performance, return the document to the debtor. If it is impossible to return, he shall be obliged to so specify this on the receipt issued to him.

The receipt may be replaced by an endorsement on the debt document returned to the debtor.

2. The location of a debt document with the debtor shall certify, insofar as not proved otherwise, the termination of the obligation.

3. In the event of the refusal of the creditor to issue a receipt concerning the performance made, to return the debt document, or to note the impossibility of the return thereof on the receipt, the debtor shall have the right to delay performance. In this event the creditor shall be considered to have delayed.

**Article 291. Performance of Obligation by Placing Debt on Deposit**

1. A debtor shall have the right in performance of an obligation to place money due from him on conditions of deposit, and securities, on conditions of keeping in the name of a notary, and in the instances established by legislative acts, in the name of a court if the obligation can not be performed as a consequence of:

(1) the absence of the creditor or person empowered by him to accept performance at the place where the obligation must be performed;

(2) the lack of dispositive legal capacity of the creditor and absence of his representative;

(3) the evident lack of specificity as to who is the creditor with regard to the obligation, in particular, in connection with a dispute in this regard between the creditor and other persons;

(4) avoidance by the creditor of accepting performance or other delay on his part.

2. The placing of money or securities on conditions of deposit or keeping in the name of a notary or court shall be considered to be performance of the obligation. The notary or court in whose name the money or securities were deposited shall notify the creditors thereof [Article as amended by Laws of 11 July 1997, No. 154-I; and of 2 March 1998, No. 211-I].

## Chapter 18. Securing Performance of Obligation

### §1. General Provisions

**Article 292. Means of Securing the Performance of Obligation**

1. The performance of an obligation may be secured by a penalty, pledge, withholding of property from the debtor, suretyship, guarantee, deposit, and other means provided for by legislation or by a contract.

The means of security performance of obligations with regard to securities shall be established by legislative acts of the Republic Kazakhstan regulating activity on the securities market.

2. The invalidity of an agreement to secure an obligation shall not entail the invalidity of this obligation (principal obligation).

3. The invalidity of the principal obligation shall entail the invalidity of the obligation securing it [Article as amended by Law of 8 July 2005, No. 72-III].

### §2. Penalty

**Article 293. Concept of Penalty**

A penalty (or fine, forfeit) shall be deemed to be a monetary amount determined by legislation or by contract which the debtor shall be obliged to pay to the creditor in the event of the failure to perform or the improper performance of an obligation, in particular in the event of the delay of performance. With regard to a demand concerning payment of a penalty the creditor shall not be obliged to prove the losses caused to him.

**Article 294. Form of Agreement on Penalty**

An agreement concerning a penalty must be concluded in written form irrespective of the form of the principal obligation.

The failure to comply with the written form shall entail the invalidity of the agreement concerning the penalty.

**Article 295. Legal Penalty**

1. A creditor shall have the right to demand the payment of a penalty determined by legislation (legal penalty) irrespective of whether the duty to pay it has been provided for by agreement of the parties.

2. The amount of a legal penalty may by agreement of the parties be increased if this is not prohibited by legislation.

**Article 296. Amounts of Penalty**

The amounts of a penalty shall be determined in a fixed monetary amount or in a percentage of the amount of the unperformed or improperly performed obligation.

**Article 297. Reduction of Amount of Penalty**

If a penalty (or fine, forfeit) subject to payment is excessively great in comparison with the losses of the creditor, a court shall have the right to reduce the penalty (or fine, forfeit), taking into account the degree of fulfilment of the obligation by the debtor and the interests of the debtor and creditor deserving of attention.

**Article 298. Grounds for Recovery of Penalty**

A penalty shall be recovered for the failure to perform or the improper performance of an obligation where conditions exist for bringing the debtor to responsibility for a violation of the obligation (Article 359 of the present Code).

*§3. Pledge*

**Article 299. Concept of Pledge**

1. That means of securing the performance of an obligation by virtue of which the creditor (pledgeholder) has the right, in the event of the failure of the debtor to perform the obligation secured by the pledge, to receive satisfaction from the value of the pledged property preferentially before other creditors of the person to whom this property (pledgor) belongs with the exceptions established by the present Code shall be deemed to be a pledge.

The pledgeholder shall have the right to receive on the same principles satisfaction from insurance compensation for loss or damage of the pledged property irrespective of to whose benefit it was insured unless the loss or damage occurred for reasons for which the pledgeholder is liable.

2. A pledge of enterprises, buildings, installations, apartments, rights to land plots, and other immovable property (mortgage ) shall be regulated by the Law of the Republic Kazakhstan on the Mortgage of Immoveables. The general rules on pledge contained in the present Code shall apply to mortgage in the instances when other rules have not been established by the Law of the Republic Kazakhstan on Mortgage.

3. A pledge subject to State registration of aircraft and marine vessels, ships of internal water navigation, ships of "river-sea" navigation (mortgage of vessel) shall be regulated by special legislative acts of the Republic Kazakhstan. The general rules on pledge contained in the present Code shall be applied to the mortgage of a vessel in instances when other rules have not been established by special legislative acts of the Republic Kazakhstan. The requirements of paragraph one of the present point also shall extend to marine vessels being built, ships of internal water navigation, and ships of "river-sea" navigation [Article as amended by Laws of 2 March 1998, No. 211-I; and of 17 January 2002, No. 285-II].

**Article 300. Grounds for Arising of Pledge**

1. A pledge shall arise by virtue of a contract. Pledge also shall arise on the basis of legislative acts when the circumstances specified therein ensue if it is provided in legislative acts which property and for securing the performance of which obligation t here is deemed to be a pledge.

2. The rules of the present Code on a pledge arising by virtue of contract shall respectively apply to a pledge arising on the basis of legislative acts unless established otherwise by legislative acts.

**Article 301. Subject of Pledge**

1. Any property, including things and property rights (or demands), may be the subject of a pledge except for things withdrawn from turnover (Article 116(2) of the present Code), demands inextricably connected with the person of the creditor, in particular, demands concerning alimony, compensation for harm caused to life or health, and other rights whose assignment to another person has been prohibited by legislative acts.

2. The right of pledge may be extended by a contract to property which comes to the ownership or economic jurisdiction of the pledgor in future.

3. The pledge of individual types of property, in particular the property of citizens against which levy of execution is not permitted, may be prohibited or limited by legislative acts.

4. [repealed by Law of 12 January 2007, No. 225-III].

5. [repealed by Law of 8 July 2005, No. 72-III] [Article as amended by Laws of 11 July 19976, No. 154-I; of 2 March 1998, No. 211-I].

**Article 302. Demands Secured by Pledge**

1. Unless provided otherwise by a contract or legislative acts, a pledge shall secure a demand in that amount which it has at the moment of actual satisfaction, including remuneration (or interest), compensation of losses caused by delay of performance, penalty (or fine, forfeit) and necessary costs for the maintenance of the pledged property, and also compensation of expenses relating to recovery.

2. A pledge may be established with respect to demands which arise in future on condition the parties agree concerning the amount of security of such demands by the pledge [Article as amended by Law of 11 July 1997, No. 154-I].

**Article 303. Types of Pledge**

1. Mortgage – is a type of pledge under which the pledged property remains in the possession and use of the pledgor or a third person.

2. The subject of a mortgage may be an enterprise, structure, building, installation, apartments in an apartment house, means of transport, space objects, goods in turnover, and other property not withdrawn from civil turnover.

Separable fruits may be the subject of a mortgage only on condition they do not become from the moment of separation the object of the rights of a third person. The mortgage of enterprises, structures, buildings, installations, apartments in an apartment house, means of transport, and space objects shall be subject to registration in agencies effectuating the registration of such objects.

2. Pawn – is a type of pledge under which the pledged property is transferred by the pledgor to the possession of the pledgeholder.

With the consent of the pledgeholder the subject of pledge may be left with the pledgor under lock and seal of the pledgeholder. The subject of pledge may be left in the possession of the pledgor with the imposition of marks testifying to the pledge (firm pledge).

3. In the event of the pledge of rights, the subject of pledge shall be the property rights which may be alienated, in particular, lease rights to an enterprise, structure, building, installation, right to

participatory share in the property of an economic partnership, debt demands, author's, inventor's, and other property rights.

The pledge of rights to a land plot, and also the rights to other natural resources, shall be permitted within the limits and on the conditions established by land and other natural resource legislation.

A short-term right may be the subject of pledge only until the expiry of the period of its operation.

The debtor of a pledged right must be informed about the pledge.

If a pledged right is confirmed by a document, the contract of pledge may be formalized by the transfer of the right-establishing document.

4. The pledge of securities shall be effectuated in accordance with legislation on the securities market.

5. Unless established otherwise by a contract on pledge, money which is the subject of a pledge shall be placed in a bank.

Remuneration (or interest) due on the said money shall belong to the pledgor.

Money may be transferred to the pledgeholder or other person in compliance with the conditions limiting the possibility of use of the pledged money by this person (or transfer for keeping to a bank safe, safe drawer, or individual premise for keeping). The failure of such person to perform the limitations for the use of pledged money shall be grounds for his responsibility for unfounded enrichment from the moment of the transfer of the money to him [Article as amended by Laws of 11 July 1997, No. 154-I; of 8 July 2005, No. 72-III; of 12 January 2007, No. 225-III].

**Article 304. Pledge of Property in Common Ownership**

Property comprising common ownership may be transferred on pledge only with the consent of all the owners. The right to a participatory share in common property may be the autonomous subject of a pledge.

**Article 305. Pledgor**

1. Either the debtor himself or a third person may be a pledgor.

2. The pledgor of a thing may be the owner thereof or, with the consent of the owner, a person having the right of economic jurisdiction over it unless provided otherwise by legislative acts.

3. The pledgor of a right may be the person to whom the pledged right belongs.

The pledge of the right of lease or other right to another's thing shall be permitted without the consent of its owner or the person having the right of economic jurisdiction over it if the alienation of this right without the consent of the said persons has been prohibited by legislative acts or by contract.

**Article 306. Insurance of Pledged Property**

1. The duty to insure pledged property transferred to his possession may be placed by contract or by legislative acts on the pledgeholder.

The insurance of pledged property which remains in the use of the pledgor shall be placed on the last.

2. When the insured event ensues, the right of demand under the contract of insurance of the pledged property which is with the pledgor shall arise only in the event of the refusal thereof by the pledgeholder.

If the amount of the insurance compensation exceeds the amount of the obligation secured by the pledge, the pledgeholder shall be obliged within three banking days from the moment of receiving it to credit the difference to the pledgor [Article as amended by Law of 18 December 2000, No. 128-II].

**Article 307. Content and Form of Contract on Pledge**

1. In the contract on pledge must be specified the subject of pledge and its valuation, the essence, amount, and period for performance of the obligation secured by the pledge. It also must contain an indication of with which of the parties the pledged property is situated and the admissibility of using it.

2. A contract on pledge must be concluded in written form.

3. The failure to comply with the rules contained in points 1 and 2 of the present Article shall entail the invalidity of the contract on pledge.

**Article 308. Registration of Pledge**

1. The pledge of property subject to State registration must be registered at the agency effectuating the registration of the particular property.

2. The agency effectuating registration shall be obliged to keep the register for the registration of pledges and to take measures relating to the defense of interests of the pledgeholders, and not permit the alienation of pledged property without the consent of the pledgeholder.

In the event of the change of character and content of the debt demand secured by a pledge, an additional registration shall be made except for instances when the possibility of a change of the amount or procedure for calculating remuneration under the contract, and also actions connected therewith and a change of the schedule for payment, including a change of the repayment periods, is provided by the parties to a contract of bank loan.

In the event of the transfer of the right of ownership to pledged property to another person, an entry shall be made in the register concerning the transfer of the pledge to the new owner.

3. The pledgor who has performed an obligation secured by a pledge shall have the right to demand the annulment in the register of the entry concerning the pledge. At the demand of the pledgor, the pledgeholder shall be obliged to submit to the agency conducting the registration the necessary documents and written applications. In the event of the failure to perform or the untimely performance by the pledgeholder of these duties the pledgor shall have the right to demand compensation of losses caused to him [Article as amended by Law of 3 June 2003, No. 426-II].

**Article 309. Property to Which Rights of Pledgeholder Extends**

1. The rights of the pledgeholder (right of pledge) to a thing which is the subject of pledge shall extend to its appurtenances and to inseparable fruits unless provided otherwise by contract or legislative acts.

The right of pledge shall extend to separable fruits, products, and revenues received as a result of the use of the pledged property in the instances provided for by contract or legislative acts.

2. In the event of the mortgage of an enterprise or other property complex as a whole the right of pledge shall extend to all of its property, movable and immovable, including the rights of demand and exclusive rights, amongst them those acquired during the period of the mortgage, unless provided otherwise by legislative acts or by contract.

3. The mortgage of a building or installation shall be permitted only with the simultaneous mortgage under the same contract of the land plot on which this building or installation is situated, or the part of this plot functionally ensuring the pledged object.

**Article 310. Arising of Right of Pledge**

1. Insofar as not provided otherwise by the contract on pledge, the right of pledge shall arise with respect to property, the pledge of which is subject to registration – from the moment of registration of the contract; with respect to other property – from the moment of the transfer of this property to the pledgeholder; and if it is not subject to transfer, then from the moment of the conclusion of the contract on pledge.

2. The right of pledge to goods in turnover shall arise in accordance with the rules of Article 327(2) of the present Code.

**Article 311. Subsequent Pledge (or Repledge)**

1. If property under pledge becomes the subject of yet another pledge to secure other demands (repledge), the demands of the subsequent pledgeholder shall be satisfied from the value of this property after the demands of preceding pledgeholders.

2. A repledge shall be permitted if it is not prohibited by the preceding contracts on pledge.

3. The pledgor shall be obliged to communicate to each subsequent pledgeholder information about all of the existing pledges of the particular property and shall be liable for losses caused to pledgeholders by the failure to fulfil this duty [Article as amended by Law of 2 March 1998, No. 211-I].

**Article 312. Content and Preservation of Pledged Property**

1. The pledgor or pledgeholder, depending upon which of them has the pledged property, shall be obliged, unless provided otherwise by legislative acts or contract, to:

(1) take measures necessary in order to ensure the preservation of the pledged property, including to defend it against infringements and demands on the part of third persons;

(2) inform immediately the other party concerning the arising of the threat of loss or damage to the pledged property.

2. The pledgeholder and the pledgor shall have the right to verify by documents the actual existence, quantity, state, and conditions of keeping the pledged property situated with the other party.

3. In the event of a flagrant violation by the pledgeholder of the duties specified in point 1 of the present Article which create a threat of loss or damage of the pledged property, the pledgor shall have the right to demand the termination of the pledge before time.

**Article 313. Consequences of Loss of or Damage to Pledged Property**

1. The pledgor shall bear the risk of accidental perishing or accidental damage to pledged property unless provided otherwise by the contract on pledge.

2. The pledgeholder shall be liable for the full or partial loss of or damage to the subject of pledge transferred to him unless it is proved that he may be relieved of responsibility in accordance with Article 359 of the present Code.

3. A pledgeholder shall be liable for the loss of the subject of pledge in the amount of its real value, and for the damaging thereof – the amount by which the value was reduced irrespective of the amount at which the subject of pledge was valued when transferring it to the pledgeholder.

4. If as a result of damage to the subject of pledge it has so changed that it can not be used for its express designation, the pledgor shall have the right to reject it and to demand compensation for the loss thereof.

5. The duty of the pledgeholder to compensate the pledgor for other losses caused by the loss of or damage to the subject of pledge may be provided for by a contract.

6. The pledgor who is a debtor with regard to the obligation secured by a pledge shall have the right to set off the demand against the pledgeholder concerning compensation of losses caused by the loss of or damage to the subject of pledge in repaying the obligation secured by the pledge.

**Article 314. Substitution and Restoration of Subject of Pledge**

1. The replacement of the subject of pledge shall be permitted with the consent of the pledgeholder unless provided otherwise by legislative acts or by contract.

2. If the subject of pledge has perished or is damaged or the right of ownership therein or the right of economic jurisdiction has been terminated on the grounds established by legislative acts, the pledgor shall have the right within a reasonable period to restore the subject of pledge or substitute other property of equal value.

**Article 315. Use and Disposition of Subject of Pledge**

1. The pledgor shall have the right, unless provided otherwise by contract and it arises from the essence of the pledge, to use the subject of pledge in accordance with its designation, including to derive fruits and revenues from it.

2. Unless provided otherwise by legislative acts or by contract and it follows from the essence of the pledge, the pledgor shall have the right to alienate the subject of pledge in ownership, economic jurisdiction, or operative management, to transfer it on lease or for use without compensation to another person, or otherwise to dispose of it only with the consent of the pledgeholder.

An agreement limiting the right of the pledgor to bequeath pledged property shall be invalid.

3. The pledgeholder shall have the right to use the subject of pledge transferred to him only in the instances provided for by contract, regularly submitting a report on use to the pledgor. The duty may

be placed by contract on the pledgeholder to derive fruits and revenues from the subject of pledge for the purposes of repaying the principal obligation or in the interests of the pledgor.

**Article 316. Defense by Pledgeholder of His Rights to Subject of Pledge**

1. The pledgeholder with whom the pledged property is situated or should be situated shall have the right to demand and obtain it from another's illegal possession, including from the pledgor himself.

2. In instances when according to the conditions of the contract the pledgeholder has been granted the right to use a subject of pledge transferred to him, he may demand from other persons, including from the pledgor, the elimination of any violations of his right, even though these violations were not linked with deprivation of possession.

**Article 317. Grounds for Levying Execution Against Pledged Property**

1. Execution may be levied against pledged property in order to satisfy the demands of the pledgeholder (creditor) in the event of the failure to perform or the improper performance by the debtor of an obligation secured by the pledge for which he is liable.

2. Levy of execution against pledged property may be refused if the violation of the obligation secured by the pledge which was permitted by the debtor is extremely insignificant and the amount of the demands of the pledgeholder as a consequence thereof is clearly incommensurate with the value of the pledged property.

**Article 318. Procedure for Levy of Execution Against Subject of Pledge**

1. The demands of a pledgeholder from the value of pledged property shall be satisfied, unless established otherwise by the present Code and other legislative acts or a contract, in a judicial procedure.

2. In the instances provided for by a contract on pledge, and also by the present Code and other legislative acts, the pledgeholder shall have the right to autonomously realize the property under pledge in a compulsory extrajudicial procedure by means of holding a public sale (or auction). A bank-pledgeholder shall have the same right with regard to the realization of the subject of pledge securing a monetary loan.

**Article 319. Realization of Pledged Property**

1. Pledged property against which execution is levied in accordance with Article 20 of the present Code shall be realized (or sold) by means of sale at a public sale in the procedure established by procedural legislation unless a different procedure has been established by legislative acts.

$1^1$. In the event of the pledge of money and rights (or demands) with regard to a monetary obligation this pledged property shall be realized by means of the transfer to the pledgeholder of the money which is the subject of pledge or under the monetary obligation due with regard to pledged rights (or demands), and when it is impossible to transfer money at the moment of levy of execution against the subject of pledge – by means of transfer to the pledgeholder of the rights of the pledgor to the subject of pledge.

If the amount of money which is the subject of pledge exceeds the amount of the demand of the pledgeholder secured by the pledge the difference shall be returned to the pledgor. If the amounts of money are insufficient to cover the demand of the pledgeholder, he shall have the right in the absence of another indication in legislative acts or contract to receive the insufficient amount from other property of the debtor without enjoying a preference based on the pledge.

2. The peculiarities of the realization of pledged property in a compulsory extrajudicial procedure shall be established by the present Code and by the Law on the Mortgage of Immoveables. The rules and procedures established by the Law on the Mortgage of Immoveables for the realization of a mortgage shall apply to the realization of property when performing other types of pledge unless established otherwise by the present Code.

3. At the request of the pledgor the court shall have the right in deciding to levy execution against pledged property to defer the sale thereof at a public sale for a period of up to one year. The deferral shall not affect the rights and duties of the parties with regard to an obligation secured by the pledge of this property and shall not relieve the debtor from compensating the losses of the creditor and amounts of penalty which grew during the period of deferral.

4. Any juridical persons and citizens, including the pledgor and pledgeholder, shall have the right to take part in public sale.

Before the commencement of the public sale, the court or entrusted person (Article 320 of the present Code) shall have the right to demand from each participant in the public sale the submission of a guarantee payment. The guarantee payments shall be subject to return upon the completion of the public sale. The guarantee payment of a participant who has succeeded at the public sale shall be deducted from the account of the final price.

The guarantee payment of the participant who has succeeded at the public sale but not paid up the final price shall not be refunded and shall remain at the disposition of the court or entrusted person.

5. When a public sale is declared to be unconstituted in view of the participation therein of less than two purchasers, a pledgeholder shall have the right either to convert the pledged property to his ownership at its current appraised value to be established by decision of the court or by the entrusted person on the basis of the opinion of a State agency for the valuation of property or to demand the designation of a new public sale.

6. If the amount received when realizing the pledged property is insufficient to cover the demand of the pledgeholder, he shall have the right in the absence of another indication in legislative acts or the contract to receive the amount in arrears from other property of the debtor without enjoying a preference based on the pledge.

If the amount received in the event of the realization of the pledged property exceeds the amount of the demand of the pledgeholder secured by the pledge, the difference shall be returned to the pledgor.

7. A debtor and pledgor who are a third person (surety of a thing) shall have the right at any time until the sale of the subject of pledge to terminate the levy of execution against it and the realization thereof, having performed the obligation secured by the pledge or that part thereof whose performance has been delayed. An agreement limiting this right shall be invalid [Article as amended by Laws of 8 November 2000, No. 96-II; of 12 January 2007, No. 225-III].

**Article 320. Realization of Pledged Property in Compulsory Extra-Judicial Procedure**

1. In the event of the realization of pledged property in a compulsory extra-judicial procedure, the public sale shall be held by an entrusted person, in the capacity of which a juridical person or citizen having a power of attorney of the pledgeholder for the realization of the pledged property shall act in the event of a violation of the obligation secured by the pledge.

2. The entrusted person shall fulfil the following procedures:

(1) draw up the notification to the pledgor concerning the failure to fulfil the obligation and register it in the agency where the contract on pledge was registered;

(2) in the event of the failure to satisfy the demands arising from the notification, but not earlier than two months from the moment of sending it to the pledgor, draw up the notification concerning the public sale of the pledge property, register it in the agency where the contract on pledge was registered, and hand it over to the pledgor;

(3) officially publish the announcement of the public sale in the local press.

**Article 321. Performance of Obligation Before Time Secured by Pledge and Levy of Execution Against Pledged Property**

1. A pledgeholder shall have the right to demand the performance before time of an obligation secured by pledge in instances of:

(1) the subject of pledge departing from the possession of the pledgor with whom it was left not in accordance with the conditions of the contract on pledge;

(2) a violation by the pledgor of the rules concerning substitution of the subject of pledge (Article 314);

(3) loss of the subject of pledge under circumstances for which the pledgeholder is not liable (Article 313(2) of the present Code) if the pledgor has not taken advantage of the right provided for by Article 314(2) of the present Code.

2. The pledgeholder shall have the right to demand the performance before time of the obligation secured by pledge and, if this demand is not satisfied, to levy execution against the subject of pledge in instances of:

(1) a violation by the pledgor of rules concerning subsequent pledge;

(2) the failure of the pledgor to fulfill the duties provided for by Article 312(1), subpoints (1) and (2) and Article 312(2) of the present Code;

(3) a violation by the pledgor of the rules concerning the disposition of pledged property (Article 315[2]).

**Article 322. Termination of Pledge**

1. A pledge shall terminate:

(1) with the termination of the obligation secured by the pledge;

(2) upon the demand of the pledgor when there exist the grounds provided for by Article 312(3) of the present Code;

(3) in the event of the perishing of the pledged thing or termination of the pledged right unless the pledgor has taken advantage of the right provided for by Article 314(2) of the present Code;

(4) in the event of the sale of pledged property at public sale, and also when the realization thereof has proved to be impossible (Article 319 of the present Code).

2. A notation in the register in which the contract on pledge was registered must be made concerning the termination of the pledge.

3. In the event of the termination of pledge as a consequence of the performance of the obligation secured by the pledge or at the demand of the pledgor (Article 312(3) of the present Code), the pledgeholder with whom the pledged property is situated shall be obliged immediately to return it to the pledgor.

**Article 323. Preservation of Pledge in Event of Transfer of Right to Pledged Property to Another Person by Way o f Legal Succession**

1. In the event of the transfer of the right of ownership to pledged property or the right of economic jurisdiction to it from the pledgor to another person as a result of the alienation with or without compensation or by way of universal legal succession, the right of pledge shall retain force.

The legal successor of the pledgor shall take the place of the pledgor and shall bear all the duties of the pledgor, unless established otherwise by an agreement with the pledgeholder.

2. If the property of the pledgor which is the subject of pledge has passed by way of legal succession to several persons, each of the legal successors (or acquirers of the property) shall bear the consequences arising from the pledge for the failure to perform the obligation secured by the pledge commensurate with the part of the said property which has passed to him. However, if the subject of the pledge is indivisible or on other grounds remains in the common joint ownership of the legal successors, they shall become joint and several pledgors.

**Article 324. Consequences of Compulsory Withdrawal of Pledged Property**

1. If the right of ownership of a pledgor to property which is the subject of pledge terminates on the grounds and in the procedure established by legislative acts as a consequence of the withdrawal (or purchase) for State needs, requisition, or nationalization, and the pledgor is granted other property or respective compensation, the right of pledge shall extend to the property provided instead or, respectively, the pledgeholder shall acquire the right of preferential satisfaction of his demand from the amount of compensation due to the pledgor. The pledgeholder also may demand the performance before time of the obligation secured by the pledge (Article 321(1) of the present Code).

2. In the instances when property which is the subject of pledge is withdrawn from the pledgor in the procedure established by legislative acts on the grounds that in reality the owner of this property is another person, or in the form of a sanction for the commission of a crime or another violation of law, the pledge with respect to this property shall terminate. In these instances the pledgeholder shall have the right to demand performance before time of the obligation secured by the pledge.

**Article 325. Assignment of Rights Regarding Contract on Pledge**

1. A pledgeholder shall have the right to transfer his rights under a contract concerning the pledge to another person while complying with the rules on the transfer of the rights of a creditor by means of the assignment of a demand (Articles 339-347 of the present Code).

2. The assignment by the pledgeholder of his rights under a contract on pledge to another person shall be valid if the rights of demand against the debtor regarding the principal obligation secured by pledge have been assigned.

3. [repealed by Law of 2 March 1998, No. 211-I].

**Article 326. Transfer of Debt Regarding Obligation Secured by Pledge**

With the transfer of a debt regarding an obligation secured by a pledge to another person, the pledge shall terminate unless the pledgor has given consent to the creditor to be liable for the new debtor.

**Article 327. Pledge of Goods in Turnover**

1. A pledge of goods while leaving them with the pledgor and granting to the pledgor the right to change the composition and natural form of the pledged property (goods reserves, raw material, materials, semi-fabricates, finished products, and the like) on condition that their total value does not become less than that specified in the contract on pledge, shall be deemed to be a pledge of goods in turnover.

A reduction of the value of the pledged goods in turnover shall be permitted commensurately with the performed part of the obligation secured by pledge unless provided otherwise by the contract.

2. Goods in turnover alienated by a pledgor shall cease to be the subject of pledge from the moment of their transfer into ownership, economic jurisdiction, or operative management of the acquirer, and goods acquired by the pledgor which are specified in the contract on pledge shall become the subject of pledge from the moment the right of the pledgor arises to ownership or economic jurisdiction.

3. The pledgor of goods in turnover shall be obliged to keep a register book of pledges in which entries are made concerning the conditions of the pledge of goods and all operations entailing a change of the composition or natural form of the pledged goods, including the processing thereof, on the day of the last operation.

4. In the event of a violation by the pledgor of the conditions of a pledge of goods in turnover, the pledgeholder shall have the right, by placing his marks and seals on the pledged goods, to suspend operations with them until the violation is eliminated.

**Article 328. Pledge of Things in Pawnshop**

1. The acceptance from citizens on pledge of movable property intended for personal consumption to secure short-term credits may be effectuated as entrepreneurial activity by juridical persons registered as pawnshops, the exclusive types of activity of which shall be:

(1) the provision of short-term loans under pledge of moveable property;

(2) the recording, keeping, and sale of jewellery articles containing precious metals and precious stones.

Pawnshops shall have the right to effectuate investment activity.

2. A contract on the pledge of things in a pawnshop shall be formalised by the issuance of a pledge ticket by the pawnshop and may contain a requirement concerning insurance of the pledged property. Insurance of pledged property shall be effectuated at the expense of the pawnshop.

3. A pawnshop shall not have the right to use and dispose of pledged things.

4. The pawnshop shall bear responsibility for loss of and damage to pledged things unless it is proved that the loss or damag e occurred as a consequence of insuperable force.

5. Pawnshops shall effectuate their activity only when there are Rules for conducting pawnshop operations which are confirmed by the highest organ of the pawnshop and must contain the following information:

(1) maximum amounts and periods for credits to be provided;

(2) maximum amounts of rates of remuneration for credits to be provided;

(3) rates and tariffs for conducting operations;

(4) rights and duties of the pawnshop and its clients and the responsibility thereof;

(5) procedure for issuance to the pledgor of duplicates in the event of loss of the pledge ticket;

(6) other conditions.

The rules for conducting pawnshop operations shall be subject to placement in a site accessible for viewing by clients of the pawnshop.

6. The conditions of a contract on pledge of things in a pawnshop limiting the rights of the pledgor in comparison with the rights granted him by the present Code shall be invalid from the moment of conclusion of the contract. In place of such conditions the respective provisions of the present Code shall be applied [Article as amended by Laws of 2 March 1998, No. 211-I; of 23 December 2005, No. 107-III].

*§4. Guarantee and Suretyship*

**Article 329. Guarantee**

1. By virtue of a guarantee the guarantor shall be obliged to the creditor of another person (debtor) to be liable for the performance of the obligation of this person wholly or partially and jointly and severally with the debtor, except for instances provided for by legislative acts [as amended by Law of 11 July 1997, No. 154-I].

2. Persons who have given a guarantee jointly shall be liable to the creditor jointly and severally, unless established otherwise by the contract of guarantee [added by Law of 11 July 1997, No. 154-I].

3. The contract of guarantee may be also concluded in order to secure an obligation which arises in future [added by Law of 11 July 1997, No. 154-I].

**Article 330. Suretyship**

By virtue of a suretyship the surety shall be obliged to the creditor of another person (debtor) to be liable for the performance of the obligation of this person, wholly or partially, jointly and severally [as amended by Law of 11 July 1997, No. 154-I].

**Article 331. Grounds and Form of Guarantee and Suretyship**

1. A guarantee and suretyship shall arise on the grounds of contracts of suretyship or guarantee. The use of a guarantee may be established by legislation [as amended by Law of 11 July 1997, No. 154-I].

2. Contracts of guarantee or suretyship must be concluded in written form. The failure to comply with the written form shall entail the invalidity of the contract of guarantee or suretyship [as amended by Law of 11 July 1997, No. 154-I].

3. The written form of contracts of guarantee or suretyship shall be considered to be complied with if the guarantor or surety has informed the creditor in writing about his responsibility for the performance of the obligation by the debtor and the creditor has not rejected the proposals of the guarantor or surety within the time normally necessary for this [as amended by Law of 11 July 1997, No. 154-I].

4. Banks of the second tier may effectuate the issuance of bank guarantees and suretyship on the basis of a license of the empowered agency in accordance with the present Code and taking into account normative legal acts of the empowered agency regulating the procedure for conducting the said operations.

The issue by banks of the second tier of bank guarantees and suretyships without complying with norms of the present Code and taking into account the requirements of normative legal acts of the empowered agency shall entail the invalidity thereof [point 4 as amended by Laws of 3 March 2001, No. 162-II; of 10 July 2003, No. 483-II; and of 12 January 2007, No. 225-III].

**Article 332. Responsibility of Guarantor and Surety**

1. Unless established otherwise by the contract, a guarantee and suretyship shall secure only a valid demand. The guarantor and surety shall not be relieved from responsibility if they have given surety for a debtor whose lack of dispositive legal capacity was previously known to them and at that time the creditor did not know of this circumstance [as amended by Law of 11 July 1997, No. 154-I].

2. The guarantor shall be liable to the creditor in the same amount as the debtor, including the payment of penalty, remuneration (or interest), court costs relating to recovery of the debt, and other losses of the creditor caused by the failure to perform or the improper performance of the obligation by the debtor unless established otherwise by the contract of guarantee [as amended by Law of 11 July 1997, No. 154-I].

3. The surety shall bear responsibility to the creditor within the limits of the amount specified in the suretyship unless provided otherwise by the conditions of the suretyship. Until demands are presented to the surety who bears subsidiary responsibility, the creditor must take reasonable measures for the satisfaction of this demand by the debtor, in particular, by means of setting off a counter demand and levying execution in the established procedure against the property of the debtor [as amended by Law of 11 July 1997, No. 154-I].

**Article 333. Rights and Duties of Guarantor in Event of Presenting of Demand Against Him by Creditor**

1. A guarantor shall be obliged before satisfaction of the demand of a creditor to warn the debtor thereof, and if a suit is brought against the guarantor, to involve the debtor in the case. Otherwise the

debtor shall have the right to advance against the counter-demand of the guarantor all the objections which he had against the creditor [as amended by Law of 11 July 1997, No. 154-I].

2. The guarantor shall have the right to advance against the demands of the creditor objections which the debtor could present unless arises otherwise from the contract of guarantee. The guarantor shall not lose the right to these objections even if the debtor waived them or has acknowledged his debt [as amended by Law of 11 July 1997, No. 154-I].

**Article 334. Rights of Guarantor and Surety Who Has Performed Obligation**

1. To a guarantor who has performed an obligation shall pass all the rights of the creditor with regard to this obligation and the rights which belonged to the creditor as pledgeholder in that amount which the guarantor satisfied the demand of the creditor. The guarantor also shall have the right to demand from the debtor the payment of a penalty and remuneration (or interest) on the amount paid to the creditor and compensation for other losses incurred in connection with responsibility for the debtor [as amended by Law of 11 July 1997, No. 154-I].

2. Upon performance by the guarantor of the obligation the creditor shall be obliged to hand over to the guarantor the documents certifying the demand against the debtor and to transfer the rights which secure this demand [as amended by Law of 11 July 1997, No. 154-I].

3. The rules established by points 1 and 2 of the present Article shall be applied unless established otherwise by legislation or by the contract of the guarantor with the debtor and arises from the relations between them [as amended by Law of 11 July 1997, No. 154-I].

4. The surety shall acquire the same rights in that part of which he has performed the obligation of the debtor to the credit or [as amended by Law of 11 July 1997, No. 154-I].

**Article 335. Notification of Guarantor and Surety about Performance of Obligation by Debtor**

The debtor who has performed an obligation secured by a guarantee or suretyship shall be obliged immediately to notify the guarantor or surety thereof. Otherwise the guarantor or surety who in turn has performed the obligation shall have the right to recover from the creditor that unjustifiably received or to present a regressive demand against the debtor. In the last instance the debtor shall have the right to recover from the creditor only that unjustly received [as amended by Law of 11 July 1997, No. 154-I].

**Article 336. Termination of Guarantee and Suretyship**

1. A guarantee and suretyship shall terminate with the termination of the obligation secured by it, and also in the event of a change of this obligation entailing an increase of responsibility or other unfavorable consequences for the guarantor and surety without the consent of the last [as amended by Law of 11 July 1997, No. 154-I].

2. A guarantee and suretyship shall terminate with the transfer to another person of the debt relating to the obligation secured by the guarantee or suretyship unless the guarantor or surety has given consent to the creditor to be liable for the new debt or [as amended by Law of 11 July 1997, No. 154-I].

3. A guarantee and suretyship shall terminate if upon the ensuing of the period for performance of the obligation secured by it the creditor has refused to accept proper performance offered by the debtor or by the guarantor and surety [as amended by Law of 11 July 1997, No. 154-I].

4. A guarantee and suretyship shall terminate upon the expiry of the period for which they were given specified in the contract of guarantee or suretyship. If such period has not been established, it shall terminate if the creditor, within one year from the date of ensuing of the period of performance of the obligation secured by the guarantee or suretyship, a suit against the guarantor or surety has not been brought. When the period of performance of the principal obligation has not been specified and can not be determined or is determined by the moment of demand, the guarantee and suretyship shall terminate if the creditor does not bring suit against the guarantor or surety within two years from the date of concluding the contract of guarantee or suretyship, unless provided otherwise by legislative acts [as amended by Law of 11 July 1997, No. 154-I].

### §5. *Deposit*

**Article 337. Concept of Deposit. Form of Agreement on Deposit**

1. A deposit shall be deemed to be a monetary amount issued by one of the contracting parties on the account under a contract of payment due from him to the other party also as security for the conclusion and performance of the contract or performance of another obligation.

2. An agreement on deposit, irrespective of the amount of the deposit, must be concluded in written form. This rule shall apply also in the event that the principal obligation must be notarially certified. The failure to comply with the written form shall entail the invalidity of the agreement on deposit [Article as amended by Law of 12 January 2007, No. 225-III].

**Article 338. Consequences of Termination and Failure to Perform Obligation Secured by Deposit**

1. In the event of the termination of the obligation before the commencement of the performance thereof by agreement of t he parties or as a consequence of the impossibility of performance which ensued without their fault the deposit must be returned.

2. If for the failure to perform the obligation the party which gave the deposit is responsible, it shall remain with the other party, and if the party which received the deposit is responsible, it shall be obliged to pay the other party twice the amount of the deposit. In addition the party responsible for the failure to perform the obligation shall be obliged to compensate the other party for losses, taking into account the amount of the deposit insofar as not provided otherwise in the contract.

### §6. *Withholding*

[added by Law of 12 January 2007, No. 225-III]

**Article 338[1]. General Provisions on Withholding**

1. A creditor with whom a thing is situated subject to transfer to a debtr or to a person specified by the debtor shall have the right in the event of the failure of the debtor to perform within the period the obligation with regard to payment for this thing or compensation to the creditor for costs and other losses connected with it to withhold it until the respective obligation is performed.

Demands also may be secured by the withholding of a thing, although not connected with payment for the thing or compensation of costs for it and other losses but arising from an obligation the parties of which act as entrepreneurs.

2. A creditor may withhold a thing situated with it even though after this thing entered the possession of the creditor the rights thereto have been acquired by a third person.

3. The rules of the present Article shall apply unless provided otherwise by a contract [Article added by Law of 12 January 2007, No. 225-III].

**Article 338$^2$. Satisfaction of Demands at Expense of Withheld Property**

Demands of a creditor who is withholding a thing shall be satisfied from the value thereof in an amount and in the procedure provided for the satisfaction of demands secured by the pledge [Article added by Law of 12 January 2007, No. 225-III].

*Chapter 19. Change of Persons in Obligation*

**Article 339. Grounds and Procedure for Transfer of Rights of Creditor to Other Person**

1. The right (or demand) belonging to a creditor on the basis of an obligation may be transferred by him to another person with regard to the transaction (assignment of demand) or pass to another person on the basis of a legislative act.

The rules concerning the transfer of the rights of a creditor to another person shall not apply to regressive demands.

2. The consent of the debtor, unless provided otherwise by legislative acts or by contract, shall not be required for the transfer of the rights of the creditor to another person.

3. If the debtor was not informed in writing about the transfer of the rights of the creditor to another person, the new creditor shall bear the risk of the unfavorable consequences caused by this for him. In this event the performance of the obligation to the initial creditor shall be deemed to be performance to a proper creditor.

4. The peculiarities of the assignment of the right of demand with regard to individual types of obligations may be established by legislative acts [point 4 added by Law of 2 March 1998, No. 211-I].

**Article 340. Rights Which May Not Pass to Other Persons**

The transfer to another person of the rights inextricably connected with the person of the creditor, in particular, demands concerning alimony and compensation of harm caused to life or health, shall not be permitted.

**Article 341. Amount of Rights of Creditor Passing to Other Person**

Unless provided otherwise by legislative acts or by contract, the right of the initial creditor shall pass to the new creditor in that amount and on those conditions which existed at the moment of transfer of the right. In particular, to the new creditor shall pass the rights securing the performance of the obligation, and also other rights connected with the demand, including the right to unpaid remuneration (or interest) [as amended by Law of 11 July 1997, No. 154-I].

**Article 342. Evidence of Rights of New Creditor**

1. The debtor shall have the right not to perform the obligation to a new creditor until the submission to him of evidence of the transfer of the demand to this person.

2. The creditor who has assigned a demand to another person shall be obliged to transfer to him the documents certifying the right of demand and to communicate information having significance for the effectuation of the demand.

**Article 343. Objections of Debtor Against Demand of New Creditor**

The debtor shall have the right to advance against the demand of a new creditor objections which he had against the initial creditor at the moment of receipt of information concerning the transfer of the rights regarding the obligation to the new creditor.

**Article 344. Transfer of Rights of Creditor to Another Person on Basis of Legislative Acts**

The rights of a creditor relating to an obligation shall pass to another person on the basis of legislative acts and ensuing of the circumstances specified therein:

(1) as a result of universal legal succession to the rights of the creditor;

(2) by decision of a court concerning the transfer of the rights of the creditor to another person when the possibility of such transfer has been provided for by legislative acts;

(3) as a consequence of the performance of the obligation by the guarantor thereof, surety, or pledgor who is not the debtor under this obligation;

(4) in the event of the subrogation to an insurer of the rights of the creditor against the debtor who is responsible for the ensuing of an insured event;

(5) in the other instances provided for by legislative acts [Article as amended by Law of 2 March 1998, No. 211-I].

**Article 345. Conditions of Assignment of Demand**

1. The assignment of a demand by the creditor to another person shall be permitted insofar as this is not contrary to legislation or a contract.

2. The assignment of the demand regarding the obligation in which the person of the creditor has material significance for the debtor without the consent of the debtor shall not be permitted.

**Article 346. Form of Assignment of Demand**

1. The assignment of a demand based on a transaction concluded in written (simple or notarial) form must be concluded in the respective written form.

2. The assignment of a demand relating to a transaction requiring State registration must be registered in the procedure established for registration of this transaction.

3. The assignment of a demand regarding an order security shall be concluded by means of an endorsement on this security (Article 132(3) of the present Code).

**Article 347. Responsibility of Creditor Who Has Assigned Demand**

The initial creditor who has assigned a demand shall be liable to the new creditor for the invalidity of the demand transferred to him but shall not be liable for the failure to perform this demand by the debtor except when the initial creditor assumed a suretyship for the debtor to the new creditor, and also unless provided otherwise by the present Code or a contract [as amended by Law of 3 June 2003, No. 426-II].

**Article 348. Transfer of Debt**

1. The transfer by the debtor of his debt to another person shall be permitted only with the consent of the creditor.

2. The new debtor shall have the right to advance against the demand of the creditor the objections based on relations between the creditor and the initial debtor.

3. The rules contained in Article 346(1) and (2) of the present Code shall apply respectively to the form of the transfer of the debt.

4. The peculiarities of the transfer of debt with regard to individual types of obligations may be established by legislative acts [point 4 added by Law of 2 March 1998, No. 211-I]

## *Chapter 20. Responsibility for Violation of Obligation*

**Article 349. Concept of Violation of Obligation**

1. By violation of obligation is understood the failure to perform it or performance improperly (untimely, goods and work with defects, violation of other conditions determined by the content of the obligation) – improper performance. In the event the impossibility of proper performance has arisen, the debtor shall be obliged to immediately notify the creditor thereof.

2. A debtor shall be brought to responsibility for the violation of an obligation at the demand of the creditor.

**Article 350. Compensation of Losses Caused by Violation of Obligation**

1. A debtor who has violated an obligation shall be obliged to compensate the creditor for losses caused by the violation (Article 9(4) of the present Code). Compensation of losses in obligations secured by a penalty shall be determined by the rules provided for by Article 351 of the present Code.

2. An agreement of the parties accepted before the violation of the obligation concerning relieving the debtor from compensation for losses caused by a violation of the obligation shall be invalid; however, the parties by mutual agreement may provide for the recovery of only real damage to property.

3. Unless provided otherwise by legislation or by contract, when determining losses the prices which existed in that place where the obligation was to have been performed on the day of voluntary satisfaction by the debtor of the demand of the creditor shall be taken into account, and if the demand was not voluntarily satisfied, on the day of presenting the suit. Proceeding from the circumstances, a court may satisfy the demand to compensate losses by taking into account the prices existing on the day of rendering the decision or the day of actual payment.

4. When determining the amount of lost advantage the measures undertaken by the creditor to receive it and the preparations made for this purpose shall be taken into account.

5. A creditor shall have the right to demand any action of a debtor to be deemed invalid if it is proved that it was performed for the purpose of evading responsibility for the violation of the obligation [Article as amended by Law of 2 March 1998, No. 211-I].

**Article 351. Losses and Penalty**

1. If a penalty has been established for the failure to perform or for improper performance of an obligation, the losses shall be compensated in the part not covered by the penalty.

Instances may be provided for by legislation or by contract: when the recovery of only a penalty is permitted, but not of losses; when losses may be recovered in full above the penalty; when at the choice of the creditor either a penalty or losses may be recovered.

2. In instances when limited responsibility was established for the failure to perform or improper performance, the losses subject to compensation in the part not covered by the penalty or above or in place of it may be recovered up to the limits established by such limitation.

**Article 352. Compensation of Moral Harm Caused by Violation of Obligation**

Moral harm caused by a violation of an obligation shall be compensated above the losses provided for by Article 350 of the present Code.

**Article 353. Responsibility for Unlawful Use of Another's Money**

1. For the unlawful use of another's money as a result of the failure to perform a monetary obligation, or delay in the payment thereof, or the unfounded receipt or savings at the expense of another person a penalty shall be subject to payment. The amount of the penalty shall be calculated by proceeding from the official refinancing rate of the National Bank of the Republic Kazakhstan on the day of performance of the monetary obligation or respective part thereof. In the event of the recovery of a debt in a judicial procedure the court may satisfy the demand of the creditor by proceeding from the official refinancing rate of the National Bank of the Republic Kazakhstan on the day of filing the suit, or on the day of rendering the decision, or on the day of the actual payment at the choice of the creditor. These rules shall apply unless new amount of penalty has been established by legislative acts or by contract [as amended by Law of 11 July 1997, No. 154-I].

2. The penalty for the use of another's money shall be recovered as of the day of payment of these monies to the creditor unless another procedure for the calculation of the amount of the penalty has been established by legislation or by a contract [as amended by Law of 11 July 1997, No. 154-I].

3. If losses caused to the creditor by the unlawful use of his money exceed the amount of the penalty due him on the basis of point 1 of the present Article, he shall have the right to demand compensation of losses from the debtor in the part exceeding this amount [Article as amended by Law of 11 July 1997, No. 154-I; and of 12 January 2007, No. 225-III].

**Article 354. Responsibility and Performance of Obligation in Kind**

1. The payment of a penalty and compensation of losses in the event of the improper performance of an obligation shall not relieve the debtor from performance of the obligation unless provided otherwise by legislative acts or by contract.

2. The compensation of losses in the event of the failure to perform an obligation and the payment of a penalty for the failure to perform shall relieve the debtor from the performance of the obligation in kind unless provided otherwise by legislative acts or by contract.

3. The refusal of a creditor to accept performance which as a consequence of delay has lost interest for him (Article 365 of the present Code), and also the payment of a monetary amount established

as release-money (Article 369 of the present Code), shall relieve the debtor from performance of the obligation in kind [Article as amended by Law of 2 March 1998, No. 211-I].

**Article 355. Consequences of Failure to Perform Obligation to Transfer Individually-Specified Thing**

1. In the event of the failure to perform an obligation to transfer an individually-specified thing in ownership, economic jurisdiction, operative management, or use to a creditor, the last shall have the right to demand that this thing be taken away from the debtor and the transfer thereof to the creditor except for instances when the third person has a preferential right to this thing.

2. The transfer of the thing shall not relieve the debtor from compensation of losses.

**Article 356. Performance of Obligation at Expense of Debtor**

In the event of the failure to perform an obligation by a debtor to manufacture and transfer a thing to a creditor, or to fulfill determined work or to render a service for him, the creditor shall have the right within a reasonable period to commission the fulfillment of the obligation to third persons for a reasonable price or to fulfill it by his own efforts unless it follows otherwise from legislation, the contract, or the essence of the obligation, and to demand from the debtor compensation for necessary expenses and other losses incurred.

**Article 357. Subsidiary Responsibility**

1. Until demands are brought against the person who in accordance with legislation or with the conditions of an obligation bears responsibility additionally to the responsibility of another person who is the principal debtor (subsidiary responsibility), the creditor must present the demand to the principal debtor.

If the principal debtor refused to satisfy or has not performed in full the demand of the creditor or the creditor has not received a reply from him within a reasonable period to the demand presented, this demand in the unperformed part may be presented to the person who bears subsidiary responsibility.

2. A creditor shall not have the right to demand satisfaction of his demand against the principal debtor from a person bearing subsidiary responsibility if this demand can be satisfied by means of the set-off of the counter demand against the principal debtor (Article 370 of the present Code).

3. The person who bears subsidiary responsibility must until satisfaction of the demand presented to him by the creditor warn the principal debtor thereof, and if suit is brought against such person, to involve the principal debtor in the case.

Otherwise the principal debtor shall have the right to advance against the regressive demand of the person subsidiarily liable objections which he had against the creditor [Article as amended by Law of 2 March 1998, No. 211-I].

**Article 358. Limitation of Amount of Responsibility for Obligations**

1. The right to full compensation of losses (limited responsibility) may be limited by legislative acts with regard to individual types of obligations and with regard to obligations connected with the determined nature of activity.

2. An agreement concerning the limitation of the amount of responsibility of a debtor under a contract of adhesion or other contract in which the citizen acting as a consumer is a creditor shall be invalid if the amount of responsibility for the particular type of obligations or for the particular violation has been determined by legislation [as amended by Law of 2 March 1998, No. 211-I].

**Article 359. Grounds of Responsibility for Violation of Obligation**

1. A debtor shall be liable for the failure to perform and/or improper performance of an obligation when there is fault unless provided otherwise by legislation or by contract. The debtor shall be deemed to be not at fault if it is proved that he has taken all measures for proper performance of the obligation.

2. The person who has not performed or who has improperly performed an obligation shall, when effectuating entrepreneurial activity, bear property responsibility unless it is proved that proper performance proved to be impossible as a consequence of insuperable force, that is, extraordinary and unavertable circumstances under the particular conditions (natural phenomena, military actions, and so forth). There shall not be relegated to such circumstances, in particular, the absence in the market of goods, work, or services necessary for performance.

Other grounds for responsibility or relief therefrom may be provided for by legislation or by contract.

3. An agreement concluded beforehand concerning the elimination or limitation of responsibility for an intentional violation of an obligation shall be invalid.

**Article 360. Entrepreneurial Risk in Obligation**

If the performance of any work has been provided by an obligation at the order of an entrepreneur, the risk of impossibility or of the inadvisability to use the work results shall be placed on the entrepreneur. The person who has properly performed the work shall have the right to receive payment commensurate with the degree of performance, except for instances when another distribution of entrepreneurial risk has been provided for by a contract.

**Article 361. Consequences of Impossibility of Performance of Bilateral Contract**

If in a bilateral contract performance for one party has become impossible as a consequence of a circumstance for which neither party is liable, then neither of the parties, insofar as not provided otherwise by a legislative act or a contract, shall have the right to demand performance of the contract. Each of the parties shall have the right to demand in this event the return of everything that it performed, not having received the respective counter performance.

**Article 362. Responsibility of Debtor for His Workers**

The actions of officials or other workers of a debtor relating to the performance of his obligation shall be considered to be the actions of the debtor. The debtor shall be liable for these actions if they entailed the failure to perform or the improper performance of the obligation.

**Article 363. Responsibility of Debtor for Actions of Third Persons**

1. A debtor shall bear responsibility to a creditor also in instances when the actions or the failure to act of third persons with regard to their obligations to the debtor served as a cause of the violation of the obligation.

A debtor shall bear responsibility also for the actions or the failure to act by third persons on whom the debtor placed performance of his duties to the creditor unless it has been established by legislation that responsibility shall be borne by the immediate performer.

2. A debtor may be relieved from responsibility for the violation of an obligation caused by the actions or failure to act of third persons, having proved the absence of their fault.

When effectuating entrepreneurial activity a debtor may be relieved from responsibility for a violation caused by the actions or failure to act of third persons if this is conditioned by insuperable force (Article 359(2) of the present Code).

3. In the event of a violation of an obligation connected with the subject of an obligation being encumbered by the rights of third persons, the debtor shall be relieved from responsibility only if such encumberments arose before the conclusion of the contract with the creditor and the last when concluding the contract was warned about them.

4. Other conditions of responsibility of a debtor for the actions of third persons may be provided for by legislation or by contract.

**Article 364. Fault of Creditor**

1. If the failure to perform or improper performance of an obligation has occurred through the fault of both parties, a court shall respectively reduce the amount of responsibility of the debtor. A court also shall have the right to reduce the amount of responsibility of the debtor if the creditor has intentionally or through negligence facilitated the increase of the amount of losses caused by the failure to perform or improper performance, or has not taken reasonable measures to reduce them.

2. The rules of point 1 of the present Article respectively shall also apply in instances when the debtor, by virtue of a legislative act or contract, bears responsibility for the failure to perform or improper performance of an obligation irrespective of his fault [Article as amended by Law of 2 March 1998, No. 211-I].

**Article 365. Delay of Debtor**

1. A debtor who has delayed performance shall be liable to the creditor for losses caused by the delay and for the consequences which incidentally ensued during the delay of the impossibility of performance.

2. If as a consequence of delay of the debtor the performance has lost interest for the creditor, he may refuse to accept performance and demand compensation of losses.

3. The debtor shall not be considered to have delayed so long as the obligation can not be performed as a consequence of delay by the creditor (Article 366 of the present Code).

**Article 366. Delay of Creditor**

1. The creditor shall be considered to have delayed if he refused to accept proper performance offered by the debtor or did not perform actions provided for by legislation or by contract or arising from the customs of business turnover or from the essence of the obligation, until the performance of which the debtor could not perform his obligation.

A creditor shall be considered to have delayed also in the event of the refusal to properly confirm performance of an obligation made by the debtor.

2. The delay of a creditor shall give the debtor the right to compensation of losses caused by the delay if the creditor does not prove that the delay occurred through circumstances for which neither he himself nor those persons on whom by virtue of legislation or the commission of the creditor acceptance of performance was placed are liable.

On a creditor who has permitted delay shall be placed all the unfavorable consequences of the incidental impossibility of performance of the obligation which ensued during the delay.

3. With regard to a monetary obligation the debtor shall not be obliged to pay remuneration (or interest) for the time of delay by the creditor [Article as amended by Law of 11 July 1997, No. 154-I].

## *Chapter 21. Termination of Obligation*

**Article 367. Grounds for Termination of Obligation**

1. Obligations shall terminate wholly or in part by performance, granting of release-money, set-off, novation, forgiveness of debt, coinciding of debtor and creditor in one person, impossibility of performance, publication of act of State agency, death of citizen, and liquidation of juridical person.

2. The termination of an obligation relating to the demand of one of the parties shall be permitted only in the instances provided for by legislation.

3. Other grounds for the termination of obligations may be provided for by legislation and by contract.

**Article 368. Termination of Obligation by Performance**

1. Proper performance shall terminate an obligation.

2. [repealed by Law of 2 March 1998, No. 211-I].

**Article 369. Release-Money**

By agreement of the parties an obligation may be terminated by granting release-money in place of performance (payment of money, transfer of property, etc.). The amount, periods, and procedure for granting release-money shall be established by the parties.

**Article 370. Termination of Obligation by Set-Off**

1. An obligation shall be terminated wholly or in part by the set-off of a counter demand of the same type, the period for which has ensued or the period of which has not been specified or is determined by the moment of demand. The statements by one party are sufficient for set-off.

2. The set-off of demands shall not be permitted:

(1) if according to the statement one of the parties the period of limitations is subject to application to the demand and this period has expired;

(2) concerning compensation of harm caused to life or health;

(3) concerning the recovery of alimony;

(4) concerning maintenance for life;

($4^1$) against a bank in the process of shutting-down or liquidation if demands of the creditor arise from the contract(s) of assignment of a right of demand ;

(5) in other instances provided for by legislation or by a contract.

3. In the event of the assignment of demand a debtor shall have the right to set-off against the demand of a new creditor his counter-demand against the initial creditor.

The set-off shall be made if the demand arose on grounds which existed at the moment of receipt by the debtor of information concerning the assignment of the demand and the period of the demand ensued before receiving it or this period was not specified or is determined by the moment of demand [Article as amended by Laws of 2 March 1998, No. 211-I; of 23 December 2005,No. 107-III].

**Article 371. Termination of Obligation by Coincidence of Debtor and Creditor in One Person**

An obligation shall terminate by the coinciding of the debtor and the creditor in one person.

**Article 372. Termination of Obligation by Novation**

1. An obligation shall be terminated by agreement of the parties concerning the substitution of the initial obligation which existed between them by another obligation between the same persons providing for another subject or means of performance (novation).

2. Novation shall not be permitted with respect to obligations relating to compensation for harm caused to life or health and relating to the payment of alimony.

3. Novation shall terminate additional obligations connected with the initial one unless provided otherwise by agreement of the parties [Article as amended by Law of 2 March 1998, No. 211-I].

**Article 373. Forgiveness of Debt**

An obligation shall be terminated by the release of the debtor by the creditor from the duties on him unless this violates the rights of other persons with respect to the property of the creditor.

**Article 374. Termination of Obligation for Impossibility of Performance**

1. An obligation shall be terminated by the impossibility of performance if it was caused by a circumstance for which the debtor is not liable. The operation of the present rule shall not extend to monetary obligations.

2. In the event of the impossibility of performance by the party to an obligation caused by a circumstance for which neither it nor the other party is responsible, it shall not have the right to demand from the other party performance regarding the obligation unless provided otherwise by legislation or

contract. In so doing each party, having performed the obligation, shall have the right to demand the return of that performed.

3. In the event of the impossibility of performance by a debtor of an obligation caused by the guilty actions of the creditor, the last shall not have the right to demand the return of that which has been performed by it under the obligation.

**Article 375. Termination of Obligation on Basis of Act of State Agency**

1. If as a result of the publication of an act of a State agency, including local representative and local agencies (public act), t he performance of an obligation becomes impossible wholly or partially, the obligation shall terminate wholly or in respective pa rt. The parties who have incurred losses as a result thereof shall have the right to demand compensation thereof in accordance w ith the present Code.

2. In the event of a public act being deemed in the established procedure to be invalid on the basis of which an obligation h as terminated, the obligation shall be restored unless it follows otherwise from an agreement of the parties or the essence of the obligation and performance has not lost interest for the creditor.

**Article 376. Termination of Obligation by Death of Citizen**

1. An obligation shall be terminated by the death of the debtor if performance can not be made without the personal participation of the debtor or the obligation is otherwise inextricably connected with the person of the debtor.

2. An obligation shall be terminated by the death of the creditor if the performance was intended personally for the creditor or the obligation was otherwise inextricably connected with the person of the creditor.

**Article 377. Termination of Obligation by Liquidation of Juridical Person**

1. An obligation shall be terminated by the liquidation of a juridical person (debtor or creditor) except for instances when by legislation the performance of an obligation of a liquidated juridical person is placed on another juridical person (relating to obligations arising as a consequence of causing harm caused to life and health, and others).

2. The termination of the activity or the reorganization of State agencies, including local representative and executive agencies, shall not entail the termination of obligations in which such agencies were debtors. The performance of the said obligations shall be entrusted to the agency at whose disposition the assets of the budget are situated unless provided otherwise by a decision concerning termination of the activity or reorganization of the respective agencies.

## SUBSECTION 2. GENERAL PROVISIONS ON CONTRACT

### *Chapter 22. Concept and Conditions of Contract*

**Article 378. Concept of Contract**

1. A contract shall be deemed to be an agreement of two or several persons concerning the establishment, change, or termination of civil rights and duties.

2. The rules concerning bilateral and multilateral transactions provided for by Chapter 4 of the present Code shall apply to a contract.

3. The general provisions on contract shall apply to contracts concluded by more than two parties (multilateral contracts) unless this is contrary to the multilateral character of such contracts.

**Article 379. Legal Relations Arising from Contract**

1. [Legal relations] of obligations, rights to a thing, authors', or other legal relations may arise from a contract.

2. The general provisions on obligations (Articles 268-377 of the present Code) shall apply to obligations which arose from the contract insofar as not provided otherwise by the rules of the present Chapter and the rules on individual types of contracts contained in the present Code.

3. To legal relations of rights to a thing, authors', and other legal relations which arise from a contract (contract on joint activity, constitutive contract, author's contract, and others) shall apply the provisions of the present Chapter unless it follows otherwise from legislation, the contract, or the essence of the legal relation.

**Article 380. Freedom of Contract**

1. Citizens and juridical persons shall be free in concluding a contract. Coercion to conclude a contract shall not be permitted except for instances when the duty to conclude a contract has been provided for by the present Code, by legislative acts, or by an obligation voluntarily accepted.

2. The parties may conclude a contract which is either provided for or is not provided for by legislation.

**Article 381. Mixed Contract**

The parties may conclude a contract which contains elements of various contracts provided for by legislation (mixed contract). The legislation on contracts whose elements are contained in a mixed contract shall apply to the relations of the parties under a mixed contract in respective parts unless it follows otherwise from the agreement of the parties or the essence of the mixed contract.

**Article 382. Determination of Conditions of Contract**

1. The conditions of a contract shall be determined at the discretion of the parties except for instances when the content of the respective conditions has been prescribed by legislation.

In instances when the condition of a contract has been provided for by a norm which in accordance with legislation operates unless established otherwise by agreement of the parties (dispositive norm), the parties may by their agreement exclude the application thereof or establish a condition different from that provided therein. In the absence of such agreement, the condition of the contract shall be determined by the dispositive norm.

2. If the condition of a contract has not been determined by the parties or by the dispositive norm, the respective condition shall be determined by the customs of business turnover applicable to the relations of the parties.

**Article 383. Contract and Legislation**

1. A contract must correspond to rules established by legislation (imperative norms) which are binding upon the parties prevailing at the moment of its conclusion.

2. If after the conclusion of a contract rules are established by legislation binding upon the parties other than those by which were prevailing when concluding the contract, the conditions of the contract concluded shall retain force except for instances when it is established by legislation that its operation extends to relations which arose from the contracts previously concluded.

**Article 384. Contract For and Without Compensation**

1. A contract under which a party must receive payment or other counter-giving for the performance of his duties shall be for compensation.

2. A contract under which one party is obliged to grant something to the other party without receiving payment from him or other counter-giving shall be deemed to be without compensation.

3. A contract shall be presupposed to be for compensation unless it arises otherwise from legislation, or the content or essence of the contract.

**Article 385. Price**

1. The performance of a contract shall be paid for at the price established by agreement of the parties.

In the instances provided for by legislative acts the prices (or tariffs, price scales, rates, etc.) established or regulated by duly empowered State agencies shall be applied.

2. The change of the price after the conclusion of a contract shall be permitted in the instances and on the conditions provided for by contract, by legislative acts, or in the procedure established by legislative acts.

3. In instances when in a contract for compensation the price has not been provided for and may not be determined by proceeding from the conditions of the contract, it shall be considered that the performance of the contract must be made at the price which at the moment of concluding the contract under comparable circumstances usually was recovered for analogous goods, work, or services.

**Article 386. Operation of Contract**

1. A contract shall enter into force and become binding for the parties from the moment of its conclusion (Article 393 of the present Code).

2. The parties shall have the right to establish that the conditions of a contract concluded by them shall apply to their relations which arose before the conclusion of the contract.

3. If the period of operation of a contract is provided by legislation or by contract, the end of this period shall entail the termination of the obligations of the parties under the contract.

A contract which lacks such a specification of the period of its operation shall be deemed to be in force until the moment of the ending of performance of the obligation by the parties determined therein.

4. The ending of the period of operation of a contract shall not relieve the parties from responsibility for the violation there of which occurred before the expiry of this period.

**Article 387. Public Contract**

1. A contract concluded by a commercial organisation and establishing its duties relating to the sale of goods, fulfillment of work, or rendering of services which this organization by the character of its activity must effectuate with respect to everyone who has recourse to it (retail trade, carriage by common-use transport, communications services, electric power supply, medical, hotel servicing, and so forth) shall be deemed to be a public contract [as amended by Law of 11 July 1997, No. 154-I].

A commercial organisation shall not have the right to prefer one person to others with respect to the conclusion of a public contract except for the instances provided by legislation.

2. The price of goods, work, and services, and also other conditions of a public contract, shall be established identically for all consumers except for instances when the granting of privileges for individual categories of consumers is permitted by legislation.

3. A refusal of a commercial organisation to conclude a public contract when it is possible to grant the respective goods (or work, services) to the consumer shall not be permitted.

In the event of an unjustified evasion by a commercial organization from the concluding of a public contract the provisions provided for by Article 399(4) of the present Code shall apply.

4. In instances provided for by legislative acts the Government of the Republic Kazakhstan may issue rules binding upon the parties when concluding and performing public contracts (standard contracts, statutes, etc.) [as amended by Law of 11 July 1997, No. 154-I].

5. The conditions of a public contract which do not correspond to the requirements established by points 2 and 4 of the present Article shall be invalid.

**Article 388. Model Conditions of Contracts**

1. It may be provided in a contract that its individual conditions shall be determined by model conditions worked out for contracts of the respective type and published in the press.

2. In instances when a reference to the model conditions is not contained in the contract, such model conditions shall apply to the relations of the parties as customs of business turnover if they correspond to the requirements established by Article 3 and by Article 382 of the present Code.

3. Model conditions may be set out in the form of a model contract or other document containing these conditions.

**Article 389. Contract of Adhesion**

1. A contract of adhesion shall be deemed to be a contract whose conditions have been determined by one of the parties in formularies or other standard forms and which may be accepted by the other party not other than by means of adhering to the contract as a whole being offered.

2. A party which has adhered to the contract shall have the right to demand dissolution of the contract if the contract of adhesion, although not contrary to legislation, deprives this party of the rights usually granted under contracts of that type, excludes or limits the responsibility of the other party for a violation of obligations, or contains other conditions clearly burdensome for the adhering party

which it, proceeding from its own reasonably understandable interests, would not accept if it had the opportunity to participate in determining the conditions of the contract.

3. When the circumstances provided for in point 2 of the present Article are present, the demand concerning dissolution of the contract presented by a party which has adhered to a contract in connection with the effectuation of its entrepreneurial activity shall not be subject to satisfaction, if the adhering party knew or should have known on what conditions the contract is concluded.

**Article 390. Preliminary Contract**

1. Under a preliminary contract the parties shall be obliged to conclude in future a contract concerning the transfer of property, fulfillment of work, or rendering of services (principal contract) on the conditions provided for by the preliminary contract.

2. The preliminary contract shall be concluded in the form established for the principal contract, and if the form of the principal contract has not been established, then in written form. The failure to comply with the rules concerning the form of the preliminary contract shall entail its invalidity.

3. A preliminary contract must contain conditions enabling the subject to be established, and also the other material conditions of the principal contract.

4. A preliminary contract shall specify the period in which the parties are obliged to conclude the principal contract.

If such period has not been determined in the preliminary contract, the contract providing for it shall be subject to conclusion within a year from the moment of concluding the preliminary contract.

5. In instances when a party which has concluded a preliminary contract evades the conclusion of the contract providing for it, it shall be obliged to compensate the other party for the losses caused thereby unless provided otherwise by legislation or by the contract.

6. Obligations provided for by a preliminary contract shall terminate if before the ending of the period in which the parties must conclude the principal contract it has not been concluded or one of the parties does not send to the other party a proposal to conclude this contract.

7. A protocol of intent (or contract of intent), unless it provides expressly for the intent of the parties to confer on it the force of a preliminary contract, shall not be a civil-law contract, and the failure to perform it shall not entail legal consequences [Article as amended by Law of 2 March 1998, No. 211-I].

**Article 391. Contract to Benefit of Third Person**

1. A contract to the benefit of a third person shall be deemed to be a contract in which the parties have established that a debtor is obliged to make performance not to the creditor, but to a third person specified or not specified in the contract and having the right to demand performance of the obligation to his benefit from the debtor.

2. Unless provided otherwise by legislation or a contract, from the moment of the expression by the third person to the debtor of an intention to take advantage of his right under the contract, the parties may not dissolve or change the contract concluded by them without the consent of the third person.

3. The debtor in the contract shall have the right to advance against the demand of the third person objections which he could have advanced against the creditor.

4. When a third person waives a right granted to him under the contract, the creditor may take advantage of this right unless this is contrary to legislation and the contract.

**Article 392. Interpretation of Contract**

1. In the event of the interpretation of the conditions of a contract by a court the literal meaning of the words and expressions contained therein shall be taken into account. The literal meaning of the condition of a contract in the event of its ambiguity shall be established by means of comparing with the other conditions and with the sense of the contract as a whole.

2. If the rules contained in point one of the present Article do not enable the content of the contract to be determined, the true common will of the parties must be elicited by taking into account the purpose of the contract. In so doing all the respective circumstances, including negotiations preceding the contract and correspondence, practice being established in the mutual relations of the parties, the customs of business turnover, and the subsequent conduct of the parties, shall be taken into account.

## *Chapter 23. Conclusion of Contract*

**Article 393. Material Conditions of Contract**

1. A contract shall be considered to be concluded when agreement regarding all of its material conditions has been reached in the form required in appropriate instances.

Conditions concerning the subject of the contract, conditions which have been deemed by legislation as material or necessary for contracts of the particular type, and also all those conditions relative to which agreement must be reached according to the statement of one of the parties, shall be material.

2. If in accordance with legislative acts the transfer of property is necessary for the conclusion of a contract, the contract shall be considered to be concluded from the moment of the transfer of the respective property.

**Article 394. Form of Contract**

1. If the parties have agreed to conclude a contract in a determined form, it shall be considered to be concluded from the moment of imparting the stipulated form to it even though such form has not been required according to legislation for contracts of the particular type.

2. The written form of the contract shall be considered to be complied with if the written offer to conclude a contract has been accepted in the procedure provided for by Article 396(3) of the present Code.

**Article 395. Offer**

1. A proposal concerning the conclusion of a contract made to one or several specific persons, if it is sufficiently definite and expresses the intention of the person who has made the proposal to consider himself to be bound in the event of the adoption ( acceptance) thereof shall be deemed to be an offer. A proposal shall be sufficiently definite if the material conditions of a contract or the procedure for determining them have been specified therein.

2. An offer shall bind the person who sent it from the moment of the receipt thereof by the addressee.

If notice of the revocation of an offer has been received earlier than or simultaneously with the offer itself, the offer shall be considered to be not received.

3. An offer received by the addressee may not be revoked within the period established for its acceptance unless otherwise stipulated in the offer itself or does not arise from the essence of the proposal or situation in which it was made.

4. An advertisement and other proposals addressed to an indefinite group of persons shall be regarded as an invitation to make offers unless expressly specified otherwise in the proposal.

5. A proposal containing all the material conditions of a contract from which the will of the person making the proposal is seen to conclude a contract on the conditions specified in the proposal with anyone who responds shall be deemed to be an offer (public offer).

**Article 396. Acceptance**

1. The reply of a person to whom an offer has been addressed concerning the acceptance thereof shall be deemed to be an acceptance.

An acceptance must be full and unconditional.

2. Silence shall not be an acceptance unless it arises otherwise from a legislative act, custom of business turnover, or former business relations of the parties.

3. The performance by a person who has received an offer within the period established for its acceptance of actions relating to the fulfillment of the conditions of the contract specified therein (shipment of goods, provision of services, fulfilment of work, payment of respective amount, etc.) shall be considered to be an acceptance unless provided otherwise by legislation or specified in the offer.

4. If notice of the revocation of an acceptance has been received by the person to whom the offer was sent earlier than or simultaneously with the acceptance itself, the acceptance shall be considered to be not received.

**Article 397. Procedure for Conclusion of Contract**

1. When an offer contains a period for acceptance, a contract shall be considered to be concluded if the acceptance was received by a person who has sent the offer within the limits of the period specified therein.

2. When a written offer does not contain the period for acceptance, the contract shall be considered to be concluded if the acceptance was received by the person who has sent the offer before the end of the period established by legislation, and if such a period has not been established, during the time normally necessary for this.

When an offer has been made orally without specifying the period for acceptance, the contract shall be considered to be concluded if the other party immediately declared its acceptance thereof.

3. In the instances when a notification of acceptance sent in good time has been received late, the acceptance shall not be considered to be late if a party who has sent the offer immediately does not inform the other party about the late receipt of the acceptance.

If a party who has sent an offer immediately communicates to the other party the accepting of its acceptance which has been received late, the contract shall be considered to be concluded.

4. A reply concerning consent to conclude a contract on conditions other than those proposed in the offer shall not be an acceptance.

Such a reply shall be deemed to be a refusal to accept and, at the same time, a new offer.

**Article 398. Place of Conclusion of Contract**

Unless the place of conclusion has been specified in the contract, a contract shall be deemed to be concluded at the place of residence of a citizen or location of the juridical person which sent the offer.

**Article 399. Conclusion of Contract in Obligatory Procedure**

1. In instances when in accordance with the present Code or other legislative acts the conclusion of a contract for one of the parties is obligatory, this party must send to the other party a notification concerning acceptance or rejection of acceptance or acceptance of the offer (or draft contract) on other conditions (protocol of disagreements to draft contract) within 30 days from the date of receipt of the offer unless another period has been established by legislation or has been agreed by the parties.

2. A party who has sent an offer and received from the party for whom the conclusion of the contract is obligatory a notification of its acceptance on other conditions (protocol of disagreements to draft contract) shall have the right to transfer disagreements which have arisen when concluding the contract for consideration of a court within thirty days from the date of receipt of such notification or the expiry of the period for acceptance unless another period has been established for individual types of con tracts.

3. If for a draft contract sent by the party for whom the conclusion of the contract is obligatory a protocol of disagreements to the draft contract has been received within the thirty-day period, this party shall be obliged within thirty days from the date of receipt of the protocol of disagreements to notify the other party about acceptance of the contract in the version thereof or about rejection of the protocol of disagreements.

In the event the protocol of disagreements is rejected or of the failure to receive notice concerning the results of the consideration thereof within the specified period, the party which sent the protocol of disagreements shall have the right to transfer the disagreements which arose when concluding the contract for the consideration of a court unless established otherwise by legislation on individual types of contracts.

4. If a party for which in accordance with the present Code or other legislative acts the conclusion of the contract is obligatory evades the conclusion thereof, the other party shall have the right to apply to a court with a demand to compel the contract to be concluded.

The party which has unjustifiably evaded the conclusion of the contract must compensate the other party for losses caused by the refusal to conclude the contract.

**Article 400. Precontractual Disputes**

In the instances provided for by Article 399(2) and (3) of the present Code, and also if disagreements which arose when concluding a contract were by agreement of the parties transferred for the consideration of a court, the conditions of the contract with regard to which the parties had disagreements shall be determined in accordance with the decision of the court.

## *Chapter 24. Change and Dissolution of Contract*

**Article 401. Grounds for Change and Dissolution of Contract**

1. A change and dissolution of a contract shall be possible by agreement of the parties unless provided otherwise by the present Code, by other legislative acts, or by contract.

2. Upon the demand of one of the parties a contract may be changed or dissolved by decision of a court only:

(1) in the event of a material violation of the contract by the other party;

(2) in other instances provided for by the present Code, by other legislative acts, or by contract.

A violation of a contract by one of the parties which entails for the other party such damage that it is deprived in significant degree of that which it had the right to count on when concluding the contract shall be deemed to be material.

3. In the event of a unilateral refusal to perform a contract (or refusal of the contract respectively partially or wholly) the contract shall be considered to be dissolved or changed (Article 404 of the present Code) [Article as amended by Law of 2 March 1998, No. 211-I].

**Article 402. Procedure for Change of and Dissolution of Contract**

1. An agreement concerning a change of or dissolution of a contract shall be concluded in the same form as the contract unless it arises otherwise from legislation, the contract, or the customs of business turnover.

2. A demand concerning a change of or dissolution of a contract may be made by a party in court only after receipt of a refusal of the other party to the proposal to change or dissolve the contract or of the failure to receive a reply within the period specified in the proposal or established by legislation or by contract, and in the absence thereof, within a thirty-day period.

**Article 403. Consequences of Dissolution of and Change of Contract**

1. In the event of the dissolution of the contract the obligations of the parties shall terminate.

2. In the event of the change of a contract, the obligations of the parties shall continue to operate in the changed form.

3. In the event of the dissolution of or change of a contract, the obligations shall be considered to be terminated or changed from the moment of the parties reaching agreement concerning the change or dissolution of the contract unless it arises otherwise from the agreement of the parties or the character of the change of the contract, and in the event of the dissolution or change of a contract in a judicial procedure, from the moment of the entry into legal force of the decision of the court on the dissolution or change of the contract.

4. The parties shall not have the right to demand the return of that which was performed by them under the obligation before the moment of dissolution or change of the contract, unless established otherwise by a law or by agreement of the parties.

5. If a material violation of the contract by one of the parties has served as the grounds for the dissolution or change of a contract, the other party shall have the right to demand compensation of losses caused by the dissolution or change of the contract [Article as amended by Law of 2 March 1998, No. 211-I].

**Article 404. Unilateral Refusal to Perform Contract [as amended by Law of 2 March 1998, No. 211-I]**

1. A unilateral refusal to perform a contract (refusal of contract) shall be permitted in instances provided for by the present Code, other legislative acts, or agreement of the parties.

2. One of the parties shall have the right to refuse to perform a contract in instances of:

(1) the impossibility of performance of an obligation based on the contract (Article 374 of the present Code);

(2) the deeming in the established procedure of the other party to be bankrupt;

(3) the change or repeal of an act of a State agency on the grounds of which the contract was concluded.

3. A unilateral refusal to perform a contract shall be permitted in instances when the contract was concluded without indication of the period unless provided otherwise by legislative acts or agreement of the parties.

4. In the event of a unilateral refusal to perform a contract the party must warn the other party thereof by not later than a month unless provided otherwise by the present Code, other legislative acts, or agreement of the parties [as amended by Law of 2 March 1998, No. 211-I].

**Article 405. Extension of Period of Operation of Contract**

The parties shall have the right to extend the operation of a contract for a new period. The period of operation of a contract shall be extended according to the rules of Article 397 of the present Code.

# CIVIL CODE OF THE REPUBLIC KAZAKHSTAN

[Adopted 1 July 1999, as amended by Law of 29 November 1999, No. 486-I; Law of 29 March 2000, No. 42-II; Law of 5 July 2000, No. 75-II; Law of 18 December 2000, No. 128-II; Law of 6 December 2001, No. 260-II; Law of 24 December 20012, No. 276-II; Law of 21 May 2002, No. 323-II; Law of 8 January 2003, No. 376-II; Law of 13 March 2003, No. 394-II; Law of 16 May 2003, No. 416-II; Law of 1 July 2003, No. 445-II; Law of 9 July 2003, No. 482-II; Law of 10 July 2003, No. 483-II; Law of 27 February 2004, No. 527-II; Law of 10 March 2004, No. 532-II; Law of 9 April 2004, No. 542-II; Law of 7 July 2004, No. 577-II; Law of 20 December 2004, No. 13-III; Law of 22 November 2005, No. 90-III; Law of 23 December 2005, No. 107-III; Law of 20 February 2006, No. 127-III; Law of 20 February 2006, No. 128-III; Law of 5 May 2006, No. 139-III; Law of 22 June 2006, No. 147-III; Law of 5 July 2006, No. 164-III; Law of 12 January 2007, No. 225-III; Law of 19 February 2007, No. 230-III; Law of 2 March 2007, No. 237-III; Law of 7 May 2007, No. 244-III; Law of 15 May 2007, No. 253-III; and Law of 19 June 2007, No. 264-III.

Introduced into operation by Law of the Supreme Soviet of the Republic Kazakhstan, 1 July 1999, No. 410-I].

## SPECIAL PART

## SECTION 4. INDIVIDUAL TYPES OF OBLIGATIONS
[AS AMENDED BY LAW OF 20 DECEMBER 2004, NO. 13-III]

### *Chapter 25. Purchase-Sale*

#### *§1. General Provisions on Purchase-Sale*

**Article 406. Contract of Purchase-Sale**

1. Under a contract of purchase-sale one party (seller) shall be obliged to transfer property (or good) to the ownership, economic jurisdiction, or operative management of the other party (purchaser), and the purchaser shall be obliged to accept this property (or good) and to pay for it the determined monetary amount (price).

2. Unless special rules have been established for the purchase-sale thereof by legislative acts, the provisions provided for by the present paragraph shall apply to the purchase-sale of securities and currency valuables.

3. In the instances provided for by the present Code or other legislative acts, the peculiarities of the purchase and sale of individual types of goods of individual types shall be determined by legislative and other normative legal acts.

4. The provisions provided for by the present paragraph shall apply to the sale of property rights unless it arises otherwise from the content or character of these rights.

5. Unless provided otherwise by rules of the present Code concerning contracts of these types, the provisions provided for by the present paragraph shall apply to individual types of contracts for purchase-sale (retail purchase-sale, delivery of goods, electric power supply, agricultural procurement, sale of enterprise).

**Article 407. Condition of Contract on Good**

1. Any thing may be a good under a contract of purchase-sale in compliance with the rules of Article 116 of the present Code.

2. A contract may be concluded for the purchase-sale of a good which the seller has at the moment of concluding the contract, and also a good which will be created or acquired by the seller in the future, unless established otherwise by legislative acts or unless it so arises from the character of the good.

3. A condition concerning a good shall be considered to be agreed if the contract enables the name and quantity of the name and quality of the good to be determined (material conditions).

**Article 408. Duties of Seller Relating to Transfer of Good**

1. The seller shall be obliged to transfer to the purchaser the good provided for by the contract.

2. Unless provided otherwise by the contract, the seller shall be obliged simultaneously with the transfer of the good to transfer to the purchaser the appurtenances thereto, as well as the documents relating thereto (documents certifying completeness, safety, quality of good, procedure for operation, and so forth) provided for by normative legal acts, or the contract.

**Article 409. Period for Performance of Duty to Transfer Good**

1. The period for the performance by the seller of the duty to transfer the good to the purchaser shall be determined by the contract, and if the contract does not enable the period to be determined, in accordance with the rules provided for by Article 277 of the present Code.

2. A contract of purchase-sale shall be deemed to be concluded with a condition of the performance thereof within a strictly determined period if it clearly arises from the contract that in the event of a violation of the period the purchaser loses interest in the performance of the contract.

The seller shall not have the right to perform such contract before the ensuing or after the expiry of the period determined therein without the consent of the purchaser.

Instances of the performance of a contract of purchase-sale by parts (or interval periods of performance of the contract) may be established by legislative acts or by the contract.

**Article 410. Moment of Performance of Duty of Seller to Transfer Good**

1. Unless provided otherwise by the contract of purchase-sale, the duty of the seller to transfer the good to the purchaser shall be considered to be performed at the moment of:

(1) handing over the good to the purchaser or person specified by him if the duty of the seller relating to the delivery of the good has been provided for by the contract;

(2) placing the good at the disposition of the purchaser if the good must be transferred to the purchaser or person specified by him at the location of the good.

A good shall be considered to be placed at the disposition of the purchaser when within the period provided for by the contract the good is ready for transfer to the proper place and the purchaser in accordance with the conditions of the contract has knowledge of the readiness of the good for transfer. A good shall not be deemed to be ready for transfer if it is not identified for the purposes of the contract by means of marking or in other form.

2. In the instances when the duty of the seller relating to delivery of a good or transfer of a good at its location to the purchaser does not arise from a contract of purchase-sale, the duty of the seller to transfer the good to the purchaser shall be considered to be performed at the moment of handing over the good to the carrier or communications organization for delivery to the purchaser, unless provided otherwise by the contract.

**Article 411. Transfer of Risk of Accidental Perishing of Good**

1. Unless provided otherwise by the contract of purchase-sale, the risk of accidental perishing or accidental damage of a good shall pass to the purchaser from the moment when in accordance with legislative acts or the contract the seller is considered to have performed his duty relating to transfer of the good to the purchaser.

2. The risk of accidental perishing or accidental damage of a good sold while en route shall pass to the purchaser from the moment of the conclusion of the contract of purchase-sale unless provided otherwise by the contract or the customs of business turnover.

The condition of the contract that the risk of accidental perishing or accidental damage of the good passes to the purchaser from the moment of handing over the good to the first carrier may, at the demand of the purchaser, be deemed by a court to be invalid if at the moment of concluding the contract the seller knew or should have known that the good has been lost or damaged and did not communicate this to the purchaser.

**Article 412. Duty of Seller With Regard to Preservation of Sold Good**

When the right of ownership, right of economic jurisdiction, or operative management passes to the purchase before the transfer of the good, the seller shall be obliged until the transfer to preserve the good without permitting the deterioration thereof.

The costs necessary for this the purchaser shall be obliged to compensate the seller unless provided otherwise by agreement of the parties.

**Article 413. Duty of Seller to Transfer Good Free from Rights of Third Persons**

1. The seller shall be obliged to transfer a good to the purchaser free from any rights of third persons, except for the instance when the purchaser has agreed to accept the good encumbered by the rights of third persons.

The failure of the seller to perform this duty shall give the purchaser the right to demand a reduction of the price of the good or dissolution of the contract and compensation of losses unless it is proved that the purchaser knew or should have known about the rights of third persons to this good.

2. The rules provided for by point 1 of the present Article shall apply respectively also when with respect to the good at the moment of its transfer to the purchaser there are claims of third persons, which were known to the seller if these claims subsequently were deemed to be lawful in the established procedure.

**Article 414. Responsibility of Seller in Event of Seizure of Good from Purchaser**

1. In the event of the seizure of the good from the purchaser by third persons on grounds which arose before the performance of the contract, the seller shall be obliged to compensate the purchaser for losses incurred by him unless it is proved that the purchaser knew or should have known about the existence of these grounds.

2. An agreement of the parties concerning relieving the seller from responsibility or limitation of responsibility in the event a good acquired is demanded and obtained from the purchaser by third persons shall be invalid.

**Article 415. Duties of Purchaser and Seller in Event of Filing of Suit Concerning Seizure of Good**

1. If a third person on grounds which arose before performance of the contract brings suit against the purchaser concerning seizure of the good, the purchaser shall be obliged to involve the seller in the case, and the seller shall be obliged to appear in this case on the side of the purchaser.

2. The failure of the purchaser to involve the seller in the case shall relieve the seller from responsibility to the purchaser if the seller proves that, having accepted to participate in the case, he could have averted the seizure of the good sold from the purchaser.

3. The seller involved by the purchaser in a case but who has not taken part therein shall be deprived of the right to prove the incorrectness of the conducting of the case by the purchaser.

**Article 416. Consequences of Failure to Perform Duty to Transfer Good**

1. If the seller refuses to transfer the good sold to the purchaser, the purchaser shall have the right to refuse to perform the contract of purchase-sale.

2. In the event of the refusal of the seller to transfer an individually-specified thing, the purchaser shall have the right to present the demand to the seller provided for by Article 355 of the present Code.

**Article 417. Consequences of Failure to Fulfill Duty to Transfer Appurtenances and Documents Relating to Good**

1. If the seller does not transfer or refuses to transfer to the purchaser appurtenances or documents relating to the good which he should transfer (Article 408(2) of the present Code), the purchaser shall have the right to designate a reasonable period to him for the transfer thereof.

2. When appurtenances or documents relating to a good have not been transferred by the seller within the specified period, the purchaser shall have the right to refuse to accept the good unless provided otherwise by the contract.

**Article 418. Quantity of Good**

The quantity of a good subject to transfer to a purchaser shall be provided for by the contract of purchase-sale in respective units of measurement or in monetary expression. The condition concerning the quantity of goods may be agreed by means of establishing in the contract the procedure for determining it.

**Article 419. Consequences of Violation of Condition of Contract Concerning Quantity of Good**

1. If the seller has transferred to the purchaser in violation of the conditions of the contract a lesser quantity of the good that has been determined by the contract, the purchaser shall have the right, unless provided otherwise by the contract, either to demand to transfer the short quantity of the good or to refuse the good transferred and the payment thereof, and if the good has been paid for, to demand the return of the monetary amount paid for it.

2. If the seller has transferred to the purchaser a good in a quantity exceeding that specified in the contract, the purchaser shall be obliged to notify the seller thereof in the procedure provided for by Article 436(1) of the present Code. If within a reasonable period after receipt of the communication of the purchaser the seller does not dispose of the respective good, the purchaser shall have the right, insofar as not provided otherwise by the contract, to accept the entire good.

3. In the event of the acceptance of the good by the purchaser in a quantity exceeding that specified in the contract, the respective good shall be paid for at the price determined for the good accepted in accordance with the contract unless another price has been determined by agreement of the parties.

**Article 420. Assortment of Goods**

If under the contract of purchase-sale goods are subject to transfer in a specified correlation with regard to types, models, dimensions, colors, or other indicia (assortment), the seller shall be obliged to transfer the goods to the purchaser in the assortment agreed by the parties.

**Article 421. Consequences of Violation of Condition of Contract on Assortment of Goods**

1. In the event of the transfer by the seller of goods provided for by the contract in an assortment which does not correspond to the contract, the purchaser shall have the right to refuse to accept and to pay for them, and if they have been paid for, to require the return of the monetary amount paid.

2. If the seller has transferred to the purchaser, together with goods whose assortment corresponds to the contract, goods in violation of the conditions of the contract concerning the assortment, the purchaser shall have the right at his choice to:

(1) accept the goods corresponding to the conditions of the contract concerning the assortment and refuse the other goods;

(2) refuse all of the goods transferred;

(3) require the replacement of the goods which do not correspond to the conditions of the contract concerning the assortment with goods in the assortment provided for by the contract;

(4) accept all the goods transferred.

3. In the event of the refusal of goods whose assortment does not correspond to the conditions of the contract, or of presenting a demand concerning replacement of the goods which do not correspond to the conditions of the contract concerning the assortment, the purchaser shall have the right also to refuse to pay for these goods, and if they have been paid for, to require the return of the amount paid.

4. Goods which do not correspond to the conditions of the contract concerning assortment shall be considered to be accepted if the purchaser within a fifteen-day period after the receipt thereof does not notify the seller concerning his refusal of the goods.

5. If the purchaser has not refused goods whose assortment does not correspond to the contract, he shall be obliged to pay for them at the price agreed with the seller. When necessary measures have not been taken by the seller to agree the price within a fifteen-day period, the purchaser shall pay for the goods at the price which at the moment of concluding the contract under comparable circumstances are usually recovered for analogous goods.

6. The rules of the present Article shall apply unless provided otherwise by the contract of purchase-sale.

**Article 422. Quality of Good**

1. The seller shall be obliged to transfer a good to the purchaser whose quality corresponds to the contract.

2. In the absence in a contract of conditions concerning the quality of a good the seller shall be obliged to transfer to the purchaser a good fit for the purposes for which a good of such nature is usually used.

If the seller when concluding the contract was given notice by the purchaser of the specific purposes for the acquisition of the good, the seller shall be obliged to transfer to the purchaser a good fit for use in accordance with these purposes.

3. In the event of the sale of a good according to a sample and/or description, the seller shall be obliged to transfer to the purchaser a good which corresponds to the sample and/or description.

4. If obligatory requirements for the quality of a good being sold have been provided in accordance with the procedure established legislative acts, then a seller effectuating entrepreneurial activity shall be obliged to transfer a good to the purchaser which corresponds to these obligatory requirements.

By agreement between the seller and the purchaser a good may be transferred which corresponds to higher quality requirements in comparison with the obligatory requirements in the procedure provided for by legislative acts.

5. A good which the seller is obliged to transfer to the purchaser must correspond to the requirements provided by the present Article at the moment of the transfer thereof to the purchaser unless another moment of determining the conformity of the good to these requirements is provided by the contract and within the limits of a reasonable period must be fit for the purposes for which a good of such nature is usually used.

**Article 423. Period of Fitness of Good**

1. A period of time upon the expiry of which a good shall be considered to be unfit for use for designation (period of fitness), and also instances when the period of fitness of a good is specified on the good, may be determined by legislation, obligatory requirements of State standards, or other obligatory rules.

2. Goods for which a period of fitness has been established the seller shall be obliged to transfer to the purchaser so calculated that it may be used for designation until the expiry of the period of fitness.

**Article 424. Calculation of Period of Fitness of Good**

The period of fitness of a good shall be determined by the period of time calculated from the day of its manufacture during which the good is fit for use or by the date until the ensuing of which the good is fit for use.

**Article 425. Guarantee of Quality of Good**

1. When by a contract the granting by the seller of a guarantee of the quality of a good has been provided for, the seller shall be obliged to transfer to the purchaser a good which must correspond to the requirements provided for by Article 422 of the present Code during the determined period of time established by the contract (guarantee period).

2. A guarantee of the quality of a good also shall extend to all parts comprising it (sets of manufacture) unless provided otherwise by the contract.

**Article 426. Procedure for Calculation of Guarantee Period**

1. A guarantee period shall begin to be calculated from the moment of the transfer of the good to the purchaser (Article 410 of the present Code) unless provided otherwise by the contract.

2. If a purchaser is deprived of the possibility to use the good with respect to which a guarantee period has been established by the contract under circumstances within the control of the seller, the guarantee period shall not run until the elimination of the respective circumstances by the seller.

Unless provided otherwise by the contract, a guarantee period shall be extended for the time during which the good could not be used because of defects discovered therein, on condition of the notification of the seller about the defects of the good in the procedure established by Article 436 of the present Code.

3. Unless provided otherwise by the contract, a guarantee period for a set of manufactures shall be considered to be equal to the guarantee period for the principal manufacture and shall begin to run simultaneously with the guarantee period on the principal manufacture.

4. In the event of the replacement of a good (or set of manufactures) the guarantee period shall begin to run anew unless provided otherwise by a contract.

**Article 427. Verification of Quality of Good**

1. If the verification of the quality of a good has been provided for by legislation or by the contract, it must be effectuated in accordance with the requirements established therein.

In instances when obligatory requirements for the verification of the quality of goods have been established by State standards and other normative documents with regard to standardization, verification of quality must be effectuated in accordance with the instructions contained therein.

2. If in the procedure established by point 1 of the present Article conditions for the verification of the quality of a good have not been provided, the quality of a good must be verified in accordance with the customs of business turnover or other ordinarily used conditions for the verification of a good subject to transfer under a contract.

3. If the duty of the seller to verify the quality of a good transferred to the purchaser (test, analysis, inspection, and so forth) has been provided for by legislative acts, obligatory requirements of State standards, other normative documents with regard to standardization, or by the contract, the seller must submit to the purchaser at the request thereof evidence of the effectuation of the verification of the quality of the good.

**Article 428. Consequences of Transfer of Good of Improper Quality**

1. If the defects of a good were not stipulated by the seller, the purchaser to whom the good of improper quality was transferred shall have the right at his choice to require from the seller:

(1) commensurate reduction of the purchase price;

(2) uncompensated elimination of defects of the good within a reasonable period;

(3) compensation of his expenses to eliminate the defects of the good;

(4) replacement of the good of improper quality with a good corresponding to the contract;

(5) refusal to perform the contract and return of the monetary amount paid for the good.

The conditions of a contract concerning the waiver by the purchaser of the rights provided for by the present point shall be invalid.

2. In the event of the improper quality of part of the goods which are part of a set (Article 432 of the present Code), the purchaser shall have the right to effectuate with respect to this part of the goods the rights provided for by point 1of the present Article.

3. When the seller of a good of improper quality is not the manufacturer thereof, demands concerning replacement or uncompensated elimination of defects of a good may be presented at the choice of the purchaser against the seller or against the manufacturer.

4. The rules provided for by the present Article shall apply unless established otherwise by the present Code or other legislative acts.

**Article 429. Defects of Good for Which Seller is Liable**

1. The seller shall be liable for the defects of a good if the purchaser proves that they arose before the transfer thereof to the purchaser or for reasons which arose before this moment.

The seller shall be liable for defects of a sold good also when he did not know about them. An agreement to relieve the seller from responsibility or to limit it shall be invalid.

2. With respect to a good for which a guarantee of quality has been granted by the seller, the seller shall be liable for defects of the good unless it is proved that the defects in the good arose after the transfer thereof to the purchaser as a consequence of a violation by the purchaser of the rules for the use of the good or the keeping thereof, or the actions of third persons, or insuperable force.

**Article 430. Periods for Discovery of Defects in Transferred Good**

1. Unless established otherwise by legislative acts or by a contract, the purchaser shall have the right to present demands connected with the defects of a good on condition that they were discovered within the periods established by the present Article.

2. If a guarantee period or a period of fitness has not been established for a good, demands connected with defects of a good may be presented by the purchaser on condition that the defects in the good sold were discovered within a reasonable period, but within the limits of two years from the date of the transfer of the good to the purchaser, unless longer periods were established by legislative acts or by contract. The period for eliciting the defects of a good subject to carriage or to dispatch by post shall be calculated from the day of delivery of the good at the place of its destination.

3. If a guarantee period has been established for a good, the purchaser shall have the right to present demands connected with defects of the good in the event the defects of the good are discovered during the guarantee period.

When a guarantee period has been established in a contract for sets of manufactures which is less in duration than the principal manufacture, the purchaser shall have the right to present demands concerning defects of the sets of manufactures in the event of their discovery during the guarantee period for the principal manufacture.

If a guarantee period has been established in a contract for a set of manufactures which is of greater duration than for the principal manufacture, the purchaser shall have the right to present demands connected with defects of the set of manufactures if the defects have been discovered during the guarantee period for it irrespective of the expiry of the guarantee period for the principal manufacture.

4. With respect to a good for which a period of fitness has been established, the purchaser shall have the right to present demands concerning defects of the good if they were discovered within the period of fitness of the good.

5. In instances when the guarantee period provided for by a contract constitutes less than two years and the defects of a good are discovered by the purchaser upon the expiry of the guarantee period but within the limits of two years from the day of transfer of the good to the purchaser, the seller shall bear responsibility if the purchaser proves that the defects of the good arose before the transfer of the good to the purchaser or for reasons which arose before this moment.

**Article 431. Completeness of Good**

1. The seller shall be obliged to transfer to the purchaser a good which corresponds to the conditions of the contract concerning completeness.

2. When the completeness of a good has not been determined by a contract, the seller shall be obliged to transfer to the purchaser a good whose completeness is determined by the customs of business turnover or other ordinarily presented requirements.

**Article 432. Complete Set of Goods**

1. If the duty of the seller to transfer to the purchaser a determined selection of goods in a complete set (complete set of goods) has been provided for by a contract, the obligation shall be considered to be performed from the moment of the transfer of all goods included in the complete set.

2. Unless otherwise provided for by the contract and does not arise from the essence of the obligation, the seller shall be obliged to transfer simultaneously to the purchaser all goods which comprise the complete set.

**Article 433. Consequences of Transfer of Incomplete Goods**

1. In the event of the transfer of an incomplete good (Article 431 of the present Code) the purchaser shall have the right at his choice to require from the seller:

(1) commensurate reduction of the purchase price;

(2) making the good complete within a reasonable period;

(3) replacement of the incomplete good by a complete [one];

(4) refuse to perform the contract and the return of the monetary amount paid for the good.

2. The consequences provided for by point 1 of the present Article shall also apply in the event of a violation by the seller of the duty to transfer a complete set of goods (Article 432 of the present Code) to the purchaser unless provided otherwise by legislation or the contract or does not arise from the essence of the obligation.

**Article 434. Packaging and Packing**

1. Unless provided otherwise by the contract and does not arise from the essence of the obligation or the character of the goods, the seller shall be obliged to transfer the good to the purchaser in packaging and/or packing.

2. Unless the requirements for packaging and packing have been determined by the contract, the good must be packaged and/or packed by the means usual for such good, and in the absence of such, by a means ensuring the preservation of goods of such nature under the usual conditions for keeping and transportation.

3. If in the procedure established by legislation obligatory requirements for packaging and/or packing have been provided for, the seller who effectuates entrepreneurial activity shall be obliged to transfer to the purchaser the good in packaging and/or packing which corresponds to such obligatory requirements.

**Article 435. Consequences of Transfer of Good Without Packaging and/or Packing or in Improper Packaging and/or Packing**

1. When a good which is subject to packaging and/or packing is transferred to the purchaser without packaging and/or packing or in improper packaging and/or packing, the purchaser shall have the right to demand of the seller to package and/or to pack the good or to replace the improper packaging and/or packing unless it arises otherwise from the essence of the obligation or the character of the good.

2. Instead of presenting the demands to the seller specified in point 1 of the present Article, the purchaser shall have the right of presenting other demands thereto which arise from the transfer of a good of improper quality (Article 428 of the present Code).

**Article 436. Notification of Seller About Improper Performance of Contract**

1. The purchaser shall be obliged to notify the seller about a violation of the conditions of the contract concerning quantity, assortment, quality, completeness, packaging and/or packing of the good within the period provided for by legislative acts, other normative legal acts, or the contract, and if a period is not established, within a reasonable period after the violation of the respective condition of the contract should have been discovered by proceeding from the character and designation of the good.

2. In the event of the failure to fulfill the rules provided for by point 1 of the present Article, the seller shall have the right to refuse satisfaction wholly or partially of the respective demands of the purchaser if it is proved that such untimely notification entailed the impossibility of satisfying the demands of the purchaser or entails for the seller incommensurate expenses in comparison with those which he would bear if he had been notified in good time about the violation of the contract.

3. If the seller knew or should have known that the goods transferred to the purchaser do not correspond to the conditions of the contract, he shall not have the right to refer to the failure of the purchaser to perform the duties provided for by point 1 of the present Article.

**Article 437. Duty of Purchaser to Accept Good**

1. The purchaser shall be obliged to accept a good transferred to him by the seller, except for instances when in accordance with the rules of the present Chapter he has the right to demand the replacement of the good or to refuse performance of the contract.

2. Unless provided otherwise by legislative acts or the contract, the purchaser shall be obliged to perform actions which in accordance with requirements usually presented are necessary on his part in order to ensure the transfer and receipt of the respective good.

3. In instances when the purchaser in violation of legislative acts or the contract does not accept a good or refuses to accept the good, the seller shall have the right to demand that the purchaser accept the good or to refuse performance of the contract.

**Article 438. Price of Good**

1. The purchaser shall be obliged to pay for a good at the price provided for by the contract or, if it is not provided for by the contract and may not be determined by proceeding from the conditions thereof, at the price determined in accordance with the rules of Article 385 of the present Code, and also to perform at his expense actions which according to legislative acts, the contract, or requirements usually presented are necessary in order to effectuate payment.

2. When the price has been established depending on the weight of the good, it shall be determined according to net weight unless provided otherwise by the contract.

3. If the contract provides that the price of a good is subject to change depending upon indicators which condition the price of the good (cost of production, expenditures, and so forth) but does not determine the means for revision of the price, the price shall be determined by proceeding from the correlation of the indicators at the moment of conclusion of the contract and at the moment of the performance of duties with regard to the transfer of the good. In the event of delay by the seller of performance of the duty to transfer the good, the price shall be determined by proceeding from the correlation of these indicators at the moment of conclusion of the contract and on the day of transfer of the good provided for by the contract, and if such day is not provided for, on the day determined in accordance with Article 277 of the present Code.

The rules provided for by the present point shall apply unless established otherwise by the present Code, another law, other legislative acts, or does not arise from the essence of the obligation.

**Article 439. Payment for Good**

1. If the duty does not arise from the conditions of the contract and legislative acts to pay the price within a determined period, the purchaser shall be obliged to pay for it without delay after the transfer of the good to him or the good-disposition documents for this good.

2. Unless payment by installment for a transferred good has been provided by the contract, the purchaser shall be obliged to pay to the seller the amount of the full price of the transferred good.

3. If the purchaser does not pay for the good transferred in accordance with the contract, the seller shall have the right to require payment for the good and the payment of a penalty for the use of another's money (Article 353 of the present Code).

4. If the purchaser in violation of the contract refuses to accept and to pay for the good, the seller shall have the right at his choice to require payment for the good or to refuse performance of the contract.

5. In instances when the seller in accordance with the contract is obliged to transfer to the purchaser not only goods which are not paid for, but also others, he shall have the right to suspend the transfer of these goods until the full payment for all goods previously transferred unless provided otherwise by legislative acts or contract.

**Article 440. Preliminary Payment for Good**

1. In instances when the duty of the purchaser to pay the price for a good wholly or partially before the transfer of the good by the seller (preliminary payment) has been provided for by the contract, the purchaser must make payment within the period provided for by the contract, and if the period has not been provided by the contract, within the period determined in accordance with Article 277 of the present Code.

2. In the event of the failure of the purchaser to perform the duty provided by the contract for preliminary payment of the good, the rules provided for by Article 284 of the present Code shall apply.

3. In instances when a seller who has received the amount of preliminary payment does not perform his duty to transfer the good within the established period (Article 409 of the present Code), the purchaser shall have the right to require the transfer of the good paid for or the return of the amount of preliminary payment for the good not transferred by the seller.

4. Unless provided otherwise by the contract of purchase-sale, in an instance when the seller does not perform the duty relating to the transfer of the good paid for in advance the amount of preliminary payment shall be subject to the payment of a penalty in accordance with Article 353 of the present Code from the day when under the contract the transfer of the good should have been made up to the day of the transfer of the good to the purchaser or the return to him of the amount paid in advance by him. The duty of the seller to pay a penalty on the amount of the preliminary payment from the day of receipt of this amount may be provided for by the contract.

**Article 441. Payment for Good Sold on Credit**

1. In instances when payment for a good over a determined time after the transfer thereof to the purchaser (sale of good on credit) has been provided for by the contract, the purchaser must make payment within the period provided for by the contract, and if the period is not provided for by the contract, within the period determined in accordance with Article 277 of the present Code.

2. In the event of the failure of the seller to perform the duty to transfer the good, the rules provided for by Article 284 of the present Code shall apply.

3. In instances when the purchaser which received the good does not perform the duty with regard to payment within the period established by the contract, the seller shall have the right to require payment of the good transferred or return of the goods not paid for.

In instances when the purchaser does not perform the duty with regard to payment for the good transferred within the period established by the contract and the present Code and contract do not provide otherwise, a penalty shall be subject to payment on the delayed amount in accordance with Article 353 of the present Code from the day when the good should have been paid for up to the day of payment for the good by the purchaser.

4. The duty of the purchaser to pay a penalty on the amount corresponding to the price of the good, commencing from the day of transfer of the good by the seller, may be provided for by the contract.

5. The sale of a good on credit shall be made at the price operating on the day of sale. A subsequent change of price for a good sold on credit shall not entail a recalculation unless provided otherwise by legislative acts or contract.

**Article 442. Payment by Installment in Event of Sale of Good on Credit**

1. Payment for a good by installment may be provided for by a contract concerning the sale of a good on credit.

A contract concerning the sale of a good on credit with a condition concerning installment payment shall be considered to be concluded if, together with the other material conditions of the contract of purchase-sale, the price of the good and the procedure, periods, and amounts of payments have been specified.

2. When a purchaser does not make a regular payment within the period established by the contract for a good sold by installment, the seller shall have the right to refuse performance of the contract and to require the return of the good sold, except for instances when the amount of payments received from the purchaser exceeds half of the price of the good unless provided otherwise by the contract.

**Article 443. Insurance of Good**

1. The duty of the seller or purchaser to insure a good may be provided for by the contract of purchase-sale unless established otherwise by legislative acts.

2. In an instance when a party obliged to insure a good does not effectuate insurance in accordance with the conditions of the contract, the other party shall have the right to insure the good and require from the obliged party compensation of expenses for the insurance or to refuse performance of the contract.

**Article 444. Preservation of Right of Ownership for Seller**

1. In instances when it is provided by a contract that the right of ownership in a good transferred to the purchaser shall be preserved for the seller until payment for the good or the ensuing of other circumstances, the purchaser shall not have the right before transfer of the right of ownership to him to alienate the good or otherwise dispose of it unless provided otherwise by legislative acts or contract or arises from the designation and properties of the good.

2. In instances when within the period provided for by the contract the transferred good is not paid for or other circumstances do not ensue under which the right of ownership passes to the purchaser, the seller shall have the right to require from the purchaser to return the good to him unless provided otherwise by the contract.

*§2. Retail Purchase-Sale*

**Article 445. Contract of Retail Purchase-Sale**

Under a contract of retail purchase-sale the seller effectuating entrepreneurial activity relating to the sale of goods on retail shall be obliged to transfer to the purchaser a good usually intended for personal, family, home, or other use which is not connected with entrepreneurial activity.

A contract of retail purchase-sale shall be a public contract (Article 387 of the present Code).

**Article 446. Form of Contract of Retail Purchase-Sale**

Unless established otherwise by legislative acts or a contract of retail purchase-sale, including the conditions of formularies or other standard forms to which the purchaser adheres (Article 389 of the present Code), a contract of retail purchase-sale shall be considered to be concluded in proper form from the moment of the issuance by the seller to the purchaser of a cashier or goods cheque or other document confirming payment of the good. The absence of the said documents with the purchaser shall not deprive him of the possibility to refer to witness testimony in confirmation of the conclusion of the contract and its conditions.

**Article 447. Public Offer of Good**

1. Exhibition of goods at the place of sale, the demonstration of models thereof, or the submission of information concerning goods being sold (descriptions, catalogs, photographs, and so forth) at the place of sale thereof shall be deemed to be a public offer irrespective of whether the price and other material conditions of the contract of purchase-sale have been specified, except for instances when the seller clearly determined that the respective goods are not intended for sale.

2. The proposal of a good specified in its advertisement, catalogs, and also other descriptions of a good addressed to an indefinite group of persons not at the place of sale of the good and not containing material conditions of the contract of purchase-sale shall not be deemed to be a public offer.

**Article 448. Granting of Information Concerning Good to Purchaser**

1. The seller shall be obliged to grant to the purchaser necessary and reliable information concerning the good proposed for sale. This information must correspond to the requirements established by legislative acts and those usually presented in retail trade for the content and means of granting such information.

2. The purchaser shall have the right before the conclusion of a contract to inspect the good and require the conducting in his presence of a verification of the properties or demonstration of the use of the good unless this is precluded in view of the character of the good and is not contrary to the rules accepted in retail trade.

3. A seller who has not provided the purchaser with the possibility of receipt of the respective information on the good shall bear responsibility also for those defects of the good which arose after the transfer thereof to the purchase with respect to which the purchaser proves that they arose in connection with his lack of information.

**Article 449. Contract with Condition Concerning Acceptance of Good by Purchaser Within Determined Period**

1. A contract with a condition concerning acceptance by the purchaser of the good within a period determined by the contract during which this good may not be sold to another purchaser may be concluded by the parties.

2. Unless provided otherwise by the contract, the failure of the purchaser to appear or the failure to perform other necessary actions in order to accept the good within the period determined by the contract may be considered by the seller as the refusal of the purchaser to perform the contract.

3. Additional expenses of the seller relating to ensuring the transfer of the good to the purchaser within the period determined by the contract shall be included in the price of the good unless provided otherwise by legislative acts or the contract.

**Article 450. Sale of Goods by Samples**

1. A contract of retail purchase-sale may be concluded on the basis of familiarizing the purchaser with a sample of the good (or description thereof, catalog of goods, and so forth) proposed by the seller.

2. Unless provided otherwise by legislative acts or the contract, a contract shall be considered to be performed from the moment of delivery of the good to the place specified in the contract, and if the place of transfer of the good is not determined by the contract, from the moment of delivery of the good to the purchaser at the place of residence of the citizen or location of the juridical person.

3. A purchaser before the transfer of the good shall have the right to refuse performance of a contract on condition of compensation to the seller for reasonable expenses connected with the performance of actions relating to performance of the contract.

**Article 451. Sale of Good With Use of Automatic Machines**

1. In the instances when a good is sold with the use of automatic machines, the possessor of the automatic machines shall be obliged to bring information to purchasers concerning the good (name, quantity, price per unit of good, and others) and the seller of the good by means of placing on the automatic machine or granting to the purchasers by other means information concerning the name (or firm name) of the seller, location, work regime, and also actions which are necessary to be performed by the purchaser in order to receive the good.

2. A contract shall be considered to be concluded from the moment of the performance of actions by the purchaser which are necessary in order to receive the good.

3. If the purchaser has not been granted a good paid for, the seller shall be obliged to ensure the immediate provision of the good to the purchaser or the return of the monetary amount paid by the purchaser for this good.

**Article 452. Contract with Condition on Delivery of Good to Purchaser**

1. In instances when a contract has been concluded with a condition concerning delivery of the good to the purchaser, the seller shall be obliged within the period established by the contract to deliver the good at the place specified by the purchaser.

2. A contract shall be considered to be performed by the seller from the moment of handing over the good to the purchaser, and in the event of his absence, to any person presenting the receipt or other document testifying to the conclusion of the contract or formalization of the delivery of the good, unless provided otherwise by legislative acts, the contract, or arises from the essence of the obligation.

**Article 453. Price and Payment for Good**

1. The purchaser shall be obliged to pay for a good at the price declared by the seller at the moment of concluding the contract unless provided otherwise by a legislative acts or arises from the essence of the obligation.

2. In instances when preliminary payment for a good (Article 440 of the present Code) has been provided for by the contract, the failure of the purchaser to pay for the good within the period established by the contract shall be deemed to be refusal of the purchaser to perform the contract unless provided otherwise by agreement of the parties.

3. The rules provided for by Article 441(3), paragraph two, of the present Code shall not be subject to application to contracts of retail purchase-sale on credit, including with a condition for payment by the purchaser for the goods by installment.

4. The purchaser shall have the right to pay up fully for the good at any time within the limits of the installment period for payment for the good established by the contract.

**Article 454. Exchange of Good of Proper Quality**

1. The purchaser shall have the right within fourteen days from the moment of the transfer to him of a non-foodstuff good, unless a longer period is declared by the seller, to exchange a purchased good bought at the place of purchase or other places declared by the seller for an analogous good of another size, form, dimension, style, color, or complement and so on, making the necessary settlement with the seller in the event of a difference in price.

2. If the seller does not have the good necessary for the exchange, the purchaser shall have the right to return the acquired good to the seller and to receive the monetary amount paid for it.

3. The demand of the purchaser concerning an exchange or return of the good shall be subject to satisfaction if the good was not used, has retained its consumer properties, and there is evidence of its acquisition from the particular seller.

4. A list of goods not subject to exchange or return on the grounds specified in the present Article shall be determined in the procedure established by legislation.

**Article 455. Rights of Purchaser in Event of Sale to Him of Good of Improper Quality**

1. A purchaser to whom a good of improper quality was sold, unless its defects were stipulated by the seller, shall have the right to effectuate actions provided for in Article 428(1) of the present Code, the purchaser at the request of the seller and at his expense must return the good of improper quality received.

2. In the event of the return to the purchaser of the monetary amount paid for the good, the seller shall not have the right to withhold from it the amount by which the value of the good was lowered because of the full or partial use of the good, loss of goods appearance, and so on.

**Article 456. Compensation of Difference in Price in Event of Replacement of Good, Reduction of Purchase Price, and Return of Good of Improper Quality**

1. In the event of the replacement of a poor-quality good not corresponding to the contract with a good of proper quality, the seller shall not have the right to demand compensation of the difference between the price of the good established by the contract and the price of the good existing at the moment of replacement of the good or rendering by a court of a decision concerning replacement of the good.

2. In the event of the replacement of a poor-quality good by an analogous good but different in dimension, style, quality, and so on, the good of proper quality shall be subject to compensation of the difference between the price of the good being replaced at the moment of replacement and the price of the good being transferred in place of the good of improper quality.

If the demand of the purchaser is not satisfied by the seller, these prices shall be determined at the moment of the rendering by a court of the decision concerning replacement of the good.

3. In the event a demand is presented concerning a commensurate reduction of the purchase price of the good in settlement, the price of the good at the moment of presenting the demand concerning

the price reduction shall be used, and if the demand of the purchase is not satisfied voluntarily, at the moment of the rendering by a court of a decision concerning the commensurate reduction of the price.

4. In the event of the return to the seller of a good of improper quality the purchaser shall have the right to require compensation for the difference between the price of the good established by the contract and the price of the respective good at the moment of voluntary satisfaction of his demand, and if the demand is not satisfied voluntarily, at the moment of the rendering of a decision by the court.

**Article 457. Responsibility of Seller and Performance of Obligation in Kind**

In the event of the failure of the seller to perform an obligation under the contract of retail purchase-sale, compensation of losses and the payment of a penalty shall not relieve the seller from performance of the obligation in kind.

*§3. Delivery*

**Article 458. Contract of Delivery**

Under a contract of delivery the seller (supplier) who is an entrepreneur shall be obliged to transfer goods produced or purchased by him within the stipulated period or periods to thepurchaser for use in entrepreneurial activity or for other purposes not connected with personal, family, home, and other similar use.

**Article 459. Settlement of Disagreements When Concluding Contract of Delivery**

1. In an instance when in concluding a contract of delivery disagreements arose between the parties with regard to individual conditions of the contract, the party proposing to conclude the contract and receiving a proposal from the other party to agree these conditions must within thirty days from the day of receipt of this proposal, unless another period has been agreed by the parties, take measures relating to agreeing the respective conditions of the contract or inform the other party in writing of the refusal to conclude it.

2. The party who received the proposal relating to respective conditions of the contract but did not take measures relating to agreeing the conditions of the contract of delivery and did not inform the other party about the refusal to conclude the contract within the period provided for by point 1 of the present Article shall be obliged to compensate the losses caused by the avoidance of agreeing the conditions of the contract.

**Article 460. Period of Operation of Contract of Delivery**

1. A contract of delivery may be concluded for one year, a period of more than one year (long-term contract), or for another period provided for by agreement of the parties.

If the period of operation thereof has not been determined in a contract and does not arise from the essence of the obligation, the contract shall be deemed to be concluded for one year.

2. If in a long-term contract the quantity of the good subject to delivery or other conditions of the contract have been determined for a year or a longer period, the procedure must be established in the contract for the parties to agree the respective conditions in subsequent periods before the end of the period of operation of the contract. In the absence in the contract of a procedure for agreeing the contract

shall be deemed to be concluded respectively for one year or for the period for which the conditions of the contract have been agreed.

**Article 461. Periods of Delivery**

1. If the delivery of goods has been provided for by the parties within the period of operation of the contract by individual lots and the periods of delivery of the individual lots (or delivery periods) have not been determined therein, the goods must be delivered in lots of equal measure monthly unless it arises otherwise from legislative acts, customs of business turnover, or the essence of the obligation.

2. Together with the determination of the periods of delivery a delivery schedule for the goods (ten-day, twenty-four hour, hour, and so on) may be established in the contract of delivery.

3. Goods may be delivered before time with the consent of the purchaser.

4. Goods delivered before time and accepted by the purchaser shall be credited to the quantity of goods subject to delivery within the following period.

**Article 462. Procedure for Delivery of Goods**

1. The delivery of goods shall be effectuated by the supplier by means of shipment (or transfer) of the goods to the purchaser under the contract or to the person specified in the contract as the recipient.

2. In instances when the right of the purchaser has been provided for by the contract to give an instruction to the supplier concerning the shipment of the goods to the recipients (shipment orders), the shipment (or transfer) of the goods shall be effectuated by the supplier to the recipients specified in the shipment order.

3. The content of a shipment order and the period for sending it by the purchaser to the supplier shall be determined by the contract. If the periods for sending the shipment order have not been provided for by the contract, it must be sent to the supplier not later than thirty days before the ensuing of the delivery period.

4. The failure of the purchaser to present the shipment order within the established period shall give the supplier the right either to refuse performance of the contract unless provided otherwise by the contract.

**Article 463. Delivery of Goods**

1. The delivery of goods shall be effectuated by the supplier by means of the shipment thereof by transport provided for by the contract and on the conditions determined by the contract.

2. If what type of transport or on what conditions the delivery shall be effectuated is not determined in the contract, the right of choice of the type of transport or determination of the conditions of delivery of the goods shall belong to the supplier unless it arises otherwise from legislative acts, the customs of business turnover, or the essence of the obligation.

**Article 464. Augmentation of Short Delivery of Goods**

1. The supplier who has permitted a short delivery of goods in an individual period of delivery shall be obliged to augment the short-delivered quantity of goods within the following period(s) within the limits of the period of operation of the contract of delivery unless provided otherwise by the contract.

2. Under a long-term contact the quantity of goods short delivered by the supplier in an individual period of delivery shall be subject to augmentation in the next period(s) within the limits of that year in which the short delivery of the good is permitted unless provided otherwise by the contract.

3. In an instance when goods have been shipped by the supplier to several recipients specified in the contract or shipment order of the recipient, the goods delivered to one recipient in excess of the quantity provided for in the contract or shipment order shall not be credited to cover the short delivery to other purchasers and shall be subject to augmentation by the supplier unless provided otherwise in the contract.

4. The purchaser shall have the right, having informed the supplier, to refuse acceptance of the good whose delivery has been delayed unless provided otherwise in the contract. The good delivered before receipt of the notice by the supplier the purchaser shall be obliged to accept and to pay for.

**Article 465. Assortment of Goods When Augmenting Short Delivery**

1. The assortment of goods whose short delivery is subject to augmentation shall be determined by agreement of the parties. In the absence of an agreement the supplier shall be obliged to augment the short-delivered quantity of the good in the assortment established for the period in which the short delivery was permitted.

2. The delivery of goods of one name in a larger quantity than is provided for the contract shall not be credited towards covering the short delivery of goods of another name within the same assortment and shall be subject to augmentation except for instances when the delivery was made with the prior written consent of the purchaser.

**Article 466. Acceptance of Good by Purchaser**

1. The purchaser (or recipient) shall be obliged to perform all necessary actions ensuring the acceptance of the good delivered in accordance with the contract of delivery.

2. A good accepted by the purchaser (or recipient) must be inspected by him within the period determined by legislative acts, the contract of delivery, or the customs of business turnover.

The purchaser (or recipient) shall be obliged within the same period to verify the quantity and quality of the good accepted in the procedure established by legislative acts, the contract, or the customs of business turnover and to inform the supplier about elicited nonconformities or short deliveries of goods immediately in writing.

3. In the event of the receipt of a good delivered from a transport organization, the purchaser (or recipient) shall be obliged to verify the conformity of the good to the information specified in the transport and accompanying documents, and also to accept this good from the transport organization in compliance with the rules provided for by legislative and other normative legal acts regulating the activity of transport.

**Article 467. Custody of Good Not Accepted by Purchaser**

1. When the purchaser (or recipient) in accordance with legislative acts or contract of delivery refuses a good transferred by the supplier, he shall be obliged to ensure the preservation of this good (custody) and immediately notify the supplier.

2. The supplier shall be obliged to remove the good accepted by the purchaser (or recipient) for custody or to dispose of it within a reasonable period.

If the supplier within this period does not dispose of the good, the purchaser shall have the right to realize the good or to return it to the supplier.

3. Necessary expenses incurred by the purchaser (or recipient) in connection with the acceptance of the good for custody, realization of the good, or the return thereof to the seller shall be subject to compensation by the supplier.

In so doing the amount received from the realization of the good shall be transferred to the supplier, deducting that due to the purchaser.

4. In instances when the purchaser does not accept a good from the supplier or refuses acceptance thereof without grounds established by legislative acts or the contract, the supplier shall have the right to require payment for the good from the purchaser.

**Article 468. Selection of Goods**

1. The receipt of goods by the purchaser (or recipient) at the location of the supplier (selection of goods) may be provided for by the contract of delivery.

2. If the period of selection is not provided by the contract, the goods must be selected by the purchaser (or recipient) within a reasonable period after receipt of notification of the supplier concerning the readiness of the goods.

3. When the selection of goods by the purchaser (or recipient) has been provided for by the contract of delivery at the location of the supplier, the purchaser shall be obliged to effectuate the inspection of the goods to be transferred to the place of their transfer unless provided otherwise by legislative acts or arises from the essence of the obligation.

4. The failure of the purchaser (or recipient) to select goods within the period established by the contract of delivery, and in the absence thereof within a reasonable period after receipt of the notification of the supplier concerning the readiness of the goods shall give the supplier the right to refuse performance of the contract or to require payment for the goods from the recipient.

**Article 469. Settlement of Accounts for Goods to be Delivered**

1. The purchaser shall pay for delivered goods in compliance with the procedure and form for the settlement of accounts provided for by the contract. If the procedure and form for the settlement of accounts has not been determined by agreement of the parties, the settlement of accounts shall be effectuated by payment orders.

2. If the delivery of a good by individual parts within a set is provided for in a contract, payment for the good by the purchaser shall be made after the shipment (or selection) of the last part within the set unless established otherwise by the contract.

3. If it is provided by a contract that the payment for a good is effectuated by the recipient (or payer) and the last unfoundedly has refused to pay or did not pay for the good within the period established by the contract, the supplier shall have the right to require payment for the good delivered from the purchaser.

**Article 470. Packaging and Packing**

1. Unless provided otherwise by the contract, the purchaser (or recipient) shall be obliged to return to the supplier reusable packaging and means of packing in which the good arrived in the procedure and within the periods established by legislative acts.

2. Other packaging and packing shall be subject to return to the supplier only in the instances provided for by the contract.

**Article 471. Consequences of Delivery of Good of Improper Quality**

1. The purchaser (or recipient) to whom a good of improper quality is delivered shall have the right to present demands to the supplier provided for by Article 428 of the present Code except for instances when the supplier who received the notification of the purchaser concerning defects of the delivered good replaces without delay the good delivered with a good of the proper quality.

2. The purchaser (or recipient) effectuating the sale of a good delivered to him at retail shall have the right to demand the replacement of the good of improper quality within a reasonable period returned by a consumer unless provided otherwise by the contract of delivery.

**Article 472. Consequences of Delivery of Incomplete Goods**

1. The purchaser (or recipient) to whom goods have been delivered in violation of the conditions of a contract of delivery, the requirements of legislative acts, or requirements usually presented for completeness shall have the right to present the demands to the supplier provided for by Article 433 of the present Code, except for the instance when the supplier who has received notification of the purchaser concerning the incompleteness of the delivered goods without delay makes the goods complete or replaces them with complete goods.

2. The purchaser (or recipient) effectuating the sale of goods at retail shall have the right to demand replacement of the incomplete goods within a reasonable period returned by a consumer with complete ones unless provided otherwise by the contract of delivery.

**Article 473. Rights of Purchaser in Event of Failure to Deliver Good, Failure to Fulfill Requirements Concerning Elimination of Defects of Good or Completing Sets of Good**

1. If the supplier does not deliver the quantity of a good provided for by the contract or did not fulfill the demands of the purchaser concerning the replacement of a poor-quality good or concerning the completion of the sets of goods within the established period, the purchaser shall have the right to acquire the nondelivered goods from other persons, relegating to the supplier all necessary and reasonable expenses for the acquisition thereof.

The calculation of the expenses of the purchaser for the acquisition of goods from other persons in the event of the short delivery thereof by the supplier or the failure to fulfill the demands of the purchaser concerning elimination of the defects of the goods or concerning the completion of sets of the goods shall be made according to the rules provided for by Article 477(1) of the present Code.

2. The purchaser (or recipient) shall have the right to refuse to pay for goods of improper quality and incomplete goods, and if such goods have been paid for, to require the return of the paid amounts until elimination of the defects and completion of the sets of the goods or the replacement thereof.

**Article 474. Penalty for Short Delivery or Delay of Delivery of Goods**

The penalty established by legislative acts or contract for the short delivery or delay of delivery of a good may be recovered from the day determined by the contract until the day of actual performance of the obligation unless another procedure for the recovery of a penalty has been established by legislative acts or the contract.

**Article 475. Cancellation of Obligations of Same Kind Under Several Contracts of Delivery**

1. In instances when the delivery of goods of the same name is effectuated by the supplier to the purchaser simultaneously under several contracts of delivery and the quantity of goods delivered is insufficient in order to cancel the obligations of the supplier under all the contracts, the goods delivered must be credited to the performance of the contract specified by the supplier when effectuating delivery or without delay after the delivery.

2. If the purchaser paid the supplier for goods of one name received under several contracts of delivery and the amounts of payment are insufficient to cancel the obligations of the purchaser under all the contracts, the amount paid must be credited to performance of the contract specified by the purchaser when effectuating payment for the goods or without delay after payment.

3. If the supplier or purchaser did not take advantage of the rights granted respectively by points 1 and 2 of the present Article, the performance of the obligation shall be credited to cancellation of the obligations under the contract whose period of performance ensued earlier. If the period of performance of obligations under several contracts has ensued simultaneously, the performance granted shall be credited in proportion to the cancellation of obligations under all the contracts.

**Article 476. Unilateral Refusal of Performance of Contract**

1. A unilateral refusal of performance of a contract (wholly or partially) or a unilateral change thereof shall be permitted in the event of a material violation of the contract by one of the parties (Article 401(2), paragraph two, of the present Code).

2. A violation of a contract of delivery by the supplier shall be presupposed to be material in instances of:

(1) the delivery of a good of improper quality with defects which can not be eliminated within a period acceptable to the purchaser;

(2) the repeated violation of the periods for delivery of goods.

3. The violation of a contract by the purchaser shall be presupposed to be material in instances of:

(1) the repeated violation of the periods for the payment of goods;

(2) the repeated failure to select goods.

4. By agreement of the parties other grounds may be provided for unilateral refusal to perform a contract or unilateral change thereof.

5. A contract of delivery shall be considered to be changed or dissolved from the moment of receipt by a party of notification by the other party concerning the change or unilateral refusal of performance of the contract unless another period for dissolution or change of the contract is provided for in the notification or has been determined by agreement of the parties.

**Article 477. Calculation of Losses in Event of Dissolution of Contract**

1. If within a reasonable period after dissolution of the contract as a consequence of a violation of an obligation by the seller the purchaser has bought from another person a good at a higher but reasonable price in place of that provided for by the contract, he may present a demand to the seller concerning compensation of losses in the form of the difference between the price established in the contract and the price of the transaction concluded in lieu.

2. If within a reasonable period after dissolution of the contract as a consequence of a violation of an obligation by the purchaser the seller has sold the good to another person at a lower but reasonable price than that provided for by the contract, the seller may present a demand to the purchaser concerning compensation of losses in the form of the difference between the price established in the contract and the price for the transaction concluded in lieu.

3. If after the dissolution of a contract on the grounds provided for by points 1 and 2 of the present Article a transaction has not been concluded in place of the dissolved contract and for the particular good there is a current price, a party may present a demand concerning compensation of losses in the form of the difference between the price established in the contract and the current price at the moment of dissolution of the contract.

The current price shall be deemed to be the price usually recovered under comparable circumstances for an analogous good at the place where the transfer of the good should have been effectuated. If a current price does not exist at that place, the current price applied in another place may be used which may serve as a reasonable replacement, taking into account the difference in expenses for the transportation of the good.

4. Satisfaction of the demands provided for by points 1 to 3 of the present Article shall not relieve the party which did not perform the obligation from compensation of other losses caused to the other party on the basis of Article 9(4) of the present Code.

*§4. Agricultural Procurement Contract*

**Article 478. Contract of Agricultural Procurement**

1. Under a contract of agricultural procurement the producer of an agricultural product shall be obliged to transfer the agricultural product grown (or produced) by him to the procurer - the person effectuating the purchase of such product for processing or sale.

2. The rules concerning the contract of delivery (Articles 458-477 of the present Code) shall apply to relations under the contract of agricultural procurement which are not regulated by the rules of the present paragraph.

**Article 479. Duties of Procurer**

1. Unless provided otherwise by the contract of agricultural procurement, the procurer shall be obliged to accept the agricultural product from the producer at the location thereof and to ensure the carriage thereof.

2. In an instance when the acceptance of an agricultural product is effectuated at the location of the procurer or other place specified by him, the procurer shall not have the right to refuse to accept the agricultural product which corresponds to the conditions of the contract of agricultural procurement and transferred to the procurer within the period stipulated by the contract.

The procurer shall be obliged to ensure the precise determination of the quality of the product in accordance with standards

3. The duty of the procurer effectuating the processing of an agricultural product may be provided for by the contract of agricultural procurement to return to the producer at his demand the wastes from the processing of an agricultural product with payment at the price determined by the contract.

**Article 480. Duties of Producer of Agricultural Product**

The producer of an agricultural product shall be obliged to transfer the agricultural product grown (or produced) to the procurer in the quantity, quality, and assortment provided for by the contract of agricultural procurement.

**Article 481. Responsibility of Producer of Agricultural Product**

The producer of an agricultural product who has not performed the obligation or has improperly performed the obligation shall bear responsibility when his fault is present.

*§5. Electric Power Supply*

**Article 482. Contract of Electric Power Supply**

1. Under a contract of electric power supply the electric power supply organization shall be obliged to provide electric power to the subscriber (or consumer) through the connected network, and the subscriber shall be obliged to pay for the electric power accepted, and also to comply with the consumption regime provided for by the contract, ensure the safety of operation of the electric power networks within its jurisdiction and the good repair of the instruments and equipment connected with the consumption of electric power used by it.

2. The contract of electric power supply shall be public (Article 387 of the present Code).

3. The conditions of a contract of electric power supply binding upon the parties shall be determined in accordance with the present Code and other legislative acts.

**Article 483. Conclusion and Extension of Contract of Electric Power Supply**

1. A contract of electric supply shall be concluded with a subscriber when he has the necessary equipment connected to the networks of the electric supply organization in the procedure established by legislation of the Republic Kazakhstan.

2. In instances when a citizen who is using electric power for domestic consumption is a subscriber under the contract of electric power supply, the contract shall be considered to be concluded from the moment of first actual connection of the subscriber in the established procedure to the connecting network.

Unless provided otherwise by agreement of the parties, such a contract shall be considered to be concluded for an indefinite period and may be changed or dissolved on the grounds provided for by Article 490 of the present Code.

3. In the absence of a statement by one of the parties concerning termination or change of the contract of electric power supply at the end of the period, it shall be considered to be extended for the same period and on the same conditions which were provided by the contract.

4. If one of the parties before the end of the period of operation of the contract has made a proposal to conclude a new contract, the relations of the parties until the conclusion of the new contract shall be regulated by the previously concluded contract [Article as amended by Law of 8 January 2003, No. 376-II].

**Article 484. Quantity of Electric Power**

1. The electric power supply organization shall be obliged to provide the subscriber with electric power through the connecting network in the quantity provided for by the contract and in compliance with the provision regime agreed by the parties. The quantity provided by the electric power organization and accepted by the subscriber of the electric power shall be determined in accordance with the record data concerning the actual consumption thereof.

2. The right of the subscriber to change the quantity of electric power used by him as determined by the contract may be provided for by the contract on condition of compensation by him of expenses incurred by the electric power supply organization in connection with ensuring the provision of electric power in a quantity not stipulated by the contract.

3. In instances when a citizen is the subscriber under the contract of electric power supply who uses electric power for domestic consumption, he shall have the right to use electric power in the quantity necessary for him. The quantity of electric power provided by the electric power supply organization and used by the subscriber shall be determined by indicators of the record instruments, and in the absence thereof, by means of accounts.

**Article 485. Consequences of Violation of Condition of Contract on Quantity of Electric Power**

If the quantity of electric power provided by the electric power organization through the network connected to the subscriber is less than provided for by the contract, the rules provided by Article 419 of the present Code shall apply unless provided otherwise by legislative acts, the contract, or arises from the essence of the obligation.

**Article 486. Quality of Electric Power**

1. The quality of electric power provided by the electric power supply organization must correspond to the requirements established by State standards and other normative documents with regard to standardization or provided for by the contract.

2. In the event of a violation by the electric power supply organization of the requirements for quality of electric power, the rules provided by Article 491 of the present Code unless provided otherwise by legislative acts, contract, or arises from the essence of the obligation.

**Article 487. Duties of Subscriber for Maintenance and Operation of Networks, Instruments, and Equipment**

1. A subscriber shall be obliged to ensure the proper technical state and safety of electric power networks being operated, instruments, and equipment, to comply with the established consumption regime for electric power, and also immediately to notify the electric power supply organization about accidents, fires, the disrepair of instruments for recording electric power, and other violations arising when using electric power.

2. In instances when a citizen is a subscriber under a contract of electric power supply who is using electric power for domestic consumption, the duty to ensure the proper technical state and safety of the electric power networks, and also the instruments for recording the consumption of electric power, shall be placed on the electric power supply organization unless established otherwise by legislative acts.

3. The requirements for the technical state and operation of electric power networks, instruments, and equipment shall be determined by legislation.

4. A subscriber shall be obliged to admit workers of electric supply organizations to instruments for control of the technical state and safety of operating electric power networks, instruments, and equipment. The procedure for the effectuation of control of compliance therewith shall be determined by legislation.

**Article 488. Payment for Electric Power**

1. Payment for electric power shall be made for the quantity of electric power actually accepted by the subscriber in accordance with the data of recording electric power unless provided otherwise by legislative acts or agreement of the parties.

2. The procedure for the settlement of accounts for electric power shall be determined by legislation or agreement of the parties.

**Article 489. Transfer by Subscriber of Electric Power to Another Person**

1. A subscriber may transfer electric power accepted by him from the electric power supply organization through the connecting network to another person (sub-subscriber) only with the consent of the electric power supply organization.

2. The rules of the present paragraph shall apply to the contract for the transfer by the subscriber of electric power to the sub-scriber unless provided otherwise by legislative acts or the contract.

3. In the event of the transfer of electric power to a sub-subscriber the subscriber shall remain liable to the electric power supply organization unless established otherwise by legislative acts.

**Article 490. Change and Dissolution of Contract**

1. An interruption in provision or the termination or limitation of provision of electric power shall be permitted by agreement of the parties, except for instances when the unsatisfactory state of electric

power devices of the subscriber certified by a State electric power supervision agency threatens an accident or creates a threat to the life and safety of citizens. The electric power supply organization must warn the subscriber in good time about an interruption in provision or the termination or limitation of provision of electric power.

2. An interruption in the provision, termination or limitation of the provision of electric power without the agreement of a subscriber and without a warning thereof but with immediate notification thereof shall be permitted when it is necessary to take urgent measures for the prevention or liquidation of an accident in the system of the electric power supply organization.

3. An interruption in the provision, termination or limitation of the provision of electric power for production entities with a continuous cycle shall not be permitted and shall be regulated by legislation.

4. In instances when a citizen acts as a subscriber under an electric power supply contract who is using electric power for domestic consumption, he shall have the right to unilaterally renounce the contract on condition of notification of the electric power supply organization thereof and payment in full for the electric power used.

5. In instances when a citizen acts as a subscriber under a contract of electric power supply who is using electric power for domestic consumption the electric power supply organization shall have the right unilaterally to suspend performance of the contract in connection with the failure of the subscriber to pay for the electric power used by him on condition of warning the subscriber not later than a month before suspension of performance of the contract.

**Article 491. Responsibility Under Contract of Electric Power Supply**

1. In instances of the failure to perform or the improper performance of obligations under a contract of electric power supply, the electric power supply organization and the subscriber shall be obliged to compensate the real damage caused by this (Article 9(4) of the present Code).

2. If as a result of the regulation of the consumption regime for electric power effectuated on the basis of legislation an interruption in the provision of electric power to the subscriber or the improper performance of contractual obligations when there is fault thereof.

**Article 492. Application of Rules on Contract of Electric Power Supply to Other Relations for Supply Through Connecting Network**

1. The rules of the present paragraph shall apply to relations for the supply of heating electric power through a connecting network unless established otherwise by legislation.

2. The rules of the present paragraph shall apply to relations for supply through a connecting network of gas, oil and oil products, water, and other goods unless established otherwise by legislation, contract, or arises from the essence of the obligation.

*§6. Sale of Enterprise*

**Article 493. Contract of Sale of Enterprise**

1. Under a contract of sale of an enterprise the seller shall be obliged to transfer to the ownership of the purchaser an enterprise as a whole as a property complex (Article 119 of the present Code), except for the rights and duties which the seller shall not have the right to transfer to other persons.

2. The rights and duties with respect to workers of an enterprise shall pass from the seller to the purchase in the procedure provided by labor legislation of the Republic Kazakhstan [as amended by Law of 15 May 2007, No. 253-III].

3. The rights for the use of the firm name, trademarks, service marks, and other means of individualization of the seller and the products thereof, work fulfilled by it or services, and also rights belonging to the seller on the basis of a license for the use of means of individualization, shall pass to the purchaser unless provided otherwise by the contract.

4. Rights received on the basis of a special authorization (or license) to engage in a respective activity shall not be subject to transfer to the purchaser of an enterprise unless established otherwise by legislative acts. The inclusion of obligations within the enterprise being transferred under the contract whose performance by the purchaser is impossible in the absence of his having a special authorization (or license) shall not relieve the seller from respective obligations to creditors. The seller and purchaser shall bear joint and several responsibility to creditors for the failure to perform obligations.

5. The peculiarities of the sale of an enterprise by way of privatization shall be determined by legislative acts on privatization.

**Article 494. Form and State Registration of Contract of Sale of Immovable**

1. A contract of sale of an enterprise shall be concluded in written form by means of drawing up one document signed by the parties with the obligatory appending thereto of the documents specified in Article 495(2) of the present Code.

2. The contract of sale of an enterprise shall be subject to State registration and shall be considered to be concluded from the moment of registration.

**Article 495. Establishment of Composition and Valuation of Cost of Enterprise Subject to Sale**

1. The composition and value of an enterprise subject to sale shall be determined by agreement of the parties unless established otherwise by legislative acts.

2. Before the signature of a contract there must be drawn up and considered by the parties: act of inventorization, bookkeeping balance sheet, audit report of an auditor organization concerning the composition and value of the enterprise, and also a list of all debts (or obligations) to be included within the composition of the enterprise, specifying creditors, and the character, amount, and periods of the demands thereof.

The property and the rights and duties specified in the said documents shall be subject to transfer by the seller to the purchaser unless arises otherwise from Article 493 of the present Code or is established by contract [Article as amended by 5 May 2006, No. 139-III].

**Article 496. Rights of Creditors in Event of Sale of Enterprise**

1. Creditors with regard to obligations included within the composition of the enterprise being sold must be notified in writing by the seller about the sale of the enterprise before the transfer thereof to the purchaser.

2. A creditor who has not communicated to the seller in writing his consent to the transfer of the debt shall have the right within three months from the day of receipt of the notification concerning the sale of the enterprise shall demand either the termination or performance before time of the obligation and compensation by the seller for losses caused by this, or the deeming of the contract of sale of the enterprise to be invalid in full or in respective part.

3. A creditor who was not notified about the sale of the enterprise in the procedure provided by point 1 of the present Article may file suit concerning the satisfaction of demands provided for by point 2 of the present Article within a year from the day when he knew or should have known about the transfer of the enterprise by the seller to the purchaser.

4. After the transfer of the enterprise to the purchaser, the seller and purchaser shall bear joint and several responsibility for the debts included within the composition of the transferred enterprise which were transferred to the purchaser without the consent of the creditor.

**Article 497. Transfer of Enterprise**

1. The transfer of an enterprise by the seller to the purchaser shall be effectuated under the act of transfer, in which shall be specified data concerning the composition of the enterprise and notice of the creditors concerning the sale of the enterprise, and also information concerning defects elicited in the property being transferred and list of property, the duties with regard to the transfer of which have not been performed by the seller in view of the loss thereof.

2. The preparation of the enterprise for transfer, including the drawing up and submission for signature of the act of transfer, shall be the duty of the seller and shall be effectuated at his expense unless provided otherwise by the contract.

3. An enterprise shall be considered to be transferred to the purchaser from the day of signature of the act of transfer by both parties.

From this moment the risk of accidental perishing or accidental spoilage of property being transferred within the enterprise shall pass to the purchaser.

**Article 498. Transfer of Right of Ownership to Enterprise**

1. The right of ownership to an enterprise shall pass to the purchaser from the moment of State registration of this right.

2. State registration of the right of ownership of the purchaser to an enterprise shall be effectuated immediately after the transfer of the enterprise to the purchaser (Article 497 of the present Code).

3. In instances when the retention by the seller of the right of ownership to an enterprise transferred to the purchaser has been provided for by the contract before payment for the enterprise or before the ensuing of other circumstances, the purchaser shall have the right until the transfer of the right of ownership to it to dispose of the property and of the rights which are part of the enterprise being transferred to that extent as is necessary to ensure the activity of the enterprise as a property complex.

**Article 499. Consequences of Transfer and Acceptance of Enterprise with Defects**

1. The consequences of the transfer by the seller and acceptance by the purchaser under an act of transfer of an enterprise the composition of which does not correspond to that provided for by the contract, including with respect to the quality of the property being transferred, shall be determined on the basis of the rules provided for by Articles 413-415, 419, 422, 428, and 432 of the present Code unless arises otherwise from the contract and is provided for by points 2-4 of the present Article.

2. In instances when an enterprise has been transferred and accepted under the act of transfer in which information concerning elicited defects of the enterprise and lost property have been specified (Article 497(1) of the present Code), the purchaser shall have the right to demand a corresponding reduction of the purchase price of the enterprise unless the right to present other demands in such instances has been provided for by contract.

3. The purchaser shall have the right to demand a reduction of the purchase price in the event of the transfer to it within the enterprise of debts (or obligations) of the seller which were not specified in the contract or act of transfer unless the seller proves that the purchaser knew about the debts (or obligations) during the conclusion of the contract and transfer of the enterprise.

4. The seller in the event of receiving notice of the purchaser concerning defects of the property being transferred within the composition of the enterprise, or the absence of individual types of property which are subject to transfer, must without delay replace the property of improper quality or provideshort-delivered property to the purchaser.

5. The purchaser shall have the right in a judicial proceeding to demand dissolution or change of the contract of sale of an enterprise and the return of that which was performed by the parties under the contract if it is established that the enterprise, in view of the defects for which the seller is liable, is unfit for the purposes named in the contract of sale and these defects have not been eliminated by the seller on the conditions, in the procedure, and within the periods established in accordance with the present Code, legislative acts, or the contract, or the elimination of the defects is impossible.

**Article 500. Application to Contract of Sale of Enterprise of Rules Concerning Consequences of Invalidity of Transactions and Concerning Change or Dissolution of Contract**

The rules of the present Code concerning the consequences of the invalidity of transactions and dissolution and change of the contract of purchase-sale providing for the return or recovery in kind of that received under the contract from one or both parties shall apply to the contract of sale of an enterprise unless such consequences materially violate the rights and the interests protected by a law of the creditors of the seller and purchaser, of other persons, and are not contrary to social interests.

## *Chapter 26. Barter*

**Article 501. Contract of Barter**

1. Under a contract of barter, each of the parties shall be obliged to transfer to the ownership, economic jurisdiction, or operative management of the other party one good in exchange for another.

2. To the contract of barter shall apply respectively the rules concerning the contract of purchase-sale insofar as this is not contrary to the rules of the present Chapter and the essence of the barter. In

so doing each of the parties shall be deemed to be the seller of the good which he is obliged to transfer and the purchaser of the good which he is obliged to accept in exchange.

3. The provisions provided by the present Chapter shall apply to the exchange of rights (or work, services) unless provided otherwise by legislative acts and arises from the essence of the respective obligations.

**Article 502. Prices and Expenses Under Contract of Barter**

1. Unless it arises otherwise from the contract, goods subject to exchange shall be offered of equal value and expenses for the transfer thereof and acceptance shall be effectuated in each instance by that party which bears the respective duties.

2. In instances when in accordance with the contract the goods to be exchanged are deemed not to be of equal value, the party obliged to transfer a good whose price is lower than the price of the good being provided in exchange must pay the difference in prices directly before or after the performance of its duty to transfer the good unless another procedure has been provided for by the contract.

**Article 503. Performance of Mutual Obligations to Transfer Good Under Contract of Barter**

In instances when in accordance with a contract the periods for the transfer of the goods to be exchanged do not coincide, the rules concerning counter performance of obligations (Article 284 of the present Code) shall apply to the performance of the obligations to transfer the good by the party which must transfer the good after the transfer of the good by the other party.

**Article 504. Transfer of Right of Ownership in Goods to be Exchanged**

Unless provided otherwise by legislative acts or by the contract, the right of ownership in the goods to be exchanged shall pass to the parties acting under the contract of barter as purchasers simultaneously after the performance of the obligations to transfer the respective goods by each of the parties.

**Article 505. Responsibility for Seizure of Good Acquired Under Contract of Barter**

The party from whom a good is seized by third persons which was acquired under a contract of barter shall have the right when there are grounds provided for by Article 414 of the present Code to require from the other party the return of the good received by the last in the exchange, and when it is impossible to receive the good in kind – the value thereof.

## *Chapter 27. Gift*

**Article 506. Contract of Gift**

1. Under a contract of gift one party (donor) transfers without compensation or is obliged to transfer to the other party (donee) a thing in ownership or a property right (or demand) against himself or against a third person or relieves or is obliged to relieve him of a property duty to himself or to a third person.

When there exists a counter transfer of a thing or right or a counter obligation the contract shall not be deemed to be a gift. The rules provided for by Article 160(2) of the present Code shall apply to such contract.

2. The promise to transfer without compensation any thing or property right whatever or to relieve someone of a property duty (promise of gift) shall be deemed to be a contract of gift and shall bind the promisor if the promise is made in the proper form (Article 508[2]) and contains a clearly expressed intention to perform in the future the transfer of the thing or right without compensation to a specific person or to relieve him from a property duty.

The promise to give all of his property or part of his property without specifying the specific subject of gift in the form of a thing, right, or relief from a duty shall be invalid.

3. A contract providing for the transfer of a gift to the donee after the death of the donor shall be invalid.

The rules of civil legislation concerning inheritance shall apply to such kind of gift.

**Article 507. Refusal of Donee to Accept Gift**

1. The donee shall have the right at any time before the transfer of the gift to him to refuse it. In this event the contract of gift shall be considered to be dissolved.

2. If the contract of gift is concluded in written form, the refusal of the gift must also be concluded in written form. In an instance when the contract of gift has been registered (Article 508[3]), the refusal to accept the gift also shall be subject to State registration.

3. If the contract of gift was concluded in written form, the donor shall have the right to demand from the donee compensation of real damage caused by the refusal to accept the gift.

**Article 508. Form of Contract of Gift**

1. A gift accompanied by the transfer of the gift to the donee may be concluded orally, except for instances provided for by points 2 and 3 of the present Article. The transfer of the gift shall be effectuated by means of handing it over, by symbolic transfer (handing over keys, and so forth) or by handing over right-establishing documents.

2. A contract of gift of moveable property must be concluded in written form in instances when:

(1) the donor is a juridical person and the value of the gift exceeds ten monthlyaccount indicators established by legislative acts;

(2) the contract contains a promise of a gift in the future.

In the instances provided for in the present point a contract of gift concluded orally shall be invalid.

3. A contract of gift of immovable property shall be subject to State registration.

**Article 509. Prohibition of Gift**

A gift shall not be permitted except for ordinary presents whose value does not exceed amounts of ten monthly account indicators established by legislative acts:

(1) in the name of youths and citizens deemed to lack dispositive legal capacity, by their legal representatives;

(2) to workers of treatment and nurturing institutions, institutions of social defense, and other analogous institutions by citizens situated therein for treatment, maintenance, or nurturing, by the spouses and relatives of these citizens;

(3) to State employees in connection with their official position or in connection with the performance by them of their official duties.

**Article 510. Limitations of Gift**

1. A juridical person to whom a thing belongs by right of economic jurisdiction or operative management shall have the right to give it with the consent of the owner unless provided otherwise by legislative acts. This limitation shall not extend to ordinary gifts whose value does not exceed the amounts of ten monthly account indicators established by legislative acts.

2. The gift of property in common joint ownership shall be permitted by consent of all the participants of joint ownership in compliance with the rules provided for by Article 220 of the present Code.

3. The gift of a right of demand belonging to the donor against a third person shall be effectuated in compliance with the rules provided for by Articles 339-343, 345, and 346 of the present Code.

4. A gift by means of the performance for the donee of his duty to a third person shall be effectuated in compliance with the rules provided for by Article 276(1) of the present Code.

A gift by means of the transfer by the donor to himself of the debt of the donee to a third person shall be effectuated in compliance with the rules provided for by Article 348 of the present Code.

5. A power of attorney to perform a gift by a representative in which the donee is not named and the subject of the gift is not specified shall be invalid.

**Article 511. Refusal of Performance of Contract of Gift**

1. The donor shall have the right to refuse performance of a contract which contains a promise to transfer a thing or right in the future to a donee, or a promise to relieve the donee from a property duty, if after conclusion of the contract the property or family status or the state of health of the donor has so changed that performance of the contract in the new conditions leads to a material reduction of his standard of living.

2. The donor shall have the right to refuse performance of a contract which contains a promise to transfer a thing or right to the donee in the future or to relieve the donee from a property duty on the grounds giving him the right to revoke the gift (Article 512(1) of the present Code).

3. The refusal of the donor of performance of the contract of gift on the grounds provided for by points 1 and 2 of the present Article shall not give a right to the donoee to demand compensation of losses.

**Article 512. Revocation of Gift**

1. The donor shall have the right to revoke a gift if the donee has committed an attempt on his life, the life of any member of his family or close relatives, or has intentionally caused bodily injuries to the donor.

In the event of the intentional deprivation of life of the donor by the donee, the right to demand revocation of the gift in court shall belong to the heirs of the donor.

2. The donor shall have the right to require revocation of the gift in a judicial proceeding if the treatment by the donee of the thing given was of great nonproperty value to the donor and creates a threat of its irretrievable loss.

3. Upon the demand of an interested person a court may revoke a gift performed by an individual entrepreneur or juridical person in violation of the provisions of legislative acts on bankruptcy at the expense of means connected with its entrepreneurial activity within the year which preceded the declaration of such person to be bankrupt.

4. The right of the donor to revoke the gift in the event he outlives the donee may be stipulated in the contract of gift.

5. In the event of revocation of a gift the donee shall be obliged to return the thing given if it has been preserved in kind at the moment of revocation of the gift.

**Article 513. Instances in Which Refusal of Performance of Contract of Gift and Revocation of Gift are Impossible**

The rules concerning the refusal of performance of a contract of gift (Article 511 of the present Code) and revocation of a gift (Article 512 of the present Code) shall not apply to gifts whose value does not exceed ten monthly account indicators established by legislative acts (Article 510(1) of the present Code).

**Article 514. Consequences of Causing Harm as Consequence of Defects of Thing Given**

Harm caused to the life, health, or property of a donee citizen as a consequence of defects of the thing given shall be subject to compensation by the donor in accordance with the rules provided for by Chapter 47 of the present Code if it is proved that these defects arose before the transfer of the thing to the donee and were not obvious and the donor, although he knew about them, did not warn the donee about them.

**Article 515. Legal Succession in Event of Promise of Gift**

1. The rights of a donee to whom a gift was promised under a contract of gift shall not pass to his heirs (or legal successors) unless provided otherwise by the contract of gift.

2. The duties of the donor who promised the gift shall pass to his heirs (or legal successors) unless provided otherwise by the contract of gift.

**Article 516. Donations**

1. The gift of a thing or right for generally useful purposes shall be deemed to be a donation.

Donations may be made to citizens, treatment and nurturing institutions, institutions of social defense, and other analogous institutions, philanthropic, scientific, and educational institutions, foundations, museums, and other institutions of culture, social and religious associations, and also to the State and other subjects of civil law specified in Articles 111 and 112 of the present Code.

2. No authorizations or consents whatever shall be required to accept donations.

3. The donation of property to a citizen must be, and to juridical persons may be, conditioned by the donor by the use of this property for a determined designation. In the absence of such a condition

the donation of the property to a citizen shall be considered to be an ordinary gift, and in other instances the donated property shall be used by the donee in accordance with the designation of the property.

A juridical person which has accepted a donation for whose use a determined designation has been established must carry out a solitary recording of all operations relating to the use of the donated property.

4. If the use of donated property in accordance with the designation specified by the donor becomes as a consequence of changed circumstances impossible, it may be used for another designation only with the consent of the donor, and in the event of the death of a citizen-donor or the liquidation of a juridical person-donor, by decision of a court.

5. The use of donated property not in accordance with the designation specified by the donor or a change of such designation in violation of the rules provided for by point 4 of the present Article shall give the right to the donor, his heirs, or other legal successor to demand revocation of the donation.

6. Articles 512 and 515 of the present Code shall not apply to donations.

## *Chapter 28. Rent and Maintenance of Dependent for Life*

### *§1. General Provisions*

**Article 517. Contract of Rent**

1. Under a contract of rent one party (recipient of the rent) shall transfer property in ownership to the other party (payer of rent), and the payer of rent shall be obliged in exchange for the property received periodically to pay to the recipient of rent in the form of a determined monetary amount or of providing means for the maintenance thereof in other form.

2. Under a contract of rent the establishment of the duty to pay rent in perpetuity (permanent rent) or for the period of life of the recipient of the rent (rent for life) shall be permitted. Rent for life may be established on conditions of the maintenance for life of a dependent citizen.

**Article 518. Form of Contract of Rent**

A contract of rent shall be subject to notarial certification, and a contract providing for the alienation of immovable property under payment of rent – also to State registration.

**Article 519. Alienation of Property Under Payment of Rent**

1. Property which is alienated under payment of rent may be transferred by the recipient of the rent to the ownership of the payer of rent for payment or free of charge.

2. In instances when the transfer of property for payment is provided for by the contract of rent, the rules concerning purchase-sale (Chapter 25 of the present Code) shall apply to relations of the parties relating to the transfer and payment, and in instances when such property is transferred free of charge, the rules concerning the contract of gift (Chapter 27 of the present Code) unless established otherwise by the rules of the present Chapter and is not contrary to the essence of the contract.

**Article 520. Encumberment of Immovable Property by Rent**

1. Rent shall encumber the right to a land plot, and also an enterprise, building, installation, or other immovable property transferred under payment thereof. In the event of the alienation of such property by the payer of the rent, his obligations under the contract of rent shall pass to the acquirer of the property.

2. The person who has transferred property encumbered by rent specified in point 1 of the present Article to the ownership of another person shall bear subsidiary responsibility (Article 357 of the present Code) with regard to the demands of the recipient of the rent which arose in connection with a violation of the contract of rent unless joint and several responsibility for this obligation has been provided for by the present Code, other legislative act, or the contract.

**Article 521. Securing Payment of Rent**

1. In the event of the transfer of rights to a land plot or other immovable property under payment of rent, the recipient of the rent shall acquire the right of pledge on this property to secure the obligation of the payer of the rent.

2. The condition establishing the duty of the payer of rent to provide security for the performance of his obligations (Article 292 of the present Code) or to insure to the benefit of the recipient of rent the risk of responsibility for the failure to perform or the improper performance of these obligations shall be a material condition of a contract providing for the transfer of a monetary amount or other moveable property under payment of rent.

3. In the event of the failure of the payer of the rent to fulfill the duties provided for by point 2 of the present Article, and also in the event of the loss of the security or worsening of the conditions thereof under circumstances for which the recipient of rent is not liable, the recipient of rent shall have the right to dissolve the contract of rent and require compensation of losses caused by dissolution of the contract.

**Article 522. Responsibility for Delay of Payment of Rent**

For a delay of payment of rent the payer of rent shall pay a penalty to the recipient of rent in the amount provided for by Article 353 of the present Code unless another amount of penalty has been established by the contract of rent.

*§2. Permanent Rent*

**Article 523. Recipient of Permanent Rent**

1. Only citizens and noncommercial organizations may be recipients of permanent rent if this corresponds to the purposes of their activity.

2. The rights of the recipient of rent under a contract of permanent rent may be transferred to the persons specified in point 1 of the present Article by means of assignment of a demand and transfer by inheritance or by way of legal succession in the event of the reorganization of juridical persons, unless provided otherwise by legislative acts or by a contract.

**Article 524. Form and Amount of Permanent Rent**

1. Permanent rent shall be paid in money in the amount established by the contract.

2. The payment of rent by means of the provision of things, fulfillment of work, or rendering of services which correspond to the value of the monetary amount of rent may be provided for by the contract.

3. Unless provided otherwise by the contract, the amount of rent to be paid shall be increased in proportion to the change of the monthly account indicator established by legislative acts.

**Article 525. Periods for Payment of Permanent Rent**

Unless provided otherwise by the contract, permanent rent shall be paid at the end of each calendar quarter.

**Article 526. Right of Payer to Purchase Permanent Rent**

1. The payer of permanent rent shall have the right to refuse the further payment of rent by means of purchasing it.

2. Such refusal shall be valid on condition that it is declared by the payer of rent in written form not later than three months before the termination of the payment of rent or longer period provided for by the contract of permanent rent. In so doing the obligation relating to the payment of rent shall not terminate until the receipt of the entire amount of the purchase by the recipient of the rent unless a different procedure of purchase has been provided for by the contract.

3. The condition of a contract concerning the waiver of the payer of permanent rent to purchase it shall be invalid.

It may be provided by a contract that the right of purchase of permanent rent may not be effectuated during the life of the recipient of rent or during another period not exceeding thirty years from the moment of conclusion of the contract.

**Article 527. Purchase of Permanent Rent at Demand of Recipient of Rent**

The recipient of permanent rent shall have the right to demand the purchase of rent by the payer in instances when:

(1) the payer of rent delayed the payment thereof by more than one year, unless provided otherwise by the contract;

(2) the payer of rent violated his obligations relating to securing the payment of rent (Article 521 of the present Code);

(3) the payer of rent is deemed to be unable to pay or other obligations have arisen which obviously testify that the rent will not be paid by him in the amount and within the periods established by the contract;

(4) the immovable property transferred under payment of rent has ensued to common ownership or been divided among several persons;

(5) in other instances provided for by the contract.

**Article 528. Purchase Price of Permanent Rent**

1. The purchase of permanent rent in the instances provided for by Articles 526 and 527 of the present Code shall be made at the price determined by the contract.

2. In the absence of a condition concerning the purchase price in a contract under which property has been transferred for payment under payment of permanent rent, the purchase shall be effectuated at the price corresponding to the yearly amount of rent subject to payment.

3. In the absence of a condition concerning the purchase price in a contract under which property has been transferred under payment of rent free of charge, the price of the transferred property shall be included in the purchase price together with the yearly amount of rent payments.

**Article 529. Risk of Accidental Perishing or Accidental Damaging of Property Transferred under Payment of Permanent Rent**

1. The risk of accidental perishing or accidental damage of property transferred free of charge under payment of permanent rent shall be borne by the payer of rent.

2. In the event of the accidental perishing or accidental spoilage of property transferred for payment under payment of permanent rent, the payer shall have the right to demand respectively termination of the obligation relating to the payment of rent or a change of the conditions for the payment thereof.

*§3. Rent for Life*

**Article 530. Recipients of Rent for Life**

1. Rent for life may be established for the period of life of a citizen transferring property under payment of rent or for the period of life of another citizen specified by him.

2. The establishment of rent for life to the benefit of several citizens whose participatory share in the right to receive rent shall be presupposed to be equal shall be permitted unless established otherwise by the contract.

In the event of the death of one of the recipients of rent his participatory share in the right to receive rent shall pass to the recipients of rent who survived him unless provided otherwise by the contract, and in the event of the death of the last recipient of rent, the obligation to pay the rent shall terminate.

3. The contract establishing rent for life to the benefit of a citizen who is deceased at the moment of concluding the contract shall be invalid.

**Article 531. Amount of Rent for Life**

1. Rent for life shall be determined in the contract as a monetary amount periodically to be paid to the recipient of rent during his life. In instances when a contract concerning maintenance for life with a dependent has been concluded by the parties, the monetary amount of such maintenance must be determined in the contract.

2. Unless provided otherwise by the contract of rent for life, the amount of rent to be paid calculated per month must be not less than the minimum earnings establishing by legislative acts.

**Article 532. Periods for Payment of Rent for Life**

Unless provided otherwise by the contract, the rent for life shall be paid at the end of each calendar month.

**Article 533. Dissolution of Contract of Rent for Life at Demand of Recipient of Rent**

1. In the event of a material violation of the conditions of a contract by the payer, the recipient of rent shall have the right to demand from the payer of rent the purchase of rent on the conditions provided for by Article 528 of the present Code or dissolution of the contract.

2. If an apartment, dwelling house, or other property under payment of rent for life has been alienated free of charge, the recipient of the rent shall have the right in the event of a material violation of the conditions of the contract by the payer of the rent to demand the return of this property, setting off the value thereof at the expense of the purchase price of the rent.

**Article 534. Risk of Accidental Perishing of Property Transferred Under Payment of Rent**

The accidental perishing or accidental spoilage of property transferred under payment of rent for life shall not relieve the payer of rent from the obligation to pay it on the conditions provided for by the contract.

*§4. Maintenance of Dependent for Life*

**Article 535. Contract of Maintenance of Dependent for Life**

1. Under a contract of maintenance of a dependent for life the recipient-citizen of rent shall transfer immovable property belonging to him to the ownership of the payer of rent, who shall be obliged to effectuate the maintenance of the dependent of this citizen for life and/or third person specified by him.

2. The rules concerning rent for life shall apply to the contract of maintenance of a dependent for life unless provided otherwise by the rules of the present paragraph.

**Article 536. Duty Relating to Granting of Maintenance of Dependent**

1. The duty of the payer of rent regarding the granting of maintenance of a dependent may include provision of the requirements for housing, nourishment, and clothing, care and necessary assistance.

The payment for ritual services by the payer of rent also may be provided for by the contract.

2. The value of the entire amount of maintenance of a dependent must be determined in the contract. In so doing the total amount of maintenance per month may not be less than two amounts of minimum earnings established by legislative acts.

3. When settling a dispute which has arisen between the parties concerning the amount of maintenance which is granted or should be granted to a citizen, the court must be guided by the principles of good faith and reasonableness.

**Article 537. Replacement of Maintenance for Life by Periodic Payments**

The possibility of replacing the granting of maintenance of a dependent in kind by the payment of periodic payments in money may be provided for by a contract.

**Article 538. Alienation and Use of Property Transferred to Secure Maintenance for Life**

1. The payer of rent shall have the right to alienate, pledge, or by other means encumber immovable property transferred to him as security for maintenance for life only with the prior consent of the recipient of rent.

2. The payer of rent shall be obliged to take necessary measures so that during the period of granting maintenance of a dependent for life the use of the said property does not lead to a reduction of the value of this property above the value of its natural wear and tear.

**Article 539. Termination of Maintenance of Dependent for Life**

1. The obligation of maintenance of a dependent for life shall terminate with the death of the recipient of rent.

2. In the event of a material violation by the payer of rent of his obligations, the recipient of rent shall have the right to demand the return of immovable property transferred to secure the maintenance for life or the payment to him of the purchase price on the conditions established by Article 528 of the present Code. In so doing the payer of rent shall not have the right to demand contributory compensation of the expenses incurred in connection with the maintenance of the recipient of rent.

## *Chapter 29. Property Rental (Lease)*

### *§1. General Provisions*

**Article 540. Contract of Property Rental**

1. Under a contract of property rental (or lease) the renter (or lessor) shall be obliged to grant to the tenant property for payment in temporary possession and use.

2. In the instances and procedure established by the present Code the tenant shall have the right to dispose of rented property.

3. Contract of finance leasing, hire, and also other types of contracts connected with the transfer of property for payment in temporary use shall be relegated to contract of property hire.

**Article 541. Objects of Property Rental**

1. Enterprises and other property complexes, land plots, buildings, installations, equipment, means of transport, and other things which do not lose their natural properties in the process of their use (nonconsumable things) may be transferred on property rental.

2. The right of land use, the right of subsoil use, and other rights to a thing also may be an object of property rental unless provided otherwise by legislative acts.

3. Types of property, the property rental out of which is not permitted or is limitedmay be established by legislative acts.

4. The peculiarities of the property rental of dwelling premises, land plots, subsoil plots, and other solitary natural objects, including on the basis of concession agreements, and also in other instances, may be established by legislative acts.

**Article 542. Conditions of Contract of Property Rental**

Data enabling the property to established which is subject to transfer to the tenant as an object of property rental must be specified in a contract of property rental.

In the absence of such data in the contract a condition concerning an object subject to transfer on property rental shall be considered to be not agreed by the parties, and the respective contract – to be not concluded.

**Article 543. Tenant**

The right to give out property on rental shall belong to its owner. Persons empowered by legislative acts or by the owner to give out property on rental also may be renters.

**Article 544. Form of Contract of Property Rental**

1. A contract of property rental for a period of not more than one year, and if one of the

parties of the contract is a juridical person, irrespective of the period, must be concluded in written form [text given with "not" as officially published in *Казахстанская правда*, 17 July 1999, although version enacted by Parliament did not contain this word].

2. A contract of property rental for immovable property shall be subject to State registration unless established otherwise by a law.

3. A contract of property rental between citizens for a period of up to one year may be concluded in oral form.

3. A contract of property rental which provides for the transfer thereafter of the right of ownership to the property to the tenant shall be concluded in the form provided for the contract of purchase-sale of such property.

**Article 545. Period of Contract of Property Rental**

1. A contract of property rental shall be concluded for the period determined by the contract.

2. If the contract of property rental has been concluded without specifying a period, it shall be considered to be concluded for an indefinite period.

Each of the parties shall have the right to renounce such contract at any time, having warned the other party thereof three months in advance – in the event of the rental of immoveable property and one month in advance – in the event of the rental of other property unless established otherwise by legislative acts of the contract.

3. Maximum periods for a contract for individual types of property rental may be established by legislative acts, as well as for the rental of individual types of property. In these instances if the period of rental is not determined in the contract and neither of the parties has renounced the contract upon the expiry of the maximum period established by legislative acts, the contract shall terminate upon the expiry of the maximum period.

In this event a contract of property rental exceeding the maximum period established by legislative acts shall be considered to be concluded for the period equal to the maximum.

**Article 546. Payment Under Contract of Property Rental**

1. Payment for the use of rented property shall be paid by the tenant in the procedure, periods, and form established by the contract unless established otherwise by legislative acts. In instances when they have not been determined by the contract it shall be considered that the procedure, periods, and form have been established as usually applied in the event of the rental of analogous property under comparable circumstances.

2. Payment shall be established for all rented property as a whole or individually for each of its constituent parts in the form of:

(1) payments determined in a fixed amount made periodically or one time;

(2) the established participatory share of the products, fruits, or revenues received as a result of the use of the rented property;

(3) the granting of determined services by the tenant;

(4) the transfer by the tenant to the renter of things stipulated by the contract in ownership or on rental;

(5) imposing on the tenant expenditures stipulated by the contract for the improvement of the leased property.

The parties may provide in the contract for combining the said forms of payment for use of the property or other forms of payment.

3. Unless provided otherwise by agreement of the parties, the amounts of payment for use of the property may be changed by agreement of the parties not more often than once a year. Other minimum periods for revision of the amount of payment for individual types of property rental, and also for the rental of individual types of property, may be provided for by legislative acts.

4. The amounts of payment may be revised at the demand of one of the parties in instances of a change of established centralized prices and tariffs.

5. Unless provided otherwise by legislative acts, the tenant shall have the right to require a respective reduction of the payment if by virtue of circumstances for which he is not liable the conditions of use provided for by the contract or the state of the property materially have worsened.

6. Unless provided otherwise by the contract, in the event of a material violation by the tenant of the periods for making payment for the use of property the renter shall have the right to require the making of payment by him before time within the period established by the renter. In so doing the renter shall not have the right to demand the making of payment before time for more than two periods in succession.

**Article 547. Granting Property to Tenant**

1. The renter shall be obliged to grant property to the tenant in a state corresponding to the conditions of the contract and designation of the property.

2. Property shall be rented out together with all of its appurtenances and documents relating thereto (documents certifying completeness, safety, quality of property, procedure for operation, and so forth), unless provided otherwise by the contract.

If such appurtenances and documents were not transferred and without them the tenant can not use the property in accordance with its designation or is to a significant degree deprived of that which he had the right to count upon when concluding the contract, he may require the granting to him by the renter of such appurtenances and documents or dissolution of the contract.

3. If the renter did not grant to the tenant property rented out within the period specified in the contract, and if such period is not specified in the contract, within a reasonable period, the tenant shall have the right to demand and obtain this property from him in accordance with Article 355 of the present Code or to require dissolution of the contract.

**Article 548. Responsibility of Renter for Defects of Property Rented Out**

1. The renter shall be liable for defects of property rented out which wholly or partially obstruct the use thereof even if during the conclusion of the contract he did not know about these defects.

In the event of the discovery of such defects the tenant shall have the right at his choice to require of the renter:

(1) the elimination of the defects of the property without compensation;

(2) the commensurate reduction of the rental payment;

(3) the withholding of the amount of expenses incurred by him for elimination of the said defects from the payment for use of the property, having informed the renter in advance thereof;

(4) the dissolution of the contract before time.

2. The renter who is notified about the demands of the tenant or about his intention to eliminate the defects of the property at the expense of the renter may without delay replace the property rented with the consent of the tenant with other analogous property in a proper state or eliminate the defects of the property without compensation.

3. If satisfaction of the demands of the tenant or withholding of expenses by him for elimination of defects from the payment for use of the property does not cover the losses caused to the tenant, he shall have the right to require compensation of the uncovered part of the losses.

4. The renter shall not be liable for those defects of property rented out which were stipulated by him when concluding the contract or were previously known to the tenant.

**Article 549. Rights of Third Persons to Property Rented Out**

1. The transfer of property on rental shall not be grounds for termination or change of the rights of third persons to such property.

2. When concluding a contract, the renter shall be obliged to warn the tenant about all the rights of third persons to the property being rented out (servitude, right of pledge, and so forth).

The failure to perform this rule shall give the tenant the right to demand a reduction of payment for use of the property or dissolution of the contract.

**Article 550. Use of Rented Property**

The tenant shall be obliged to use the property in accordance with the conditions of the contract, and if such conditions have not been determined in the contract – in accordance with the designation of the property.

**Article 551. Limits of Disposition by Tenant of Rented Property**

1. The tenant shall have the right with the consent of the renter to subrent (or sublease) and to transfer his rights and duties under the contract of property rental to another person (re-hire), to grant the rented property for use without compensation, and also to pledge these rights and contribute them as a contribution to the charter capital of economic partnerships and joint-stock societies or a contribution to a production cooperative unless established otherwise by the legislative acts. In the said instances, except for re-hire, the tenant shall remain responsible under the contract to the renter.

2. The contract concerning the transfer of property to other persons may not be concluded for a period exceeding the period of the contract of rental.

3. The rules concerning the contract of property rental, unless established otherwise by legislative acts, shall apply to a contract of subrental.

**Article 552. Duties of Renter With Regard to Maintenance of Rented Property**

1. The renter shall be obliged to perform at his own expense capital repair to the property transferred on rental within the periods agreed by the parties unless provided otherwise by legislative acts or the contract.

2. The renter shall be obliged to perform a repair at his expense caused by urgent necessity which arose by virtue of circumstances for which the tenant is not liable within reasonable periods unless established otherwise by legislative acts or the contract.

3. The failure of the renter to perform duties with regard to capital repair shall give the tenant the right at his choice to:

(1) perform the repair autonomously and recover from the renter the cost of the repair;

(2) set-off the cost of the repair on account of the payment under the contract;

(3) require a corresponding reduction of payment under the contract;

(4) renounce the contract.

**Article 553. Duties of Tenant With Regard to Maintenance of Rented Property**

The tenant shall be obliged to maintain the property in a proper state, to perform current repair at his own expense, and to bear expenses for the maintenance of the property unless otherwise established by legislation or by the contract.

**Article 554. Right of Ownership of Tenant to Product, Fruits, and Other Revenues from Rented Property**

A product, fruits, and other revenues received by the tenant as a result of use of rented property shall be his ownership unless provided otherwise by legislative acts or the contract.

**Article 555. Improvements of Property**

1. Separable improvements of rented property made by the tenant shall be his ownership unless provided otherwise by the contract.

2. In an instance when a tenant has made improvements at the expense of own means and with the consent of the renter which are not separable without harm to the rented property, he shall have the right after termination of the contract to compensation of the cost of these improvements unless provided otherwise by the contract.

3. The cost of inseparable improvements made by the tenant without the consent of the renter shall not be subject to compensation unless provided otherwise by legislative acts or the contract.

**Article 556. Change and Dissolution of Contract of Property Rental at Demand of One of Parties**

1. Upon the demand of one of the parties a contract of property rental may be changed or dissolved before time in a judicial proceeding in the instances provided for by the present Code, other legislative acts, or the contract.

2. Upon the demand of the renter the contract of property rental may be dissolved and the property returned to the renter in the following instances:

(1) if the tenant uses the property with material violation of the conditions of the contract or the designation of the property despite a written warning of the renter concerning the termination of such actions;

(2) if the tenant intentionally or through negligence materially worsens the property;

(3) if the tenant does not make payment more than two times upon the expiry of the period of payment established by the contract for use of the property;

(4) if the tenant does not make capital repair of the property within the periods established by the contract, and in the absence thereof in the contract within reasonable periods in those instances when in accordance with legislative acts or the contract the duty of capital repair lies on the tenant.

The renter shall have the right to demand dissolution of the contract before time only after providing the tenant the possibility to perform his obligation within a reasonable period.

3. A contract may be dissolved before time at the demand of the tenant in the following instances:

(1) the renter does not grant property for use to the tenant or creates obstacles to the use of the property in accordance with the conditions of the contract or the designation of the property;

(2) the renter does not perform within the periods established by the contract, and in the absence thereof in the contract – within reasonable periods the duty of capital repair of the property placed on him;

(3) property transferred to the tenant has defects which obstruct its use which were not stipulated by the renter when concluding the contract, were not known to the tenant in advance, and could not have been discovered by him during the inspection of the property or verification of its good repair when concluding the contract;

(4) if the property by virtue of circumstances for which the tenant is not liable turns out to be in a state not fit for use.

**Article 557. Preferential Right of Tenant to Conclude Contact for New Period**

1. Unless provided otherwise by legislative acts or by the contract, the tenant who has properly performed his duties shall have upon the expiry of the period of the contract a preferential right under equal conditions before other persons to conclude a contract of property rental for a new period. The tenant shall be obliged to inform the renter in writing about the wish to conclude such contract within the period specified in the contract of property rental, and if such period is not specified in the contract, within a reasonable period before the end of the operation of the contract.

2. When concluding a contract of property rental for a new period, the conditions of the contract may be changed by agreement of the parties.

3. If the renter has refused the tenant to conclude a contract for a new period, but within a year from the day of expiry of the period of the contract has concluded a contract of property rental with another person, the tenant shall have the right at his choice to demand in court the transfer to himself of the rights and duties under the contract concluded and compensation of losses caused by the refusal to renew the contract with him or only compensation of losses.

**Article 558. Renewal of Contract of Property Rental**

If the tenant continues to use the property after the expiry of the period of the contract in the absence of objections on the part of the renter, the contract shall be considered to be renewed on the same conditions for an indefinite period. In so doing each of the parties shall have the right at any time to renounce the contract, having warned in writing the other party thereof not less than three months in advance – in the event of the rental of an immoveable and one month – in the event of the rental of other property unless provided otherwise by legislative acts or the contract.

**Article 559. Preservation of Contract of Property Rental in Force in Event of Change of Parties**

1. Transfer of the right of ownership, right of economic jurisdiction, or right of operative management to property rented out to another person shall not be grounds for a change of or dissolution of the contract of property rental.

2. In the event of the death of a citizen who is a tenant of immovable property, his rights and duties under the contract of property rental shall pass to the heir unless provided otherwise by legislative acts or by the contract.

The renter shall not have the right to refuse such heir from entering into the contract for the remaining period of its operation except for instances when the conclusion of the contract was conditioned by the personal qualities of the tenant.

**Article 560. Dependence of Contract of Subrental on Basic Contract of Property Rental**

1. Unless provided otherwise by the contract of property rental, the termination before time of a contract of property rental shall entail termination of the contract of subrental concluded in accordance therewith.

2. If a contract of property rental is invalid on the grounds provided for by the present Code, the contract of subrental concluded in accordance with it shall be invalid.

**Article 561. Return of Property to Renter in Event of Termination of Contract**

1. After the termination of the contract of property rental the tenant shall be obliged to return property to the renter in that state in which he received it, taking into account normal wear and tear or in the state stipulated by the contract.

2. If the state of the returned property at the end of the contract does not correspond to the conditions provided for in point 1 of the present Article, the tenant shall compensate the renter for damage caused. If property rented out is not serviceable before the period of service provided for in the contract, the tenant shall compensate the renter for the residual value of the property unless provide otherwise by the contract.

3. If the tenant has not returned the rented property or returned it not in good time, the renter shall have the right to demand the making of payment for use of the property for the entire time of the delay. In an instance when the said payment does not cover the losses caused to the renter, he may demand the compensation thereof.

4. In an instance when a penalty has been provided for by the contract for the untimely return of the rented property, losses may be recovered in the full amount above the penalty unless provided otherwise by the contract.

**Article 562. Transfer of Property to Ownership of Tenant**

1. It may be provided in a contract of property rental that the rented property shall pass to the ownership of the tenant on the conditions determined by agreement of the parties.

2. If a condition concerning the purchase of rented property is not provided in the contract, it may be established by an additional agreement of the parties which in so doing shall have the right to agree concerning a set-off of the previously paid payment for use of the property in the purchase price.

3. Instances of the purchase of rental property may be established by legislative acts.

**Article 563. Defense of Rights of Tenant**

Defense of his rights to rental property equally with the defense of the right of ownership shall be ensured to a tenant. Responsibility to the tenant for a violation of the use which third persons perform by their coercive actions not having any rights to rental property shall not lie on the renter.

The tenant shall have the right to bring suit and otherwise defend the rights belonging to him in his own name.

**Article 564. Peculiarities of Individual Types of Property Rental and Rental of Individual Types of Property**

The provisions provided for by the present paragraph shall apply to individual types of contract of property rental and to contracts of rental of individual types of property (finance lease, lease of enterprises, lease of buildings and installations, lease of means of transport, hire) unless established otherwise by legislative acts and the rules of the present Code concerning them [Article as amended by Law of 5 July 2000, No.75-II].

*§2. Finance Leasing*

**Article 565. Contract of Finance Lease**

1. According to a contract of finance leasing, the finance lessor shall be obliged to acquire in ownership property specified by the finance lessee from a seller and to grant this property to the finance lessee in temporary possession and use for entrepreneurial purposes for payment.

2. It may be provided by the contract of finance leasing that the choice of seller and property to be acquired shall be effectuated by the finance lessee.

3. The peculiarities of individual types of contract of finance leasing may be established by legislative acts of the Republic Kazakhstan [point 3 added by Law of 10 March 2004, No. 532-II].

**Article 566. Subject of Contract of Finance Leasing**

Buildings, installations, machines, equipment, tools, means of transport, land plots, and any other non-consumer things may be the subject of finance leasing.

Securities and natural resources may not be the subject of finance leasing.

**Article 567. Material Conditions of Contract of Finance Leasing**

A contract of finance leasing must, besides the conditions specified in Article 542 of the present Code, contain the following conditions:

(1) name of the seller of the property;

(2) conditions and period for transfer of property to finance lessee;

(3) amount and periodicity of payments;

(4) period of contract;

(5) conditions of transfer of property to ownership of finance lessee if such transfer is provided for by the contract.

**Article 568. Notification of Seller About Handing Over Property on Finance Leasing**

The finance lessor in acquiring property for the finance lessee must notify the seller that the property is intended for transfer thereof on finance leasing to a determined person.

**Article 569. Risk of Accidental Perishing or Spoilage of Property**

The risk of accidental perishing or spoilage of property which is the subject of finance leasing shall pass to the finance lessee at the moment of the transfer of the property unless provided otherwise by the contract.

**Article 570. Payments Under Contract of Finance Leasing**

Periodic payments subject to payment in accordance with the contract of finance leasing may be calculated by taking into account amortization of all or the material part of the value of the property at the price at the moment of concluding the contract.

**Article 571. Transfer to Finance Lessee of Subject of Contract of Finance Leasing**

1. Unless provided otherwise by the contract or arises from the essence of the obligation, the property which is the subject of the contract of finance leasing shall be transferred by the seller directly to the finance lessee at the location of the last.

2. In an instance when property which is the subject of a contract of finance leasing is not transferred to the finance lessee within the period specified in this contract, the finance lessee shall have the right if the delay was permitted under circumstances for which the finance lessor is liable to demand dissolution of the contract and compensation of losses.

**Article 572. Responsibility of Seller**

1. The finance lessee shall have the right to present demands directly to the seller of the property which is the subject of the contract of finance leasing and which arise from the contract of purchase-sale concluded between the seller and the finance lessor, in particular, with respect to the quality and completeness of the property, the periods for the delivery thereof, and in other instances of improper performance of the contract by the seller. In so doing the finance lessee shall have the rights and bear the duties provided for by the present Code for a purchaser except the duties to pay for the property acquired as if he were a party to the contract of purchase-sale of the said property.

In relations with the seller the finance lessee and finance lessor shall act as joint and several creditors.

2. Unless provided otherwise by the contract of finance leasing, the finance lessor shall not be liable to the finance lessee for the fulfillment by the seller of demands arising from the contract of purchase-sale, except for instances when the right of choice of the seller lies on the finance lessor. In the last instance the finance lessee shall have the right at his choice to present demands arising from the contract of purchase-sale both directly to the seller of the property and to the finance lessor, who shall bear joint and several responsibility.

§3. *Lease of Enterprise*

**Article 573. Contract of Lease of Enterprise**

1. Under the contract of lease of an enterprise the lessor shall be obliged to grant to the lessee for payment in order to effectuate entrepreneurial activity in temporary possession and use an enterprise as a whole as a property complex (Article 119 of the present Code), including the right to the firm name and/or commercial designation of the rightholder to protected commercial information, and also other

objects of exclusive rights provided for by the contract – trademark, service mark, and so on (complex of exclusive rights), except for those rights and duties which the lessor does not have the right to transfer to other persons.

2. The rights of the lessor received by it on the basis of a license to engage in a respective activity shall not be subject to transfer to the lessee unless established otherwise by legislative acts. The inclusion in the composition of the enterprise to be transferred under the contract of obligations whose performance by the lessee is impossible in the absence of such special authorization (or license) shall not relieve the lessor from the respective obligations to creditors.

3. The rights and duties with respect to workers of the enterprise shall pass from the lessor to the lessee in the procedure provided for by labor legislation of the Republic Kazakhstan [point 3 as amended by Law of 15 May 2007, No. 253-III].

**Article 574. Rights of Creditors in Event of Lease of Enterprise**

1. The lessor shall be obliged to notify in writing its creditors about the transfer of debts to the lessee before the conclusion of the contract of lease, which in the event of non-consent to such transfer shall have the right within three months from the day of receipt of notification to demand from the lessor termination or performance before time of respective obligations and compensation of losses. If within the said period any of the demands is not presented, the creditor shall be deemed to have given consent to the transfer of the respective debt to the lessee.

2. An enterprises may be transferred to the lessee only after completion of the settlement of accounts with creditors which have demanded from the lessor the termination or performance of obligations before time.

3. After the transfer of an enterprise as a property complex on lease the lessor and lessee shall bear joint and several responsibility for debts included within the composition of the transferred enterprise which were transferred to the lessee without the consent of the creditor.

**Article 575. Form and State Registration of Contract of Lease of Enterprise**

1. The contract of lease of an enterprise shall be concluded in written form by means of drawing up a single document signed by the parties.

2. The failure to comply with the form of the contract of lease of an enterprise shall entail the invalidity of the contract.

3. The contract of lease of an enterprise shall be subject to State registration and shall be considered to be concluded from the moment of such registration.

**Article 576. Transfer of Leased Enterprise**

The transfer of an enterprise to the lessee shall be effectuated under an act of transfer. The preparation of the enterprise for transfer, including the drawing up and submission for signature of the act of transfer, shall be the duty of the lessor and shall be effectuated at his expense unless provided otherwise by the contract.

**Article 577. Duties of Lessee with Regard to Maintenance of Enterprise and Payment of Expenses for Operation Thereof**

1. The lessee of an enterprise shall be obliged during the entire period of operation of the contract to maintain the enterprise in a proper technical state, including the current and capital repair thereof, unless provided otherwise by the contract.

2. Expenses connected with the operation of the leased enterprise shall be placed on the lessee unless provided otherwise by the contract.

**Article 578. Use of Property of Leased Enterprise**

Unless provided otherwise by legislative acts or the contract, the lessee shall have the right without the consent of the lessor to sell, exchange, grant for temporary use, or loan material valuables which are part of the property of the leased enterprise, sublease them, and transfer their rights and duties under the contract of lease with respect to such valuables to another person on condition that this does not entail a reduction of the value of the enterprise and does not violate other provisions of the contract of lease.

**Article 579. Making of Changes and Improvements by Lessee in Leased Enterprise**

1. The lessee shall have the right without the consent of the lessor to make changes in the composition of the lease property complex, to conduct the reconstruction thereof, expansion, and technical re-equipping increased the value thereof unless provided otherwise by the contract of lease of the enterprise.

2. The lessee of an enterprise shall have the right to compensation for the cost to him of inseparable improvements of the leased property irrespective of the authorization of the lessor for such improvements unless provided otherwise by the contract of lease of the enterprise.

3. The lessor may be relieved by a court from the duty to compensate the lessee for the cost of such improvements of a leased enterprise if it is proved that the costs of the lessee for such improvements exceeds the value of the leased property incommensurately to the improvement of its operational properties or when effectuating such improvements the principles of good faith and reasonableness were violated.

**Article 580. Return of Leased Enterprise**

In the event of the termination of a contract of lease, the enterprise as a whole as a property complex must be returned to the lessor in compliance with the rules provided for by Articles 573, 574, and 576 of the present Code. The preparation of the enterprise for transfer to the lessor, including the drawing up and submission for signature of the act of transfer, shall in this event be the duty of the lessee and shall be effectuated at his expense unless provided otherwise by the contract.

*§4. Lease of Buildings and Installations*

**Article 581. Contract of Lease of Building or Installation**

1. Under the contract of lease of a building or installation the lessor shall be obliged to transfer a building or installation in temporary possession and use to the lessee.

2. The rules of the present paragraph shall apply to the lease of enterprises unless provided otherwise by the rules of the present Code concerning the lease of an enterprise.

**Article 582. Form and State Registration of Contract of Lease of Building or Installation**

1. A contract of lease of a building or installation shall be concluded in written form by means of drawing up one document signed by the parties.

2. The failure to comply with the form of the contract of lease of a building or installation shall entail its invalidity.

3. The contract of lease of a building or installation concluded for a period of not less than one year shall be subject to State registration and shall be considered to be concluded from the moment of such registration.

**Article 583. Amount of Lease Payment**

1. A contract of lease of a building or installation must provide for the amount of lease payment. In the absence of the condition concerning the amount of lease payment agreed by the parties in written form, the contract of lease of a building or installation shall be considered to be not concluded. In so doing the rules for determining price provided for by Article 385(3) of the present Code shall not apply.

2. In instances when the payment for lease of a building or installation has been established in the contract per unit of space of the building (or installation) or other indicator of the dimension thereof, the lease payment shall be determined by proceeding from the actual dimension of the building or installation transferred to the lessee.

**Article 584. Transfer of Building or Installation**

1. The transfer of a building or installation by the lessor and the acceptance thereof by the lessee shall be effectuated under an act of transfer or other document concerning the transfer to be signed by the parties.

2. The avoidance by one party of signature of the document concerning the transfer of the building or installation on the conditions provided for by a contract shall be considered as a refusal respectively of the lessor to perform the duty with regard to the transfer of property and of the lessee to accept the property.

3. In the event of the termination of the contract of lease of a building or installation, the leased building or installation must be returned to the lessor in compliance with the rules provided for by points 1 and 2 of the present Article.

*§5. Lease of Means of Transport*

**Article 585. Contract of Lease of Means of Transport with Crew**

1. Under a contract of lease (time-charter) of a means of transport with the provision of services for management and technical operation (contract of lease of means of transport with crew) the lessor shall grant the means of transport to the lessee in temporary possession and use for payment in

temporary possession and use and render services with his own forces with regard to the management and technical operation thereof.

2. The rules of the present Chapter concerning the preferential right of the lessee to renewal of a contract of lease and concerning renewal of a contract of lease for an indefinite period (Articles 557 and 558 of the present Code) shall not apply to the contract of lease of means of transport with a crew.

**Article 586. Form of Contract of Lease of Means of Transport with Crew**

A contract of lease of means of transport with a crew must be concluded in written form irrespective of the period thereof.

**Article 587. Duty of Lessor Relating to Maintenance of Means of Transport**

The lessor throughout the entire period of the contract shall be obliged to maintain the proper state of the means of transport leased, including the effectuation of current and capital repair and the granting of necessary appurtenances.

**Article 588. Duties of Lessor With Regard to Management and Technical Operation of Means of Transport**

1. The amount of services with regard to management and technical operation of means of transport granted by the lessor to the lessee must ensure its normal and safe operation in accordance with the purposes of the lease specified in the contract. A more extensive group of services to be granted to the lessee may be provided for by the contract of lease of means of transport with a crew.

2. The composition of the crew of means of transport and the skills thereof must correspond to the rules and conditions of the contract which are binding upon the parties, and if such requirements have not been established by rules and conditions of the contract which are binding upon the parties, the requirements of usual practice for the operation of means of transport of the particular type and the conditions of the contract.

3. Members of the crew shall preserve labor relations with the lessor. They shall be subordinate to the regulations of the lessor with respect to the management and technical operation and to the regulations of the lessee affecting the commercial operation of the means of transport.

4. Unless provided otherwise by the contract of lease, expenses relating to the payment for services of members of the crew, and also expenses for the maintenance thereof, shall be borne by the lessor.

**Article 589. Duty of Lessee Relating to Payment of Expenses Connected with Commercial Operation of Means of Transport**

Unless provided otherwise by the contract of lease of means of transport with a crew, the lessee shall bear expenses for the payment of fuel and other materials expended in the process of use of materials, with regard to payment of fees, and other expenses arising in connection with the commercial operation of the means of transport.

**Article 590. Insurance of Means of Transport**

Unless provided otherwise by a contract of lease of means of transport with a crew, the duty to insure the means of transport and/or to insure responsibility for damage which may be caused by it or in connection with its operation shall be placed on the lessor in those instances when such insurance is obligatory.

**Article 591. Contracts With Third Persons Concerning Use of Means of Transport**

The lessee within the framework of effectuating commercial operation of leased means of transport shall have the right without the consent of the lessor to conclude in his own name with third persons contracts of carriage and other contracts unless they are contrary to the purposes of the use of means of transport specified in the contract of lease, and if such purposes have not been established, the designation of the means of transport.

**Article 592. Responsibility for Harm Caused to Means of Transport**

In the event of the perishing or damage of leased means of transport, the lessee shall be obliged to compensate the lessor for losses caused if the last proves that the perishing or damage of the means of transport occurred with regard to circumstances for which the lessee is liable in accordance with legislative acts or the contract.

**Article 593. Responsibility for Harm Caused by Means of Transport**

Responsibility for harm caused to third persons by leased means of transport, mechanisms thereof, devices, equipment, and so on shall be borne by the lessee in accordance with the rules of Article 931 of the present Code.

**Article 594. Peculiarities of Lease of Individual Types of Means of Transport**

Peculiarities of the lease of individual types of means of transport with the granting of services relating to management and technical operation may be established, besides those provided for by the present paragraph, by legislative acts.

The lease of means of transport without the granting of services relating to management and technical operation (lease of means of transport without a crew) shall be subordinated to the general provisions of the present Code on the contract of property rental.

*§6. Hire*

**Article 595. Contract of Hire**

1. Under a contract of hire, the hirer effectuating the rental of moveable property as permanent entrepreneurial activity shall be obliged to provide property to the hiree for payment in temporary possession and use.

Property provided under a contract of hire shall be used for consumer purposes unless provided otherwise by the contract or arises from the essence of the obligation.

2. A contract of hire shall be concluded in written form.

3. A contract of hrie shall be public (Article 387 of the present Code).

**Article 596. Period of Contract of Hire**

1. A contract of hire shall be concluded for a period of up to one year.

2. Rules concerning the preferential right of the hiree to renewal of a contract of property rental and renewal of a contract of property rental for an indeterminate period (Articles 557 and 558 of the present Code) shall not apply to the contract of hire.

3. The hiree shall have the right to renounce the contract of hire at any time unless provided otherwise by the contract.

**Article 597. Granting of Property to Hiree**

The hirer concluding a contract of hire shall be obliged in the presence of the hiree to verify the good repair of the property being rented, and also to familiarize the hiree with the rules of operation of the property or issue to him written instructions concerning the use of this property.

**Article 598. Elimination of Defects of Rented Property**

In the event of the discovery by the hiree of defects of the rented property wholly or partially obstructing its use, the hirer shall be obliged within a ten-day period from the day of declaration of the hiree concerning the defects unless a shorter period is established by the contract to eliminate the defects of the property without compensation on site or to replace the particular property with other analogous property in a proper state.

If the defects of the rented property were a consequence of a violation by the hiree of the rules of operation and maintenance of the property, the hiree shall pay the hirer the cost of repair and transporting of the property.

**Article 599. Payment for Use of Property**

1. Payment for the use of property under a contract of hire shall be established in the form of payments determined in a fixed amount to be made periodically or at one time.

2. In the event of the return of the property before time by the hiree the hirer shall refund to him a respective part of the payment received for use of the property, calculating it from the day following the day of actual return of the property.

3. [repealed by Law of 29 March 2000, No. 42-II].

**Article 600. Use of Rented Property**

1. Capital and current repair of property rented under a contract of hire shall be the duty of the hirer.

2. Subrental of property granted to the hiree under a contract of hire, transfer by the hiree of his rights and duties under the contract of hire to another person, granting this property for uncompensated use, pledge of the rights of the hiree and contribution thereof as a property contribution to economic partnerships, joint-stock societies, and contribution to production cooperatives shall not be permitted.

## *Chapter 30. Rental of Dwelling*

### Article 601. Contract of Rental of Dwelling

1. Under a contract of rental of a dwelling the owner of the dwelling or person empowered by him (landlord) shall be obliged to grant to a citizen (tenant) and members of the family thereof a dwelling in use for payment.

2. A contract of rental of dwelling must be concluded in written form, and in instances provided for by legislative acts is subject to registration.

### Article 602. Contract of Rental of Dwelling in Houses of State Housing Fund

1. A contract of rental of a dwelling in houses of the State housing fund shall be concluded on the basis of a decision of the local executive agency on granting a dwelling.

2. The conditions of granting a dwelling, the rights and duties of the parties, and the grounds for a change and dissolution of a contract of rental of a dwelling in houses of the State housing fund shall be established by housing legislation.

### Article 603. Contract of Rental of Dwelling in Houses of Private Housing Fund

The conditions of the rental of a dwelling in houses of the private housing fund shall be determined by agreement of the parties unless provided otherwise by housing legislation.

## *Chapter 31. Uncompensated Use of Property*

### Article 604. Contract of Uncompensated Use of Property

1. Under a contract of uncompensated use of property (or contract of loan), one party (the lender) shall transfer for temporary uncompensated use to the other party (loan recipient), and the last is obliged to return this same property in the same state in which it was received, taking into account normal wear and tear, or in a state stipulated by the contract.

2. The rules provided for by Article 541, Article 545(1) and (2), paragraph one, Article 550, Article 555, and Article 556(2), subpoint (1)(2) and (4), and Article 558 of the present Code shall apply respectively to the contract of uncompensated use of property.

### Article 605. Lender

1. The right to transfer property for uncompensated use shall belong to the owner thereof and to other persons empowered to do so by legislative acts or by the owner.

2. A commercial organization shall not have the right to transfer property form uncompensated use to a person who is the founder, participant (or stockholder), director, or member of the management or control organs thereof.

### Article 606. Granting Property for Uncompensated Use

1. The lender shall be obliged to grant property in a state corresponding to the conditions of the contract of uncompensated use and the designation thereof.

2. Property shall be granted for uncompensated use with all of its appurtenances and documents relating thereto (documents certifying completeness, safety, quality of property, procedure for operation, and so on) unless provided otherwise by the contract.

If such appurtenances and documents were not transferred and without them the thing can not be used for the designation or its use to a significant degree loses value for the loan recipient, the last shall have the right to require such appurtenances and documents be granted to him or to dissolution of the contract and compensation for real damage incurred by him.

**Article 607. Responsibility for Defects of Property Transferred for Uncompensated Use**

1. The lender who has transferred for uncompensated use shall be liable for defects of this property which he intentionally or through gross negligence did not stipulate when transferring the property if in so doing real damage is caused to the loan recipient.

2. The lender notified about the demands of the loan recipient or of his intention to eliminate the defects of the property at the expense of the lender may without delay replace the thing in disrepair with another analogous thing which is in a proper state.

3. The lender shall not be liable for defects of property which were stipulated by him when concluding the contract or were known to the loan recipient beforehand or should have been discovered by the loan recipient during the inspection of the property or verification of its good repair when concluding the contract or when transferring the thing.

**Article 608. Rights of Third Persons to Property Being Transferred for Uncompensated Use**

The transfer of property for uncompensated use shall not be grounds for the change or termination of the rights of third persons to this property.

When concluding a contract of uncompensated use the lender shall be obliged to warn the loan recipient about all the rights of third persons to this property (servitude, right of pledge, and so forth). The failure to perform this duty shall give the loan recipient the right to demand dissolution of the contract and compensation for real damage incurred by him.

**Article 609. Duties of Loan Recipient With Regard to Maintenance of Property**

The loan recipient shall be obliged to maintain the property received for uncompensated use in a correct state of repair, including the effectuation of current and capital repair, and bear all expenses for the maintenance thereof unless provided otherwise by the contract of uncompensated use.

**Article 610. Risk of Accidental Perishing or Accidental Damaging of Property**

The loan recipient shall bear the risk of accidental perishing or accidental damage of property received for uncompensated use if the property perished or was spoiled in connection with the fact that he used it not in accordance with the contract of uncompensated use or designation of the property or transferred it to a third person without the consent of the lender.

The loan recipient also shall bear the risk of accidental perishing or accidental damage of the property if, taking into account the actual circumstances, he could prevent the perishing or spoilage thereof by having sacrificed his property but preferred to preserve his property.

**Article 611. Responsibility for Harm Caused to Third Person as Result of Use of Property**

The lender shall be liable for harm caused to a third person as a result of the use of the property unless it is proved that the harm was caused as a consequence of the intent or gross negligence of the loan recipient or person from whom this property is situated with the consent of the lender.

**Article 612. Dissolution Before Time of Contract**

1. The lender shall have the right to require dissolution before time of a contract of uncompensated use in instances when the loan recipient:

(1) uses the property not in accordance with the contract or designation of the

thing;

(2) does not fulfill duties with regard to maintenance of the property in a proper state of repair or the maintenance thereof;

(3) materially worsens the state of the property;

(4) has transferred the property without the consent of the lender to a third person.

2. The loan recipient shall have the right to demand the dissolution before time of the contract of uncompensated use:

(1) in the event of the discovery of defects making the normal use of the property impossible or encumbered, concerning the existence of which he did not know and could not have known at the moment of concluding the contract;

(2) if the property by virtue of circumstances for which he is not liable proves to be in a state not fit for use;

(3) if when concluding the contract the lender did not warn him about the rights of third persons to the property being transferred;

(4) in the event of the failure of the lender to perform the duty to transfer the property or appurtenances thereof and documents relating to it.

**Article 613. Renunciation of Contract**

1. Each of the parties shall have the right at any time to renounce the contract of uncompensated use concluded without specification of the period, having notified the other party thereof one month beforehand unless a different period of notice has been provided for by the contract.

2. Unless provided otherwise by the contract, the loan recipient shall have the right at any time to renounce the contract concluded with specification of the period in the procedure provided for by point 1 of the present Article.

**Article 614. Change of Parties in Contract**

1. The lender shall have the right to alienate the property or transfer it for compensated use to a third person. In so doing to the new owner or user shall pass the rights relating to the previously concluded contract of uncompensated use, and his rights with respect to the property shall be encumbered by the rights of the loan recipient.

2. In the event of the death of a citizen-lender or the reorganization or liquidation of a juridical person-lender the rights and duties of the lender under the contract of uncompensated use shall pass to the heir (or legal successor) or to another person to whom the right of ownership has passed to the property or other right on the basis of which the thing was transferred in uncompensated use.

In the event of the reorganization of a juridical person-loan recipient its rights and duties under the contract shall pass to the juridical person which is the legal successor thereof unless provided otherwise by the contract.

**Article 615. Termination of Contract**

A contract of uncompensated use shall terminate in the event of the death of the citizen-loan recipient or liquidation of the juridical person-loan recipient unless provided otherwise by the contract.

## *Chapter 32. Independent Work*

### *§1. General Provisions on Independent Work*

**Article 616. Contract of Independent-Work**

1. Under a contract of independent-work one party (the independent-work contractor) shall be obliged to fulfill according to the assignment of the other party (customer) determined work and to hand over the result thereof to the customer within the established period, and the customer shall be obliged to accept the result of the work and to pay for it (or to pay the price of the work). The work shall be fulfilled at the risk of the independent-work contractor unless provided otherwise by legislative acts or by the contract.

2. Unless provided otherwise by the contract the independent-work contractor autonomously shall determine the means of fulfilling the assignment of the customer.

3. The provisions provided for by the present paragraph shall apply to individual types of contract of independent-work (domestic independent-work, construction independent-work, independent-work for the fulfillment of design and survey work, independent-work for scientific-research, experimental-construction design, and technological work) unless established otherwise by the rules of the present Code concerning contracts of these types.

4. Relations with regard to individual types of independent-work contract may be regulated together with the present Code also by legislative acts on individual types of independent-work contracts.

**Article 617. Fulfillment of Work by the Means of Independent-Work Contractor**

1. Unless provided otherwise by the contract, the work shall be fulfilled by the means of the independent-work contractor - from his materials and by his forces and means.

2. The independent-work contractor shall bear responsibility for the improper quality of materials and equipment granted by him, and also for granting materials and equipment encumbered by the rights of third persons.

**Article 618. Risk of Accidental Perishing of Materials**

Unless provided otherwise by legislative acts or by the contract the risk of accidental perishing or accidental damage of materials until the ensuing of the period for handing over the work by the independent-work contractor stipulated by the contract shall be borne by the party which granted the materials.

In the event of the delay of the transfer or acceptance of the result of the work the risk shall be borne by the delaying party unless otherwise established by legislative acts or by the contract.

**Article 619. General Independent-Work Contractor and Subindependent-Work Contractor**

1. Unless arises otherwise from legislative acts or the contract, the independent-work contractor shall have the right to involve other persons in the performance of a contract (subindependent-work contractors). In this event the independent-work contractor shall act as the general independent-work contractor to the customer and as the customer to the subindependent-work contractor.

2. The general independent-work contractor shall bear responsibility to the subindependent-work contractor for the failure to perform or improperty performance of an obligation by the customer, and to the customer – responsibility for the failure to perform or improper performance of an obligation by the subindependent-work contractor.

3. Unless provided otherwise by legislative acts or the contract, the customer and the subindependent-work contractor shall not have the right to present to one another demands connected with a violation by them of the contracts with the general independent-work contractor.

4. With the consent of the general independent-work contractor the customer shall have the right to conclude a contract for the fulfillment of individual work with third persons. In this event the third person shall bear responsibility for the failure to perform or the improper performance of work directly to the customer.

5. If a contract is concluded simultaneously with two or more independent-work contractors and the subject of the obligation is indivisible, the independent-work contractors shall be deemed with respect to the customer to be joint and several debtors and respectively joint and several creditors. In the event of the divisibility of the subject of the obligation, and also in other instances provided for by legislative acts or agreement of the parties, each of the independent-work contractors shall acquire the rights and bear the duties with respect to the customer within the limits of his participatory share.

**Article 620. Periods for Fulfillment of Work**

1. The beginning and ending periods of fulfillment of the work shall be specified in the contract of independent-work. By agreement between the parties periods for completing individual stages of work (intermediate periods) also may be provided for in the contract.

Unless established otherwise by the contract, the independent-work contractor shall bear responsibility for a violation of both the beginning and ending, and also the intermediate, periods for the fulfillment of work.

2. The beginning, ending, and intermediate periods for the fulfillment of work specified in the contract of independent-work may be changed in the instances and in the procedure provided for by the contract.

**Article 621. Price of Work**

1. In the contract of independent-work the price of the work subject to fulfillment and the means of determining it shall be specified. In the absence of such indications in the contract and the failure of the parties to reach agreement the price shall be established by a court by proceeding from prices usually applied for analogous work taking into account necessary expenses incurred by the parties.

2. The price of the work may be determined by means of drawing up an estimate.

In instances when work is fulfilled in accordance with the estimate drawn up by the independent-work contractor, the estimate shall acquire force and become part of the contract from the moment of the confirmation thereof by the customer.

The price of the work (or estimate) may be approximate or firm. In the absence of other indications in the contract the price of the work (or estimate) shall be considered to be firm.

3. If the necessity arose for carrying out additional work and for this reason the price of the work (or approximate estimate) determined approximately materially increases, the independent-work contractor shall be obliged to warn the customer thereof in good time and to suspend work. The customer who has not agreed to the increase of the price of the work (or estimate) shall have the right to renounce the contract. In this event the independent-work contractor may demand payment from the customer to him of the price for the part of the work fulfilled.

4. An independent-work contractor who has not warned the customer in good time about the necessity of increasing the price (or estimate) specified in the contract shall be obliged to fulfill the contract, retaining the right to payment for the work at the price determined in the contract.

5. An independent-work contractor shall not have the right to demand an increase of a firm price (or firm estimate), nor the customer to reduce it, including in an instance when at the moment of concluding the contract the possibility to provide for the full amount of work subject to fulfillment or the expenses necessary for this was excluded.

In the event of the material growth after conclusion of the contract of the cost of materials and equipment which must be granted by the independent-work contractor, and also of services rendered to him by third persons, the independent-work contractor shall have the right to demand an increase of the established price (or estimate), and in the event of the refusal of the customer to fulfill this demand, dissolution of the contract.

**Article 622. Economies of Independent-Work Contractor**

1. In instances when the actual expenses of the independent-work contractor prove to be less than those which were taken into account when determining the price (or drawing up the estimate) of the work, the independent-work contractor shall retain the right to payment for the work at the price provided for by the contract (or estimate) unless the customer proves that the economies received by the independent-work contractor negatively influenced the quality of the work fulfilled.

2. A distribution of the economies received by the independent-work contractor between the parties may be provided for in the contract of independent-work.

**Article 623. Procedure for Payment of Work**

1. Unless preliminary payment for work fulfilled or individual stages thereof has been provided for by the contract of independent-work, the customer shall be obliged to pay the independent-work contractor the stipulated price after the final handing over of the results of the work, on condition that the work is properly fulfilled and within the agreed period, or with the consent of the customer before time.

2. The independent-work contractor shall have the right to demand the payment to him of an advance or a deposit only in the instances and in the amount specified in legislative acts or in the contract.

**Article 624. Right to Withholding**

1. In the event of the failure of the customer to perform the duty to pay the established price or other amount due to the independent-work contractor in connection with the fulfillment of the contract, the independent-work contractor shall have the right to withhold the result of the work, and also the equipment belonging to the customer transferred for processing the thing, the balance of the unused materials, and other property of the customer which proves to be with him until the payment by the customer of the respective amounts.

2. Withholding by the customer of part of the remuneration due to the independent-work contract in order to cover expenses for the elimination of defects discovered within the limits of the period provided for in Article 630 of the present Code may be provided for by the contract.

**Article 625. Fulfillment of Work with Use of Materials of Customer**

1. The independent-work contractor shall be obliged to use the materials granted by the customer economically and carefully, after the ending of the work to submit a report to the customer concerning the expenditure of the materials, and also to return the balance thereof or with the consent of the customer to reduce the price of the work by taking into account the cost of the unused material remaining with the independent-work contractor.

2. The independent-work contractor shall bear responsibility for the improper fulfillment of work caused by defects of materials granted by the customer unless it is proved that defects could not be discovered by him during a proper acceptance of these materials.

**Article 626. Responsibility of Independent-Work Contractor for Non-Preservation of Property Granted by Customer**

The independent-work contractor shall bear responsibility for the non-preservation of materials, equipment, the thing transferred for processing, or other property granted by the customer which turned out to be in the possession of the independent-work contractor in connection with the performance of the contract of independent-work.

**Article 627. Rights of Customer During Fulfillment of Work**

1. The customer shall have the right at any time to verify the course and quality of the work without interfering in the activity of the independent-work contractor.

2. If the independent-work contractor does not embark upon the timely performance of the contract or fulfills the work so slowly that the ending thereof within the period clearly becomes impossible, the customer shall have the right to renounce the contract and to require compensation of losses.

3. If during the fulfillment of work it becomes evident that it will not be properly fulfilled, the customer shall have the right to designate a reasonable period to the independent-work contractor for elimination of the defects and in the event of the failure to perform this demand by the independent-work contractor within the designated period to renounce the contract or to assign rectification of the work to a third person at the expense of the independent-work contractor, and also to require compensation of losses.

4. Unless provided otherwise by a contract, the customer may at any time before the handing over of the work to him to renounce the independent-work contract, having paid the independent-work contractor for work fulfilled before receipt of notification concerning renunciation of the contract by the customer. The customer also shall be obliged to compensate losses to the independent-work contractor caused by termination of the contract within the limits of the difference between the part of the price paid for the work fulfilled and the price determined for the entire work.

**Article 628. Circumstances of Which Independent-Work Contractor is Obliged to Warn Customer**

1. The independent-work contractor shall be obliged immediately to warn the customer and until receiving instructions from him to suspend the work in the event of discovering:

(1) the unfitness or poor quality of the materials, equipment, technical documentation, or thing transferred for conversion granted by the customer;

(2) possible consequences unfavorable for the customer of the fulfillment of his instructions concerning the means of performance of the work;

(3) other circumstances beyond the control of the independent-work contractor which threaten the fitness or stability of the results of the work to be fulfilled or create the impossibility of completing it within the period.

2. An independent-work contractor who has not warned the customer about the circumstances specified in point 1 of the present Article or who has continued the work without awaiting the expiry of a reasonable period for reply to the warning or despite the timely instruction of the customer concerning suspension of the work, shall not have the right to refer to the said circumstances in the event of the presentation to him or by him to the customer of respective demands.

3. If the customer, notwithstanding a timely and substantiated warning on the part of the independent-work contractor concerning the circumstances specified in point 1 of the present Article, within a reasonable period does not replace unfit or poor-quality material, does not change instructions concerning the means of fulfilling the work, or does not take other necessary measures in order to eliminate the circumstances threatening the fitness or stability thereof, the independent-work contractor shall have the right to renounce the contract and to require compensation of losses caused by its termination.

**Article 629. Assistance of Customer**

1. The customer shall be obliged to render assistance to the independent-work contractor in the fulfillment of the work in the amount and in the procedure provided by the contract of independent-work.

In the event of the failure of the customer to perform this duty the independent-work contractor shall have the right to demand compensation of losses caused, including additional costs caused by idle-time, or to carry over the periods for performance of the work, or to increase the price of the work.

2. In instances when performance of the work under the contract of independent-work has become impossible as a consequence of actions or omissions of the customer, the independent-work contractor shall retain the right to payment to him of the price established, taking into account the part of the work fulfilled.

**Article 630. Acceptance by Customer of Work Fulfilled**

1. The customer shall be obliged within the periods and in the procedure which are provided for by the contract of independent-work to inspect and accept, with the participation of the independent-work contractor, the result of the work fulfilled, and in the event of discovering deviations from the contract which worsen the work or other defects in the work, to immediately declare this to the independent-work contractor.

2. The customer who has discovered defects in the work when receiving it shall have the right to refer to them in instances when in the act or in the other document certifying acceptance these defects or the possibility of subsequent presentation of a demand concerning their elimination were stipulated.

3. The customer who has accepted work without verification shall be deprived of the right to refer to defects of the work which could have been established by ordinary means of the acceptance thereof (obvious defects).

4. The customer who has discovered after acceptance of the work deviations therein from the contract or other defects which could not be established by ordinary means of acceptance (latent defects), including those which were intentionally concealed by the independent-work contractor, shall be obliged to notify the independent-work contractor thereof within a reasonable period with regard to the discovery thereof.

5. The maximum period for notification of the independent-work contractor about latent defects discovered by the customer shall constitute one year, and with respect to work connected with buildings and installations, and also irrespective of the type of work – with respect to defects which were intentionally concealed by the independent-work contractor, – three years from the day of acceptance of the work.

Periods (or guarantee periods) of greater duration may be established by legislative acts or by contract.

If in accordance with the contract work is accepted by the customer in parts, the period established by the present point shall commence from the day of acceptance of results of the work as a whole.

6. In the event a dispute arises between the customer and the independent-work contractor on the occasion of defects of the work fulfilled or the reasons therefor, an expert examination must be designated at the demand of any of the parties. The expenses with regard to conducting the expert examination shall be borne by the independent-work contractor except for instances when the expert examination established the absence of violations by the independent-work contractor of the contract or a causal link between the actions of the independent-work contractor and the defects discovered. In these instances the expenses for the expert examination shall be borne by the party which required the designation of the expert examination, and if it was designated by agreement between the parties, both parties equally.

7. Unless provided otherwise by the contract, in the event the customer evades accepting the results of the work fulfilled, the independent-work contractor shall have the right upon the expiry of one month from the day when according to the contract the result of the work should have been transferred to the customer, and a subsequent warning twice of the customer, to sell the result of the work, and to deposit with a notary the amount received less all payments due to the independent-work contractor in the name of the customer.

8. If the evasion of the customer of acceptance of the results of the work fulfilled entailed delay in handing over the work, the right of ownership to a manufactured (or processed) thing shall be deemed to have passed to the customer at the moment when the transfer occurred.

**Article 631. Settlement of Accounts Between Parties in Event of Perishing of Subject of Independent-Work or Impossibility of Finishing Work**

If the subject of independent-work before the handing over thereof has perished or the ending of the work has become impossible not through the fault of the parties, the independent-work contractor shall not have the right to demand remuneration for work.

If the perishing of the subject of independent-work or impossibility of ending the work occurred as a consequence of the defects of material delivered by the customer, or his instructions concerning the means of fulfillment of the work, or occurred after the ensuing of delay of acceptance by the customer of the work fulfilled, the rules of Article 628 of the present Code having been complied with by the independent-work contractor, the independent-work contractor shall retain the right to receive remuneration for the work.

**Article 632. Quality of Work**

1. The work fulfilled by the independent-work contractor must correspond to the conditions of the contract, and in the absence or incompleteness thereof, to the requirements ordinarily presented for work of the respective nature.

2. If obligatory requirements for work to be fulfilled under a contract of independent-work have been provided for by legislative acts or in the procedure provided by them, the independent-work contractor acting as an entrepreneur shall be obliged to fulfill the work while complying with these obligatory requirements.

The independent-work contractor may accept the duty to fulfill work under the contract which meets the requirements for quality that are higher in comparison with the established obligatory requirements.

**Article 633. Guarantee of Quality of Work**

1. In an instance when the granting of a guarantee for the quality of work to the customer by the independent-work contractor is provided for by legislative acts or by the contract, the independent-work contractor shall be obliged to transfer to the customer the result of the work, which must correspond during the entire guarantee period to the requirements of Article 632 of the present Code.

2. The guarantee of quality of the result of work, unless provided otherwise by the contract, shall extend to all elements comprising the result of the work.

**Article 634. Procedure for Calculation of Guarantee Period**

Unless provided otherwise by the contract of independent-work, the guarantee period shall commence to run from the moment when the results of the fulfilled work were accepted or should have been accepted by the customer.

**Article 635. Responsibility of Independent-Work Contractor for Improper Quality of Work**

1. If work is fulfilled by an independent-work contractor with deviations from the contract which worsen the work, or with other defects which make it unfit for the use provided for in the contract or in the event of the absence in the contract of a corresponding condition, for ordinary use, the customer shall have the right, insofar as notestablished otherwise by legislative acts or the contract, at his choice to require from the independent-work contractor:

(1) elimination of the defects of work without compensation within a reasonable period;

(2) commensurate reduction of the price established for the work;

(3) compensation of his expenses for elimination of the defects when the right of the customer to eliminate them has been provided for in the contract.

2. The independent-work contractor shall have the right instead of eliminating the defects of work for which he is liable to fulfill the work without compensation anew with compensation to the customer of losses caused by the delay of performance. In this event the customer shall be obliged to return the results of the work previously transferred to him to the independent-work contractor if by the character of the work such return is possible.

3. If deviations in the work from the conditions of the contract of or other defects of the work are material and ineradicable or andwithin a reasonable period established by the customer have not been eliminated, the customer shall have the right to renounce the contract and to require compensation of losses caused.

4. The relieving of the independent-work contractor of responsibility for determined defects may be provided by the contract. The said condition shall not operate if the customer proves that the defects arose as a consequence of guilty actions or the failure to act of the independent-work contractor.

5. The independent-work contractor who has granted material to fulfill work shall be liable for the quality thereof according to the rules concerning responsibility of the seller for goods of improper quality (Article 428, subpoints (1)-(3) and (5) of the present Code).

**Article 636. Limitation With Regard to Suits Concerning Improper Quality of Work**

The period of limitations for demands caused by the improper quality of work to be fulfilled under the contract of independent-work shall commence to run from the discovery of the defects which the customer declared within the limits of the period provided for by Article 630 of the present Code.

**Article 637. Duty of Independent-Work Contractor to Transfer Information to Customer**

An independent-work contractor shall be obliged to transfer to the customer together with the result of the work information affecting the operation or other use of the subject of the contract if this is provided for by the contract or the character of the information is such that without it the use of the results of the work is impossible for the purposes specified in the contract.

**Article 638. Confidentiality of Information Received by Parties**

If a party thanks to the performance of his obligation under the contract has received information from the other party concerning new solutions and technical knowledge, including not enjoying legal protection, and also information which might be considered as a commercial secret, he shall not have the right to communicate this to third persons without the consent of the other party.

The procedure and conditions for the use of such information shall be determined by agreement of the parties.

**Article 639. Return to Customer of Materials and Equipment**

In instances when the customer on the basis of Article 627(4) or Article 635(3) of the present Code renounces a contract of independent-work, the independent-work contractor shall be obliged to return the materials, equipment, thing transferred for processing, and other property granted by the customer or to transfer them to the person specified by the customer, and if this proved to be impossible, to compensate the cost of the materials, equipment, and other property received from the customer.

*§2. Peculiarities of Domestic Independent-Work*

**Article 640. Contract of Domestic Independent-Work**

Under a contract of domestic independent-work, the independent-work contractor effectuating entrepreneurial activity shall be obliged to fulfill according to the assignment of a citizen-customer the work determined which is intended to satisfy the domestic or other personal requirements of the customer, and the customer shall be obliged to accept the results of the work and to pay for it.

2. The contract of domestic independent-work shall be a public contract (Article 387 of the present Code).

**Article 641. Guarantees of Rights of Customer**

1. An independent-work contractor shall not have the right to bind the customer to include additional compensated work or services in the contract of domestic independent-work. In the event of a violation of this requirement the customer shall have the right to refuse payment for such work or services.

2. The customer shall have the right at any time before the results of the work are handed over to him to renounce the contract of domestic independent-work, having paid to the independent-work

contractor the part of the established price for the work fulfilled before receipt of the notification of the renunciation of the contract by the customer, and the customer shall be obliged to compensate the independent-work contractor for expenses made up to this moment. Conditions of a contract depriving the customer of this right shall be invalid.

**Article 642. Form of Contract**

1. Unless provided otherwise by legislative acts or the contract, including the conditions of standards contracts or other standard forms to which the customer has acceded (Article 389 of the present Code), the contract of domestic independent-work shall be considered to be concluded in proper form from the moment of the issuance by the independent-work contractor to the customer of a receipt or other document confirming conclusion of the contract.

2. The absence of the said documents with the customer shall not deprive him of the right to refer to witness testimony in conformation of the fact of the conclusion of the contract or the conditions thereof.

**Article 643. Granting Information to Customer About Results of Work**

When handing over the result of the work to the customer, the independent-work contractor shall be obliged to communicate to him requirements which it is essential to comply with for the effective and safe use of the thing manufactured or transferred or other result of the work fulfilled, and also about possible consequences for the customer himself and other persons of the failure to comply with the respective requirements.

**Article 644. Submission of Information to Customer Concerning Work**

1. The independent-work contractor shall be obliged before conclusion of the contract of domestic independent-work to submit to the customer necessary and reliable information concerning the proposed work, the types thereof, and peculiarities, the price and form of payment for the work, and also notify the customer at his request of other information relating to the contract and respective work. If by the character of the work this has significance, the independent-work contractor must indicate to the customer the specific person who will fulfill it.

2. The customer shall have the right to demand dissolution of the contract of domestic independent-work and compensation of losses in instances when as a consequence of the incompleteness or unreliability of the information received from the independent-work contractor a contract was concluded for the fulfillment of work not possessing the properties which the customer had in view.

**Article 645. Fulfillment of Work from Material of Independent-Work Contractor**

1. If work under the contract of domestic independent-work is fulfilled from material of the independent-work contractor, the material shall be paid for by the customer when concluding the contract wholly or in the part specified in the contract, with the final settlement of accounts when the results of the work fulfilled by the independent-work contractor is received by the customer.

In accordance with the contract the material may be granted by the independent-work contractor on credit, including with a condition of payment for the material by the customer on installment.

2. A change of price of the material granted by the independent-work contractor after the conclusion of a contract of domestic independent-work shall not entail a resettlement of accounts.

**Article 646. Fulfillment of Work from Material of Customer**

If work under the contract of domestic independent-work is fulfilled from the material of the customer, the precise name, quantity, description, and price of the materials determined by agreement of the parties must be specified on the receipt or other document issued by the independent-work contractor to the customer when concluding the contract. A valuation of the material on the receipt or other analogous document may be subsequently contested by the customer in a court by means of the submission of written evidence.

**Article 647. Price and Payment for Work**

The price of work in a contract of domestic independent-work shall be determined by agreement of the parties and may not be higher than that specified on a price-list declared by the independent-work contractor. The work shall be paid for by the customer after the final handing over of the results thereof by the independent-work contractor. By agreement of the parties the work may be paid for by the customer when concluding the contract in full or by means of issuance of an advance.

**Article 648. Consequences of Discovery of Defects in Work Fulfilled**

1. The customer may effectuate one of the rights provided for in Article 635 of the present Code in the event he has discovered defects during acceptance of the results of the work or during the use of the subject of the independent-work – within the general periods provided for in Article 630 of the present Code, and when there are guarantee periods – within these periods. or to require.

2. A demand concerning the uncompensated elimination of such defects of work fulfilled under a contract of domestic independent-work which may represent a danger for life or health of the customer himself and other persons may be presented by the customer or legal successor thereof within three years form the moment of acceptance of the work unless other periods (or service periods) have been provided in the procedure established by legislative acts. Such demand may be presented irrespective of when these defects were discovered, including in the event of their discovery at the end of the guarantee period.

In the event of the failure of the independent-work contractor to fulfill the said demand, the customer shall have the right within this same period to require either the return of part of the price paid for the work or compensation of expenses incurred for the elimination of defects by his forces or with the assistance of third persons

**Article 649. Consequences of Failure of Customer to Appear for Receipt of Results of Work Fulfilled**

1. In the event of the failure of the customer to appear for the receipt of the results of the work fulfilled or other evasion of the customer from acceptance thereof, the independent-work contractor shall have the right, having warned the customer in writing, upon the expiry of two months from the day of such warning to sell the subject of the independent-work for a reasonable price and to place the amount received, less all payments due to the independent-work contractor, on deposit with a notary in the name of the customer in accordance with Article 291 of the present Code.

2. In the instances specified in point 1 of the present Article the independent-work contractor may instead of the sale of the subject of independent-work take advantage of the right to withhold it (Article 624 of the present Code) or to recover losses caused from the customer.

### Article 650. Consequences of Death of One of Parties in Contract

In instances of the termination of a contract of domestic independent-work on the grounds of the death of one of the parties (Article 376 of the present Code), the consequences of termination of the contract shall be determined by agreement between the legal successor of the respective party and contracting party thereof, and in the event of their failure to reach agreement – by a court taking into account the amount of work fulfilled and the prices thereof, the cost of material expended and preserved, and also other material circumstances.

*§3. Peculiarities of Construction Independent-Work*

### Article 651. Contract of Construction Independent-Work

1. Under a contract of construction independent-work the independent-work contractor shall be obliged within the period established by the contract to build a determined object according to the assignment of the customer or to fulfill other construction work, and the customer shall be obliged to create necessary conditions for the independent-work contractor in order to fulfill the work, accept the result thereof, and to pay the stipulated price.

2. The contract of construction independent-work shall be concluded for the construction or reconstruction of an enterprise, building (including dwelling house), installation, or other object, and also for the fulfillment of assembly, launching, and other work inextricably connected with the object being built. The rules of the present paragraph shall also apply in the event of the capital repair of buildings and installations unless provided otherwise by the contract.

If this is provided for by the contract, the independent-work contractor shall assume the duty to ensure the operation of the object after its acceptance by the customer during the period specified in the contract.

3. Under a contract concerning "turn-key" construction an independent-work contractor shall assume all duties with regard to construction and the provision thereof and must hand over to the customer an object ready for operation according to the contractual conditions.

4. The independent-work contractor shall be the owner of the uncompleted construction until handing over to the customer and payment for work.

5. In instances when, under the contract of construction independent-work, work is fulfilled in order to satisfy domestic or other personal requirements of a citizen (or customer), the rules concerning the rights of the customer under the contract of domestic independent-work shall apply respectively to such contract.

### Article 652. Distribution of Risk Under Contract of Construction Independent-Work

1. In the event of the destruction of or damaging of an object of construction as a consequence of insuperable force before the expiry of the period established by the contract for handing over the work the customer shall be obliged unless provided otherwise by the contract to pay for the cost of work fulfilled and/or restored.

2. Unless provided otherwise by legislative acts or the contract, the risk of the impossibility of performing work accidentally ensuing before the handing over thereof shall be borne by the customer.

3. The risk of incidental increase in the cost of the work shall be borne by the independent-work contractor.

4. The carrying over of all possible construction risks ("turn-key" construction) to the independent-work contractor may be provided for by a contract.

5. Insurance of the risks of the independent-work contractor may be provided by a contract. In this event expenses for insurance shall be include din the costs for construction to be taken into account when determining remuneration for the work fulfilled.

**Article 653. Responsibility for Safety of Work Conducted**

Responsibility for the safety of work conducted shall be borne by the independent-work contractor.

**Article 654. Design-Estimate Documentation**

1. The independent-work contractor shall be obliged to effectuate construction and work connected therewith in accordance with the design documentation determining the amount and content of the work and other requirements for the work presented to him and with the estimate determining the price of the work.

In the absence of other instructions in the contract it shall be presupposed that the independent-work contractor is obliged to fulfill all the work specified in the design documentation and in the estimate (design-estimate documentation).

2. Unless provided otherwise by the contract, the design-estimate and other technical documentation drawn up in a foreign language shall be transferred to the independent-work contractor translated into the State or Russian language. Units of measurement must correspond to the metric system established by legislative acts.

3. The composition and content of design-estimate documentation must be determined by the contract of construction independent-work, and it also must be provided which of the parties and within what period the respective documentation must be provided.

4. An independent-work contractor who has discovered in the course of construction work which is not taken into account by the design-estimate documentation and in connection therewith the need to conduct additional work and increase the estimate cost of the construction shall be obliged to inform the customer thereof.

In the event of the failure to receive a reply from the customer to his communication within ten days, unless another period for this has been provided by a legislative acts or by the contract, the independent-work contractor may suspend the respective work with relegation of the losses caused by the idleness to the account of the customer.

5. An independent-work contractor who has not fulfilled the duties established by point 4 of the present Article shall be deprived of the right to demand payment from the customer for the additional work fulfilled by him and compensation of losses caused thereby unless it is proved that the necessity for immediate actions in the interests of the customer, in particular in connection with the fact that the suspension of work could lead to the perishing or damaging of the object of construction.

6. In the event of the consent of the customer to the additional work and payment thereof, the independent-work contractor shall have the right to refuse the fulfillment of the said work only in

instances when such is not within the sphere of the professional activity of the independent-work contractor or may not be fulfilled by the independent-work contractor for reasons beyond his control.

**Article 655. Making Changes in Design-Estimate Documentation**

1. The customer shall have the right to demand the making of changes in the design-estimate documentation not connected with additional expenses for the independent-work contractor and/or lengthening of the periods for fulfillment of the work.

2. Changes of design-estimate documentation requiring additional expenses for the independent-work contractor shall be effectuated at the expense of the customer on the basis of an additional estimate agreed by the parties.

3. The independent-work contractor shall have the right to demand a revision of the estimate if for reasons beyond his control the cost of the work exceeded the estimate by not less than 10%.

4. The independent-work contractor shall have the right to demand compensation of reasonable expenses which were incurred by him in connection with the establishment and elimination of defects in the design-estimate documentation except for instances when such documentation was drawn up according to his order.

**Article 656. Material Provision for Work**

1. The duties relating to provision of the construction with materials, including parts and construction designs, as well as equipment, shall be borne by the independent-work contractor unless it is provided by the contract that the material provision of construction as a whole or in determined part shall be effectuated by the customer.

2. The independent-work contractor within whose duty is the material provision of the construction shall bear the risk for the impossibility being discovered of using the materials (of partes, construction designs) or the equipment granted by the independent-work contractor without worsening the quality of the work to be fulfilled.

3. In instances of the impossibility being discovered of the use of the materials (or parts, construction designs) or equipment granted by the customer without worsening the quality of the work to be fulfilled, the independent-work contractor shall be obliged to demand the replacement thereof by the customer within a reasonable period, and in the event of the refusal of the customer to fulfill this demand, the independent-work contractor shall have the right to renounce the contract and to require from the customer the payment of the price of the contract in proportion to the part of the work fulfilled, and also compensation of losses not covered by this amount.

**Article 657. Payment for Work**

1. Payment for the work fulfilled shall be made by the customer in the amount provided for by the estimate, within the periods, and in the procedure which has been established by legislative acts or by the contract. In the absence of respective instructions in legislative acts or in the contract the payment for work fulfilled by the independent-work contractor shall be made in accordance with Article 623 of the present Code.

2. In the event of "turn-key" construction the price specified in the contract shall be paid, unless provided otherwise by agreement of the parties, in full after acceptance of the object by the customer.

**Article 658. Granting of Land Plot for Construction**

The customer shall be obliged to grant in a timely manner a land plot for construction of such space and in such a state as specified in the contract. In the absence in the contract of such instructions, the space and state of the land plot must ensure the timely commencement of work and the normal conducting and completion thereof within the period.

**Article 659. Additional Duties of Customer in Contract of Construction Independent-Work**

The customer shall be obliged in the instances and procedure provided for by the contract of construction independent-work to transfer for use to the independent-work contractor buildings and installations necessary in order to effectuate the work, ensure transportation of goods to the address of the independent-work contractor, the temporary laying of the network for electric power supply, water, and steam and to render other services. Payment shall be made on the conditions provided for by the contract.

**Article 660. Control and Supervision of Customer Over Fulfillment of Work under Contract**

1. The customer in the contract of construction independent-work shall have the right to effectuate control and supervision over the course and quality of work being fulfilled, compliance with the periods for the fulfillment (or schedule) thereof, the quality of materials granted by the independent-work contractor, and also the correctness of the use of the materials of the customer by the independent-work contractor without interfering in so doing in the operational-economic activity of the independent-work contractor.

2. The customer who has discovered when effectuating control and supervision over the fulfillment of work deviations from the conditions of the contract which may worsen the quality of work or other defects therein shall be obliged immediately to state this to the independent-work contractor. The customer who has not made such statement shall lose the right thereafter to refer to the defects discovered by him.

3. The independent-work contractor shall be obliged to perform instructions of the customer received in the course of the construction if such instructions are not contrary to the conditions of the contract of and do not represent interference in the operational-economic activity of the independent-work contractor.

4. The independent-work contractor who has improperly fulfilled work shall not have the right to refer to the fact that the customer did not effectuate control and supervision over the fulfillment thereof except for instances when the duty to effectuate such control and supervision is placed on the customer by legislative acts or by the contract.

**Article 661. Duties of Independent-Work Contractor For Protection of the Environment and Safety of Conducting of Construction Work**

An independent-work contractor shall not have the right to use in the course of the effectuation of work materials (or parts, construction designgs) and equipment granted by the customer or to fulfill the instructions thereof if this may lead to a violation of requirements binding for the parties concerning protection of the environment and safety of the conducting of construction work.

**Article 662. Duties of Parties When Shutting Down Construction**

If for reasons beyond the control of the parties work under a contract of construction independent-work has been suspended and the object of construction has been shut down, the customer shall be obliged to pay the independent-work cotractor in full for work fulfilled up to the moment of shutting down the work, and also to compensate expenses caused by the need to terminate work and the shutting down of construction.

**Article 663. Handing Over and Acceptance of Results of Work**

1. The customer who has received the communication of an independent-work contractor concerning the readiness for handing over the work fulfilled under the contract of construction independent-work shall be obliged or, if this is provided for by the contract, stage of work, immediately to embark upon the acceptance of the results thereof.

2. The customer shall organize and effectuate the acceptance of the results of work at his expense unless provided otherwise by the contract. In the instances provided for by legislative acts the representatives of State agencies and agencies of local self-government must participate in the acceptance of the results of the work.

3. The customer, having accepted individual stages of work in advance, shall bear the risk of the consequences of the perishing or damaging thereof not through the fault of the independent-work contractor, including also in instances when the fulfillment of work at the risk of the independent-work contractor has been provided by the contract.

4. The handing over of the results of the work by the independent-work contractor and the acceptance thereof by the customer shall be formalized by an act signed by both parties, and in instances provided by legislative acts – also by representatives of State agencies and agencies of local self-government. In the event of the refusal of one of the parties to sign the act, a notation shall be made thereon concerning this and the act shall be signed by the other party.

A unilateral act of handing over and acceptance of the results of work may be deemed by a court to be valid only if the reasons for the refusal to sign the act are deemed by it to be not substantiated.

5. In instances when this has been provided for by legislative acts or contract or arises from the character of the work to be fulfilled under the contract of construction independent-work, preliminary tests must precede acceptance of the results thereof. In these instances acceptance of the results of the work may be effectuated only in the event of a positive result of the preliminary tests.

6. The customer shall have the right to refuse acceptance of the results of the work in the event of the discovery of defects which exclude the possibility of using the results of the work for the purpose specified in the contract and can not be eliminated by the independent-work contractor, by the customer, or by a third person.

In the event of the discovery during acceptance of other defects they must be specified in the act provided for by point 4 of the present Article.

7. In instances provided for by legislative acts constructed objects must be accepted by a State commission.

The Government of the Republic Kazakhstan shall establish the procedure for the State acceptance of constructed objects and determine the possibility of the participation of State agencies and intermediate acceptances.

**Article 664. Responsibility of Independent-Work Contractor for Quality of Work**

The independent-work contractor shall bear responsibility to the customer for deviations permitted from the requirements provided for by the contract, design, and construction norms and rules obligatory for the parties, and also for the failure to achieve the indicators of the object of construction specified in the design-estimate documentation, including those such as the production capacity of the enterprise.

In the event of the reconstruction (renewal, restructuring, restoration, and so forth) of a building or installation, the responsibility shall be placed on the independent-work contractor for a reduction or the loss of firmness, stability, or reliability of the building, installation, or part thereof.

**Article 665. Guarantees of Quality in Contract of Construction Independent-Work**

1. The independent-work contractor, unless provided otherwise by the contract of construction independent-work, shall guarantee the achievement by the object of construction of the indicators specified in the design-estimate documentation and the possibility of operation of the object in accordance with the contract throughout the extent of the guarantee period. The guarantee period shall comprise ten years from the day of acceptance of the object by the customer unless another guarantee period has been provided by legislative acts or by the contract.

2. The independent-work contractor shall bear responsibility for defects discovered within the limits of the guarantee period unless it is proved that they arose as a consequence of normal wear and tear of the object or parts thereof, the incorrect operation thereof or the incorrectness of the instructions for its operation worked out by the customer himself or by third persons involved by him, or improper repair of the object made by the customer himself or third persons involved by him.

3. The running of the guarantee period shall be suspended for the entire time during the extent of which the object could not be operated as a consequence of the defects (or faults or incompleteness) for which the independent-work contractor is liable.

4. In the event of the discovery during the guarantee period of the defects specified in Article 630(4) of the present Code, the customer must state them to the independent-work contractor within a reasonable period of the discovery thereof.

5. The right of the customer to withhold part of the price specified in the contract for work until completion of the guarantee period may be provided for by the contract of construction independent-work.

**Article 666. Elimination of Defects at Expense of Customer**

1. The duty of the independent-work contractor to eliminate defects (or faults or incompleteness) at the demand of the customer and at the expense of the customer for which the independent-work contractor does not bear responsibility may be provided for by the contract of construction independent-work.

2. The independent-work contractor shall have the right to refuse fulfillment of the work specified in point 1 of the present Article in instances when it is not connected directly with the subject of the contract or cannot be fulfilled by the independent-work contractor for reasons beyond his control.

*§4. Peculiarities of Independent-Work forDesign and Survey Work*

**Article 667. Contract of Independent-Work for Design and Survey Work**

1. Under a contract of independent-work for design and survey work the independent-work contractor (or designer, surveyor) shall be obliged to work out design-estimate documentation according to the assignment of the customer and/or to fulfill the survey work, and the customer shall be obliged to accept and to pay for them.

2. Unless provided otherwise by legislative acts oк the contract for design and/or survey work, the risk of accidental impossibility to perform the contract for design and survey work shall lie on the customer.

**Article 668. Base Data for Design and Survey Work**

1. Under a contract of independent-work for design and survey work the customer shall be obliged to transfer to the independent-work contractor an assignment for the design, and also other base data necessary in order to draw up the design-estimate documentation. The assignment for the design work may be prepared on behalf of the customer by the independent-work contractor. In this event the assignment shall become obligatory for the parties from the moment of its confirmation by the customer.

2. The independent-work contractor shall be obliged to comply with the requirements contained in the assignment and other base data for the design and the fulfillment of the survey work and shall have the right to deviate from them only with the consent of the customer.

**Article 669. Duties of Customer**

Under an independent-work contract for design and survey work the customer shall be obliged, unless provided otherwise by the contract, to:

(1) pay the independent-work contractor the established price after the completion of all work or to pay for it in parts after the completion of individual stages of work;

(2) use design-estimate documentation received from the independent-work contractor only for the purposes provided for by the contract, not transfer the design-estimate documentation to third persons, and not divulge the data contained therein without the consent of the independent-work contractor;

(3) render services to the independent-work contractor in the fulfillment of design and survey work to the extent and on the conditions provided for in the contract;

(4) participate together with the independent-work contractor in agreeing the finished design-estimate documentation with competent State agencies and agencies of local self-government;

(5) compensate the independent-work contractor for additional expenses caused by a change of base data for the design and survey work as a consequence of the circumstances beyond the control of the independent-work contractor;

(6) involve the independent-work contractor to participate in the case with regard to a suit brought against the customer by a third person in connection with shortcomings in the design documentation drawn up or survey work fulfilled.

**Article 670. Duties of Independent-Work Contractor**

Under a contract of independent-work for design and survey work the independent-work contractor shall be obliged to:

(1) fulfill work in accordance with the base data for the design transferred to him when concluding the contract;

(2) agree the finished design-estimate documentation with the customer, and, when necessary, together with the customer, with competent State agencies and agencies of local self-government;

(3) transfer the finished design-estimate documentation to the customer and the results of the survey work simultaneously unless provided otherwise by the contract;

(4) not transfer design-estimate documentation to third persons without the consent of the customer.

**Article 671. Guarantees of Independent-Work Contractor**

The independent-work contractor under a contract of independent-work for design and survey work shall guarantee to the customer the absence in third persons of the right to obstruct or limit the fulfillment of work on the basis of the design-estimate documentation prepared by the independent-work contractor.

**Article 672. Responsibility of Independent-Work Contractor for Defects of Design-Estimate Documentation and Survey Work**

1. The independent-work contractor under a contract of independent-work for design and survey work shall bear responsibility for the defects of design-estimate documentation and survey work, including defects discovered subsequently in the course of construction, and also in the process of the operation of the object created on the basis of fulfilled design-estimate documentation and the data of survey work.

2. In the event of the discovery of defects in the design-estimate documentation or in the survey work the independent-work contractor shall be obliged at the demand of the customer to redo the design-estimate documentation without compensation and respectively perform necessary additional survey work, and also to compensate the customer for losses caused unless established otherwise by legislative acts or by the contract.

3. Demands arising from defects of design documentation may be presented by the person using the design documentation even though he is not the customer for the manufacture thereof.

*§5. Peculiarities of Independent-Work for Scientific-Research, Experimental-Construction Design, and Technological Work*

**Article 673. Contracts for Scientific-Research Work, Experimental-Construction Design and Technological Work**

1. Under a contract for scientific-research work the independent-work contractor (or executor) shall be obliged to carry on the scientific research stipulated by the assignment of the customer, and under a contract for experimental construction design and technological work – to work out the model of a new manufacture, construction design documentation for it, new Technology, or to manufacture a model, and the customer shall be obliged to issue to the independent-work contractor (or executor) the technical assignment, to accept the results of the work, and to pay for it.

2. A contract with the independent-work contractor (or executor) may encompass both the entire cycle of conducting the research, development, and manufacture of the models, or individual elements thereof.

**Article 674. Fulfillment of Work**

1. The independent-work contractor (or executor) shall be obliged to conduct scientific research personally. Unless provided otherwise by the contract, he shall have the right to involve third persons to perform the contract for scientific-research work only with the consent of the customer.

2. In the event of the fulfillment of experimental-construction design or technological work the independent-work contractor shall have the right, unless provided otherwise by the contract, to involve third persons in the performance thereof as subindependent-work contractors.

**Article 675. Handing Over, Acceptance, and Payment for Work**

An independent-work contractor (or executor) shall be obliged to hand over, and the customer to accept and to pay for in full the completed scientific research, experimental-construction design, and technological work. The acceptance and payment for individual stages of work or other means of payment may be provided for by the contract.

**Article 676. Confidentiality of Information Concerning Contract**

Unless provided otherwise by the contract for scientific-research work, experimental-construction design, and technological work:

(1) the independent-work contractor (or executor) and the customer shall be obliged to ensure the confidentiality of information affecting the subject of the contract, the course of its performance, and the results received. The amount of information deemed to be confidential shall be determined in the contract;

(2) the independent-work contractor shall have the right to effectuate the patenting of the results of the work received under the said contracts only with the consent of the customer.

**Article 677. Rights of Parties to Results of Work**

1. The customer under a contract for scientific-research work, experimental-construction design, and technological work shall have the right to use the results of the work transferred to him within the limits and on the conditions provided for by the contract.

2. Unless provided otherwise by the contract, the independent-work contractor (or executor) shall have the right to use the results of work received for himself.

3. The right of the independent-work contractor (or executor) to realize the results of the work to third persons may be provided by the contract.

**Article 678. Duties of Customer**

1. The customer under a contract for scientific-research work or for experimental-construction design and technological work shall be obliged to:

(1) issue a technical assignment to the independent-work contractor (or executor) and agree with him the program (or technical-economic parameters) or theme of the work;

(2) transfer to the independent-work contractor (or executor) information necessary for the fulfillment of the work;

(3) accept the results of the work fulfilled and pay for them (Article 623 of the present Code).

**Article 679. Duties of Independent-Work Contractor (or Executor)**

1. The independent-work contractor (or executor) under a contract for scientific-research work or for experimental-construction design and technological work shall be obliged to:

(1) fulfill work in accordance with the program (or technical-economic parameters) or theme agreed with the customer and transfer to the customer the result within the period provided for by the contract;

(2) comply with the requirements connected with the legal protection of intellectual property;

(3) eliminate with his own forces and at his expense defects permitted through his fault in the technical documentation which might entail deviations from the technical-economic parameters provided for in the technical planning task or in the contract;

(4) immediately inform the customer about the impossibility discovered of receiving the anticipated results or the inadvisability of continuing the work;

(5) guarantee to the customer the absence in third persons of exclusive rights to the results to be transferred on the basis of such contract.

2. Unless provided otherwise by contracts for scientific research or for experimental-construction design or technological work the independent-work contractor (or executor) shall be obliged to:

(1) refrain from the publication without the consent of the customer of scientific-technical results received when fulfilling the work;

(2) take measures for the defense of results received when fulfilling work capable of legal protection and inform the customer thereof;

(3) grant to the customer an exclusive license for use of the scientific-technical results possessing legal defense to be applied in the work to be fulfilled.

**Article 680. Consequences of Impossibility to Achieve Result in Contract for Scientific Research Work**

If in the course of scientific research work the impossibility of achieving a result is discovered as a consequence of circumstances beyond the control of the independent-work contractor (or executor), the customer shall be obliged to pay for the cost of the work carried on until eliciting the impossibility of receiving the results provided for by the contract, but not higher than the respective part of the price of the work specified in the contract.

**Article 681. Consequences of Impossibility to Achieve Result in Contract for Experimental-Construction Design and Technological Work**

If in the course of the fulfillment of experimental-construction design and technological work the impossibility or inadvisability of continuing work is discovered that arose not through the fault of the independent-work contractor, the customer shall be obliged to pay for the expenditures incurred by the executor.

**Article 682. Responsibility of Independent-Work Contractor (or Executor) for Violation of Contract**

1. The independent-work contractor (or executor) shall bear responsibility to the customer for a failure to perform or improper performance of a contract for scientific-research work or for experimental-construction design and technological work unless it is proved that the violation of the contract occurred not through the fault of the independent-work contractor (or executor).

2. The independent-work contractor (or executor) who has violated the contract shall be obliged to compensate losses of the customer in the form of real damage unless provided otherwise by the contract.

## *Chapter 33. Compensated Rendering of Services*

**Article 683. Contract of Compensated Rendering of Services**

1. Under a contract of compensated rendering of services the executor shall be obliged under the assignment of the customer to render services (or perform determined actions or effectuate a determined activity), and the customer shall be obliged to pay for these services.

2. The rules of the present Chapter shall apply to contracts for the rendering of communications, medical, veterinary, auditor, consulting, and informational services, services relating to teaching, tourist servicing, and others, except for services rendered under contracts provided for by Chapters 32, 34, 35, 39, 41, 43, and 44 of the present Code.

**Article 684. Performance of Contract of Compensated Rendering of Services**

Unless provided otherwise by the contract of compensated rendering of services, the executor shall be obliged to render the services personally.

**Article 685. Payment for Services**

1. The customer shall be obliged to pay for services rendered to him within the periods and in the procedure which has been specified in the contract of compensated rendering of services.

2. In the event of the impossibility of performance which arose through the fault of the customer, the services shall be subject to payment in full unless provided otherwise by legislative acts or by the contract of compensated rendering of services.

3. In an instance when impossibility of performance arose through circumstances for which neither of the parties is liable, the customer shall compensate the executor for the expenses actually incurred by him unless provided otherwise by legislative acts or by the contract.

**Article 686. Unilateral Refusal to Perform Contract of Compensated Rendering of Services**

1. The customer shall have the right to refuse performance of a contract of compensated rendering of services on condition of payment to the executor of expenses actually incurred by him.

2. The executor shall have the right to refuse performance of obligations under a contract of compensated rendering of services only on condition of the full compensation of losses to the customer caused by dissolution of the contract except when this occurred through the fault of the customer.

**Article 687. Legal Regulation of Contract of Compensated Rendering of Services**

The general provisions on independent-work (Articles 616-639 of the present Contract) and the provisions on domestic independent-work (Articles 640-650) shall apply to the contract of compensated rendering of services unless this is contrary to Articles 683-686 of the present Code, and also to the peculiarities of the subject of the contract of compensated rendering of services.

## *Chapter 34. Carriage*

**Article 688. General Provisions**

1. The carriage of goods, passengers, and baggage shall be effectuated on the basis of the contract of carriage.

2. The general conditions of carriage shall be determined by legislative acts on transport, other legislative acts, and rules issued in accordance with them.

The conditions for the carriage of goods, passengers, and baggage by individual types of transport shall be determined by agreement of the parties unless established otherwise by the present Code, legislative acts on transport, other legislative acts, and rules issued in accordance with them.

**Article 689. Contract of Carriage of Good**

1. Under a contract for the carriage of goods one party (carrier) shall be obliged to deliver the goods entrusted to him by the other party (consignor) to the point of destination and to issue the goods to the person (or recipient) empowered to receive, and the consignor shall be obliged to pay the payment for the carriage of the goods according to the contract or tariff.

2. The contract of carriage of goods shall be formalized by drawing up a transport waybill, bill of lading, goods-transport waybill, or other document for goods provided for by legislative acts on transport.

**Article 690. Contract of Carriage of Passenger**

1. Under the contract of carriage of a passenger, the carrier shall be obliged to carry the passenger to the point of destination, and in the event of the passenger handing over baggage, also to deliver the baggage to the point of destination and to issue it to the person empowered to receive the baggage; the passenger shall be obliged to pay the payment for the travel, and in the event of handing over baggage, also for the carriage of the baggage.

2. The contract of carriage of a passenger and baggage shall be formalized respectively by a travel ticket and baggage receipt. The form of travel ticket and baggage receipt shall be established in the procedure provided for by legislative acts on transport.

**Article 691. Contract of Affreightment (or Charter)**

Under a contract of affreightment (or charter) one party (owner) shall be obliged to grant to the other party (charterer) for payment all or part of the capacity of one or several means of transport for one or several voyages for the carriage of passengers, baggage, and goods.

The procedure for the conclusion of the contract of affreightment, and also the form of the contract and the types thereof, shall be established by legislative acts on transport.

**Article 692. Contracts on Organization of Carriages**

The carrier and consignor may when the effectuation of systematic carriages is necessary conclude long-term contracts concerning the organization of carriages.

Under a contract concerning the organization of carriages the carrier shall be obliged within the established periods to accept, and the consignor – to present for carriage goods in the stipulated amount.

The amounts, periods, and quality of carriages and other conditions for the provision of means of transport and presentation of goods for carriage, and also other conditions for the organization of carriage not provided for by legislative acts, shall be determined in the contract on the organization of carriages.

**Article 693. Contracts Between Transport Organizations**

Contracts concerning the organization of work for ensuring carriages of goods (junction agreements, contracts for the centralized delivery (or removal) of goods, and others) may be concluded between organizations of various types of transport.

The procedure for the conclusion of such contracts shall be determined by legislative acts on transport.

**Article 694. Direct Mixed Transport**

The mutual relations of transport organizations in the event of the carriage of goods, passengers, and baggage by various types of transport under a single transport document (direct mixed transport), and also the procedure for the organizations of these carriages, shall be determined by agreements between the organizations of the respective types of transport concluded in accordance with legislative acts on direct mixed carriages.

**Article 695. Carriage by Transport of Common Use**

1. Carriage being effectuated by a commercial organization shall be deemed to be carriage by transport of common use if from legislative acts or other normative legal acts or a license (or patent) issued to this organization it arises that this organization is obliged to effectuate the carriage of passengers, goods, and/or baggage upon the recourse of any citizen or juridical person.

2. The contract of carriage by transport of common use shall be a public contract (Article 387 of the present Code).

**Article 696. Supply of Means of Transport, Loading (or Unloading) of Goods**

1. The carrier shall be obliged to supply to the consignor of goods for loading within the period established by the accepted application (or order) means of transport in good repair in a state fit for carriage of the respective goods.

The consignor of goods shall have the right to refuse the means of transport supplied which are not fit for the carriage of the respective goods.

2. The loading (or unloading) of the goods shall be effectuated by the transport organization or consignor (or recipient) in the procedure and within the periods provided for by the contract in compliance with the requirements established by legislative acts on transport and by the rules issued in accordance with them.

3. The loading (or unloading) of goods effectuated by the forces and means of the consignor (or recipient) of the goods must be done within the periods provided for by the contract unless such periods have been established by legislative acts on transport and with the rules issued in accordance therewith.

**Article 697. Fare**

1. Payment shall be recovered for the carriage of goods, passengers, and baggage established by agreement of the parties unless provided otherwise by legislative acts.

2. Payment for the carriage of goods, passengers, and baggage by transport of common use shall be determined on the basis of tariffs confirmed in the procedure established by legislative acts on transport.

3. Work and services being fulfilled at the demand of the goods possessor and not provided for by the tariffs shall be paid by agreement of the parties.

4. The carrier shall have the right to withhold goods and baggage transferred to it for carriage to secure the fare due thereto and other payments relating to carriage (Article 292 of the present Code) unless established otherwise by legislation, the contract of carriage, or does not arise from the essence of the obligation.

**Article 698. Period of Delivery of Goods, Passenger, and/or Baggage**

The carrier shall be obliged to deliver goods, passenger, and/or baggage to the point of destination within the period determined by legislative acts on transport and rules of transport established in accordance with them. If a period of delivery for goods, a passenger, or baggage has not been established and the parties have not provided this period in the contract, the delivery must be made within a reasonable period.

**Article 699. Right with Regard to Disposition of Goods** [as amended by Law of 6 December 2001, No. 260-II]

1. A consignor or possessor of a disposition document for goods may demand from the carrier the termination of the carriage or return of the goods or make another disposition. In this event the carrier shall have the right to demand payment for the carriage already made, and also compensation for expenses incurred by it in connection with the disposition made.

2. A consignor shall lose the rights specified in the preceding point at the moment of transfer of the goods to the recipient after arrival of the goods at the place of destination.

3. In the event of the recipient evading the performance of obligations with regard to receipt of the goods requiring special conditions for keeping (or perishable), in the absence of instructions of the consignor concerning how to dispose of such goods, when the keeping thereof is impossible and may lead to the spoilage there of, the carrier shall have the right to realize the goods.

The amount derived from realization of the goods shall be placed on conditions of deposit in the name of a notary, deducting the amounts due to the carrier.

**Article 700. Rights of Passengers**

A passenger shall have the right in the procedure provided for by legislative acts on transport to:

(1) carry children with him free of charge or on other privileged conditions;

(2) carry hand luggage with him free of charge within the limits of established norms;

(3) hand over baggage for carriage for payment according to the tariff.

**Article 701. Responsibility for Violation of Obligations Relating to Carriage**

1. In the event of the failure to perform or the improper performance of obligations relating to carriage, the parties shall bear responsibility established by the present Code, legislative acts on transport, other legislative acts, and also by agreement of the parties.

2. The agreements of transport organizations with passengers and goods possessors (or goods recipients) concerning the limitation or elimination of the responsibility established by legislative acts shall be invalid except for instances when the possibility of such agreements in carriages of goods has been provided for by legislative acts on transport.

**Article 702. Responsibility of Carrier for Failure to Provide Means of Transport and of Consignor for Failure to Use Means of Transport Provided**

1. The carrier shall bear the responsibility established by legislative acts, and also by agreement of the parties, for the failure to supply means of transport for the carriage of goods in accordance with an accepted application (or order) or other contract, and the consignor for the failure to present the goods or failure to use the means of transport supplied for other reasons.

2. The carrier and the consignor of goods shall be relieved of responsibility in the event of the failure to supply or the untimely supply of means of transport or the failure to use the means of transport if this occurred as a consequence of:

(1) insuperable force;

(2) termination or limitation of the carriage of goods in determined directions established in the procedure provided for by legislative acts on transport;

(3) in other instances provided for by legislative acts.

**Article 703. Responsibility of Carrier in Direct Mixed Transport**

For the loss, spoilage, damaging, or short delivery of goods the carriers in direct mixed transport shall be liable to the consignor (or consignee) jointly and severally.

Responsibility for delay shall be borne by the last carrier unless it is proved that the delay occurred not through the fault of the carriers.

**Article 704. Responsibility of Carrier for Delay of Departure of Passenger**

1. For a delay of the departure of the means of transport carrying a passenger, or for the late arrival of such means of transport at the point of destination (except for carriages on city and suburban transport) the carrier shall pay to the passenger a fine in the amount established by legislative acts on transport unless it is proved that the delay or lateness occurred as a consequence of insuperable force.

2. In the event of the refusal of the passenger of carriage by reason of delay of the departure of the means of transport, the carrier shall be obliged to return the fare to the passenger in full, and also to compensate the passenger for losses incurred in connection with such delay.

**Article 705. Responsibility of Carrier for Loss, Shortage, and Damage (or Spoilage) of Goods or Baggage**

1. The carrier shall ensure the preservation of goods or baggage from the moment of the acceptance thereof for carriage and until the issuance to the recipient or person empowered by him or person empowered to receive the baggage.

2. The carrier shall be liable for the loss of goods or baggage unless it is proved that the loss, shortage, or damage (or spoilage) of the goods or baggage not through its fault.

3. Damage caused during the carriage of goods or baggage shall be compensated by the carrier:

(1) in the event of the loss or shortage of goods or baggage - in the amount of the value of the lost or short goods or baggage;

(2) in the event of damage (or spoilage) of the goods or baggage - in the amount by which its value was reduced, and if it is impossible to restore the damaged good or baggage – in the amount of its value;

(3) in the event of the loss of the goods or baggage handed over to the carrier with a declaration of the value thereof – in the amount of the declared value of the goods or baggage.

The value of the goods or baggage shall be determined by proceeding from the price thereof specified on the account of the seller or provided for by the contract, and in the absence of the account or specification of the price in the contract by proceeding from the price which under comparable circumstances usually is recovered for analogous goods.

4. The carrier shall together with compensation of the established damage caused by the loss, shortage, or damage (or spoilage) of the goods or baggage return to the consignor (or recipient) the fare recovered for carriage of the lost, short delivered, spoiled, or damaged goods or baggage unless this payment is part of the value of the goods.

5. The documents concerning the reasons for the failure to preserve the goods or baggage (commercial act, act of general form, and so forth) drawn up by the carrier unilaterally shall be subject in the event of a dispute to valuation by the court together with other documents certifying the circumstances which might serve as grounds for the responsibility of the carrier, consignor, or recipient of the goods or baggage.

### Article 706. Claims and Suits With Regard to Carriages of Goods

1. Before bringing suit against a carrier arising from the carriage of goods the presentation to it of a claim in the procedure provided for by legislative acts shall be obligatory.

2. The period of limitations with regard to demands arising from the carriage of goods shall be established as one year.

3. The rules of the present Article shall not extend to demands arising from the carriage of a passenger and baggage.

### Article 707. Responsibility of Carrier for Causing Harm to Life or Health of Passenger

The responsibility of a carrier for obligations arising as a consequence of the causing of harm to the life or health of a passenger shall be determined according to the rules of Chapter 47 of the present Code unless increased responsibility of the carrier has been provided for by legislative acts or by the contract of carriage.

## *Chapter 35. Transport Expediting*

### Article 708. Contract of Transport Expediting

1. Under a contract of transport expediting one party (expeditor) shall be obliged for remuneration and at the expense of the other party (client - consignor or consignee) to fulfill or organize the fulfillment of the services connected with the carriage of goods determined by the contract of expediting, including to conclude in the name of the client or in its own name a contract(s) for the carriage of goods.

The effectuation of such operations necessary for the delivery of goods as the receipt of documents required for export or import, the fulfillment of customs and other formalities, verification of the quantity and state of goods, the loading and unloading thereof, the payment of duties, charges, and other expenses placed on the consignor, the keeping of goods, the receipt thereof at the point of destination, and also the fulfillment of other operations and services, may be provided for by the contract of transport expediting as additional services.

With the consent of the consignor of the goods the expeditor may itself determine by what type of transport to carry the goods of the consignor, taking into account the interests of the consignor, level of tariffs, and periods of delivery.

2. The provisions of Chapter 41 of the present Code shall apply respectively in the part not regulated by the present Chapter to relations under the contract of expediting if the expeditor under the conditions of the contracts acts in the name of the client, and the provisions of Chapter 43 of the present Code – if it acts in its own name.

**Article 709. Form of Contract**

1. The contract of transport expediting shall be concluded in written form.

2. The consignor (or recipient) must issue a power of attorney to the expeditor if it is necessary for the fulfillment of his duties.

**Article 710. Documents and Other Information Granted to Expeditor**

1. The consignor (or recipient) of the goods shall be obliged to grant to the expeditor documents and other information concerning the properties of the goods, conditions of carriage thereof, and also other information necessary for the performance of the duty by the expeditor provided for by the contract.

2. The expeditor shall be obliged to communicate to the consignor (or recipient) of the goods information received about defects discovered, and in the event of the incompleteness of the information to request necessary additional data from the consignor (or recipient) of the goods.

3. In the event of the failure of the consignor (or recipient) of the goods to grant the necessary information, the expeditor shall have the right not to embark upon performance of the respective duties until such information is granted.

4. The consignor (or recipient) shall bear responsibility for losses caused to the expeditor in connection with the violation of the duties relating to the granting of the information specified in point 1 of the present Article.

**Article 711. Performance of Duties of Expeditor by Third Person**

1. Unless the duty of the expeditor arises from the contract of expediting to perform his duties personally, the expeditor shall have the right to involve other persons in the performance of his duties.

2. The imposition of the performance of an obligation on a third person shall not relieve the expeditor from responsibility to the client for the fulfillment of the contract.

**Article 712. Right of Withholding**

The expeditor shall have the right to withhold goods only in connection with the failure to pay the remuneration which he should receive for expediting services.

**Article 713. Responsibility of Expeditor Under Contract of Transport Expediting**

1. For the failure to perform or the improper performance of duties under the contract of expediting the expeditor shall bear responsibility on the grounds and in the amount which is determined in accordance with the rules of Chapter 20 of the present Code.

2. If the expeditor proves that a violation of the obligation has been caused by the improper performance of the contracts of carriage, the responsibility of the expeditor to the consignor (or recipient) shall be determined by the same rules under which the respective carrier is liable to the expeditor.

**Article 714. Unilateral Refusal of Performance of Contract of Transport Expediting**

1. The consignor (or recipient) of goods or the expeditor shall have the right to refuse to perform a contract of transport expediting, having warned the other party thereof within a reasonable period.

2. In the event of the unilateral refusal to perform the contract, the party which has declared the refusal shall compensate the other party for losses caused by the dissolution of the contract.

## *Chapter 36. Loan*

**Article 715. Contract of Loan**

1. Under a contract of loan one party (lender) shall transfer, and in the instances provided for by the present Code or contract, shall be obliged to transfer to the ownership (or economic jurisdiction, operative management) of the other party (borrower) money or things determined by generic indicia, and the borrower shall be obliged to return to the lender in a timely way the same amount of money or equal quantity of other things of the same kind and quality.

2. The granting of a loan may be provided for by contracts whose performance is connected with the transfer of money or things determined by generic indicia, including in the form of an advance, prior payment, deferral and installment payment of goods (or work and services) unless established otherwise by legislative acts and is not contrary to the essence of the respective obligations.

3. The attraction of money in the form of a loan from citizens as entrepreneurial activity shall be prohibited for juridical persons and citizens, and such contracts shall be deemed to be invalid from the moment of the conclusion thereof.

This prohibition shall not extend to instances when the lenders are banks having a license of an empowered State agency for the receipt of deposits, and also in instances of the acceptance of money in exchange for securities whose issue has been registered in the procedure established by legislation [Article as amended by Law of 10 July 2003, No. 483-II].

**Article 716. Form of Contract of Loan**

1. A contract of loan must be concluded in the form corresponding to the rules of Articles 151-152 of the present Code.

2. A contract of loan shall be deemed to be concluded in proper written form also when there is a bond, receipt of the borrower or other document certifying the transfer to him by the lender of a determined amount or determined quantity of things.

**Article 717. Conclusion of Contract of Loan**

A contract of loan shall be considered to be concluded from the moment of the transfer of money or thing unless provided otherwise by the present Code or agreement of the parties.

In instances when the transfer of money or a thing in parts (or installment) is provided for by the contract it shall be considered to be concluded from the moment of the transfer of the first part thereof unless provided otherwise by the contract.

**Article 718. Remuneration Under Contract of Loan**

1. Unless provided otherwise by legislative acts or by contract, the borrower shall pay remuneration to the lender in the amounts determined by the contract for the use of the subject of the loan.

2. If under a contract of loan things are transferred to the borrower the payment of remuneration shall be performed when the amount and form (monetary or in kind) thereof have been provided for by the contract.

3. The procedure and periods for the payment of remuneration shall be established by the contract of loan.

If the procedure and periods for the payment of remuneration have not been established by contract, it shall be paid monthly.

4. If the borrower does not return the subject of the loan within the period, remuneration shall be paid for the entire period of use of the subject of the loan.

**Article 719. Granting Subject of Loan**

1. The subject of a loan shall be granted within the periods, amount, and on the conditions provided for by the contract.

Unless provided otherwise by the contract, the subject of loan shall be considered to be granted at the moment of the transfer thereof to the borrower or crediting of the espective money to his bank account.

2. A borrower shall have the right to refuse to receive the subject of loan in full or in part, having notified the lender thereof before the period established by the contract for granting it unless established otherwise by legislative acts or by contract.

3. In the event of granting things on loan determined by generic indicia the performance of conditions concerning the quantity thereof, assortment, completeness, quality, packing and/or packaging must be effectuated in accordance with the rules concerning contracts of purchase-sale of goods (Articles 406-492 of the present Code) unless provided otherwise by the contract.

**Article 720. Special-Purpose Loan**

1. Unless provided otherwise by the contract, a loan shall be presupposed to be without a special purpose, and the borrower shall use the subject of the loan received at his discretion.

2. In instances when a contract was concluded on conditions of the use by the borrower of the subject of the loan for determined purposes (special-purpose loan), the lender shall have the right to effectuate control over the special-purpose use of the loan, and the borrower shall be obliged to ensure the possibility of the effectuation by the lender of such control.

3. In the event of the failure to fulfill the duties by the borrower concerning the special-purpose use of the subject of the loan, and also the duties provided for by point 2 of the present Article, the lender shall have the right to refuse performance of the contract respectively in the part of the subject of the loan not granted and to demand of the borrower return of the subject of the loan before time and remuneration with regard to it.

**Article 721. Security of Performance of Obligations of Borrower**

1. Performance of obligation with regard to return of the subject of a loan and payment of remuneration may be secured by means provided for by the present Code. In this event the borrower shall be obliged to grant to the lender the possibility of control over the securedness of the loan unless established otherwise by legislative acts or by contract.

2. In the event of the failure of the borrower to fulfill duties with regard to security of the return of the subject of the loan and payment of remuneration, and also in the event of the loss of security or worsening of its conditions with regard to obligations for which the lender is not liable, the lender shall have the right to refuse performance of the contract respectively for the part of the subject of the loan not granted and to demand from the borrower the return of the subject of the loan before time and remuneration with regard to it.

**Article 722. Return of Subject of Loan**

1. The borrower shall be obliged to return the subject of the loan in the procedure and within the periods provided for by the contract.

Unless provided otherwise by the contract, the subject of loan shall be considered to be returned at the moment of the transfer thereof to the lender or crediting of the respective money in his bank account.

If the period of return of the subject of loan is not established by the contract, it must be returned by the borrower within thirty days from the day of presentation of the demand concerning this by the lender.

The subject of a loan granted without a condition concerning the payment of remuneration may be returned before time. The subject of a loan granted with the condition of payment of remuneration may be returned before time with the consent of the lender or if this has been provided by the contract.

Remuneration for a loan may be paid before time at any time unless established otherwise by the contract.

2. With the consent of the lender, obligations of the borrower may be fulfilled: under a contract of the loan of money – by the acceptance of things determined by generic indicia on the account of the debt; under a contract for the loan of a thing – by the acceptance of money on the account of the debt. The value of the said things shall be determined by agreement of the parties.

3. If return of the subject of a loan in parts (or by installment) is provided for by the contract, in the event of a violation by the borrower of the period established for return of the next part of the subject of loan the lender shall have the right to demand return of the entire remaining part before time of the subject of the loan together with the remuneration due.

4. If payment of remuneration under a loan is provided by a contract within the periods exceeding the periods of return of the subject of loan itself, in the event of a violation of the period establishment for the payment of remuneration the lender shall have the right to demand from the borrower the return of the subject of loan before time together with the remuneration due.

**Article 723. Period of Satisfaction of Demand Concerning Return of Subject of Loan Before Time**

In the event of the lender presenting a demand concerning the return of the subject of loan before time on the grounds provided for by Article 720(3), Article 721(2), and Article 722(3) and (4), the new period for return of the subject of loan and payment of remuneration with regard to it shall be calculated according to the rule established by Article 722(1) of the present Code.

**Article 724. Contesting Contract of Loan**

1. The borrower shall have the right to contest a contract of loan, proving that the subject of loan (money or things) in reality was not received by him from the lender or was received in a lesser amount or quantity than specified in the contract.

2. In those instances when the contract of loan was concluded in written form (Article 716 of the present Code), the contesting thereof by means of witness testimony shall not be permitted, except for instances when the contract was concluded under the influence of fraud, coercion, threat, or ill-intentioned agreement of representatives of the parties with the lender or the confluence of grave circumstances (Article 159(9) and (1) of the present Code).

**Article 725. Novation of Obligation into Contract of Loan**

1. By agreement of the parties any obligation which has arisen from transactions of purchase-sale, lease of property, or other grounds may be formalized by a contract of loan.

2. The formalization of an obligation into a contract of loan shall be effectuated in compliance with the requirements concerning novation (Article 372 of the present Code) and concluded in the form provided for a contract of loan (Article 716 of the present Code).

**Article 726. Contract of State Loan**

1. Under a contract of State loan the borrower is the State, and the lender is a citizen or juridical person.

2. State loans shall be voluntary.

3. A contract of State loan shall be concluded by means of the acquisition by the lender of issued State bonds, and also other State securities (documentary or paperless) certifying the right of the lender to receive from the borrower the money granted to it on loan or, depending upon the conditions of the loan, other property equivalent, established remuneration, or other property rights within the periods provided for by the conditions of the issue of the loan into circulation.

4. The borrower shall be liable with property of the State treasury for its obligations arising from a contract of State loan.

5. The peculiarities of the participation of the Republic Kazakhstan in relations of a State loan may be established by legislative acts.

**Article 727. Contract of Bank Loan**

1. Under a contract of bank loan the lender shall be obliged to transfer money on loan to the borrower on conditions of payment, periodicity, and repayment.

2. The rules concerning a contract of loan shall apply to the contract of bank loan with the peculiarities provided for by Article 728 of the present Code [as amended by Law of 23 December 2005, No. 107-III].

**Article 728. Peculiarities of Contract of Bank Loan**

1. A contract of bank loan shall have the following peculiarities:

(1) a bank or other juridical person having a license of an empowered State agency for the granting of loans in monetary form shall act as the lender;

(2) the subject of the loan shall be money which may be granted in future. In the last instance the contract shall be considered to have entered into force from the moment of the conclusion thereof (Article 393(1) of the present Code) unless provided otherwise by this contract.

(3) the contract must be concluded in written form. Failure to comply with the written form shall entail the invalidity of the contract of bank loan;

(4) [repealed by Law of 23 December 2005бТщю 107-III].

(5) the provisions of Article 722(2) of the present Code shall not apply to the contract of bank loan except for instances provided for by banking legislation.

Banks shall be prohibited from the issuance of loans secured by stocks whose emitent is the particular bank or loans for the purchase of the said stocks [Article as amended by Law of 10 July 2003, No. 483-II].

## *Chapter 37. Financing Under Assignment of Monetary Demand (Factoring)*

**Article 729. Contract of Financing Under Assignment of Monetary Demand**

1. Under a contract of financing under assignment of a monetary demand one party (financial agent) shall transfer or shall be obliged to transfer to the other party (client) money to the disposition of the other party (client), and the client shall assign or shall be obliged to assign this monetary demand to the financial agent against a third person arising from relations of the client (creditor) with this third person (debtor).

A monetary demand against a debtor may be assigned by the client to a financial agent also for the purpose of securing the performance of an obligation of the client to the financial agent.

2. The obligations of the financial agent under a contract of financing under assignment of monetary demand may include the keeping of bookkeeping records for the client and the presentation

of documents with respect to monetary demands (or submission of accounts for monetary demands) which are the subject of assignment, and also the granting to the client of other financial services connected with these demands.

3. The general rules concerning the assignment of a demand established by the present Code (Articles 339-347 of the present Code) shall apply to financing under assignment of monetary demand unless provided otherwise by the present Chapter.

**Article 730. Form of Contract on Financing Under Assignment of Monetary Demand**

A contract of financing under assignment of monetary demand must be concluded in written form in compliance with the requirements established by Article 346 of the present Code.

**Article 731. Monetary Demand Assigned for Purposes of Receiving Financing**

1. Both a monetary demand, the period for the payment of which has already ensued (existing demand) and the right to receive money which arises in the future (future demand) may be the subject of an assignment under which financing is granted.

A monetary demand which is the subject of an assignment must be determined in the contract of the client with the financial agent such that it enables the existing monetary demand to be identified at the moment of conclusion of the contract, and a future demand, not later than at the moment it arises.

2. An existing monetary demand shall be considered to have passed to the financial agent from the moment of conclusion of the contract unless provided otherwise by this contract.

When assigning a future monetary demand, it shall be considered to have passed to the financial agent after the right itself arose to receive the money from the debtor which is the subject of assignment of the demand provided for by the contract.

If the assignment of a monetary demand is conditioned by a determined event, it shall enter into force after the ensuing of this event. In these instances additional formalization of the assignment of the monetary demand shall not be required.

**Article 732. Responsibility of Client to Financial Agent**

1. Unless provided otherwise by the contract, the client shall bear responsibility to the financial agent for the invalidity of the monetary demand which is the subject of the assignment.

2. A monetary demand which is the subject of assignment shall be valid if the client possesses the right to transfer the monetary demand and at the moment of assignment of this demand circumstances were not known to him as a consequence of which the debtor has the right not to perform it.

3. A client shall not be liable for the failure to perform or the improper performance by the debtor of a demand which is the subject of an assignment in the event of the presentation thereof by the financial agent for performance unless provided otherwise by the contract between the client and the financial agent.

**Article 733. Invalidity of Prohibition of Assignment of Demand**

The assignment of a monetary demand to a financial agent shall be valid even if an agreement exists between the client and the debtor thereof concerning the prohibition or limitation thereof.

**Article 734. Subsequent Assignment of Monetary Demand**

Unless the contract of financing under assignment of monetary demand provides otherwise, subsequent assignment of the monetary demand by the financial agent shall not be permitted.

In instances when subsequent assignment of a monetary demand is permitted by the contract, the provisions of the present Chapter shall apply to it respectively.

**Article 735. Performance of Monetary Demand by Debtor to Financial Agent**

1. The debtor shall be obliged to make payment to a financial agent on condition that he received from the client or from the financial agent written notification concerning the assignment of the monetary demand to the particular financial agent.

The monetary demand subject to performance must be determined specifically in the notification, and also the financial agent to whom payment must be made specified.

2. At the request of the debtor, the financial agent shall be obliged within a reasonable period to submit evidence to the debtor that the assignment of the monetary demand to the financial agent has actually occurred. If the financial agent has not fulfilled this duty, the debtor shall have the right to make payment with regard to the particular demand to the client in performance of his obligation to the last.

3. The performance of a monetary demand by the debtor to the financial agent in accordance with the rules of the present Article shall relieve the debtor from the respective obligation to the client.

**Article 736. Rights of Financial Agent to Amounts Received from Debtor**

1. If under the conditions of a contract of financing under assignment of a monetary demand the financing of a client is effectuated by means of the purchase from him of this demand by the financial agent, the last shall acquire the right to all the amounts which he receives from the debtor in performance of the demand, and the client shall not bear responsibility to the financial agent for the amounts received by him which prove to be less than the amount which the agent paid to the client.

2. If the assignment of a monetary demand to a financial agent is effectuated as a means of securing the performance by the client of his obligation to the financial agent and it is not provided otherwise by the contract of financing under assignment of monetary demand, the financial agent shall be obliged to submit a report to the client and to transfer to him the amount exceeding the amount of the obligation of the client secured by the assignment of the demand. If the money received by the financial agent from the debtor proved to be less than the amount of the obligation of the client to the financial agent secured by the assignment of the demand, the client shall bear responsibility for the remaining part of the obligation.

**Article 737. Counter Demands of Debtor**

1. In the event of the financial agent applying to the debtor with a demand to make payment, the debtor shall have the right in accordance with Article 370 of the present Code to present his own monetary demands as set-off which are based on the contract with the client that the debtor already had at the time when notification was received by him concerning the assignment of the demand to the financial agent.

2. A financial agent shall have the right to refuse set-off if the client has not notified him about the existence of obligations to the debtor.

**Article 738. Return to Debtor of Amounts Received by Financial Agent**

1. In the event of a violation by the client of his obligations under the contract concluded with the debtor, the last shall not have the right to demand from the financial agent the return of amounts already paid to him under the demand transferred to the financial agent if the debtor has the right to receive such amounts directly from the client.

2. A debtor who has the right to receive amounts directly from the client paid to the financial agent as a result of the assignment of a demand nonetheless shall have the right to demand the return of these amounts by the financial agent if it is proved that the last did not perform his obligation to effectuate his financing under assignment of demand to the client or made such financing knowing about the violation by the client of the obligation to the debtor to which the financing relates connected with the assignment of the demand.

**Article 738[1]. Assignment of Monetary Demand in Event of Securitization [added by Law of 20 February 2006, No. 127-III]**

The peculiarities of financing under assignment of monetary demand in the event of securitization shall be established by a legislative act of the Republic Kazakhstan on securitization. The provisions of the present Chapter shall apply to securitization transactions unless established otherwise by a legislative act of the Republic Kazakhstan on securitization.

## *Chapter 38. Bank Servicing*

### *§1. General Provisions*

**Article 739. Contract of Bank Servicing**

1. Under a contract of bank servicing one party (bank) shall be obliged on behalf of the other party (client) to render banking services, and the client shall be obliged to pay for these services unless provided otherwise by a contract.

2. The contract of bank servicing shall be subdivided into:

(1) contract of bank account;

(2) contract of transfer of money;

(3) contract of bank deposit;

(4) other types of contracts provided for by legislation or by agreement of the parties.

3. A bank may used money existing in an account while guaranteeing the right of the client to dispose of his money without obstruction.

**Article 740. Limitations on Disposition of Money in Bank**

1. Arrest may be imposed in money of juridical persons and citizens in banks not other than by courts, agencies of investigation and inquiry, and execution proceeding agencies with regard to criminal

and civil cases under proceedings and cases of an execution proceeding in the procedure and on the grounds established by criminal procedure and civil procedure legislation and legislation on an execution proceeding.

2. The period of arrest of money of juridical persons and citizens in banks may not exceed the periods established for conducting the respective cases by criminal procedure and civil procedure legislation.

3. Decisions of agencies of investigation and inquiry concerning the imposition of arrest on money of a client may be appealed to a court in the procedure established by legislative acts [Article as amended by Law of 29 March 2000, No. 42-II].

**Article 741. Removal of Money Without Consent of Client**

The removal of money of juridical persons and citizens without their consent in banks and other organizations effectuating individual types of banking operations may be done only on the basis of a judicial act which has entered into legal force, and also in instances provided for by the Tax and Customs codes of the Republic Kazakhstan and by legislative acts of the Republic Kazakhstan on pension security and on obligatory social insurance [as amended by Laws of 29 March 2000, No. 42-II; of 24 December 2001, No. 276-II, of 13 March 2003, No. 394-II, of 8 April 2004, No. 542-II, and of 22 June 2006, No. 147-III].

**Article 742. Priority of Removal of Money of Client**

1. In the event of the sufficiency of money of the client in the bank for the satisfaction of all demands presented against the client the removal of money shall be effectuated in the procedure of receipt of instructions of the client or other persons (calendar priority) unless provided otherwise by legislative acts.

2. In the event of the insufficiency of money of the client in the bank for the satisfaction of the next demand presented against the client the bank shall accumulate money arriving to the benefit of the client, the amount of which is sufficient for the satisfaction of the said demand, except for instances provided for by legislative acts of the Republic Kazakhstan. When several demands are presented against the client the bank shall remove the money of the client in the following priority:

(1) in first priority shall be effectuated the removal of money with regard to execution documents providing for the satisfaction of demands concerning compensation of harm caused to life and health, and also demands for the recovery of alimony;

(2) in second priority shall be made the removal of money with regard to execution documents providing for the removal of money for the settlement of accounts with regard to the payment of severance benefits and payment of labor for persons working under a labor contract, payment of remuneration under an author's contract, obligations of the client for the transfer of obligatory pension payment to accumulation pension funds and social deductions to the State Social Insurance Fund [as amended by Law of 15 May 2007, No. 253-III];

(3) in third priority shall be made the removal of money for obligations of the client to the budget;

(4) in fourth priority shall be made the removal of money with regard to execution documents providing for the satisfaction of other monetary demands;

(5) in fifth priority shall be made the removal of money for the satisfaction of other demands presented against the client by way of calendar priority.

The removal of money from the bank with regard to demands relating to one priority shall be made in priority of time of receipt of the respective documents.

3. In the event of the liquidation of a juridical person which is a client, satisfaction of demands of creditors shall be made in the priority provided for by Article 51 of the present Code [Article as amended by Laws of 29 March 2000, No. 42-II; of 13 March 2003, No. 394-II; of 9 July 2003, No. 482-II; of 8 April 2004, No. 542-II; and of 15 May 2007, No. 253-III].

**Article 743. Rendering of Banking Services by Organizations Effectuating Individual Types of Banking Operations**

Organizations effectuating individual types of banking operations shall have the right to render individual types of banking services.

The rendering of individual types of banking services by such organizations shall be effectuated in the procedure established by the present Code and by legislative acts of the Republic Kazakhstan [as amended by Law of 23 December 2005, No. 107-III].

**Article 744. Payment of Services of Bank**

A client shall pay for the services of a bank rendered thereto under a contract of bank servicing on the conditions and in the procedure provided by the contract.

**Article 745. Banking Secret**

A bank shall guarantee the nondivulgence of a banking secret.

A list of information comprising a banking secret and the grounds for the issuance thereof shall be determined by legislative acts regulating banking activity.

**Article 746. Responsibility for Violation of Conditions of Bank Servicing of Clients**

For the commission of violations connected with the bank servicing of clients, banks and organizations effectuating individual types of banking operations shall bear responsibility within the limits established by legislative acts of the Republic Kazakhstan regulating banking activity and by contracts of bank servicing [as amended by Law of 29 March 2000, No. 42-II].

§2. *Bank Account*

**Article 747. Contract of Bank Account**

1. Under a contract of bank account one party (bank) shall be obliged to accept money coming to the benefit of the other party (client), fulfill instructions of the client concerning the transfer (or issuance) to the client or third persons of respective amounts of money and render other services provided for by the contract of bank account.

Under the contract of bank account an individual identification code of the client shall be conferred on the client or person specified by him for the purposes of recording the money of the client in the bank on the conditions agreed by the parties. The procedure for the conferment and annulment of the individual identification code of the client, keeping of the recording of the money of the client by the bank shall be determined by banking legislation.

2. Juridical persons and citizens autonomously shall select banks for servicing and shall have the right to conclude contracts of bank account with one or with several banks.

3. A contract of bank account shall be in perpetuity unless established otherwise by legislative acts or by agreement of the parties [as amended by Law of 29 November 1999, No. 486-I].

**Article 748. Form of Contract of Bank Account**

1. A contract of bank account must be concluded in written form.

2. The failure to comply with the written form of a contract of bank account shall entail the invalidity of this contract.

**Article 749. Disposition of Money of Client**

1. A bank shall effectuate the removal of money of the client in a bank on the basis of an instruction of the client unless provided otherwise by legislative acts or by the contract of bank account.

A bank shall not have the right to determine and control the orientation of the use of money by the client and establish other limitations not provided by legislation of his right to dispose of money at his discretion unless provided otherwise by legislation or by the contract of bank account.

2. If money was deposited by a citizen, then the right of disposition of money in a bank shall be enjoyed by the citizen himself or a person to whom he has entrusted this right.

If money was deposited by a juridical person, the right of disposition of the money in the bank shall be enjoyed by the executive of this juridical person and/or other persons empowered by him.

3. The rights of persons effectuating the disposition of money in the name of the client in a bank shall be confirmed by the client by means of the submission to the bank of documents provided for by legislation and by the contract.

4. A procedure for the disposition of money in a bank may be established by the contract of bank account. The requirements for such procedure shall be established by legislative acts regulating banking activity.

**Article 750. Operations to be Fulfilled by Bank Under Contract of Bank Account**

1. In accordance with a contract of bank account a bank shall be obliged to:

(1) ensure the existence of money when demands of the client are presented;

(2) accept money coming to the benefit of the client;

(3) fulfill instructions of the client concerning the transfer of money to the benefit of third persons;

(4) perform the instructions of third persons concerning the removal of money of the client if this is provided by the contract of bank account;

(5) effectuate the acceptance from the client and issuance thereto of cash money in the procedure established by the contract of bank account;

(6) present information at the demand of the client concerning the amount of money of the client in the bank and operations performed in the procedure provided by the contract;

(7) perform other bank servicing of the client provided by the contract, by legislation, and by customs of business turnover applicable in banking practice.

2. A bank shall be obliged to accept money coming to the benefit of the client, and also to perform the removal or issuance of money of the client, reflecting such operations according to the individual identification code thereof not later than the day following the day of receipt of the respective instruction in the bank unless other periods have been provided by legislative acts and normative legal acts of the National Bank of the Republic Kazakhstan issued in accordance therewith.

**Article 751. Remuneration for Use of Money**

For the use of money in a bank the bank shall pay remuneration in the amount and in the procedure determined by the contract [as amended by Law of 29 November 1999, No. 486-I].

**Article 752. Dissolution of Contract of Bank Account**

1. A contract of bank account shall be dissolved upon the application of the client at any time unless provided otherwise by legislation or by the contract.

2. Dissolution of a contract of bank account shall be grounds for the annulment of the annulment of the individual identification code of the client.

3. Money remaining in the bank shall be issued to the client or at his instruction shall be transferred (or withdrawn) to the benefit of third persons.

**Article 753. Bank Accounts of Banks**

The rules of the present Chapter shall extend to bank accounts of banks unless provided otherwise by legislative acts or by normative legal acts of the National Bank of the Republic Kazakhstan adopted in accordance therewith.

*§3. Transfer of Money*

**Article 754. Contract on Transfer of Money**

1. Under a contract concerning the transfer of money one party (bank) shall be obliged on behalf of the other party (client) to transfer money to a third person without the conferment on the client of an individual identification code.

2. The procedure for the transfer of money by a bank without the conferment on the client of an individual identification code shall be established by legislative acts regulating banking activity.

**Article 755. Conclusion of Contracts on Transfer of Money**

A contract on the transfer of money without opening a bank account shall be considered to be concluded if the bank accepts for execution an assignment of the client at the moment of recourse of the client with a proposal to render him such banking service unless provided otherwise by legislative acts regulating banking activity.

*§4. Bank Deposit*

**Article 756. Contract of Bank Deposit**

Under a contract of bank deposit one party (bank) shall be obliged to accept from the other party (depositor) money (deposit), to pay remuneration with regard to it in the amount and procedure provided for by the contract of bank account, to return the deposit on the conditions and in the procedure provided for the deposit of the particular type by legislative acts and by the contract.

For each of the types of deposits banks shall for the purposes of recording money of the client confer an individual identification code thereon. The procedure for the conferment and annulment of an individual identification code, keeping of a record by the bank of money of the client shall be determined by banking legislation of the Republic Kazakhstan [as amended by Law of 9 July 2003, No. 482-II].

**Article 757. Types of Bank Deposits**

1. Depending on the conditions of the return of deposits they shall be subdivided into the following types:

(1) demand deposit;

(2) fixed-term deposit;

(3) conditional deposit.

2. A demand deposit shall be subject to return in full or partially upon the first demand of the depositor.

A fixed-term deposit shall be for a determined period.

A conditional deposit shall be until the ensuing of circumstances determined by the contract of bank deposit.

3. In instances when a fixed-term deposit is demand by the depositor before the expiry of the established period, and a conditional deposit – before the ensuing of the circumstances determined by the contract of bank account, remuneration for the deposit shall be paid in the amount established for the demand deposit unless provided otherwise by the contract of bank deposit.

**Article 758. Form of Contract of Bank Deposit**

1. A contract of bank deposit must be concluded in written form meeting the requirements established by legislative acts, normative legal acts of the National Bank of the Republic Kazakhstan, and customs of business turnover applicable in banking practice.

2. Upon the demand of the depositor the document certifying the deposit made may be formalized either in his name or in the name of a determined third person.

3. The failure to comply with the written form of the contract of bank deposit shall entail the invalidity of this contract [Article as amended by Law of 12 January 2007, No. 225-III].

**Article 759. Period of Operation of Contract of Bank Deposit**

1. A contract of bank deposit shall be considered to be concluded from the day of receipt of the amount of the deposit in the bank.

2. A contract of bank demand deposit shall be in perpetuity.

3. When a depositor does not demand the amount of a fixed-term deposit after the expiry of the period thereof, and also the amount of a conditional deposit after the ensuing of those circumstances with which the contract of bank deposit links the return of the deposit, the contract of bank deposit shall be considered to be prolonged on the conditions of a demand deposit unless provided otherwise by the contract.

**Article 760. Remuneration Under Contract of Bank Deposit**

1. A bank shall pay remuneration to the deposit on the amount of the deposit in the amount determined by the contract of bank deposit.

2. A bank shall not have the right to change the amount of remuneration on deposits unilaterally unless provided otherwise by the contract of bank deposit [Article as amended by Law of 29 November 1999, No. 486-I].

**Article 761. Procedure for Payment of Remuneration Under Contract of Bank Deposit**

1. Remuneration under a contract of bank deposit shall be paid by the bank in the procedure and in the amount established by the contract of bank deposit.

2. Unless provided otherwise by the contract of bank deposit, remuneration for a bank deposit shall be paid to the depositor at his demand upon the expiry of each quarter separately from the amount of deposit, and the amount of remuneration not demanded in this period shall increase the amount of the deposit for which remuneration is paid.

In the event of the return of the deposit to the depositor remuneration shall be paid a all due to him at this moment.

3. With regard to demand deposits a depositor shall have the right to receive the remuneration due to him on the deposit separately from the amount of the deposit.

Under fixed-term deposits the depositor also shall have the right to receive the remuneration due to him separately from the amount of the deposit upon the expiry of the period thereof, but in so doing unless provided otherwise by the contract of bank deposit the amount of remuneration shall be recalculated according to that amount which is applied by the bank for demand deposits. Upon the expiry of the period of the deposit the depositor shall have the right to receive the remuneration due to him in full irrespective of whether he demands and obtains the deposit or not (Article 759(3) of the present Code).

Under conditional deposits the receipt by the depositor of remuneration due to him separately from the amount of the deposit shall be in the procedure established by the contract of bank account.

4. Remuneration shall be paid within the periods and in the form provided for the return of the deposit (Article 765 of the present Code).

5. In the event of the full return of the deposit to the depositor all remuneration due to him at this moment shall be paid.

**Article 762. Making of Deposits**

1. Unless provided otherwise by a contract of bank deposit, the depositor shall make deposits either as cash money or by means of non-cash transfers.

2. In the event of a demand deposit the money may be deposited by the depositor by individual deposits in any amounts and any periodicity. In so doing the settlement of remuneration for newly arrived amounts shall be made according to that amount of remuneration which is applied by the bank on the day of receipt of the money.

In the event of fixed-term deposits, and also conditional deposits, money shall be deposited by the depositor in the form of a one-off deposit unless provided otherwise by the contract of bank deposit.

**Article 763. Deposit of Money by Third Persons in Deposit**

Money received in a bank in the name of the depositor from third persons specifying the necessary data concerning the individual identification code thereof shall be deposited in the deposit.

**Article 764. Deposits to Benefit of Third Persons**

A deposit may be made to a bank in the name of a determined third person.

An indication of the name of the citizen (Article 15 of the present Code) or name of the juridical person (Article 38 of the present Code) to whose benefit the deposit is made shall be a material condition of the respective contract of bank deposit.

The contract of bank deposit to the benefit of a citizen deceased at the moment of conclusion of the contract or to a juridical person which does not exist at this moment shall be invalid.

2. In the event of the written refusal of a third person of the rights of depositor the person who has concluded the contract of bank deposit may take advantage of the rights of the depositor with respect to money deposited by him on deposit.

3. In the event of depositing a conditional deposit to the benefit of a third person, he shall have the right to dispose of it only in compliance with the conditions provided by the contract of bank deposit. Until the ensuing of these conditions a third person may dispose of the deposit only upon the written authorization of the person who made the deposit.

A condition with regard to the deposit must be fixed in writing in the contract of bank deposit, not be contrary to legislative acts, and not have ambiguities which make difficult the issuance of the deposit.

In order to receive a conditional deposit the third persons hall submit to the bank the documents confirming the fulfillment of the established condition.

A person who has made a condition deposit to the benefit of a third person shall have the right to: change the condition established by him in the event the third person has not submitted the document confirming the fulfillment of this condition, dispose of the deposit in the event of the failure of the third person to fulfill the condition specified when making the deposit, or the death thereof before the fulfillment of the condition provided by the contract of bank deposit.

4. The rules concerning the contract to the benefit of a third person (Article 391 of the present Code) shall apply to the contract of bank deposit to the benefit of a third person if this is not contrary to the rules of the present Article.

**Article 765. Return of Bank Deposits**

1. A bank shall be obliged to issue a deposit or part thereof upon the first demand of the depositor:

(1) with regard to demand deposits – upon receipt of the demands of the depositor;

(2) with regard to fixed-term deposits – upon the ensuing of the period provided for by the contract of bank deposit;

(3) with regard to conditional deposits – when there are circumstances with the ensuing of which the contract of bank deposit links the return of the deposit.

2. A depositor shall have the right to return of a fixed-term deposit before time.

In so doing the bank shall be obliged to issue the deposit or part thereof not later than 5 days from the moment of receipt of the demand of the depositor.

3. With regard to conditional deposits the depositor shall have the right to return of the deposit before the ensuing of circumstances with which the contract of bank deposit links return of the deposit. In so doing the bank shall be obliged to issue the deposit or part thereof within the periods provided for by point 2 of the present Article.

4. The provision of a contract of bank deposit concerning the refusal of the depositor of the right to receive a fixed-term deposit before time, and also a conditional deposit before the ensuing of the conditions provided for, shall be invalid.

5. A deposit made in foreign currency must be returned in this same currency unless provided otherwise by legislative acts, contract of bank deposit, or additional agreement of the parties.

6. In the event of the failure of the bank to fulfill the demand of the depositor concerning return of the deposit or part thereof within the periods provided by points 2 and 3 of the present Article the payment of remuneration shall continue on the conditions provided for by the contract of bank deposit.

$6^1$. The rules of the present Article shall not extend to deposits which are the subject of pledge and made in the bank to secure obligations of the depositor [point added by Law of 29 March 2000, No. 42-II].

**Article 766. Securing Return of Deposit**

The means and methods which a bank is obliged to use in order to secure the return of deposits received by it shall be determined by legislative acts, normative legal acts of the National Bank of the Republic Kazakhstan, and the contract of bank deposit.

**Article 767. Payment of Services of Bank for Performance of Operations With Regard to Bank Deposit**

A depositor shall pay for services of a bank with regard to the performance of operations relating to a bank deposit in the procedure determined by the contract.

## *Chapter 39. Keeping*

### *§1. General Provisions on Keeping*

**Article 768. Contract of Keeping**

1. Under a contract of keeping one party (keeper) shall be obliged to keep a thing transferred to it by the other party (transferor) and to return this thing intact.

2. A contract of keeping shall be deemed to be concluded from the moment of the transfer of the thing for keeping.

3. The operation of the present Chapter shall not extend to the protection of immoveable property.

**Article 769. Contract on Acceptance of Thing for Keeping**

1. A keeper effectuating keeping as entrepreneurial activity may assume under the contract the obligation to accept things for keeping of the transferor and to keep things transferred by the transferor in accordance with the provisions of the present Chapter.

2. A keeper who has assumed under a contract the obligation to accept a thing for keeping shall not have the right to demand the transfer of this thing to him for keeping. However, a transferor who has not transferred a thing for keeping within the period provided for by the contract shall bear responsibility to the keeper for losses caused in connection with the unconstituted keeping unless provided otherwise by legislative acts or by the contract.

3. The transferor shall be relieved of responsibility for the failure to transfer a thing for keeping if he declares the refusal of services of the keeping within a reasonable period.

4. Unless provided otherwise by the contract, the keeper shall be relieved form the duty to accept a thing for keeping in instances when within the period stipulated by the contract the thing is not transferred for keeping, and when this period is not determined – upon the expiry a twenty-four hours from the day of conclusion of the contract.

**Article 770. Duty to Accept Thing for Keeping**

The keeper effectuating keeping by virtue of his entrepreneurial activity shall not have the right to refuse to accept things for keeping when there are technical possibilities unless established otherwise by legislative acts. In such instances contracts of keeping shall be deemed to be public (Article 387 of the present Code).

**Article 771. Keeping of Things with Pooling**

1. When keeping things with pooling, things accepted for keeping from one transferor may be mixed with things of the same kind and quality of other transferors. The quantity of things of the same kind and quality shall be returned to the transferor equally or as stipulated by the parties.

2. When keeping things with pooling things must be isolated from things of the same kind and quality if this is established by legislative acts or by agreement of the parties.

**Article 772. Form of Contract of Keeping**

1. A contract of keeping must be concluded in written form, except for handing over a thing for short-term keeping in cloakrooms and check-rooms of stations, airports, institutions, enterprises, theaters, museums, stadiums, cafeterias, and so on with the issuance by the keeper of numbers, tokens, and other legitimizing marks.

2. The written form shall be considered to be complied with if the acceptance of a thing for keeping is certified by the keeper by means of the issuance to the transferor of a retained personal receipt, receipt, certificate, or other document signed by the keeper.

3. A contract of keeping in the form of a domestic service may be concluded in oral form.

4. In the event of a dispute concerning the identity of a thing accepted for keeping and thing returned by the keeper witness testimony shall be permitted.

5. The transfer of a thing for keeping under extraordinary circumstances (fire, flood, and others) may be proved by witness testimony irrespective of the value of the thing handed over for keeping.

**Article 773. Period of Keeping**

1. If a thing is handed over for keeping on demand or without indicating the period, the keeper shall have the right upon the expiry of the period of keeping a thing usual under these circumstances to require the acceptance of the thing back by the transferor but shall be obliged to grant the transferor a reasonable period sufficient for acceptance of the thing.

2. The transferor shall have the right at any time to demand the thing from the keeper even if under the contract another period of keeping was provided. However, in this event the transferor shall be obliged to compensate the keeper for losses caused by termination before time of the obligation unless provided otherwise by the contract.

**Article 774. Remuneration and Compensation of Expenses for Keeper**

1. The amount of remuneration for the keeper under a contract of keeping shall be determined by agreement of the parties. In instances established by legislative acts the amount of remuneration may be determined by fees, rates, and tariffs.

2. Keeping without compensation may be stipulated by agreement of the parties or by legislative acts. In the event of keeping without compensation the transferor shall be obliged to compensate the keeper for necessary and actual expenses made for keeping a thing.

3. Unless provided otherwise by legislative acts or by agreement of the parties, remuneration for keeping must be paid to the keeper at the end of keeping, and if payment is provided for by periods

– upon the expiry of each period. If keeping is terminated before the expiry of the period of keeping determined in the contract, the keeper must be paid the commensurate part of remuneration.

4. If upon the expiry of the period provided for by the contract a thing in keeping is not taken back by the transferor, he shall be obliged to pay the keeper remuneration for the further keeping of the thing in the previous amount.

5. Unless provided otherwise by the contract, expenses for keeping shall be included in the amount of remuneration. It shall be presupposed that extraordinary expenses are not included in the amount of remuneration or in the composition of expenses provided for by the contract.

**Article 775. Duties of Keeper to Ensure Preservation of Thing**

1. A keeper shall be obliged to take all necessary measures provided by the contract and also others in order to ensure the preservation of the thing transferred to him.

2. If keeping is effectuated without compensation the keeper shall be obliged to be concerned about a thing accepted for keeping as though his own thing.

3. A thing must be returned in that state in which it was accepted for keeping, taking into account its natural deterioration or natural decrease.

4. A keeper shall not have the right to use a thing, except for instances when this is provided for by the contract, and also if the use of the thing is necessary in order to ensure the preservation thereof.

5. Simultaneously with the return of a thing the keeper shall be obliged to transfer the fruits and revenues received for the time of keeping thereof unless provided otherwise by the contract.

**Article 776. Change of Conditions of Keeping**

1. When a change of conditions of keeping of a thing is necessary provided for by the contract of keeping, the keeper shall be obliged immediately to notify the transferor thereof and to await his reply.

2. When the danger has arisen of the loss or damaging ot a thing, the keeper shall be obliged to change the means and place of keeping provided by the contract without waiting for the reply of the transferor (point 1 of the present Article).

3. If a thing during keeping is subjected to spoilage or other circumstances arose not allowing the preservation thereof to be ensured and one can not wait to take measures on the part of the transferor, the keeper shall have the right to realize the thing or part thereof with compensation of its expenses for keeping and realization.

**Article 777. Transfer of Thing for Keeping to Third Person**

1. Unless provided otherwise by legislative acts or by the contract, a keeper shall not have the right without the consent of the transferor to transfer a thing for keeping to a third person unless the need has arisen in the interests of the transferor and the keeper is deprived of the possibility to obtain his consent. The keeper shall be obliged immediately to notify the transferor about the transfer of the thing to a third person.

2. The keeper shall be liable for the actions of a third person to whom he transferred the thing for keeping.

**Article 778. Responsibility of Keeper for Non-Preservation of Thing**

A keeper shall be liable for the loss, shortage, or damaging of a thing accepted for keeping.

He shall be relieved from responsibility if it is proved that the loss, shortage, or damaging of a thing occurred not through his fault.

**Article 779. Responsibility of Keeper-Entrepreneur**

1. A person effectuating keeping by virtue of his entrepreneurial activity shall be relieved from responsibility for the non-preservation of a thing only in instances when the loss, shortage, or damaging of the thing was caused by insuperable force or by the properties of the thing itself, or by the intent or gross negligence of the transferor.

2. If upon the expiry of the period of keeping provided for in the contract or the period specified by the keeper in the procedure established in Article 773 of the present Code a thing is not taken back by the transferor, the keeper shall be liable for loss, shortage, or damaging of this thing only when there is intent or gross negligence on his part.

**Article 780. Amount of Responsibility of Keeper**

1. Losses caused to the transferor by the loss, shortage, or damaging of a thing shall be compensated by the keeper in accordance with Article 350 of the present Code unless provided otherwise by legislative acts or the contract.

2. If when handing over for keeping a valuation was made of a thing which is specified in the contract or other written document issued by the keeper, responsibility of the keeper shall be determined by proceeding from the amount of the valuation.

3. In the event of keeping without compensation, the losses caused to the transferor by the loss, shortage, or damaging of the thing shall be compensated:

(1) for loss or shortage of the thing: in the amount of the value of the lost or short-delivered things;

(2) for the damaging of a thing: in the amount by which the value thereof was reduced.

4. If as a result of the damage for which the keeper is liable the quality of the thing has been so changed that it can not be used for its initial designation, the transferor shall have the right to refuse it and to require compensation from the keeper for the value of this thing, and also compensation of other losses, unless provided otherwise by legislative acts or by the contract.

**Article 781. Consequences of Violation of Periods for Receipt of Thing**

1. A transferor shall be obliged upon the expiry of the period specified in Article 773 of the present Code to take back the thing handed over for keeping.

2. In the event of the evasion by the transferor of receiving his thing the keeper shall have the right to demand after a warning of not less than a month the realization of the thing in the procedure provided for by the Code of Civil Procedure of the Republic Kazakhstan unless provided otherwise by legislative acts or by the contract.

3. Amounts received from the realization of the thing shall be transferred to the transfer, deducting the amounts due to the keeper.

**Article 782. Compensation of Losses Caused to Keeper**

The transferor shall be obliged to compensate losses to the keeper caused by the properties of a think if the keeper, in accepting a thing for keeping, did not know and should not have known about these properties.

**Article 783. Application of General Provisions on Keeping to Individual Types Thereof**

General provisions on keeping shall apply to individual types thereof unless the rules on individual types of keeping provided for by Articles 784-802 of the present Code and/or other legislative acts establish otherwise.

*§2. Individual Types of Keeping*

**Article 784. Keeping in Pawnshop**

1. A contract of keeping in a pawnshop of a thing shall be formalized by an inscribed deposit receipt.

2. A thing handed over for keeping to a pawnshop shall be subject to valuation by agreement of the parties in accordance with the prices for a thing of that type and quality usually established in trade at the moment and at the place of its acceptance for keeping.

3. A pawnshop shall be obliged to insure to the benefit of the transferor a thing accepted for keeping in the full amount of their valuation made in accordance with point 2 of the present Article.

**Article 785. Thing Not Demanded from Pawnshop**

1. In the event of the evasion by the transferor from receving a thing back a pawnshop shall be obliged to keep it for three months. Upon the expiry of this period a thing not demanded may be sold by the pawnshop in the procedure established by Article 781(2) of the present Code.

2. From the amount received from the sale of the thing, payment for the keeping and other payments due to the pawnshop shall be paid. The balance of the amount shall be returned by the pawnshop to the possessor of the deposit receipt upon the presentation thereof.

**Article 786. Keeping of Valuables in Bank**

1. A bank may accept securities, precious metals and stones, and other valuables, and also documents, for keeping.

2. The contract of keeping for valuables in a bank shall be formalized by the issuance by the bank to the transferor of an inscribed deposit document, the presentation of which shall be grounds for the issuance by the bank of the valuables being kept to the transferor or the representative thereof.

3. A contract for the keeping of valuables with the use of an individual bank safe (safe box, individual premise for keeping) may be concluded by means of the performance by the bank of actions for the acceptance of valuables for keeping and issuance to the transferor of a key for the safe, card identifying the transferor, or other mark or document which certifies the right of the transferor of access to the safe and receipt of valuables from it.

4. Unless provided otherwise by the contract, the transferor shall have the right at any time to take valuables from the safe, return them, and work with documents being kept. A bank in so doing shall have the right to record the receipt and return of valuables by the transferor.

5. In the event of the receipt by the transferor, including temporary, of part of the valuables form the safe the bank shall bear responsibility for the preservation of the remaining part of the valuables.

6. The rules established by the present Article for keeping valuables in a banks safe shall not extend to an instance when the bank provides its own safe (or safe box, individual premise for keeping) to another person for use on conditions of property rental.

**Article 787. Keeping in Left Luggage Rooms of Transport Organizations**

1. Left luggage rooms within the jurisdiction of transport organizations shall be obliged to accept for keeping the things of passengers and other citizens irrespective of whether they have travel documents. A contract for keeping in left luggage rooms of transport organizations shall be deemed to be a public contract (Article 387 of the present Code).

2. In confirmation of the acceptance of a thing for keeping in a left luggage room (except for automatic rooms) a receipt or numbered token shall be issued to the transferor. In the event of the loss of the receipt or token the thing handed over to the left luggage room shall be issued to the transferor upon presentation of evidence of the affiliation of these things to him.

3. The amount of losses incurred by the transferor as a consequence of the loss, shortage, or damaging of a thing handed over to a left luggage room shall be paid to the transferor within a twenty-four hour period if when handing over a thing for keeping a valuation was made thereof or the parties came to an agreement relative to the amount subject to compensation for losses.

4. Things may be handed over to a left luggage room for a period within the limits established by special rules or by agreement of the parties. Things not demanded within the said periods the left luggage room shall be obliged to keep for three months. Upon the expiry of this period things not demanded may be sold, and the amounts received from the sale distributed in accordance with Article 781 of the present Code.

**Article 788. Keeping in Check Rooms of Organizations**

1. Keeping in check rooms of organizations shall be presupposed to be without compensation if remuneration for keeping is not stipulated when handing over a thing for keeping.

2. In confirmation of the acceptance of a thing for keeping in a check room the keeper shall issue to the transferor a numbered token or other mark confirming the acceptance of the think for keeping.

3. A think handed over to a check room shall be issued to the bearer of the token. In so doing the keeper shall not be obliged to verify the powers of the bearer of the token to receive the thing. However, the keeper shall have the right to delay the return of the thing to the bearer of the token if he has doubts about the affiliation of the token to the bearer thereof.

4. A keeper shall have the right to issue a thing from the check room also when the transferor has lost the token but the fact of his handing over the thing to the checkroom or affiliation thereof to the transferor does not give rise to doubts with the keeper or has been proved by the transferor.

**Article 789. Keeping in Hotel**

1. A hotel shall be liable as keeper and without a special agreement concerning this for loss or damaging of things, except for money, other currency valuables and securities deposited in the hotel by a person residing therein except for instances when the loss or damaging occurred as a consequence of insuperable force, properties of the thing itself, or through the fault of the person residing himself, persons accompanying him, or visitors thereof.

2. A hotel shall be liable for the loss of money, other currency valuables, and securities only on condition that they were accepted for keeping.

3. The person residing in the hotel who has discovered a loss or damaging of his things shall be obliged without delay to declare this to the administration of the hotel. Otherwise, the hotel shall be relieved from responsibility for the failure to preserve the things.

4. A hotel shall not be relieved from responsibility for the failure to preserve things of persons residing therein even if it makes an announcement that it does not assume this responsibility.

5. The rules of the present Article shall apply also with respect to keeping of things in motels, rest homes, sanatoriums, dormitories, and similar organizations, and also in organizations having specially allotted places for keeping outer clothing, headwear, and other similar things of citizens visiting the organization.

**Article 790. Keeping of Contested Things (Sequestration)**

1. Under a contract on sequestration two or several persons between whom a dispute has arisen concerning the right to a thing shall transfer the contested thing to a third person who shall be obliged upon the settlement of the dispute to return the thing to that person to whom it was awarded by decision of a court or by agreement of all the disputing persons (contractual sequestration).

2. A contested thing may be transferred for keeping by way of sequestration by decision of a court (judicial sequestration).

Either a person designated by a court or a person determined by mutual consent of the disputing parties may be the keeper under judicial sequestration. In both instances the consent of the keeper shall be required unless provided otherwise by legislative acts.

3. Both moveable and immovable things may be transferred for keeping by way of sequestration.

*§3. Keeping in Goods Warehouse*

**Article 791. Goods Warehouse**

A goods warehouse shall be deemed to be a commercial organization effectuating the keeping of goods and rendering services connected with keeping as entrepreneurial activity.

**Article 792. Goods Warehouse of Common Use**

1. A goods warehouse shall be deemed to be a warehouse of common use if in accordance with legislative acts it is not relegated to warehouses which may accept goods for keeping from a limited group of persons.

2. A contract of warehouse keeping concluded by a goods warehouse of common use shall be deemed to be a public contract (Article 387 of the present Code).

**Article 793. Duties of Goods Warehouse**

1. A goods warehouse shall be obliged to comply with the conditions (or regime) of keeping established in standards, technical conditions, technological instructions, instructions for keeping, and rules for keeping of individual types of goods and other special normative documents binding for the warehouse.

2. A goods warehouse shall be obliged to carry out at its expense an inspection of goods when accepting for keeping.

3. A goods warehouse shall be obliged to grant to the goods-possessor the possibility to inspect goods or samples thereof if keeping is effectuated with pooling, to do tests, and to take measures necessary to ensure the preservation of the goods.

4. When in order to ensure the preservation of goods it is required to urgently change the conditions of keeping a goods warehouse shall have the right to take the required urgent measures autonomously. He shall be obliged to notify the goods-possessor about the measures taken.

5. In the event of the discovery of damage to a good the warehouse shall be obliged immediately to draw up an act and to inform the goods-possessor at the address declared by it to the goods warehouse.

**Article 794. Requirements of Goods-Possessor for Goods Warehouse**

Unless provided otherwise by the contract, a goods-possessor shall be obliged to declare to the goods warehouse the loss, shortage, or damaging of a good which arose as a result of improper keeping when receiving the good from the warehouse, and latent damage – within the usual period necessary for the discovery thereof. If damage and shortage of a good is not declared within the respective periods to the warehouse, the goods warehouse shall not bear responsibility for losses, except for instances when the losses were caused as a consequence of the intent or gross negligence thereof.

**Article 795. Compensation of Expenses of Goods Warehouse for Keeping**

A warehouse shall have the right to compensation at rates of expenses provided for by the contract or established by legislative acts for additional operates effectuated in the interests of the transferor (insurance of goods, loading-unloading work, payment of customs duties, and so on). This right shall be secured by the right of the warehouse to withhold the kept good.

**Article 796. Renunciation by Goods Warehouse of Contract of Keeping**

A goods warehouse shall have the right to refuse performance of a contract of keeping in instances when the transferor has concealed the dangerous character of the good, which threatens the infliction of material damage.

**Article 797. Warehouse Documents**

1. Goods warehouses may issue in confirmation of the acceptance of goods for keeping the following warehouse documents:

(1) simple warehouse certificate;

(2) dual warehouse certificate.

1[1]. In instances provided for by legislative acts of the Republic Kazakhstan goods warehouses shall be obliged to issue dual or simple warehouse certificates in confirmation of the acceptance of goods for keeping in pooling.

2. A dual warehouse certificate, each part thereof, and a simple warehouse certificate shall be securities.

3. A dual and simple warehouse certificates may be the subjects of pledge [Article as amended by Law of 12 January 2007, No. 225-III].

**Article 798. Simple Warehouse Certificate**

1. A simple warehouse certificate shall be issued to bearer.

2. A simple warehouse certificate must contain the information provided for by Article 799(2), subpoints (2), (3), and (5)-(10) of the present Code, and also an indication that it was issued to bearer.

**Article 799. Dual Warehouse Certificate**

1. A dual warehouse certificate shall consist of a warehouse certificate and a pledge certificate (or warrant) which are identical in content and, when necessary, have been separated from one another.

2. On each part of a dual warehouse certificate there must be indicated:

(1) the name of the respective part of the dual warehouse certificate;

(2) the name and address of the goods warehouse which accepted the good for keeping;

(3) the current number of the warehouse certificate according to the register of the warehouse;

(4) the name of the organization or the name of the citizen from which the good was accepted for keeping, and also the location (or place of residence) of the goods-possessor;

(5) the name and quantity of the good and the number of pieces of the good;

(6) the amount of good accepted unless established otherwise by legislative acts of the Republic Kazakhstan;

(7) the period for which the good is accepted for keeping, if such is established;

(8) the tariffs and procedure for payment for keeping;

(9) the date of issuance of the warehouse certificate;

(10) the signature of the empowered person and seal of the goods warehouse.

Additional requirements for the form and content of a dual warehouse certificate may be established by legislative acts of the Republic Kazakhstan [as amended by Law of 12 January 2007, No. 225-III].

**Article 800. Rights of Holder of Dual Warehouse Certificate for Good**

1. The holder of a dual warehouse certificate shall have the right to dispose of the good being kept in the warehouse in full.

2. The holder of the warehouse certificate separated from the pledge certificate shall have the right to dispose of the good, but may not take it from the warehouse until payment of the credit issued under the pledge certificate. The holder of the warehouse certificate may effectuate the transfer of the right of ownership to the warehoused good by means of making an endorsement of transfer (endorsement) and handing over the document itself but without the movement of the good.

3. The purchaser who has received by endorsement a warehouse certificate with a pledge certificate not separated from it shall become the owner of the warehouse good free of a pledge. In the event of the acquisition of a warehouse certificate without a pledge certificate it shall be presupposed that the right of ownership to the good is encumbered by a right of pledge. Information concerning the conditions of the pledge (or the amount and period of established of the pledge right on the good) may be received in the register of the warehouse open for viewing by interested persons.

4. The holder of a pledge certificate shall have the right of pledge to the good in the amount of the loan issued under this certificate and remuneration with regard to it. In the event of the establishment of pledge rights for goods, a notation thereof shall be made on the warehouse certificate.

5. The purchaser or seller may release a good from pledge by depositing the respective amount secured by the pledge to the pledgeholder (or creditor) or to the goods warehouse, which shall be obliged to transfer it to the legal holder of the pledge certificate.

6. The holder of a pledge certificate in the event of the failure to satisfy his demand secured by the pledge within the period shall have the right to sell the good pledged to him under the pledge certificate in the procedure established by legislative acts and to cover his demand preferentially before other creditors of the pledgor. In the event of the insufficiency of the amount received the holder of the pledge certificate may recover the part not received form all endorsees bearing joint and several responsibility for payment of the demand secured by the pledge certificate [as amended by Law of 12 January 2007, No. 225-III].

**Article 801. Transfer of Warehouse and Pledge Certificates**

The warehouse certificate and the pledge certificate may be transferred together or separately under inscriptions of endorsements (or endorsements).

**Article 802. Issuance of Good Under Dual Warehouse Certificate**

1. A goods warehouse shall issue the good to the holder of the warehouse and pledge certificates (dual warehouse certificate) in exchange for both these certificates together.

The holder of a warehouse certificate who does not have the pledge certificate but who has deposited the amount of debt with regard to it shall be issued the good by the warehouse not other than in exchange for the warehouse certificate and on condition of the contribution of the entire amount of the debt under the pledge certificate.

2. The holder of warehouse and pledge certificates shall have the right to demand the issuance of the good in parts. In so doing new certificates for the good remaining in the warehouse shall be issued to him in exchange for the initial certificates.

3. A goods warehouse, notwithstanding the requirements of the present Article, which has issued a good to the holder of a warehouse certificate who does not have the pledge certificate and has not deposited the amount of the debt with regard to it shall bear responsibility to the holder of the pledge certificate for payment of the entire amount due under it.

## *Chapter 40. Insurance*

### Article 803. Contract of Insurance

1. Under a contract of insurance one party (insurant) shall be obliged to pay the insurance premium, and the other party (insurer) shall be obliged in the event of the ensuing of the insured event to effectuate an insurance payment to the insurant or other person to whose benefit the contract was concluded (beneficiary) within the limits of the amount (insured amount) determined by the contract [as amended by Law of 18 December 2000, No. 128-II].

2. Insurance shall be effectuated on the basis of a contract of insurance [as amended by Law of 5 July 2006, No. 164-III].

### Article 804. Insurance Relations Regulated by Present Code

Relations between the insurer and insurant, and also their relations with insured persons and beneficiaries which arise in the process of the conclusion and performance of a contract of insurance, shall be regulated by the present Code.

### Article 805. Forms of Insurance

1. The forms of insurance shall be:

(1) by degree of obligatoriness – voluntary and obligatory;

(2) by object of insurance – personal and property;

(3) by grounds of effectuation of insurance payment – accumulative and nonaccumulative.

2. For the purposes of licensing insurance activity a different classification may be provided by legislative acts [Article as amended by Law of 18 December 2000, No. 128-II].

### Article 806. Obligatory and Voluntary Insurance

1. Obligatory insurance – insurance effectuated by virtue of the requirements of legislative acts, the conditions of which shall be determined by agreement of the parties unless established otherwise by legislative acts regulating obligatory types of insurance [as amended by Law of 7 May 2007, No. 244-III].

2. [repealed by Law of 7 May 2007, No. 244-III].

3. The duty to insure his life or health may not be placed on a citizen either by legislative acts or by a contract.

Obligatory insurance shall be effectuated at the expense of the insurant.

4. In the event of obligatory insurance the insurant shall be obliged to conclude a contract with the insurer on conditions determined by agreement of the parties unless established otherwise by

legislative acts regulating the particular type of insurance [as amended by Law of 7 May 2007, No. 244-III].

5. A contract of obligatory insurance may be concluded only with the insurer having a license for the effectuation of the particular type of insurance. The conclusion of a contract of obligatory insurance, the procedure and conditions of which have been established by legislative acts regulating the obligatory type of insurance shall be binding upon the said insurer unless provided otherwise by the particular legislative acts [as amended by Law of 7 May 2007, No. 244-III]..

6. Voluntary insurance – insurance effectuated by virtue of the will of the parties.

The types, conditions, and procedure for voluntary insurance shall be determined by agreement of the parties.

**Article 807. Object of Insurance**

1. Any property interests of citizens and juridical persons may be objects of property and personal insurance, including connected with:

(1) citizens living until a determined age or period established by the contract of insurance, death, ensuring of determined events in the life of citizens;

(2) the causing of harm to life and health of citizens as a result of accidents and other events, illnesses;

(3) the possession, use, and disposition of property;

(4) the duty to compensate harm caused to other persons, including as a result of the violation of a contract (or obligations).

The object of insurance with regard to obligatory types of insurance shall be determined by legislative acts [as amended by Laws of 20 February 2006, No. 128-III, and of 7 May 2007, No. 244-III].

2. Unlawful property interests of the insurant shall not be subject to insurance [as amended by Law of 20 February 2006, No. 128-III].

3. Contracts of insurance whose object are property interests provided for by point 2 of the present Article shall be invalid.

**Article 808. Consequences of Violation of Rules on Obligatory Insurance**

1. A person to whose benefit in accordance with legislative acts must be effectuated obligatory insurance shall have the right if it became known to him that he is not insured to demand in a judicial proceeding insurance from the person on whom the duty is placed.

2. If a person on whom the duty of insurance is placed has not effectuated it or has concluded a contract of insurance on conditions worsening the position of the insured in comparison with that provided by legislative acts, this person if the insured event ensues shall bear responsibility to the insured on the same conditions on which the insurance would have been effectuated under proper insurance [as amended by Law of 18 December 2000, No. 128-II].

3. A person on whom the duty is placed by legislative acts to act as an insurant shall have the right to demand in a judicial proceeding compulsion of the insurer obliged in accordance with Article 806(5)

of the present Code to effectuate insurance but evades this to conclude a contract of insurance on the conditions provided for by legislative acts.

4. Evasion of insurance by a person obliged to effectuate it as an insurant, and also by an insurance organization obliged to act as an insurer, shall entail the responsibility provided for by legislative acts.

**Article 809. Personal and Property Insurance**

1. To personal insurance shall be relegated the insurance of life, health, capacity to labor, and other property interests connected with the person.

Under a contract of personal insurance the insurant himself may be insured and another person named in the contract (insured) [as amended by Law of 20 February 2006, No. 128-III].

2. To property insurance shall be relegated the insurance of property and property interests connected with it [as amended by Law of 20 February 2006, No. 128-III].

3. When insuring property the risk of the loss (or perishing0, shortage, or damaging of property and other property benefits and rights provided for by Article 115 of the present Code shall be insured.

4. A contract of insurance of property concluded in the absence of an interest of the insurant or beneficiary to preserve the insured property shall be invalid [as amended by Law of 18 December 2000, No. 128-II].

5. When insuring civil-law responsibility the risk of responsibility under obligations arising as a consequence of the causing of harm to life, health, or property of third persons, and also responsibility under obligations arising from contracts, shall be insured [as amended by Law of 20 February 2006, No. 128-III].

**Article 809[1]. Accumulative Insurance** [added by Law of 20 February 2006, No. 128-III]

1. Insurance provided for the effectuation of an insurance payment when an insured event ensues, including upon the expiry of a period established by the contract of insurance or other event provided for by the contract of insurance, depending upon which of them first ensues, shall be accumulative insurance.

2. Insurance providing for the effectuation of insurance payment only when the insured event ensues possessing the indicia of probability and incidentalness of the ensuing thereof shall be non-accumulative insurance.

3. A contract of annuity insurance – a contract of insurance according to which the insurer shall be obliged to effectuate insurance payment in the form of periodic payments to the benefit of the beneficiary during a period established by the contract.

4. Contracts of accumulative insurance may be concluded exclusively with regard to personal insurance.

5. A contract of annuity insurance shall be relegated to contracts of accumulative insurance.

**Article 810.** [repealed by Law of 20 February 2006, No. 128-III].

**Article 811.** [repealed by Law of 20 February 2006, No. 128-III].

**Article 812.** [repealed by Law of 20 February 2006, No. 128-III].

**Article 813. Insurant**

1. An insurant – person who has concluded a contract of insurance with an insurer.

2. Juridical persons and citizens may be insurants.

3. An insurance shall be free in the choice of insurer both under voluntary and under obligatory forms of insurance [as amended by Law of 18 December 2000, No. 128-II].

**Article 814. Insurer**

1. An insurer – person effectuating insurance, that is, obliged when an insured event ensues to make insurance payment to the insurant or other person to whose benefit a contract has been concluded (beneficiary) within the limits of the amount (insured amount) determined by the contract.

2. Only a juridical person registered as an insurance organization and having a license for the right to effectuate insurance activity or a mutual insurance society in accordance with a legislative act of the Republic Kazakhstan on mutual insurance may be an insurer [Article as amended by Laws of 18 December 2000, No. 128-II and of 5 July 2006, No. 164-III].

**Article 815. Insured**

1. An insured – a person with respect to whom nsurance is effectuated.

Unless provided otherwise by a contract an insurant simultaneously shall be an insured.

2. The duty to effectuate the insurance of a third person may be placed on an insurant by legislative acts. In the event of voluntary insurance an insurant may in the contract of insurance determine the third person as insured. In these instances either the person of the insured and interests thereof connected with him (personal insurance of insured) or property of the insured and property interests (property insurance of insured) shall be the object of insurance.

When insuring property the insured who is not the insurant must have an interest in the preservation of this property [point 2 as amended 7 May 2007, No. 244-III].

3. If under the conditions of a contract determined duties are placed on an insured who is not the insurant, the insurant must receive the consent of the insured for the conclusion of the particular contract.

In the event of obligatory insurance, and also under group pooled insurance, the consent of a third person to the conclusion of a contract in which he will be determined as an insured shall not be required.

In the event of voluntary insurance the objection of a person with regard to his personal or property insurance shall entail the impossibility of the conclusion of the contract, and if it already has been concluded – dissolution of the contract.

4. If a duty lies on an insurant to insure a third person, the said person shall have the right to demand from the insurant a report concerning the fulfillment of this duty, and in instances provided for by legislative acts – receipt of a document certifying that he is an insured.

In the event of the failure to fulfill or the improper fulfillment by the insurant of his duty with regard to insurance of a third person, the last shall have the right to apply measures provided for by Article 808(1) and (2) of the present Code.

5. If a minor citizen is an insured, his rights shall be realized in the procedure provided for by Articles 22-24 of the present Code.

6. The conclusion of a contract to the benefit of an insured shall not relieve the insurant from the fulfillment of the duties under this contract.

Insurance of a third person shall be effectuated at the expense of the insurant.

7. If an insured has refused to receive insurance payment due to him in accordance with the contract, the right to receive insurance payment shall pass to the insurant.

8. In the event of the death of an insured who is not an insurant with respect to whom a contract of personal insurance is concluded not providing for such instance, this contract shall be subject to termination unless substitution of the insured is provided for by legislative acts or by the contract.

If the death of the insured was that insured event which is provided for by the contract of insurance, this contract shall be performed on the conditions provided for by it.

In the event of the death of an insured who is not an insurant with respect whom a contract of property insurance has been concluded, the rights and duties of the insured with the consent of the insurant shall pass to the heirs of that property and those property rights of the insured which were the object of insurance unless provided otherwise by legislative acts or by contract.

If the insurant does not consent to substitution of the deceased insured or the heirs of the insured do not consent to accept his rights and duties arising from the contract of insurance, this contract shall be subject to termination.

9. The provisions of Article 391 of the present Code shall extend in that part in which they are not contrary to the provisions of the present Article to a contract of insurance to the benefit of a third person (or insured) [Article as amended by Law of 18 December 2000, No. 128-II].

**Article 816. Beneficiary**

1. A beneficiary – person who in accordance with a contract of insurance or legislative acts on obligatory insurance is the recipient of an insurance payment.

Both a juridical person and a citizen may be a beneficiary.

A beneficiary may be designated either under personal or property insurance.

With regard to obligatory types of insurance the beneficiary shall be determined by legislative acts regulating this type of insurance, and with regard to voluntary types – shall be designated by the insurant.

2. Unless provided otherwise by legislative acts on obligatory insurance or a contract on voluntary insurance, the insurant shall be the beneficiary.

If the insurant is not the insured, the beneficiary must be the insured or he shall be designated with the written consent of the insured.

If the beneficiary in a contract of insurance is not indicated, the insured shall be presupposed to be him.

3. [repealed in accordance with Law of 20 February 2006, No. 128-III].

4. [repealed in accordance with Law of 18 December 2000, No. 128-II].

5. When an insured is simultaneously a beneficiary, to the last shall extend the provisions provided for by Article 815 of the present Code.

6. In the event of the death of the beneficiary who is not an insured, or of his renunciation of the rights of beneficiary, the rights of the last shall pass to the insurant.

In the event of the death of the beneficiary who is an insured, the consequences ahll ensue provided for by Article 815(8) of the present Code.

7. If the death of the insured was that event which is provided by the contract of insurance, then when such insured is not an insurant or is such but is not designated the beneficiary in the contract, the heirs of the insured shall be deemed to be beneficiaries.

8. When the insured event ensues the beneficiary shall have the right to present a demand directly to the insurer concerning the payment to him of the insurance payment provided for by the contract of insurance.

9. The conclusion of a contract to the benefit of a beneficiary shall not relieved the insurant from the fulfillment of duties under this contract [Article as amended by Law of 18 December 2000, No. 128-II].

**Article 817. Insured Event**

1. An insured event – an event with the ensuing of which a contract of insurance provided for the effectuation of an insurance payment.

2. Types of insured events with regard to obligatory insurance shall be determined by legislative acts on obligatory insurance, and with regard to voluntary insurance – by agreement of the parties.

3. An event considered as an insured event must possess the indicia of probability and incidentalness of the ensuing thereof except for events which may be provided for under a contract of accumulative insurance.

4. Proving the ensuing of an insured event, and also the losses caused by it, shall lie on the insurant [Article as amended by Law of 18 December 2000, No. 128-II].

**Article 818. Insurance Premiums**

1. An insurance premium – an amount of money which the insurant shall be obliged to pay to an insurer for the acceptance by the last of obligations to make an insurance payment to the insurant (or beneficiary) in the amount determined by the contract of insurance.

The insurance premiums receiveв by the insurer from the insurant shall belong to it by right of ownership [point as amended by Law of 20 February 2006, No. 128-III].

2. The amounts of insurance premiums shall be established by a contract. In the event of obligatory types of insurance they shall be established by legislative acts.

The procedure and periods for the payment of insurance premiums shall be determined by a contract. With regard to obligatory types of insurance they may be determined by legislation [point as amended by law of 7 May 2007, No. 244-III].

3. The parties when determining the amount of insurance premiums subject to payment under a contract of insurance may apply insurance tariffs worked out by the insurer determining the rate of insurance premium to be recovered per unit of insured amount taking into account the object of insurance and the character of the insured risk.

4. Payment of an insurance premium by installment in the form of periodic insurance contributions may be provided for by a contract.

5. If the payment of an insurance premium by installment is provided for by the contract of insurance, the consequences of the failure to pay within the established periods of regular insurance contributions, including dissolution of the contract before time, may be provided for by the contract of insurance.

6. If an insured event has ensued before the payment of a determined insurance contribution, the making of which was delayed, the insurer shall have the right when determining the amount of insurance payment to set off the amount of delayed insurance contribution [Article as amended by Law of 18 December 2000, No. 128-II].

**Article 819. Insured Amount**

1. An insured amount – an amount of money for which the object of insurance is insured and which represents the maximum amount of responsibility of the insurer when the insured event ensues.

2. The amounts of insured amounts shall be established by a contract. In the event of obligatory types of insurance they may not be less than the amounts established by legislative acts [point as amended by Law of 18 December 2000, No. 128-II].

3. In the event of the insurance of property, the insured amount may not exceed its true value at the moment of the conclusion of the contract (insured value) [point as amended by Law of 20 February 2006, No. 128-III].

4. The parties may not contest the value of the property determined in the contract of insurance, except for instances when the insurer proves that he was intentionally deluded by the insurant. If the insured amount determined by the contract of insurance exceeds the insured value, it shall be invalid in that part of the insured amount which exceeds the insured value at the moment of conclusion of the contract.

5. [repealed by Law of 20 February 2006, No. 128-III].

**Article 820. Insurance Payment**

1. Insurance payment – the amount of money to be paid by the insurer to the insurant (or beneficiary) within the limits of the insured amount when the insured event ensues or when the period ensues determined in a contract of accumulative insurance.

Insurance payment shall be effectuated by a one-time payment, except for insurance payments under contracts of annuity insurance [point as amended by Law of 20 February 2006, No. 128-III].

2. The procedure for determining the amounts of insurance payment shall be established by a contract. In the event of obligatory types of insurance the procedure for determining the amounts of insurance payment shall be determined by legislative acts of the Republic Kazakhstan.

3. The procedure and periods for the effectuation of insurance payments shall be determined by the contract.

With regard to obligatory types of insurance they may be determined by legislative acts.

4. Insurance payment with regard to the insurance of property and civil-law responsibility may not exceed the amount of real damage incurred by the insurant (or insured) as a result of the ensuing of the insured event.

5. Insurance payment with regard to personal insurance shall be effectuated to the insurant (or insured) irrespective of amounts due thereto under social security and other contracts of insurance and by way of compensation of harm.

6. The substitution of an insurance payment by contributory compensation of damage in kind within the limits of the amount of the insurance payment may be provided for by the conditions of the contract of property insurance.

7. When effectuating an insurance payment the insurer shall have the right to make a set-off of the insurance premiums or insurance contributions due thereto from the insurant.

8. For the untimely effectuation of an insurance payment the insurer shall bear responsibility in accordance with Article 353 of the present Code unless a higher amount of responsibility is provided for by the contract or legislative acts on obligatory insurance [Article as amended by Law of 18 December 2000, No. 128-II].

**Article 821. Double Insurance**

1. Double (or multiple) insurance – insurance of the same object by several insurers under autonomous contracts with each.

2. In the event of double insurance of property each insurer shall bear to the insurant responsibility within the limits of the contract concluded with it; however, the total amount of insurance payments received by the insurant from all insurers may not exceed the real damage.

In so doing the insurant shall have the right to receive the insurance payment from any insurer in the insured amount provided for by the contract concluded with it. If the insurance payment received does not cover the read damage, the insurance shall have the right to receive the amount lacking from another insurer.

An insurer wholly or partially relieved from insurance payment by virtue of the fact that the damage caused is compensated by other insurers shall be obliged to return to the insurant the respective part of the insurance premiums, deducting expenses incurred [point 2 as amended by Law of 18 December 2000, No. 128-II].

3. Under dual (or multiple) personal insurance each insurer shall fulfill its insurance obligations to the insurant autonomously irrespective of the fulfillment thereof by other insurers.

**Article 822. Group Insurance**

1. In the event of group insurance several insureds who are simultaneously beneficiaries shall be encompassed by one contract of insurance.

2. Group insurance may be personal or property, either personified or pooled, encompassing a determined category of persons.

In the event of pooled insurance the group of insureds must be made specific in the contract of insurance to the extent to which this is necessary for individualization of the insured event, consequences thereof with respect to each insured and the amount of insurance payment due thereto [point 2 as amended by Law of 18 December 2000, No. 128-II].

3. Collective insurance by an employer of its workers may be only personal insurance.

**Article 823. Co-Insurance**

1. An object of insurance may be insured under one contract jointly by several insurers (co-insurance). In so doing conditions determining the rights and duties of each insurer in agreed participatory shares must be contained in the contract.

If the rights and duties of each of the insurers have not been determined in such contract, they jointly and severally shall be liable to the insurant (or beneficiary) for the effectuation of insurance payment [point as amended by Law of 18 December 2000, No. 128-II].

2. Co-insurers may create on the basis of a contract of joint activity simple partnerships (or insurance pools) for the joint insurance of large-scale or especially large-scale risks.

3. When there is a respective agreement between co-insurers one of them may represent all the co-insurers in mutual relations with the insurant, while remaining responsible to the last only in its participatory share.

**Article 824. Reinsurance**

1. An insurer shall have the right by means of reinsurance to ensure the coverage of the risk of performance of all or part of its obligations to the insurant with another insurer (or reinsurer).

2. An insurer who has concluded a contract of reinsurance with a reinsurer (reinsurant) shall remain responsible to the insurance in full in accordance with the contract of insurance concluded with it.

3. The conditions of reinsurance shall be determined by legislative acts of the Republic Kazakhstan and by a contract of reinsurance between the reinsurant and reinsurer.

A contract of reinsurance must meet the requirements presented by the present Code for a contract of insurance. In so doing the insurer under the principal contract of insurance shall be considered the reinsurant in the contract of reinsurance [point as amended by Law of 20 February 2006, No. 128-III].

4. In order to organize reinsurance the reinsurers may join together on the basis of a contract on joint activity into simple partnerships (or reinsurance pools).

5. The consecutive conclusion or two or several contracts of reinsurance shall be permitted [Article amended by Law of 10 July 2003, No. 483-II].

**Article 825. Form of Contract of Insurance**

1. A contract of insurance shall be concluded in written form by means of:

(1) drawing up by the parties of a contract of insurance [point as amended by Law of 20 February 2006, No. 128-III];

(2) accession of the insurant to standard conditions (or rules of insurance) worked out by the insurer unilaterally (or contract of accession) and issuance by the insurer to the insurant of an insurance policy;

(3) [repealed in accordance with Law of 10 July 2003, No. 483-II];

(4) [repealed in accordance with Law of 20 February 2006, No. 128-III].

2. The form of a written contract with regard to obligatory insurance shall be determined by legislative acts of the Russian Federation on obligatory insurance, and with regard to voluntary insurance – by the insurer or by agreement of the parties.

3. The failure to comply with the written form of the contract of insurance shall entail the invalidity thereof [Article as amended by Law of 18 December 2000, No. 128-II; of 1 July 2003, No. 445-II; and of 10 July 2003, No. 483-II].

**Article 825[1]. Rules of Insurance** [added by Law of 18 December 2000, No. 128-II]

1. The rules of insurance shall be worked out by the insurer and subject to agreement with an empowered State agency in instances established by legislative acts of the Republic Kazakhstan. The rules of insurance with regard to a specific type of insurance must correspond to the requirements of the present Article.

2. The rules of insurance must contain:

(1) list of objects of insurance;

(2) procedure for determining insured amounts;

(3) list of insured events [as amended by Law of 20 February 2006, No. 128-III];

(4) exclusion from insured events and limitation of insurance;

(5) period and place of operation of contract of insurance;

(6) procedure for conclusion of contract of insurance;

(7) rights and duties of the parties;

(8) actions of insurant when insured event ensues;

(9) list of documents confirming ensuing of insured event and amount of losses;

(10) procedure and conditions of effectuation of insurance payments;

(11) period of adoption of decision concerning insurance payment or refusal of insurance payment;

(12) conditions of termination of contract of insurance;

(13) procedure for settlement of disputes;

(14) [repealed by Law of 20 February 2006, No. 128-III];

(15) additional conditions [as amended by Law of 20 February 2006, No. 128-III].

3. [repealed by Law of 10 July 2003, No. 483-II].

4. By agreement between the insurant and insurer on the basis of the rules of insurance contracts of insurance may be concluded providing for additional conditions to be determined when concluding the contract of insurance. In the event of a repetition of the same additional conditions more than three times, the insurer shall be obliged in the procedure established by legislation to change the rules for the determined type of insurance.

5. When changes are made in the rules of insurance the insurer must provide these changes to the empowered State agency for agreement [Article as amended by Laws of 18 December 2000, No. 128-II; of 10 July 2003, No. 483-II].

**Article 826. Content of Contract of Insurance**

1. A contract of insurance must contain:

(1) name, location, and banking requisites of insurer;

(2) surname, forename, patronymic (if there is one) and place of residence of insurant (if a natural person) or name, location, and banking requisites (if a juridical person);

(3) indication of object of insurance;

(4) indication of insured event;

(5) amounts of insured amount and procedure and periods for effectuation of insurance payment;

(6) amount of insurance premium and procedure and periods for payment thereof;

(7) date of conclusion and period of operation of contract;

(8) indications concerning insured and beneficiary if they are participants of the insurance relation;

(9) number and series of contract (or insurance policy);

(10) instances and procedure for making changes in conditions of contract;

(11) conditions of payment and amount of redemption amount (for accumulative insurance);

(12) indication of registration number of taxpayer (if there is one), indicator of residence, and sectors of economy of insurant;

(13) indication of registration number of taxpayer (if there is one), indicator of residence, and sectors of economy of insured (or beneficiary) if it is not an insurant under the contract of insurance;

(14) type of currency of insured amount, insurance payment, and insurance premium.

2. By agreement of the parties other conditions may be included in the contract.

$2^1$. Franchise – relieving of insurer provided for by conditions of insurance from compensation of damage not exceeding a determined amount [added by Law of 20 February 2006, No. 128-III].

Franchise occurs as nondeductible (non-subtracted) and deductible (subtracted)

In the event of nondeductible franchise the insurer shall be relieved from compensation of damage not exceeding the established amount of the franchise but must compensate damage in full if the amount thereof is greater than this amount.

In the event of deductible franchise the damage in all instances shall be compensated with the deduction of an established amount.

Franchise shall be established either in percentages of the insured amount or in an absolute extent.

3. If a contract of insurance contains conditions worsening the position of the insurant in comparison with those which are provided by legislative acts, the rules established by these legislative acts shall operate.

4. The period of responsibility of the reinsurer under a contract of reinsurance must correspond to the period of responsibility of the insurer under the contract of insurance, obligations with regard to which have been transferred in the reinsurance unless provided otherwise by the contract of reinsurance.

5. Responsibility for the incompleteness of conditions subject to indication in a contract of insurance shall be borne by the insurer. In the event a dispute arises under a contract of insurance as a consequence of the incompleteness of individual provisions thereof the dispute shall be decided in favor of the insurant. Conditions of the present point shall not extend to contracts of reinsurance [Article as amended by Laws of 18 December 2000, No. 128-II; and of 12 January 2007, No. 225-III].

**Article 826[1]. Deferral of Payment of Insurance Premium Under Contract of Accumulative Insurance [added by Law of 18 December 2000, No. 128-II]**

1. In the event of the failure of the insurant to comply twice in succession with the conditions for payment of an insurance contribution under contracts of accumulative insurance the insurer within the period established by the contract of accumulative insurance shall be obliged to notify the insurant about the necessity to pay the insurance contribution [point as amended by law of 20 February 2006, No. 128-III].

2. The notification must contain:

(1) period during which it is necessary to pay the insurance contribution (or period of deferral of insurance premium);

(2) amount of forfeit for delay of payment of insurance contribution;

(3) right of insurer unilaterally to terminate operation of the contract in the event of failure to pay the insurance contribution during the period of deferral of the insurance premium.

3. The period of deferral of an insurance premium may not be less than 30 calendar days.

4. When an insured event ensues in the period of deferral of an insurance premium under a contract of accumulative insurance the insurer shall be obliged to effectuate the insurance payment, having withheld in so doing the amount of indebtedness.

5. Notification concerning the necessity to pay an insurance contribution shall be sent to the insurant by a means enabling the sending of the notification to be confirmed.

**Article 826[2]. Restoration of Operation of Contract of Accumulative Insurance [added by Law of 18 December 2000, No. 128-II]**

1. If the operation of a contract of accumulative insurance was suspended or terminated on the grounds of the failure of the insurant to pay the insurance contribution, the insurer shall be obliged to restore the operation of the contract in the event of payment by the insurant:

(1) [repealed by Law of 20 February 2006, No. 128-III];

(2) deferred insurance contributions;

(3) forfeit for deferral of payment of insurance contributions in the amount provided for by Article 353 of the present Code.

2. An insurant shall have the right to restore the operation of a contract of accumulative insurance within one year from the date of termination of the operation of the contract or suspension of performance by the parties to the contract of their obligations.

3. An insurer shall have the right when restoring the operation of a contract of accumulative insurance to perform a medical expert examination of the state of health of the insured person.

In the event of a worsening of the state of health of an insured person the insurer shall have the right to recalculate the amounts of insurance payment and/or insurance premium. In the event of the refusal of the insurant to restore the operation of the contract on the new conditions, the contract shall not be subject to restoration [as amended by Law of 20 February 2006, No. 128-III].

4. An insurer shall have the right to refuse to restore the operation of a contract of accumulative insurance if the operation of such contract was terminated before time and the redemption amount was paid by the insurer [as amended by Law of 20 February 2006, No. 128-III].

**Article 826[3]. Insurance Under Contract by Means of Formalization of General Policy [added by Law of 18 December 2000, No. 128-II]**

1. By agreement of the insurant with the insurer the systematic insurance of various lots of a homogeneous property (goods, cargoes, and so on) under similar conditions during a determined period may be effectuated on the basis of a single contract of insurance by means of issuance of a general policy to the insurant.

2. An insurant shall be obliged with respect to each lot of property falling under the operation of the contract specified in point 1 of the present Article to communicate to the insurer information stipulated by such contract within the period provided by it, and if it is not provided, immediately upon the receipt thereof. An insurant shall not be relieved from this duty even if at the moment of receipt of such information the possibility of losses subject to compensation by the insurer already has disappeared.

3. Upon the demand of the insurant an insurer shall be obliged to issue insurance policies with regard to individual lots of property falling under the operation of the contract specified in point 1 of the present Article.

In the event of the failure of the content of an insurance policy to conform to the general policy, preference shall be given to the insurance policy.

**Article 827. Operation of Contract of Insurance**

1. A contract of insurance shall enter into force and become binding upon the parties from the moment of payment by the insurant of the insurance premium, and in the event of the payment thereof by installment – the first insurance contribution unless provided otherwise by contract or by legislative acts on obligatory insurance.

2. A contract of insurance shall terminate its operation from the moment of the effectuation of insurance payment with regard to the first insured event which has ensued unless provided otherwise by the contract or by legislative acts on obligatory insurance.

3. The period of operation of insurance defense shall coincide with the period of operation of the contract unless provided otherwise by the contract or by legislative acts on obligatory insurance [Article as amended by Law of 18 December 2000, No. 128-II].

**Article 828. Duties of Insurer**

1. An insurer shall be obliged to:

(1) when an insured event ensues to make the insurance payment in the amount, procedure, and period established in the contract of insurance or legislative acts;

($1^1$) familiarize the insurant with the rules of insurance [added by Law of 18 December 2000, No. 128-II];

(2) compensate the insurant (or insured) for expenses made by him in order to reduce losses in connection with the insured event;

(3) ensure the secrecy of insurance.

2. Other duties of the insurer may be provided by legislative acts on insurance and insurance activity, and also by the contract of insurance [Article as amended by Law of 18 December 2000, No. 128-II].

**Article 829. Compensation of Expenses Directed Towards Reduction of Losses from Insured Event**

1. In the event the insured event ensues which is provided for by the contract of property insurance, the insurant (or insured) shall be obliged to take reasonable and available measures under the circumstances which formed in order to prevent or reduce possible losses, including measures to rescue and preserve insured property.

In taking such measures, the insurant (or insured) must follow the instructions of the insurer if they have been communicated to the insurant (or insured).

2. Expenses incurred by the insurant (or insured) for the purpose of preventing or reducing losses shall be subject to compensation by the insurer if such expenses were necessary or were made in order to fulfill instructions of the insurer, even if the respective measures proved to be unsuccessful.

Such expenses shall be compensated in actual amounts, provided that the total amount of an insurance payment and contributory compensation of expenses shall not exceed the insured amount provided for by the contract of insurance, but if the expenses arose as a result of the performance by the insurant (or insured) of instructions of the insurer, they shall be compensated in full irrespective of the insured amount.

3. The insurer shall be relieved from the effectuation of insurance payment in the part of those losses which arose as a consequence of the fact that the insurant (or insured) intentionally did not take reasonable and available measures in order to reduce possible losses [Article as amended by Laws of 18 December 2000, No. 128-II; and of 1 July 2003, No. 445-II].

**Article 830. Secrecy of Insurance**

1. The secrecy of insurance shall include information concerning the amounts of the insured amount, redemption amount, and insurance premiums paid, and other conditions of the contract of insurance (or reinsurance) relating to the person of the insurant, insured, or beneficiary. Information concerning contracts of insurance (or reinsurance) concluded of an insurance (or reinsurance) organization in the process of liquidation shall not be relegated to the secrecy of insurance.

$1^1$. Other conditions and the procedure for the divulgence of information comprising a secret of insurance may be provided by legislative acts on obligatory insurance [added by Law of 20 February 2006, No. 128-III].

2. Professional participants of the insurance market and insurance agent shall not have the right to divulge information received by them as a result of their professional activity to another professional participant of the insurance market or insurance agent connected with the conclusion of a contract of reinsurance or with relations regarding co-insurance, and also instances provided by points 4, 5, and 6 of the present Article.

3. Officials, workers of an insurance (or reinsurance) organization, insurance brokers, insurance agents, and other persons who by virtue of the effectuation of their employment duties have received access to information comprising a secret of insurance shall bear responsibility for the divulgence thereof provided for by legislative acts of the Republic Kazakhstan.

4. A secret of insurance may be disclosed to a third person on the basis of the written consent of the insurant (or insured, beneficiary).

5. Information containing a secret of insurance shall be granted to:

(1) a representative of the insurant (or beneficiary) – on the basis of a notarially certified power of attorney;

(2) agency of inquiry and preliminary investigation – for criminal cases in the proceedings thereof;

(3) to a court – for cases on the basis of a ruling of a court in the proceedings thereof;

(4) to a procurator – on the basis of a decree concerning a proceeding of verification within the limits of its competence with regard to the consideration of materials with him;

(5) to an empowered State agency – with regard to questions connected with the effectuation of supervision over insurance activity;

(6) other persons in accordance with legislative acts of the Republic Kazakhstan on obligatory insurance.

6. Information containing a secret of insurance in the event of the death of an insurant, insured, or beneficiary shall be issued to:

(1) heirs;

(2) courts and notaries with regard to inheritance cases within their proceedings on the basis of a ruling, decree of a court, or written inquiry of a notary attested by the seal thereof. A copy of the certificate concerning the death of the insurant must be appended to the written inquiry of the notary;

(3) foreign consular institutions – with regard to cases on inheriting in the proceedings thereof.

7. General conditions of the effectuation of insurance activity, a list of the proposed insurance services, insurance tariffs, periods of insurance, and also other grounds of the condition of a contract of insurance (or reinsurance) shall be open information and may not be the subject of a secret of insurance and a commercial secret.

8. In the event of the divulgence by the insurer of information comprising a secret of insurance, the insurant (or insured, beneficiary) shall have the right to demand compensation of losses caused, and in proper instances – contributory compensation of moral harm [Article as amended by Laws of 18December 2000, No. 128-II; of 10 July 2003, No. 483-II; and of 27 February 2004, No. 527-II].

**Article 831. Duties of Insurant**

1. An insurant shall be obliged to:

(1) pay insurance premiums in the amount, procedure and periods established by the contract of insurance;

(2) inform the insurer about the state of insured risk;

(3) notify the insurer about the ensuing of the insured event;

(4) take measure to reduce losses from the insured event (Article 829(1) of the present Code);

(5) ensure the transfer to the insurer of the right of demand against the person responsible for the ensuing of the insured event (Article 840 of the present Code) [point 1 as amended by Law of 18 December 2000, No. 128-II].

2. Other duties of the insurant may be provided also by the contract of insurance.

**Article 832. Information to be Provided by Insurant When Concluding Contract**

1. When concluding a contract an insurant shall be obliged to inform the insurer of circumstances known to the insurant having material significance for determining the probability of the ensuing of the insured event and amount of possible losses from the ensuing thereof (insured risk) if these circumstances are not known and should not be known to the insurer.

Circumstances definitely stipulated in the rules of insurance worked out by the insurer, or in a written questionnaire of the insurer sent to the insurant during the period of conclusion of the contract shall be deemed in any event to be material [point 1 as amended by Law of 18 December 2000, No. 128-II].

2. If a contract of insurance was concluded in the absence of replies of the insurant to any questions of the insurer, the last may not subsequently demand dissolution of the contract or deeming thereof to be invalid on the grounds that the respective circumstances were not communicated by the insurant.

3. If after the conclusion of a contract it is established that the insurant communicated to the insurer information known to be false concerning circumstances specified in point 1 of the present Article, the

insurer shall have the right to demand the deeming of the contract to be invalid and application of circumstances provided for by Article 844(1), paragraphs two and three, of the present Code.

An insurer may not demand the deeming of a contract to be invalid if the circumstances concerning which the insurant was silent have already disappeared.

**Article 833. Evaluation of Insured Risk and Harm Caused**

1. When concluding a contract of insurance of property, the insurer shall have the right to view and evaluate the property to be insured and, when necessary, to designate an expert examination for the purposes of establishing the true value thereof.

The evaluation of the property to be insured and harm caused effectuated by the insurer shall be an integral part of the insurance and shall not require additional licensing.

2. When concluding a contract of personal insurance an insurer shall have the right to perform an examination of the person to be insured in order to evaluate the actual state of the health thereof.

3. An evaluation of the insured risk by an insurer on the basis of the present Article shall not be binding for the insurant, who shall have the right to prove otherwise.

4. The amount of harm caused as a result of the ensuing of an insured event the insurer shall determine upon the application of the insurant or representative thereof. When necessary, the evaluation of the amount of harm caused shall be carried out by a valuer (or independent expert). In the event of disagreement with the results of the evaluation of harm caused the parties shall have the right to prove otherwise [points 1 to 4 as amended by Law of 1 July 2003, No. 445-II].

5. In the event of obligatory types of insurance the procedure and conditions for conducting an evaluation of the amount of harm caused as a result of the ensuing of the insured event may be determined by legislative acts of the Republic Kazakhstan [point 5 added by Law of 7 May 2007, No. 244-III].

**Article 834. Consequences of Increase of Insured Risk in Period of Operation of Contract**

1. In the period of operation of a contract of property insurance the insurant (or insured) shall be obliged immediately to communicate to the insurer significant changes in the circumstances communicated to the insurer when concluding the contract which have become known to him, if these changes may materially influence the increase of the insured risk.

Changes shall be deemed to be significant in any event which are stipulated in the contract of insurance.

2. An insurer who has been notified about circumstances entailing an increase of the insured risk shall have the right to demand a change of the conditions of the contract of insurance or payment of an additional insurance premium commensurate to the increase of risk.

If the insurant or insured objects to changes of the conditions of the contract of insurance or additional payment of the insurance premium, the insurer shall have the right to demand dissolution of the contract in accordance with the rules provided for by Chapter 24 of the present Code [point 2 as amended by Law of 18 December 2000, No. 128-II].

3. In the event of the failure of the insurant or insured to fulfill the duty provided for in point 1 of the present Article, the insurer shall have the right to demand dissolution of the contract and compensation of losses caused by dissolution of the contract.

4. The insurer shall not have the right to demand dissolution of the contract if the circumstances entailing an increase of the insured risk have disappeared.

5. In the event of personal insurance, the consequences of a change of insured risk in the period of operation of the contract specified in points 2 and 3 of the present Article may ensue only if they are expressly provided for in the contract.

**Article 835. Informing Insurer About Ensuing of Insured Event**

1. An insurant shall, after the ensuing of the insured event became known to him, be obliged immediately to inform the insurer or his representative about the ensuing thereof. If a period and/or means of informing has been provided for by the contract or legislative act of the Republic Kazakhstan on obligatory insurance, it must be made within the stipulated period and by the means specified in the contract or legislative act of the Republic Kazakhstan.

Such duty shall lie on the insured if the insurant is not the insured.

If in the event of personal insurance the insured event is the death of the insured, the duty of notifying the insurer about the insured event shall lie on the insurant, and if he is simultaneously the insured – than on the beneficiary. In so doing the period of notification of the insurer established by the contract may not be less than thirty days.

2. The beneficiary shall have the right to notify the insurer about the ensuing of the insured event under all circumstances irrespective of whether the insurant or insured has done so or not.

3. The failure to inform the insurer about the ensuing of the insured event shall give it the right to refuse insurance payment unless it is proved that the insurer simultaneously knew about the ensuing of the insured event or the lack of information with the insurer about this could not affect its duties to effectuate the insurance payment [Article as amended by Laws of 18 December 2000, No. 128-II and of 1 July 2003, No. 445-II].

**Article 836. Replacement of Insurant**

1. In the event of the death of the insurant who has concluded a contract of insurance of property, the rights and duties of the insurant shall pass to the person who has accepted this property by way of inheriting. In other instances of the transfer of the right of ownership (or other rights to a thing), the rights and duties of the insurant shall pass to the new owner (or possess of other rights to a thing) with the consent of the insurer unless established otherwise by the contract of legislative acts.

2. In the event of the death of the insurant who has concluded a contract of personal insurance to the benefit of the insured, the rights anв duties determined by this contract shall pass to the insured with his consent. When the fulfillment by the insured of duties under the contract of insurance is impossible, his rights and duties may pass to persons effectuating in accordance with legislative acts duties with regard to the protection of his rights and legal interests.

3. In the event of the reorganization of the insurant which is a juridical person during the period of operation of a contract of insurance his rights and duties under this contract shall pass with the consent of the insurer to the respective legal successor in the procedure determined by the present Code.

**Article 837. Replacement of Insured**

1. In an instance when under a contract of insurance of responsibility for causing harm (Article 811 of the present Code) the responsibility of a person other than the insurant has been insured, the last shall have the right, unless provided otherwise by the contract, at any time before the ensuing of the insured event to replace this person by another, having informed the insurer thereof in writing.

2. The insured named in the contract of personal insurance, and also property insurance, may be replaced by another only with the consent of the insured himself (except for group personal insurance) and the insurer [point 2 as amended by Law of 18 December 2000, No. 128-II].

3. If insurance of a third person arises from the requirements of legislative acts on obligatory insurance, replacement of the insured shall be effectuated in the procedure established by the said legislative acts and the contract based on them.

**Article 838. Replacement of Beneficiary**

1. An insurant shall have the right before the ensuing of the insured event to replace the beneficiary, who is not an insured, named in the contract of insurance by another person, having informed the insurer thereof in writing.

2. The beneficiary may not be replaced by another person after he has fulfilled determined duties under the contract of insurance arising from his agreement with the insurant or presented to the insurer a demand for the effectuation of insurance payment [point 2 as amended by Law of 18 December 2000, No. 128-II].

3. Replacement of a beneficiary who is an insured shall be in the procedure provided for by Article 837 of the present Code.

**Article 839. Grounds for Relief of Insurer from Effectuation of Insurance Payment**

1. An insurer shall have the right fully or partially to refuse insurance payment to the insurant if the insured event has ensued as a consequence of:

(1) intentional actions of the insurant, insured, and/or beneficiary directed towards the arising of the insured event or facilitating the ensuing thereof, except for actions committed in a state of necessary defense and extreme necessity;

(2) actions of the insurant, insured, and/or beneficiary deemed in the procedure established by legislative acts to be intentional crimes or administrative violations in a causal link with the insured event.

An insurer shall not be relieved from the effectuation of insurance payment under contracts of insurance of civil-law responsibility if the insured event occurred through the fault of the person whose responsibility is the object of insurance.

An insurer shall not be relieved from the effectuation of insurance payment which under a contract of personal insurance is subject to payment in the event of the death of the insured if the death ensued as a consequence of suicide and by this time the contract of insurance had operated not less than two years [point 1 as amended by Law of 20 February 2006, No. 128-III].

2. Insofar as not provided otherwise by a contract of voluntary insurance and legislative acts on obligatory insurance, the insurer shall be relieved from the effectuation of insurance payment if the insured event ensued as a consequence of:

(1) the impact of nuclear explosion, radiation, or radioactive contamination;

(2) military actions;

(3) civil war, popular uprising of any type, mass disorders, or strikes.

3. Insofar as not provided otherwise by a contract of property insurance an insurer shall be relieved from the effectuation of insurance payment for losses which arose as a consequence of the seizure, confiscation, requisition, arrest, or destruction of insured property at the instruction of State agencies.

4. The grounds for the refusal of an insurer to effectuate an insurance payment may be also the following:

(1) communication by the insurant to the insurer of information known to be false concerning the object of insurance, insured risk, insured event, or consequences thereof;

(2) intentional failure to take measures by the insurant for the reduction of losses from the insured event (Article 829 of the present Code);

(3) receipt by the insurant of respective compensation of loss with regard to property insurance from the person at fault in causing the loss;

(4) obstruction by the insurant of the insurer in investigation the circumstances of the ensuing of the insured event and in establishing the amount of losses caused thereto;

(5) failure to notify the insurer about the ensuing of the insured event (Article 835 of the present Code);

(6) renunciation of the insurant of his right of demand against the person responsible for the ensuing of the insured event, and also a refusal to transfer documents to the insurer necessary for the transfer to the insurer of the right of demand (Article 840 of the present Code). If insurance compensation already has been paid, the insurer shall have the right to demand the return thereof fully or partially;

(7) other instances provided for by legislative acts.

5. Relieving the insurer from insured responsibility to an insurant for reasons of the unlawful actions thereof provided for by the present Article shall simultaneously relieve the insurer from the effectuation of insurance payment to an insured or beneficiary.

6. Other grounds for a refusal of insurance payment, unless this is contrary to legislative acts, may be provided for by the conditions of a contract of insurance.

7. A decision concerning a refusal of insurance payment shall be adopted by the insurer and communicated to the insurant in written form with a reasoned substantiation of the reasons for the refusal.

8. A refusal of an insurer to make insurance payment may be appealed by the insurant to a court [Article as amended by Law of 18 December 2000, No. 128-II].

**Article 840. Transfer to Insurer of Rights of Insurant to Compensation of Losses (Subrogation)**

1. Unless provided otherwise by the contract of property insurance, to the insurer who has effectuated the insurance payment shall pass within the limits of the amount paid the right of demand which the insurant (or insured) has against the person responsible for the losses compensated as a result of the insurance. However, a condition of the contract excluding the transfer to the insurer of the right of demand against a person who intentionally caused losses shall be invalid.

2. The right of demand which has passed to the insurer shall be effectuated by him in compliance with the rules regulating relations between the insurant (or insured) and the person responsible for the losses.

3. An insurant (or insured) shall be obliged when receiving the insurance payment to transfer to the insurer all documents and evidence and to communicate to him all information necessary for the effectuation by the insurer of the right of demand which has passed to him.

4. If the insurant (or insured) has waived his right of demand against the person responsible for losses compensated by the insurer, or the effectuation of this right has become impossible through the fault of the insurant (or insured), the insurer shall be relieved from the effectuation of the insurance payment of in full or in respective part and shall have the right to demand the return of the amount of compensation paid in excess [Article as amended by Law of 18 December 2000, No. 128-II].

**Article 841. Termination of Contract of Insurance Before Time**

1. Besides the general grounds for the termination of obligations provided for by the present Code a contract of insurance shall be terminated before time in instances:

(1) when the object of insurance ceased to exist;

(2) the death of the insured who is not an insurant when a replacement did not occur (Article 815(8) of the present Code);

(3) alienation by the insurant of the object of property insurance if the insurer objects to replacement of the insurant and is not established otherwise by the contract or by legislative acts on obligatory insurance (Article 836(1) of the present Code);

(4) termination in the established procedure of entrepreneurial activity by an insurant who has insured his entrepreneurial risk or civil-law responsibility connected with this activity;

(5) when the possibility of the ensuing of the insured event has disappeared and the existence of the insured risk has terminated for circumstances other than the insured event;

(6) entry into legal force of a decision of a court concerning the compulsory liquidation of the insurer. In so doing the organization effectuating the guarantee of insurance payments under obligatory types of insurance shall fulfill its obligations under the contracts of insurance guaranteed by it in the procedure and within the periods which have been established by legislative acts of the Republic Kazakhstan [as amended by Law of 10 July 2003, No. 483-II].

(7) entry into force of a decision of an empowered agency concerning the issuance of authorization for the voluntary liquidation of an insurer [as amended by Law of 20 February 2006, No. 128-III].

In the said instances the contract shall be considered to be terminated from the moment of arising of circumstances provided for as grounds for the termination of the contract, of which the interested party must immediately notify the other.

1[1]. If an insurant under a contract of accumulative insurance dissolves it unilaterally within a period of from fourteen to thirty days from the date of conclusion of the contract, the insurer shall be obliged to return the amount of insurance premiums received to the insurant, deducting expenses not exceeding twenty percent of the amount of insurance premiums received incurred by the insurer when concluding the contract of accumulative insurance [added by Law of 20 February 2006, No. 128-III].

2. An insurant shall have the right to renounce the contract of insurance at any time [Article as amended by Law of 10 July 2003, No. 483-II].

**Article 842. Consequences of Termination of Contract of Insurance Before Time**

1. In the event of the termination before time of a contract of accumulative insurance with regard to circumstances provided for in Article 841(1) of the present Code, an insurer shall have the right to part of the insurance premium in proportion to the time during which the insurance operated.

In the event of the termination before time of a contract of accumulative insurance for a circumstances specified in Article 841(1), subpoints (6) and (7), of the present Code, the redemption amount in the amounts established by legislation shall be subject to return.

The return of insurance premiums (or contributions) in the event of the liquidation of an insurer shall be effectuated in accordance with the priority of satisfaction of demands of creditors established by legislation of the Republic Kazakhstan on insurance and insurance activity [point 1 as amended by Law oa 20 February 2006, No. 128-III].

2. In the event of the renunciation of the contract by an insurance (Article 841(2) of the present Code), if this is not connected with the circumstances specified in Article 841(1) and (1[1]) of the present Code, the insurance premium or insurance contributions paid to the insurer shall not be subject to return unless provided otherwise by the contract [point 2 as amended by Law of 20 February 2006, No. 128-III].

3. In instances when termination before time of a contract of insurance is caused by the failure to fulfill its conditions through the fault of the insurer, the last shall be obliged to return to the insurant the insurance premium paid by him or the insurance contributions in full [Article as amended by Law of 18 December 2000, No. 128-II].

**Article 843. Invalidity of Contract of Insurance**

1. Besides the general grounds of invalidity of transactions provided for by the present Code a contract of insurance shall be deemed to be invalid in instances of:

(1) at the moment of conclusion of the contract the object of insurance did not exist;

(2) unlawful property interests are the object of insurance (Article 807(2)) [as amended by Law of 20 February 2006, No. 128-III];

(3) property subject to confiscation on the basis of a respective decision which has entered into legal force or property acquired by criminal means or which is the subject of a crime is the object of insurance;

(4) an event is provided for an the insured event which lacks the indicia of probability and incidentalness of the ensuing thereof (Article 817(3) of the present Code) and which is inevitable and objectively must occur within the limits of operation of the contract, of which the parties or, at least, the insurant knowingly knew;

(5) an insurant when concluding a contract knowingly pursued the purpose of extracting unlawful advantage, including the conclusion of a contract after the ensuing of the insured event;

(6) [repealed by Law of 20 February 2006, No. 128-III];

(7) [repealed by Law of 20 February 2006, No.128-iII];

(8) consent is lacking of the insured in those instances when receiving the consent thereof is obligatory;

(9) the written form of the contract has not been complied with (Article 825(3) of the present Code).

2. Other grounds of deeming a contract to be invalid may be provided by legislative acts on obligatory insurance with regard to individual types of insurance.

**Article 844. Consequences of Deeming Contract of Insurance to be Invalid**

1. In the event of deeming a contract of insurance to be invalid an insurer shall be obliged to return to the insurant the insurance premium received therefrom or insurance contributions, and the insurant (or beneficiary) – to return to the insurer the insurance payment received from it.

If a contract is deemed to be invalid on the grounds which arose as a consequence of unlawful actions of the insurant, of which the insurer at the moment of conclusion of the contract and also in the process of performance thereof did not know and should not have known, the insurer shall also return to the insurant the insurance premium or instruction contributions for the unexpired period of the contract, deducting expenses incurred, and if an insurance payment was made – shall have the right to demand return of the paid amount.

The same consequences shall ensue in the event of deeming a contract of insurance to be invalid for the reasons giving grounds to the insurer to refuse the insurance payment (Article 839 of the present Code) [point 1 as amended by Law o 18 December 2000, No. 128-II].

If the contract of insurance was directed towards achieving a criminal purpose, the consequences shall be ensue provided for by Article 157(4)-(6) of the present Code.

**Article 845. Mutual Insurance**

1. Citizens and juridical persons may insure their property interests specified in Article 807(1) of the present Code on a mutual basis by means of combining in mutual insurance societies the means necessary for this [point 1 as amended by Law of 20 February 2006, No. 128-III].

2. The mutual insurance societies shall effectuate the insurance of property interests of their members and shall be noncommercial organizations.

The peculiarities of the effectuation of mutual insurance, the legal status of mutual insurance societies, and the conditions of their activity shall be determined in accordance with the present Code and by legislative acts on mutual insurance [point 2 as amended by Law of 20 February 2006, No. 128-III, and of 5 July 2006, No. 164-III].

3. Insurance of property interests of their members by mutual insurance societies shall be effectuated on the basis of membership and contracts of insurance [point 3 as amended by Laws of 20 February 2006, No. 128-III, and of 5 July2006, No. 164-III].

4. The effectuation of obligatory insurance by means of mutual insurance shall be permitted in the instances provided for by legislative acts on mutual insurance.

5. [repealed by Law of 20 February 2006, No. 128-III].

## *Chapter 41. Commission*

### Article 846. Contract of Commission

1. Under a contract of commission one party (the attorney) shall be obliged to perform in the name of and at the expense of another party (the principal) determined legal actions. The rights and duties with regard to the transaction concluded by the attorney shall arise directly with the principal.

2. A contract of commission shall be concluded in written form.

### Article 847. Performance of Commission in Accordance with Instructions of Principal

1. An attorney shall be obliged to perform the commission given to him in accordance with the instructions of the principal. The instructions of the principal must be specific, lawful, and practicable.

2. An attorney shall have the right to deviate from instructions of the principal if under the circumstances of the case this is necessary in the interests of the principal and the attorney could not inquire in advance of the principal or did not receive a timely reply to his enquiry. In this event an attorney shall be obliged to inform the principal about deviations permitted as soon as notice became possible.

3. By agreement of the parties a commercial representative may be relieved from the performance of a duty specified in point 2 of the present Article.

### Article 848. Duties of Attorney

An attorney shall be obliged to:

(1) personally perform the commission given to him;

(2) communicate to the principal at his demand all information concerning the course of the performance of the commission;

(3) transfer to the principal without delay everything received under the transaction;

(4) upon the performance of the commission return without delay the power of attorney to the principal, the period of operation of which has not expired, and submit a report with documents of justification appended, if this is required according to the character of the commission.

### Article 849. Duties of Principal

The principal shall be obliged, unless provided otherwise by the contract to:

(1) provide the attorney with means necessary for the performance of the commission;

(2) compensate the attorney for costs incurred which were necessary for performance of the commission.

2. The principal shall be obliged without delay to accept everything performed by the attorney in accordance with the contract.

3. The principal shall be obliged upon the performance of the commission to pay remuneration to the attorney in accordance with Article 850 of the present Code.

**Article 850. Remuneration in Contract of Commission**

1. The principal shall be obliged to pay remuneration to the attorney if this is provided for by legislative acts or the contract.

If a contract of commission is connected with the effectuation of entrepreneurial activity by both parties or one of them, the principal shall be obliged to pay remuneration to the attorney unless provided otherwise by the contract.

2. If the contract of legislative acts contain an indication of the compensatoriness of the fulfillment of a contract but do not specify the amount of remuneration, it shall be determined by taking into account the usually-accepted prices for services of such nature.

3. Remuneration shall be subject to payment also when at attorney proves that all required actions were duly performed, but the commission was not fulfilled not through his fault.

**Article 851. Transfer**

1. An attorney shall have the right to transfer the performance of a commission to another person (deputy) if this has been provided by the contract or if the attorney is forced to do so by circumstances for the purposes of protection of the interests of the principal.

2. An attorney who has transferred performance to another person shall be obliged immediately to notify the principal thereof. A principal shall have the right to remove the deputy chosen by the attorney except for instances when such deputy was named in the contract.

3. If a deputy of the attorney is named in the contract, the attorney shall not be liable for the conducting of affairs by his deputy.

4. If the conducting of affairs by a deputy has been provided in the contract, but the deputy is not named therein, the attorney shall not be liable for the guilty actions of his deputy.

5. If the conducting of affairs by the deputy of an attorney has not been provided in the contract, the attorney shall be liable for any actions of his deputy.

**Article 852. Termination of Contract of Commission**

1. A contract of commission shall be terminated, besides the general grounds of termination of obligations, as a consequence of:

(1) revocation of the commission by the principal;

(2) refusal of the attorney;

(3) death of the principal or attorney, deeming either of them to lack dispositive legal capacity, have limited dispositive legal capacity, or to be missing.

2. If the attorney did not know and should not have known about the termination of a contract of commission, his actions performed at the instruction of the principal shall oblige principal (or legal successor thereof) with respect to third persons and the attorney.

3. A party renouncing the contract with the attorney operating as an entrepreneur must inform the other party about the termination of the contract one month in advance unless a longer period has been provided for by the contract.

**Article 853. Consequences of Termination of Contract of Commission**

1. If a contract of commission is terminated before the commission is performed by the attorney in full, the principal shall be obliged to compensate the attorney for the costs incurred when performing the commission, and when remuneration was due to the attorney, also to pay remuneration to him commensurate with the work fulfilled by him. This rule shall not apply to the performance by the attorney of the commission after he knew or should have known about the termination of the commission.

2. The revocation of the commission by the principal shall not be grounds for compensation of losses due to the attorney by the termination of the contract, except for instances of termination of the contract with an attorney acting as an entrepreneur.

3. The refusal of the attorney to perform the commission of the principal shall not be grounds for the compensation of losses caused to the principal by the termination of the contract, except for instances of the refusal of an attorney in conditions when the principal is deprived of the possibility to otherwise ensure his interests, and also instances of the termination of a contract by an attorney acting as an entrepreneur.

**Article 854. Legal Succession in Contract of Commission**

1. In the event of the death of an attorney, his heirs or other persons on whom ensuring the preservation of inheritance property has been placed shall be obliged to notify the principal about the termination of the contract of commission and take measures necessary in order to protect the property of the principal, in particular, to preserve the things, and also the documents, of the principal, and them to him.

The same duty shall lie on the liquidator of a juridical person which is an attorney.

2. In the event of the reorganization of a juridical person operating as a representative the principal must be immediately informed about this in accordance with Article 48 of the present Code. In the said instance the rights and duties of such juridical person shall pass to the legal successor thereof unless the principal within a reasonable period communicates his renunciation of the contract.

*Chapter 42. Actions in Another's Interest Without Commission*

**Article 855. Conditions of Actions in Another's Interest**

1. Actions without a commission, other instruction, or consent of the interested person promised in advance for the purpose of preventing harm to his person or property, performance of his obligation or in his other not unlawful interests (actions in another's interest) must be performed by proceeding from

the obvious advantage or benefit and actual or probable intentions of the interested person and with the necessary concern and circumspection under the circumstances of the case.

2. The rules provided for by the present Chapter shall not apply to actions in the interest of other persons to be performed by State agencies for which such actions are one of the purposes of their activity.

**Article 856. Notification of Interested Person Concerning Actions in His Interest**

1. The person acting in another's interest shall be obliged at the first opportunity to notify the interested person thereof and await his decision within a reasonable period concerning approval or disapproval of the actions undertaken if only the waiting does not entail serious damage for the interested person.

2. It shall not be required to specially notify the interested citizen about actions in his interest if such actions are undertaken in his presence.

**Article 857. Consequences of Approval by Interested Person of Actions in His Interest**

If a person in whose interest actions are undertaken without his commission approves these actions, the rules concerning the contract of commission or other contract corresponding to the character of the actions undertaken, even if approval was oral, shall apply to relations of the parties thereafter.

**Article 858. Consequences of Failure of Interested Person to Approve Actions in His Interest**

1. Actions in another's interest performed after it became known to he who performed them that they are not approved by the interested person shall not entail for the last duties either with respect to those actions performed or with respect to third persons.

2. Actions for the purpose of preventing danger for the life of a person who has turned out to be in danger shall be permitted also against the will of this person, and performance of a duty with respect to the maintenance of someone – against the will of he on whom this duty lies.

**Article 859. Compensation of Losses to Person Who Acted in Another's Interest**

1. Necessary expenses and other real damage incurred by the person who acted in another's interest in accordance with the rules provided for by the present Chapter shall be subject to compensation by the interested person, except for expenses which were caused by the actions specified in Article 858(1) of the present Code.

The right to compensation of necessary expenses and other real damage shall also be preserved when the actions in another's interest did not lead to the result presupposed. However, in the event of the prevention of damage to the property of another person the amount of compensation must not exceed the value of the property.

2. Expenses and other losses of the person who acted in another's interest incurred by him in connection with actions which were undertaken after receiving the approval of the interested person (Article 857 of the present Code) shall be compensated according to the rules on the contract of the corresponding type.

**Article 860. Remuneration for Actions in Another's Interest**

The person whose actions in another's interest led to a positive result for the interested person shall have the right to receive remuneration if such right is provided for by legislative acts, agreement with the interested person, or the customs of business turnover.

**Article 861. Consequences of Conclusion of Transaction in Another's Interest**

Duties with regard to a transaction concluded in another's interest shall pass to the person in whose interests it was concluded on condition of the approval by him of this transaction and if the other party does not object to such transfer or when concluding the transaction knew or should have known that the transaction was concluded in another's interest.

In the event of the transfer of duties under the transaction to the person in whose interests it was concluded, to the last must be transferred also the rights with regard to this transaction.

**Article 862. Unfounded Enrichment as Consequence of Actions in Another's Interest**

If actions directly not directed towards ensuring the interests of another person, including in an instance when the person who performed them mistakenly presupposed that he acts in his own interest, led to the unfounded enrichment of the other person, the rules provided for by Chapter 48 of the present Code shall apply.

**Article 863. Compensation of Harm Caused by Actions in Another's Interest**

Relations with regard to compensation of harm caused by actions in another's interest to the interested person or to third persons shall be regulated by the rules provided for by Chapter 47 of the present Code.

**Article 864. Report of Person Who Acted in Another's Interest**

The person who acted in another's interest shall be obliged to submit to the person in whose interests such actions were effectuated a report specifying the revenues received and expenses incurred and other losses.

## *Chapter 43. Commission Agency*

**Article 865. Contract of Commission Agency**

1. Under a contract of commission agency, one party (commission agent) shall be obliged on behalf of another party (committent) to conclude for remuneration one or several transactions in his own name, but at the expense of the committent.

2. The contract of commission agency must be concluded in written form.

**Article 866. Commission Agency Remuneration**

The committent shall be obliged to pay remuneration to the commission agent, and in the event provided for by Article 868(2) of the present Chapter, also additional remuneration in the amount established in the contract. If the amount has not been provided for by the contract and can not be determined by proceeding from the conditions thereof, the amount of remuneration shall be established in accordance with Article 385(3) of the present Code.

If the contract of commission agency was not performed for reasons dependent upon the committent, the commission agent shall retain the right to the commission agency remuneration, and also to compensation for expenses incurred.

**Article 867. Rights and Duties of Commission Agent Under Transaction with Third Person**

1. Under a transaction concluded by a commission agent with a third person a commission agent shall acquire rights and come to be obliged even though the committent also was named in the transaction or entered with the third person into direct relations under the transaction.

2. With regard to a demand of the committent a commission agent shall be obliged to transfer rights under such transaction thereto, having notified the third person about the transfer with whom the transaction is concluded. The last shall not have the right to advance against demands of the committent objections based on his demands against the commission agent not arising from the particular transaction.

**Article 868. Performance of Commission Agency Commission**

1. A commission agent must fulfill all duties and effectuate all rights arising from the transaction concluded by him with a third person.

2. A commission agent shall be obliged to perform the commission assumed in accordance with the instructions of the committent, and in the absence of such instructions in the contract, in accordance with the customs of business turnover or other requirements ordinarily presented on conditions most advantageous for the committent. If the commission agent has concluded a transaction on conditions more advantageous than those which were specified by the committent, the advantage shall be divided between parties equally unless provided otherwise by the contract.

3. A commission agent shall not be liable to the committent for the failure to perform a transaction by a third peson concluded by him at the expense of the committent except for instances when the commission agent did not manifest necessary attentiveness in the selection of this person or assumed a guaranty for performance of the transaction (del credere).

4. In the event of a violation by a third person of a transaction concluded by the commission agent with him the commission agent shall be obliged immediately to inform the committent thereof and to collect and ensure the necessary evidence.

5. A committent notified about a violation by a third person of a transaction concluded with him by the commission agent shall have the right to demand the transfer of the demands of the commission agent against this person under such transaction.

**Article 869. Sub-Commission Agency**

1. Unless provided otherwise by the contract, the commission agent shall have the right to conclude a contract of sub-commission agency with another person while remaining responsible for the actions of the sub commission agent to the committent.

Under a contract of sub-commission agency, the commission agent shall acquire the rights and duties of the committent with respect to the sub-commission agent, except for the rights provided for by Article 867(2) of the present Code.

In instances when the conclusion of any transactions is permitted by legislative acts only by specially empowered persons, a contract of sub-commission agency may be concluded only with such person.

2. Until the termination of the contract of commission agency, the committent shall not have the right to enter into direct relations with the sub-commission agent, unless provided otherwise by the contract of the committent with the commission agent.

**Article 870. Deviation from Instructions of Committent**

1. The commission agent shall have the right to deviate from the instructions of the committent in the instances provided for by Article 847(2) of the present Code.

2. A commission agent who has sold property at a price lower than agreed with the committent shall be obliged to compensate the last for the difference unless it is proved that he had no possibility to sell the property at the agreed price and the sale for a lower price prevented more losses, and also that he did not have the possibility to receive the prior consent of the committent for the deviation from his instructions.

3. If the commission agent purchases property at a price higher than agreed with the committent, the committent, not wishing to accept such purchase, shall be obliged to declare this to the commission agent without delay upon receipt of notice thereof concerning the conclusion of a transaction with a third person. Otherwise, the purchase shall be deemed to be accepted by the committent.

If the commission agent communicates that he accepts the difference in price at his own expense, the committent shall not have the right to renounce the transaction concluded for him.

**Article 871. Rights to Property Which is Subject of Commission Agency**

1. Property which has ensued to the commission agent from the committent or acquired by the commission agency at the expense of the committent shall be the ownership of the committent.

2. A commission agent shall have the right to withhold property subject to transfer to the committent or to a third person under a transaction concluded by the commission agent until payment of the amounts due to him under the contract of commission agency.

**Article 872. Withholding by Commission Agent of Amounts Due Thereto**

A commission agent shall have the right to withhold amounts due to him under a contract of commission agency from all amounts which were received by him at the expense of the committent.

**Article 873. Responsibility of Commission Agent for Loss, Shortage, or Damage to Property of Committent**

1. A commission agent shall be liable to the committent for loss, shortage, or damage to the property of the committent situated with him.

2. If the commission agent accepts the property sent by the committent or which comes to the commission agent for the committent, and this property proves to be damaged or have other defects,

which may be noted from an external inspection, and also damage has been caused by someone to the property of the committent situated with the commission agent, the commission agent shall be obliged to take measures for the protection of the rights of the committent, to gather the necessary evidence, and immediately to notify the committent about everything. When fulfilling the said conditions the commission agent shall not be liable for losses of the committent.

3. A commission agent who has not insured property of the committent situated with him shall be liable for this only in instances when the committent instructed him to insure the property or the insuring of this property is obligatory by virtue of a law.

**Article 874. Transaction for Self**

1. Unless a committent has stipulated otherwise, a contract of commission agency may be effectuated by a commission agent so that he himself delivers a good as the seller which he must purchase or himself as the purchaser accepts the good which he must sell.

2. A commission agent who autonomously has delivered a good as a seller or accepted it as a purchaser shall have the right to usual commission agency fees and may submit an account with regard to compensation of expenses arising from commission agency transactions.

**Article 875. Acceptance by Committent of That Performed Under the Contract of Commission Agency**

The committent shall be obliged to:

(1) accept from the commission agent everything performed under the contract;

(2) inspect the property acquired for him by the commission agent and notify the last without delay about the defects discovered in this property;

(3) relieve the commission agent from obligations assumed by him to a third person with regard to the performance of the commission agency commission.

**Article 876. Compensation of Expenses for Performance of Commission Agency Commission**

1. The committent shall be obliged, in addition to payment of the commission agency remuneration, and in respective instances also additional remuneration for del credere, to compensate the commission agent for amounts expended by him for performance of the commission.

2. The commission agent shall not have the right to compensation of expenses for the keeping of property of the committent situated with him, unless established otherwise in legislative acts or in the contract.

**Article 877. Revocation of Commission by Committent**

The committent shall have the right at any time to revoke the particular commission to the commission agent. In so doing the losses caused by the revocation of the commission shall be compensated on the general grounds.

In the event of the revocation of the commission, the committent shall be obliged within a month to dispose of the property situated with the commission agent unless another period has been established by the contract. If the committent does not fulfill this duty, the commission agent shall have the right either to hand over the property for keeping or to sell it at the price as advantageous as possible for the committent.

**Article 878. Refusal of Commission Agent to Perform Commission**

1. A commission agent shall not have the right, unless provided otherwise by the contract, to refuse the performance of a commission accepted, except for instances when the violation by the committent of his duties entails the impossibility of performance of the commission in accordance with instructions of the committent or the impossibility of performance arises as a consequence of other circumstances for which the commission agent is not liable.

The commission agent shall be obliged to notify the committent in writing about the refusal and take measures to preserve the property of the committent situated with him.

The committent placed on notice concerning the refusal of the commission agent to perform the commission shall be obliged to dispose of property situated with the commission agent within a month from the day of receipt of the refusal unless another period is established by the contract. If he does not fulfill this duty, the commission agent shall have the right to either hand over the property for keeping or to sell it at the price as advantageous as possible for the committent.

3. A commission agent who has refused to perform a commission as a consequence of a violation by the committent of his duties shall retain the right to commission agency remuneration, and also to compensation of expenses incurred.

**Article 879. Termination of Contract of Commission Agency**

1. In the event of the revocation by the committent of all commission provided for by a contract of commission agency the contract shall terminate.

2. A contract of commission agency shall terminate, besides on the general grounds, as a consequence of:

(1) refusal of the commission agent to perform the contract;

(2) death of the commission agent, deeming him to lack dispositive legal capacity, limited dispositive legal capacity, or to be missing or to be insolvent (or bankrupt).

**Article 880. Renunciation by Committent of Contract Concluded Without Specification of Period**

A committent shall have the right at any time to renounce a contract of commission agency concluded with specification of a period, having notified the commission agent concerning the renunciation not later than one month unless a longer period for notification has been provided by the contract.

In this event the committent shall be obliged to pay the commission agent remuneration for transactions concluded by him before termination of the contract, and also to compensate the commission agent for expenses incurred by him before termination of the contract.

**Article 881. Renunciation by Commission Agent of Contract Concluded Without Specification of Period**

1. A commission agent shall have the right at any time to renounce a contract of commission agency concluded without specification of the period, having notified the committent concerning the refusal not later than one month unless a longer period of notification has been provided by the contract.

In this event the commission agent shall be obliged to take measures for the preservation of property of the committent situated with him. A committent shall be obliged until the moment of termination of the contract to dispose of the property situated with the commission agent. If he does not fulfill this duty, the commission shall have the right to hand over the property for keeping or to sell it as the price most advantageous for the committent.

2. A commission agent who has renounced the contract shall have the right to receive the commission agency remuneration and compensation of expenses due to him at the moment of termination of the contract.

**Article 882. Legal Succession in Contract of Commission Agency**

1. In the event of the reorganization of a juridical person-commission agent the rights and duties thereof shall pass to the legal successors unless within a month from the day of receipt of the notification concerning the reorganization which has occurred a committent does not communicate the dissolution of the contract.

2. In the event of the death of a committent-citizen, deeming thereof to lack dispositive legal capacity, to be of limited dispositive legal capacity, to be missing, and also in the event of the liquidation of a juridical person-committent the commission agent shall be obliged to continue performance of the commission given thereto until proper instructions are coming from the heirs or representatives of the committent.

## *Chapter 44. Trust Management of Property*

**Article 883. Concept and Grounds of Arising of Trust Management of Property** [as amended by Law of 12 January 2007, No. 225-III]

1. In the event of founding trust management of property the trustee manager shall be obliged to effectuate in his name the management of property transferred to his possession, use, and disposition unless provided otherwise by contract or legislative acts in the interests of the beneficiary.

2. Trust management of property shall arise (or be founded) on the basis of a:

(1) transaction (in particular, under a contract or under a will in which the executor of the will is appointed (trustee manager);

(2) judicial act (in the event of the appointment of a bankruptcy or rehabilitation manager in the procedures of bankruptcy, establishment of a trusteeship over property of a citizen lacking dispositive legal capacity, missing, or declared to be deceased and in other instances provided for by legislative acts);

(3) administrative act (when establishing a trusteeship over property of a minor or deceased; enrollment of an entrepreneur in State service, and in other instances provided for by legislative acts) [as amended by Law of 12 January 2007, No. 225-III].

**Article 884. Subjects of Trust Management of Property**

1. An owner, and also a subject of another right to a thing or competent agency empowered to transfer property to trust management, may be a founder.

2. Any person may be a trustee manager unless provided otherwise by legislative acts.

The appointment of a trustee manager may be made only with the consent thereof.

3. Any person who is not a trustee manager, and also the State or administrative-territorial entity, may be a beneficiary (or person in whose interests the management of property is effectuated).

4. Unless provided otherwise by legislative acts or by a contract of trust management of property the founder of the trust management of property shall be a beneficiary.

**Article 885. Objects of Trust Management of Property**

1. Any property, including money, securities, and property rights, unless provided otherwise by legislative acts, may be an object of trust management.

2. Trust property shall be subject to recording by the trustee manager separately from property belonging thereto by right of ownership (or economic jurisdiction, operative management).

3. Property acquired and/or received by the trustee manager in the process of the effectuation of duties placed on him shall be included in the composition of the trust property.

4. Levy of execution for debts of the founder against property transferred by him to trust management shall not be permitted except for instances provided for by Article 1081 of the present Code, and also the insolvency (or bankruptcy) of this person. In the event of bankruptcy of the founder the trust management of this property shall terminate, and it shall be included in the bankruptcy mass.

5. The transfer of pledged property to trust management shall not deprive the pledgeholder of the right to levy execution against this property.

**Article 886. Contract of Trust Management of Property**

1. Under a contract of trust management of property one party (founder of trust management) shall transfer to the other party (trustee manager) property in trust management, and the other party shall be obliged to effectuate the management of this property in the interests of the founder or person (beneficiary) specified by the founder.

During the period of operation of the contract of trust management of property the founder of trust management shall not have the right to effectuate any actions with respect to property in trust management unless established otherwise by legislative acts of the Republic Kazakhstan or by the said contract.

2. The contract of trust management of property must provide for:

(1) subject and period of the contract of trust management of property;

(2) composition of property being transferred to trust management;

(3) indication of the beneficiary;

(4) periods and form of report of trustee manager;

(5) indication of the person receiving trust property in the event of the termination of a contract of trust management of property.

For individual types of contract other material conditions also may be provided for by legislative acts.

A contract may provide also other conditions, including the amount and forms of remuneration for the manager.

The rights of third persons to property being transferred to trust management must be specified in the contract.

3. Norms concerning a contract of trust management of property shall extend to relations arising on other grounds of the establishment of trust management of property unless arises otherwise from legislative acts or the essence of relations which arose [Article as amended by Law of 16 May 2003, No. 416-II].

**Article 887. Form of Contract of Trust Management of Property**

1. A contract of trust management of property shall be concluded in written form.

2. A contract of trust management of immovable property shall be concluded in the form and procedure provided for the contract of alienation of immovable property.

The failure to comply with the form of the contract or the absence of registration of the contract for immovable property shall entail the invalidity thereof.

**Article 888. Rights and Duties of Trustee Manager**

1. The trustee manager shall have the right to perform any actions which the owner might perform with the trust property for the purpose of the proper management thereof.

The rights of a trustee manager to trust property may be limited by legislative acts, contract, or other act on the basis of which trust management of the property arose.

A trustee manager shall have the right to perform the alienation and pledge of immoveable property only in instances when this is expressly provided in the act on the founding of trust management.

2. A trustee manager shall have the right to compensation of necessary expenses made by him during the trust management of property at the expense of the founder (or beneficiary) or at the expense of the trust property, or at the expense of revenues from use of the trust property.

A trustee manager shall have the right to remuneration if this is provided for by the act on founding the trust management of property.

3. A trustee manager shall have the right to demand and obtain property entrusted thereto from another's illegal possession, and also to demand the elimination of a violation of his right to management even though these violations are not connected with a violation of possession.

4. A trust manager shall submit to the founder and beneficiary a report concerning his activity within the periods and in the procedure established by the contract of trust management of property. Upon the demand of the founder and/or beneficiary the report concerning the activity of the trust manager must be submitted immediately also in other instances.

5. A transaction concluded by a trustee manager with a violation of the limitations established for him shall be deemed to be invalid if third persons participating in the transaction did not know and should not have known about such limitations. In this event the trust manager shall bear responsibility to the founder in accordance with the contract and legislative acts.

Obligations under a transaction concluded by a trustee manager in excess of the powers granted to him or with a violation of the limitations established for him shall be borne by the trustee manager at the expense of his own property.

**Article 889. Transfer at Initiative of Trustee Manager**

1. The trustee manager shall effectuate trust management of property personally.

2. The trustee manager may charge another person to perform actions which are necessary for the management of the property entrusted to him if he is empowered to do so by the act concerning the founding of trust management of property, or is forced to do so by virtue of circumstances in order to ensure the interests of the beneficiary and does not have in so doing the possibility to request instructions of the founder. In so doing the trustee manager shall be liable for actions of the entrusted person he selected as though for his own.

The trustee manager shall be obliged at first possibility to notify the founder about the transfer. The founder, unless provided otherwise by legislative acts, in this event shall have the right to declare the termination of trust management of property, having compensated the trustee manager for expenses previously made, and if the trust management is entrepreneurial activity, also to compensate losses.

**Article 890. Responsibility of Trustee Manager**

1. In the event of the improper management of property the founder or beneficiary may present in court a demand concerning the termination of trust management and compensation of losses. In so doing the trustee manager shall be presupposed to be at fault in the improper performance of duties unless it is proved that he took all measures within his control for the proper performance of the duties.

2. The trust manager shall bear to third persons subsidiary responsibility with his property for losses caused by improper actions with regard to the management of property.

**Article 891. Termination of Contract of Trust Management of Property**

1. A contract of trust management of property shall, together with the general grounds, be terminated:

(1) by the death of a citizen-trustee manager who has been declared to be deceased, deeming thereof to lack dispositive legal capacity, be of limited dispositive legal capacity, or missing; or the liquidation of the juridical person-trustee manager;

(2) the renunciation of the trustee manager or founder in connection with the impossibility for the trustee manager personally to effectuate the management of the trust property;

(3) the refusal of the founder to perform the contract on condition of the payment to the trustee manager of losses and remuneration if it has been provided by the contract;

(4) the renunciation of the trustee manager in the event of the failure to communicate to him remuneration if it has been provided for by the contract.

2. The transfer of the right of ownership to trust property shall not terminate the trust management of the property.

3. In the event of the termination of a contract of trust management of property, the trust property shall be transferred to the person specified in the contract.

4. In the event of the bankruptcy of the founder the trust management of property shall be terminated and trust property shall be transferred to the bankruptcy mass.

In the event of the death of a natural person-founder the trust property shall go to the inheritance mass.

5. When terminating a contract at the initiative of one of the parties, the other party must be notified by not less than 3 months in advance (except for instances provided for by point 1, subpoints (2) and (4) of the present Article) unless provided otherwise by legislative acts or by the contract.

**Article 892. Trust Management of Stocks and Other Securities**

1. A trustee manager shall have the right to effectuate operations with stocks and other securities transferred to trust management and/or acquired at the expense of trust property or at the expense of revenues from the use of trust property.

2. Information concerning the trustee manager of emission securities shall be subject to reflection on the account of the founder of trust management open to professional participants of the securities market in the procedure established by legislation of the Republic Kazakhstan.

3. A trustee manager when managing stock(s) entrusted thereto shall unless provided otherwise by the act on founding the trust management of property:

(1) participate in the management of the joint-stock society;

(2) receive dividends due on the stocks and transfer them to the beneficiary;

(3) in the event of the liquidation of the joint-stock society receive property due for the stocks and transfer it in accordance with the contract to the beneficiary or founder;

(4) effectuate the alienation of stocks and other operations with them, including pledge.

4. The peculiarities of trust management of securities shall be established by legislation of the Republic Kazakhstan [Article as amended by Law of 16 May 2003, No. 416-II].

**Article 893. Trust Management of Assets of Investment Funds**

The peculiarities of trust management of assets of investment funds shall be effectuated on the conditions and in the procedure established by a legislative act of the Republic Kazakhstan on investment funds [as amended by Law of 7 July 2004, No. 577-II].

**Article 894. Trust Management of Enterprise as Property Complex**

Trust management of an enterprise as a property complex shall be effectuated on the conditions and in the procedure provided for by the act on founding trust management of property unless provided otherwise by legislative acts.

**Article 895. Trust Management of Property of State Employee**

The property of a State employee used for entrepreneurial activity shall be subject to transfer on trust management in the instances and in the procedure provided by legislative acts.

*Chapter 45. Integrated Entrepreneurial License (Franchising)*

**Article 896. Concept of Contract of Integrated Entrepreneurial License**

1. Under a contract of integrated entrepreneurial license one party (integrated licensor) shall be obliged to grant to the other party (integrated licensee) for remuneration a complex of exclusive rights (license complex) including, in particular, the right of use of the firm name of the licensor and protected commercial information, and also other objects of exclusive rights (trademark, service mark, patent, and so on) provided for by the contract for use in entrepreneurial activity of the licensee.

2. A contract of integrated entrepreneurial license shall provide for the use of the license complex, business reputation, and commercial experience of the licensor to a determined amount (in particular, with the establishment of a minimum and/or maximum amount of use), specifying or without specifying the territory of use applicable to the determined sphere of activity (sale of goods received from the licensor or produced by the user, effectuation of other commercial activity, fulfillment of work, and rendering of services).

3. Limitations with regard to the application of a contract of integrated entrepreneurial license in individual spheres of entrepreneurial activity shall be established by legislative acts.

**Article 897. Form of Contract of Integrated Entrepreneurial License**

A contract of integrated entrepreneurial license must be concluded in written form.

**Article 898. Duties of Licensor**

A licensor shall be obliged within the period and in the amount provided for by the contract to transfer to the licensee technical and commercial documentation and to submit other information necessary for the licensee to effectuate the rights granted thereto under the contract, and also to conduct the instruction and consulting of the licensee with regard to questions connected with the effectuation of these rights.

**Article 899. Duties of Licensee**

Unless provided otherwise by the contract, the licensee shall be obliged to:

(1) use when effectuating the activity provided for by the contract the license complex of the licensor in the way specified in the contract;

(2) admit the licensor to his production territory, submit to him necessary documentation and render assistance in obtaining information necessary for the effectuation of control over the proper use of the exclusive rights granted;

(3) comply with all instructions and directions of the licensor with respect to the character, means, and conditions of use of the exclusive rights transferred for use;

(4) not divulge secrets of production, of the licensor and other confidential commercial information received from him;

(5) inform purchasers (or customers) by a means most obvious for them of the fact that he is using a firm name, trademark, service mark, or other means of individualization on the basis of a contract of integrated entrepreneurial risk.

**Article 900. Limiting Conditions**

1. Limiting (or exclusive) conditions may be provided by a contract of integrated entrepreneurial license, in particular:

(1) obligation of the licensor not to issue analogous integrated entrepreneurial licenses for their use on the territory consolidated to the licensee or to refrain from direct autonomous activity on this territory;

(2) obligation of the licensor not to compete with the licensee on the territory of use of the integrated entrepreneurial license with respect to entrepreneurial activity effectuated by the licensee with the use of the exclusive rights belonging to the licensor;

(3) renunciation of the licensee to receive other integrated entrepreneurial licenses from competitors (or potential competitors) of the licensor;

(4) obligation of the licensee to agree with the licensor the location of premises to be used when effectuating exclusive rights granted under the contract, and also their external and internal formalization.

2. Limiting conditions of a contract of integrated entrepreneurial license shall be invalid by virtue of which:

(1) the licensor shall have the right to determine the price of sale of the good by the licensee or price of work (or services) to be fulfilled (or rendered) by the licensee, or to establish the upper or lower limit of the said prices;

(2) the licensee shall have the right to sell goods, fulfill work, or render services exclusively to a determined category of purchasers (or customers) or exclusively to purchasers (or customers) having a location (or place of residence) on a territory determined in the contract.

**Article 901. Responsibility of Licensor for Demands Presented to Licensee**

A licensor shall bear subsidiary responsibility for demands presented to the licensee concerning the failure of the good (or work, service) to conform to quality which are to be sold (or fulfilled, rendered) by the licensee under the contract of integrated entrepreneurial license.

**Article 902. Integrated Entrepreneurial Sublicense**

1. The right may be provided by a contract of integrated entrepreneurial license of the licensee to authorize the use of all or individual exclusive rights granted to him to other persons on conditions agreed by him with the licensor or determined in the contract.

2. The duty may be contained in the contract of integrated entrepreneurial license of the licensee to issue within a determined period of time a determined quantity of sublicenses with specification or without specification of the territory of the use thereof.

3. The rules of the basic contract of the licensor with the licensee shall apply to contracts of integrated entrepreneurial sublicense unless arises otherwise from the peculiarities of the contract of integrated entrepreneurial sublicense.

**Article 903. Dependence of Integrated Entrepreneurial Sublicense on Basic Contract of Licensor with Licensee**

1. A contract of integrated entrepreneurial sublicense may not be concluded for a longer period than the basic contract of the licensor with the licensee.

2. Termination of the contract of integrated entrepreneurial license shall terminate all contracts of integrated entrepreneurial sublicense concluded in accordance with them.

3. If the basic contract of the licensor with the licensee on the grounds provided for by legislative acts is invalid, the contracts of integrated entrepreneurial sublicense concluded in accordance with it also shall be invalid.

**Article 904. Peculiarities of Relations of Licensor, Licensee, and Sublicensee**

1. Unless provided otherwise by the contract of integrated entrepreneurial license, in the event of the termination thereof before time the rights and duties of the licensee under the contract of integrated entrepreneurial sublicense shall pass to the licensor.

2. A licensee shall bear subsidiary responsibility for harm caused to the licensor by the actions of sublicensees unless provided otherwise by the contract of integrated entrepreneurial license.

**Article 905. Preservation of Contract in Force in Event of Change of Firm Name**

In the event of a change by the licensor of its firm name the contract of integrated entrepreneurial license shall be preserved and operate with respect to the new firm name of the licensor unless the licensee demands dissolution of the contract and compensation of losses. In the event of the preservation of the operation of the contract the licensee shall have the right to demand commensurate reduction of the remuneration due to the licensor.

**Article 906. Preservation of Contract in Force in Event of Change of One or Several Exclusive Rights Transferred for Use**

In the event of a change by the licensor of one or several exclusive rights transferred for use, the contract of integrated entrepreneurial license shall be preserved and operate with respect to the new exclusive rights of the licensor unless the licensee demands dissolution of the contract and compensation of losses. In the event of preservation of the operation of the contract the licensee shall have the right to demand commensurate reduction of the remuneration due to the licensor.

**Article 907. Consequences of Termination of Exclusive Right Transferred for Use**

If within the period of operation of a contract of integrated entrepreneurial license the period of operation of any exclusive right within the complex transferred for use under the contract has expired, or such right was terminated on other grounds, the contract shall be preserved except for provisions relating to the right being terminated, and the licensee, unless provided otherwise by the contract, shall have the right to demand commensurate reduction of the remuneration due to the licensor.

**Article 908. Termination of Contract of Integrated Entrepreneurial License**

1. A contract of integrated entrepreneurial license concluded with a specification of the period may be dissolved in accordance with the rules of the present Code.

2. A party to a contract shall have the right to renounce a contract in perpetuity of an integrated entrepreneurial license, having notified the other party six months in advance, unless a longer period of notification has been provided by the contract.

**Article 909. Legal Succession in Contract of Integrated Entrepreneurial License**

1. The transfer to any person of any separate exclusive right within the license complex shall not be grounds for a change or dissolution of the contract. The new rightholder shall enter into the contract in the part of the rights and duties relating to the transferred exclusive right.

2. In the event of the death of a citizen-licensor, his rights and duties under a contract of integrated entrepreneurial license shall pass to the heir on condition that the last has been registered or within six months from the day of opening the inheritance is registered as an entrepreneur. Otherwise the contract shall terminate.

The management of a license complex during the period before acceptance by the heir of respective rights and duties or until registration of the heir as an entrepreneur shall be effectuated by a trustee manager appointed by a notary in the established procedure.

*Chapter 46. Competition Obligations*

**Article 910. Content of Competition Obligation**

1. Competition obligations arising from a public promise of remuneration and obligations arising on the basis of a tender, auction, or other forms of public sale established by legislative acts of the Republic Kazakhstan shall be regulated by the present Chapter.

Competition obligations may be regulated also by other legislative acts of the Republic Kazakhstan.

2. In a competition obligation the initiator thereof on the basis of a subject determined by him and initial conditions of the competition shall make a proposal to accept participation therein to an indefinite or definite group of persons and shall be obliged to pay the established remuneration to the winner of the competition and/or conclude with him the contract corresponding to the content of the competition obligation.

3. The proposal to take part in a competition may be made by the initiator of the competition directly or through an intermediary-organizer of the competition.

The rights and duties of the intermediary shall be determined by the contract thereof with the initiator of the competition.

4. A competition may be open when the proposal of the initiator of the competition to take part in the competition is addressed to all who wish by means of an announcement in the press and other mass media or closed, when the proposal to take part in the competition is sent to a determined group of persons at the choice of the initiator of the competition.

5. An open competition may be conditioned by a preliminary qualification of the participants thereof when a preliminary selection of persons who wished to take part in the competition is conducted by the initiator of the competition [Article as amended by Law of 21 May 2002, No. 323-II].

**Article 911. Public Promise of Remuneration**

1. Any person who has publicly announced the payment of remuneration in monetary or other form for the better fulfillment of work or achievement of other results must perform the obligation to the person who in accordance with the conditions of the competition deemed to be the winner thereof.

2. A public promise of remuneration must obligatorily contain conditions providing for the essence of the assignment, criteria and procedure for the submission of results, amount and form of remuneration, and also the procedure and periods of announcing the results.

3. A decision concerning payment of remuneration and the payment itself must be accepted and realized within the periods established by the promise.

4. If the competition is announced for the creation of a work of science, literature, or art, the person giving the public promise shall acquire a preferential right to conclude with the creator of the work a contract for the use thereof with payment of a royalty unless established otherwise by the public promise of remuneration.

5. A person who has given a public promise of remuneration shall be obliged to return the works not awarded remuneration to the creators thereof unless provided otherwise by the conditions of the competition.

**Article 912. Revocation of Public Promise of Remuneration**

1. A person who has announced publicly the payment of remuneration shall have the right in the same form to retract the promise given except for instances when in this announcement it is provided or the inadmissibility of a retraction arises from it or a determined period has been given for the performance of an action for which the remuneration is promised, or at the moment of the announcement concerning the retraction one of the persons being revoked has already fulfilled the actions specified in the announcement.

2. Revocation of a public promise of remuneration shall not relieve he who announced the remuneration from compensating the person being revoked for expenses incurred by him in connection with the performance of the action provided for by the announcement. The amount of compensation in all instances may not exceed the remuneration specified in the announcement.

**Article 913. Peculiarities of Conducting Lotteries, Totalizers, and Other Games**

1. Relations between the State, administrative-territorial entity, or person who has received a license from an empowered State agency for conducting a lottery, totalizers, and other games based on risk

with a participant of these games based on a contract. Such contract shall be formalized by the issuance of a lottery ticket, receipt, or other document and shall be deemed to be concluded from the moment of payment by the participant of games of the cost of the lottery ticket or other payment for participation in the game.

2. Persons who in accordance with the conditions of conducting the lottery, totalizer, or other games are deemed to be winners must be paid by the initiator (or organizer) of the games the winnings in the amount, form (monetary or in kind), and periods provided for by the conditions of conducting the games, and if the period was not specified in these conditions – not later than ten days from the moment of totaling up the results of the games.

3. In instances of the failure of the initiator (or organizer) of the games to perform the duty specified in point 2 of the present Article, the participant who has won in the lottery, totalizer, or in other games shall have the right to demand the payment of winnings to him, and also compensation for losses due thereto.

**Article 914. Demands Connected with Conducting Games and Betting and Participation Therein**

Demands of citizens and juridical persons connected with the organization and conducting of games or betting based on risk (gambling and betting), or with the participation therein, shall not be subject to judicial defense except for demands arising from relations specified in Article 913 of the present Code.

**Article 915. Tender**

1. In the event of competition public sales in the form of a tender the initiator (or organizer) thereof shall be obliged on the basis of initial conditions proposed by him to conclude a contract (as seller, purchaser, customer, independent-work contractor, lessor, lessee, and so on) with he of the participants of the tender who proposes the best conditions of a contract for the initiator of the tender.

2. The participants of the tender within the limits of the periods established by the conditions thereof shall send to the initiator of the tender or organizer thereof their proposals in written form with all documentation stipulated by the tender appended. The sending of proposals in sealed envelopes and under symbols may be provided for by the conditions of the tender.

A violation of the periods for filing proposals shall entail exclusion of the person who permitted lapse of the period from among the participants of the tender unless the initiator or organizer thereof notifies this person in writing about admittance to participation in the tender.

3. The selection of a winner of a tender from among the participants thereof shall be made by the initiator of the tender or tender commission created by him in a closed or, according to the conditions of the tender, open procedure.

4. A tender may be deemed by the initiator to be unconstituted if less than two participants took part therein or the proposals of the participants of the tender were deemed by the initiator to not satisfy the conditions of the tender.

5. The initiator thereof shall conclude a respective contract with the winner of the tender. In the event of the refusal of the initiator of the tender to conclude a respective contract with the winner, the winner of the tender shall have the right to recover losses caused to him.

6. The making by each participant of a tender of a guarantee contribution which shall be returned to participants after totaling up the results of the tender may be provided by the conditions of the tender. The guarantee contribution shall not be returned if the participant of the tender retracts his proposal or changes it before the expiry of the period of the tender.

A guarantee contribution shall not be returned to the winner of the tender in the event of the refusal of the winner to conclude a respective contract with the initiator of the tender on the conditions meeting the proposal of the winner of the tender.

**Article 916. Auction**

1. In the event of competition public sales in the form of an auction the seller shall be obliged to sell the subject of the auction to that participant of the auction who proposes the highest price for it.

2. An auction may be conducted on conditions of raising or lowering the price from that declared by the seller.

3. A minimum price for which the subject may be sold may be provided for by the conditions of an auction conducted by lowering the price.

4. Any moveable or immoveable property not withdrawn from civil turnover, including objects of intellectual property, contracts and property rights, including import, export, and other quotas and licenses, may be the subject of an auction.

5. Proposals concerning participation in an auction must contain information concerning the subject of the auction and the place and time of conducting it.

6. Persons who wished to take part in an auction must before the commencement of the auction, unless established otherwise by the conditions of conducting it, submit an application to participate in the auction and make the established amount of auction contribution.

7. An auction may be constituted if not less than two participants (or purchasers) take part therein.

8. If none of the participants thereof wished to acquire the subject of an auction, the initial price may be reduced or the subject of the auction removed from the particular auction.

9. Unless established otherwise by the conditions of an auction, a contract concerning the sale thereto of the subject of an auction shall be concluded with the participant of the auction who proposed the highest price.

10. If the purchaser refused to conclude a contract provided for by point 9 of the present Article he shall be excluded from among the participants of the auction, the guarantee contribution shall not be returned to him, and the subject of the auction from the acquisition of which the purchaser refused may be again offered for public sale.

11. The amount of the guarantee contribution shall be returned to persons who took part in the auction but purchased nothing at it.

The amount of the guarantee contribution shall be set off on the account of the purchase price paid to persons who purchased any of the articles of the auction.

## *Chapter 47. Obligations Arising as a Consequence of Causing Harm*

### *§1. General Provisions*

**Article 917. General Grounds of Responsibility for Causing of Harm**

1. Harm (property and/or nonproperty) caused by unlawful actions (or failure to act) to property and nonproperty benefits and rights of citizens and juridical persons shall be subject to compensation in full by the person who caused the harm.

The duty of compensation of harm may be placed by legislative acts on a person who is not the causer, and also a higher amount of compensation established.

2. A person who has caused harm shall be relieved from compensation thereof if it is proved that the harm was caused not through his fault, except for instances provided for by the present Code.

3. Harm caused by lawful actions shall be subject to compensation in the instances provided for by the present Code and other legislative acts.

**Article 918. Prevention of Causing of Harm**

1. The danger of causing harm in the future may be grounds for a suit concerning the prohibition of actions creating such a danger.

2. If the harm caused is the consequence of the operation of an enterprise, installation, or other production activity which continues to cause harm or threatens new harm, a court shall have the right to oblige the defendant, in addition to compensation of harm, to suspend or terminate the respective activity.

A court may reject a suit concerning the termination of the respective activity only if the termination thereof is contrary to social interests. The refusal to terminate such activity shall not deprive the victim of the right to compensation for the harm caused by this activity.

**Article 919. Causing Harm in State of Necessary Defense**

Harm caused in a state of necessary defense, unless the limits thereof were exceeded, shall not be subject to compensation.

**Article 920. Causing Harm in State of Extreme Necessity**

Harm caused in a state of extreme necessity, that is, in order to eliminate a danger threatening the causer of the harm himself or other persons, if this danger under the given circumstances could not be eliminated by other means, must be compensated by the person who caused the harm.

Taking into account the circumstances under which such harm was caused, a court may place the duty of compensating it on a third person in whose interests the causer of the harm acted or on this third person and the causer of harm by way of participatory shares, and also relieve both this third person and the causer of the harm fully or partially from compensation of the harm.

**Article 921. Responsibility of Juridical Person or Citizen for Harm Caused by Worker Thereof**

1. A juridical person or citizen shall compensate harm caused by a worker thereof when performing labor (or employment, official) duties.

2. With regard to the provisions of the present Chapter concerning obligations as a consequence of causing harm, workers shall be deemed to be citizens fulfilling work on the basis of a labor contract, and also on the basis of a civil-law contract, if in so doing they acted or should have acted under an assignment and under the control of the respective juridical person or citizen for the safe conducting of work [as amended by Law of 15 May 2007, No. 253-III].

Economic partnerships, joint-stock societies, and production cooperatives shall compensate harm caused by their participants (or members) when the last effectuate entrepreneurial, production, or other activity of the partnership or cooperative.

**Article 922. Responsibility for Harm Caused by State Agencies, Agencies of Local Self-Government, and Also the Officials Thereof**

1. Harm caused as a result of the publication by State agencies of acts not corresponding to legislative acts shall be subject to compensation on the basis of a decision of a court irrespective of the fault of the agencies and officials who issued the act. Harm shall be compensated at the expense of the State treasury. Financial agencies or other agencies and citizens by special assignment shall act as the representative of the treasury.

2. Agencies of local self-government shall be liable for harm caused by the agencies and officials thereof in a judicial proceeding.

3. Harm caused by illegal actions (or failure to act) of officials of State agencies in the domain of administrative management shall be compensated on the general grounds (Article 917 of the present Code) at the expense of money at the disposition of these agencies. In the event of the insufficiency thereof, harm shall be compensated subsidiarily at the expense of the State treasury.

**Article 923. Responsibility for Harm Caused by Illegal Actions of Agencies of Inquiry or Preliminary Investigation, Procuracy, and Court**

1. Harm caused to a citizen as a result of the illegal conviction, illegal bringing to criminal responsibility, illegal application of confinement under guard, house arrest, or written undertaking not to leave as a measure of restraint, or the illegal imposition of an administrative sanction in the form of arrest or correctional tasks, illegal placement in a psychiatric or other treatment institution shall be compensated by the State in full irrespective of the fault of the officials of the agencies of inquiry or preliminary investigation, procuracy, and court in the procedure established by legislative acts.

2. Harm caused to a citizen or juridical person as a result of other illegal activity of agencies of inquiry or preliminary investigation, and procuracy shall be compensated on the grounds and in the procedure which has been provided for by Article 922 of the present Code.

3. The harm caused by the illegal actions (or failure to act) by a judge and other workers of a court when effectuating justice, except for instances provided for by point 1 of the present Article, shall be compensated on the general grounds and in the procedure established by Article 922(3) of the present Code.

**Article 924. Compensation of Harm by Person Who Has Insured His Responsibility**

A juridical person or citizen who has insured his responsibility by way of voluntary or obligatory insurance, when the insured amount is insufficient for the full compensation of the harm caused, shall compensate the difference between the insured amount and the actual amount of damage.

**Article 925. Responsibility for Harm Caused by Minors Up to Fourteen Years of Age**

1. For harm caused by a minor who has not attained fourteen years of age (youth) his parents (or adoptive parents) or trustees shall be liable unless it is proved that the harm arose not through their fault.

2. If a youth who needs trusteeship is situated in a respective nurturing or treatment institution, institution for the social defense of the population, or other analogous institution which by virtue of a law is his trustee, this institution shall be obliged to compensate the harm caused by the youth unless it is proved that the harm arose not through the fault thereof.

3. If a youth has caused harm at the time when he was under the supervision of an educational, nurturing, treatment, or other institution obliged to effectuate supervision over him, and also a person obliged to effectuate supervision on the basis of a contract, this institution and person shall be liable for the harm unless it is proved that the harm arose not through their fault in effectuating the supervision.

4. The duty of the parents (or adoptive parents), trustees, educational, nurturing, treatment, and other institutions relating to compensation of harm caused to a youth shall not terminate with the attainment by the youth of majority or receipt by him of property sufficient to compensate the harm.

If the parents (or adoptive parents) or trustees have died or they, as well as other citizens specified in point 3 of the present Article, do not have sufficient means in order to compensate the harm caused to the life or health of the victim, and the causer himself having full dispositive legal capacity possesses such means, the court shall have the right, taking into account the property status of the victim and the causer of the harm, and also other circumstances, to adopt a decision concerning compensation of harm fully or partially at the expense of the causer of the harm himself.

**Article 926. Responsibility for Harm Caused by Minors in Age from Fourteen to Eighteen Years**

1. A minor from fourteen to eighteen years of age shall bear responsibility on the general grounds autonomously for harm caused.

2. In an instance when a minor from fourteen to eighteen years of age has no property or other sources of revenues sufficient to compensate harm, the harm must be compensated fully or in the insufficient part by his parents (or adoptive parents) or guardian unless they prove that the harm arose not through their fault.

If a minor from fourteen to eighteen years of age who needs guardianship is situated in a respective nurturing or treatment institution, institution for the social defense of the population, or other analogous institution which by virtue of a law is his guardian, these institutions shall be obliged to compensate the harm fully or in the insufficient part unless it is proved that the harm arose not through its fault.

3. The duty of parents (or adoptive parents), guardian, and respective institution with regard to the compensation of harm shall terminate upon the attainment of majority by the causer of the harm or when upon attaining majority he has property and other sources of revenues sufficient to compensate the harm or when he before attaining majority has acquired dispositive legal capacity (Article 17(2), Article 22[1] of the present Code).

**Article 927. Responsibility of Parents Deprived of Parental Rights for Harm Caused by Minors**

A court may place on a parent deprived of parental rights responsibility for harm caused by the minor children thereof for three years after the deprivation of the parent of parental rights if it is established that the behavior of the child which entailed the causing of the harm was a consequence of the improper effectuation of parental duties with regard to nurturing the child.

**Article 928. Responsibility for Harm Caused by Citizen Deemed to Lack Dispositive Legal Capacity**

1. Harm caused by a citizen deemed to lack dispositive legal capacity (Article 26 of the present Code) shall be compensated by his trustee or the organization obliged to effectuate supervision over him unless they prove that the harm arose not through their fault.

2. The duty of a trustee or the organization with regard to compensation of harm caused by a citizen deemed to lack dispositive legal capacity shall not terminate also in the event of the restoration of his dispositive legal capacity.

3. If the trustee is deceased or does not have sufficient means for the compensation of harm, and the causer of harm himself possesses such means, the court shall have the right, taking into account the property status of the victim and the causer of the harm, and also other circumstances, in particular the restoration of the dispositive legal capacity of the causer of harm, to adopt a decision concerning compensation of harm caused to life and health of the victim fully or partially at the expense of the causer of the harm himself.

**Article 929. Responsibility for Harm Caused by Citizen Deemed to Have Limited Dispositive Legal Capacity**

Harm caused by a citizen limited in dispositive legal capacity as a consequence of the abuse of alcoholic beverages or narcotic substances (Article 27 of the present Code) shall be compensated by the causer of the harm himself on the general grounds.

**Article 930. Responsibility for Harm Caused by Citizen Not Capable of Understanding Significance of His Actions**

1. A citizen who has dispositive legal capacity, and also a minor from fourteen to eighteen years of age, who has caused harm in such a state that he could not understand the significance of his actions or direct them shall not be liable for the harm caused by him.

If harm is caused to the life or health of the victim, the court may, taking into account the property status of the victim and the causer of the harm, and also other circumstances, place the duty with regard to compensation of harm fully or partially on the causer of the harm.

2. The causer of harm shall not be relieved from responsibility if he has brought himself into such a state by the use of alcoholic beverages, narcotic substances, or other means.

3. If the harm was caused by a person who could not understand the significance of his actions or direct them as a consequence of mental disturbance or feeble-mindedness, the duty to compensate the harm may be placed by a court on those residing jointly with this person who have labor capacity: a spouse, parents, or children who have reached majority and who knew about such state of the causer of the harm but did not raise the question of deeming him to lack dispositive legal capacity and instituting a trusteeship over him.

**Article 931. Responsibility for Harm Caused by Activity Creating Increased Danger for Surrounding Persons (Source of Increased Danger)**

1. Juridical persons and citizens whose activity is connected with an increased danger for surrounding persons (transport organizations, industrial enterprises, construction sites, possessors of means of transport, and others) shall be obliged to compensate the harm caused by a source of increased danger unless it is proved that the harm arose as a consequence of insuperable force or the intent of the victim.

The duty of compensation of harm shall be placed on the juridical person or citizen who possesses the source of increased danger by right of ownership, right of economic jurisdiction, or right of operative management, or any other legal basis (contract of property rental, power of attorney for the right to drive means of transport, by virtue of the regulation of a respective agency concerning the transfer of the source, and the like).

2. The possessors of sources of increased danger shall bear joint and several responsibility for harm caused as a result of the interaction of sources (collision of means of transport, and so on) to third persons on the grounds provided for by point 1 of the present Article.

The harm caused as a result of the interaction of the sources of increased danger to their possessors shall be compensated on the general grounds. In so doing:

(1) harm caused through the fault of one party shall be compensated in full to this party;

(2) harm caused through the fault of both or several parties shall be compensated commensurately with the degree of fault of each of them.

In the event of the impossibility to establish the degree of fault of each of the parties, responsibility shall be distributed among them equally.

In the absence of fault of the parties in causing harm neither of them shall have the right to demand compensation of harm. Each of the parties shall bear in this event the risk of losses incurred by it

3. The possessor of a source of increased danger shall not be liable for harm caused by this source if it is proved that the source left the possession of the possessor as a result of the unlawful actions of other persons. Responsibility for harm caused by a source of increased danger shall be borne in such instances who unlawfully possessed the source. When there is fault of the possessor in the unlawful removal from his possession of a source of increased danger responsibility may be placed both on the possessor and on the persons who took possession of the source of increased danger.

**Article 932. Responsibility for Jointly Caused Harm**

Persons who have caused harm jointly shall be liable to the victim jointly and severally.

Upon the application of the victim and in his interests a court shall have the right to place on the persons who have caused harm jointly responsibility in participatory shares.

**Article 933. Right of Regression Against Person Who Caused Harm**

1. The person who has compensated harm caused by another person (or by a worker when performing his labor (or employment, official) duties, by a person driving means of transport, and so forth) shall have the right of counter demand (regression) against this person in the amount of the compensation paid unless another amount has been established by legislative acts.

2. The causer of harm who has compensated harm jointly caused shall have the right to demand from each of the other causers of harm a participatory share of the compensation paid to the victim in the amount corresponding to the degree of fault of this causer of harm. If it is impossible to determine the degree of fault, the participatory shares shall be deemed to be equal.

3. The State which has compensated harm caused by officials of agencies of inquiry or preliminary investigation, the procuracy, or a court (Article 923(1) of the present Code) shall have the right of regression against these persons in instances when the fault of such persons has been established by the judgment of a court which has entered into legal force.

4. The persons who have compensated harm on the grounds specified in Articles 925-928 of the present Code shall not have the right of counter-demand (regression) against the person who caused the harm.

**Article 934. Means of Compensation of Property Harm**

In satisfying the demand concerning compensation of harm, the court in accordance with the circumstances of the case shall oblige the person responsible for the harm to compensate the losses caused in full or to compensate it in kind (to provide a thing of the same kind and quality, to rectify a damaged thing, and so forth).

**Article 935. Taking Account of Fault of Victim and Property Status of Person Who Caused Harm**

1. Harm which arose as a consequence of the intent of the victim shall not be subject to compensation.

2. If the gross negligence of the victim himself furthered the arising or the increasing of the harm, depending on the degree of fault of the victim and the causer of the harm the amount of compensation must be reduced.

3. In the event of gross negligence of the victim and the absence of fault of the causer of the harm in instances when his responsibility ensues irrespective of fault, the amount of compensation must be reduced or compensation of harm may be refused unless provided otherwise by legislative acts. In the event of causing harm to the life or health of a citizen, the complete refusal of compensation shall not be permitted.

4. The fault of the victim shall not be taken into account when compensating additional expenses (Article 937 of the present Code), when compensating harm to persons who have incurred damage as a result of the death of a citizen (Article 940 of the present Code), and also when compensating expenses for burial (Article 946 of the present Code).

5. A court may reduce the amount of compensation of harm caused by a citizen by taking into account his property status, except for instances when the harm was caused by actions committed intentionally.

*§2. Compensation of Harm Caused to Life and Health of Citizen*

**Article 936. Compensation of Harm Caused to Life or Health of Citizen When Performing Contractual and Other Obligations**

Harm caused to the life or health of a citizen when performing contractual obligations, labor (or employment) duties, and duties of military service shall be compensated according to the rules of the present Chapter unless a higher responsibility has been provided by legislative acts or by contract.

**Article 937. Amount and Character of Compensation of Harm Which Caused Impairment of Health**

1. When mutilation or other impairment of health is caused to a citizen, the earnings (or revenue) lost by the victim which he had or could be determined to have, and also expenses caused by the impairment of health (for treatment, additional nourishment, acquisition of medicines, prosthetics, outside care, sanatorium-resort treatment, the acquisition of special means of transport, and training for another profession, and so on) shall be subject to compensation if it is deemed that the victim needs these types of assistance and care and does not receive them free of charge.

2. When determining lost earnings (or revenue), the disability pension assigned to the victim in connection with the mutilation or other impairment of health, other types of benefits assigned both before and after the causing of harm to health, and also pension payments at the expense of compensation shall not be set-off. Earnings received by the victim after the impairment of health also shall not be set-off at the expense of compensation of harm.

3. The extent and amount of compensation of harm due to the victim in accordance with the present Article may be increased by legislative acts or by a contract.

**Article 938. Determination of Earnings (or Revenue) Lost as Result of Impairment of Health**

1. The amount of earnings (or revenue) lost which is subject to compensation shall be determined in percentages of his average monthly earnings (or revenue) before the mutilation or other impairment of health or before the ensuing of the loss of labor capacity, of the respective degree of loss by the victim of professional capacity to labor, and in the absence thereof, general capacity to labor.

2. Within lost earnings (or revenue) shall be included all types of payment for labor under labor and civil-law contracts both at the principal place of work and second jobs levied with income tax. Payments of a one-off character (contributory compensation for unused leave, severance benefit in the event of dismissal, and others) shall not be taken into account. The benefit paid for the period of temporary lack of labor capacity or pregnancy and birth leave shall be taken into account. Revenues from entrepreneurial activity, and also author's royalty, shall be included in the lost earnings, the revenues from entrepreneurial activity being included on the basis of tax agency data.

All types of earnings (or revenue) shall be taken into account in the amounts credited before the withholding of taxes.

3. The average monthly earnings (or revenue) shall be calculated by means of dividing the total amount of his earnings (or revenue) for the twelve months of work which preceded the impairment of health or ensuing of the loss of labor capacity by twelve. In an instance when the victim at the time of causing the harm worked less than twelve months, the average monthly earnings (or revenue) shall be calculated by means of dividing the total amount of earnings (or revenue) for the number of months actually worked which preceded the impairment of health by the number of these months.

Months not worked in full by the victim shall at his wish be replaced by the preceding months fully worked or by excluding them from the calculation when it is impossible to substitute them.

4. In an instance when the victim at the moment of causing of the harm was not working, the earnings before dismissal or the usual amount of remuneration of a worker of his qualifications in the particular locality shall, at his wish, be taken into account, but not less than ten time the monthly account indicator established by legislative acts.

5. If stable changes improving his financial status (increase of earnings in the post held, he was transferred to higher-paid work, took up the job after completing an educational institution, and in other instances when the stability of the change or possibility of change of payment of labor of the victim is proved) occurred in the earnings (or revenue) of the victim before the mutilation or other impairment of health was caused to him, when determining his average monthly earnings (or revenue) only the earnings (or revenue) which he received or should have received after the respective changes shall be taken into account [Article as amended by Law of 24 December 2001, No. 276-II].

**Article 939. Compensation of Harm in Event of Impairment of Health of Person Who Has Not Attained Majority**

1. In the event of the mutilation or other impairment of health of a minor who has not attained fourteen years and does not have earnings, the persons responsible for the harm shall be obliged to compensate the expenses connected with the impairment of health.

2. Upon the attainment of fourteen years by a victim, and also in the event of the causing of harm to a minor of from fourteen to eighteen years in age who does not have earnings (or revenue), the persons responsible for the harm shall be obliged to compensate the victim for, in addition to the expenses caused by the impairment of health, also the harm connected with the loss of or reduction of his labor capacity by proceeding from ten times the monthly account indicator established by legislative acts.

If at the moment of the impairment to health a minor had earnings, the harm shall be compensated by proceeding from the amount of these earnings, but not lower than ten times the monthly account indicator established by legislative acts.

After the commencement of labor activity a victim shall have the right to demand an increase of compensation of harm by proceeding from the earnings received by him, but not lower than the amount of remuneration established for the post occupied by him or the earnings of a worker of the same qualifications at his place of work.

**Article 940. Compensation of Harm to Persons Who Have Incurred Damage as Result of Death of Citizen**

1. In the event of the death of a citizen the right to compensation of harm shall be had by persons who were dependent on the deceased or had on the day of his death the right to receive maintenance from him; a child of the deceased born after his death; and also one of the parents, spouse, or other member of the family, irrespective of labor capacity, who does not work and cares for the children, grandchildren, brothers and sisters who had not attained fourteen years who were dependent on him or although they had attained the said age but in the opinion of medical agencies need outside care by reason of their state of health.

2. Persons dependent on the deceased citizen and who come to lack labor capacity within 5 years after his death also shall have the right to compensation.

One of the parents, spouse, or other member of the family who does not work and cares for children, grandchildren, brothers, and sisters of the deceased specified in point 1 of the present Article and came to lack labor capacity during the period of effectuating care shall retain the right to compensation of harm after ending the care of these persons.

3. The harm shall be compensated to: a minor – until attaining eighteen years of age; pupils eighteen years of age and older – until completion of study in day educational institutions, but not more than up to twenty-three years of age; women older than fifty-eight years and men older than sixty-three years – for life; disabled persons – for the period of disability; one of the parents, spouse, or other member of the family engaged in caring for children, grandchildren, brothers, and sisters dependent on the deceased – until they attain fourteen years of age or the state of health changes.

**Article 941. Amount of Compensation of Harm Incurred in Event of Death of Citizen**

1. Harm shall be compensated to persons who have the right to compensation for harm in connection with the death of a citizen in the amount of that participatory share of earnings (or revenue) of the deceased calculated according to the rules of Article 938 of the present Code which they have received or had the right to receive for their maintenance during his life. When determining the compensation for harm to these persons within the revenues of the deceased, together with earnings shall be included a pension, maintenance for life, and other similar payments being received by them while alive.

2. When determining the amount of compensation for harm, benefits assigned to persons in connection with the death of a breadwinner, other types of benefits assigned both before and after the death of a breadwinner, and also earnings, stipend, and pension benefits shall not be taken into account.

3. The amount of compensation established for each of those having the right to compensation for the loss of a breadwinner shall not be subject to further recalculation except for instances of the birth of a child after the death of a breadwinner; the assignment (or termination) of the payment of compensation to persons caring for children, grandchildren, brothers, and sisters of a deceased breadwinner.

The extent and amount of compensation may be increased by a legislative act or by a contract.

**Article 942. Change of Amount of Compensation of Harm**

1. A victim who has partially lost labor capacity shall have the right at any time to require from the person on whom the duty of compensation of harm has been placed a respective increase of the amount of his compensation if his labor capacity has decreased in connection with the causing of impairment of health in comparison with that which remained at the moment of awarding compensation for harm to him.

2. Persons on whom the duty to compensate harm has been placed which was connected with the impairment of health of the victim shall have the right to demand a respective reduction of the amount of compensation if the labor capacity of the victim increased in comparison with that which he had at the moment compensation for harm was awarded.

3. The victim shall have the right to demand an increase of the amount of compensation of harm if the property status of the citizen on whom the duty to compensate harm was placed has improved, and the amount of compensation was reduced in accordance with Article 935(5) of the present Code.

4. A court may at the demand of a citizen who caused harm reduce the amount of compensation for harm if his property status in connection with disability or attainment of pension age was worsened in comparison with the status at the moment of awarding compensation for harm (Article 935(5) of the present Code).

**Article 943. Increase of Compensation of Harm in Connection with Increased Cost of Living and Increase of Monthly Account Indicator**

Amounts of compensation for harm to be paid to citizens in connection with impairment of health or death of a victim shall be subject to indexation in the procedure established by legislative acts in the event of an increase of the cost of living.

In the event of an increase in the procedure established by legislative acts of the minimum amount of earnings, the amounts of compensation for lost earnings (or revenue) and other payments awarded in connection with impairment of health and death of the victim shall be increased in proportion to the increase of the monthly account indicator (Article 283 of the present Code).

**Article 944. Payments for Compensation of Harm**

1. Compensation of harm connected with a reduction of labor capacity or the death of a victim shall be made by monthly payments.

When there are justifiable reasons, the court, taking into account the possibilities of the causer of harm, may at the demand of the citizen who has the right to compensation award him the payments due as a single payment, but for not more than three years.

2. Additional expenses may be recovered for a future period within the limits of periods established on the basis of an opinion of a medical expert examination, and also when preliminary payment is necessary for the cost of services and property (acquisition of passes, payment for travel, and payment for special means of transport and so on).

3. In instances when the victim in accordance with legislative acts has the right to demand the termination or performance before time of an obligation, such demand shall be satisfied by means of the capitalization of the respective timepayments.

**Article 945. Compensation of Harm in Event of Termination of Juridical Person**

1. In the event of the reorganization of a juridical person deemed in the established procedure to be responsible for harm caused to life or health, the duty relating to the payment of the respective payments shall be borne by its legal successor. Demands concerning compensation of harm shall also be presented to it.

2. In the event of the liquidation of a juridical person deemed in the established procedure to be responsible for harm caused to life or health, the respective payments must be capitalized for the payment thereof to the victim according to the rules established by legislative or other normative legal acts.

3. In instances when the capitalization of payments can not be made in view of the absence or insufficiency of property with the juridical person being liquidated, the amounts awarded shall be paid to the victim by the State in the procedure determined by legislative acts.

**Article 946. Compensation of Expenses for Burial**

Persons responsible for harm connected with the death of the victim shall be obliged to compensate necessary expenses for the burial to the person who incurred those expenses.

The benefit for burial received by citizens who incurred these expenses shall not be set-off at the expense of compensation of harm.

*§3. Compensation of Harm Caused as Consequence of Defects of Goods, Work, or Services*

**Article 947. Grounds for Compensation of Harm Caused as Consequence of Defects of Good, Work, or Services**

Harm caused to the life, health, or property of a citizen or the property of a juridical person as a consequence of design, prescription, or other defects of a good (or work, service), and also as a consequence of unreliable or insufficient information concerning the good (or work, service), shall be subject to compensation by the seller or the manufacturer (or executor) irrespective of their fault and whether the victim was in contractual relations with them or not. The present rule shall apply only in instances of the acquisition of the good (or work, service) for consumption purposes.

**Article 948. Persons Responsible for Harm Caused as Consequence of Defects of Good, Work, or Service**

1. Harm caused as a consequence of the defects of a good shall be subject to compensation at the choice of the victim by the seller or the manufacturer of the good.

2. Harm caused as a consequence of the defects of work or services shall be subject to compensation by the executor thereof.

3. Harm caused as a consequence of the failure to submit full or reliable information concerning the properties and rules for use of the good (or work, service) shall be subject to compensation in accordance with the rules of points 1 and 2 of the present Article.

**Article 949. Periods for Compensation of Harm Caused as Result of Defects of Good, Work, or Service**

1. Harm caused by defects of a good (or work, service) shall be subject to compensation if it is caused during the established period of fitness (or service) of a good (or work, service), and if the period of fitness (or service) is not established, within ten years from the day of production of the good (or work, service).

2. Beyond the limits of the periods specified in point 1 of the present Article harm shall be subject to compensation if:

(1) in violation of the requirements of legislative acts the period of fitness (or service) has not been established;

(2) the purchaser (or consumer) was not warned about necessary actions upon the expiry of the period of fitness (or service) and possible consequences in the event of the failure to fulfill the said actions.

**Article 950. Grounds for Relief from Responsibility for Harm Caused as Consequence of Defects of Good, Work, or Service**

The seller or manufacturer of a good or executor of work or service shall be relieved from responsibility if it is proved that the harm arose as a consequence of insuperable force or a violation by the consumer of the rules for the use of the good (or the results of the work, service) or keeping thereof.

*§4. Compensation of Moral Harm*

**Article 951. Compensation of Moral Harm**

1. Moral harm – a violation, diminution, or deprivation of personal nonproperty benefits and rights of natural and juridical persons, including moral or physical sufferings (humiliation, irritation, depression, hatred, shame, despair, physical pain, detriment, discomfort, and so on) experienced (or endured, survived) by the victim as a result of a violation of law committed against him.

2. Moral harm shall be compensated by the causer when the fault of the causer is present, except for instances provided for by point 3 of the present Article.

3. Moral harm shall be compensated irrespective of the fault of the causer in instances if:

(1) the harm was caused to the life and health of a citizen by a source of increased danger;

(2) the harm was caused to a citizen as a result of his unlawful conviction, illegal bringing to criminal responsibility, illegal application of confinement under guard as a measure of restraint, house arrest, or undertaking not to leave, illegal imposition of an administrative sanction in the form of arrest, illegal placement in a psychiatric treatment institution, or other treatment institution;

(3) the harm was caused by the dissemination of information defaming the honor, dignity, and business reputation;

(4) other instances provided for by legislative acts.

4. Moral harm caused by actions (of failure to act) violating the property rights of a citizen not subject to compensation except for instances provided for by legislative acts.

**Article 952. Amount of Compensation of Moral Harm**

1. Moral harm shall be compensated in monetary form.

2. When determining the amount of moral harm, both the subjective evaluation of the gravity of moral harm by the victim caused to him and the objective data testifying to the degree of moral and physical sufferings of the victim shall be taken into account: the vital importance of the benefit which was the object of the infringement (life, health, honor, dignity, freedom, inviolability of dwelling, and so on); gravity of consequences of the violation (homicide of close relatives, causing of bodily injuries which entailed disability, deprivation of freedom, deprivation of work or dwelling, and so on); character and sphere of dissemination of false defamatory information; vital conditions of the victim (employment, family, domestic, material, state of health, age, and others), and other circumstances deserving attention.

3. Moral harm shall be compensated irrespective of the property harm subject to compensation.

*Chapter 48. Obligations as Consequence of Unfounded Enrichment*

**Article 953. Duty to Return Unfounded Enrichment**

1. A person (acquirer) who without grounds established by legislation or transaction acquired or saved property (unfoundedly enriched) at the expense of another person (victim) shall be obliged to return to the last property unfoundedly acquired or saved, except for instances provided for by Article 960 of the present Code.

2. The duty established by point 1 of the present Article also shall arise if the grounds under which the property was acquired or saved subsequently disappeared.

3. The rules of the present Chapter shall be applied irrespective of whether the unfounded enrichment is a result of the behavior of the acquirer of the property, the victim himself, third persons, or as the consequence of an event.

**Article 954. Correlation of Demands Concerning Return of Unfounded Enrichment with Other Demands Concerning Defense of Civil Rights**

Unless established otherwise by the present Code, other legislative acts, and does not arise from the essence of the respective relations, the rules of the present Chapter shall be subject to application also to demands:

(1) concerning the return of that performed under an invalid transaction;

(2) concerning the demanding and obtaining of property by the owner from another's illegal possession;

(3) by one party in an obligation to the other concerning the return of that performed in connection with this obligation;

(4) concerning compensation of harm, including that caused by the behavior not in good faith of the enriched person.

**Article 955. Return of Unfounded Enrichment in Kind**

1. Property comprising unfounded enrichment of the acquirer must be returned to the victim in kind.

2. The acquirer shall be liable to the victim for any, including also for any accidental, shortage or deterioration of the unfoundedly acquired or saved property which occurred after he knew or should have known about the unfoundedness of the enrichment. Before that moment he shall be liable only for intent and gross negligence.

**Article 956. Compensation of Value of Unfounded Enrichment**

1. In the event it is impossible to return in kind property unfoundedly received or saved, the acquirer must compensate the victim for the real value of this property at the moment of its acquisition, and also compensate the losses caused by the subsequent change of the value of this property if the acquirer did not compensate its value immediately after he knew about the unfounded enrichment.

2. A person who unfoundedly and temporarily used another's property (without the intention to acquire it) or another's services must compensate the victim for that which he saved as a consequence of such use at the price which existed at the time when the use ended and in that place where it occurred.

**Article 957. Consequences of Unfounded Transfer of Right to Another Person**

A person who has transferred by means of assignment of a demand or otherwise a right belonging to him to another person on the basis of a nonexistent or invalid obligation shall have the right to demand the restoration of his previous position, including the return to him of documents certifying the transferred right.

**Article 958. Compensation to Victim of Revenues Not Received**

1. The person who unfoundedly received or saved property shall be obliged to return or to compensate the victim for all revenues which he derived or should have derived from this property from the time when he knew or should have known about the unfounded enrichment.

2. A penalty shall be subject to being calculated on the amount of unfounded monetary enrichment for the use of another's money from the time when the acquirer knew or should have known about the unfoundedness of the receipt or savings of money.

**Article 959. Compensation of Expenditures on Property Subject to Return**

In the event of the return of property unfoundedly received or saved

(Article 955 of the present Code) or compensation of the value thereof (Article 956 of the present Code), the acquirer shall have the right to demand compensation from the victim of necessary expenditures incurred for the maintenance and preservation of property from the time from which he is obliged to return revenues (Article 958 of the present Code), setting off the advantages received by him. The right to compensation of expenditures shall be lost in an instance when the acquirer intentionally withheld property which is subject to return.

**Article 960. Unfounded Enrichment Not Subject to Return**

There shall not be subject to return as unfounded enrichment:

(1) property transferred in performance of an obligation before the ensuing of the period of performance unless provided otherwise by the obligation;

(2) property transferred in performance of an obligation upon the expiry of the period of limitations;

(3) monetary amounts and other property granted to a citizen, in the absence of lack of good faith on his part, as a means for existence (earnings, author's remuneration, compensation of harm to life or health, pension, alimony, and so on) and used by the acquirer;

(4) monetary amounts and other property granted in performance of a nonexistent obligation if the acquirer proves that the person requiring the return of the property knew about the absence of the obligation or granted the property for the purposes of philanthropy.

## SECTION 5. LAW OF INTELLECTUAL PROPERTY

### *Chapter 49. General Provisions*

**Article 961. Objects of Right of Intellectual Property**

1. There shall be relegated to objects of the right of intellectual property:

(1) results of intellectual creative activity;

(2) means of individualization of participants of civil turnover, goods, work, or services;

2. There shall be relegated to results of intellectual creative activity:

(1) works of science, literature, and art;

(2) performances, stagings, phonograms, and broadcasts of air and cable broadcasting organizations;

(3) inventions, utility models, industrial designs;

(4) selection achievements;

(5) topologies of integral microcircuits;

(6) undisclosed information, including secrets of production (know-how);

(7) other results of intellectual creative activity in instances provided for by the present Code or other legislative acts.

3. There shall be relegated to means of individualization of participants of civil turnover, goods, work, or services:

(1) firm names;

(2) trademarks (or service marks);

(3) names of places of origin (or indications of origin) of goods;

(4) other means of individualization of participants of civil turnover, goods, and services in instances provided for by the present Code and legislative acts [Article as amended by Law of 22 November 2005, No. 90-III].

**Article 962. Grounds of Arising of Rights to Objects of Intellectual Property**

Rights to objects of intellectual property shall arise by virtue of the fact of their creation or as a consequence of granting legal protection by an empowered State agency in the instances and in the procedure provided for by the present Code and other legislative acts.

**Article 963. Personal Nonproperty and Property Rights to Objects of Intellectual Property**

1. Personal nonproperty and property rights shall belong to the authors of the results of intellectual creative activity with respect to these results.

Personal nonproperty rights shall belong to an author irrespective of the property rights thereof and shall be preserved for him in the event of the transfer of his property rights to the results of intellectual creative activity to another person.

2. To the possessors of rights to means of individualization of participants of civil turnover, goods, or services (hereinafter – means of individualization) shall belong the property rights with respect to these means.

3. The right to be recognized as the author of a result of intellectual activity (right of authorship) shall be a personal nonproperty right and may belong only to the person whose creative labor created the results of intellectual creative activity.

The right of authorship shall be inalienable and nontransferable.

If the result was created by the joint creative labor of two or more persons, they shall be deemed to be coauthors. With respect to individual objects of intellectual property the group of persons who are deemed to be coauthors of a work as a whole may be limited by legislative acts.

**Article 964. Exclusive Rights to Objects of Intellectual Property**

1. The property right of the possessor thereof to use an object of intellectual property by any means at his discretion shall be deemed to be the exclusive right to the result of intellectual creative activity or means of individualization.

The use of an object of exclusive rights by other persons shall be permitted only with the consent of the right-possessor.

2. The possessor of an exclusive right to an object of intellectual property shall have the right to transfer this right to another person fully or partially and to authorize the use of the object of intellectual property and otherwise dispose of it unless this is contrary to the rules of the present Code and other legislative acts.

3. Limitations of exclusive rights, deeming these rights to be invalid, and the termination (or annulment) thereof shall be permitted in instances, within the limits, and in the procedure established by the present Code and other legislative acts.

**Article 965. Transfer of Exclusive Rights to Another Person**

1. Exclusive rights to an object of intellectual property, unless provided otherwise by the present Code or other legislative acts, may be transferred by the right-possessor thereof wholly or partially under a contract to another person, and also transfer by way of universal legal succession by inheritance and as a result of the reorganization of a juridical person which is a right-possessor.

The transfer of exclusive rights should not limit the effectuation of the right of authorship and other nonproperty rights. The conditions of a contract on the transfer or limitation of such rights shall be invalid.

2. To a contract providing for the granting of an exclusive right for the period of operation thereof to another person for a limited time the rules on a license contract (Article 966 of the present Code) shall apply.

**Article 966. License Contract**

1. Under a license contract the party possessing the exclusive right to a result of intellectual creative activity or means of individualization (licensor) shall grant to the other party (licensee) the right to temporarily use the respective object of intellectual property by a determined means.

A license contract shall be presupposed to be compensated.

2. A license contract may provide for the granting to a licensee:

(1) rights of use of an object of intellectual property with retention for the licensor of the possibility of the use thereof and rights to issue licenses to other persons (simple, nonexclusive license);

(2) rights of use of an object of intellectual ownership with retention for the licensor of the possibility of the use thereof but without the right to issue licenses to other persons (exclusive license);

(3) other conditions not contrary to legislative acts for use of the object of intellectual property.

Unless provided otherwise in the license contract a license shall be presupposed to be simple (nonexclusive).

3. A contract concerning the granting by the licensee of the right of use of an object of intellectual property to another person shall be deemed to be a sublicense contract. The licensee shall have the right to conclude a sublicense contract only in the instances provided for by the license contract.

Responsibility to the licensor for actions of the sublicense shall be borne by the licensee unless provided otherwise by the license contract.

**Article 967. Contract on Creation and Use of Results of Intellectual Creative Activity**

1. An author may assume under a contract the obligation to create a work, invention, or other result of intellectual creative activity and to grant to the customer who is not the employer thereof exclusive rights to the use thereof.

2. A contract provided for in point 1 of the present Article must determine the character of the results of intellectual creative activity subject to creation, and also the purposes or means of the use thereof.

3. The conditions of a contract limiting the right of the author to create results of intellectual creative activity of a determined type or within a determined domain shall be invalid.

**Article 968. Exclusive Right and Right of Ownership**

The exclusive right to a result of intellectual creative activity or means of individualization shall exist irrespective of the right of ownership to the material object in which such result or means of individualization is expressed.

**Article 969. Period of Operation of Exclusive Rights**

1. An exclusive right to objects of intellectual property shall operate during the period provided for by the present Code or other legislative acts.

Legislative acts may provide for the possibility of extending such period.

2. Personal nonproperty rights to results of intellectual creative activity shall operate in perpetuity.

3. In instances provided for by legislative acts the operation of an exclusive right may terminate as a consequence of the failure to use it within a determined time.

**Article 970. Means of Defense of Exclusive Rights**

1. The defense of exclusive rights shall be effectuated by the means provided by Article 9 of the present Code. The defense of exclusive rights may be effectuated also by means of:

(1) seizure of material objects with the use of which exclusive rights have been violated and material objects created as a result of such violation;

(2) obligatory publication concerning the violation permitted with the inclusion therein of information concerning he to whom the violated right belongs;

(3) other means provided for by legislative acts.

2. In the event of a violation of contracts concerning the use of results of intellectual creative activity and means of individualization the general rules shall apply concerning responsibility for a violation of obligations (Chapter 20 of the present Code).

## *Chapter 50. Author's Right*

**Article 971. Works Protected by Author's Right (Objects of Author's Right)**

1. Author's right shall extend to works of science, literature, and art which are the result of creative activity irrespective of their designation, content, and merit, and also means and forms of expression.

2. Author's right shall extend both to promulgated (or published, issued publicly performed, publicly shown) and to nonpromulgated works existing in any objective form:

(1) written (manuscript, typewritten, musical recording, and so on);

(2) oral (public utterance, public performance, and so on);

(3) sound or video recording (mechanical, digital, magnetic, optical, and so on);

(4) depiction (drawing, sketch, picture, map, blueprint, film, tele, video, or photo frame, and so on);

(5) volumetric-spatial (sculpture, model, layout, installations, and so on);

(6) other forms.

3. Part of a work (including the name thereof and names of personages) which possess the indicia specified in point 1 of the present Article and may be used autonomously shall be an object of author's right.

4. Author's right shall not extend to own ideas, conceptions, principles, methods, systems, processes, discoveries, and facts [Article as amended by Law of 22 November 2005, No.90-III].

**Article 972. Types of Objects of Author's Right**

1. There shall be objects of author's right:

(1) literary works;

(2) dramatic and musical-dramatic works;

(3) film scripts;

(4) works of choreography and pantomime;

(5) musical works with and without text;

(6) audiovisual works;

(7) works of painting, sculpture, graphics, and other works of the decorative art;

(8) works of applied art;

(9) works of architecture, urban construction, and garden-park art;

(10) photographic works and works received by means analogous to photography;

(11) maps, plans, sketches, illustrations, and three-dimensional works relating to geography, topography, and other sciences;

(12) computer programs;

(13) other works.

2. The protection of computer programs shall extend to all types of computer programs (including operational systems) which may be expressed in any language and in any form, including base text and object code.

3. There shall also be relegated to objects of author's right:

(1) derivative works (translations, processing, annotations, abstracts, summaries, surveys, dramatizations, musical arrangements, and other reworkings of works of science, literature, and art);

(2) collections (encyclopedias, anthologies, data bases) and other compiled works representing by selection and/or positioning of materials a result of creative labor.

Derivative and compiled works shall be protected by author's right irrespective of whether the works on which they are based or which they include are objects of author's right [Article as amended by Law of 22 November 2005, No. 90-III].

**Article 973. Legal Regulation of Author's Relations**

Author's relations shall be regulated by the present Code and other legislative acts on author's right and neighboring rights, and in instances provided for by them, also by other legislative acts.

**Article 974. Works Which are Not Objects of Author's Right**

There shall not be objects of author's right:

(1) official documents (laws, judicial decisions, other texts of legislative, administrative, judicial, and diplomatic character), and also official translations thereof;

(2) State symbols and marks (flags, arms, orders, banknotes, and other State symbols and marks);

(3) works of folk creativity;

(4) communications concerning events and facts having an information character.

**Article 975. Rights to Draft Official Documents, State Symbols, and Marks**

1. The right of authorship to draft official documents, State symbols, and marks shall belong to the person who created the drafts (draftsman).

The draftsmen of draft official documents, symbols, and marks shall have the right to publish such drafts unless this is prohibited by the agency on whose behalf the elaboration was produced. In the event of publication of the draft, the draftsmen shall have the right to indicate their name.

2. The draft may be used by the competent agency to prepare an official document without the consent of the draftsman if this draft was published by the author or sent by him to the respective agency.

In the event of the preparation of official documents, State symbols, or marks on the basis of a draft additions and changes may be made therein at the discretion of the agency effectuating the preparation of the official document, State symbol, or mark.

3. After adoption of the draft by the competent agency it may be used without indicating the name of the draftsman and without payment of author's remuneration [Article as amended by Law of 22 November 2005, No. 90-III].

**Article 976. Protection Mark of Author's Right**

1. The possessor of an exclusive author's right may in order to notify his rights use a protection mark of author's right which shall be placed on each example of a work and consist of three elements:

(1) the Latin letter "C" encircled;

(2) the name of the possessor of the exclusive author's rights;

(3) the year of first publication of the work.

2. Unless proved otherwise, the person designated in the protection mark shall be considered to be the possessor of the exclusive author's right.

**Article 977. Personal Nonproperty Rights of Author**

1. To the author of a work shall belong the following personal nonproperty rights:

(1) the right to be recognized as the author of a work and demand such recognition in the event of the use thereof excluding the authorship of other persons for this same work (right of authorship);

(2) the right to use a work under his own name, under a pseudonym, or anonymously (right to author's name);

(3) right to make changes in and additions to his work and to defense of the work, including the name thereof, against making any changes and additions without the consent of the author in the event of publication, public performance, or other use of the work (right to inviolability of the work).

It shall be forbidden without the consent of the author to supply his work in the event of publication with illustrations, prefaces, afterwords, commentaries, or any other explanations.

After the death of the author defense of the inviolability of the work shall be effectuated by the person specified in the will, and in the absence of such instructions – by the heirs of the author, and also persons on whom in accordance with legislative acts the protection of author's rights has been placed;

(4) right to open access to the work to an indeterminate number of persons (right to promulgation).

2. An author shall have the right to renounce a decision previously adopted concerning promulgation of a work (right of recall) on condition of compensation to the user of losses caused by this decision, including lost advantage. If the work has already been promulgated, the author shall be obliged publicly to notify the recall thereof. In so doing he shall have the right to remove at his expense from circulation examples of the work previously manufactured.

The provisions of the present Article shall not apply to employment work.

3. An agreement of the author with anyone or a statement of the author renouncing the effectuation of personal nonproperty rights shall be invalid.

**Article 978. Property Rights of Author**

1. To the author shall belong the exclusive rights to use a work in any form and by any means.

2. When using a work the author shall have the right to authorize or to prohibit third persons to effectuate the following actions:

(1) reproduce the work (right to reproduction);

(2) disseminate the original or examples of the work by any mans: sell, exchange, hire out (or rent) and perform other operations (right to dissemination);

(3) publicly show the work (right to public showing);

(4) publicly perform the work (right to public performance);

(5) publicly communicate the work for general information, including communication on the air or by cable (right to public communication);

(6) broadcast a work (transmit by radio or television), including transmit by cable or satellite connection (right to communicate on the air);

(7) translate a work (right of translation);

(8) rework, arrange, or otherwise process a work (right to reprocess);

(9) practically realize urban construction, architectural, and design project;

(10) effectuate other actions not contrary to legislative acts.

3. The second imparting to a work of objective form which it had in the original (publication of a work, reproduction of a sound or video recording, and so on) shall be reproduction.

4. If examples of a work lawfully published have been introduced into civil turnover by means of the sale thereof, their further dissemination shall be permitted without the consent of the author and without the payment of author's remuneration, except for instances provided for by legislative acts of the Republic Kazakhstan.

5. A work shall be considered to be used irrespective of whether it is realized for the purpose of deriving revenue or the realization thereof was not directed to this.

6. The practical application of the provisions comprising the content of a work (inventions, other technical, economic, organizational, and so on solutions) shall not comprise the use of a work in the sense of author's right [Article as amended by Law of 22 November 2005, No. 90-III].

**Article 979. Depositing of Works**

1. The depositing of manuscripts of works, other works on a material carrier, including machine, shall be deemed to be the use of a work if such depositing was done in each depository open for access and permits the receipt under contract with the depository of an example of a work by any person.

2. Depositing a work shall be effectuated on the basis of a contract of the right-possessor with the depository establishing the conditions of use of a work. Such contract and the contract of the depository with the user shall be public (Article 387 of the present Code).

**Article 980. Operation of Author's Right on Territory of Republic Kazakhstan**

1. Author's right to a work first promulgated on the territory of the Republic Kazakhstan or not promulgated but the original of which is situated on the territory thereof in any objective form shall operate on the territory of the Republic Kazakhstan. In this event author's right shall be recognized for the author and/or heirs thereof, and also for other legal successors of the author irrespective of their citizenship.

2. Author's right shall also be recognized for citizens of the Republic Kazakhstan whose works were first promulgated or is in any objective form on the territory of a foreign State, and likewise the legal successors thereof.

3. When granting the protection of author's right to the possessor in accordance with international treaties, the fact of promulgation of a work on the territory of a foreign State shall be determined according to the provisions of the respective international treaty.

4. For the purposes of protection of a work on the territory of the Republic Kazakhstan the author of a work shall be determined according to the laws of the State on whose territory whose work became first protected.

**Article 981. Commencement of Operation of Author's Right**

Author's right to a work shall commence to operate from the moment of imparting objective form to the work accessible for perception of third persons irrespective of the promulgation thereof. Author's right to an oral work shall operate from the moment of its communication to third persons.

If a work does not fall under the operation of Article 980 of the present Code, author's right to such work shall be protected from the moment of first promulgation of the work if this is effectuated in the Republic Kazakhstan.

**Article 982. Period of Operation of Author's Right**

1. Author's right shall operate during the entire life of the author and seventy years after the death thereof, counting from the first of January of the year following the year of death of the author.

2. The author's right to a work created in coauthorship shall operate during the entire life of the coauthors and seventy years after the death of the last author who survived the other coauthors.

3. Author's right to a work first issued under a pseudonym or anonymously shall operate for seventy years, counting from the first of January of the year following the year of issuance of the work.

If during the said year the anonomity or pseudonimity is disclosed, the periods established by point 1 of the present Article shall operate.

4. During the period specified in point 1 of the present Article author's right shall belong to the heirs of the author and shall pass by inheritance, belong to legal successors who received the right under a contract with the author, heirs thereof, and subsequent legal successors.

5. Author's right to a work first issued during the thirty years after the death of the author shall operate for seventy years after the issuance thereof, counting from the first of January of the year following the year of issuance of the work.

6. Authorship, name of the author, and inviolability of the work shall be protected in perpetuity [Article as amended by Law of 22 November 2005,No. 90-III].

**Article 983. Transfer of Work to Common Weal**

1. Upon the expiry of the period of the operation of an author's right to a work it shall become the common weal.

2. Works which are common weal may be used freely by any person without the payment of author's remuneration. In so doing the right of authorship, right to author's name, and right to inviolability of the work must be complied with [Article as amended by Law of 22 November 2005, No. 90-III].

**Article 984. Management of Author's Rights**

1. The right-possessor shall have the right to effectuate the rights belonging to him personally at his discretion. Other persons may manage author's rights only with the consent of the right-possessor and within the limits of the powers granted to him, except for rights provided for by Article 977 of the present Code when a legal representative effectuates representation.

2. The possessors of authors' and neighboring rights may in the procedure established by legislative acts create organizations on which the management of authors' and neighboring rights is placed.

## *Chapter 51. Neighboring Rights*

### Article 985. Objects of Neighboring Rights

Neighboring rights shall extend to the staging, performance, phonogram, and transmission by a broadcast and cable organization irrespective of the designation thereof, content, and merit, and also the means and form of expression thereof.

### Article 986. Subjects of Neighboring Rights

1. Performers, producers of phonograms, and broadcasting and cable organizations shall be subjects of neighboring rights.

2. A producer of a phonogram and broadcasting and cable organization shall effectuate the rights provided for by the present Chapter within the limits of the rights received under the contract with the performer and author of the work recorded on the phonogram or transmitted by the broadcasting or cable organization.

3. The performer shall effectuate the rights provided for by the present Chapter on condition of compliance with the rights of authors of the work being performed.

4. The registration of works or compliance with any other formal requirements shall not be required for the arising and effectuation of neighboring rights.

5. The producer of a phonogram and/or performer in order to notify his rights shall have the right to use a protection mark of neighboring rights which shall be placed on each example of the recording of the performance, phonogram and/or on each envelope containing it and shall consist of three elements:

(1) the Latin letter "P" encircled;

(2) the name of the possessor of the exclusive neighboring rights;

(3) the year of first publication of the recording of the performance, phonogram.

6. Unless proved otherwise, a natural or juridical person whose name is designated on the phonogram and/or envelope containing it shall be deemed to be the producer of the phonogram [Article as amended by Law of 22 November 2005, No. 90-III].

### Article 987. Operation of Neighboring Rights

1. The right of a performer to a performance which first occurred on the territory of the Republic Kazakhstan shall operate on the territory of the Republic Kazakhstan. In this event the right shall be recognized for the performer and heirs thereof, and also for other legal successors of the performer irrespective of citizenship.

The right of the performer shall also be recognized for him in instances when the performance first was effectuated on the territory of a foreign State, and likewise for his legal successors.

2. The rights of the producer of a phonogram shall operate on the territory of the Republic Kazakhstan if this recording was first publicly reproduced or examples thereof were publicly disseminated in the Republic Kazakhstan.

The rights of the producer of a phonogram also shall be recognized for citizens of the Republic Kazakhstan or juridical persons having a place of residence or location on the territory of the Republic Kazakhstan.

3. The rights of a broadcasting or cable organization shall be recognized for it if the organization has an official location on the territory of the Republic Kazakhstan and effectuate the transmission with the assistance of transmittors situated on the territory of the Republic Kazakhstan.

4. The rights of other foreign performers, producers of phonograms, and broadcasting and cable organizations shall be protected on the territory of the Republic Kazakhstan in accordance with international treaties ratified by the Republic Kazakhstan [Article as amended by Law of 22 November 2005, No. 90-III].

**Article 988. Regulation of Rights of Subjects of Neighboring Rights**

The amount and content of exclusive rights and other rights of the performer, producer of a phonogram, and broadcasting and cable organization, and also instances and limits of the limitation of exclusive rights of the said subjects and responsibility for their violation shall be regulated by legislative acts [Article as amended by Law of 22 November 2005, No. 90-III].

**Article 989. Period of Operation of Neighboring Rights**

1. Neighboring rights with respect to a performer shall operate for seventy years after the first performance or staging. The rights of the performer to a name and to defense of the performance or staging against distortion shall be protected in perpetuity.

2. Neighboring rights with respect to the producer of a phonogram shall operate for seventy years after first promulgation of the phonogram or for seventy years after the first recording thereof unless the phonogram was promulgated during this period.

3. Neighboring rights with respect to a broadcasting organization shall operate for seventy years after the effectuation by this organization of the first broadcast.

4. Neighboring rights with respect to cable organizations shall operate for seventy years after the effectuation by such organization of the first transmission by cable.

5. The calculation of the periods provided for by points 1 to 4 of the present Article shall commence from 1 January of the year following the year in which the legal fact occurred which is grounds for the commencement of the running of the period [Article as amended by Law of 22 November 2005, No. 90-III].

**Article 990. Rights of Performers, Producers of Phonograms, Broadcasting and Cable Organizations Which Are Foreign Citizens or Foreign Juridical Persons**

The rights of performers and producers of phonograms and broadcasting and cable organizations which are foreign citizens or foreign juridical persons, if they have effectuated the first staging, performance, recording, or broadcast outside the territory of the Republic Kazakhstan, shall operate on the territory thereof in accordance with international treaties ratified by the Republic Kazakhstan [Article as amended by Law of 22 November 2005, No. 90-III].

### *Chapter 52. Right to Invention, Utility Model, Industrial Design*

**Article 991. Conditions of Legal Protection of Invention, Utility Model, Industrial Design**

1. Rights to an invention shall be protected by an innovation patent or patent, and for a utility model and industrial design – by a patent.

2. A technical solution which is new, having an inventive standard, and industrially applicable shall be deemed to be an invention to which protection is granted.

3. The structural fulfillment of means of production and articles of consumption which are new and industrially applicable shall be deemed to be a utility model to which legal protection is granted.

4. An artistic-construction design solution of a manufacture determining its external appearance and which is new, original, and industrially applicable shall be deemed to be an industrial design to which legal protection is granted.

5. The requirements for an invention, utility model, and industrial design under which the right arises to receive an innovation patent and patent, the procedure for the issuance thereof by the empowered State agency (hereinafter – patent agency (or organization)) shall be established by a legislative act.

6. A List of nonpatentable technical solutions, structural fulfillments of means of production, and articles of consumption and artistic-construction design solutions of manufactures shall be determined by legislative acts [Article as amended by Law of 2 March 2007, No. 237-III].

**Article 992. Right of Use of Invention, Utility Model, Industrial Design**

1. To the patentholder shall belong the exclusive right of use of a defended innovation patent or patent for an invention, utility model, and industrial design at his discretion, including the right to produce a product with the use of defended solutions, use the technological processes defended by an innovation patent or patent in own production, sell or offer for sale the manufactures containing defended solutions and import respective manufactures.

2. Other persons shall not have the right to use an invention, utility model, and industrial design without the authorization of the patentholder, except for instances when such use in accordance with the present Code or other legislative acts is not a violation of the rights of the patentholder.

3. A violation of an exclusive right of a patentholder shall be deemed to be the unsanctioned manufacture, application, import, proposal for sale, sale, other introduction into civil turnover or keeping for this purpose of a manufacture manufactured with the use of the patented invention, utility model, or industrial design, and also the use of a means protected by an innovation patent or patent for an invention, or introduction into civil turnover, or keeping for this purpose of the manufacture manufactured directly by the means protected by the innovation patent or patent for an invention.

A manufacture shall be considered to be manufactured by a patented means so long as not proved otherwise [Article as amended by Law of 2 March 2007, No. 237-III].

**Article 993. Disposition of Right for Patent and Innovation Patent**

The right to receive a patent and innovation patent, rights arising from the registration of the application, right to possess a patent and innovation patent, and rights arising from a patent and innovation patent may be transferred wholly or partially to another person [Article as amended by Law of 2 March 2007, No. 237-III].

**Article 994. Right of Authorship**

1. The right of authorship and right to confer a special name on an invention, utility model, and industrial design shall belong to the author of the invention, utility model, and industrial design.

2. The right of authorship and other personal rights for an invention, utility model, and industrial design shall arise from the moment of the arising of the rights based on the protection document.

3. Legislative acts may consolidate special rights, privileges, and advantages of a social character for the author of an invention, utility model, and industrial design.

4. A person specified in an application as an author shall be considered to be the author insofar as not proved otherwise. Only facts and circumstances which existed before the arising of the right may be involved as evidence [Article as amended by Law of 2 March 2007, No. 237-III].

**Article 995. Coauthors of Invention, Utility Model, Industrial Design**

1. The mutual relations of coauthors of an invention, utility mode, and industrial design shall be determined by agreement between them.

2. Noncreative assistance in the creation of an invention, utility model, and industrial design (technical, organizational, or other assistance, facilitating the formalization of rights and so on) shall entail coauthorship.

**Article 996. Employment Inventions, Utility Models, Industrial Designs**

The right to an innovation patent, patent for an invention, utility model, and industrial design created by the worker when fulfilling his employment duties or a specific assignment of the employer (employment invention) shall belong to the employer unless provided otherwise in a contract between them [Article as amended by Law of 2 March 2007, No. 237-III].

**Article 997. Right of Author to Remuneration for Employment Invention, Utility Model, and Industrial Design**

The amount, conditions, and procedure for the payment of remuneration to an author for an employment invention, utility model, and industrial design shall be determined by an agreement between them and the employer. In the event of the failure to reach an agreement the decision shall be adopted by a court. If it is impossible to commensurate the contribution of the author and employer in the creation of an employment invention, utility model, or industrial design the right shall be recognized for the author of half of the advantage which the employer received or should have received.

**Article 998. Operation of Innovation Patent and Patent on Territory of Republic Kazakhstan**

1. An innovation patent, patent for an invention, patent for a utility model, and industrial design issued by an empowered agency shall operate on the territory of the Republic Kazakhstan.

2. Patents issued in a foreign State or by an international organization shall operate on the territory of the Republic Kazakhstan in instances provided for by international treaties of the Republic Kazakhstan.

2. Foreign citizens and foreign juridical persons or the legal successors thereof shall have the right to receive in the Republic Kazakhstan an innovation patent and patent for an invention and patent for a utility model and industrial design if the solution applied for in the established procedure meets the requirements presented by legislative acts of the Republic Kazakhstan respectively for inventions, utility model, or industrial designs [Article as amended by Law of 2 March 2007, No. 237-III].

**Article 999. Period of Operation of Innovation Patent and Patent**

1. An innovation patent and patent shall operate from the date of filing the application at the patent agency (or organization) and shall retain force on condition of compliance with the requirements established by legislative acts:

(1) an innovation patent for an invention – for three years with possible extension of this period by the patent agency (or organization) upon the petition of the patentholder, but for not more than two years;

(2) patent for an invention – for twenty years;

(3) patent for utility model – for five years with possible extension of this period by the patent agency (or organization) upon the petition of the patentholder, but for not more than three years;

(4) [repealed by Law of 2 March 2007, No. 237-III];

(5) patent for industrial design – for ten years with possible extension of this period by the patent agency (or organization) upon the petition of the patentholder, but for not more than five years.

2. The protection of an invention, utility model, and industrial design shall operate from the date of filing the application at the patent agency (or organization). Defense of the rights may be effectuated after the issuance of an innovation patent or patent. In the event of a refusal to issue a patent or innovation patent protection shall be considered to have not ensued.

3. The priority of an invention, utility model, and industrial design shall be determined in the procedure provided by legislative acts [Article as amended by Law of 2 March 2007, No. 237-III].

**Article 1000. Contract on Transfer of Patent Rights**

Contracts concerning the assignment of the right to receive an innovation patent and patent, and also assignment of an innovation patent and patent, must be concluded in written form and shall be subject to registration at the patent agency (or organization). The failure to comply with the written form or requirements concerning registration shall entail the invalidity of the contract [Article as amended by Law of 2 March 2007, No. 237-III].

**Article 1001. License Contract on Use of Invention, Utility Model, and Industrial Design**

1. A license contract and sublicense contract for use of an invention, utility model, and industrial design shall be concluded in written form and shall be subject to registration in a patent agency (or organization). The failure to comply with the written form or requirement concerning registration shall entail the invalidity of the contract.

2. The content of a license contract must correspond to the requirements set out in Article 966 of the present Code.

**Article 1002. Open License**

1. A patentholder may file at the patent agency (or organization) an application concerning the granting to any person of the right to receive a license for use of the invention, utility model, or industrial design (open license).

2. A person who has expressed the wish to take advantage of an open license shall be obliged to conclude a contract with the patentholder on patents. Disputes concerning the conditions of such contract shall be settled by a court.

An application of the patentholder concerning the granting of the right to an open license shall not be subject to review.

**Article 1003. Responsibility for Violation of Innovation Patent and Patent**

Upon the demand of the patentholder a violation of an innovation patent and patent must be terminated, and the violator shall be obliged to compensate the patentholder for losses incurred by him (Article 9 of the present Code). Instead of losses incurred the patentholder shall have the right to recover revenues from the violator received by him as a consequence of unlawful use of the invention, utility model, or industrial design [Article as amended by Law of 2 March 2007, No. 237-III].

**Article 1004. Right of Prior Use**

1. Any person who before the date of priority of an invention, utility model, or industrial design in good faith used on the territory of the Republic Kazakhstan an identical solution created independently of the author or made preparations necessary for this shall retain the right to the further uncompensated use thereof without expanding the amount of use.

2. A person who has commenced in good faith the use of an invention, utility model, or industrial design after the date of priority but before the date of official publication of information concerning the issuance of an innovation patent or patent on an invention, utility model, or industrial design shall be obliged at the demand of the patentholder to terminate further use. However, such person shall not be obliged to compensate the patentholder for losses incurred by him as a result of such use [Article as amended by Law of 2 March 2007, No. 237-III].

**Article 1005. Limitation of Rights of Patentholder**

The grounds for the limitation of the rights of a patentholder and conditions for the termination (or annulment) of a patent, deeming thereof to be invalid, termination of the operation thereof, issuance of compulsory licenses and compulsory alienation of patents shall be established by legislative acts.

## *Chapter 53. Rights to Selection Achievements*

### Article 1006. Conditions of Protection of Rights to New Species of Flora and New Breeds of Fauna

1. The rights to new species of flora and new breeds of fauna (selection achievements) shall be protected on condition of the issuance of a patent. The patent shall certify the exclusive right of the patentholder to use of the selection achievement, priority thereof, and authorship of the selectioner.

A species of flora received by artificial means or by means of selection and having one or several economic indicia which distinguish it from existing species of flora shall be deemed to be a selection achievement in plant-growing.

A breed, that is, an integral numerous group of fauna of common origin created by man and having a genealogical structure and properties which enable it to be distinguished from other fauna of the same type and quantatively sufficient for multiplication as a single breed shall be deemed to be a selection achievement in animal husbandry.

2. The conditions of legal protection of selection achievements, procedure for formalization and issuance of a patent for a species of flora and breed of fauna shall be established by legislative acts.

3. To relations connected with rights to selection achievements and protection of these rights shall apply respectively the rules of Articles 992-998 and 1000-1004 shall be established by legislative acts [Article as amended by Law of 22 November 2005, No. 90-III].

### Article 1007. Right of Author to Determine Name of Selection Achievement

1. The author of a selection achievement shall have the right to determine the name thereof which must meet the requirements established by legislation.

2. In the event of production, regeneration, proposal for sale, sale, and other types of sale of protected selection achievements the use of the names registered for them shall be obligatory. The conferment of names differing from the registered on seeds and pedigree material to be produced and/or sold shall not be permitted.

3. The conferment of a name of a registered selection achievement not relevant to seeds and pedigree material to be produced and/or sold shall be a violation of the rights of the patentholder and selectioner.

### Article 1008. Rights of Author of Selection Achievement for Remuneration

1. The author of a selection achievement who is not the patentholder shall have the right to receive remuneration from the patentholder for the use of the selection achievement during the period of operation of the patent.

2. The amount and conditions of payment of remuneration to the author of a selection achievement shall be determined by the contract concluded between him and the patentholder. In so doing the amount of remuneration must not comprise more than five percent of the amounts of annual receipts received by the patentholder for use of the selection achievement, including receipts from the sale of the license.

Remuneration shall be paid to the author during six months after the expiry of each year in which the selection achievement was used unless provided otherwise by the contract of the author with the patentholder.

**Article 1009. Rights of Possessor of Patent for Selection Achievement**

The exclusive right to use of this achievement within the limits established by legislative acts on the protection of selection achievements shall belong to the possessor of the patent for a selection achievement.

**Article 1010. Duties of Patentholder**

The holder of a patent for a selection achievement shall be obliged to:

(1) introduce into turnover the species and breed admitted for use in production;

(2) maintain the respective species of flora or respective breed of fauna during the period of operation of the patent so that the indicia are preserved specified in the official description of the species or breed established by the expert agency.

**Article 1011. Period of Operation of Patent for Selection Achievement**

The operation of a patent for a selection achievement shall commence from the day of filing the application at the patent agency (or organization) and shall continue for twenty-five years.

Longer period of the operation of a patent for individual types of selection achievements, and also the possibility of their extension by the patent agency (or organization), may be established by legislative acts on selection achievements.

**Article 1012. Admittance of Selection Achievements for Use**

1. Selection achievements which have been granted legal protection (or there is a patent) and information concerning which has been included in the State Register of Selection Achievements admitted for use in production shall be admitted for use.

2. The inclusion of species of flora and breeds of fauna in the State Register of Selection Achievements admitted for use in production shall be effectuated by the State agency conducting expert examination and tests of selection achievements with regard to the results of State tests for economic usefulness.

*Chapter 54. Rights to Topology of Integral Microcircuits*

**Article 1013. Conditions of Protection of Rights to Topology of Integral Microcircuits**

1. The legal protection provided for by the present Chapter and other legislative acts shall extend only to original topologies of integral microcircuits.

An original topology of an integral microcircuit shall be deemed to be spatial-geometric location fixed on a material carrier of the aggregate elements of an integral microcircuit and the links between them created as a result of the creative activity of the author.

2. Legal protection granted by Articles of the present Section shall not extend to ideas, means, systems, technology, or encoded information which might be embodied in the topology.

3. The rules of Articles 994-997 of the present Code shall apply to relations connected with the right to a topology of integral microcircuits and the protection of these rights respectively.

**Article 1014. Exclusive Right to Topology of Integral Microcircuits**

1. The exclusive right to use this topology at his discretion, in particular, by means of the manufacture of an integral microcircuit with such topology, including the right to prohibit the use of such topology by other persons without the respective authorization, shall belong to the author or other right-possessor of the topology of the integral microcircuit.

2. The procedure for the use of rights belonging to several authors of the topology or other right-possessors shall be determined by the contract between them.

3. The commission without the authorization of the author of the following actions shall be a violation of the exclusive right:

(1) copying of the topology as a whole or part thereof by means of inclusion in an integral microcircuit or otherwise except for that part thereof which is not original;

(2) application, bringing in, proposal for sale, sale, and other introduction into turnover of the topology or integral circuit with this topology.

4. A list of actions which are not a violation of the exclusive rights of the possessor of rights to a topology shall be established by legislative acts.

**Article 1015. Registration of Topologies**

1. The author of a topology of an integral microcircuit or other right-possessor shall have the right to register the topology by means of filing an application for registration at the empowered State agency.

2. The filing of an application for registration may be effectuated within a period not exceeding two years from the date of first use of the topology if this occurred.

3. The procedure for registration of topologies, and also contracts concerning the full or partial assignment of rights to them, shall be established by legislative acts.

**Article 1016. Period of Operation of Exclusive Right to Use of Topology**

1. An exclusive right to the use of a topology shall operate for ten years commencing from the date of registration of the topology.

If registration of the topology has not been made, the said ten-year period shall be calculated from the documentarily confirmed date of first use in any country of the world of this topology or integral circuit with this topology.

2. The emergence of an identical, original topology independently created by another author shall not interrupt and shall not terminate the running of the period of exclusive rights specified in point 1 of the present Article.

## *Chapter 55. Right to Defense of Undivulged Information Against Illegal Use*

### Article 1017. Conditions of Legal Protection of Undivulged Information

1. A person lawfully possessing technical, organizational, or commercial information, including secrets of production (know-how) unknown to third persons (undivulged information) shall have the right to defense of this information against illegal use if the conditions established by Article 126(1) of the present Code are complied with.

2. The right to defense of undivulged information against illegal use shall arise irrespective of the fulfillment with respect to this information of any formalities (registration thereof, receipt of certificates, and so on).

3. The rules concerning the defense of undivulged information shall not apply with respect to information which in accordance with legislative acts may not comprise an employment or commercial secret (or information concerning juridical persons, rights to property and transactions therewith; information subject to submission as State statistical reports, and others).

4. The right to defense of undivulged information shall operate so long as the conditions provided for by Article 126(1) of the present Code are preserved.

### Article 1018. Responsibility for Illegal Use of Undivulged Information

1. A person who without legal grounds has received or disseminated undivulged information or using it shall be obliged to compensate he who lawfully possesses this information for losses caused by the illegal use thereof.

2. If a person illegally using undivulged information has received it from the person who did not have the right to disseminate it, of which the acquirer of the information did not know and should not have known (good-faith acquirer), the lawful possession of undivulged information shall have the right to demand from him compensation of losses caused by use of the undivulged information after the good-faith acquirer knew that the use thereof is illegal.

3. A person lawfully possessing undivulged information shall have the right to demand from he who illegally uses it the immediate termination of the use thereof. However, a court, taking into account the means expended by the good-faith acquirer of undivulged information for the use thereof, may authorize the further use thereof on conditions of an compensated exclusive license.

4. A person who autonomously and lawfully has received information comprising the content of undivulged information shall have the right to use this information irrespective of the rights of the possessor of the respective undivulged information and shall not be liable to him for such use.

### Article 1019. Transfer of Right to Defend Undivulged Information Against Illegal Use

1. A person possessing undivulged information may transfer all or part of the information comprising the content of this information to another person under a license contract (Article 966 of the present Code).

2. The licensee shall be obliged to take proper measure to protect the confidentiality of the information received under the contract and shall have those same rights for the defense thereof against illegal use by third persons as the licensor. Unless provided otherwise in the contract, the duty

to preserve the confidentiality of the information shall lie on the licensee also after the termination of the license contract if the respective information continues to remain undivulged information.

## *Chapter 56. Means of Individualization of Participants of Civil Turnover, Goods, and Services*

### *§1. Firm Name*

**Article 1020. Right to Firm Name**

1. A juridical person shall have the exclusive right to use a firm name (Article 38 of the present Code) on official letterheads, printed publications, advertising, billboards, prospectuses, invoices, on goods and the packaging thereof, and in other instances necessary for the individualization of a juridical person.

2. A firm name of a juridical person shall be determined when confirming the charter thereof. Under the determined firm name a juridical person shall be included in the State Register of Juridical Persons.

3. A firm name similar to the firm name of a juridical person already registered so that this may lead to the identity of the respective juridical persons, and also delude relative to goods issued by them and services rendered, may not be used.

**Article 1021. Use of Firm Name of Juridical Person in Trademark**

A firm name of a juridical person may be used in a trademark belonging thereto.

**Article 1022. Operation of Right to Firm Name**

1. The exclusive right to a firm name registered in the Republic Kazakhstan as a designation of a juridical person shall operate on the territory of the Republic Kazakhstan.

An exclusive right on the territory of the Republic Kazakhstan shall operate in the instances provided by legislative acts for a firm name registered or generally-recognized in a foreign State.

2. The operation of the right to a firm name shall terminate with the liquidation of a juridical person and with a change of the firm name thereof.

**Article 1023. Alienation of Right to Firm Name**

1. The alienation and transfer of the right to the firm name of a juridical person shall not be permitted except for instances of the reorganization of the juridical person and alienation of the enterprise as a whole.

2. The possessor of the right to a firm name may authorize (or issue a license) to another person to use its name by means stipulated in the contract. In so doing measures must be provided in the license contract excluding delusion of the consumer.

§2. *Trademark*

**Article 1024. Conditions of Legal Protection of Trademark**

1. Legal protection of a trademark shall be granted on the basis of the registration thereof or without registration on the basis of international treaties of which the Republic Kazakhstan is a participant.

A trademark (or service mark) shall be deemed to be a registered or protected without registration by virtue of an international treaty verbal, figurative, volumetric, or other designation serving to distinguish goods or services of one person from homogeneous goods and services of other persons.

2. Designations whose registration as a trademark shall not be permitted, the procedure for the registration of trademarks, termination of their operation and deeming a registration to be invalid, and also instances in which the legal protection of unregistered trademarks may be permitted shall be determined by legislative acts on trademarks.

3. The right to a trademark shall be certified by a certificate.

**Article 1025. Right of Use of Trademark**

1. The possessor of a right to a trademark shall have the exclusive right of use and disposition of the mark belonging to him.

2. Use of a trademark shall be considered to be any introduction thereof into turnover: manufacture, application, bringing in, keeping, proposal for sale, sale of trademark or good designated by this mark, use on billboards, advertisement, printed product, or other business documentation.

3. The peculiarities of the advertisement of trademarks and goods designated by trademarks shall be determined by laws of the Republic Kazakhstan [point 3 added by Law of 19 June 2007, No. 264-III].

**Article 1026. Legal Protection of Trademark on Territory of Republic Kazakhstan**

On the territory of the Republic Kazakhstan legal protection shall be granted to a trademark registered by the patent agency (or organization) of the Republic Kazakhstan or international organization by virtue of a ratified international treaty of the Republic Kazakhstan.

**Article 1027. Period of Operation of Right to Trademark**

1. The priority of a trademark shall be established according to the date of receipt of the application at the patent agency (or organization) unless provided otherwise by legislative acts on trademarks.

2. The right to a trademark shall operate for ten years from the moment of registration of the application.

Upon the application of the possessor of the right to a trademark filed at the patent agency (or organization) during the last year of operation of the trademark the extension of the period of the operation of the trademark for ten years may be registered. The extension may be made an unlimited number of times.

**Article 1028. Consequences of Failure to Use Trademark**

In the event of the failure to use a trademark without a justifiable reason continuously during five years, the registration thereof may be annulled at the request of any interested person.

The conclusion of a license contract for use of a trademark shall be considered to be the use thereof.

**Article 1029. Transfer of Right to Trademark**

1. The right to a trademark with respect to all the classes of goods and services specified in the certificate or part thereof may be transferred by the right-possessor to another person under a contract.

2. The transfer of a right to a trademark shall not be permitted if it may be the cause of delusion with respect to the good or the manufacturer thereof.

3. The transfer of the right to a trademark, including the transfer thereof under a contract or by way of legal succession, must be registered at the patent agency (or organization).

**Article 1030. Authorization for Use of Trademark**

1. The right to use a trademark may be granted by the possessor of the right to the trademark to another person with respect to all classes of goods and services specified in the certificate or part thereof under the license contract (Article 966 of the present Code).

2. A license contract authorizing the licensee use of a trademark must contain a condition concerning the fact that the quality of goods or services of the licensee will not be lower than the quality of goods or services of the licensor and that the licensor shall have the right to effectuate control over the fulfillment of this condition.

3. In the event of the termination of the operation of a right to a trademark, the operation of the license contract shall terminate.

4. The transfer of the right to a trademark to another person shall not entail itself the termination of the license contract.

**Article 1031. Form and Registration of Contracts on Transfer of Right to Trademark and License Contracts**

A contract concerning the right to a trademark or a license contract must be concluded in written form and registered at the patent agency (or organization).

The failure to comply with the written form and requirements concerning registration shall entail the invalidity of the contract.

**Article 1032. Responsibility for Violation of Right to Trademark**

A person unlawfully using a trademark or designation similar to it to the degree of confusion shall be obliged to terminate the violation and compensate the possessor of the trademark for losses incurred by him (Article 9 of the present Code).

A person unlawfully using a trademark shall be obliged to destroy the manufactured image of the trademark and remove the illegally used trademark or designation from the good or packaging thereof similar to it to the degree of confusion.

In the event it is impossible to fulfill the requirements established by paragraph two of the present Article the respective good shall be subject to destruction.

*§3. Name of Place of Origin of Good*

**Article 1033. Condition of Legal Protection of Name of Place of Origin of Good**

1. The legal protection of a name of place of origin of a good shall be granted on the basis of the registration thereof, except for instances provided for in legislative acts.

The name of a country, population center, locality, or other geographic object used to designate a good whose special properties solely or chiefly are determined by natural conditions or other factors or a combination of natural conditions and these factors characteristic for this geographic object.

An historical name of a geographic object may be a name of a place of origin of a good.

2. A designation, although representing or containing the name of a geographic object but in universal use in the Republic Kazakhstan as the designation of a good of a determined type not connected with the place of its manufacture shall not be deemed to be a name of place of origin of a good and shall not be subject to registration for the purposes of the legal protection thereof in accordance with the rules of the present paragraph. This, however, shall not deprive the person whose rights have been violated by the use not in good faith of such name the possibility of their defense by other means provided for by legislative acts, including on the basis of rules concerning unfair competition.

3. Registration of a name of place of origin of a good shall be effectuated by the patent agency (or organization).

A certificate on the right of use of a name of place of origin of a good shall be issued on the basis of registration.

The procedure and conditions of registration and issuance of a certificate, the deeming thereof to be invalid, and termination of the operation of registration and certificates shall be determined by legislative acts on trademarks, service marks, and names of places of origin of goods.

**Article 1034. Right of Use of Name of Place of Origin of Good**

1. A person possessing the right of use of a name of place of origin of a good shall have the right to place this name on a good, packaging, advertisement, prospectuses, invoices, and to use it otherwise in connection with the introduction of this good into civil turnover.

2. The name of a place of origin of a good may be registered by several persons both jointly and independently of one another to designate a good meeting the requirements specified in Article 1033(1) of the present Code. The right of use of a name of place of origin of a good shall belong to each of such persons.

3. A person who in good faith used a geographic designation identical or similar to a registered name of a place of origin of a good not less than six months before the day of first registration thereof shall preserve the right for its further use during a period established by the patent agency (or organization), but not less than seven years counting from the date of the said registration.

4. The alienation and other transactions concerning assignment of the right of use of a name of place of origin of a good and granting of the use of it on the basis of a license shall not be permitted.

**Article 1035. Sphere of Operation of Legal Protection of Name of Place of Origin of Good**

1. In the Republic Kazakhstan legal protection shall be granted to names of places of origin of goods on the territory of the Republic.

2. Legal protection of a name of place of origin of a good in another State shall be granted in the Republic Kazakhstan if this name was registered in the country of origin of the good, and also in the Republic Kazakhstan in accordance with the present Code.

**Article 1036. Period of Operation of Certificate for Right of Use of Name of Place of Origin of Good**

A certificate for the right of use of a name of place of origin of a good shall operate for ten years, counting from the date of receipt of the application at a patent agency (or organization).

The period of operation of a certificate may be extended upon the application of the possessor thereof filed during the last year of operation of the certificate for ten years with preservation of the conditions giving the right to use the name. The extension shall be possible for an unlimited number of times.

**Article 1037. Responsibility for Unlawful Use of Name of Origin of Good**

1. A person having the right of use of a name of a place of origin of a good, and also organizations for the protection of consumer rights, may demand that he who illegally uses this name the termination of use thereof, removal from the good, packaging thereof, letterheads, and other documentation illegally using the name or designation similar with it to the degree of confusion, destruction of manufactured images of the name or designation, and if this is impossible – the seizure and destruction of the good and/or packaging.

2. A person possessing the right of use of a name of origin of a good shall have the right to demand from the violator of this right compensation of losses incurred (Article 9 of the present Code).

## SECTION 6. INHERITANCE LAW

### *Chapter 57. General Provisions on Inheriting*

**Article 1038. Inheriting**

1. Inheriting – the transfer of property of the deceased citizen (decedent) to another person(s) – heir(s).

2. The inheritance of a deceased citizen shall pass to other persons on conditions of universal legal succession as a single whole at the same moment unless arises otherwise from the rules of the present Section.

3. Inheriting shall be regulated by the present Code, and in instances expressly established by it, also by other legislative acts.

**Article 1039. Grounds of Inheriting**

1. Inheriting shall be effectuated by will and/or by operation of law.

2. Inheriting by operation of law shall occur when a will is lacking or determines the fate not of the entire inheritance, and also in other instances established by the present Code.

**Article 1040. Composition of Inheritance**

1. Property belonging to the decedent, and also rights and duties whose existences do not terminate with his death, shall be within the composition of an inheritance.

2. The rights and duties inextricably connected with the person of the decedent shall not be within the composition of an inheritance.

(1) rights of membership in organizations which are juridical persons unless established otherwise by legislative acts or contract;

(2) right to compensation of harm caused to life or health;

(3) rights and duties deriving from alimony obligations;

(4) rights to pension payments, benefits, and other payments on the basis of labor legislation of the Republic Kazakhstan and laws of the Republic Kazakhstan in the sphere of social security [as amended by Law of 15 May 2007, No. 253-III];

(5) personal nonproperty rights not connected with property.

3. Personal nonproperty rights and other nonmaterial benefits which belonged to the decedent may be effectuated and defended by heirs.

**Article 1041. Inheriting of Property Which is Common Joint Ownership**

1. The death of a participant of common joint ownership shall be grounds for the determination of his participatory share in the ownership and division of common property or partition from it of the participatory share of the deceased participant in the procedure established by Article 218 of the present Code. In this event the inheritance shall be opened for the participatory share of the deceased participant in common property, and when the division of property in kind is impossible – with respect to the value of the participatory share.

2. The participant of common joint ownership shall have the right to bequeath his participatory share in common property which will be determined after his death in accordance with point 1 of the present Article.

**Article 1042. Opening of Inheritance**

1. An inheritance shall be opened as a consequence of the death of a citizen or declaration thereof to be deceased.

2. The time of opening an inheritance shall be the day of death of the decedent, and in the event of the declaration thereof to be deceased – the day of entry into force of a judicial decision concerning the declaration of a citizen to be deceased, unless another day has been specified in the decision of a court.

3. If on the same day the persons died who have the right to inherit one after the other, they shall be deemed to have died simultaneously and the inheritance shall be opened after each of them, and the heirs of each of them shall be called to inherit.

**Article 1043. Place of Opening Inheritance**

The last place of residence of the decedent, unless it is unknown – the location of property or the principal part thereof, shall be the place of opening an inheritance.

**Article 1044. Heirs**

1. Citizens alive at the moment of opening an inheritance, and also conceived during the life of the decedent and born alive after the opening of the inheritance may be heirs by will or by operation of law.

2. Juridical persons created before the opening of an inheritance and existing at the time of opening an inheritance, and also the State, may be heirs by will.

**Article 1045. Elimination of Unworthy Heirs from Inheriting**

1. Persons who intentionally deprived the decedent of life or any of the possible heirs or committed an attempt on their life shall not have the right to inherit either by will or by operation of law. An exception shall comprise persons with respect to whom the testator drew up the will after the commission of the attempt on his life.

2. Persons who intentionally obstructed the effectuation by the decedent of his last volition and thereby facilitated the calling of themselves or persons close to them to inherit or an increase in the participatory share of the inheritance due to them also shall not have the right to inherit either by will or by operation of law.

3. Parents shall not have the right to inherit by operation of law after children with respect to whom they have been deprived of parental rights and were not restored in these rights at the moment of opening the inheritance, and also the parents (or adoptive parents) and children (or adopted) who have reached majority who evaded the fulfillment of duties for the maintenance of the decedent placed on them by virtue of a law.

4. Circumstances serving as grounds for the elimination from inheriting of unworthy heirs shall be established by a court.

$4^1$. A person who does not have the right to inherit or eliminated from inheriting on the basis of the present Article (unworthy heir) shall be obliged to return all property unfoundedly received by him from the composition of the inheritance.

When the return of inherited property is impossible, an unworthy heir shall be obliged to compensate the market value thereof.

5. The rules of the present Article also shall apply to a testamentary legacy (Article 1057 of the present Code).

When the subject of a testamentary legacy was the fulfillment of a determined work for the unworthy recipient of a legacy or rendering to him of a determined service, the last shall be obliged to compensate the heir who performed the testamentary legacy the value of the work fulfilled or service rendered to him.

6. The rules of the present Article shall extend to all heirs, including to those having the right to an obligatory participatory share [Article as amended by Law of 12 January 2007, No. 225-III].

## *Chapter 58. Inheriting by Will*

### Article 1046. General Provisions

1. The expression of will of a citizen with regard to a disposition of property belonging thereto in the event of death shall be deemed to be a will.

1[1]. A will shall be concluded by a citizen possessing at the moment of concluding it dispositive legal capacity in full.

2. A citizen may bequeath all of his property or part thereof to one or several persons both within and without the group of heir by operation of law, and also to juridical persons and to the State.

3. A will must be concluded personally. The conclusion of a will through a representative shall not be permitted.

4. A testator shall not have the right without an explanation of the reasons to deprive of an inheritance one, several, or all heir by operation of law. Deprivation of an heir by operation of law of an inheritance shall not extend to descendants thereof inheriting by right of representation unless arises otherwise from the will.

5. A decedent shall have the right to conclude a will containing a disposition concerning any of his property, including that which he may acquired in future.

A testator may by any means determined the participatory share of heirs in the inheritance, dispose of his property or any part thereof, having drawn up one or several wills concerning various property.

6. A decedent shall be free to revoke or change a will drawn up at any moment after the conclusion thereof and shall not be obliged to specify reasons for the revocation or change.

7. A decedent shall not have the right to impose on persons designated by him as heirs in a will a duty in turn to dispose of property in a determined way bequeathed by him in the event of their death [Article as amended by Law of 12 January 2007, No. 225-III].

### Article 1047. Will with Condition

1. The testator shall have the right to condition the receipt of an inheritance by a determined condition relative to the character of behavior of the heir.

2. Unlawful conditions included in a disposition concerning the designation of an heir or deprivation of the right of inheriting shall be invalid.

3. Conditions included in a will which are unfulfillable by the heir by reason of his state of health or by virtue of other objective reasons may be deemed invalid upon the suit of the heir.

**Article 1048. Subdesignation of Heirs**

1. A testator may, if the heir specified in the will dies before the opening of the inheritance, does not accept it or refuses it or is eliminated from inheriting as an unworthy heir by way of Article 1045 of the present Code, and also in the event of the failure of the heir by will to fulfill lawful conditions of the decedent, designate another heir (subdesignation of heir).

2. Any person who in accordance with Article 1044 of the present Code may be an heir may be a subdesignated heir.

3. A refusal of an heir by will not to the benefit of a subdesignated heir shall not be permitted.

**Article 1049. Inheriting Part of Property Remaining Unbequeathed**

1. Part of property remaining unbequeathed shall be distributed among the heirs by operation of law called to inherit by way of Article 1061-1064 of the present Code.

2. Among these heirs are those heirs by operation of law to whom the other part of the property was left by will [Article as amended by Law of 12 January 2007, No. 225-III].

**Article 1050. General Rules Concerning Form of Will**

1. A will must be drawn up in written form and notarially certified with an indication of the place and time of drawing it up.

2. There shall be deemed to be duly formalized:

(1) notarially-certified wills;

(2) wills equated to notarially-certified.

3. A will must be signed by the testator in own hand.

If the testator by virtue of physical defects, illness, or illiteracy can not sign a will in own hand, it at his request may be signed in the presence of a notary or other person certifying the will or other citizen, specifying the reasons by virtue of which the testator could not sign the will in own hand.

4. In instances when in accordance with the rules of the present Code witnesses must be present when drawing up, signing, or certifying a will there may not be witnesses, and also may not sign a will instead of the testator:

(1) notary or other person certifying the will;

(2) person to whose benefit the will is drawn up or a testamentary legacy made, spouse thereof, children thereof, parents, grandchildren, and great-grandchildren, and also heirs of the testator by operation of law;

(3) citizens not possessing full dispositive legal capacity;

(4) illiterate and other persons not capable of reading out the will;

(5) persons having a record of conviction for giving false testimony.

**Article 1051. Notarially-Certified Will**

1. A notarially-certified will must be written out by the testator or written down from the words of the testator by a notary. When writing down the will from the words of the testator, technical means (typewriter, personal computer, and so on) may be used by the notary.

2. A will written down by a notary from the words of the testator must before signature of the will be read out in full by the testator in the presence of the notary.

If the testator is not in a state personally to read out the will by virtue of physical defects, illness, or illiteracy, the text thereof shall be read aloud for him by a witness in the presence of the notary, concerning which a respective notation shall be made on the will specifying the reasons for which the testator could not personally read out the will.

3. If a notarially-certified will is drawn up in the presence of a witness, the surname, forename, and permanent place of residence of the witness must be specified in the will. Such information must be included in the will with respect to a person who signed the will in place of the testator.

4. At the wish of the testator, a will shall be certified by a notary without familiarization with the content thereof (secret will).

A secret will, on pain of the invalidity thereof, must be written in own hand and signed by the testator, sealed in an envelope in the presence of two witnesses and a notary on which the witnesses place their signatures. The envelope signed by the witnesses shall be sealed in the presence of the witnesses and notary in another envelope on which the notary shall place a certifying signature.

5. Wills of persons residing in population centers where there is no notary shall be certified by an official empowered by legislative acts for the performance of notarial actions.

**Article 1052. Wills Equated to Notarially-Certified**

1. There shall be equated to notarially-certified wills:

(1) wills of citizens situated for care in hospitals, sanatoriums, and other treatment-prophylactic institutions, and also residing in homes for the aged and disabled certified by chief doctors and duty doctors of these hospitals, sanatoriums, and other treatment-prophylactic institutions, and also directors and chief doctors of homes for the aged and disabled;

(2) wills of military servicemen and other persons situated for care in military hospitals, sanatoriums, and other military treatment institutions certified by heads and deputies thereof for the medical unit and senior and duty doctors of these military hospitals, sanatoriums, and other military treatment institutions;

(3) wills of citizens situated during voyages on maritime vessels or vessels of internal navigation sailing under the State Flag of the Republic Kazakhstan certified by the masters of these vessels;

(4) wills of citizens on prospecting and other expeditions certified by the heads of those expeditions;

(5) wills of military servicemen, and in stationing centers for military units, formations, institutions, and military instructional institutions where there are no notaries and officials empowered to perform notarial actions, and also the wills of civilian persons working in those units, members of

their families, and members of the families of military servicemen, certified by the commanders (or heads) of the military units, formations, institutions, and educational institutions;

(6) wills of citizens in places of deprivation of freedom certified by the heads of places of deprivation of freedom.

2. Wills provided for in point 1 of the present Article must be signed by the testator in the presence of a witness, who also shall sign the will.

Officials enumerated in point 1 of the present Article shall be obliged to transfer one example of the certified will for keeping to a notary in accordance with legislation on the notariat.

The rules of Article 1051 of the present Code shall apply to such wills in other respects, except for the requirement concerning notarial certification of the will.

**Article 1053. Revocation and Change of Will**

1. A testator shall have the right to revoke or change a will made by him.

2. A will may be revoked by means of:

(1) filing in a notarial office a statement concerning revocation wholly of the will previously made by him;

(2) drawing up a new will.

3. A will may be changed by means of:

(1) filing in a notarial office a statement concerning a change in determined part of a will previously made by him;

(2) drawing up a new will changing the will previously made in part.

4. A will previously made that is revoked wholly or partially by a subsequent will shall not be restored if the last is in turn revoked or changed by the testator.

**Article 1054. Secrecy of Will**

A notary, other person certifying a will, witnesses, and also citizen signing a will in place of the testator, shall not have the right before the opening of an inheritance to divulge information concerning the content of the will, drawing up thereof, revocation, or change.

**Article 1055. Interpretation of Will**

When a will is interpreted by a notary, executor of the will, or by a court the literal meaning of the words and expressions contained therein shall be taken into account. In the event of an ambiguity in the literal meaning of any provision of a will, it shall be established by means of contrasting this provision with other provisions and the meaning of the will as a whole.

**Article 1056. Invalidity of Will**

1. A will concluded in improper form shall be invalid. The invalidity of a will shall also be based on the rules of Chapter 4 of the present Code on the invalidity of transactions.

2. A will may be deemed to be invalid upon the suit of the person for whom the deeming of a will to be invalid shall have property consequences as a result of a violation by the procedure established by the present Code for drawing up, signature, and certification of a will.

Slips of the pen and other insignificant violations of a technical character permitted when during the drawing up thereof, signature, or certification, if it is established by a court that they do not influence the understanding of the expression of will of the testator, may not serve as grounds for invalidity of a will.

3. The invalidity of individual dispositions contained in a will shall not affect the validity of the remaining part of the will.

4. In the event of deeming a will to be invalid the heir who under this will was deprived of an inheritance shall receive the right to inherit by operation of law in the procedure established by Article 1060 of the present Code [Article as amended by Law of 12 January 2007, No. 225-III].

**Article 1057. Testamentary Legacy**

1. A testator shall have the right to place on an heir by will the performance at the expense of the inheritance of any obligation (testamentary legacy) to the benefit of one or several persons (recipient of legacy), who shall acquire the right to demand performance of the testamentary legacy.

The recipients of a legacy (legatees) may be persons within or not within the heirs by operation of law.

2. The subject of a testamentary legacy may be the transfer to the recipient of a legacy in ownership, in use, or another right to a thing, things within the composition of an inheritance,

for him of determined work or the rendering to him of a determined service, and so on.

3. The heir on whom a testamentary legacy has been placed by the testator must perform it only within the limits of the actual value of the inheritance which has passed to him and deducting the part of the debts of the decedent which fall on him.

If the heir on whom a testamentary legacy has been placed has the right to an obligatory participatory share in the inheritance, his duty to perform the legacy shall be limited to the value of the inheritance which has passed to him exceeding the value of his obligatory participatory share.

If a testamentary legacy is placed on all or several heirs, it shall encumber each of them commensurately to the participatory share in the inheritance unless the will provided otherwise.

4. On a heir to whom a dwelling house or dwelling premise passes the testator shall have the right to place the obligation to provide to another person the use for life of a dwelling premise or a determined part thereof. In the event of subsequent transfer of the right of ownership to the dwelling premise, the right of use for life shall retain force.

The right of use for life shall be inalienable, nontransferable, and shall not pass to the heirs of the recipient of the legacy.

The right of use for life granted to the recipient of a legacy shall not be grounds for members of his family to reside unless specified otherwise in the will.

5. In the event of the death of the heir on whom a testamentary legacy has been placed, or in the event of his failure to accept the inheritance, performance of the testamentary legacy shall pass to

the other heirs who received a participatory share thereof, or to the State if the property has become escheat.

A testamentary legacy shall not be performed in the event of the death of the recipient of the legacy before the opening of the inheritance or after the opening but before the moment when the heir by will succeeded in accepting it.

6. The recipient of a legacy shall not be liable for debts of the decedent.

**Article 1058. Imposition**

1. A testator may in a will place on an heir by will the duty to perform any action or refrain therefrom without granting to anyone the right to demand as a creditor the performance of this duty. In order to effectuate a generally-useful purpose such duty also may be placed on the executor of the will in the event of the separation out by the decedent of part of the property for execution of the imposition.

2. The rules of Article 1074 of the present Code shall apply respectively to an imposition whose subject is actions having a property character.

3. The duty to execute an imposition shall terminate if under the obligations provided for by the present Code the participatory share of the inheritance due or belonging to an heir onwhom the duty lay to execute the imposition passes to other heirs.

**Article 1059. Execution of Will**

1. A testator may assign the execution of a will to a person specified in the will who is not an heir (executor of will, performer). Consent of this person to be an executor must be expressed by him either in his own hand on the will itself or in a statement appended to the will.

If the executor has not been specified in a will, the heirs by agreement among them shall have the right to assign the execution of the will to one of the heirs or to another person. In the event of the failure to reach such agreement, the executor of the will may be appointed by a court upon the demand of one or several heirs.

The executor of a will shall have the right at any time to refuse to execute the duties placed on him by the testator, having notified beforehand the heirs by operation of law thereof. Relieving the executor of the will from his duties also shall be possible by decision of a court upon the application of the heirs.

2. The executor of a will must:

(1) effectuate the protection and management of the inheritance;

(2) take all possible measures so as to notify all heirs and recipients of a legacy about the opening of an inheritance to their benefit;

(3) receive monetary amounts due to the decedent;

(4) issue to the heirs property due to them in accordance with the volition of the decedent and legislative acts;

(5) ensure the execution by heirs of testamentary legacies imposed on them (Article 1057 of the present Code);

(6) execute testamentary impositions or demand from heirs by operation of law the execution of a testamentary imposition (Article 1058 of the present Code);

(7) clear the inheritance from debts.

3. The executor of a will shall have the right to act in his own name in judicial and other cases connected with the management of the inheritance and execution of the will, and also may enlist to participate in such cases.

4. The executor of a will shall effectuate his functions within the period reasonably necessary to clear the inheritance of debts, recover amounts due to the decedent, and entry of all heirs into possession of the inheritance.

5. The executor of a will shall have the right to compensation at the expense of the inheritance of necessary expenses for the management of the inheritance and execution of the will. The payment of remuneration to the executor of the will at the expense of the inheritance may be provided for in the will.

6. Upon execution of the will the executor of the will shall be obliged to provide to the heirs a report at their demand.

## *Chapter 59. Inheriting by Operation of Law*

### Article 1060. General Provisions

1. Heirs by operation of law shall be called to inherit by way of the priority provided for by Articles 1061-1064 of the present Code.

2. When inheriting by operation of law an adopted person and his descendants, on one hand, and the adoptive person and his relatives, on the other, shall be equated to blood relatives.

Adopted persons and their descendants shall not inherit by operation of law after the death of blood parents of the adopted person and other of his blood relatives.

Parents of an adopted person and other of his blood relatives shall not inherit by operation of law after the death of the adopted person and his descendants.

3. Each subsequent priority of heirs by operation of law shall receive the right to inherit in the event of the absence of heirs of the preceding priority, the elimination thereof from the inheritance, their failure to accept the inheritance or refusal thereof, except for instances specified in Article 1074(5) of the present Code.

4. The rules of the present Code concerning priority of recognition of heirs by operation of law to inherit and the amount of their participatory shares in the inheritance may be changed by a notarially certified agreement of interested heirs concluded after the opening of the inheritance. This agreement must not affect the rights of heirs not participating therein, and also heirs having the right to an obligatory participatory share [Article as amended by Law of 12 January 2007, No. 225-III].

### Article 1061. First Priority of Heirs by Operation of Law

1. Children of the decedent, including those born alive after his death, and also the spouse, and parents of the decedent, shall receive the right to inherit by operation of law in equal participatory shares in first priority.

2. Grandchildren of the decedent and descendants thereof shall inherit by right of representation [Article as amended by Law of 12 January 2007, No. 225-III].

**Article 1062. Second Priority of Heirs by Operation of Law**

1. If there are no heirs of the first priority, the heirs of the second priority by operation of law, the full or half brothers and sisters of the decedent, grandfather and grandmother thereof both on the side of the father and on the side of the mother shall receive the right to inherit by operation of law.

2. Children of full and half brothers and sisters of the decedent (nephews and nieces of the decedent) shall inherit by right of representation [Article as amended by Law of 12 January 2007, No. 225-III].

**Article 1063. Third Priority of Heirs by Operation of Law**

1. If there are no heirs of the first and second priorities, the heirs of the third priority by operation of law shall be full uncles and aunts of the decedent in equal participatory shares.

2. First cousins of the decedent shall inherit by right of representation [Article as amended by Law of 12 January 2007, No. 225-III].

**Article 1064. Heirs of Subsequent Priorities**

1. If there are no heirs of the first, second, or third priorities, relatives of the decedent of the third, fourth, and fifth degrees of kinship who are not relegated to heirs of the preceding priorities shall receive the right to inherit by operation of law.

The degree of kinship shall be determined by the date of births separating the relatives one from the other. The birth of the decedent himself shall not be within this number.

2. In accordance with point 1 of the present Article there shall be called to inherit:

as heirs of the fourth priority, relatives of the third degree of kinship – great-grandfather and great-grandmother of the decedent;

as heirs of the fifth priority, relatives of the fourth degree of kinship – children of full cousins of the decedent (grandchildren once removed), and children of own brothers and sisters of his grandfather and grandmother (grandfathers and grandmothers once removed);

as heirs of the sixth priority, relatives of the fifth degree of kinship – children of grandchildren once removed of the decedent (great-grandchildren once removed), children of his brothers and sisters once removed (nephews and nieces once removed), and children of his grandfathers and grandmothers once removed (uncles and aunts once removed).

3. If there are no heirs of the preceding priorities, stepchildren, stepdaughters, step-father, and step-mother of the decedent shall be called to inherit as heirs of the seventh priority by operation of law if they resided jointly with the decedent as one family for not less than ten years [Article as amended by Law of 12 January 2007, No. 225-III].

**Article 1065.** [repealed by Law of 12 January 2007, No. 225-III].

**Article 1066.** [repealed by Law of 12 January 2007, No. 225-III].

**Article 1067. Inheriting by Right of Representation**

1. The participatory share of an heir by operation of law who has died before the opening of an inheritance or simultaneously with the decedent shall pass by right of representation to his respective descendants in the instances provided for by Article 1061(2), Article 1062(2), and Article 1063(2) of the present Code, and shall be divided between them equally.

2. Descendants of an heir who dies before the opening of the inheritance or simultaneously with the decedent and who did not have the right to inherit in accordance with Article 1045 of the present Code shall not inherit by right of representation [Article as amended by Law of 12 January 2007, No. 225-III].

**Article 1068. Dependents Not Having Labor Capacity of Decedent**

1. Citizens relegated to heirs by operation of law specified in Articles 1062, 1063, and 1064 of the present Code who lack labor capacity on the day of opening the inheritance but are not within the group of heirs of that priority which is called to inherit shall inherit by operation of law together and equally with the heirs of that priority if not less than a year before the death of the decedent they were dependent on him, irrespective of whether they resided jointly with the decedent or not.

2. Heirs by operation of law who are not within the group of heirs specified in Articles 1062, 1063, and 1064 of the present Code but on the day of opening the inheritance did not have labor capacity and not less than a year before the death of the decedent were dependent on him and resided jointly with him shall inherit together and equally with heirs of that priority which is called to inherit.

3. In the absence of other heirs by operation of law dependents not having labor capacity of the decedent specified in point 2 of the present Article shall inherit autonomously as heirs of the eighth priority [Article as amended by Law of 12 January 2007, No. 225-III].

**Article 1069. Right to Obligatory Participatory Share in Inheritance**

1. Minors and children not having labor capacity of the decedent, and also the spouse and parents thereof not having labor capacity, shall inherit irrespective of the content of the will not less than half of the participatory share which would have been due to each of them when inheriting by operation of law (obligatory participatory share).

2. To an obligatory participatory share shall be credited all that an heir having the right to such participatory share receives from the inheritance by will and/or by operation of law, including the value of property consisting of ordinary domestic household articles and the value of a testamentary legacy established to the benefit of such heir.

3. Any limitations and encumberments established in the will for an heir having the right to an obligatory participatory share in the inheritance shall be valid only with respect to that part of the inheritance passing to him which exceeds the obligatory participatory share.

**Article 1070. Rights of Spouse When Inheriting**

1. The right to inherit belonging to a spouse by virtue of a will or law shall not affect the other rights thereof connected with being in marriage with the decedent, including the right of ownership to part of the property jointly acquired in the marriage.

2. By decision of a court a spouse may be removed from inheriting by operation of law if it is proved that the marriage with the decedent actually had terminated before the opening of the inheritance and the spouses during not less than five years before the opening of the inheritance resided separately.

**Article 1071. Protection of Inheritance and Administration Thereof in Event of Inheritance by Operation of Law**

1. If part of property is inherited by will, the executor of the will appointed by the decedent shall effectuate the protection of all the property and manage it, including that part of the inheritance which passes by way of inheriting by operation of law.

The executor of a will appointed in accordance with Article 1059 of the present Code by heirs by will or by a court shall effectuate functions for the protection of the entire inheritance as a whole and management thereof unless the heirs by operation of law require the appointment of a trustee manager of the inheritance to perform the said functions with regard to that part of the property of the inheritance passing by way of inheriting by operation of law.

2. A trustee manager of an inheritance shall be appointed by a notary at the place of opening the inheritance at the request of one or several heirs by operation of law. An heir by operation of law who does not agree with the appointment of the manager of the inheritance or the selection thereof shall have the right to contest the appointment of the trustee manager of the inheritance in court.

3. If heirs by operation of law are lacking or unknown, the apparatus of the akim of the district in city, city of district significance, rural settlement, aul (or rural village) of an aul (or rural) area must apply to a notary with a request to appoint a trustee manager of the inheritance. In the event heirs by operation of law appear, the trustee manager of the inheritance may be recalled at their request with compensation to him of necessary expenses and the payment of reasonable remuneration at the expense of the inheritance.

4. A trustee manager of an inheritance shall effectuate the powers provided for by Article 1059 of the present Code with regard to the executor of a will unless arises otherwise from the peculiarities of inheritance by operation of law.

5. A trustee manager of an inheritance shall have the right to compensation at the expense of the inheritance of necessary expenses for protection of the inheritance and management thereof, and unless provided otherwise by his agreement with the heirs – also to remuneration [Article as amended by Law of 20 December 2004, No. 13-III].

## *Chapter 60. Acquisition of Inheritance*

**Article 1072. Acceptance of Inheritance**

1. In order to acquire an inheritance an heir must accept it.

In order to acquire escheat property (Article 1083) acceptance of an inheritance shall not be required.

2. Acceptance by an heir of part of the inheritance shall mean acceptance of the entire inheritance due to him.

When calling an heir to inherit simultaneously on several grounds, an heir may accept the inheritance due to him with regard to one of these grounds, several of them, or all grounds.

Acceptance of an inheritance on condition or with reservations shall not be permitted.

3. Acceptance of an inheritance by one or several heirs shall not mean acceptance of the inheritance by remaining heirs.

4. An accepted inheritance shall be deemed to belong to the heir from the day of opening the inheritance irrespective of the time of actual acceptance, and also irrespective of the moment of State registration of the right of the heir to inherited property when such right is subject to State registration [Article as amended by Law of 12 January 2007, No. 225-III].

**Article 1072[1]. Means of Acceptance of Inheritance** [added by Law of 12 January 2007, No. 225-III]

1. The acceptance of an inheritance shall be effectuated by the filing at the place of opening the inheritance with a notary or official empowered in accordance with a law to issue a certificate on the right to an inheritance an application of the heir to accept the inheritance or application of an heir concerning the issuance of a certificate on the right to an inheritance.

If the application of the heir is transferred to the notary by another person or is sent by post, the signature of the heir on the application must be certified by a notary, official empowered to perform notarial actions (Article 1051(5) of the present Code), or person empowered to certify powers of attorney in accordance with Article 167(3) of the present Code.

The acceptance of an inheritance through a representative shall be possible if the power to accept an inheritance is specially provided for in the power of attorney. A power of attorney shall not be required for the acceptance of an inheritance by a legal representative.

2. It shall be deemed, so long as not proved otherwise, that an heir has accepted an inheritance if he has performed actions testifying to the actual acceptance of the inheritance, in particular if the heir:

entered into possession or management of inheritance property;

took measure with regard to preservation of inheritance property and defense thereof against infringements or claims of third persons;

made expenses at his own account for maintenance of inheritance property;

paid debts at his own account of the decedent or received money from third persons due to the decedent.

**Article 1072[2]. Period for Acceptance of Inheritance** [added by Law of 12 January 2007, No. 225-III]

1. An inheritance may be accepted within six months from the day of opening the inheritance.

In the event of the opening of an inheritance on the day of the supposed death of a citizen or declaration of him to be deceased (Article 1042(2) of the present Code), the inheritance may be accepted within six months from the day of the death of the citizen, and when declaring him to be deceased – from the day of entry into legal force of the decision of the court declaring the citizen to be deceased unless another day has been specified in the decision of the court.

2. If the right to inherit arises for other persons as a consequence of a refusal by an heir of an inheritance, failure to accept an inheritance by another heir, or elimination from the inheritance of an heir on the grounds established by Article 1045 of the present Code, such persons may accept the inheritance within six months from the day the right to inherit arose with them.

**Article 1072$^3$. Acceptance of Inheritance Upon Expiry of Established Period** [added by Law of 12 January 2007, No. 225-III]

Upon the application of the heir who has allowed the period to lapse established for acceptance of an inheritance (Article 1072$^2$ of the present Code), a court may restore this period and deem the heir to have accepted the inheritance if the heir allowed this period to lapse for other justifiable reasons and on condition that the heir who allowed the period to lapse established for acceptance of an inheritance had recourse to a court within six months after the reasons for the lapse of this period disappeared.

In the event of deeming an heir to have acceptance an inheritance, the court shall determine the participatory share of all heirs in the inheritance property and, when necessary – the measures with regard to defense of the rights of the new heir to receive the participatory share of the inheritance due to him. Previously issued certificates on the right to an inheritance shall be deemed by the court to be invalid.

**Article 1072$^4$. Transfer of Right to Accept Inheritance (Inheritance Transmission)** [added by Law of 12 January 2007, No. 225-III]

If an heir by operation of law or by will dies after the opening of an inheritance without succeeding in accepting it within the period established by Article 1072$^2$ of the present Code, the right to accept the participatory share of the inheritance due to him shall pass to his heirs.

This right of a deceased heir may be effectuated by his heirs on the general grounds during the remaining part of the period for acceptance of the inheritance.

If the remaining part of the period is less than three months, he shall be extended by up to three months.

Upon expiry of the period established for acceptance of an inheritance, the heirs of the deceased heir may be deemed by a court to have accepted an inheritance in accordance with Article 1072$^3$ of the present Code if the court finds the reasons for the lapsing of this period by them to be justified.

The right of an heir to accept part of an inheritance as an obligatory participatory share in accordance with Article 1069 of the present Code shall not pass to the heirs thereof [Article added by Law of 12 January 2007, No. 225-III].

**Article 1073. Issuance of Certificate on Right to Inheritance**

1. A notary at the place of opening the inheritance shall be obliged at the request of an heir to issue to him a certificate on the right to an inheritance.

2. A certificate on the right to an inheritance shall be issued upon the expiry of six months from the day of opening the inheritance.

In the event of inheriting either by will or by operation of law, a certificate may be issued upon the expiry of the said period if the notary has reliable data concerning the fact that besides the persons who had recourse for the issuance of a certificate there are no other heirs with respect to the respective property or the entire inheritance.

**Article 1074. Right to Refuse Inheritance**

1. An heir shall have the right to refuse an inheritance within six months from the day when he knew or should have known about his being called to inherit. When there are justifiable reasons this period may be extended by a court; however for not more than two months.

2. The refusal of an inheritance shall be performed by the filing by the heir of a statement to a notary at the place of opening the inheritance.

The refusal of an inheritance through a representative shall be possible if the power to refuse is specially provided in a power of attorney.

3. A refusal of an inheritance may not be subsequently revoked or taken back.

4. An heir shall lose the right to refuse an inheritance upon the expiry of the period granted to him for this. He shall lose this right also upon the expiry of the said period if he actually entered into possession of the inheritance property or disposed of it, or applied to receive documents certifying his rights to this property.

5. In the event of the refusal of an inheritance the heir shall have the right to specify that he refuses it in favor of other persons from among the heirs by will or by operation of law of any priority, including in favor of those who have been called to inherit by right of representation.

Refusal of an inheritance in favor of heirs deprived by the testator of an inheritance shall not be permitted.

6. If an heir is called to inherit either by will or by operation of law, he shall have the right to refuse the inheritance due to him under one of these grounds or on both grounds.

7. An heir shall have the right to refuse an inheritance due to him by right of increment (Article 1079 of the present Code) irrespective of the inheriting of the remaining part of the inheritance.

8. Except for instances provided for in the present Article the refusal of part of an inheritance, refusal of an inheritance with reservations, or on condition shall not be permitted [Article as amended by Law of 12 January 2007, No. 225-III].

**Article 1075. Right to Refuse Receipt of Testamentary Legacy**

1. The recipient of a legacy shall have the right to refuse receipt of a testamentary legacy. A partial refusal, refusal with reservations, on condition, or to the benefit of another person shall not be permitted.

2. The right provided for by the present Article shall not depend on the right of the recipient of the legacy who is simultaneously an heir to refuse the inheritance.

3. If the person who received the legacy took advantage of the right provided for by the present Article the heir encumbered by the testamentary legacy shall be relieved from the duty to perform it.

**Article 1076. Division of Inheritance**

1. Any of the heirs by operation of law who accepted the inheritance shall have the right to demand division of the inheritance.

An inheritance shall be divided by agreement of the heirs in accordance with participatory shares due thereto, and in the event of the failure to reach an agreement – in a judicial proceeding.

2. The rules of the present Article shall apply to a division of the inheritance between the heirs by will in instances when the entire inheritance or part thereof has been bequeathed to heirs in participatory shares without specifying specific property.

**Article 1077. Rights of Absent Heirs**

1. If among the heirs there are persons whose whereabouts is unknown, the remaining heirs, executor of the will (or administrator of the inheritance) and notary shall be obliged to take reasonable measures for the establishment of their whereabouts and calling thereof to inherit.

2. If an absent heir called to inherit whose whereabouts is established does not refuse the inheritance within the period provided for by Article 1074 of the present Code, the remaining heirs shall be obliged to notify him about their intention to divide the inheritance.

If within three months from the moment of notification provided for by the preceding paragraph the absent heir does not inform the remaining heirs of his wish to participate in the agreement concerning the division of the inheritance, the remaining heirs shall have the right to make the division by agreement between themselves, having singled out the participatory share due to the absent heir.

3. If within one year from the day of opening the inheritance the whereabouts of the absent heir is not established and there is no information concerning his refusal of the inheritance, the remaining heirs shall have the right to make a division according to the rules of point 2, paragraph two, of the present Article.

4. When there is a conceived but unborn heir the division of the inheritance may be made only after the birth of such heir.

When there is a conceived heir born alive, the remaining heirs shall have the right to make a division of the inheritance only by separating out the inheritance participatory share due thereto. In order to protect the interests of the newly-born to participate in the division a representative of the trusteeship and guardianship agency may be invited.

**Article 1078. Preferential Right of Individual Heirs to Property Within Inheritance**

1. Heirs within a year before the opening of an inheritance who resided jointly with the decedent shall have a preferential right to inheritance of the dwelling, and also ordinary domestic household articles.

2. Heirs possessing together with the decedent the right of common ownership in property shall have a preferential right of inheritance of the property in common ownership.

3. When effectuating preferential rights specified in points 1 and 2 of the present Article the property interests of other heirs participating in the division must be complied with. If property forming an inheritance is insufficient for granting the participatory shares due to them, the heir effectuating the preferential right must grant him respective monetary or property contributory compensation.

**Article 1079. Increment of Inheritance Participatory Shares**

1. In the event of a refusal of an inheritance by an heir or the falling away thereof for circumstances specified in the present Code, the part of the inheritance which would have been due to such heir shall go to the heirs by operation of law called to inherit and shall be distributed among them in proportion to their inheritance participatory shares.

If the decedent bequeathed all property to the heirs designated by him, part of the inheritance which is due to those who refused the inheritance or an heir who fell away shall go to other heirs by will and shall be distributed between them in proportion to their inheritance participatory shares insofar as not provided otherwise by the will.

2. The rules contained in point 1 of the present Article shall not apply:

(1) if the person who refused or the heir who fell away subdesignated an heir;

(2) in the event of the refusal of an inheritance by an heir to the benefit of a determined person;

(3) in instances when in the event of an inheritance by operation of law the refusal or falling away of an heir shall entail the calling of the heirs of the next priority to inherit.

**Article 1080. Expenses Subject to Payment at Expense of Inheritance**

Demands concerning compensation of necessary expenses caused by the last illness before death of the decedent, expenses for burial of the decedent, expenses connected with the protection and administration of the inheritance, execution of the will, and also payment of remuneration to the executor of the will or trustee manager of the inheritance shall be subject to satisfaction at the expense of the inheritance before the distribution thereof among the heirs.

**Article 1081. Recovery of Debts of Decedent by Creditors**

Creditors of the decedent shall have the right to present their demands arising from obligations of the decedent to the executor of the will (or trust manager of the inheritance) or to heirs who are liable as joint and several debtors within the limits of the value of the property which has passed to each heir.

**Article 1082. Inheriting in Peasant or Farmer Economy**

In the event of the death of a member of a peasant or farmer economy an inheritance shall be opened according to the general rules. Heirs shall have the right to receive monetary contributory compensation commensurate with the participatory share thereof in the common ownership to this property.

**Article 1083. Escheat Property**

1. If there are no heirs either by will or by operation of law, or none of the heirs has the right to inherit (Article 1045 of the present Code), or they all have refused the inheritance (Article 1074 of the present Code), the inheritance shall be considered to be escheat.

2. An escheat inheritance shall pass to municipal ownership at the place of opening the inheritance.

The organization of work with regard to the recording, keeping, valuation, further use, and realization of escheat property which has ensued to municipal ownership shall be effectuated by the agency empowered to manage municipal ownership.

The procedure for recording, keeping, valuation, further use, and realization of escheat property which has ensued to State ownership shall be determined by the Government of the Republic Kazakhstan.

3. An inheritance shall be deemed to be escheat by a court on the basis of an application of the apparatus of an akim of a district in city, city of district significance, rural settlement, aul (or settlement), aul (or rural) district at the place of opening the inheritance upon the expiry of one year from the day of opening the inheritance. An inheritance may be deemed to be escheat upon the expiry of the said period if the expenses connected with the protection of an inheritance and management thereof exceed the value thereof.

4. The protection of escheat property and management thereof shall be effectuated in accordance with Article 1071 of the present Code.

## SECTION 7. INTERNATIONAL PRIVATE LAW

### *Chapter 61. General Provisions*

#### Article 1084. Determination of Law Subject to Application to Civil-Law Relations Complicated by Foreign Element

1. The law subject to application to civil-law relations with the participation of foreign citizens or foreign juridical persons or complicated by another foreign element shall be determined on the basis of the present Code, other legislative acts, international treaties ratified by the Republic Kazakhstan, and recognized international customs.

2. If in accordance with point 1 of the present Article it is impossible to determine the law subject to application, the law most closely connected with the civil-law relations complicated by a foreign element shall be applied.

3. The rules of the present Section concerning the determination of the law subject to application by a court shall be applied respectively also by other agencies endowed with the powers to decide a question concerning a law subject to application.

#### Article 1085. Classification of Legal Concepts (Legal Classification)

1. The classification of legal concepts (legal classification) by a court shall be based on the interpretation thereof in accordance with the law of the country unless provided otherwise by legislative acts.

2. If legal concepts are unknown to the law of the country of the court or known by another name or with other content and can not be determined by means of interpretation under the law of the country of the court, then when classifying legal concepts (legal classification) the law of a foreign State also may be applied.

**Article 1086. Establishment of Content of Norms of Foreign Law**

1. When applying foreign law, a court shall establish the content of its norms in accordance with their official interpretation, practice of application, and doctrine in the respective foreign State.

2. For the purposes of establishing the content of norms of foreign law a court may apply in the established procedure for assistance and explanation to the Ministry of Justice of the Republic Kazakhstan and other competent agencies and institutions of the Republic Kazakhstan, including abroad, or enlist experts.

3. Persons participating in a case shall have the right to submit documents confirming the content of norms of foreign law to which they refer in substantiation of their demands or objections and otherwise assist the court in establishing the content of these norms.

4. If the content of norms of foreign law, notwithstanding the measures undertaken in accordance with the present Article, is not established within reasonable periods, the law of the Republic Kazakhstan shall be applied.

**Article 1087. Renvoi and Reference to Law of Third Country**

1. Any reference to foreign law in accordance with the rules of the present Section, except for instances provided for by the present Article, must be considered as a reference to material, and not to conflicts, law of the respective country.

2. Renvoi to the law of the Republic Kazakhstan and reference to the law of a third country shall be applied in instances of the application of foreign law according to Article 1094, Article 1095(2)(3) and (5), and Article 1097 of the present Code.

**Article 1088. Consequences of Evasion of Law**

Agreements and other actions of participants of relations regulated by the present Code directed so as to evade rules of the present Section concerning the law subject to application to subordinate the respective relations to another law shall be invalid. In this event the law subject to application in accordance with the present Section shall apply.

**Article 1089. Reciprocity**

1. A court shall apply foreign law irrespective of whether the law of the Republic Kazakhstan is applied in the respective foreign State to analogous relations, except for instances when the application of foreign law on the principle of reciprocity is provided for by legislative acts of the Republic Kazakhstan.

2. If the application of foreign law depends on reciprocity, it shall be presupposed that it exists unless proved otherwise.

**Article 1090. Clause Concerning Public Policy**

1. Foreign law shall not apply in instances when the application thereof would be contrary to the foundations of the legal order of the Republic Kazakhstan (public policy of the Republic Kazakhstan). In these instances the law of the Republic Kazakhstan shall be applied.

2. A refusal to apply foreign law may not be based only on the distinction of the political or economic system of the respective foreign State from the political or economic system of the Republic Kazakhstan.

**Article 1091. Application of Imperative Norms**

1. The rules of the present Section shall not affect the operation of imperative norms of legislation of the Republic Kazakhstan which as a consequence of the indication in the imperative norm itself or in view of their special significance to ensure rights and interests protected by a law of participants of civil turnover regulate respective relations irrespective of the law subject to application.

2. When applying the law of any country according to the rules of the present Section, a court may apply imperative norms of law of the other country having a close connection with the relation if according to the law of this other country such norms must regulate the respective relations irrespective of the law subject to application. In so doing the court must take into account the designation and character of such norms, as well as the consequences of their application.

**Article 1092. Application of Law of Country with Multiplicity of Legal Systems**

In instances when the law of a country is subject to application in which several territorial or legal systems operate, the legal system shall apply in accordance with the law of this country.

**Article 1093. Retorsion**

Retaliatory limitations (retorsion) with respect to the rights of citizens and juridical persons of those States in which there are special limitations of the rights of citizens and juridical persons of the Republic Kazakhstan may be established by the Republic Kazakhstan.

## *Chapter 62. Conflicts Norms*

### *§1. Persons*

**Article 1094. Personal Law of Natural Person**

1. The law of the country whose citizenship this person has shall be considered to be the personal law of a natural person. When a person has two or more citizenships, the law of the country with which the person is most closely connected shall be considered to be the personal law.

2. The personal law of a stateless person shall be considered to be the law of the country in which this person permanently resides.

3. The personal law of a refugee shall be considered to be the law of the country which granted asylum.

**Article 1095. Legal Capacity and Dispositive Legal Capacity of Natural Person**

1. The civil legal capacity of a natural person shall be determined by the personal law thereof. In so doing foreign citizens and stateless persons shall enjoy in the Republic Kazakhstan civil legal capacity equally with citizens of the Republic Kazakhstan, except for instances established by legislative acts of the Republic Kazakhstan or by international treaties ratified by the Republic Kazakhstan.

2. The dispositive legal capacity of a natural person shall be determined by the personal law thereof.

3. The civil dispositive legal capacity of a natural person with respect to transactions and obligations arising as a consequence of the causing of harm shall be determined according to the law of the country of the place of the conclusion of transactions or arising of obligations from the causing of harm.

4. The capacity of a natural person to be an individual entrepreneur and to have rights and duties connected therewith shall be determined according to the law of the country where the natural person is registered as an individual entrepreneur. In the absence of a country of registration the law of the country of the principal place of the effectuation of individual entrepreneurial activity shall be applied.

5. Deeming a natural person to lack dispositive legal capacity or to have limited dispositive legal capacity shall be subordinate to the law of the country of the court [Article as amended by Law of 21 January 2007, No. 225-III].

**Article 1096. Deeming Natural Person to be Missing and Declaration Thereof to be Deceased**

The deeming of a natural person to be missing and declaration thereof to be deceased shall be subordinate to the law of the country of the court.

**Article 1097. Name of Natural Person**

The rights of a natural person to a name, the use and defense thereof, shall be determined by the personal law thereof unless arises otherwise from the rules provided for by Article 15(5) and (7) and Articles 1103 and 1120 of the present Code.

**Article 1098. Registration of Acts of Civil Status of Citizens of Republic Kazakhstan Beyond Limits of Republic Kazakhstan**

The registration of acts of civil status of citizens of the Republic Kazakhstan residing beyond the limits of the Republic Kazakhstan shall be effectuated in consular institutions of the Republic Kazakhstan. In so doing legislative acts of the Republic Kazakhstan shall apply.

**Article 1099. Deeming Documents Issued by Agencies of Foreign State in Certification of Acts of Civil Status**

Documents issued by competent agencies of foreign States in certification of acts of civil status performed beyond the limits of the Republic Kazakhstan under laws of the respective States with respect to citizens of the Republic Kazakhstan, foreign citizens, and stateless persons shall be deemed to be valid in the Republic Kazakhstan when there is legalization.

**Article 1100. Law of Juridical Person**

The law of a juridical person shall be considered to be the law of the country where this juridical person is founded.

**Article 1101. Legal Capacity of Juridical Person**

1. The civil legal capacity of a juridical person shall be determined by the law of the juridical person.

2. A foreign juridical person may not refer to a limitation of powers of an organ thereof or representative to conclude transactions not known to the law of the country in which the organ or representative of the foreign juridical person concluded the transaction.

3. The civil legal capacity of foreign organizations which are not a juridical person under foreign law shall be determined under the law of the country where the organization is founded.

To the activity of such organizations if the law of the Republic Kazakhstan is applicable shall apply the rules of the present Code which regulate the activity of juridical persons that are commercial organizations unless arises otherwise from legislation of the Republic Kazakjhstan or the essence of the obligation.

**Article 1102. Participation of State in Civil-Law Relations with Foreign Element**

The rules of the present Section shall apply on general grounds to civil-law relations with a foreign element with the participation of the State unless provided otherwise by legislative acts of the Republic Kazakhstan.

*§2. Personal Nonproperty Rights*

**Article 1103. Defense of Personal Nonproperty Rights**

The law of the country where the action or other circumstance occurred which served as grounds for a demand concerning the defense of such rights shall apply to personal nonproperty rights.

*§3. Transactions, Representation, Limitations*

**Article 1104. Form of Transaction**

1. The form of a transaction shall be subordinate to the law of the place of the conclusion thereof. However, a transaction concluded abroad may not be deemed to be invalid as a consequence of the failure to comply with the form if the requirements of the law of the Republic Kazakhstan have been complied with.

2. A foreign economic transaction, if one of the participants to which is a juridical person of the Republic Kazakhstan or a citizen of the Republic Kazakhstan, shall be concluded irrespective of the place of the conclusion of the transaction, in written form.

3. The form of a transaction with respect to immoveable property shall be subordinate to the law of the country where this property is situated, and with respect to immoveable property which has been entered in a State register in the Republic Kazakhstan, – to the law of the Republic Kazakhstan.

**Article 1105. Power of Attorney**

The form and period of operation of a power of attorney shall be determined according to the law of the country where the power of attorney is issued. However, a power of attorney may not be deemed to be invalid as a consequence of the failure to comply with the form if the last satisfies the requirements of the law of the Republic Kazakhstan.

**Article 1106. Limitations**

1. Limitations shall be determined according to the law of the country being applied to regulate the respective relation.

2. Demands to which the limitations do not extend shall be determined according to the law of the Republic Kazakhstan if one of the participants to the respective relation is a citizen of the Republic Kazakhstan or juridical person of the Republic Kazakhstan.

*§4. Rights to Thing*

**Article 1107. General Provisions on Law Applicable to Rights to Thing**

1. The right of ownership and other rights to a thing to immoveable and moveable property shall be determined according to the law of the country where this property is situated unless provided otherwise by legislative acts of the Republic Kazakhstan.

2. The affiliation of property to immoveable and moveable things, and also other legal classification of property, shall be determined according to the law of the country where this property is situated.

**Article 1108. Arising and Termination of Rights to Thing**

1. The arising and termination of rights to a thing in property shall be determined according to the law of the country where this property is situated at the moment when the action or other circumstance occurred which served as grounds for the arising or termination of rights to a thing unless provided otherwise by legislative acts of the Republic Kazakhstan.

2. The arising and termination of rights to a thing in property which is the subject of a transaction shall be determined according to the law of the country to which the particular transaction is subordinated unless established otherwise by agreement of the parties.

3. The arising of the right of ownership to property as a consequence of acquisitive prescription shall be determined by the law of the country where property was situated at the moment of the ending of the period of acquisitive prescription.

**Article 1109. Rights to Thing in Means of Transport and Other Property Subject to Entry in State Registers**

Rights to a thing in means of transport and other property subject to State registration shall be determined according to the law of the country where these means of transport or property have been entered in a State register.

**Article 1110. Rights to Thing in Moveable Property en Route**

The right of ownership and other rights to a thing in moveable property en route under a transaction shall be determined according to the law of the country from which this property was dispatched unless established otherwise by agreement of the parties.

**Article 1111. Defense of Rights to Thing**

1. The law of the country where property is situated or the law of country of the court shall apply at the choice of the applicant to the defense of the right of ownership and other rights to a thing.

2. The law of the country in which this property is situated shall apply to the defense of the right of ownership and other rights to a thing in immoveable property. The law of the Republic Kazakhstan shall apply with respect to property which has been entered in the State register of the Republic Kazakhstan.

*§5. Contractual Obligations*

**Article 1112. Choice of Law by Agreement of Parties to Contract**

1. A contract shall be regulated by the law of the country chosen by agreement of the parties unless provided otherwise by legislative acts of the Republic Kazakhstan.

2. An agreement of the parties concerning the choice of the law subject to application must be clearly expressed or directly arise from the conditions of the contract and circumstances of the case being considered in their aggregate.

3. The parties to a contract may select an applicable law either for the contract as a whole or for individual parts thereof.

4. The choice of applicable law may be made by the parties to the contract at any time both when concluding the contract and subsequently. The parties also may at any time agree concerning a change of the law applicable to a contract.

**Article 1113. Law Applicable to Contract in Absence of Agreement of Parties**

1. In the absence of an agreement of the parties to a contract concerning the law subject to application to this contract the law of the country shall apply where the party is founded, has a place of residence, or principal place of activity is:

(1) the seller – in a contract of purchase-sale;

(2) the donor – in a contract of gift;

(3) the lessor or renter – in a contract of property rental (or lease);

(4) the lender – in a contract of uncompensated use of property;

(5) the independent-work contractor – in a contract of independent work;

(6) the carrier – in a contract of carriage;

(7) the expeditor – in a contract of transport expedition;

(8) the creditor – in a contract of loan or other credit contract;

(9) the attorney – in a contract of commission;

(10) the commission agent – in a contract of commission agency;

(11) the keeper – in a contract of keeping;

(12) the insurer – in a contract of insurance;

(13) the surety – in a contract of suretyship;

(14) the pledgor – in a contract of pledge;

(15) the licensor – in a license contract on the use of exclusive rights.

2. The law of the country where this property is situated, and with respect to property which is entered in a State register in the Republic Kazakhstan – the law of the Republic Kazakhstan, shall apply to the rights and duties under a contract, the subject of which is an immoveable, and also under a contract concerning trust management of property.

3. In the absence of an agreement of the parties to a contract concerning the law subject to application there shall apply irrespective of the provisions of point 1 of the present Article:

(1) to contracts on joint activity and construction independent-work the law of the country where such activity is effectuated or the results provided for by the contract are created;

(2) to a contract concluded according to the results of competitive public sales (or tender, auction) or on the stock market – the law of the country where the competitive public sales are conducted or the stock exchange is situated.

4. To contracts not enumerated in points 1 to 3 of the present Article, in the absence of agreement of the parties concerning the law subject to application the law of the country shall apply where the parties is founded, has a place of residence, or principal place of activity which effectuated performance having decisive significance for the content of such contract. When it is impossible to determine the performance having decisive significance for the content of a contract the law of the country shall apply with which the contract is most closely connected.

5. With respect to the acceptance of performance under a contract the law of the place of conducting such performance shall be taken into account insofar as not agreed otherwise by the parties.

6. If trade terms accepted in international turnover have been used in the contract, then in the absence in the contract of other indications it shall be considered that the application to their relations of customs of business turnover has been agreed by the parties which exist with respect to the respective trade terms.

**Article 1114. Law Applicable to Contract on Creation of Juridical Person with Foreign Participation**

1. The law of the country where a juridical person is being founded or is founded shall apply to a contract concerning the creation of a juridical person with foreign participation.

2. Relations regulated by the present Article shall include relations with regard to the creation and termination of the juridical person, transfer of participatory share of participation therein and other relations between participants of the juridical person connected with their mutual rights and duties (including determined by subsequent agreements).

3. The provisions of the present Article shall also apply in the event of the establishment of mutual rights and duties of participants of the juridical person with foreign participation by other constitutive documents.

**Article 1115. Sphere of Operation of Applicable Law**

1. The law applicable to a contract by virtue of the provisions of the present paragraph shall encompass, in particular:

(1) interpretation of the contract;

(2) rights and duties of the parties;

(3) performance of the contract;

(4) consequences of failure to perform or improper performance of the contract;

(5) termination of the contract;

(6) grounds and consequences of invalidity of the contract;

(7) assignment of a demand and transfer of debt in connection with the contract.

2. With respect to the means and procedures of performance, and also measures which must be taken in the event of improper performance, in addition to the applicable law the law of the country in which performance occurs shall also be taken into account.

*§6. Extracontractual Obligations*

**Article 1116. Obligations from Unilateral Transactions**

To obligations from unilateral transactions (public promise of reward, activity in another's interest without commission, and others) shall apply the law of the place of conclusion of the transaction. The place of conclusion of a unilateral transaction shall be determined according to the law of the Republic Kazakhstan.

**Article 1117. Obligations as Consequence of Causing of Harm**

1. Rights and duties with regard to obligations arising as a consequence of the causing of harm shall be determined according to the law of the country where the action or circumstance occurred which served as grounds for the demand concerning compensation of harm.

2. Rights and duties with regard to obligations arising as a consequence of the causing of harm abroad, if the parties are citizens or juridical persons of the same State, shall be determined according to the law of this State.

3. Foreign law shall not apply if the action or other circumstance serving as grounds for the demand concerning compensation of harm is not unlawful according to legislative acts of the Republic Kazakhstan.

**Article 1118. Responsibility for Damage Caused to Consumer**

To demands concerning compensation of damage which arose with the consumer in connection with the purchase of a good or rendering of a service there shall apply at the choice of the consumer:

(1) the law of the country where the place of residence of the consumer is situated;

(2) the law of the country where the place of residence or location of the producer or person who rendered the service is situated;

(3) the law of the country where the consumer acquired the good or service was rendered to him.

**Article 1119. Unfounded Enrichment**

1. To obligations arising as a consequence of unfounded enrichment shall apply the law of the country where the enrichment occurred.

2. If unfounded enrichment arises as a consequence of the disappearance of the grounds for which the property is acquired or saved, the applicable law shall be determined according to the law of the country to which this grounds was subordinated.

3. The concept of unfounded enrichment shall be determined according to the law of the Republic Kazakhstan.

*§7. Intellectual Property*

**Article 1120. Rights to Intellectual Property**

1. The law of the country where the defense of these rights is requested shall apply to rights to intellectual property

2. Contracts having as their subject rights to intellectual property shall be regulated by the law to be determined according to the provisions of the present Section on contractual obligations.

*§8. Inheritance Law*

**Article 1121. Relations with Regard to Inheriting**

Relations with regard to inheriting shall be determined according to the law of the country where the decedent had his last permanent place of residence insofar as not provided otherwise by Articles 1122 and 1123 of the present Code unless the law of the country of which he is a citizen is chosen by the decedent in a will.

**Article 1122. Capacity of Person to Draw Up and Revoke Will, Form of Will, and Act of Revocation Thereof**

The capacity of a person to draw up and revoke a will, and also the form of the will and act of revocation thereof, shall be determined according to the law of the country where the decedent had a permanent place of residence at the moment of drawing up the act unless the law of the country of which he is a citizen is selected by the decedent in a will. However, a will or the revocation thereof may not be deemed to be invalid as a consequence of the failure to comply with the form if the last satisfies the requirements of the law of the place of drawing up the act or requirements of the law of the Republic Kazakhstan.

**Article 1123. Inheriting Immoveable Property and Property Subject to Entry in State Register**

Inheriting immoveable property shall be determined according to the law of the country where this property is situated, and property which is entered in a State register in the Republic Kazakhstan – according to the law of the Republic Kazakhstan. The capacity of a person to draw up or revoke a will, and also the form of the last, if the said property is bequeathed, shall be determined by the same law.

*§9. Trusteeship and Guardianship*

**Article 1124. Trusteeship and Guardianship**

1. Trusteeship and guardianship over minors and persons who have reached majority and lack dispositive legal capacity or are limited in dispositive legal capacity shall be established and vacated under the personal law of the person with respect to which the trusteeship and guardianship is established or vacated.

2. The duty of a trustee (or guardian) to accept a trusteeship (or guardianship) shall be determined under the personal law of the person appointed as trustee (or guardian).

3. Legal relations between the trustee (or guardian) and the person under trusteeship (or guardianship) shall be determined according to the law of the country whose institution appointed the trustee (or guardian). However, if a person under trusteeship (or guardianship) resides in the Republic Kazakhstan the law of the Republic Kazakhstan shall apply if it is more favorable for this person.

4. A trusteeship (or guardianship) established over citizens of the Republic Kazakhstan residing beyond the limits of the Republic Kazakhstan shall be deemed to be valid in the Republic Kazakhstan unless there are objections against the establishment of the trusteeship (or guardianship) or against the recognition thereof based on a law of a respective consular institution of the Republic Kazakhstan.

## ON THE INTRODUCTION INTO OPERATION OF THE CIVIL CODE OF THE REPUBLIC KAZAKHSTAN (GENERAL PART)

[Decree of the Supreme Soviet of the Republic Kazakhstan, 27 December 1994 No. 269-XII, as amended 30 December 1995, No. 2837, and 2 March 1998, No. 211-I]

The Supreme Soviet of the Republic Kazakhstan decrees:

1. To introduce the Civil Code of the Republic Kazakhstan (General Part) into operation from 1 March 1995.

2. The Civil Code (General Part) shall apply to civil law relations which arose after the introduction into operation of the Civil Code, that is, from 1 March 1995.

With regard to civil law relations which arose before 1 March 1995, the Civil Code shall apply to those rights and duties which arise after the introduction into operation of the Civil Code (General Part).

3. Until legislation of the Republic Kazakhstan is brought into conformity with the Civil Code of the Republic Kazakhstan (General Part) the legislation of the Republic Kazakhstan shall apply insofar as it is not contrary to the Civil Code (General Part).

In so doing the edicts and decrees of the President of the Republic Kazakhstan, and also decrees of the President of the Republic Kazakhstan, as well as decrees of the Government of the Republic Kazakhstan relating to questions which according to the Civil Code (General Part) may be regulated only by legislative acts, shall operate until the introduction of the respective legislative acts into operation.

4. To economic partnerships and production cooperatives created before the official publication of the Civil Code (General Part) shall apply the norms thereof concerning the respective type of economic partnership and production cooperative.

Juridical persons formed before the official publication of the Civil Code (General Part) in organizational-legal forms not provided for by the Civil Code (General Part) shall be subject to transformation into organizational-legal forms provided for by the Civil Code (General Part) before 1 January 1998.

Juridical persons shall be relieved from the payment of a registration charge in the event of their registration and reregistration in connection with bringing into conformity with norms of the Civil Code (General Part).

5. New periods of limitation provided for by the Civil Code shall apply to disputes, the grounds for which served circumstances which arose after 1 March 1995.

6. New grounds for the invalidity of transactions and the consequences of invalidity established by the Civil Code (General Part) shall apply to transactions concluded after 1 March 1995.

7. The operation of Article 240 of the Civil Code (General Part) (acquisitive prescription) shall also extend to instances when the possession of property commenced before 1 March 1995 and continued until the introduction of the present Code into operation.

8. A judicial proceeding relating to cases concerning the termination of the right of ownership on grounds not provided for by the Civil Code (General Part) shall be subject to termination.

Judicial decisions rendered but not executed with regard to such cases must not be compulsorily executed after 1 March 1995.

9. Cases relegated by the Civil Code (General Part) to the jurisdiction of a court or arbitrazh court and not completed by a proceeding in administrative and other agencies by 1 March 1995 shall be subject to consideration by the courts or arbitrazh courts in accordance with their jurisdiction.

10. From the moment of the introduction into operation of the Civil Code of the Republic Kazakhstan (General Part) to deem to have lost force: the preamble and Articles 1-223 of the Civil Code of the Kazakh SSR (*Ведомости Верховного Совета и Правительства Казахской ССР* (1964), no. 2);

Articles 1-73 of the Fundamental Principles of Civil Legislation of the USSR and Republics (*Ведомости Съезда народных депутатов СССР и Верховного Совета СССР* (1991), no. 26, item 733).

Laws of the Republic Kazakhstan:

"On Ownership" (*Ведомости Верховного Совета Казахской ССР* (1991), no. 1, item 18; *Ведомости Верховного Совета Республики Казахстан* (1993), no. 8, item 204);

"On Enterprises" (*Ведомости Верховного Совета Казахской ССР* (1991), no. 8, item 96; *Ведомости Верховного Совета Республики Казахстан* (1992), no. 24, item 594; (1993), no. 8, item 179; (1993), no. 10, item 253);

"On Pledge" (*Ведомости Верховного Совета Казахской ССР* (1991), no. 52, item 638).

11. To charge the Cabinet of Ministers of the Republic Kazakhstan before 1 October 1995:

- to work out and submit in the established procedure draft laws on registration of the rights to immovable property and transactions with it, on the mortgage of immovable property, on the State enterprise, on economic partnerships, on the procedure for the registration of juridical persons, and on the production cooperative;

- to submit for the consideration of the Supreme Soviet of the Republic Kazakhstan proposals concerning the bringing of legislative acts of the Republic Kazakhstan into conformity with the Civil Code of the Republic Kazakhstan (General Part);

- to bring into conformity with the Civil Code of the Republic Kazakhstan (General Part) the decrees and regulations of the Government of the Republic Kazakhstan.

## LAW ON THE TEMPORARY DELEGATION OF ADDITIONAL POWERS TO THE PRESIDENT OF THE REPUBLIC KAZAKHSTAN AND THE HEADS OF LOCAL ADMINISTRATIONS

[Law of the Republic Kazakhstan, adopted 10 December 1993. *Ведомости Верховного Совета Казахской ССР* (1993), no. 23-24, item 513]

Article 1. To grant to the President of the Republic Kazakhstan the right for the period up to the commencement of the work of the first session of the newly elected Supreme Soviet of the Republic Kazakhstan to issue, on the basis of and in execution of the Constitution, acts having the force of a law.

To establish that these acts shall operate until the adoption of respective laws of the Republic Kazakhstan.

Article 2. To grant to the President of the Republic Kazakhstan the right for the period up to the commencement of the work of the first session of the newly elected Supreme Soviet and with subsequent confirmation by it to effectuate, when necessary , the powers of the Supreme Soviet provided for by Article 64(12-15) and (20) of the Constitution of the Republic Kazakhstan.

Article 3. To grant to the President of the Republic Kazakhstan the right for the period up to the commencement of the work of the first session of the newly elected Supreme Soviet to autonomously effectuate the powers provided for by Article 78(3)( 7) and (16) of the Constitution.

Article 4. To grant to the President of the Republic Kazakhstan the right to conform the advance Republic budget for the first half-year with allocations for the first quarter of 1994, with subsequent submission thereof for the consideration of the first session of the newly elected Supreme Soviet.

Article 5. To grant to the heads of local administrations the right to confirm the advance budgets of the respective administrative-territorial entities for the first half-year with allocations for the first quarter of 1994, with subsequent submission there of for the consideration of the newly elected respective local representative agencies.

Article 6. To grant to the heads of administrations of the regions the right to form aul (or rural) districts within the boundaries of the existing aul and rural soviets which incorporate several population centres.

The present Law shall enter into force from the day of its publication.

## EDICT ON ACTS OF THE SUPREME SOVIET OF THE REPUBLIC KAZAKHSTAN

[Edict of the President of the Republic Kazakhstan Having the Force of a Law, 23 March 1995. *Ведомости Верховного Совета Республики Казахстан*, 29 March 1995]

[Excerpt]

In accordance with Article 1 of the Law of the Republic Kazakhstan of 10 December 1993 "On the Temporary Delegation of Additional Powers to the President of the Republic Kazakhstan and the Heads of the Local Administrations" and in connection with the need to recognize as prevailing and having legal force certain acts of the Supreme Soviet of the Republic Kazakhstan, I issue the following Edict.

Article 1. To recognize as prevailing and having legal force the following acts as from the date of introduction into operation:

...

Civil Code of the Republic Kazakhstan (General Part) of 27 December 1994; Decree of the Supreme Soviet of the Republic Kazakhstan of 27 December 1994 "On the Introduction into Operation of the Civil Code of the Republic Kazakhstan (General Part)"; ...

Article 2. The present Edict shall enter into force from the day of publication.

## ON THE INTRODUCTION INTO OPERATION OF THE CIVIL CODE OF THE REPUBLIC KAZAKHSTAN (SPECIAL PART)

[Law of the Republic Kazakhstan, 1 July 1999,
No. 410-I]

1. To introduce the Civil Code of the Republic Kazakhstan (Special Part) into operation from 1 July 1999.

2. To deem to have lost force from 1 July 1999: ...

10. The norms of Section VI "Inheritance Law" shall apply to an inheritance opened after the introduction into operation of the Civil Code of the Republic Kazakhstan (Special Part).

# Truth and Beauty

## The Art of Sophie Chang

UNICORN *Art Solos*

# Truth and Beauty

## The Art of Sophie Chang

Ian Strathcarron

Ian Strathcarron.

UNICORN

*I would like to thank my dear husband Morris Chang who has helped me discover my love for art and has unconditionally supported my painting endeavors.*

Published in 2020 by
Unicorn, an imprint of Unicorn Publishing Group LLP
5 Newburgh Street
London
W1F 7RG
www.unicornpress.org



ISBN 978 1 912690 97 8

10 9 8 7 6 5 4 3 2 1

Designed by Nick Newton Design
Printed in the EU for Latitude Press Ltd.

*Front cover:* enlarged detail of **Our Inner World** (see pp. 12–13)

*Back cover:* enlarged detail of **Flowerfall** (see pp. 130–1)

*Frontispiece:* **Stability**, 116.5 × 91 cm, 2019, oil on canvas

# Contents

# Truth and Beauty

## The Art of Sophie Chang

We are in Sophie Chang's studio, high on the 30th floor of an apartment block overlooking Taiwan's capital, Taipei. Not too far above us winter clouds, menacing rain, sail westward across the sky toward Zhangzhou on the Chinese mainland. Below us, way below us, a private, silver jetplane takes off from the city airport and heads north towards Japan. Beyond that sits the mid-level concrete slab of the city, uniform, square and dull, old concrete, drab with cold tones. Under us the Dahan River, moulded into shape by more cement, reflects backs to the open mind the dull grey matter it sees all around it.

In contrast, Sophie's studio is a madness of colour. There are so many of her paintings, vivid with energy and light, hanging on the walls, lying on the floor, resting on easels or stored in racks that it looks more like an art gallery than a studio. Light comes in from three sides. Debussy's *String Quartet* plays on the Sonos. On the table is the Green Tara deity abstract, she is currently working on. Around the table are dozens of oil tubes, paintbrushes, ink bottles, colour charts, scalpels, knives, spray cans and paper rolls. We are talking about her art and her Buddhism, the former intrinsically linked to the latter, and the latter the biggest influence on her life and art, especially Tibetan Buddhism, especially its more mystical branches.

*Splat!* Using the scalpel like a spatula she wallops a dollop of ochre oil onto the canvas, lifts the flat scalpel quickly to leave behind a mini-squall of oil paint. The virgin rain forest green underneath is now transformed into a wild orange grove. Next she places a series of small pats, almost kisses, of deep red around the ochre and the fruit copse in the jungle now has its sunset. Or sunrise, as the imagination divines. "Art is the daughter of the divine", as the anthroposophist Rudolph Steiner once said.

One of the paintings in progress on an easel is *Our Inner World*, inspired by Tibetan Buddhist mandalas and recently finished, and finding pride of place on the cover of this book. Even unfinished it inspires the title of the book, *Truth and Beauty*. The Tibetan mystics hold that all we know is only gathered through experience and is filtered through three elements: the intellect – so knowledge, thoughts and memories; the emotions; and perceptions – the five senses. All these three, thoughts, feelings and perceptions have at their source the divine: the intellect's essential nature is Truth, the emotions' is Love and perceptions' is Beauty. Thus as in philosophy, so in art: the *Our Inner World* mandala is painted with Love and speaks of Truth and resides in Beauty.

---

On the walls of the adjoining rooms are works from Sophie's past as well as her current experiments with ink wash and freewheeling forms of calligraphy. The contrast between these earlier works and the pieces she is working on now show clearly her evolution as an artist. Unsurprisingly, her art embraces both Chinese and Western traditions. The Chinese tradition to which she belongs stretches back to the Tang Dynasty (618–97 AD), that is to say for more than a millennium. The Western narrative, to which her work also relates, has a much shorter span, having its roots in

American Abstract Expressionism. The dialogue between these two forms of artistic expression varies according to the mediums she uses. Works in ink alone, or in mixed media on paper, tend towards the calligraphic. What one sees in them is the quintessential link, to be found in much scholarly Chinese art made by revered masters, between the act of representing something in art and the act of describing it in writing by using characters that are images in their own right. Yet one also finds in Sophie's Eastern works the influence of Western gestural abstraction.

Her early work is clearly influenced by Monet and Cézanne, in fact her first stabs at painting (literally stabs as she learned to paint before learning to draw) was to copy works by these great artists. As one would expect much of the work is derivative: a necessity given that she is largely autodidact. She recalls how she would go to MoMA to see, for example, a Monet exhibition and copy works from the catalogue as part of her self-teaching. In other works we can see echoes of Constable, Pissarro, Van Gogh, Degas, Manet, Renoir, Seurat and Mackintosh.

If Truth and Beauty shine out of Sophie's current work as shown in this book, seeing her earlier work hanging in the studio, some going back a dozen or so years, shows feelings of Love, the third element of the mystic's world. Here her art shows the compassion she brings to her life as leader of Taiwan's largest philanthropic initiative, meeting the pastoral and spiritual needs of the less fortunate of the nation without any sense of vainglory.

Then, about four years ago, something strange happened. Sophie just stopped painting. Partly it was frustration at the limitations of copying great works by others; if not literally painting by numbers, philosophically painting by rote. But I suspect a cause even closer to her heart called her to arms: the Fo Guang Shan Buddhist monastic order, whose dharma for humanity concentrates on the relief of all kinds of material suffering, asked her to lead the fundraising to build the new Buddha Museum on their site in Kaohsiung in the south of Taiwan. "Museum" barely describes this enormous endeavour: a 110-metre high Shakyamuni Buddha looks down on four stupas that symbolize the Four Noble Truths, below which the Memorial Hall holds several shrines including the Jade Buddha Shrine, then down to the Bodhi Square, surrounded by statues of the Buddha's main disciples. Beyond that are eight pagodas that lead down to the Welcoming Hall. The site cover over 100 hectares. Sophie is too modest to say how much money was needed, but it must have been tens of millions of any currency you care to mention. With considerable trepidation about its critical acceptance, she auctioned all her art to raise their first funds, then tirelessly rounded up other Taiwanese and Chinese Buddhist philanthropists to play their parts too.

And then there was the devastating 2016 Taiwan earthquake and its sixty-five aftershocks, also near Kaohsiung. Most of the 115 deaths were caused by poorly built residential buildings collapsing. Sophie as ever led the volunteer rescue effort, mobilising one of the largest civilian aid missions in Asia.

Museum and earthquake missions accomplished, she returned to her art three years ago. Without determining why, she changed her approach entirely, or as she says, "the approach just changed itself". No longer painting objectively what she saw with her eyes, she was now creating subjectively, and abstractly, onto the canvas that which arose each morning after meditation. This is the work we now see: spiritual abstract art. As she says, "I start with love, then the colours just come. My hand, my mind, my love. Like that."

Whereas Christian art uses illustration to depict a religious narrative, up to and including such elusive fellows as the

Holy Ghost and even the Abrahamic, personalised God himself, Tibetan Buddhist art goes beyond illustration, using forms that have no inherent, intrinsic meaning or even tangible reality; thus speaking directly to qualities like Truth, Beauty and Love that not only cannot be represented literally, but lose all their meaning if rendered representationally. Sophie believes that art lives when it creates such a spiritual experience. As an artist she wants to eliminate the distance between herself and the world, and she wants their paintings to do the same for us.

If Sophie's earlier work was influenced by Cézanne's paintings her current work has clearly been influenced by his philosophy. Cézanne famously said, "Everything vanishes, falls apart doesn't it? Nature is always the same, but nothing in her that appears to us lasts. Our art must render the thrill of her permanence, along with her elements, the appearance of all her changes. It must give us a taste of her Eternity." As he was standing in front of one of his favourite scenes, the distinctly unvanishing and un-falling apart Mont St. Victoire at the time, as we discussed Sophie has an instinctive mystic's understanding of what he meant.

Everything that Cézanne saw could only be known by the act of seeing it and the only way the seeing of it could be known was through consciousness. When he saw that mountain, he only saw it because it appeared in consciousness; there is nothing that humans know that is ever outside consciousness. If it appeared in consciousness, it follows that the experience of seeing it is made out of consciousness; it simply couldn't be otherwise.

If he were to close his eyes for a few moments, whatever he had been seeing would disappear, would "vanish and fall apart". When he reopens them the mountain is still there, but it is a new perception, and so to consciousness, a new mountain. The mind will link the two and tell itself that is the same mountain, but the artist will know that it's a new perception of the mountain, subtly different, redefined by light and time. This is what he means by "everything vanishes". The seemingly permanent mountain is made impermanent with this understanding and the realisation that what is being seen is actually a series of fleeting and different impressions. It is in this sense that "everything falls apart".

Yet as a human being Cézanne was just as much a part of "nature" as the mountain. The subjective and objective, mind and matter, are ultimately One. Objectively, he acknowledges that the sense of permanence in nature cannot come from "the appearance of all her changes", because "nothing in her that appears to us lasts". Here he recognizes the existence of nature, "which is always the same"; and the appearance of nature, in which "nothing lasts". And there is the "us", the consciousness, the knowing in which all this appears.

In Cézanne's world there was no separate subject, separate verb and separate object, all acting independently of each other looking at Mont St. Victoire. He, the act of looking at the view, and calling the object Mont St. Victoire are all concepts of the finite mind, which can only understand these thoughts and perceptions in linear time and discovered space. He, like a Buddhist mystic, knew that time is limitless consciousness objectified by thoughts and space is infinite consciousness objectified by perceptions. In other words, he painted the "viewness" of the view rather than just the view itself.

Likewise Sophie, fresh from her morning meditation, conjures up for example the mandala *Our Inner World* or the Green Tara work in progress. Without using the filter of the finite mind, free from the limitations of time and space, with creativity necessarily free from the past, she applies oil to canvas. She works quickly yet unhurriedly, spontaneously, at the pace her art requires. There is no conversation or interruption. There is no separate Sophie as the subject, painting as the verb, on a canvas as the object; there is just art arting. She is in touch with what Kandinsky called the *innerer Klang*, especially, this very morning, with Debussy keeping time so colourfully.

---

How do we judge what we see in the book? The viewer can easily interpret dramatic images of changing landscape. Nature in motion is her signature theme, movement all around, nothing standing still on the canvas, while stillness resides in the artist. The compositions are titled as abstractly as the art, but still leave an impression of the world surrounding the artist: *Our Inner World* as on the front cover, *Flowerfall* as on the back cover, *Epiphany* and *Autumn Harvest* on the front and back endpapers respectively. This, if one thinks further, tends to focus one's attention on a particular characteristic of these paintings, which is that they offer a vision of a world that is never stable, but which is, on the contrary, constantly in a state of becoming. This is nature in movement, sometimes benignly, as in *Flowerfall*, sometimes in turmoil as in *Epiphany*.

When one looks at them with eyes conditioned by familiarity with Western art, what these canvases suggest are some of the radical late compositions of the British Romantic J.M.W. Turner, particularly those that Turner himself described as Colour Beginnings. The similarity is also in the effect the art has on the viewer, in each case one gently drifts into it, it takes time and trust, the opposite of the instant result of a selfie, for example. There's the same freedom of handling, the shades of colour that transform the solid into the ethereal, as if the light and sensitivity of the ethereal become the focus of the art rather than the backdrop.

In traditional Chinese paintings this characteristic is present in horizontal landscape scrolls, where the panorama represented is never meant to be seen complete. The viewer unrolls, and simultaneously rolls up the scroll, as he or she looks along it. The relationship between the viewer and the composition is not static but dynamic. Sophie reaches for this mutability by other means: for example by layering new paint on top of old. As the new layer dries, the surface splits offering glimpses of what lies beneath.

The real dynamic, however, is supplied by her compositional choices. An example is the composition entitled *Light Break*, with its looming mountain forms, placed very close to the surface of the picture. One's gaze struggles to escape, to find a way through. The title of the work indicates that this is exactly what the artist intended. Most often, however, one is offered sweeping panoramas. We find ourselves floating above these landscapes, like some kind of winged creature.

---

Back in Sophie's studio she is revisiting *Spring Ploughing*. The day before her assistant had taken if off the table and absent-mindedly placed it upside down on an easel. For fun, she asked him to place it through the ninety degree quadrants. We all agree it looks more haunting as placed by accident the day before. Now she works on the deeper lemons as seen on the lower right side of the painting; it now becomes even more haunting, evoking an almost chilling excitement of the unforeseen.

Here we can see how Sophie's approach to spiritual abstract art occupies a somewhat different sphere from the more reductive Western version. At first glance, the forms used in both cases easily register as being "abstract", in other words non-descriptive, but Sophie's still has some traces inherited from the traditions of Chinese scholarly ink-painting.

In this tradition, the basic concern is not with the human image, but with landscape. That is to say, with the image of nature. Mankind, in scholarly ink-painting, is an incident – a phenomenon within nature. Not independent, a thing in itself, but something given meaning by what surrounds the figure or figures depicted, which, if they appear at all, do so on a much smaller scale than that which surrounds them.

While contemporary Chinese art has in recent years been ready to absorb ideas and techniques from Western models, more especially from the varieties of Western art that are escribed as either Modern or Post-Modern, fundamental differences of approach and sensibility remain. These are what we see here in Sophie's art: even when entirely abstract, her work always carries within itself echoes of representation.

By contrast, Western spiritual abstract artists like Malevich or Mondrian make a point of wanting to avoid any reference to figuration. One might even say that the radical avoidance of anything resembling representation is the whole essence of the work, which aims to place itself in a sphere that is entirely distinct from the surrounding world of images – images that exist naturally without human intervention, as well as images that exist within the existing sphere of art.

Sophie's spiritual abstract art, even when it rejects figuration and presents itself as entirely abstract, does not do this. There is always within it a remote echo of forms that belong to the long, continuous history of Chinese culture and spirituality. These traditions of art and mysticism present a sequence of unbroken development which does not exist in any other sphere. All other major human cultures and religions – European, Middle Eastern, African, North and South American – have been subject to violent disruptions at some point or points in their history and have been obliged to begin again. Even the Cultural Revolution failed to entirely break the thread of art and worship, and now those dark days are fast receding, artists like Sophie are entirely free to truly represent what is best from her artistic and spiritual heritage. The result is evocative and inspiring in equal measure, distinct in its own right yet representing universal Truth and Beauty.

*Ian Strathcarron*

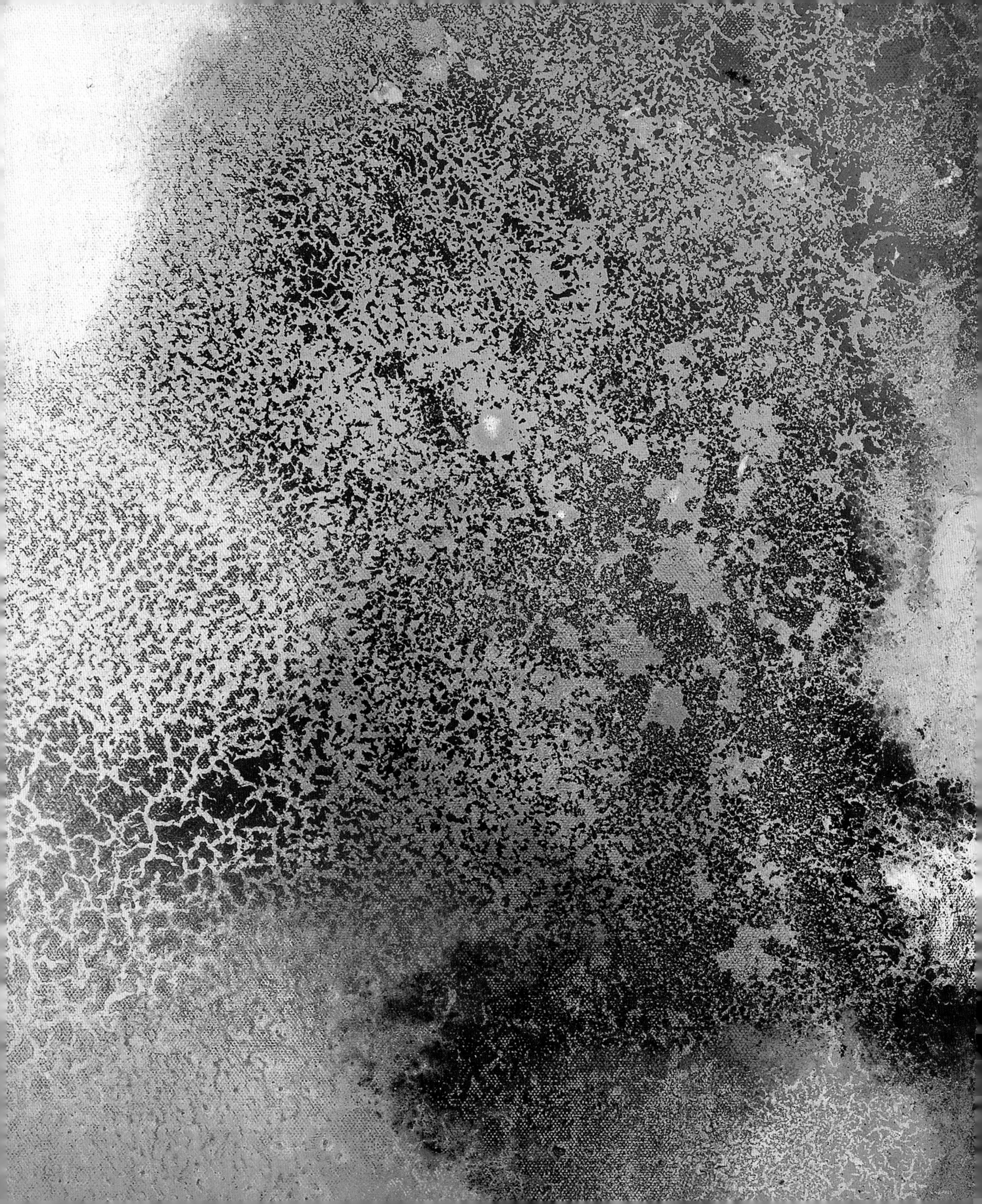

Chapter One

# A Religious Spirit

Religious experience has always played a key role in Sophie Chang's painting. For her, creating a work that has religious significance does not mean just interpreting Buddhist scriptures or conveying a believer's sense of reverence. Instead, through the use of abstract techniques, she attempts to communicate an understanding, gained through many years of spiritual cultivation.

The road that led to Sophie Chang's involvement with religion began in the 1980s when she returned from the US to Taiwan. From a routine and ordinary life in the States, she entered the warmer and more lively Taiwanese society. Yet in the midst of the excitement, she felt a number of troubling contradictions that led her to seek a truer sense of belonging in religion. Belief in Tibetan Buddhism has exerted an especially important influence on her. She began by reading books by the Dalai Lama and practising Zen meditation, and each year she went to Tibet and Nepal to experience the tranquil atmosphere of the temples. In 2007, she travelled to New Delhi, India, where she met the Dalai Lama in person. He taught her about "compassion and wisdom", that is, how to reach out to the world by doing good works based on compassion and wisdom.

Based on these experiences, Chang found a peaceful resolution to the contradictions she felt after her return to Taiwan. She began to promote social charity work, and spiritual experience became the most important subject of her later paintings; her meditation practice in particular allowed her to capture with sensitivity the various moods flowing through her. For these reasons, the abstract styles that arose in Europe and the US in the 20th century became the principle style in which Chang worked after resuming painting again in 2016. In particular, the abstract style of the post-war period, with its examination of the inner self and its ability to portray inner mental images, became important as she projected her feelings about religious experience in her works.

Four of Chang's works, her 2018 *Echoes* (pp. 38–9) and *Blessing* (pp. 14–15), her 2019 *Source of Hope* (pp. 10–11), and her 2019–2020 *Our Inner World* (pp. 12–13), can be seen as a series that she produced as an ode to the positive inner power of the human spirit. The latter two share similar compositions, with colourful pigments that spread across the entire canvas. *Source of Hope* further adds a shining image that stands out in the centre of the canvas, whereas a circular area of orange appears in *Our Inner World*. Both are based on the religious symbolism of the mandala. The Sanskrit word *Mandala* indicates a symbolic drawing, one that illustrates the truth of the universe and its energies, forming a Zen circle in which "all phenomena are governed by order, and subsumed in harmonious understanding".

Chang's *Source of Hope* represents the endless warmth she feels inside when visualizing the Green Tara goddess. Legend has it that the Green Tara was born from a teardrop shed by Avalokitesvara out of his compassion for the world. She is thus the embodiment of compassion, a goddess who gives succour to all and offers liberation in the cycle of birth, death, and reincarnation. Starlight flickers in the centre of the painting, symbolizing the light of the Green Tara's merciful and open heart that illuminates all under heaven. In *Our Inner World*, the circular orange area at the centre reveals many subtly layered colours; viewers will sense that they are exploring a scene of unlimited depth, in the same way that we search our inner self during the practice of internal observation. In Buddhism, our intrinsic nature is considered to be the Buddha nature. The essence of our minds is intrinsically pure, and it is intrinsically free from either becoming or annihilation; hence, for everyone, the essence of mind is intrinsically self-sufficient. Reality is emptiness, it is selflessness; it is the Buddha-nature (Tathagatagarbha). Yet within reality, there is endless love and compassion, and any search we make for our inner, intrinsic nature often serves to augment our understanding of the greater spirit of the universe.

Chang's *Echoes* and *Blessing* date from the previous year. In the centre of *Echoes* she has painted the "seed syllables" "Om", "Au", and "Hum" from Tibetan Buddhism. The power of the true word seems to reverberate between the larger world of the universe and the smaller world of the human heart, as the vibration between the two calls forth the deep power of reality. In *Blessing*, unique brushwork spreads across the canvas like waves of sound, while from this universe a band of light seems to emerge, leading viewers into a different kind of space and time, filled with love, blessing, and tranquillity.

Sophie Chang's years of religious experience have enabled her, in her painting, to consistently delve into the deepest layers of her spiritual world. This ongoing, sincere dialogue with her inner self often gives her works a deep and impactful power. In retrospect, we can see this search for the inner self consistently as the artist developed her abstract painting style. We see it already in her 2014 work, *Abstract Atmosphere* (pp. 64–5). In both form and colour the painting appears somewhat hazy and indeterminate, yet an orange-red lustre slowly emerges from the darkness, as if a process of realization has taken place that reveals the bright nature of the original self. Chang's *Sunburnt Dusk* (pp. 60–1), dating from 2016, her year of explosive creativity in the abstract mode, along with her *Calm Day Ahead with Immense Red Sky* (pp. 48–9) from the following year, both feature bright and powerful red pigments that gradually fill the entire painting. Not only are these paintings more mature and confident in technique; they also show us how the artist reveals to us parts of her inner world.

The backgrounds of three works from 2018, *Daylight* (pp. 42–3), *Epiphany* (pp. 36–37), and *Light Break* (pp. 18–19), all suggest deep valleys and dense mists; we seem to be immersed in an endless darkness from somewhere deep inside. But a miraculous light appears, and all the dark chaos of the past is dispelled by this deep halo of light, and a sense of new life suddenly appears. In this artist's work, the glow of the inner self that she depicts often urges us to re-embrace the beauty of life. In Chang's 2019 *Shaking Water* (pp. 22–3), she layers colours in three tones that suggest deep, strong moods, yet smudges of paint are freely spattered and swirled on top; we can see how her respect for life and for the inner strength of the human heart grow out of her devout religious beliefs.

In Sophie Chang's new "gold colour" series from 2019, which includes the works *Glacial Waterfalls* (pp. 26–7) and *Dancers in the Sand* (pp. 20–1), we feel even more the sense of inner peace, of "a thousand sails passing by". The two paintings do more than depict the wonderful feeling of peace, however. As she builds up layers of gold pigment, the different textures and veins that she produces ultimately lead the viewer to sense a special kind of tranquility, which we find only after our hearts have been tempered by the long and arduous journey through this earthly realm. Buddhism has always stressed the wisdom of "emptiness"; once we realize that the essence of reality is found in the emptiness of all phenomena, we can then embrace complete insight into ourselves and the universe, and finally achieve ultimate peace. Through the paintings of Sophie Chang, we come to sense the influence of her religious beliefs and training, and the many different aspects of her truthful dialogue with her inner self and the universe.

**Source of Hope**

116.5 × 91 cm

2019

Oil on canvas

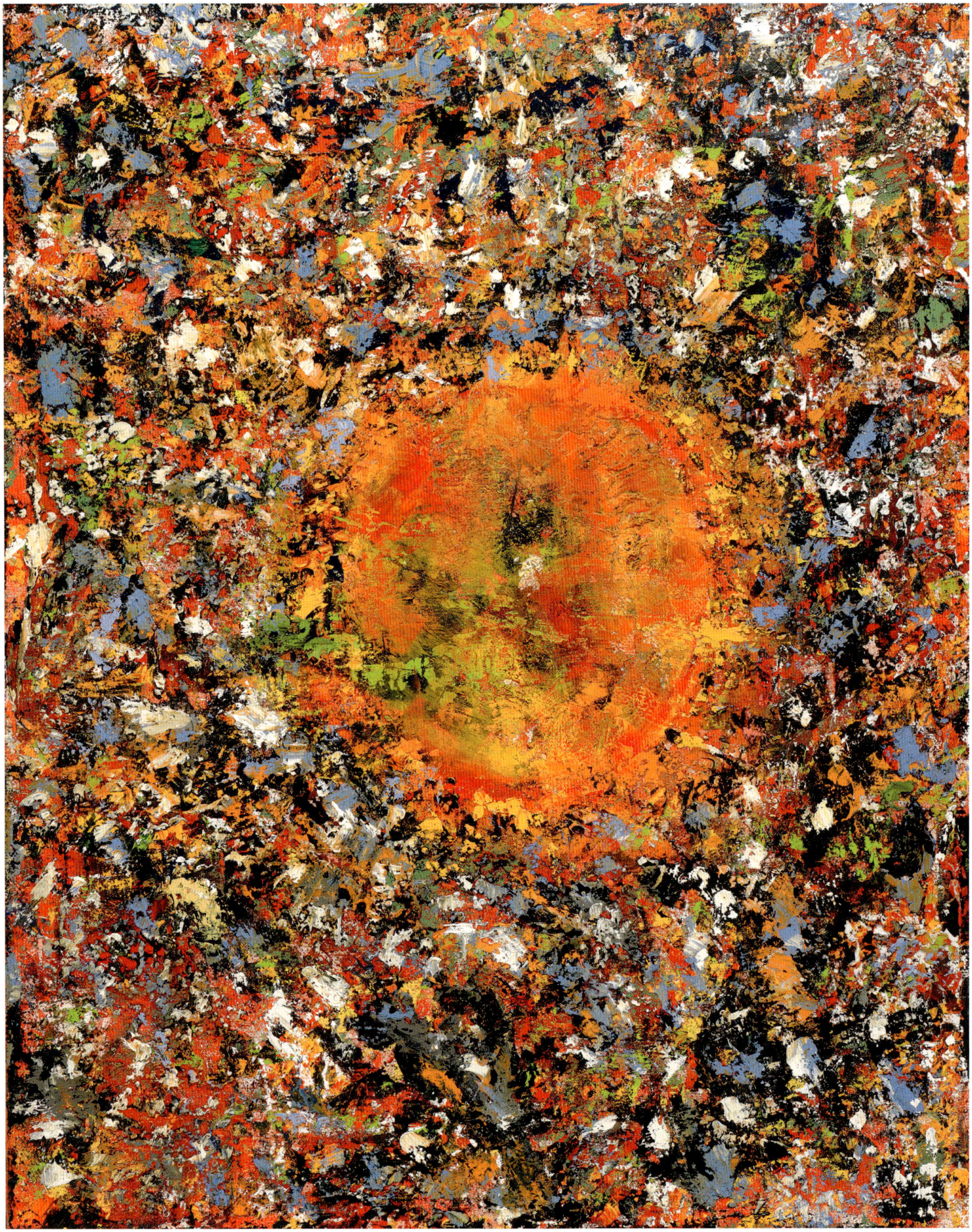

**Our Inner World**

116.5 × 91 cm

2019/20

Oil on canvas

**Blessing**

90.2 × 116.8 cm

2018/19

Oil on canvas

"*On Auction:
Sotheby's Hong Kong Modern Art-Evening Sale

*Enlarged detail on next spread*

**Light Break**

150 × 150 cm

2019

Acrylic, oil on canvas

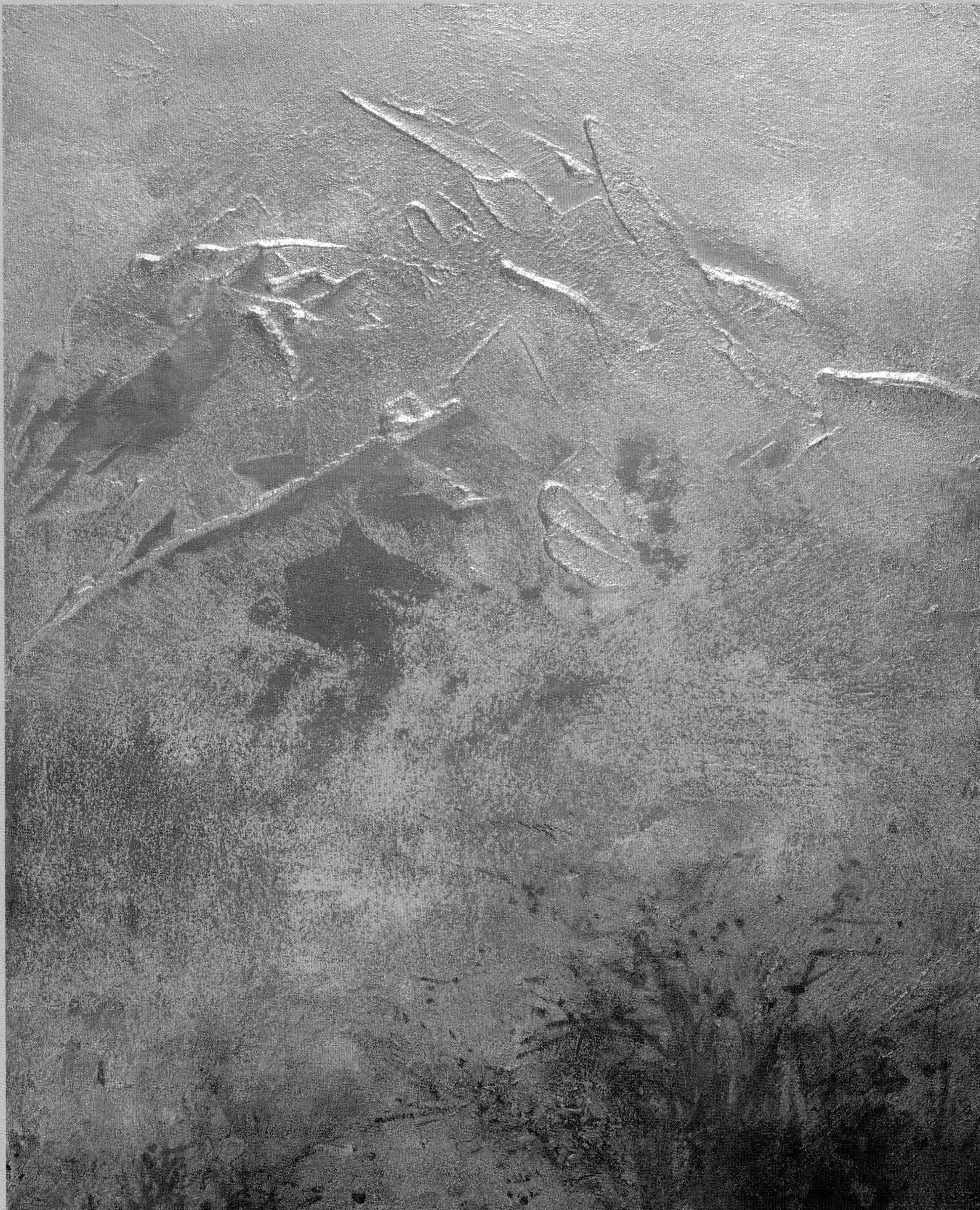

**Dancers in the Sand**

91 × 72.5 cm

2019

Mixed media on canvas

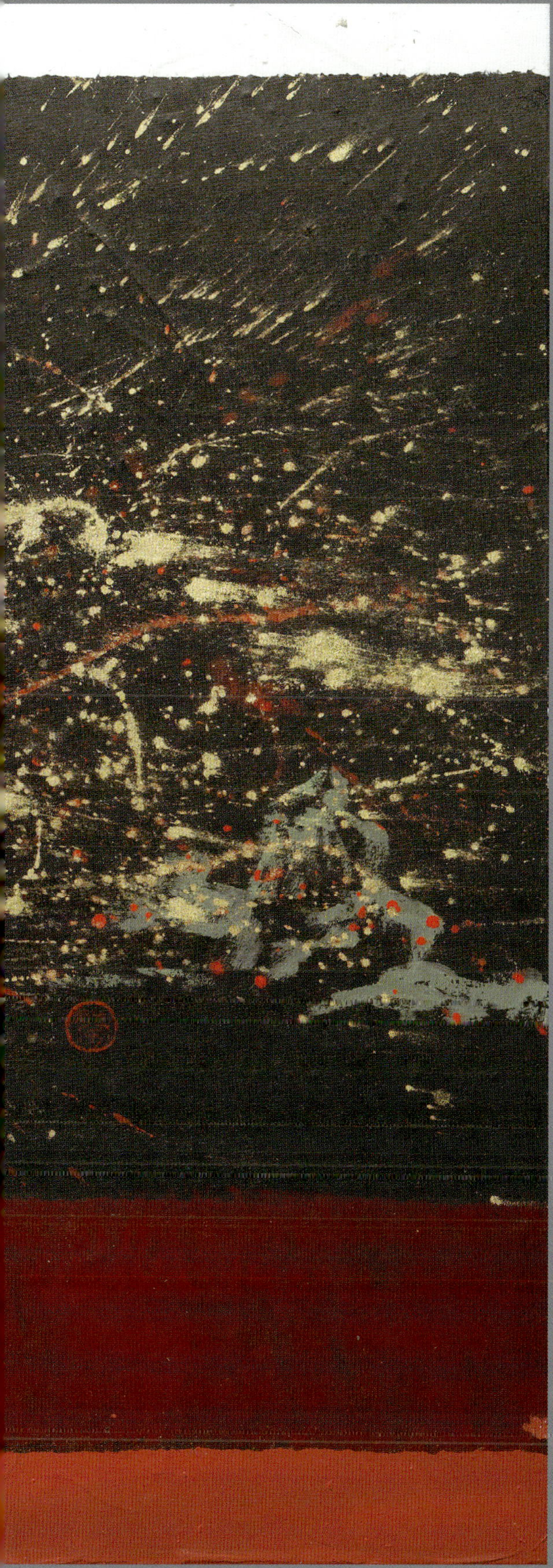

**Shaking Water**

80 × 100 cm

2019

Ink and colour on paper

*Enlarged detail on next spread*

**Glacial Waterfalls**

53 × 65 cm

2019

Mixed media on canvas

*Enlarged detail on next spread*

Sophie
2016

**The Greatest Sound Is Hard to Hear**

100 × 80 cm

2018

Oil on canvas

**Heaven and Earth**

95 × 190 cm

2018

Oil on canvas

*Enlarged detail on next spread*

**Epiphany**

130 × 162 cm

2018

Oil on canvas

*See front endpaper for enlarged detail*

**Echoes**

91 × 116.5 cm

2018

Oil on canvas

*Enlarged detail on next spread*

**Daylight**

162 × 130 cm

2018

Oil on canvas

**Holy Light**

130 × 162 cm

2017

Oil on canvas

*Enlarged detail on next spread*

## Calm Day Ahead with Immense Red Sky

130 × 162 cm

2017

Oil on canvas

*Enlarged detail on next spread*

**Intangible Boundary**

116.5 × 91 cm

2017

Oil on canvas

**Aurora**

72 × 91 cm

2017

Oil on canvas

## Endless Mist

72.5 × 91 cm

2017

Oil on canvas

*Enlarged detail on next spread*

**Sunburnt Dusk**

91 × 116.5 cm

2016

Oil on canvas

*Enlarged detail on next spread*

**Abstract Atmosphere**

91 × 116.5 cm

2014

Oil on canvas

*See page 175 for enlarged detail*

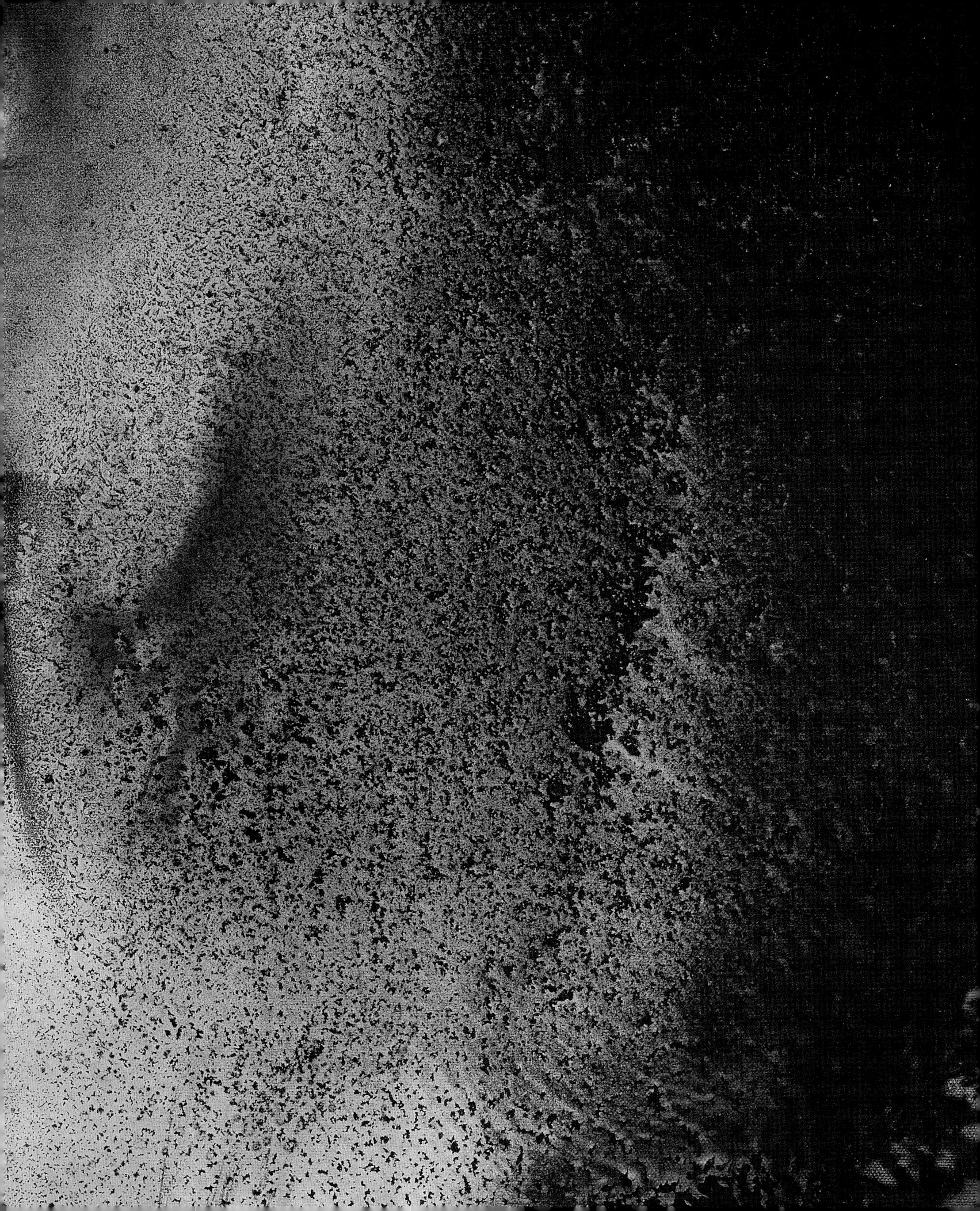

Chapter Two

# Grand Journeys Between Heaven and Earth

## Mental Images of the Universe – the World of Sophie Chang's Abstract Landscapes

The subjects Sophie Chang most loves to paint have always been "mountains" and "the universe".

Sophie Chang once expressed how much she loves seeing deep rows of mountain peaks, towering between heaven and earth with their solemn and venerable presence. That became especially true as her involvement with religion grew, and she visited the sacred Buddhist regions of India, Nepal and Tibet. It was there, among grand natural vistas of mountains and skies, that she awoke to the nature of inner personal experience and felt the impact of those seemingly limitless spaces. In particular, her many years of meditation required careful attention to the fleeting changes of mood in each passing moment, and it is from this state of mindfulness that she responds to others and encounters the Earth. For that reason, her abstract paintings always exude a feeling for the grandeur of the Earth and the universe: Often, we seem to be viewing Earth's grandeur from a point in space, looking down on the towering peaks of a mountain range, or gazing at the endless folds of a far shore. She reminisces how once, during early morning meditation at a Buddhist temple in the Nepalese mountains, the early light of dawn began to slowly emerge as she faced the ridgeline of the Himalayas. From deep, quiet darkness, the sky first turned grey, then a streak of red light emerged, and finally, filled the entire sky until she seemed to be sitting between heaven and earth. The experience had such an impact that, even today, she uses it as a centring image during meditation.

For these reasons, the external scenes presented in her abstract landscapes often merge with her own inner realizations. These images of her inner thoughts gradually take shape on canvas during a process in which she applies layer after layer of oils. For Sophie Chang, painting is not just something she uses to capture her inner moods; the process of painting is an opportunity to reappraise the mountains and rivers, the Earth, the universe, and the human heart. Her abstract landscapes often convey a sense of the fullness and abundance that one may feel after gaining insight into and understanding of reality. That, coupled with her bold, free use of colour and the buildup of clashing pigments on the canvas, projects a sweeping, dazzling "mental image of the universe" – a kind of "mental image" that reflects her immediate perception of the inner self, the world, the universe. The resulting creation projects from her inner heart a state in which "the mind and the universe are one and the same". In her art, even as we undertake these grand visual journeys across her boundless landscapes, there is always an intriguing sense of mystery, a unique feeling for the land, the world, and the universe, touched with a special sense of love and yearning affection. It is as if the artist's brush has lit gently upon everything in the world, and she paints the reality of that world as sensed and understood in her own heart.

In late 2016, the artist developed an abstract vocabulary based on her almost accidental discovery of the "Chang

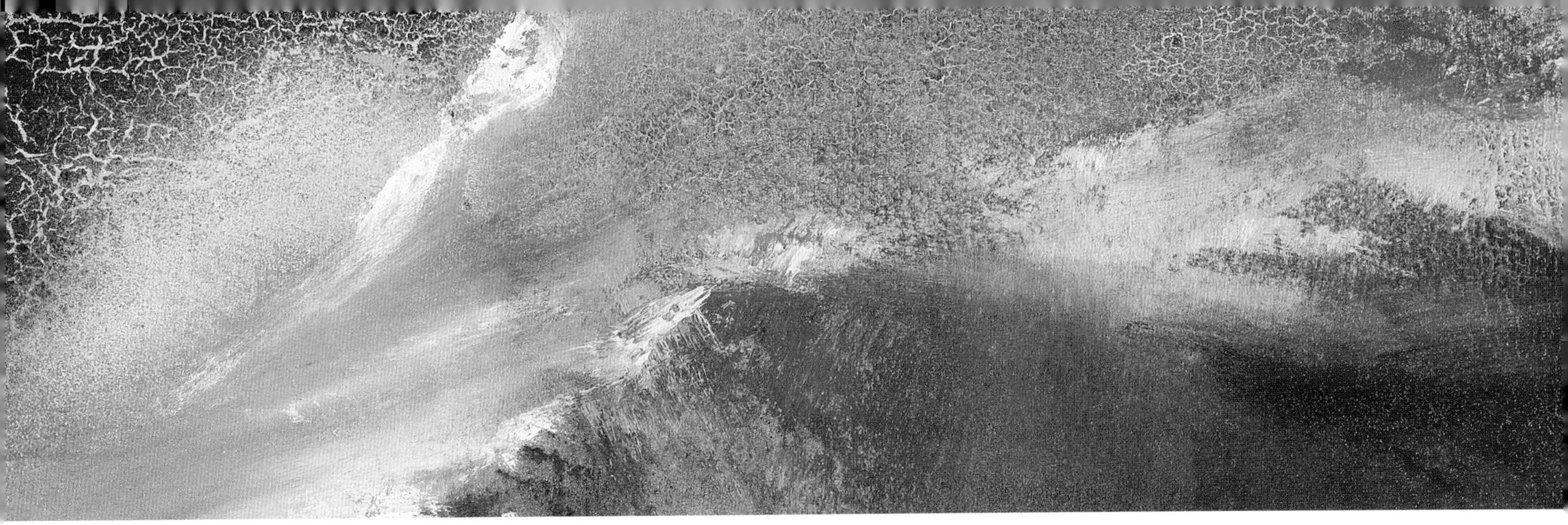

technique", which further enriched the "mental images of the universe" that welled up in her heart. At times she builds up veins and textures in muscular layers of pigment, emphasizing the powerful, buckling folds of mountains; at other times criss-cross patterns of cracks stretch out, reminiscent of the "cracked" texture strokes in traditional Chinese landscape painting, which add detail and texture to the mountainous terrain. Chang customarily employs this effect in paintings with many layers of pigments, letting the cracks expose the colours of the bottom layers. The effect may seem accidental, but Chang's use of it is brings the layers alive. In her philosophy, life shows us an endless stream of pictures, and its dazzling beauty is ultimately revealed in the endless colours that are layered over the deepest hues at the bottom.

Chang has found other insights in nature too: In addition to the blue, green, and black tones she favours, she also has a special fondness for white, a kind of white that is distilled and purified by the passage of time. She once said that, as a young girl, she liked the atmosphere of cemeteries, since they represented a kind of ultimate tranquillity after all the tumultuous events of life. Seeing a tomb always helped her feel calm. And living in the US for many years, the heavy snows she saw each year from her home facing Central Park in New York City left her well-acquainted with blizzards and snowstorms. For that reason, when she returned to painting in 2016 and once again began producing abstract works, snow scenes became the first theme to attract her interest. Early on, she depicted snowfall with a flurry of rapid strokes across the canvas, but found the results disappointing. Then, after 2018, images of white snow gradually entered the mountainous scenes in her abstract visions of the universe. There, they came to represent a hazy region between heaven and earth, a kind of pure, wintry realm formed from the condensation of ice and snow. It is as if, when her inner self views our world, a world filled with noise and clamour and the riotous colour of human activity, she must still find that sliver of white, that peaceful scene, that exists somewhere amid the heavens and the earth. These patches of pure, tranquil white, evolving from her earlier snow scenes, in fact represent Chang's original intent to cultivate her mind in the midst of the daily world; they suggest as well a state of quiet observation achieved amid all of life's disorder and complications. In this way, they recall how, amid the sounds of chanting, drums, and bells in Nepal, she once experienced a deep sense of the tranquillity of the heavens and the earth. Circling around the Buddhist tower, turning again and again, she delved into the deepest levels of her mind to find that pure white, with its profound quietness and tranquillity.

**Deep Sea Paradise**

91 × 116.7 cm

2019

Oil on canvas

*Enlarged detail on next spread*

**Soaring Beyond**

each: 130 × 97 cm
overall: 130 × 194 cm

2018

Oil on canvas, diptych

"*On Charity Auction:
Presented by Sophie Chang & Save the Children Hong Kong, 27 May 2018
(the work wasdonated by the artist)"

Sophie
2018

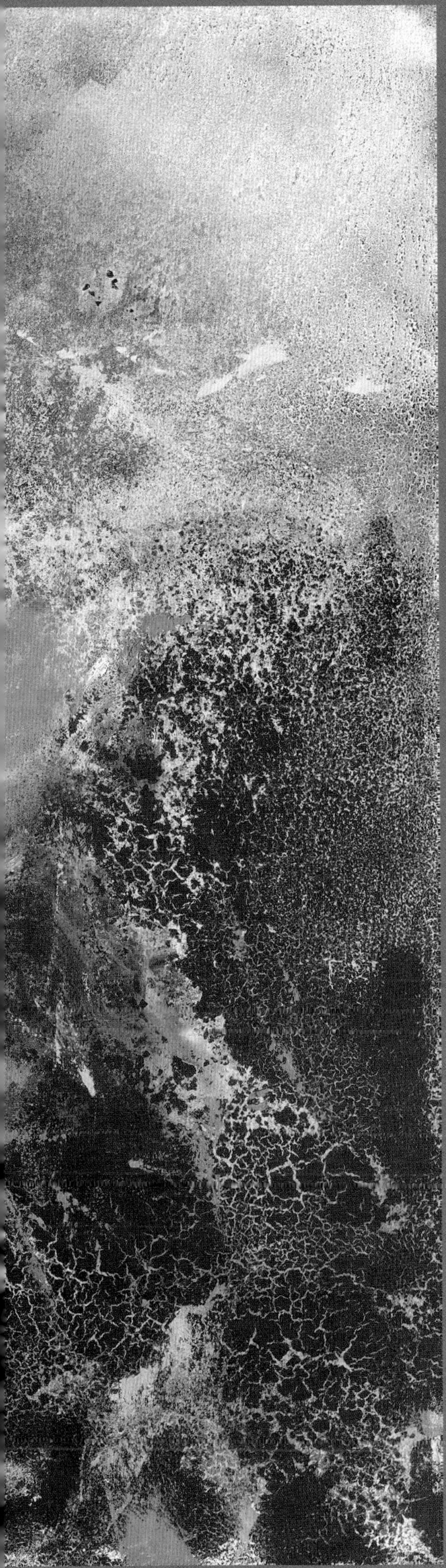

**Between Ourselves**

130 × 162 cm

2018

Oil on canvas

*Enlarged detail on next spread*

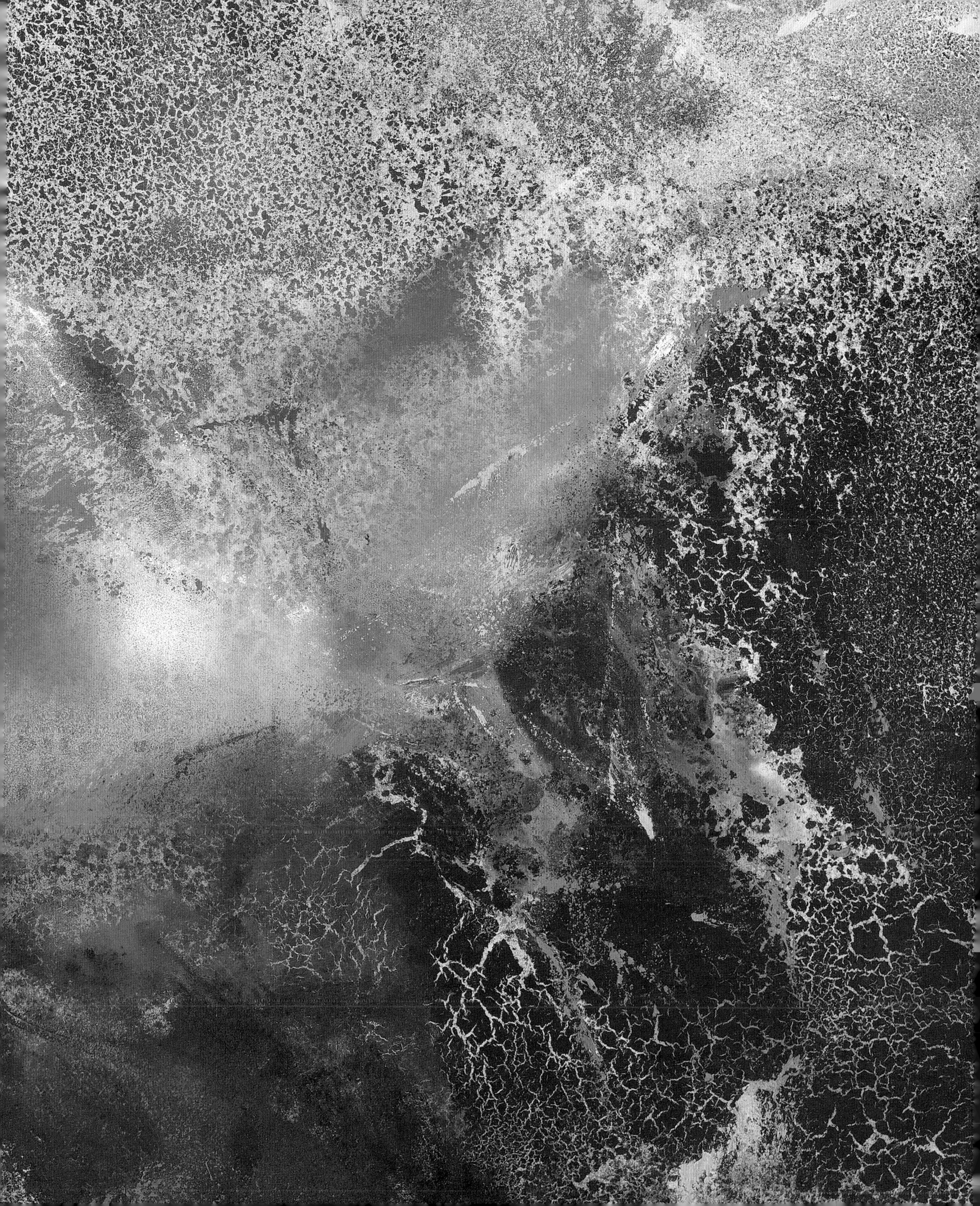

**Reflection of Nature**

130 × 89 cm

2018

Oil on canvas

**Hand of Life**

145 × 112 cm

2018

Oil on canvas

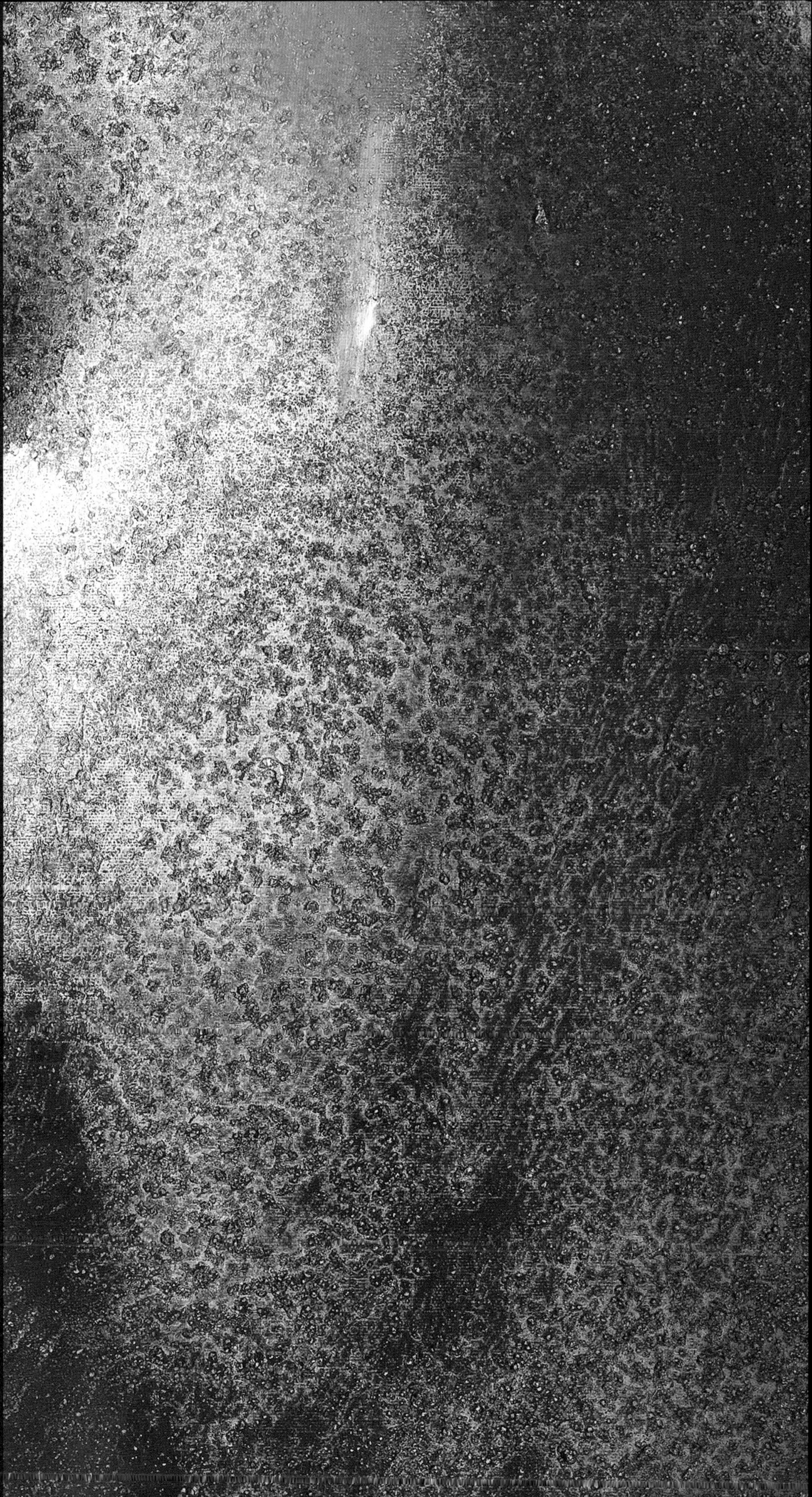

**Silent Valley**

145.5 × 112 cm

2018

Oil on canvas

**Frozen Path**

130 × 162 cm

2017

Oil on canvas

*Enlarged detail on next spread*

## Green Mountain Mist No. 1.2.3.4

each: 112 × 145.5 cm
overall: 224 × 291 cm

2017

Oil on canvas

*Enlarged details on next spread*

**Mountain Restructure**

130 × 162 cm

2017

Oil on canvas

*Enlarged detail on next spread*

**Emerald Ridge**

130 × 97 cm

2017

Oil on canvas

**Emerald Ridge**

130 × 162 cm

2017

Oil on canvas

*See opposite page 1 for enlarged detail*

**Sky Light**

91 × 116.5 cm

2017

Oil on canvas

*Enlarged detail on next spread*

**Snow Dance**

72.5 × 91 cm

2016

Oil on canvas

*Enlarged detail on next spread*

## Peak of the Mountain

110 × 163 cm

2010

Oil on canvas

"*On Auction:
Ravenel Taipei Modern and Contemporary Asian Art
on 3 Decober 2017."

*See page 178 for enlarged detail*

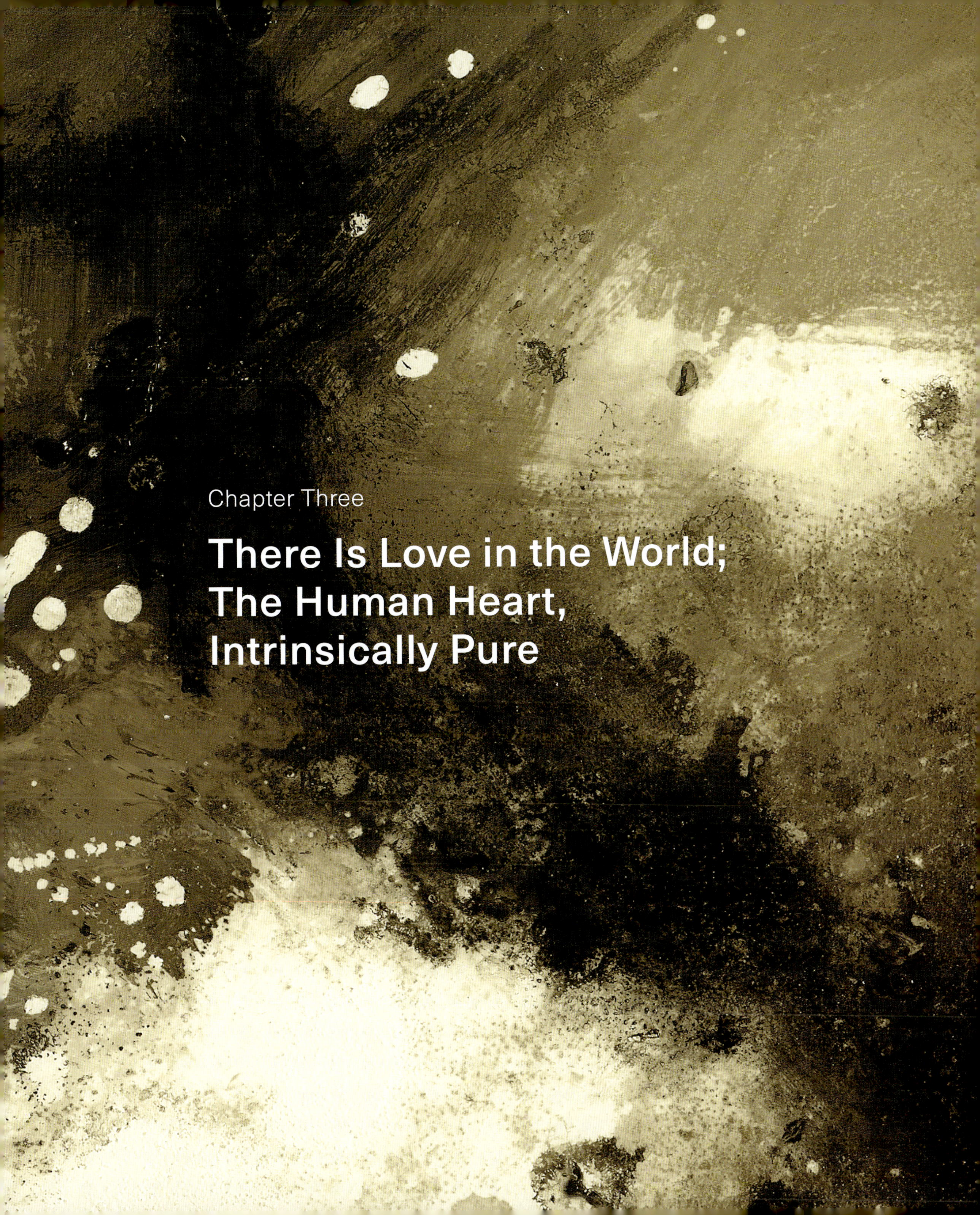

Chapter Three

# There Is Love in the World; The Human Heart, Intrinsically Pure

In Sophie Chang's creative work, there is first her spiritual practice – cultivating attentiveness to experience, perceiving the truth of the universe, and conveying the multitude of images from her inner heart. But the joy she derives from completion of a charity project also fills her with creative energy and motivation. Her status as a broadly-recognized figure in society, as the spouse of Taiwan Semiconductor's founder and former chairman, and from her own position as chairwoman of the TSMC Charity Foundation, go together like oil on canvas. Since 2004, she has promoted public welfare and charity work, with an overwhelmingly positive response from society. During a series of natural and man-made catastrophes, including the 2009 Morakot Typhoon, the 2014 gas-line explosions in Kaohsiung, and the 2018 Hualian earthquake, she led the TSMC Volunteer Program immediately following into the disaster areas to assess local conditions, integrating a platform of resources to provide disaster assistance. Her efforts have been universally recognized in the disaster areas, and the Foundation has now become the best-known and respected of Taiwan's philanthropic organizations. Chang has played a leadership role in promoting these efforts, frequently visiting disaster areas in person, using her network of personal connections to draw on resources from many sectors, and uniting her team of volunteers. It has been said that all people possess some degree of good will, but if everyone's good will, no matter how large or small, can only be guided and harnessed, then many small trickles of good will join together like a vast ocean.

As she gives her full efforts to philanthropy, Sophie Chang has in recent years focused on providing care to elderly persons living alone, promoting a culture of respect and care for one's family elders, concern for the disadvantaged, and strengthening environmental protection. Her sense of concern derives from the awareness, as part of the Bodhisattva mind, that all humanity shares in the suffering of any of its members. "Loving kindness brings happiness; compassion offers liberation from suffering." With charity as a starting point, people will respond with love, and through the great goal of spreading love, we can continue to bring change to people's hearts. The fullness Chang felt at the completion of a charity project, or during a lull in her charity work, has often inspired her to take up her brush and depict on canvas the happiness and satisfaction she feels. In her 2017 *Dawn of Spring* (pp. 134–5), and her *Flowerfall* (pp. 130–1) from the following year, deep, inchoate backgrounds serve to set off showers of maple leaves and flower petals. These two paintings, Chinese in conception, exude a clear vein of joy and happiness. In her 2018 *Hand of Life* (pp. 86–7), beneath what seems to be a cold

mountain spring, we see a flash of colour and life. Tender green leaves, poignant flowers of lavender, and arresting mangroves all work together to remind the viewer of the beauty of life, and to convey a sense of the happiness the artist feels in all things in the world as a result of her work.

If the three paintings above, reflecting the spiritual happiness of Buddhism, seem to convey the bliss of private, inner contemplation, then Sophie Chang's *Spring Ploughing* (pp. 120–1) and *Autumn Harvest* (pp. 124–5), from 2019, are simply unreserved songs of praise, the heart's inner happiness sung aloud. Rich with colour, their broad-brush calligraphic lines dance across the paintings, and the hearty, outgoing mood of the artist virtually leaps from the canvas.

Chang herself has said, however, that while charity is performed in the name of love, as one extends the love of one's own heart to call forth the common love shared among all, it is impossible at the same time to avoid seeing a darker side of avarice, ill-will, and ignorance. But a Bodhisattva does not abandon others to misery, and with experience and wisdom, she has always found a way to handle matters properly; such experiences in fact simply become another opportunity to practice forbearance and to reflect on human nature. Recently, as typhoons and earthquakes continue, natural disasters seem more common than ever. As she faces a ravaged Earth, marshalling the faith and strength of the public to work together for the common good has become a focus of her reflection and practice. In Chang's large-scale 2017 tetraptych *Green Seeding* (pp. 126–7), she sends her benevolent gaze down toward a land of rivers and mountains, with the constant hope that seeds of life will take root everywhere. Our eyes crave the blue that we find in the lake in the heart of the mountains, which is a spring, a source that gives birth to all of life. In her charity work, this artist firmly believes that "As we pass through layer after layer of green, each footstep is planted more deeply than the last." As she takes each step with the correct mindfulness, she at the same time upholds her belief in the grand order of all things in the universe.

Sophie Chang's favourite sights, of bright flowers and green leaves blown in the breeze, serve not only to remind viewers of the beauty of the world, but also to remind us of this artist's consistent belief in the inherent purity of the human heart.

**Floating Life**

91 × 116.7 cm

2019

Oil on canvas

*Enlarged detail on next spread*

**Spring Ploughing**

50 × 70 cm

2019

Oil on canvas

*Enlarged detail on next spread*

**Autumn Harvest**

50 × 70 cm

2019

Oil on canvas

*See back endpaper for enlarged detail*

2018

## Green Seeding

each: 97 × 130 cm
overall: 194 × 260 cm

2018

Oil on canvas

*Enlarged details on next spread*

**Flowerfall**

145 × 112 cm

2018

Oil on canvas

**Untitled**

72.7 × 60.4 cm

2018

Oil on canvas

"*On Auction:
Sotheby's Hong Kong Modern
Art-Evening Sale on 5 Octber
2019."

**Dawn of Spring**

145 × 112 cm

2017

Oil on canvas

"*On Auction:
Ravenel Taipei Modern and Contemporary Asian Art on 3 Decober 2017."

**Green Foliage**

97 × 130 cm

2016

Oil on canvas

*Enlarged detail on next spread*

Chapter Four

# A Salute to the Great Masters

Once Sophie Chang received her basic instruction in painting, she very quickly demonstrated an excellent grasp of colour, form, and projecting feeling into her paintings. Despite her non-traditional background, her work matured rapidly, and her surprising talent was evident from her earliest efforts, when she produced work in an Impressionist vein. As early as her third year of painting, while learning contrasting colour values, Chang went beyond the requirement of depicting an "image" and took her first steps toward abstraction. She developed a style based on pure line and colour, using abstraction to express her inner feelings.

During the three years between 2013 and 2015, when she paused her public charity activities, she also set aside her paintbrush and other creative work. Following the sabbatical, however, she found that the abstract style, a style which has given expression to the soul and spirit of artists since the 20th century, was liberating. A new stream of abstract works poured out as she set down on canvas the insights derived from her spiritual cultivation and her reflections on life and the human world.

Even more crucial for Chang was a bold personality with limited restrictions, so that once she set out on the road to abstraction, she quickly adopted a multi-faceted approach. She learned from a number of different sources, in particular spending many hours in the museums of New York, viewing works by the great abstract painters of Europe and the US. She was deeply struck by the scepticism of those painters in the aftermath of World War II, their brash emphasis on the individual spirit, and their search for an ultimate inner peace. She was also greatly inspired by the work of German painter Gerhard Richter (1932–), who used a homemade squeegee to scrape away layers of accumulated paint, letting old and new layers collide in a kind of fusion emerging from conflict. The sharp marks left by his scraper, and the mottled hues of the old picture surface underneath, speak of the tension and anxiety rife in human society following the industrialization and globalization of the 20th century. Then there were the Chinese artists who travelled to France, such as Zao Wou-ki (1921–2013), Chu Teh-Chun (1920–2014), and Wu Guanzhong (1919–2010), and Taiwanese artists such as Liu Guosong (1932–). The spirit of the East was deeply rooted in each of those artist's work, and given her own similar cultural experiences, they are ones to whom Sophie Chang feels closest. Rather than blindly copying, as she emulates the styles of such masters from previous generations, she adds her own ideas and feelings, telling a fresh, new story that reveals her true inner feelings.

When Chang once again took up the brush in 2016, continuing her earlier experiments with abstraction, she subtly integrated into her work the Impressionists' handling of light and shadow. In her 2016 *Snow Dance* (pp. 106–1), we can see in her flurries of snow an Impressionist conception, along with the short brushstrokes that characterized their work. In *Green Foliage* (pp. 136–7) from the same year, however, it is as if the blue tones of Claude Monet's (1840–1926) lily ponds have been replaced with green; the green in the upper part of the painting especially recalls the beautiful hues of that artist. But *Green Foliage* also shows the gradual development of a new element of Chang's style, the "falling leaf pattern", an image seen in the subtle patterns that float above the water. In the blue at the bottom of the painting we can also see her using a scraping technique, similar to Richter's, to produce horizontal streaks on the water's surface. The contrasts revealed through this process, between the darker and lighter areas of new and old pigments, suggest the patterns of rippling light on the pond's surface. Though the painting as a whole suggests an Impressionist style, Sophie Chang borrows freely from the techniques of different great artists, ingeniously combining them in an original creation of her own. In *Mirrored Pond* (pp. 146–7), from 2018, what might be Monet's water lilies now appear as if in a dream, blending seamlessly as they reveal the inner panorama of the artist's mind and heart.

Sophie Chang had previously experimented with the pointillist style of the Impressionist painter Georges-Pierre Seurat (1859–91), and produced some scenic depictions in that style. But as was the case with the influence of Monet, pointillism gradually became simply one of the constituent elements that fed into her own abstract style. In the four small works making up the tetraptych *Starry Night Sky* (pp. 152–3), Chang incorporates various textural cracking effects, along with tiny drops of dripped paint; even on these small canvases, viewers can visually roam through images of vast star fields, and we still see an ingenious use of Seurat-style pointillist effects. Chang's 2019 *Glimpse of Heaven* (pp. 144–5) offers a dreamlike version of Seurat's pointillism, its rich scattering of large and small stars throwing off a halo of light, as if all individual lives have been gathered together to burst forth in a brilliant radiance.

As for the German Richter, Chang had been carefully emulating his works, especially those with the scraping strokes that reveal their multi-layered, variegated colours. That technique has helped Chang express the ineffable quality of some of her deepest mental dimensions. Chang's 2018 *Blessing* (pp. 14–15) is a very important work, reflecting the artist's religious experience, in which the powerful influence of Richter can be seen.

But for Sophie Chang, with her love of the magnificent mountains, the mysterious depths found in the works of Zao Wou-ki best represent her "images of the cosmic mind". Chang once confessed that she most loves the sense of imposing power and boundless scope she finds in Zao Wou-ki, and for that reason she carefully studied his special use of colour. In her 2017 work *Sky Light* (pp. 102–3), we find a painting full of Chang's own inner individuality, yet stylistically, in terms of colour, texture, and conception, it remains a transformation of stylistic elements from Zao's work.

Two of Chang's powerful works from 2018, *The Greatest Sound is Hard to Hear* (pp. 30–1) and *Epiphany* (pp. 36–7), feature compositions and delicate layering effects that also approach Zao Wou-ki stylistically. Yet in borrowing from this influence, Chang manages to penetrate an even deeper feeling for the universe, producing a powerful impact on the viewer. It is only because the two artists possess a shared breadth of spirit that Sophie Chang, is able to express herself in that idiom with such ease and confidence.

By contrast, Sophie Chang admires another of the leading Chinese artists who sojourned in France, Chu Teh-Chun, for the joyful feeling of his rich, light, and flowing compositions. Chang's 2018 *Kaleidescope* (pp. 148–9) and *Untitled* (pp. 132–3) possess Chu Teh-Chun's pleasing and eye-catching colours. Her 2019 *Spring Ploughing* (pp. 120–1), *Autumn Harvest* (p. 124–5), and *Floating Life* (pp. 116–17) blend flowing, calligraphic lines with richness and variety of colour, showing how Chang's expression of positive inner energy was inspired by her influences.

For any painter, studying and copying the great masters of previous generations is a necessary part of artistic growth, helping them hone their technique while also drawing sustenance from the spiritual world of those great artists. For Sophie Chang, her long experience with internal observation in her religious pursuit has given her the ability to quickly grasp the unique spirit that lies behind any particular style. Each of these artists' styles and techniques have become outlets for expressing the many and varied emotions of the human world, and ultimately, in Sophie Chang's work, they are fused together to produce the rich, diverse variety of her painting today. Her work, beyond paying tribute to these masters, also allows their spirit to once again shine in our contemporary world.

**Glimpse of Heaven**

116.5 × 91 cm

2019

Oil on canvas

**Mirrored Pond**

91 × 72.5 cm

2018

Oil on canvas

**Kaleidescope**

97 × 130 cm

2018

Oil on canvas

*Enlarged detail on next spread*

Sophie

**Starry Night Sky**

each: 53 × 45.5 cm
overall: 106 × 91 cm

2017

Oil on canvas

*Enlarged details on next two spreads*

Sophie

Chapter Five

# The Spirit of the East

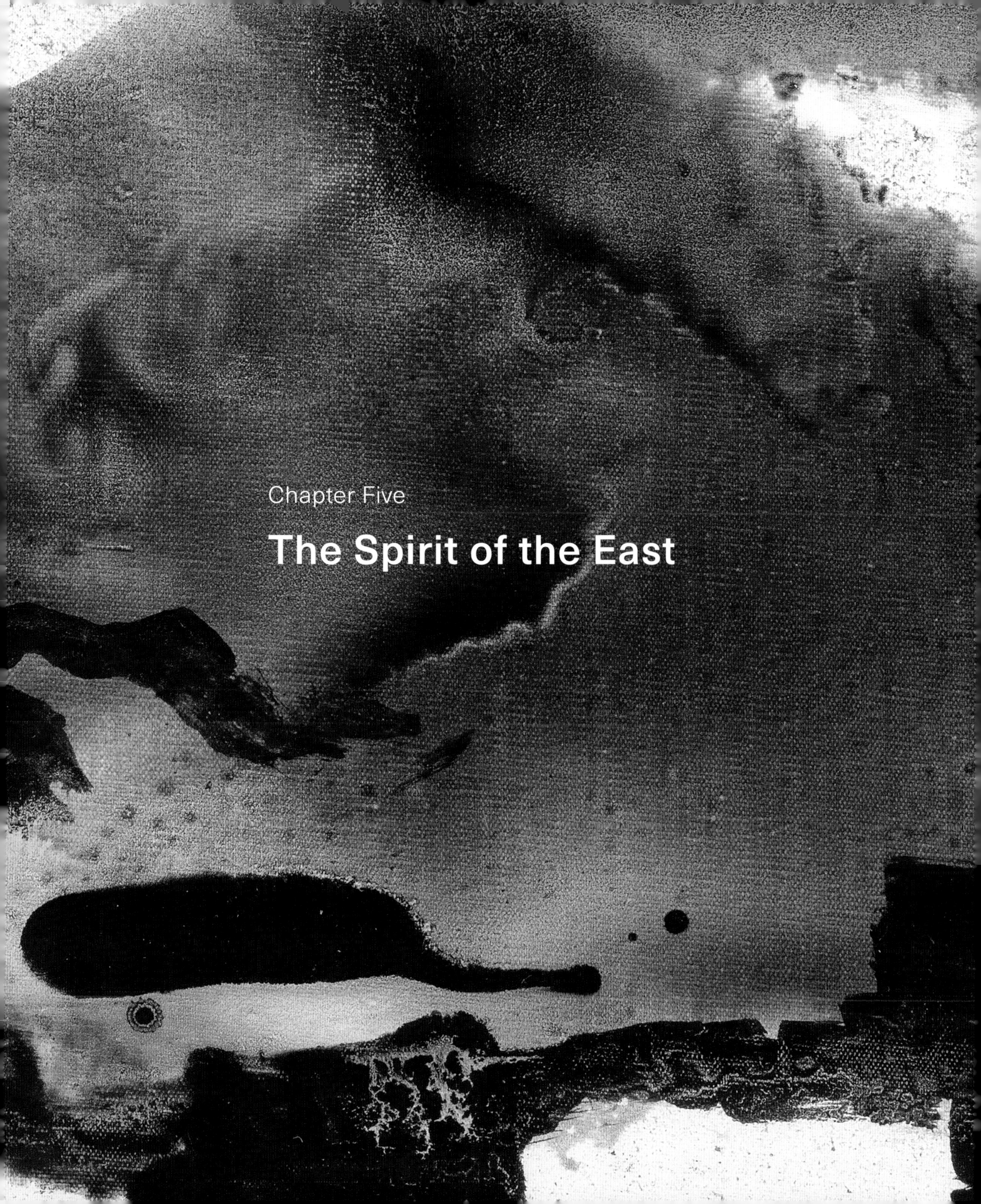

In addition to painting in oils, Sophie Chang has recently found a new format to express her emotions in ink painting. Oil painting, with its great scope, its complex layering, and its exceptional variations in texture, still remains for her a great instrument. But by contrast, Chinese ink-wash painting is more of a vehicle for personal expression and release, making possible her personal discovery of a new domain – the spirit of the East. With the multi-facet nature of oils, she becomes a poet; with ink and brush, she finds insight into her own culture.

Chang did not receive the typical training in the ink and brush techniques of Chinese painting; if anything, her experience during the many years she spent abroad in the US dictated a more Westernized approach. For that reason, she took to oil medium immediately, creating rich and varied imaginative realms on canvas. But traditional ink-wash painting of China has been, for thousands of years, a vehicle for the expression of ideas and sentiments by its poets and educated classes, embodying their appreciation for and insights into the principles of Confucianism or Daoism. Much attention was given to knowledge imparted by the instructor, the proper use of the brush and ink, and the origin and development of different styles; in fact, great attention was given to any connection with the great teachers of the past and their methods of instruction. Ink-wash painting is more than just a kind of Eastern artistic vocabulary; instead, it embodies and expresses the spiritual meanings of the entire network of cultural traditions that lie behind its development. Chang's experimentation with ink-wash painting, in the seemingly Eastern conceptions that inform her style, can find a variety of new insights into this millennia-old culture.

First, Chang's materials: Initially, in creating her series, Mental Images of the Universe, the artist was most influenced by Zao Wou-ki. But, encountering the world with her own sensibilities, she developed her own new style, and then, almost accidentally as she was applying paints to canvas, her experiments yielded results. She produced a new world of mellow, inky tones, reminiscent of Zhang Daqian (1899–1983) and his splashed ink and colour paintings of the 1960s. An example is Chang's 2017 *Between Heaven and Earth* (pp. 170–1). Painted entirely in oils, it possesses to a surprising degree the charm and flavour of ink, and a conception that evokes the use of empty space in traditional Chinese painting. In particular, the lightly brushed swath of yellow ochre across the upper part of the canvas seems as if it were done with a single sweep of the calligraphy brush, and the softness of the colour suggests a spreading halo of ink, creating a world of dense, flowing mists. From this point on, Chang's landscapes, conceived as if for the Chinese ink medium but painted in Western oils, have been a greatly anticipated new aspect of her artistic output. This new series also includes a work from 2018, *Beneath the Surface* (pp. 168–9).

The use of the Western oil medium to portray Chinese-style conceptions or to evoke a kind of "Zen spirit" has already stretched the barriers separating East and West. In Chang's work, the resemblance between her oils and Chinese ink-wash painting is far from accidental. Such resemblance shows how, as the artist was steeped in Chinese culture during her formative years, it exerted a subconscious influence that is now quietly emerging, bringing a new recognition of the Eastern spirit behind the ink forms she finds so appealing. Traditional Chinese landscapes, most often painted by scholars or officials, were grand, hazy depictions that idealized their notion of seclusion from the world, but were painted amid the temples and markets of the mundane, common world. They provided those individuals with sustenance for the mind and a place of spiritual retreat. Similarly, as Sophie Chang daringly depicts on canvas her broad, rich mental images of the universe, she also seems to have used these paintings, with their Chinese conceptions, to settle her mind and feelings. By allowing her to connect on her own with the world of Zen, they let her retain some of that steadying feel in the midst of a full, busy life.

Following this path, she has also explored, step by step, more deeply in the world of traditional Chinese-style ink paintings. Perhaps most intriguing, in addition to the way these paintings recall the splashed ink-and-colour works of Zhang Daqian, is their use of freely flowing, calligraphic lines. This closely resembled calligraphic abstract style was first foreshadowed in the work of Franz Kline (1910–62), who in 1950s New York refined and abstracted elements of industry and architecture into the black, linear motifs of his paintings. Chang likewise responds to the power of line, and here she launches yet another wave of appealing black-and-white motifs, working on Chinese *xuan* paper with printer's ink and wielding the calligraphy brush. The subtle shifts in these works between wet and dry effects, between movement and repose, equal the efforts of many calligraphers who have wielded their brushes for a lifetime, and her own training in abstract styles allows her to capture even more intuitively in these lines the motion of her far-ranging thoughts.

Some other works, such as lotuses in ink, landscapes, and floral and fauna paintings, bring her even closer to Chinese ink-wash, and clearly seem playful experiments growing from the artist's sense of curiosity. Chang's 2019 *Lotus* (pp. 166–7), painted on *xuan* paper with a heavily ribbed texture, presents the cool, fresh world of the lotus in broad washes of colour. Her style at first may seem to reflect the freehand approach of the old literati painters, but on closer inspection, it can be seen as an abstract arrangement of denser and lighter areas of colour. She also boldly employs a kind of collage effect, introducing what seem to be suitable elements of other paintings, or lines of calligraphy couplets not written by the artist herself. The result enhances the depth and dimensionality of the work even as it suggests a free and playful approach. Zhang Daqian spent the first part of his life imitating the old masters, and the second part trying to escape their influence; summing up his life's experience, he once said, "Learning brush technique is easy, but applying ink is hard; yet applying ink is easy, next to learning the secrets of water." For Chang too, the world of brush and ink has found its way into her soul. In these dialogues with her inner self, Chang handles with confidence themes and materials deriving from thousands of years of Chinese history, and she manages with ease to create a separate world in her washes of ink, a place where she knows the sensations and feelings as her own. Here, we enter into a pure world of ink-wash creation, like stepping directly into a realm of Buddhist enlightenment. For Chang, both mediums, Western oils and Chinese inks, are ones she finds amenable for expressing an Eastern spirit, and for appreciating and celebrating the spirit of Zen. In fact, the use of different mediums only has only added greater breadth to her expressions of this special realm. And for her works in the ink medium, it has imbued them with a character that is personal and contemporary.

**First Bloom** or **Flower Box**

94 × 76 cm

2019

Ink and colour on paper

般若波羅蜜多心經 五蘊皆空度一切苦厄
金剛般若波羅蜜經 應無所住而生其心
波羅蜜心經 觀自在菩薩

**Mysterious Valley**

145.5 × 112 cm

2019

Ink and colour on paper

Sophie '19

**Lotus**

85.5 × 94 cm

2019

Ink and colour on paper

"*On Auction:
Sotheby's Hong Kong Modern Asian Art on 6 October 2019."

## Beneath the Surface

80 × 100 cm

2018

Oil on canvas

Sophie
2017

**Between Heaven and Earth**

112 × 145.5 cm

2017

Oil on canvas

*Enlarged detail on next spread*

## About the Artist

The artist Sophie Chang is better known for her other roles: as wife of the founder of Taiwan Semiconductor Manufacturing Company (TSMC) and chairwoman of the TSMC Charity Foundation, in which role she has been publicly acclaimed for her social and charity work. While charity remains Chang's most important mission in life, her role as artist, a role which she discovered unexpectedly in her sixties and which is still very new, has become an important and obsessive outlet of expression. She began painting as a hobby in the time afforded to her by – and with the unconditional support of – her husband Morris Chang. With the warm and edifying support of his love, Sophie immersed herself in the world of art.

When Chang first started painting in 2006, she was attracted by Impressionism, exploring the changes of light and shadow in colour. As she built confidence, she broke away from representational art and toward broadening her use of colour with simpler lines, and exploring the expression of emotion available through abstract art.

Sophie is a dedicated student and has studied many twentieth-century Abstract masters. Her lifelong commitment to Buddhism and decades of charitable endeavour enables her to show on canvas a mental image of her beliefs and observations of current events. Combining the experience of Eastern Zen and the Abstract techniques of Western painting, Chang has created a personalised poetic abstract with its own distinctive style.

# Index of Titles